JEWISH LAW AND CONTEMPORARY ISSUES

Organized as a series of authoritative discussions, this book presents the application of Jewish law – or *Halakhah* – to contemporary social and political issues. Beginning with the principle of divine revelation, it describes the contents and canons of interpretation of Jewish law. Though divinely received, the law must still be interpreted and "completed" by human minds, often leading to the conundrum of divergent but equally authentic interpretations. Examining topics from divorce to war and from rabbinic confidentiality to cloning, this book carefully delineates the issues presented in each case, showing the various positions taken by rabbinic scholars, clarifying areas of divergence, and analyzing reasons for disagreement.

Written by widely recognized scholars of both Jewish and secular law, this book will be an invaluable source for all who seek authoritative guidance in understanding traditional Jewish law and practice.

J. David Bleich is a professor of Talmud (Rosh Yeshiva) at Rabbi Isaac Elchanan Theological Seminary, as well as Professor of Law at the Benjamin N. Cardozo School of Law, and Tenzer Professor of Jewish Law and Ethics at Yeshiva University. A prolific writer and an authority on Jewish law and ethics, he is widely known as author of the six-volume *Contemporary Halakhic Problems*.

Arthur J. Jacobson is Max Freund Professor of Litigation and Advocacy at the Benjamin N. Cardozo School of Law, Yeshiva University. He is the author of numerous articles and books on legal theory and contracts law, including *Weimar: A Jurisprudence of Crisis* (with Bernhard Schlink, 2002). Professor Jacobson received his J.D. from Harvard Law School.

Jewish Law and Contemporary Issues

J. DAVID BLEICH
Benjamin N. Cardozo School of Law,
Yeshiva University

ARTHUR J. JACOBSON
Benjamin N. Cardozo School of Law,
Yeshiva University

CAMBRIDGE
UNIVERSITY PRESS

CAMBRIDGE
UNIVERSITY PRESS

32 Avenue of the Americas, New York, NY 10013-2473, USA

Cambridge University Press is part of the University of Cambridge.

It furthers the University's mission by disseminating knowledge in the pursuit of education, learning, and research at the highest international levels of excellence.

www.cambridge.org
Information on this title: www.cambridge.org/9780521765473

First published 2015

A catalog record for this publication is available from the British Library.

ISBN 978-0-521-76547-3 Hardback

Contents

Preface *page* vii

1 The Nature and Structure of Jewish Law 1

2 Divorce 18

3 Jewish Law and the State's Authority to Punish Crime 100

4 The Sotheby Sale 130

5 Torture and the Ticking Bomb 174

6 War 206

7 Dead or Alive? 252

8 Rabbinic Confidentiality 325

9 Cloning 357

A Note on Halakhic Sources 397

Transliteration Style 401

Index of Passages Cited 403

Index of Names and Subjects 407

Preface

Judaism is a religion of law and its legal system, known as Halakhah, is unique in that it has survived as a living system for millennia without being the law of any sovereign jurisdiction. Courses in Jewish law have of late become a staple of comparative law offerings in law schools and universities. Unhappily, as has been stated in a different context, "The students are many, but the knowledgeable are few."

Mastery of Jewish law requires years and years of long and arduous study. The Midrash (*Va-Yikra Rabbah* 2:1) declares: "A thousand [students] enter . . . but only one emerges" as a proficient scholar. For the uninitiated, the language barrier is itself a formidable obstacle. Rabbinic texts are written in a linguistic style dubbed by one classical commentator as a language of its own, "the language of the Talmudists" – a curious amalgam of rabbinic Hebrew and Aramaic with frequent incorporations of allusions to biblical and rabbinic texts of antiquity and replete with idioms and literary metaphors beyond the ken of all but the cognoscenti. Until relatively recently, recognized rabbinic scholars eschewed presentation of serious scholarship in the vernacular.

In order to appreciate the nature of Jewish law, it is necessary to recognize that it constitutes a self-contained system. It is founded upon a complex set of axiological premises, or *grundnorms*, that serve as the matrix of its internal coherence. A philosopher of science understands full well that the entire complement of the laws of nature as posited by science cannot be tested simultaneously. Any given hypothesis can be confirmed or disconfirmed only by assuming, at least for the purposes of that investigation, the constancy of all other axioms comprising the corpus of scientific knowledge. Thus, it can readily be shown that parallel lines do not converge, but that is true only of Euclidean space. Euclidean geometry is cogent and demonstrably certain only if basic premises regarding the nature of the universe are assumed. Much the same is true of the nature of halakhic discussion and dialectic. Little wonder, then, that persons trained primarily in other, quite different, legal systems and ideological traditions are ill-equipped to serve as exponents of Jewish law.

This volume constitutes an attempt to present Jewish law as it has been understood by its devotees and transmitted from generation to generation over a span of centuries, *viz.*, as an internally consistent system essentially impervious to external, historical and sociological influences.

The work is designed to introduce the contemporary reader to Jewish law as it was – and continues to be – understood in rabbinic academies. It is, after all, that system of Jewish law that divine providence has guided and caused to flourish and thrive.

American students are fully familiar with the casebook method. Law, in the United States, is not taught as a disembodied system of principles and statutes. Instead, the law is extracted from analysis of concrete applications. For a variety of reasons, a pure version of that method is not a feasible approach to an introductory study of Jewish law. But the method that is employed in the discussions undertaken herein is a reasonable approximation thereof. Those discussions are in the form of a quest for resolution of a series of concrete modern-day questions from the vantage point of Jewish law. The student will readily perceive the methodological similarity to the casebook method with which he or she is familiar. Common to both systems is the pedagogic device of extrapolation and elucidation of basic principles from their application in the analysis of identified problems.

Much of the material in this work has appeared in a somewhat different form in various volumes of J. David Bleich's *Contemporary Halakhic Problems* and *Bioethical Dilemmas*, vol. II. We extend our appreciation to the publishers of those volumes, Ktav Publishing House and Targum Press. Significant portions of Chapter 2 appeared in Volume 5 (2015) of the *International Journal of the Jurisprudence of the Family*, edited by Professor Scott FitzGibbon, to whom thanks are due for his valuable and incisive comments.

We are indebted to Professor Bernhard Schlink, of the faculty of law, Humboldt University in Berlin, who urged us to collaborate on this book. Without his encouragement this enterprise would not have become a reality.

We also wish to express our thanks to John Ludwig for preparing the index, to Hadassah Gurwitz for her meticulous proofreading, and to Kaaron Saphir and Sharon Thomas for their secretarial assistance.

It has been a singular pleasure to work with the editorial and production team of the Cambridge University Press. Our particular gratitude to John Berger for his patience, graciousness, and friendship.

1

The Nature and Structure of Jewish Law

Every legal system must grapple with a fundamental meta-legal question: Why should any person feel bound to obey its laws? This question is more commonly addressed in a graduate school philosophy seminar than in a class in law school. Law schools not only take notice of the existence of a system of laws but also presume that it is legitimate and that it commands obedience. The philosopher wants to know why *any* system of law should command obedience. Over millennia multiple answers have been formulated in response to this crucial meta-legal question.

Perhaps the most down-to-earth answer is the one Plato places in the mouth of Thrasymachus in the *Republic*, namely, that "might makes right."[1] Certainly, the only motive that prompts obedience to the law on the part of a citizen who lacks a commitment to a value system is that failure to obey will result in a significant financial penalty, incarceration or perhaps even more severe punishment. Such a person faces no moral dilemmas; he must simply choose between obeying the law and accepting the penalty for non-obedience: "You did the crime, you do the time." If one does not want "to do the time," then one must be scrupulous in avoiding the crime in the first place. The major flaw in terms of gaining acceptance of a legal system on that basis is that a person who believes that he is clever enough to avoid detection and consequent punishment really has very little reason to be law-abiding.

Immanuel Kant dealt with the problem by formulating the notion of the categorical imperative.[2] In effect, he argued, even a person who behaves immorally does not want others to emulate his conduct. Such a person

[1] Plato, *Republic*, book 3.

[2] Immanuel Kant, *Fundamental Principles of the Metaphysics of Morals*, trans. by Thomas Kingsmill Abbott (Seaside, OR, 1969); *Kant's Critique of Practical Reason and Other Works on the Theory of Ethics*, 6th ed., trans. by Thomas Kingsmill Abbott (London, 1909), pp. 32–42.

recognizes full well that were everyone to behave in a similar way life would be untenable. Therefore, he argues, a person must eschew any form of conduct that he would not be prepared to endorse as a universal norm. The flaw in that theory is quite similar to that inherent in the notion that "might makes right." Suppose a person could convince himself that others will remain ignorant of, or unaffected by, his conduct; all other people would remain law-abiding and moral. If that person could indeed flout the law without his conduct becoming universalized, why should he not do so?

Utilitarians would assert that acceptance of the rule of law is the only way to assure the greatest happiness of the greatest number of people. If the state maintains law and order, then a greater number of people are happier than if it does not. If the state does not maintain law and order, then some may indeed be able to secure disproportionate benefits and hence greater happiness but only at the expense, suffering and disproportionate unhappiness of others. Such a theory assumes that a person ought to be no less concerned for the happiness of others than for his own happiness. That proposition is far from self-evident.

Philosophers of natural law claim that notions of right and wrong, the moral and the immoral, are ingrained in the human psyche. It is noteworthy that the common law definition of insanity is an inability to comprehend the categories of right and wrong and to distinguish between them. Common law did not posit the ability to perceive particular acts or modes of conduct as moral and other acts or modes of conduct as immoral as the criteria of mental competence but it did equate failure to recognize the morally dichotomous nature of right and wrong as constituting a mental deficiency sufficient to preclude meting out penal sanctions for deviant behavior. Clearly, the ability to distinguish between right and wrong was regarded as innate in the normal human intellect just as the axioms of logic are grasped as *a priori* truths.

Natural law theorists go beyond that position in maintaining that not only is the perception of the existence of dichotomous categories of right and wrong innate but also that the content of each category can be grasped by the light of reason alone. In effect, these theorists believe that a person can intuitively recognize that X is good and Y is evil just as he or she can recognize that a rose is red and the sky is blue. Man is "programmed" to distinguish between good and evil just as he is programmed to distinguish between colors. But natural law goes far beyond positing a natural awareness of moral principles comparable to recognition of simple qualities such as X is red and Y is blue. Recognizing that X is red and Y is blue does not command the selection or the preference of X over Y or of Y over X; choosing between X and Y remains a matter of unconstrained individual choice. Proponents of natural law, however, maintain that the psyche does more than recognize that X is good and Y is evil; it transforms the "is" into an "ought" in legislating that I must choose X and eschew Y. The human intellect not only knows *a priori* that X is good and Y is evil but it also intuitively recognizes that a person *ought* to choose X and renounce Y. Accordingly, a person who disobeys the command of the intellect and makes the wrong moral choice deserves punishment. He or she has been forewarned and put on notice by his or her own moral consciousness.

Opponents of natural law respond by saying that they have examined their consciences and fail to discern any compelling intellectual force commanding them to recognize specific actions as good or bad or as commanding them to behave one way rather than another. Opponents of natural law reject the notion that the human conscience has binding legislative authority.

Is there or is there not an *a priori* moral awareness? A twentieth-century philosopher, William Frankena, categorized the natural law debate as one in which natural law theorists effectively depict their detractors, who assert that despite having plumbed their psyches they cannot discover the moral propositions posited by natural law theorists, as suffering from moral blindness, while philosophers who reject such *a priori* notions claim that natural law theorists suffer from moral hallucination.[3]

Perhaps the simplest answer advanced in response to the question, why one should obey the law, is theological: human beings ought to be law-abiding because it is divine will that humans obey the law. God has commanded man to obey the law. The sole remaining question is what law God has commanded us to obey. God has certainly commanded us to obey any law revealed by Him. The notion of the divine right of kings endows the king's law with the same status as divine law. In effect, the divine right of kings confers untrammeled legislative authority upon the monarch by divine authority. A more moderate version of divine right would limit the king's authority to measures designed to promote the welfare of society.

Of course, invoking obedience to the will of God to explain obedience to the law simply pushes the question back one step. Instead of asking, "Why should I obey the law?" one must ask, "Why should I obey God?" The answer likely to be forthcoming is simply a different form of one or another of the answers formulated as a response to the original question: God is all-powerful; God rewards and punishes. Moreover, there is no possibility for concealment and hence no escape from divine retribution. In effect, divine might gives rise to divine right. Alternatively, it might be suggested that human beings are endowed

[3] William K. Frankena, "The Naturalistic Fallacy," *Mind*, vol. 48, no. 192 (October 1939), pp. 474–76.

with an *a priori* awareness that they ought to obey the commands of the Deity. An eleventh-century Jewish philosopher, Baḥya ibn Pakuda, asserted that children recognize and appreciate the benefits that parents shower upon them and should reciprocate by endeavoring to please their parents. According to Baḥya, *a fortiori*, people should recognize that they are the beneficiaries of extraordinary divine largesse and intuitively apprehend a reciprocal obligation to please God by obeying His laws.[4]

Any attempt to understand the nature and content of the corpus of Jewish law – known in Hebrew as "Halakhah" – must begin with the awareness that it is a self-contained system predicated upon the axiological assumption that both its contents and canons of interpretation are the product of divine revelation. Thus it follows that man has no legal or moral right to manipulate the system in order to support predetermined conclusions, no matter how appealing or desirable they may seem. To be sure, human intellect may, and indeed must, be employed in order to apply Halakhah to novel or previously unexamined situations. But that process must be both intellectually honest and rigorous. In applying theory to practice the decisor must pursue the law to its logical conclusion. The underlying nature of the legal system is modified only by the narrowly defined and severely circumscribed legislative powers of properly constituted rabbinic bodies to create "fences" around the law, to promulgate social welfare legislation and to issue emergency *ad hoc* rulings.

In analyzing and applying any system of law, a scholar need not necessarily accept the basic principles of the system as wise or prudent. Thus, for example, an American constitutional law scholar need not accept the doctrine of separation of powers as either socially beneficial or politically pragmatic. But intellectual honesty compels him to analyze the legal status of an executive order or of a congressional enactment against the backdrop of that principle.

"You don't have to be Jewish to love Levy's Real Jewish Rye," read a New York subway advertisement of the 1960's and 70's. Similarly, one does not have to be Jewish to study or appreciate Halakhah. One need not necessarily be a professing Jew or accept the phenomenon of revelation at Sinai as a historical fact in order to engage in an analysis of Halakhah. But one must recognize that divine revelation at Sinai is the *grundnorm* of Halakhah. Perhaps more importantly, the student must recognize that, most assuredly, the scholars who over millennia served as exponents of Halakhah were men of intellectual honesty as well as moral probity and that their halakhic determinations were based upon the sincerely held assumption that the law was theirs to interpret only objectively, rather than subjectively, and certainly that they were powerless to

4 See Baḥya ibn Pakuda, *Ḥovot ha-Levavot, Sha'ar Avodat Elokim*, introduction.

modify the law other than in accordance with the very limited power conferred upon them.

Consistent with the notion that the ultimate source of Halakhah is revelation at Sinai is the recognition that the Pentateuch – the first five books of the Hebrew Bible – is primarily a legal document encapsulating that corpus of law. Rabbi Shlomoh Yitzchaki (1040–1105), better known as Rashi, and undoubtedly the foremost and most popular biblical commentator, makes the point quite eloquently. In his very first comment upon the Book of Genesis, Rashi observes that the Bible should properly have commenced with the commandments announced in Exodus 12, which is the beginning of the substantive legal material included in the Pentateuch. His point is cogent only in light of the assumption that the Pentateuch is a legal work. If so, it follows that the narratives and the historical information presented in the Book of Genesis and in the opening sections of Exodus are incongruous.

Rashi's response is perhaps even more striking. He informs us that ascription of the creation of the universe to God and the recounting of early human history is necessary to make the point that the entire world we inhabit belongs to the Deity. Those early sections of the Bible inform us how God apportioned the geographical areas of the known world among the nations of antiquity and established the Promised Land as the inheritance of the people of Israel. Thus, the early chapters of the Pentateuch are also a legal document but of a nature quite different from the ensuing text. Unlike the bulk of the Pentateuch, which is a record of divine legislation, those introductory sections constitute Israel's deed to the Land of Israel.

From recognition of the Pentateuch as a legal document it follows that every phrase and every word has legal significance. Students of law know that a word used in a statute sometimes has a meaning that is not synonymous with the meaning one would find in a dictionary. Thus, for example, everyone knows the difference in common parlance between a hospital and a nursing care facility. Nevertheless, for the purpose of some public health statutes, nursing care facilities are categorized as hospitals. Those statutes incorporate a preamble that is, in effect, a short glossary declaring that, for the purposes of that particular statute, a "hospital" is defined as including, *inter alia*, nursing care facilities. Accordingly, when endeavoring to understand any word in the Bible, it is necessary to appreciate the precise legal meaning of the word. When the contents of the Pentateuch were revealed to Moses he was, in effect, also given a glossary that would enable him to define each and every word. Those definitions were passed on together with the written text as part of the Oral Law.

An obvious example is explication of the meaning of Exodus 20:13. A common fundamentalist argument for abolishing the death penalty is that the Bible commands "Thou shalt not kill" (Exodus 20:13). In point of fact, such a verse does not exist. The Hebrew text reads "*lo taharog.*" The verse should be translated as "Thou shalt not commit an act of homicide." Not every act of killing is an act of homicide; homicide is carefully defined by statute. Self-defense is not homicide; the taking of human life in the course of legitimate warfare is not homicide; execution of a person convicted of a capital crime is not homicide. Quite obviously, a homicide statute must contain a precise definition of the nature of the action decreed to be a capital offense and, indeed, in Halakhah all such matters are defined very precisely.

This point may also be illustrated by examining Halakhah's definition of death. As is the case with every word used in human discourse, people may agree to use a word any way they wish. Different societies may use the same word in different ways; the same people may assign different meanings to a single word in different contexts. Thus, for example, there is a classical common law definition of death and a more recent neurological definition of death, while Rastafarians recognize only putrefaction as a criterion of death.

A precise formulation of the halakhic definition of death occurs for the first time in a nineteenth-century responsum by Rabbi Moses Sofer,[5] one of the most prominent rabbinic scholars of the day. Rabbi Sofer spells out in a clear and precise way the criteria of death as culled from much earlier halakhic sources. He then turns to the question of associating those criteria with the term "death" as used in the Bible. Essentially, his problem is how did the Sages of the Talmud arrive at their definition? Generally, such definitions are part of the Oral Law tradition. But one of the theories Rabbi Sofer advances is that the criteria of death reflect the received wisdom of the scientists of the biblical era. In effect, Rabbi Sofer says that the word "death" as it occurs in the Bible means what the physicians of antiquity would have understood by the term at that time in history. The meaning associated with the word then becomes enshrined in the biblical system of law, which uses the term in an immutable manner. The word retains that meaning for halakhic purposes for posterity even though its connotation in common parlance may have changed. It retains that meaning simply because that meaning was enshrined in the relevant statutes.

Recognition that biblical terms have a precise technical meaning points to the intrinsic link that exists between the Written Law and the Oral Law. Obviously, Moses had to be told how particular words should be understood and that information was conveyed to him at Sinai. In that sense, the Oral Law

[5] R. Moses Sofer, *Teshuvot Ḥatam Sofer, Yoreh De'ah*, no. 338.

serves as the preamble to the written text but was not committed to writing at Sinai.

It cannot be overemphasized that the Oral Law is in no way secondary to the Written Law. The Oral Law is no less valid, no less significant and no less authoritative than the Written Law. Together they constitute twin fonts of revelation. Indeed it may be said that the Oral Law is paramount because the Written Law means only what the Oral Law says it means. The notion that the Constitution of the United States means what the Supreme Court says it means is roughly analogous. The crucial difference is that the Written Law is not subject to untrammeled, subjective interpretation but is understood in light of a received tradition.

The Oral Law explains, amplifies and even modifies the plain meaning of the Written Law. Indeed, in many instances, it is virtually impossible to understand the Written Law without Oral Law interpretation. Take for example the verse "and they shall be for *totafot* between your eyes" (Deuteronomy 6:8). The King James translation of "*totafot*" as "frontlets" has no relationship to the Hebrew. In fact, the term "*totafot*" has no known Hebrew meaning; it appears in no other context. The Oral Law tradition declares the word to be a combination of two foreign words, each of which has the meaning "two" in different exotic languages. Two plus two equals four. Accordingly, the verse is interpreted as meaning that a four-chambered box must be placed upon the scalp above the eyes. Absent that explanation the verse would be devoid of meaning.

In some cases the Oral Law serves to define. In other cases it applies various principles of hermeneutic interpretation to uncover meanings not evident upon a literal reading. The principles to be utilized in interpreting a text are themselves part of the Oral Law tradition. Proper application of those canons of interpretation yields additional rules and principles. And, of course, both deductive reasoning and common sense are involved in the process of halakhic dialectic.

Not infrequently the contributors to the Talmud disagreed about how those principles should he applied and consequently they differed about the rules and regulations to be derived on their basis. Each scholar was certainly convinced that his position was correct and that of his colleagues untenable. Is there any way to adjudicate between such competing opinions?

The halakhic attitude to such controversies is encapsulated in the maxim "*Elu va-elu divrei Elokim ḥayyim* – These and those are the words of the living God" (*Eruvin* 13b and *Gittin* 6b). That notion reflects recognition that reasoning processes differ from person to person. Different persons can accept a single set of propositions, agree on the general canons of interpretation and yet reach mutually exclusive conclusions for the simple reason that "Just as their countenances are not alike so are their thought processes not alike" (Palestinian Talmud, *Berakhot* 9:5). When interpretive reasoning is entered into in a *bona fide* manner the human intellect cannot be "wrong." Different minds may reach different conclusions. The conclusions reached by the inquiring mind of a qualified scholar are, in a fundamental sense, infallible.

But how can two individuals reach contradictory conclusions and both be infallible? There is an apocryphal story of a rabbi who heard a dispute between two litigants. The plaintiff presented his case and the rabbi turned to him and said, "You are right." Thereupon the defendant presented his case and the rabbi turned to him and said, "You are right." At that point the rabbi's wife, who had been eavesdropping behind the door, entered the room and exclaimed, "But how can they both be right?" The rabbi turned to her and said, "You too are right!"

Paradoxical as it may seem, each of two conflicting views may be correct. The very nature of ambiguity is that it allows differing interpretations. In plumbing the meaning of a text, it must be recognized that if the text admits of a given interpretation that interpretation cannot be "wrong." By the same token if the text admits of a different interpretation that interpretation cannot be wrong either. Both interpretations are correct.

At times, human texts are drafted with deliberate ambiguity. During the events leading to adoption of Resolution 242 of the United Nations General Assembly concerning the return of territories controlled by Israel pursuant to the Six-Day War there was a debate about whether the resolution should call for return of all the territories or whether it should require return only of some of them. The compromise was to refer simply to "territories" without a modifier. Does the resolution, as drafted, call for return of all territories or only some? If some territories, does the resolution mean the lion's share of the territories or only limited areas? At times, such texts are purposely left ambiguous in order to achieve timely agreement among the parties while allowing disputed matters to be cloaked in ambiguities to be resolved at a later date. For the same reason, statutes are often drafted ambiguously because the legislature does not want to address certain issues. The legislator is perfectly willing to leave such issues for adjudication by the courts or to be resolved in some other way. At times, ambiguities that later arise in application of a statute may simply never have occurred to the draftsmen.

Similarly, many issues in American constitutional law hinge upon the interpretation of a phrase or clause in the Constitution. In at least some cases it is clear that the Framers purposely created ambiguity because protracted debate over every issue would have defeated all attempts to reach a consensus. As a result, many issues had to be resolved at a later time through either legislation or judicial interpretation.

The examination of issues in constitutional law with a view to determining whether one or another constitutional interpretation is correct leads to a conclusion that is not terribly different from examination of similar problems in Halakhah. Does provision of separate but equal educational facilities satisfy the requirement of the Equal Protection clause of the Fourteenth Amendment or is "separate" inherently unequal? There was a time before *Brown v. Board of Education* when the accepted doctrine was that the Equal Protection clause does not preclude racial segregation. Separate but equal satisfied the equal protection requirement because, after all, everybody was treated equally. The Supreme Court's decision in *Brown v. Board of Education* declares that separate is in its very nature unequal and, accordingly, that separate can never be equal. Does this now mean that the earlier decision in *Plessy v. Ferguson* was wrong, but earlier courts simply were not sagacious enough to realize that racial segregation is *ipso facto* antithetical to equality? Perhaps. If it can be demonstrated that the psychological burden of segregation necessarily creates inequality then, of course, the earlier doctrine was incorrect. If, on the other hand, the question whether separation inherently constitutes inequality is a matter of judgment, we then have a situation in which different people have made different judgment calls and there is no way to say who is right and who is wrong. We then have a legitimate disagreement between those who espoused the original doctrine and the court that issued the later decision.

To consider a mundane parallel, were one to be mistakenly convinced that there is some sort of transcendental truth embodied in the text of the Constitution, it would become necessary to formulate a doctrine to the effect that "*elu va-elu*– 'these and those' are the words of the Framers," i.e., "these and those" are both correct in the sense that each is consistent with the meaning imbedded in the Constitution by its authors. Indeed, if the framers of the Fourteenth Amendment had contemplated a dispute of the nature later addressed in *Plessy v. Ferguson* but could not agree upon whether separate was, or was not, inherently unequal, it is quite conceivable that they might have intended the ambiguity and purposely left the issue unresolved. Whether they did or did not is irrelevant; the text acquires a life and meaning or meanings of its own.

Jewish tradition is based upon the premise that the divinely dictated text of the Pentateuch was designed to be ambiguous and subject to multiple interpretations. This too reflects a fundamental principle of Halakhah and was recognized as such by the Sages. *Midrash Shoḥar Tov* 12:4 reports:

> Rabbi Yan'ai declared, "The words of the Torah were not given in final form (*ḥatukhin*). Rather, with regard to every single matter that the Holy One, blessed be He, told Moses, He enunciated forty-nine considerations [to render it] pure and forty-nine considerations [to render it] impure. Moses exclaimed before Him, 'Sovereign of the Universe, when shall we arrive at a clarification of Halakhah?' God said to him, 'According to the majority shall you decide (Exodus 23:2). If those who declare it impure are more numerous, it is impure; if those who declare it pure are more numerous, it is pure.'"

Clearly, the "matters" to which the Midrash refers are not those presented to Moses in an unequivocal manner in the context of the corpus of either the Written or the Oral Law. They are, then, matters with regard to which human intelligence must seek answers by grappling with principles and precedents firmly established within the system of Halakhah. Such endeavors constitute a dynamic and ongoing process.

Conflicting results were clearly the divine intention. The very fact that God allowed the text to be ambiguous means that He intended it to be so. But why should divine language be anything but unequivocal? That is not a legal question; it is a metaphysical or theological question.

The only cogent answer to that question is that God intended man to be His partner in the interpretation and development of Halakhah. Striking as it may seem, this is not a terribly novel theological notion – at least not in the Jewish tradition. Jewish tradition embraces the notion that the universe is not complete; rather, it is a work in progress. There is a well-known aggadic statement[6] to the effect that in the eschatological era the earth will produce baked foods and linen clothing. Putting aside the obvious prognostication inherent in the statement, that prediction reflects a profound theological insight: There was nothing to prevent God from creating a universe in which it would not be necessary to harvest wheat, thresh the grain, grind the kernels into flour and then knead the dough and bake the bread in an oven. God could have created a universe in which climate conditions cause winds to blow when kernels of wheat have developed to maturity. Such winds might be endowed with velocity sufficient to pulverize grain. That phenomenon might, in turn, be followed by rains capable of transforming the powder into a kind of dough whereupon the sun might emerge and shine so brightly that the dough would become baked into bread – all without human intervention. Instead of going out into the field and harvesting kernels of wheat man would harvest breadfruit ready for the table. God could have done the same thing with the flax plant. Instead of producing flax, the plant might have produced tiny strands of fabric capable

6 *Shabbat* 60b.

of weaving themselves into jackets, dresses and the like. But God chose not to. He chose not to create such a universe because, in effect, He chose to make man a partner in the process of creation. God is the Creator and man, in *imitatio Dei*, is bidden to engage in the labor necessary to complete the marvel of creation.[7]

Indeed, virtually all the biblical restrictions regarding human activity on the Sabbath are restrictions upon activities that bring to completion the work that God abruptly interrupted *in medias res* on the sixth day. God rested on the seventh day and left an unfinished and incomplete universe. Beginning on the eighth day, Adam was empowered to continue where God left off. Only in the end of days will man be relieved of that chore in order to be enabled to devote himself entirely to spiritual pursuits.[8]

Man is the partner of God not only in bringing the process of creation to fruition but also in the workings of God's providential guardianship of man. Man is commanded to engage in efforts to further his own interests, to preserve and restore his own health and to provide for his own needs. In doing so, man is assisting God in the exercise of providence and in the fulfillment of divine will.

God similarly made man His partner in the development of the corpus of Halakhah. Ambiguities abound; issues are left unaddressed; novel situations arise. Man must use the intellectual gifts bestowed upon him to complete the process of establishing a comprehensive system of Halakhah.

Since human intellect figures so prominently in this process disagreement is certainly to be anticipated. Disagreement is certainly legitimate and opinions of both "these and those," if arrived at conscientiously and with intellectual honesty, are equally valid. Nevertheless, clear determinations of law must be made in order to guide human conduct. Just as there are canons of interpretation there must also be canons of judicial decision-making.

In a world of transcendental truth there may well be contradictory propositions that are both true. But in the very real terrestrial world inhabited by human beings there must be a way to resolve ambiguities. Or to put the matter a bit differently, putting aside matters of legitimacy of interpretation, there must be canons of judicial decision-making. People must know how to act when scholars disagree. In the American legal system there are clearly formulated methods for making such determinations. If the majority of the members of a court are of one opinion and the minority are of another and both positions involve the interpretation of a phrase in the Constitution there is no absolute

7 R. Joseph Dov ha-Levi Soloveitchik, *Bet ha-Levi, Parashat Lekh Lekha*.

8 Cf. R. Jacob Zevi Mecklenburg, *Ha-Ketav ve-ha-Kabbalah*, Exodus 35:1.

right or absolute wrong. Nevertheless, offering a choice between the two opinions would result in legal and social chaos. To prevent that from happening we have adopted the principle of majority rule, i.e., the decision of the majority will be implemented. Does that mean that the majority is always correct? Let us assume that each of the five members of the majority was on academic probation throughout his or her law school career, failed to establish any scholarly credentials before being appointed to the bench and, moreover, was named to the judiciary only as the result of political influence. Let us further assume that each of the four members of the minority was an outstanding law student, had previously been a highly regarded professor of constitutional law at one of the leading law schools in the United States and was recognized as a leading legal scholar. Our legal system declares that all votes are counted equally: One man, one vote; five to four, the majority wins. Neither an epistemologist nor a legal scholar is likely to agree that the five are "right" and the four are "wrong" in any abstract sense of right and wrong. But we are dealing with rules of judicial decision-making, not rules of truth-determination. We might have had different canons. Surely, we could conceive of a system in which nine people are appointed to the Supreme Court and in every case before the court each justice is entitled to one vote for every law review article that he has published in the course of his lifetime with the result that the justice who has authored fifty law review articles is given fifty votes and the justice who has written only a single law review article receives only one vote. To be sure, that would be a rather crude way of measuring scholarship but it would certainly represent an attempt to assign weight to erudition and scholarship and a negation of the extension of the democratic notion of one man one vote to the judicial arena. Certainly in other areas, e.g., medical treatment, no one would accept the mode of treatment embraced by the majority of general practitioners over a mode of treatment advocated by a smaller number of preeminent specialists.

Halakhah certainly recognizes the need to establish rules of judicial decision-making. The Talmud declares, "These and those are the words of the living God but the law is in accordance with the House of Hillel" (*Eruvin* 13b). Halakhah incorporates a number of rules of decision-making, some of which are virtually intuitive and some of which are not at all obvious. The first rule is that the judiciary established in any given jurisdiction is the ultimate authority for that jurisdiction unless and until there is a binding rule announced by the supreme judicial body, which then becomes binding on all of Jewry. As a result, in times of yore, there were conflicting practices in different jurisdictions.

The Mishnah, *Shabbat* 130a, records that there was a difference of opinion between Rabbi Eliezer and Rabbi Akiva with regard to whether preparations necessary in order to carry out a circumcision on the Sabbath might be undertaken on the Sabbath itself when those acts involve what would otherwise constitute desecration of the Sabbath. The letting of blood, although ordinarily forbidden on the Sabbath, is intrinsic to the act of circumcision and is expressly permitted on the Sabbath because it cannot be performed prior to the eighth day following parturition. But preparations for the procedure can be made in advance. In antiquity, instead of sterilizing instruments it was the practice to "sterilize" the infant. Bathing the baby in hot water was mandatory before one would dare to perform the act of circumcision. Circumcision without bathing the baby in hot water was prohibited as posing an undue risk to the infant. But what is the rule in a situation in which people neglected to boil water in advance? Is it permissible to boil the water on the Sabbath in order not to delay the circumcision? Suppose there is no fuel or that there is no fire. May one chop down a tree and build a fire to boil the water to bathe the baby in order to carry out the circumcision?

The majority opinion, and hence the normative rule, is that it is only the act of circumcision itself that may be performed on the Sabbath; any antecedent act of Sabbath desecration that might have been performed before the Sabbath dare not be performed on the Sabbath even if, through negligence or otherwise, those responsible for carrying out the circumcision failed to do so before the Sabbath. However, Rabbi Eliezer dissented and ruled that such acts are indeed permitted and consequently he sanctioned that practice in his jurisdiction. The talmudic narrative tells us that in the city in which Rabbi Eliezer served as the chief rabbinic judge this was done on a regular basis. In a neighboring town someone who acted in a similar manner would have been charged with a capital offense. Differing rules were adopted in different jurisdictions.

The jurisdiction of local authorities flows directly from the biblical verse "Judges and court officers you shall appoint to yourselves in all of your gates" (Deuteronomy 16:18). Every city is required to appoint its own judicial authority and the citizenry may and must act in reliance upon that authority unless the issue has been resolved by a decision of the Great Court, i.e., the Sanhedrin sitting in the Temple precincts in Jerusalem. The decision of that body is, in effect, a Supreme Court decision that is binding upon all inferior courts. However, unless and until such a decision is forthcoming there is no single uniform and monolithic ruling binding on everyone. Disagreements among members of a particular court, including disagreement among members of the Sanhedrin, are resolved on the basis of majority rule.

Unlike other systems of law, in Halakhah policy considerations are irrelevant and not a factor to be taken into consideration in judicial decision-making.

A civil court dealing with a human system of law may well seek guidance in legislative history, may consider how social policies fostered by the statute may best be implemented, may examine relevant values and institutions, etc., and then interpret the statute in a manner that will best reflect those considerations and advance those particular goals.

Decision-making in Halakhah does not operate that way. Indeed, it could not operate that way for the simple reason that it is often extremely difficult and even impossible to determine what the relevant "policy considerations" might be. Delineation of policy considerations would require that man fathom the reason or the rationale underlying any particular legal provision. Although it is perfectly legitimate for man to endeavor to understand why certain laws were promulgated, nevertheless, when the underlying rationale is not announced in either the Written Law or the oral tradition, it remains at best a matter of speculation and hence cannot be accepted as part of the legal corpus. The result is that, in its application, particular provisions of Halakhah are often quite divorced from what one might presume to be their underlying rationale.

A halakhic scholar who is attempting to understand and apply the law must not begin with a determination that he regards as wise or the goal that he assumes the legal system seeks to advance and then work back and try to substantiate that conclusion on the basis of legal argumentation. In other systems of law, it may be perfectly legitimate to assume that certain results are compatible with the thrust of a statute or with the nature of the legal system and then to proceed to seek justification using various forms of legal dialectic. In Halakhah, that is not a legitimate mode of procedure. In Halakhah the principle is that a scholar must begin with the given, i.e., the raw material, the legal principles and statutes as they are formulated, then apply canons of interpretation and deductive reasoning in a *bona fide* manner in order to reach the necessary conclusion. The conclusion will not necessarily be the conclusion that the scholar might wish to reach but it will be the one he feels compelled to reach on the basis of the legal evidence. That methodological principle is captured in the rabbinic aphorism "*Yikov ha-din et ha-har*" (*Yevamot* 92a and *Sanhedrin* 5a), which translated literally means, "Let the law pierce the mountain!"

Obviously, lack of authority to modify the legal system by means of innovative interpretation can lead to situations in which corrective measures of some type are necessary, or at least are perceived as being necessary, because the purpose of the law seems to have been thwarted. However, that does not mean that the halakhic decisor has the right to engage in intellectual gymnastics in order to reach what he believes to be a more satisfactory conclusion. The practical or the social problems that may arise are addressed by means of applying rabbinic authority to promulgate *takkanot*, i.e., rabbinic legislation, or by constructing devices designed to harness provisions of the law as a means that makes it possible to escape the harshness or the onus of the law that would result if the law were allowed to run its own course.

Thus there are situations in which it is quite evident that the ultimate purpose of the law is not being advanced by applying the technicalities of the law, e.g., the law that provides that the firstborn of domestic animals be offered as a sacrifice in the Temple. Today, with the destruction of the Temple, that is no longer a possibility. But since there is no license to dispense with the law itself the only expedient available is to modify circumstances so that different provisions of law will apply, i.e., to sell the pregnant animal to a non-Jew to whose animals such rules do not pertain. Contemporary use of a "device" to avoid transgressing the letter of the law is probably best exemplified in the development of the *hetter iska*. That device is designed to transform what otherwise would have been a simple loan agreement into a joint venture in order to allow the financier to profit from the enterprise without running afoul of the prohibition against interest-taking. The effect of a *hetter iska* is to transform the technical nature of a transaction so that a different set of rules will apply.

The maxim "These and those are the words of the living God" has as its concomitant the notion that revelation, or more precisely, legal revelation, is a once in an eternity phenomenon. That is clearly a very profound theological doctrine. It is unique to Judaism and it explains why, insofar as Judaism is concerned, there cannot be a second, superseding revelation. Revelation at Sinai was unique and there never will a comparable revelation that will result in a new covenant.[9] The Sinaitic code will not be repealed in whole or in part; it will not be amended, modified or supplemented. Nor is it subject to further divine interpretation or resolution of ambiguities.

That principle is not simply theological in nature; it speaks directly to the core of the system of Halakhah itself. The principle is based upon the biblical verse "*lo ba-shamayim hi*– [the Torah] is not in Heaven" (Deuteronomy 30:12). Literally, the verse means that the Torah is not beyond human comprehension: "It is not in Heaven that you should say, 'Who will go to Heaven and bring it down to us?' . . . Neither is it beyond the ocean that you shall say, 'Who will cross the ocean to bring it back to us?' . . . But the matter is close to you, in your mouth and in your heart to fulfill" (Deuteronomy 30:12–14). Rabbinic exegesis understands the phrase "it is not in Heaven" as meaning that now that the contents of the Pentateuch have been presented to man, God has surrendered

9 Rambam, *Mishneh Torah, Hilkhot Yesodei ha-Torah* 9:1.

His law-giving prerogative together with all further authority with regard to development of the law or its interpretation.

Before revelation at Sinai the Torah was in Heaven but now it has been given to man in its entirety. As Rambam (Maimonides) carefully spells out in his *Mishneh Torah, Hilkhot Yesodei ha-Torah* 9:1, the notion that the Torah has been given to man means: (1) it cannot be recalled, rescinded, changed, annulled or abrogated; and (2) it cannot be modified by God because modification is a form of change. Not only can the Torah not be modified but if there is a matter requiring clarification or interpretation God will not perform that function.

The principle "it is not in Heaven" means that after revelation at Sinai the Torah is in the hands of man, i.e., interpretation of the laws contained in the Pentateuch, resolution of any ambiguity and application to novel circumstances are left to man. The revealed corpus of law contains many broad principles applicable to situations that could not have been envisioned by the human intellect at the time of revelation at Sinai. It may be presumed that if Moses were to have been asked whether it is permissible to open a refrigerator door on the Sabbath he would have been at a loss to answer unless an explanation of the workings of an electric motor and the nature of a refrigerator would have been forthcoming. Yet the answer, and perhaps even multiple, contradictory answers, was already inherent in the Torah that he presented to the ancient Israelites. The principles were already present; it is issue analysis that is necessary in order to discover the answer.

One ramification of that doctrine is that, were an individual to establish himself as a prophet and then claim that he had received a prophetic revelation enabling him to adjudicate between two conflicting views with regard to a matter of Halakhah or were he to claim to interpret a certain principle or provision of Halakhah[10] on the basis of prophetic insight, he would be condemned by his own mouth as a false prophet. Since prophecy of that nature is impossible any person making such a claim is clearly lying; he is a false prophet because he is prophesying in a sphere in which there can be no prophecy and hence is guilty of a capital transgression.

The legal corpus revealed at Sinai is a unitary whole. Thus, Halakhah is first and foremost a comprehensive, self-contained legal system. Yet it is a legal system that also presumes profound faith commitments that fashion its methodology. No wonder, then, that rabbinic scholars have always felt that they bear an awesome responsibility. Their charge is to navigate new waters with utmost fidelity to received instructions and to resolve novel issues on

[10] *Loc. cit.*

the basis of ancient sources. In doing so they have always been keenly aware that they must strive to sublimate subjective predilections in endeavoring to uncover the mysteries of divine reason. But above all, they have always recognized that they must be ever mindful of their unique role as delegates of the Deity in interpreting and transmitting the eternal verities of the Torah. But it is precisely because of those considerations that the study of Halakhah is an intellectual experience *par excellence*.

2

Divorce

Jews loyal to the teachings and practice of their faith are not free to enter into a marriage unless any prior marriage has been terminated by the death of the spouse or dissolved by the execution of a divorce in the form recognized by Jewish law. In Jewish law, divorce is effected by means of a *get* delivered by the husband (or his agent) to the wife (or her agent). A *get* is a document, usually written by a scribe at the behest of the husband, reciting the names of the parties, the date and place of its drafting, and containing a statement declaring the document to be a bill of divorce that serves to dissolve the marital relationship. The source of the *get* is Deuteronomy 24:3: "... and he shall write her a bill of divorce [*get*] and give it into her hand and send her from his house." Myriad technicalities must be observed both in drafting and delivery in order for the *get* to be effective.

In recent times, there have been an increasing number of cases in which a couple obtains a divorce in civil court, but one of the parties subsequently refuses to cooperate in the execution of a *get*. The refusal is often motivated by animosity or by a desire to use the *get* to extract financial or custodial concessions.

During much of the medieval period European Jewish communities constituted a virtual *imperium in imperio* in their host countries. Jews were denied many of the rights and freedoms enjoyed by the general population. Paradoxically, it was their status as an alien and despised community that served as the basis for granting Jewish communities judicial autonomy. Jewish communities were commonly authorized to establish independent judicial systems for adjudicating monetary disputes among members of the community. At times these courts had jurisdiction over criminal matters as well. But of greatest social and religious significance was the absolute authority of the courts over matters of marriage and divorce. No Jew, male or female, could enter into a marriage without their acquiescence. Hence, no Jew, male or female, could enter into a second marriage unless any first marriage was terminated by death of the spouse or by execution of a religious divorce. Civil marriage did not exist.

With emancipation and the conferral of civil rights upon Jews, a process that began in the Napoleonic era, the courts of the Jewish communities lost exclusive authority over marriage and divorce. Thus, a secular court could terminate a marriage valid under religious law and thus authorize remarriage of the parties. Although valid under civil law, civil divorce decrees have no religious significance.

When both spouses profess allegiance to Jewish law and both wish to be free to enter into a new marriage, they can readily execute a *get*, and thus satisfy the requirements of Jewish law. But one spouse may be unconcerned with religious law and thus with religious proscriptions against remarriage without a prior *get*, or may not contemplate remarriage and by reason of acrimony or malice or greed seek to prevent the other from entering into a new marriage.

Typically it is the husband who refuses to participate in execution of the *get*, not the wife. To be sure, since an eleventh-century edict issued by Rabbenu Gershom of Mainz (960–1040), no religious divorce may be effected without the consent of the wife,[1] and thus, by refusing to accept a *get* a wife may prevent the remarriage of her estranged husband. However, in practice, it typically proves much easier to secure the compliance of a recalcitrant wife than that of a recalcitrant husband. Although plural marriages are now banned by another of Rabbenu Gershom's edicts, biblical law does permit polygamy. In certain limited circumstances, e.g., insanity or mental incapacity of the first wife, a man may marry a second wife even after Rabbenu Gershom's edict. Another exception to the ban against polygamous marriage permits a husband whose wife has abandoned him to remarry if the wife refuses to accept a bill of divorce. Since the Bible does not prohibit polygamy and it is the wife who caused the marriage to disintegrate, and since it is she who refuses to accept a divorce, it would be inequitable for rabbinic legislation (*takkanah*) to bar the husband from establishing a viable marital relationship. However, the edict of Rabbenu Gershom does require that a minimum of one hundred Torah scholars domiciled in at least three different jurisdictions certify that the second marriage is justified by one of the grounds for dispensation to commit polygamy. The rationale underlying this exception to the ban against plural marriage is particularly compelling if the purpose of the edict against plural marriage was to safeguard the welfare and status of the wife. A woman who has

[1] See Rema, *Shulḥan Arukh, Even ha-Ezer* 119:6.

abandoned her husband and home without leave of a *bet din* (rabbinic court) is not entitled to such protection. Hence, unless the wife professes a desire to reunite with her husband, the wife's refusal to accept a subsequent *get* may entitle the husband to a dispensation to remarry – a *hetter me'ah rabbanim* (dispensation by one hundred rabbis). Often realization that, in light of her own intransigence, the husband's petition for a *hetter me'ah rabbanim* is likely to be granted is enough to make the wife willing to negotiate the execution of a religious divorce.

Since biblical law forbids polyandry, no provision equivalent to the *hetter me'ah rabbanim* could be granted to the wife. In the absence of a valid *get* a marriage subsequently contracted by the wife would, from the perspective of Jewish law, be adulterous and its issue would suffer the stigma of bastardy. Since no device similar to the *hetter me'ah rabbanim* could be devised to enable the wife to remarry, it is not surprising that the number of women prevented from remarrying for religious reasons far exceeds the number of men.

Post-emancipation Jewish communities increasingly confront the problem of the *agunah*, the "chained" woman denied consortium and other marital prerogatives but unable to enter into a new marriage because her husband refuses to give her a *get*. In an age of increasing divorce rates what was once the tragic plight of the few has become a significant societal problem. The husband's own desire to be free to enter into a second marriage once provided a measure of self-interest sufficiently strong to guarantee cooperation. Moreover, an autonomous judiciary had other coercive measures available. With the loss of formal judicial authority there remains only the power of moral persuasion. But moral authority too has eroded, leaving little or no recourse against a recalcitrant husband. As a result there has arisen a pressing need to find a way to ensure that a Jewish husband will not avail himself of civil divorce while refusing to make it possible for his estranged wife to remarry with ecclesiastic blessing.

Yet courts in the United States and other Western countries have often misconceived Jewish divorce and consequently taken the position that judicial process is incapable of compelling a recalcitrant husband to give his wife a *get*. Divorce in the United States is reserved to the jurisdiction of the states, none of which recognizes the authority of ecclesiastic tribunals. Moreover, the First Amendment to the U.S. Constitution bars judicial entanglement in religion, and religious divorce would seem to require just such entanglement.

More considered examination, however, suggests a different perspective. (1) A *get* is not a decree of a rabbinic court but an instrument that gains effect solely by action of the parties themselves. It is in effect the rescission of a contract by mutual consent. (2) The giving of the *get* is not a sacerdotal or religious act. It is not an act of worship; it does not invoke the Deity; it involves neither profession of creed nor confession of faith. A court would not construe the execution of a contract or promissory note in accordance with the forms and procedures of Jewish law as a religious act. Indeed, Judaism itself regards execution of the *get* as a mundane act comparable to the rescission of a contract.

I. RELIGIOUS DIVORCE EXECUTED IN A FOREIGN COUNTRY

American courts have consistently recognized the validity of a religious divorce obtained in another country and valid according to its laws.

Leshinsky v. Leshinsky[2] was the first American case to consider recognition of a foreign religious divorce. A husband married in Illinois sought to annul his marriage on the grounds that the wife still had a husband from a prior marriage. She had been married in Russia. She and her first husband had dissolved their marriage by means of a Jewish divorce in Russia before she immigrated to America. Her second husband argued that because religious divorce is invalid in the United States, their marriage in Illinois was a nullity. The court (a New York trial court) rejected the argument. Although the state religion of Russia did not recognize divorce, Russian law delegated authority to other religious groups to grant divorce to their members. Applying a principle of comity, the court ruled "that a divorce regularly obtained, according to the laws of the country where the marriage is celebrated, and where the parties are domiciled, (both ingredients concurring,) will be held a complete dissolution of the marriage contract in every other country . . . and this, whether the ground for divorce be one recognized as such in this state or not."[3] Thus, because Russian law recognized the validity of a Jewish divorce, the courts of New York must recognize its validity as well. "There is nothing in the mode of divorce," said the court, "repugnant to our institutions, or detrimental to society. On the contrary, such matters must be considered fully as safe in the hands of the church to which the parties belong as in any judicial branch of government."[4]

Every decision since *Leshinsky* has agreed: When a married couple executes a Jewish divorce in a foreign jurisdiction whose laws recognize the validity of the divorce, American courts will also recognize its validity.[5] However,

[2] 5 Misc. 495, 25 N.Y.S. 841 (Sup. Ct. 1893).

[3] *Id.* at 496, 25 N.Y.S.2d at 842.

[4] *Id.*

[5] See Miller v. Miller, 70 Misc. 368, 128 N.Y.S. 787 (Sup. Ct. 1911); *In re* Spondre, 98 Misc. 524, 162 N.Y.S. 943 (Sur. Ct. 1917); Machransky v. Machransky, 31 Ohio App. 482, 166 N.E. 423 (1927).

recognition of a Jewish divorce executed *within* the United States is quite a different matter.

II. A *GET* EXECUTED IN THE UNITED STATES

In *Kantor v. Bloom*,[6] an American court for the first time addressed the legal impact of a *get* executed in the United States. A woman appearing before a Connecticut probate court as Sarah Kantor had married her first spouse, Solomon Rubin, in Russia. They subsequently immigrated to America and continued to live together as husband and wife until they executed a religious divorce before a rabbi in Brooklyn. Shortly after, both parties remarried in religious ceremonies, apparently without benefit of a civil license. Solomon then died intestate. Sarah sued the administrator of his estate in probate court claiming to be Solomon's lawful widow and hence entitled to a statutory share of the estate. At the time of her appearance before the court, Sarah had been continuously living with Kantor, her second spouse, for seventeen years and had borne him two children. A Connecticut statute deprived a surviving spouse, "who, without sufficient cause, had abandoned the other, and had continued such abandonment to the time of the other's death," of his or her share of the other's estate. The probate court ruled against Sarah on the grounds that she had abandoned Solomon without cause and continued the abandonment until his death.

On appeal, the Supreme Court of Errors of Connecticut agreed:

> This plaintiff has twice solemnly and ceremonially renounced all her marital rights and duties towards Rubin, once by the rabbinical divorce of 1893, and again by the rabbinical marriage to Kantor in the same year, and for 17 years has lived with Kantor as his wife, has borne him children, and still continues to live with him. A more complete case of an actual abandonment of the lawful husband cannot well be imagined.[7]

Sarah's argument was that separation by mutual consent does not constitute desertion,[8] and that "the rabbinical divorce of 1893 was in legal effect an agreement by the parties for a permanent separation, with permission to marry again according to the custom of their religion."[9] Therefore, her subsequent marriage to Kantor followed by seventeen years of married life

6 90 Conn. 210, 96 A. 974 (1916).

7 *Id.* at 213, 96 A. at 975.

8 "A married partner who concurs in the other's going away cannot complain of the going. In consequence whereof, a separation by the mutual consent of the parties is not desertion in either." *Bishop on Marriage and Divorce* (1891), vol. I, § 1690.

9 90 Conn. at 213, 96 A. at 975.

in Kantor's home all took place with the consent of her first husband. The court rejected the argument. "A voluntary separation," it said, "is not a license to commit adultery."[10] Adultery following a voluntary separation constitutes abandonment. The court noted that even were it to agree with Sarah that execution of a *get* is tantamount to consent, the "plaintiff, by throwing aside the mantle of her religion and claiming now to be the lawful widow of Rubin, necessarily characterizes her rabbinical marriage with Kantor as adulterous."[11]

Two years after *Kantor*, a similar question came before a New York trial court in *Shilman v. Shilman*[12] and resulted in a very different ruling. Max and Lizza Shilman married in Odessa, Russia and immigrated to the United States. They separated and obtained a religious (but not a secular) divorce. Lizza returned to Odessa and remarried. Max petitioned for divorce on grounds of adultery. Citing language in the *get* freeing the wife to marry any man of her choosing, the trial court dismissed the petition. "The offense complained of...," said the court, "was committed by the procurement or with the connivance of the plaintiff."[13] The Appellate Division, followed by the New York Court of Appeals, affirmed on appeal, both without opinion.[14] Only one justice, in the Appellate Division, dissented:

> Of course the law does not recognize the so-called "get" or Hebrew divorce, but it does not seem to me that the consent of these ignorant people in going through this sort of a procedure can be held either as matter of fact or in law as constituting *per se* the connivance or procurement which the law brands as a bar to the legal remedy of divorce on account of a subsequent adultery...

10 *Id.* at 216, 96 A. at 976 (quoting Franklin v. Franklin, 154 Mass. 515, 517, 28 N.E. 681, 682 (1891)).

11 *Id.*

12 105 Misc. 461, 174 N.Y.S. 385 (Sup. Ct. 1918), *aff'd*, 188 A.D. 908, 175 N.Y.S. 681 (1919), *aff'd*, 230 N.Y. 554, 130 N.E. 890 (1920) (per curiam).

13 105 Misc. at 461, 174 N.Y.S. at 385.

14 230 N.Y. 554, 130 N.E. 890 (1920) (per curiam). See also Preger v. Preger, [1926] 42 T.L.R. 281, an English case in which there is the suggestion that, if one party consented to a *get* knowing that the other party contemplated living with another person of the opposite sex, acquiescence in the *get* might be evidence of conniving at the adultery. This suggestion is reiterated in another English case, Leeser v. Leeser. For a discussion of these two British cases, see Susan Maidment, "The Legal Effect of Religious Divorces," *Modern Law Review*, vol. 37 (1974), pp. 611, 617. Maidment argues:

> [W]hile the two decisions are correct on their facts, it is undesirable to allow consent to a Get ever to amount to connivance or conduct conducing, for it allows ignorance of the civil law to operate against the petitioner. Whether the parties are aware of the fact or not, a Get cannot have the effect of dissolving the marriage, and can therefore not have the effect of allowing the parties to remarry and to commit adultery.

> So far as appears by this record the husband and wife merely separated by consent and she went back to Russia. I am at a loss to find any basis for the proposition that thereby the plaintiff contemplated that his wife would commit adultery and certainly not that he connived at or procured such act.
>
> It seems to me that the statute denying the aid of the court in an action for divorce contemplates evil intent and active participation in bringing about the defilement of the spouse and that mere voluntary separation is not sufficient.[15]

The decisions in *Shilman* and *Kantor* stand in sharp contradiction to one another. In *Kantor*, the Connecticut court rejected Sarah's claim to the statutory share in her first husband's estate because it refused to acknowledge execution of a *get* as "a license to commit adultery." In *Shilman*, the court described execution of a *get* as "connivance" at adultery. In fact, the Connecticut court in *Kantor*, although correct in result, was inaccurate in its characterization of sexual relationships pursuant to the granting of a *get*, whereas the New York court in *Shilman* was entirely accurate. Execution of a *get* is, in fact, a "mutual license" to commit what in the absence of a secular divorce the secular law calls adultery. The phrase incorporated in the text of the *get*, "and you are permitted to every man" (literally, "and you are unfettered with regard to every man"), is an explicit and unequivocal license to seek a new husband. Thus, if the state refuses to recognize the efficacy of a *get* in dissolving a marriage, execution of a *get* may well be seen as condoning behavior that the state regards as adulterous.

The *Kantor* court did raise an issue that it did not unequivocally resolve: Does execution of a *get* by itself establish abandonment or merely consensual separation? To be sure, the court did accord the *get* in *Kantor* a quasi-legal status, either as a separation agreement or as an instrument establishing abandonment. But the court's finding of abandonment rested upon more than execution of the *get*; it rested also upon Sarah's religious remarriage to Kantor, together with her living with him as his wife for seventeen years and bearing him two children. It was in light of the totality of these facts that the Connecticut court, both in equity and as a consequence of legislative intent, treated Sarah's behavior as abandonment. To permit her, said the court, "to share in the estate which Rubin accumulated during the seventeen years while she was living as the wife of another man, and so to diminish the share of Rubin's children, would be to perpetuate the very injustice which the legislature intended to prevent."[16] It would, from that perspective, have been a miscarriage of justice to allow Sarah to claim a statutory share despite subsequent marriage

[15] 188 A.D. at 909, 175 N.Y.S. at 681–82 (Clarke, J., dissenting).
[16] 90 Conn. at 217, 96 A. at 976.

to another man. This conclusion rests upon firm legal grounds that are quite independent of the nature of a *get*. As noted by the court, the crucial issue in determining abandonment is the presence or absence of intent to return to the spouse, resume marital duties and claim marital rights. In *Kantor*, both parties had subsequently remarried in religious ceremonies. Scripture explicitly forbids a remarried divorcee to return to her first husband even following dissolution of the second marriage.[17] Sarah, who was scrupulous in following Jewish law in arranging for a religious divorce and remarriage even while ignoring civil law, could not have envisioned resuming marital rights and duties as the wife of her former husband. Hence, in *Kantor*, a state of abandonment based upon intent never to resume marital rights or duties certainly did exist. The court was correct in its crucial finding that "the rabbinical divorce between Rubin and the plaintiff was a separation with intent never to resume their marital rights or duties, and that intent was clinched by the subsequent rabbinical marriages of both parties."[18]

The unresolved issue is whether religious divorce, absent "subsequent rabbinical marriage" to "clinch" the parties' intent, would have constituted abandonment. Although the state cannot recognize a *get* as an instrument effecting dissolution of a marriage, the language of the *get* does establish that there exists "a separation with intent never to resume . . . marital rights or duties."[19] As such, the *get* might well be recognized as evidence, not of voluntary separation or of a license to commit adultery, but of mutual recognition that a state tantamount to "abandonment" exists.[20]

[17] Deuteronomy 24:1–4.

[18] 90 Conn. at 216–17, 96 A. at 976.

[19] *Id.*

[20] Although the court in *Kantor* described the *get* itself as establishing mutual separation or abandonment by the wife, it is uncertain that a similar conclusion would have been reached had the husband exerted pressure upon the wife to accept a *get*.

The related question of whether execution of a *get* defeats divorce on grounds of abandonment was raised in an English case. In Joseph v. Joseph, [1953] 2 All E.R. 710, a wife petitioned for divorce alleging that her husband had deserted her for the period required by statute. However, during that period the husband had acceded to the wife's request and granted her a *get*. The court ruled that as a result of the *get* the parties were thereafter living apart by consent and so a divorce could not be granted on grounds of desertion. In construing the wife's attempt to secure a *get* as consent to desertion Jenkins, L.J., said: "I cannot accept the position that where a Get . . . has been given by a husband to a wife with the approval of the *Beth Din* . . . it could be consistent with the religious obligations of those two persons to ignore the *Get* and live together as man and wife." *Id.* at 712.

However, in Corbett v. Corbett, [1957] W.L.R. 486, the court held that the wife's consent to a *get* did not terminate the husband's desertion. In *Corbett* the wife, at the instigation of the husband, acceded to the *get* but did not, according to the evidence, really consent to her

The Connecticut decision, however, was not the end of the matter. Despite her defeat in Connecticut, Sarah Kantor asserted dower rights the very next year in litigation in New York against a purchaser of real estate conveyed by Rubin before his death.[21] In that action, Sarah claimed that her religious divorce had no legal effect, but that both parties wrongly regarded the *get* as sufficient in law to dissolve their marriage. Despite this contention, the trial court ruled that she might be estopped from exercising her rights against the innocent purchaser because she "must be deemed a party to the creation of a situation which without her participation the husband, it must be assumed, would not have entered into."[22] Interestingly, the court did not deny Sarah dower rights in the estate of her husband – a matter that was not directly before the court. On the contrary, it recognized her right of dower and the applicability of the law requiring a wife to join in her husband's conveyance of real estate,[23] but as a matter of equity, the trial court estopped her from asserting those rights against an innocent purchaser.

On appeal, the Appellate Division upheld the verdict against Sarah, but in the process extended a certain recognition of the *get* absent in the decision of the trial court. The court found estoppel upon combined grounds: "(a) the rabbinical divorce, wherein she was the complainant; (b) her knowledge of Rubin's remarriage with her acquiescence; (c) her own remarriage, followed by 23 years consortium with Kantor."[24] Thus far the court was concerned

husband leaving her. The court found that the wife's consent was merely technical and she did not want her husband to leave her. *Joseph* was distinguished on its facts.

Indeed, there is no reason why acceptance of a *get* should defeat a petition for divorce based on abandonment. A petition based on abandonment does not in itself constitute an agreement to separate even though, if granted, the divorce would endow the separation with permanence. Were such an action to constitute an agreement to separate, divorce based on abandonment would effectively be precluded, since presentation of a petition based on abandonment would nullify the very grounds of the petition. The logic underlying the validity of such a petition must reside in a distinction between recognition and acquiescence. Recognition that abandonment has occurred does not entail consent to its occurrence. Hence a petition for divorce based on abandonment does not connote agreement to separate: it signifies only a preference for the status of divorcee over the status of abandonee. Although the *get* has no civil effect in terminating the marriage, it should be construed by the courts as an instrument designed to accomplish for purposes of religious law precisely the same results that are attendant upon a divorce in civil law. Thus, consent to execution of a *get* does not constitute consent to the existing separation any more than a petition for divorce under such circumstances constitutes an agreement to separate.

[21] Kantor v. Cohn, 98 Misc. 355, 164 N.Y.S. 383 (Sup. Ct. 1917), *aff'd*, 181 A.D. 400, 168 N.Y.S. 846 (1918).

[22] 98 Misc. at 359, 164 N.Y.S. at 385.

[23] *Id.* at 362–63, 164 N.Y.S. at 387–88.

[24] 181 A.D. at 403, 168 N.Y.S. at 848.

only with the question of equitable estoppel and the natural consequences of Sarah's own actions, which led to strangers being misled in purchasing land from Rubin. However, the court proceeded to declare: "But the solemn acts performed under the sanction of Jewish communal usage, followed by a daily conduct consistent with such renunciation for 23 years, debar this divorcee from now undoing her renunciation of her husband, and casting dishonor on her later family, and clouding the parentage of innocent children."[25] The legal impact of this statement is unclear. Certainly, the *get* did not dissolve Sarah's marriage civilly. Yet, she was restrained from claiming the *get* to be nugatory if that would dishonor her later family and cloud the parentage of innocent children. The Appellate Division appears to have granted even greater recognition to a *get* than did the Connecticut court in *Kantor*. The New York court would not allow an inequitable challenge that could wreak harm upon others, preferring, rather, to let sleeping dogs lie in legal peace.

III. A *GET* DELIVERED IN A FOREIGN JURISDICTION

The previously cited cases consistently affirm the principle that religious divorces executed in jurisdictions in which their efficacy is recognized by the civil government will be recognized by United States courts, but that religious divorces executed in the United States do not serve to sever the matrimonial relationship in the eyes of the state. In the early twentieth century it was not uncommon for a husband to immigrate to the United States and leave his family behind. Often the marital relationship did not survive the separation and the parties sought to dissolve the marriage by means of a trans-Atlantic religious divorce.

The procedure usually followed involved drafting a *get* in the United States at the behest of the husband. The husband then appointed an agent, who, under the supervision of a rabbi, delivered the *get* into his wife's hands while she continued to live in the foreign jurisdiction. The validity in American law of a *get* executed in this manner was challenged in New York courts on several occasions. The decisions failed to recognize the validity of a *get* written in the United States but delivered in a foreign jurisdiction. These rulings had a significant impact not only upon family law but also upon the right of certain individuals to obtain United States citizenship. These rulings were later cited and applied by federal courts in naturalization proceedings. The cases rested upon a fundamental misunderstanding of Jewish law.

[25] *Id.* at 403, 168 N.Y.S. at 848–49.

One such case, *Chertok v. Chertok*,[26] involved an action for annulment brought by Eva Chertok against her husband, Morris. In 1910 Morris married a woman in Warsaw, then under Russian rule. He subsequently left his first wife and immigrated to America. In 1917, before his marriage to Eva, Morris appeared before a rabbi in Brooklyn to draw up a bill of divorce that was delivered to his wife in St. Petersburg (then Petrograd) under the auspices of the Petrograd rabbi, David Tevel Katzenellenbogen. Rabbi Katzenellenbogen testified in a deposition that the Russian government recognized such a divorce. In her petition for annulment, Eva argued that a religious divorce is invalid in New York and hence her marriage to Morris should be annulled on the grounds that Morris' first marriage had not been dissolved. The Appellate Division agreed.

The court described the *get* as a "rabbinical divorce obtained by defendant from a rabbi in the borough of Brooklyn, New York City"[27] and concluded:

> [W]e must hold that the writing, purporting to be a divorce obtained from a rabbi in Brooklyn, cannot be recognized as having any effect in this state, or as having been validated by what was done in Russia . . . Although a divorce may have been perfected in Russia, according to the law prevailing there, by the delivery of the alleged divorce granted by a rabbi in New York City, the act of the local rabbi in granting it was not thereby rendered consonant with law prevailing here. The rabbinical divorce must be rendered as having had its inception in the paper issued by the Brooklyn rabbi, and, although the Russian government may recognize it, the divorce is void in its inception under our law.
>
> We cannot regard it as a divorce obtained in Russia. The record indicates that what was done in that country was intended merely to give effect there to the rabbinical divorce obtained in Brooklyn.[28]

The New York court completely misunderstood the nature of a *get*. The *get* is not a judicial decree. It takes effect upon delivery to the wife[29] and the place of effect is the place of delivery.[30] Even after the *get* has been written and attested to by witnesses it is revocable and voidable until the

[26] 208 A.D. 161, 203 N.Y.S. 163 (1st Dep't 1924).
[27] *Id.* at 162, 203 N.Y.S. at 164.
[28] *Id.* at 162–63, 203 N.Y.S. at 164.
[29] Moses Maimonides, *Mishneh Torah, Hilkhot Gerushin* 1:1; *Shulḥan Arukh, Even ha-Ezer* 133:1 & 138:1–2.
[30] For this reason the *get* is written using the names by which the parties are known at the place of delivery rather than those by which they are known at the place of drafting. See *Shulḥan Arukh, Even ha-Ezer* 129:4.

moment of the wife's acceptance.[31] When the husband and wife are not in the same locale, the husband appoints an agent to act in his stead to deliver the *get* to his wife.[32] Language referring to "a divorce obtained from a rabbi in Brooklyn," "the paper issued by the Brooklyn rabbi" and "what was done . . . to give effect there to the rabbinical divorce obtained in Brooklyn" is grossly inaccurate. The Brooklyn rabbi issued no paper and granted no divorce. He merely supervised the drafting of an instrument, i.e., the writing of the *get*. The divorce proceedings themselves were supervised by the rabbi in Petrograd. The delivery of a *get* is not simply the transmission of a decree already issued by a rabbinic court. Delivery is the essence of the *get* proceedings. Morris could just as readily have designated an agent in Petrograd to serve as his proxy not only for delivery of the *get*, but also for its drafting. From the language of the decision it appears that under the latter circumstances the court would have accepted the validity of the divorce. Because the wife was domiciled in Russia and the divorce would have been executed in the country of domicile, comity would have demanded recognition of the divorce. Although the bill of divorce was drafted in Brooklyn, to the extent that Jewish law associates divorce with a judicial act, the act took place in Petrograd. Jewish judicial procedure provides that following the execution of a *get* the *bet din* issues a document known as a *petur*. This document recites the facts contained in the bill of divorce, certifies that the divorce proceedings have indeed been completed and authorizes the parties to remarry. The *petur* is invariably issued by the *bet din* that presides over delivery of the *get* to the wife. In *Chertok*, the rabbi in Petrograd issued the *petur*. In recognizing the *get*, the Russian government was not extending recognition to a divorce issued by a Brooklyn rabbi, but rather recognizing an act of the Petrograd rabbi. Russian law required that the crown rabbi enter all divorces upon a public record kept by him for that purpose; in the absence of an entry the religious divorce would have been invalid under Russian law.[33] The Russian government, in conformity with Russian law, was recognizing a divorce executed in its own jurisdiction on behalf of a woman domiciled in Russia. It was not recognizing a divorce perfected outside Russia under the laws of a different jurisdiction. Were the Russian government actually to have extended validity to divorce proceedings outside of its jurisdiction, such recognition would properly have been of no consequence in American law.[34]

[31] See *Shulḥan Arukh, Even ha-Ezer* 141:63 and *Even ha-Ezer* 154, *Seder ha-Get* §§ 23 & 76.

[32] *Shulḥan Arukh, Even ha-Ezer* 140:1.

[33] See Miller v. Miller, 70 Misc. 368, 128 N.Y.S. 787 (Sup. Ct. 1911). See *supra* note 5.

[34] In *Chertok*, the court held not only that a *get* was invalid under American law but also that the rabbi issuing the *get* in the absence of a prior civil divorce decree was guilty of a misdemeanor. Consistent with its misunderstanding of the *get*, the court observed that even the drafting of

Chertok was not the first case in which a New York court failed to recognize that a Jewish divorce is not a judicial decree but is effected by the parties themselves, at the time when and in the place where the *get* is delivered to the wife, not when and where it is drafted. *Saperstone v. Saperstone*[35] presented the converse of *Chertok* – the husband remaining abroad, in Odessa, and the wife immigrating to the United States. At the wife's request Rabbi Franklin of Buffalo contacted the Chief Rabbi of Odessa to arrange a religious divorce. Rabbi Franklin soon received a *get*. The Chief Rabbi of Odessa directed Rabbi Franklin not to deliver it to the wife until she executed a notarized document in Russian, countersigned by Rabbi Franklin, acknowledging receipt of the *get*. Presumably, the husband needed the document so that Russian authorities would recognize his divorce and permit him to remarry. Rabbi Franklin kept the *get* for several months before he delivered it and never executed the document acknowledging receipt of the *get*.

The court held the religious divorce invalid for two reasons: (1) The condition stipulated by the Chief Rabbi was not fulfilled – no Russian-language acknowledgment of receipt was executed; (2) although prima facie the domicile of the husband is the domicile of the wife, in view of the fact that the couple had separated permanently and the wife had abandoned her Russian home, New York was her legal domicile. Hence, the Russian rabbinic authority lacked jurisdiction.

The court in *Saperstone* failed to recognize that a *get* is not a judicial decree but an instrument executed solely by the divorcing couple. In Judaism, both marriage and divorce flow from the acts of the parties and not from rabbinic judicial authority.[36] Failure to fulfill the directions of the rabbi in Odessa

the *get* by a rabbi in New York for the purpose of subsequent delivery in Russia constituted a violation of New York penal law. However, no criminal action has ever been brought against an officiant in proceedings involving the execution of a religious divorce. New York law, certainly as currently in effect, provides penal sanctions only for the purported issuance of a decree of *civil* divorce. *McKinney's Penal Law*, § 255.05.

35 73 Misc. 631, 131 N.Y.S. 241 (Sup. Ct. Monroe Equity Term 1911).

36 See David Werner Amram, *The Jewish Law of Divorce* (Charleston, SC, 2009) (1897); Peter Elman, ed., *Jewish Marriage* (Jewish Marriage Education Council) (London, 1967); Louis M. Epstein, *The Jewish Marriage Contract: A Study in the Status of the Woman in Jewish Law* (Clark, NJ, 2004) (1927); Ze'ev Wilhelm Falk, *Jewish Matrimonial Law in The Middle Ages* (London, 1966); Joseph Prader, *Das Religiöse Ehericht der Christlichen Kirchen, der Mohammedaner und der Juden* 72–83 (Frankfurt am Main, 1973); Morris (Moshe) Swift, *Jewish Marriage and Divorce* (London, 1962); Abraham Zagouri, *Le divorce d'après la loi talmudique chez les Marocains de confession israélite et les réformes actuelles en la matièr* (Paris, 1958); Menachem Elon, "Marriage" and "Divorce," in Menachem Elon, ed., *The Principles of Jewish Law* (Jerusalem, 1975); Samuel Daiches, "Divorce in Jewish Law," *Jouranl of Comparative Legislation*, vol. 8 (1926), p. 215; Mességa-Fara, "Le divorce juif en droit international privé,"

requiring acknowledgment of receipt (unless made a condition of the *get* by the husband, which it was not)[37] in no way affected the validity of the *get*. The rabbi supervising a religious divorce is not a party to the proceedings in any legal sense. He has no authority to impose a condition precedent affecting the validity of the *get*. Hence, Rabbi Frankel's directive was no more than an equitable request on behalf of the husband. Moreover, the principle of comity would not require recognition of a religious divorce executed in the United States simply because its validity is recognized by a foreign government. This principle, whose theory (but not whose application) was correctly explained in *Chertok*, is limited to divorces issued pursuant to the jurisdiction of a foreign state. A divorce must be valid in the jurisdiction where issued; only then is comity applicable. As already stated, the *get* in *Saperstone* was not a judicial decree issued by the Chief Rabbi of Odessa but an instrument executed by the parties themselves that had legal effect only upon delivery. Accordingly, because the *get* was delivered to the wife in Buffalo, an American court could not properly have recognized it, even if the court had found Russia to have remained her country of domicile. In *Saperstone*, the decision was correct, but was reached on faulty grounds.

Eleven years after *Chertok*, yet a third New York court misunderstood the operation of a *get*. In *In re Estate of Goldman*,[38] as in *Chertok*, the husband drafted the *get* in New York, and the wife received delivery of it in Russia. As in *Chertok*, the court – this time the Surrogate's Court of King's County – wrongly believed that the husband's preparation of the *get*, not the wife's receipt of it, effectuated the divorce, and that the validity of the *get* under Jewish, and hence Russian law, was predicated upon a decree of an ecclesiastic court in New York. The court went further, however. It said that the "wife had no notice of [the husband's] application for a divorce, and the only information of its granting which she received arose from the fact that a certificate thereof was subsequently delivered to her in Russia where she still resided."[39] That

Nouvelle revue de droit international privé, vol. 9 (1936), p. 685; Julian D.M. Lew, "Jewish Divorces," *New Law Journal*, vol. 123 (1973), p. 829; Israel T. Naamani, "Marriage and Divorce in Jewish Law," *Journal of Family Law*, vol. 3 (1963), p. 177; Isaac S. Shiloh, "Marriage and Divorce in Israel," *Israel Law Review*, vol. 5 (1970), p. 479.

37 The decision refers only to "the formalities or conditions pointed out by the rabbi in Odessa, which he required to be observed," 73 Misc. at 633, 131 N.Y.S. at 242. It is unthinkable that in presiding over the conveyance of a conditional divorce a rabbinic authority would issue a *petur* unless a condition affecting the validity of the instrument had been fulfilled. Also, there is a strong aversion among rabbinic authorities to execution of a conditional divorce. See Rema, *Shulḥan Arukh, Even ha-Ezer* 145:9.

38 156 Misc. 817, 282 N.Y.S. 787 (Sur. Ct. King's Co. 1935).

39 *Id.* at 818, 282 N.Y.S. at 789.

conclusion is absurd under a system of law that demands consent of the wife. The assertion that the wife's only information of the divorce arose from "a certificate thereof" reflects the same ignorance. The "certificate thereof" was nothing other than the instrument of divorce itself, which acquired halakhic (and hence legal) significance only upon its delivery to the wife in the presence of rabbinic authorities in Russia. The rabbis in New York merely supervised the writing of a bill of divorce; any "transactions purporting to grant the divorce"[40] were performed in Russia, not in New York.[41]

IV. JUDICIAL INVOLVEMENT IN RELIGIOUS DIVORCE

A. *Enforcement of Voluntary Undertakings*

Absent specific statutory authority, no American court could recognize the validity of a religious divorce executed in the United States as a means of terminating a legally valid marriage.[42] Nevertheless, courts have on occasion

[40] *Id.* at 819, 282 N.Y.S. at 790.

[41] Ignorance of the operation of a *get* has not been confined to New York courts. In Falkoff v. Sugerman, 26 Ohio N.P. (n.s.) 81 (Ct. Common Pleas, Sterk Co. 1925), the husband of a couple married in Russia emigrated to America. He remarried, claiming that he had executed a *get* under the supervision of a rabbi in St. Louis. Upon his death the first wife sued for dower rights claiming that she was the lawful widow and that the second marriage was void. The husband, she said, had never executed a *get*. The court agreed that the husband had never executed a *get*, but went on to say that even had a *get* existed, "it was absolutely void. So far as this court knows, no state in this union permits any ecclesiastical authority to grant divorces. It is an un-American doctrine." *Id.* at 87. Just like the courts in New York, the Ohio court ignored the fact that the first wife was domiciled in Russia, that the religious divorce, had it happened, would have taken place in Russia upon delivery of the *get* and would have been given civil efficacy under the laws of Russia, and that the husband's domicile upon execution of the *get* was irrelevant.

Regrettably, the court's misunderstanding was reinforced by the testimony of a Rabbi Pelchrovist who stated: "[N]o rabbi in this country would grant a Rabbinical divorce unless the parties had already been divorced in the civil courts, or that a condition be written into the 'Get' providing that it should not become effective until a civil divorce was obtained." *Id.* His testimony was wrong on three counts: (1) Religious authorities, despite the dictum to the contrary in *Chertok*, had no reason to feel constrained in the issuance of religious divorces for purely religious purposes; (2) It is at variance with normative practice, to say the least, for *any* condition to be "written into the 'Get.'" See Rema, *Shulḥan Arukh, Even ha-Ezer* 145:9. At most, a statement would be inserted in the *petur* admonishing the parties, and by implication any rabbi called upon to solemnize a future marriage, that a civil divorce is required by the law of the land; (3) Since, in Russia, religious divorces were civilly valid, there would have been no reason not to transmit a *get* to Russia for delivery to the wife.

[42] It was for this reason that in Shikoh v. Murff, 257 F.2d 306 (2d Cir. 1958), the Second Circuit refused to grant a Pakistani citizen permanent residence on the basis of marriage to an American citizen. The marriage was ruled to be void because of the invalidity of the alien's prior divorce

addressed the problem posed by the absence of a *get*: that one of the parties cannot remarry without violating religious scruples. In the vast majority of cases, the issue brought before the court was enforcement of an agreement between the parties to execute a religious divorce. Such an action poses a significant constitutional question: May the assistance of a court be invoked in order to enforce a contract when the contract is designed to accomplish a religious objective? The question is whether the First Amendment creates a barrier between Church and State so strong that the courts may never involve themselves in matters that are essentially religious,[43] or whether such matters may be litigated before the courts because the issue at stake is a civil one, namely, enforcement of a contractual right, with the subject matter of the contract being merely collateral.[44] Indeed, failure to enforce such a contract may violate the Free Exercise Clause of the First Amendment. Freedom to enter into a contract with another party is a civil right; to exclude from contract areas that impinge upon religious practice is to interfere with the free exercise of religion.[45]

from a wife living in Pakistan. The divorce was a *talaq* conducted in Brooklyn in accordance with Islamic law and practice. The petitioner had received a document signed by a Moslem clergyman declaring the parties to be divorced by virtue of "the authority vested in him in accordance with the laws of Islam and in conformity with the laws of the Government of the United States of America." *Id.* at 307. The court repudiated this claim. It conceded that the divorce was valid in Pakistan and would have been recognized by United States courts had it been granted in Pakistan, even though the parties were physically present in the United States, because Pakistan remained the matrimonial domicile of the parties. Nevertheless, the divorce could not be recognized because it was granted, not in Pakistan, but in the United States. *Id.* at 309.

43 Shelley v. Kraemer, 334 U.S. 1, 14–18 (1948), established that enforcement action by a state court is tantamount to action by the state itself.

44 See Weinberger v. Van Hessen, 236 A.D. 14, 257 N.Y.S. 738, *aff'd*, 260 N.Y. 294, 183 N.E. 429 (1932).

45 See Donald A. Giannella, "Religious Liberty, Nonestablishment and Doctrinal Development. Part II. The Nonestablishment Principle," *Harvard Law Review*, vol. 81 (1968), p. 513:

> Where the State does no more than extend to religion the benefits of the prevailing social order, it does not lend the kind of support forbidden by the principle of voluntarism. Indeed, to deny religion such benefits would place it at a handicap inconsistent with the values of free self-development.

Id. at 518.

Ira Ellman made the identical point in a more recent article on judicial involvement in church disputes that are not doctrinal. Ellman observes:

> When a court refuses to adjudicate church disputes, it may sacrifice members' contractual interests and religious freedom. Immunity from judicial dispute resolution may also burden the organizational efforts of religious groups by denying them the benefit of secular rules that facilitate the creation and growth of private, voluntary associations. There

This issue also arises in other areas, most significantly the enforcement of antenuptial agreements concerning the religious rearing of children. In 1961, an Illinois appellate court enforced an antenuptial agreement requiring children to be raised as Jews.[46] Similarly, litigation has tested employment agreements imposing certain religious requirements.[47]

The resolution of this question in the setting of a contract to execute a *get* has a checkered history. In *Koeppel v. Koeppel*,[48] the earliest case in which an

> is thus a tension between autonomy for the church and some of the very values that such autonomy might at first be assumed to further. This tension colors the constitutional question differently than appears on initial examination.

Ira Mark Ellman, "Driven From the Tribunal: Judicial Resolution of Internal Church Disputes," *California Law Review*, vol. 69 (1981), pp. 1378, 1383.

Ellman's comments are cited with approval by New York Supreme Court Justice Martin Rodell in an opinion issued in Zimbler v. Felber, 111 Misc.2d 867, 445 N.Y.S.2d 366 (1981). The issue before the court was the propriety of judicial involvement in a dispute within a congregation regarding renewal of a rabbinic contract. Ruling in the affirmative, Justice Rodell commented:

> There is no question that the dispute involves rights ordinarily recognized under corporation and contract law. Complete autonomy for the organization – total immunity from judicial dispute resolution – would thus require denying church members ordinarily available judicial remedies, solely because of the religious nature of the organization in which the contractual or corporate dispute arose.

Id. at 877, 445 N.Y.S.2d at 372. This conclusion was reached despite the fact that Justice Rodell, in the same opinion, sharply criticized the finding in Kupperman v. Congregation Nusach Sfard, 39 Misc.2d 107, 240 N.Y.S.2d 315 (Sup. Ct. 1963), that within the Jewish faith the appointment and tenure of an ordained spiritual leader does not involve questions of discipline and doctrine but is a temporal matter. In this well-documented opinion, Justice Rodell concluded that "the Kupperman decision simply misstated 'the nature of the structure of the religious faith' and de minimis, the appointment and tenure of an ordained spiritual leader of the Jewish faith certainly involves questions of discipline and doctrine, and is not merely a temporal matter." Zimbler, 111 Misc.2d at 876, 445 N.Y.S.2d at 372.

The *Zimbler* decision establishes that although it is "not merely a temporal matter" the civil courts may involve themselves in litigation concerning rabbinic tenure to the extent that mundane matters of contract and corporate law must be resolved. Total immunity from judicial dispute would serve to deny "ordinarily available judicial remedies" and would serve to deny both due process and free exercise. The same reasoning should apply, *mutatis mutandis*, to enforcement of a voluntary undertaking to execute a religious divorce. Resolution of the contractual aspects of a dispute concerning specific performance need not at all involve the court in theological matters. "Denying the benefit of secular rules" in facilitating enforcement of such contracts can only serve to impede freedom of religious practice and certainly "colors the constitutional question differently than appears on initial examination." See generally Zimbler v. Felber, 111 Misc.2d 867, 445 N.Y.S.2d 366 (1981).

46 Gottlieb v. Gottlieb, 31 Ill. App. 2d 120, 175 N.E.2d 619 (1961). Ironically, this case involved a situation in which the mother was not Jewish and hence the children were non-Jews in the eyes of Jewish law.

47 See, e.g., Fisher v. Congregation B'nai Yitzhok, 177 Pa. Super. 359, 110 A.2d 881 (1955).

48 138 N.Y.S.2d 366 (Sup. Ct. 1954), *affd.* 3 A.D.2d 853, 161 N.Y.S.2d 694 (1957).

action was brought to enforce such a contract, a New York trial court dismissed the complaint but held the contract enforceable. While an action brought by the wife for annulment of the marriage was pending, the Koeppels entered into an agreement providing

> that he and she will, whenever called upon, and if and whenever the same shall become necessary, appear before a Rabbi or Rabbinate selected and designated by whomsoever of the parties who shall first demand the same, and execute any and all papers and documents required by and necessary to effectuate a dissolution of their marriage in accordance with the ecclesiastical laws of the Faith and Church of said parties.[49]

The wife went to court for an order compelling her husband to abide by the terms of the agreement. The trial court rejected the husband's contention that enforcement would interfere with his constitutionally protected freedom of religion:

> Complying with his agreement would not compel the defendant to practice any religion . . . His appearance before the Rabbinate to answer questions and give evidence needed by them to make a decision is not a profession of faith. Specific performance herein would merely require the defendant to do what he voluntarily agreed to do.[50]

49 138 N.Y.S.2d at 370.

50 *Id.* at 373. Again, a court failed to understand the nature of a *get*. The husband answers questions put to him by the *bet din*, but he does not "give evidence," nor does the *bet din* "make a decision" on the merits of the case. However, the salient point, that no "profession of faith is involved," is entirely true.

The crucial point is that a *get* is an instrument that dissolves a contractual relationship; its execution is not a sacerdotal act. The Talmud itself, *Kiddushin* 41b, states this in a discussion of the scriptural basis of the law of agency. The efficacy of agency with regard to execution of a bill of divorce is established on the basis of explicit biblical authority. The Talmud remarks that agency with regard to divorce cannot be inferred from a parallel provision recognizing agency in setting aside the gift-offering presented the priests (*terumah*) because divorce is "secular" or "mundane" (*ḥol*) while the gift offering is "sacred."

Justice Haim Cohn placed divorce, and indeed the matrimonial relationship itself, in perspective in a decision of the Israeli Supreme Court in Riegenfeld v. Jacobson, *Piskei Din shel Bet ha-Mishpat ha-Elyon le-Yisra'el*, vol. 17 (1963), pp. 1009, 1018:

> Unlike English Common Law, Jewish law does not confer on spouses the "status" of marriage which, once entry thereinto has been decided upon and solemnized, cannot be abandoned except by legislation or divine decree. Marriage in Jewish law is a contractual tie, although of a most solemn kind, between a man and a woman which, if they so wish, they can enter into and, if they so wish, may dissolve and terminate. Where a consenting couple so desire, the only task of the courts is to supervise and carry into effect the entry into marriage or its dissolution. In this very difference of Jewish law from Christian marriage law lies its greatness and, if you will, its modernity, not the rigidity of status but freedom of contract, not the incontestable determination of status but the right of spouses to choose in their discretion between marriage and divorce.

The judge ordered compliance. On appeal,[51] the Appellate Division, Second Department, noted that the wife had remarried in a ceremony "at which a duly ordained rabbi of her own faith officiated."[52] The court pointed to a clause in the agreement requiring the parties to appear before a rabbi to execute a religious divorce "if and whenever the same shall be necessary."[53] The court found itself "unable to determine . . . what circumstances the parties intended to be sufficient to establish the necessity of the dissolution of the marriage in accordance with Jewish ecclesiastical law."[54] It thus dismissed the wife's complaint on the grounds that the agreement was "too indefinite to support a judgment of specific performance."[55]

In *Koeppel* the court did not address the question of whether the U.S. Constitution would prevent enforcement of an agreement to execute a religious divorce. The court denied relief to the wife solely because it found the condition triggering religious divorce – "if and whenever the same shall become necessary" – to be indefinite. There is little doubt, however, that the parties' primary intent was to guarantee acquiescence and cooperation when and if either of them wanted to remarry. The court presumably reasoned that because the wife had remarried with benefit of clergy "of her own faith"[56] the contractual requirement of necessity could not be demonstrated. Yet, a *get* is necessary not simply to permit religious remarriage but, more importantly, to remove the stigma of bastardy[57] from future issue, as well as to relieve the conjugal partners from the guilt associated with adultery. A *get* is necessary for these two purposes no less than for persuading a Jewish clergyman to perform

Translation from *Selected Judgments of the Supreme Court of Israel* (1963), vol. 5, pp. 96, 104.

Justice Cohn contrasts this view with "the odour of Catholic sacrament" that pervades the common law view of marriage. *Selected Judgments of the Supreme Court of Israel*, vol. 5, p. 102. The presumption that termination of marriage by means of a *get* in the presence of a rabbinic tribunal is a religious act is undoubtedly rooted in an unwarranted assumption of the existence of a Judeo-Christian tradition concerning marriage, which yields the erroneous notion that marriage, and hence divorce, are essentially sacramental in Judaism as well.

51 3 A.D.2d 853, 161 N.Y.S.2d 694 (1957).

52 *Id.* at 853, 161 N.Y.S.2d at 695.

53 *Id.*

54 *Id.* at 853, 161 N.Y.S.2d at 695–96.

55 *Id.*

56 *Id.*

57 In Jewish law a *mamzer*, or bastard, is defined as the issue of an incestuous union or of an adulterous relationship, e.g., a child of a married woman fathered by a man other than her husband. No stigma of bastardy or illegitimacy attaches to the child of an unwed mother (provided the child is not born of an incestuous union). See *Shulḥan Arukh, Even ha-Ezer* 4:13. Jewish law forbids marriage between a bastard and a person of legitimate birth. The child of a *mamzer* is also a *mamzer*. *Shulḥan Arukh, Even ha-Ezer* 4:1.

a marriage. The court addressed only the last purpose. However, even granting such a narrow construction of necessity, the fact that the parties entered into a contract to execute a religious divorce suggests that they deemed it necessary that a marriage ceremony be performed by a rabbi who adheres to the provisions of Jewish law and that the marriage be recognized as valid under Jewish law. A *get* is unnecessary for securing the services of a Reform rabbi who does not feel bound by Jewish law;[58] in that case a contract binding the parties to execute a *get* would be superfluous. However, a *get* is necessary for a marriage to be valid under Jewish law and it was undoubtedly this necessity that the Koeppels contemplated. A *get* constitutes a "necessity," therefore, because it makes possible the performance of a marriage ceremony in the manner contemplated by the Koeppels.

Sixteen years after *Koeppel*, in *Margulies v. Margulies*,[59] the Appellate Division, First Department, refused to order a husband to give a *get* but upheld a fine the trial judge had imposed upon him for contempt of court. After a

58 The requirement of a *get* for dissolving a marriage was abolished by Reform Judaism in a resolution adopted at the Philadelphia Conference in 1869. *Protokolle der Rabbiner-Conferenz Abgehalten zu Philadelphia* (1869), pp. 26–36 [hereinafter cited as *Protokolle*] (quoted in Moses Mielziner, *The Jewish Law of Marriage and Divorce in Ancient and Modern Times and its Relation to the Law of the State* (Cincinnati, OH, 1884), p. 135). See also David Philipson, *The Reform Movement in Judaism* (London, 1907), p. 484, n. 38. This position has been universally accepted by the Reform Movement. Wolf Gunther Plaut, *The Rise of Reform Judaism: A Sourcebook of its European Origins* (New York, 1963), pp. 222–23. See also 1928 *Central Conference of American Rabbis, Rabbi's Manual* (Cincinnati, OH, 1928), p. 184; Frederic Aubrey Doppelt and David Polish, *A Guide for Reform Jews* (Cincinnati, OH, 1957), p. 74.

It may be noted that the resolution adopted by the Philadelphia Conference provided for recognition of civil divorce provided "it can be ascertained from the judicial documents that both parties consented to the divorce." However, when the decree is issued "by constraint," the validity of the divorce is to be recognized only "if the cause assigned is sufficient in conformity with the spirit of the Jewish religion." *Protokolle, supra*, at 36 (quoted in Mielziner, *supra*, at 135). The requirement for consent has been understood, not as a requirement for a mutual agreement of the parties to be divorced, "but to a final consent on both sides, in a case where one of the parties, on some complaint, petitions for a divorce, and the other party, without contesting the allegations, is willing to accept the divorce." *Protokolle, supra*, at 36 (quoted in Mielziner, *supra*, at 136). Mielziner asserts that the proceedings of the Conference indicate that this reservation was necessary because of the laxity in granting divorces that existed in some territories and states. At times, a decree of divorce was obtained by one of the parties on very loose grounds and, on occasion, without the knowledge of the other party. The effect of the resolution was to charge the rabbi with a duty to refrain from giving religious sanction to a second marriage where the former one was frivolously dissolved. Mielziner, *supra*, at 136. Reference to this reservation is omitted in the current edition of the *Rabbi's Manual* and the sources cited therein grant unqualified recognition to divorce decrees issued by civil courts. 1961 *Central Conference of American Rabbis, Rabbi's Manual* (Cincinnati, OH, 1961), pp. 137–39.

59 42 A.D.2d 517, 344 N.Y.S.2d 482 (1973).

divorce, the Margulieses began to quarrel about visitation rights and the division of personal property. As part of a stipulation in open court resolving their differences, the husband voluntarily agreed to appear before a rabbi to execute a religious divorce.[60] This, however, he later refused to do, leading the trial court to hold him in contempt and fine him subject to his purging himself of contempt by payment of the fine and appearing before a Jewish court to execute a religious divorce.

The husband raised the First Amendment on appeal: "It is argued," wrote the First Department, "that the court was without power to direct defendant to participate in a religious divorce, as such is a matter of one's personal convictions and is not subject to the court's interference."[61] The court did not respond to that argument directly, apparently because it believed the constitutional issue to be moot: "We are told further, that since a Jewish divorce can only be granted upon the representation that it is sought by the husband of his own free will, any such divorce, if obtained under compulsion by the court, would in any event be a nullity."[62]

The court evidently felt powerless to direct specific performance because it believed that a religious divorce to which the husband gives his consent only in order to purge himself of contempt would be invalid. Nor did the court find it necessary to resolve the constitutional issue in order to find the husband's behavior contumacious because, "even if the orders were erroneous, the defendant was obligated, in the absence of a stay, to obey the court's mandate until vacated or reversed."[63] The court thus allowed the fines to stand.

Margulies, then, deals with neither the constitutional nor the contractual issues but solely with the contemptuous behavior of a husband who, when agreeing to participate in a religious divorce, knew "that it could only be obtained upon his assertion to the rabbinical court that it was being sought of his own free will."[64]

In *Margulies* there may well have been grounds for forcing the husband to execute a religious divorce. Jewish law provides that in certain situations a wife may sue for an injunction directing her husband to execute a religious divorce.[65] The decision in *Margulies* notes that the defendant had remarried.

60 *Id.* at 517, 344 N.Y.S.2d at 484.
61 *Id.*
62 *Id.*
63 *Id.*
64 *Id.* at 517, 344 N.Y.S.2d at 485.
65 In Rubin v. Rubin, 75 Misc.2d 776, 348 N.Y.S.2d 61 (Fam. Ct. 1973), Judge Stanley Gartenstein correctly notes that the statement in *Margulies* that a *get* can be obtained only on consent "refers only to so-called 'no-fault' decrees" but that when certain grounds exist execution of a

The husband's civil marriage was either invalid under Jewish law or bigamous. Under such circumstances, the wife might have sought to compel the husband to divorce her on the grounds that he was "a frequenter of prostitutes," grounds entitling the wife to divorce.[66] In such cases, Jewish law would find

get can be compelled "against the will of one or even both parties." He does not say whether such grounds existed in *Margulies*. *Id.* at 781 n.3, 348 N.Y.S.2d at 66 n.3.

66 Rema, *Shulḥan Arukh, Even ha-Ezer* 154:1, cites a ruling that, upon application of the wife, a "frequenter of prostitutes" may be compelled to divorce his wife provided that the allegation is supported by the testimony of eyewitnesses or by the husband's own confession. The source of this statement is R. Alexander Suslin ha-Kohen, *Sefer ha-Agudah, Yevamot* 65a (Jerusalem, 1979), which advances two arguments in support of this ruling: (1) The behavior of the husband in frequenting prostitutes undoubtedly causes the wife embarrassment and emotional anguish, which she is not obliged to bear; (2) "He who frequents harlots will waste his fortune," Proverbs 29:3, and hence the husband will ultimately become incapable of providing for the support and maintenance of his wife. Yechiel Michel Epstein, *Arukh ha-Shulḥan, Even ha-Ezer* 154:16, advances additional justification for this ruling by arguing that a "frequenter of prostitutes" undoubtedly fails to fulfill his marital duties. He may therefore be forced to grant a *get* because denial or diminution of consortium constitutes grounds for compelling a divorce. However, each of the reasons advanced is problematic. Although *Shulḥan Arukh, Even ha-Ezer* 154:3, does indeed rule that inability to provide for support and maintenance constitutes grounds for compelling the husband to execute a *get*, Rema, *Shulḥan Arukh, Even ha-Ezer* 154:21, rules that coercion predicated upon these and similar considerations must be limited to sanctions such as refusing the husband any and all favors and privileges, refusing to engage in business dealings with him, etc., but may not take the form of corporal punishment or formal excommunication. Later authorities have accepted his position as normative. See *Teshuvot Noda bi-Yehudah, Mahadurah Tinyana, Even ha-Ezer*, no. 90; R. Shabbetai ben Meir ha-Kohen, *Gevurot Anashim*, §§ 28 & 48; *Pithei Teshuvah, Even ha-Ezer* 154:7, 154:8 & 154:31; see also *Piskei Din shel Batei ha-Din ha-Rabbaniyim* (Rabbinical District Court of Haifa, 1970), vol. 8, pp. 124, 126. These authorities similarly refuse to sanction overt coercion on grounds of denial of consortium. Although some authorities sanction coercion when all marital obligations, including maintenance and consortium, are denied, *Gevurot Anashim* refuses to sanction coercion even under such circumstances. Later rabbinic authorities give particular deference to the ruling of *Gevurot Anashim* due to the high esteem in which they hold the author of that work, R. Shabbetai ha-Kohen. He is renowned as the author of *Siftei Kohen* (*Shakh*), a standard commentary on *Shulḥan Arukh*, *Ḥoshen Mishpat* and *Yoreh De'ah*. *Gevurot Anashim* § 72, also disallows any formal edict imposing any sanction other than a simple declaration that the husband is a transgressor. *Teshuvot Ḥakham Ẓevi*, no. 133, disagrees with the ruling of *Sefer ha-Agudah* and opines that only actual non-support constitutes grounds for coercion according to the authorities cited, but that for no authority does fear of non-support at some future time constitute grounds for immediate coercion. Embarrassment and mental anguish resulting from such a situation are apparently not considered by this authority the grounds for coercion and are expressly rejected in the opinion issued by the Rabbinical District Court of Haifa.

Nevertheless, in a 1970 case before the Haifa rabbinical court, the *bet din* did issue a ruling compelling the husband to execute a *get*. The case involved a husband sentenced to a prison term of fourteen years on several counts of rape and sexual incest involving minors. *Piskei Din shel Batei ha-Din ha-Rabbaniyim* (Rabbinical District Court of Haifa, 1970), vol. 8, pp. 124, 126. It would appear that each of the arguments raised in this case are applicable, *mutatis mutandis*, to a situation in which the husband avails himself of a civil decree and enters into a subsequent

it appropriate for a secular court to order the husband, under threat of incarceration, to appear before a *bet din* and comply with any directive it might issue. Jewish law sanctions employment of the coercive authority of secular courts and recognizes the validity of a religious divorce issued on the basis of such threat when (1) there is a finding by the *bet din* under Jewish law that the husband may be compelled to divorce his wife and (2) the secular court does not itself compel the execution of the *get* but simply coerces the husband to "do what the Jew[ish *bet din*] tells you."[67] Even when Jewish law mandates the husband to give a *get*, it must be executed pursuant to an order of a rabbinical tribunal, which is empowered to request a civil court to enforce its decree. The action of a civil court under such circumstances is deemed ancillary to the decree of the ecclesiastical body, hence valid.

The enforceability of an undertaking to execute a religious divorce was examined on the merits for the first time in *Pal v. Pal*.[68] Sidney Pal obtained a divorce judgment in 1973. He and his wife Cipora stipulated in open court that:

> [E]ach of the parties hereto hereby submit themselves to a Rabbinical Tribunal on the question of whether the Plaintiff shall be directed to take all steps necessary to grant a Jewish divorce [*Get*] and the parties shall be bound

marriage, particularly if the husband fails to provide for the support and maintenance of his first wife in accordance with the standard demanded by Jewish law. Under such circumstances, the willful action of the husband effectively denies his first wife consortium. The denial is likely to be permanent because consortium with the first wife would, from the civil perspective, constitute the crime of adultery. In addition, the facts are such that a complaint in the nature of "he is disdainful to me" is immediately perceived to be objective and hence would arguably serve as independent grounds for compelling a divorce.

Moreover, even *Gevurot Anashim* concedes that one form of coercion is warranted in such circumstances, i.e., *kefiyah derekh bereirah*, meaning coercion, not in the form of directing the husband to execute a *get*, but in enforcing an order directing the husband to fulfill his marital obligations of support and/or consortium or, at his option, to relieve himself of such obligations by executing a *get*. An order of the *bet din* directing the husband to satisfy his wife's claim for consortium may be enforced by any means available to the *bet din*. See *Gevurot Anashim*, § 48, and *Pithei Teshuvah, Even ha-Ezer* 154:8.

In addition, it should be noted that *Gevurot Anashim*, § 28, freely concedes that the Talmud explicitly mandates coercion if the wife is childless. Denial of consortium coupled with refusal to grant a religious divorce effectively precludes the possibility of the wife ever bearing children. Under such circumstances a wife may compel a *get* upon the plea that she wishes to bear a child because "I wish a staff in my hand and a spade for burial," i.e., to provide support in her declining years and dignified burial upon death. *Ketubot* 64a.

67 *Bava Batra* 48a; see also *Mishneh Torah, Hilkhot Gerushin* 2:20; *Shulḥan Arukh, Even ha-Ezer* 134:9.

68 N.Y.L.J., July 25, 1973 at 13, col. 5, rev'd, 45 A.D.2d 738, 356 N.Y.S.2d 672 (1974).

> by the decision of said Rabbinical Tribunal in accordance with Article 75 of the CPLR.[69]

They also agreed that:

> [I]n the event that either of the parties fails to choose a Rabbi . . . or in the event that the two Rabbis chosen by the parties . . . should fail to select a third Rabbi, then this court shall . . . select any competent Rabbi for the one that failed to so choose a third Rabbi.[70]

This stipulation was incorporated into the judgment.

Sidney proved uncooperative. Also, the rabbi he designated to serve as a member of the *bet din* withdrew. In response to a motion by Cipora the court appointed a rabbi to replace Sidney's designee and directed the replacement together with the rabbi designated by Cipora to select the third member of the tribunal.[71]

In a statement requesting that "Rabbi Bleich and Rabbi Scharfman select a third Rabbi and convene a Jewish Tribunal,"[72] the trial court said:

> Parenthetically, the court notes that the plaintiff has remarried and that his second wife is now pregnant. In other words, the plaintiff has taken advantage of the provisions of a secular judgment of divorce, which gave him the opportunity to reorganize his life and another chance to achieve a happy life. He has denied this to his former wife by his refusal to release her from the religious consequences of his marriage to her. Unfortunately, this court has no jurisdiction over the plaintiff's conscience or over the powers granted to him because of his status as a Jewish male. However, it is within the power of this court to compel all parties to comply with the provisions of the judgment of divorce and will insist that the parties proceed expeditiously with the formation of a Rabbinical Tribunal so that the matter of a Get may be speedily resolved.[73]

The Appellate Division, Second Department, citing the First Department's decision in *Margulies* but ignoring its own decision in *Koeppel*, reversed the order of the lower court, saying that "Special Term had no authority to, in effect, convene a rabbinical tribunal."[74]

[69] N.Y.L.J., July 25, 1973 at 13, col. 5.
[70] *Id.*
[71] *Id.*
[72] *Id.*
[73] *Id.*
[74] 45 A.D.2d at 739, 356 N.Y.S.2d at 673.

Between the trial court's decision in *Pal* and its reversal on appeal, a related decision was handed down in New York Family Court in *Rubin v. Rubin*.[75] The opinion of Judge Stanley Gartenstein, who holds ordination from Mesivta Torah Vodaath, represents the first reasonably accurate analysis in an American decision of the Jewish law of divorce and the operation of a *get*. *Rubin* discusses the First Amendment issue. It also represents a rare instance in which a husband sought the cooperation of the wife, rather than a wife the cooperation of the husband.

Leah Rubin sued her former husband, Phillip, after he fell into arrears for weekly payments due under an Alabama divorce decree. Eventually the parties entered into a consent order for monthly payments and payment of the arrears with the understanding that Leah cooperate in securing a religious divorce. Phillip subsequently refused to pay the arrears, saying that Leah had refused to cooperate. Leah sought enforcement of the arrears.

In a hearing before Judge Gartenstein, Leah refused to appear before a *bet din* but said she had no reservations about accepting a *get*. Noting that Leah's presence before a *bet din* was unnecessary so long as she manifested assent to the *get*,[76] the court directed compliance with the consent order and adjourned to enable completion of its requirements. On the adjournment date, however, Leah refused consent to the *get*. Judge Gartenstein, correcting the mistaken views of his predecessors, noted that under talmudic law marriage is a contract and the *get* "a simple act of release nominally executed by the husband for delivery to the wife 'freeing' her for marriage to anyone else."[77] He dismissed as "fallacious"[78] the view that the *get* is a judicial decree.

[75] 75 Misc.2d 776, 348 N.Y.S.2d 61 (Fam. Ct. 1973). The performance of the Appellate Court of Illinois in *In re* the Marriage of Kenneth I. Goldman v. Annette C. Goldman, 196 Ill. App. 3d 785, 554 N.E.2d 1016 (1990), is of comparable quality, both in its account of the Jewish law of divorce and in its understanding of the constitutional consequences of ordering a spouse to participate in the execution of a Jewish divorce.

[76] Judge Gartenstein's assertion, 75 Misc.2d at 781, 348 N.Y.S.2d at 66, is not entirely correct. The wife must be willing to accept delivery of the bill of divorce either personally or through an agent specifically designated for that purpose. Her acceptance or designation of an agent must be in the presence of qualified witnesses and for all practical purposes must be under the supervision of a *bet din*. Hence appearance before a tribunal, or, alternatively, before two witnesses, is an absolute requirement. See *infra* note 108.

[77] 75 Misc.2d at 779, 348 N.Y.S.2d at 64.

[78] *Id.* at 780, 348 N.Y.S.2d at 65. In a civil divorce, the party seeking the divorce petitions the court to dissolve the marriage. However, neither the petitioning party nor the respondent dissolves the marriage. The parties merely bring the question before the court. It is the state, acting through the court, which dissolves the marriage. In Jewish law, however, the husband grants the divorce with the consent of the wife; the court merely supervises the proceedings. See *supra* text accompanying notes 29, 37 & 77 and *infra* note 108 and accompanying text.

Judge Gartenstein noted that asking a court to act in a matter that might interfere with religious disciplines or is the subject of litigation before an ecclesiastical court raises a First Amendment issue. He cited *Koeppel* as support for the contention that a contract to effectuate a *get* may be enforced in a civil court. (The trial judge overcame constitutional objections to order specific performance of the parties' agreement, and the Second Department reversed only because it found the agreement indefinite.) He distinguished *Margulies* – which he apparently and incorrectly thought to be a case in which a court was called upon to command specific performance and enforce a religious discipline upon a recalcitrant party – from the facts of the case before him. In *Rubin* it was not the innocent party asking the court to direct the defaulting party to comply with an undertaking to execute a *get*, but rather the defaulting party was seeking to enforce a financial agreement to which the religious act constituted a condition precedent. The fact that fulfillment of the condition is a religious act, Judge Gartenstein argued, in no way prevents the court from recognizing that the condition has not been fulfilled and hence the obligation is not enforceable. The court's involvement, he reasoned, is not with the religious practice but with the obligations made contingent upon it.[79] To recast this distinction in an idiom that has gained judicial currency, the two cases are distinguishable in that *Margulies* required "excessive entanglement" by the court in the execution of the *get* and *Rubin* did not.[80]

Just three years after its decision in *Pal*, in *Waxstein v. Waxstein*[81] the Second Department tacitly followed its decision in *Koeppel* by affirming without opinion a trial court decision to grant specific performance of a husband's promise in a separation agreement to provide his wife with a *get*. The trial judge in *Waxstein* found that *Koeppel* had upheld the enforceability of a promise to give a *get* and that neither *Margulies* nor *Pal* contradicted *Koeppel*.[82] He found further that both the First Department in *Margulies* and the Second

79 75 Misc.2d at 782, 348 N.Y.S.2d at 67. But cf. Steinberg v. Steinberg, 1982 WL 2446 (Ohio App. 8 Dist. June 24, 1982), where the appellate court held that conditioning an obligation to pay alimony to the wife upon her fulfilling her agreement to cooperate in obtaining a *get* violated Article I, § 7 of the Ohio Constitution, which prohibits the intervention by courts in religious matters. The court said that the trial court attempted to do indirectly what it could not do directly, inducing the wife to perform a religious act. Thus the trial court's order was declared unconstitutional and void.

80 The "excessive entanglement" criterion was first stated in Walz v. Tax Comm'n of New York, 397 U.S. 664, 675 (1970), and later in Lemon v. Kurtzman, 403 U.S. 602, 612–13 (1971). See also Presbyterian Church v. Mary Elizabeth Blue Hull Memorial Presbyterian Church, 393 U.S. 440 (1969).

81 90 Misc.2d 784, 395 N.Y.S.2d 877 (Sup. Ct. 1976), *aff'd*, 57 A.D.2d 863, 394 N.Y.S.2d 253 (1977).

82 *Id.* at 789, 395 N.Y.S.2d at 881. One judge had dissented in *Pal*, on the same grounds, that *Koeppel* had enforced a promise to give a *get*, 45 A.D.2d at 741, 356 N.Y.S.2d at 676.

Department in *Pal* had at least inferentially decided the constitutional issue in favor of enforcement: in *Margulies* the First Department "upheld the underlying orders of contempt and the fines imposed and permitted the husband to purge his contempt by paying the fines or by complying with the stipulation,"[83] and in *Pal* the Second Department refused to punish a wife for depriving her husband of visitation rights on the grounds that the husband had not complied with the terms of a stipulation in a divorce judgment that required the husband to give his wife a *get*.[84] Going beyond the decision in *Rubin*, the trial judge maintained that all three cases – *Koeppel*, *Margulies* and *Pal* – establish that a court may grant specific performance of a promise to effect a religious divorce. He construed *Margulies* and *Pal* only as precluding enforcement by imprisonment and as forbidding the court to convene a rabbinic tribunal. This was the decision that on appeal the Second Department affirmed.[85]

[83] 90 Misc.2d at 788, 395 N.Y.S.2d at 881.

[84] 45 A.D.2d at 739, 356 N.Y.S.2d at 673.

[85] 57 A.D.2d 863, 394 N.Y.S.2d 253 (1977). See also Scholl v. Scholl, 621 A.2d 808 (Del. Fam. Ct. 1992) (enforcing husband's promise to cooperate in giving a *get* pursuant to a separation agreement).

Nevertheless, it can hardly be stated that enforceability of a contract providing for satisfaction of a religious requirement or practice has been firmly established even in the state of New York. In an earlier case, not involving a religious divorce, the appellate division declined to order a Jew to comply with his contractual obligation to abide by Jewish law. In Wener v. Wener, 59 Misc.2d 957, 301 N.Y.S.2d 237 (Sup. Ct. 1969), *aff'd.* 35 A.D.2d 50, 312 N.Y.S.2d 815 (1970), a case involving an infant whose "adoption" had not been formalized in accordance with New York law, the trial court held a husband liable for child support based on common law and also on the court's interpretation of Jewish law, to which the court found the parties had bound themselves in their *ketubah*. 59 Misc.2d at 959, 301 N.Y.S.2d at 240. Justice Multer's decision, however, may be challenged for two reasons. (1) Nowhere does the *ketubah* provide explicitly for support of children, either adopted or natural. The *ketubah* is also silent about divorce in accordance with Jewish law. But, as a contract, it is certainly limited to the obligations of a husband towards his wife. (2) It is far from clear that there is an obligation in Jewish law to support an adopted child even when there exists a formal undertaking. The sources and arguments cited by Justice Multer are not germane, reflecting a lack of awareness of both the sources and methodology of Jewish law. For a discussion of this complex issue, see R. Abraham Rudner, *Imuẓ Yeled u-Mitḥayev la-Zon Ḥavero*, *No'am* (1961), vol. IV, p. 61; R. Moshe Findling, *Imuẓ Yeladim*, *No'am*, vol. IV, p. 65; Rabbi B.N. Ezrachi, *Gidrei Hitḥayevut be-Imuẓ Yeladim*, *No'am*, vol. IV, p. 94; and the cursory discussion of R. Mordecai ha-Kohen, *Imuẓ Yeladim lefi ha-Halakhah*, 48 *Sinai* 204 (1961), reprinted in *Torah she-be-al Peh* (1961), vol. III, p. 73.

The appellate division, nevertheless, affirmed the trial court decision, but on common law grounds only. It declined to apply Jewish law, declaring that "[a]pplication of religious law would raise grave constitutional problems of equal protection and separation of Church and State." 35 A.D.2d at 54, 312 N.Y.S.2d at 819. This statement is open to challenge on the grounds that the particular law to be applied in enforcing the contractual agreement is hardly "religious." It requires no profession of belief or performance of ritual. The parties could have spelled out the particular financial obligations without hint of subscription to religious practice and, hence, incorporation by reference to Jewish law of a mundane matter should

B. *Submission to Arbitration*

In 1983 a dispute over a husband's refusal to appear before a *bet din* reached the New York Court of Appeals, the state's highest court. In *Avitzur v. Avitzur*[86]

not be precluded. This distinction was clearly formulated in S. S. & B. Live Poultry Corp. v. Kashruth Ass'n, 158 Misc. 358, 360, 285 N.Y.S. 879, 883 (Sup. Ct. 1936).

Similar issues have been raised regarding the validity of antenuptial agreements concerning religious upbringing and education of children. The courts have consistently ruled that the welfare of the child is the overriding and determining factor. These decisions are discussed in Annot., 25 A.L.R.2d 928, 939 (1952) (Divorce-Race, Religion or Politics), and in Annot., 66 A.L.R.2d 1410, 1432 (1959) (Custody of Child-Religion as Factor). A number of cases contain dicta supporting enforcement of an agreement pertaining to religious matters. Denton v. James, 107 Kan. 729, 193 p. 307 (1920); Ramon v. Ramon, 34 N.Y.S.2d 100 (Fam. Ct. 1942); *In re* Luck, 10 Ohio Dec. 1 (Prob. Ct. 1900); Commonwealth v. McClelland, 70 Pa. Super. 273 (1918). In several cases, the courts declared such agreements to be unenforceable under the Free Exercise Clause. McLaughlin v. McLaughlin, 20 Conn. Supp. 278, 132 A.2d 420 (1957); Brewer v. Cary, 148 Mo. App. 193, 127 S.W. 685 (1910); Boerger v. Boerger, 26 N.J. Super. 90, 97 A.2d 419 (1953); Hackett v. Hackett, 78 Ohio L. Abs. 485, 150 N.E.2d 431, appeal dismissed, 168 Ohio St. 373, 154 N.E.2d 820 (1958).

The appellate division in *Wener* further said that "New York cannot apply one law to its Jewish residents and another law to all others." 35 A.D.2d at 54, 312 N.Y.S.2d at 819. However, as argued in Note, "Enforceability of Religious Law In Secular Courts – It's Kosher, But Is It Constitutional?," *Michigan Law Review*, vol. 71 (1973), p. 1641:

> [T]he application of Jewish law by the trial court in *Wener* was predicated not upon the parties' religion or race but upon the marriage contract... There was no indication that a Jew would be required to enter into such a contract by New York law; nor did the trial court rule that a non-Jew who entered into a similar contract would not be bound by the substantive provisions referring to Jewish law.

Id. at 1643.

Similarly, Judge Multer, in an unusual defense of his decision in the pages of a law journal, "Further Comment on Wener v. Wener," *Israel Law Review*, vol. 5 (1970), p. 463, wrote: "[I]t was proper to look to Jewish law for evidence of the intent of the parties. The *Ketuba*, the marriage agreement of the parties, established that intent as forcefully as their acts and conduct did." *Id.* at 464.

Parties to a contract may provide that disputes arising out of the contract must be adjudicated according to the laws of a specified jurisdiction, and subject to certain limitations other jurisdictions will enforce that agreement. The contract thus effectively incorporates by reference the relevant laws of the chosen jurisdiction. Thus an agreement to abide by Jewish law is no more than incorporation by reference of the corpus of Jewish law into the agreement. Accordingly, it is not Jewish law *per se* that the court applies to the parties, but the parties' own agreement. It was in line with this reasoning that the court in Hurwitz v. Hurwitz, 216 A.D. 362, 215 N.Y.S. 184 (1926), determined that a *ketubah* could be enforced as a contract insofar as its provisions are not contrary to the laws of New York and, accordingly, granted a widow the right to remain in the matrimonial abode.

No later case concerning enforcement of a contract to give a *get* discusses *Wener*, and despite *Wener*, New York courts in several subsequent cases have upheld the *ketubah* as a binding contract.

86 58 N.Y.2d 108, 446 N.E.2d 136, 459 N.Y.S.2d 572 (1983).

the parties, as part of their marriage ceremony, signed a marriage contract – a *ketubah*. Following a form common in Conservative Judaism, the *ketubah* used by the couple contained a clause binding the parties to submit to the jurisdiction of "the Beth Din of the Rabbinical Assembly and the Jewish Theological Seminary," and granted that body the right "to summon either party at the request of the other in order to enable the party so requesting to live in accordance with the standards of the Jewish law of marriage throughout his or her lifetime."[87] After obtaining a civil divorce, the wife sought an order, based on that clause, to compel her husband to appear before the *bet din*. The husband moved to dismiss the complaint on the grounds that the lawsuit involved religion and the court's assumption of jurisdiction would unconstitutionally entangle Church and State. The trial court granted the order. On appeal, the Third Department reversed, describing the *ketubah* as a "liturgical agreement," beyond the jurisdiction of the civil courts, and enforcement of its terms "a dangerous precedent."

By four votes to three the Court of Appeals in turn reversed the Third Department. The majority recognized that the issue before them was enforcement of an agreement to arbitrate, not specific performance of a promise to execute a *get*. They rejected the conclusion that the *ketubah* is a "liturgical agreement," and found the secular clauses of the *ketubah* to be enforceable:[88] "Viewed in this manner," they wrote,

> the provisions of the ketubah relied upon by plaintiff constitute nothing more than an agreement to refer the matter of a religious divorce to a nonjudicial forum. Thus, the contractual obligation plaintiff seeks to enforce is closely analogous to an antenuptial agreement to arbitrate a dispute in accordance with the law and tradition chosen by the parties. There can be little doubt that a duly executed antenuptial agreement, by which the parties agreed in advance of the marriage to the resolution of disputes that may arise after its termination, is valid and enforceable [citations omitted]. This agreement – the ketubah – should ordinarily be entitled to no less dignity than any other civil contract to submit a dispute to a non-judicial forum, so long as its enforcement violates neither the law nor the public policy of this State . . .[89]

[87] *Id.* at 112, 446 N.E.2d at 137, 459 N.Y.S.2d at 573.

[88] *Id.* at 115, 446 N.E.2d at 139, 459 N.Y.S.2d at 575.

[89] *Id.* at 113–14, 446 N.E.2d at 138, 459 N.Y.S.2d at 574. Furthermore, Section 7501 of the New York Civil Practice Law and Rules provides that "[a] written agreement to submit any controversy thereafter arising or any existing controversy to arbitration is enforceable *without regard to the justiciable character of the controversy . . .*" CPLR § 7501 (emphasis added). The New York statute is unambiguous in declaring that disputes do not become non-arbitrable simply because they differ from controversies that are ordinarily capable of judicial determination. See, e.g.,

The Court of Appeals found that an agreement to arbitrate the issue of religious divorce could be enforced "upon application of neutral principles of contract law, with no reference to any religious principle"[90] and hence that enforcement of such an agreement does not involve judicial entanglement in religious matters. Because the issue was not before it, the court did not decide whether a neutral principles doctrine would permit enforcement of an agreement to execute a *get*.[91]

The Court of Appeals focused its constitutional discussion on the Establishment Clause, not the Free Exercise Clause. Since Boaz Avitzur had conceded that as a practicing Jew he had no religious objection to executing a *get*, no free exercise issue was before the court.[92] The constitutional issue was whether judicial intervention for the purpose of enforcing a promise to submit to arbitration by a *bet din* constitutes an "establishment" of religion. Whether executing a *get* constitutes a religious practice and whether a promise to execute a *get* is enforceable were questions left unresolved.[93]

Siegel v. Ribak, 43 Misc.2d 7, 14, 249 N.Y.S.2d 903, 909 (Sup. Ct. 1964); Board of Educ. v. Cracovia, 36 A.D.2d 851, 852, 321 N.Y.S.2d 496, 497 (1971).

90 *Id.* at 115, 446 N.E.2d at 138, 459 N.Y.S.2d at 574–75.

91 Relying on *Avitzur* suggests that an agreement should submit disputes over the granting of a *get* to a *bet din* for arbitration rather than commit the husband to granting a *get*. The agreement should specify the *bet din* or, at a minimum, provide a mechanism for choosing its members lest a future court find, as did the appellate court in *Pal*, that civil courts lack the authority to convene a *bet din*. See *supra* notes 74 & 85 and accompanying text. Drafting such an agreement as a separate instrument, independent of the *ketubah*, would also obviate the objection expressed in the dissenting opinion in *Avitzur* that the *ketubah* is religious and not civil. For a form of such an agreement see J. David Bleich, "A Suggested Antenuptial Agreement: A Proposal in the Wake of *Avitzur*," *The Journal of Halacha and Contemporary Society*, vol. 7 (1984), pp. 25, 38–41; and J. David Bleich, "Jewish Divorce: Judicial Misconceptions and Possible Means of Civil Enforcement," *Connecticut Law Review*, vol. 16 (1984), pp. 201, 249–51, note 164.

92 To date, only one court has addressed the viability of a free exercise claim in refusing cooperation in the execution of a *get*. See Aflalo v. Aflalo, 295 N.J. Super. 527, 685 A.2d 523 (Ch. Div. 1996), discussed in text accompanying notes 134–136 *infra*. However, the order sought in *Aflalo* was not based on a contract to execute a *get*. Cf. Price v. Price, 16 Pa. D. & C. 290 (Pa. Com. Pl. 1932), discussed *infra* note 137.

93 146. *Id.* at 115–16, 446 N.E.2d at 139, 459 N.Y.S.2d at 575. It may be assumed that an order of the *bet din* to execute a *get* pursuant to a judicially mandated appearance before that tribunal would also be enforced by the *Avitzur* court. Indeed, the minority dissented in part because it viewed such an order as unenforceable: "[T]he evident objective of the present action . . . is to obtain a religious divorce, a matter well beyond the authority of any civil court." *Id.* at 121, 446 N.E.2d at 142, 459 N.Y.S.2d at 578 (Jones, J., dissenting). The majority must have recognized that arbitration is pointless unless the decision of the arbitrators is enforceable in a civil court. Hence, the majority should have been willing to enforce a decision of the arbitrators for specific performance even though it might not order specific performance directly, in the absence of a decision by the arbitrators. However, it should be noted that in Board of Education v.

C. *Non-Performance as Grounds for Invalidating a Divorce Decree*

In an unreported case, a New York trial judge, without directly enforcing an agreement to execute a *get*, used an indirect strategy to achieve the same result. In *B v. B*,[94] a trial judge adopted the view that the First Department's decision in *Margulies* barred him from ordering specific performance. Nonetheless, he reasoned that *Margulies* did not prevent him from exploring the circumstances surrounding the secular divorce. In the case before him, the wife withdrew her opposition to the husband's action for a divorce decree upon his agreement to cooperate in her obtaining a *get*. Accordingly, the judge scheduled a hearing to determine whether the husband, a Conservative clergyman and spiritual leader of a New York temple, had perpetrated a fraud in obtaining a secular divorce by reneging on his agreement to provide his wife with a religious divorce. A finding of fraud would have invalidated the divorce.

As in *Pal*, the judge was contemptuous of the husband's conduct, stating that "[h]e has reaped the fruits of the secular divorce and has carved out a new life for himself. He refuses to make it possible for the plaintiff to do the same. He has thus condemned her to a dismal future of never being free to marry."[95] The tactic apparently served its purpose. The scheduled hearing never took place, presumably because the husband recognized that failure to comply would result in invalidation of the divorce decree on grounds of fraud.

D. *Enforcement of the* Get *as an Obligation Established by the* Ketubah

1. In Civil Courts

In recent years, two decrees have required a husband to execute a religious divorce even in the absence of a specific undertaking. In *Stern v. Stern*[96] a New York trial court ordered a husband to deliver a *get* to his wife based on provisions of the *ketubah* he had executed at the time of his wedding. In granting the wife's motion for specific performance the trial judge wrote that "[t]he upholding of such contracts is favored by our courts and will be enforced

Cracovia, 36 A.D.2d 851, 321 N.Y.S.2d 496 (1971), the Second Department held an arbitration agreement to seek an advisory opinion to be enforceable pursuant to CPLR § 7501. Hence, it is possible, although unlikely, that a future court might find confirmation of an arbitration decision ordering the husband to grant a *get* to be unenforceable and construe *Avitzur* as mandating only that the parties seek the advice of the *bet din*.

94 N.Y.L.J., May 4, 1978 at 1, col. 2.

95 *Id.* at col. 3.

96 N.Y.L.J., Aug. 8, 1979, at 13, col. 5

according to the purpose and intentions of the parties."[97] The judge rejected an argument that the First Amendment prohibits enforcement:

97 *Id.* at col. 6. The enforceability of a *ketubah* in civil courts has a long and checkered history. In the first case, Goldstein v. Goldstein, 87 N.J. Eq. 601, 101 A. 249 (1917), the court ruled that, although the "marriage articles" of the *ketubah* employed unusual terminology, the *ketubah* was nevertheless enforceable. In a subsequent New York case, Hurwitz v. Hurwitz, 216 A.D. 362, 215 N.Y.S. 184 (1926), the *ketubah* was recognized as a valid contract despite the absence of signatures of the parties. This position was reaffirmed in Kaplan v. Kaplan, 69 Misc.2d 198, 329 N.Y.S.2d 750 (Sup. Ct. 1972), and by the trial court in Wener v. Wener, 59 Misc.2d 957, 301 N.Y.S.2d 237 (Sup. Ct. 1969). Although the decision of the lower court in *Wener* was sustained on appeal, 35 A.D.2d 50, 312 N.Y.S.2d 815 (1970), the appellate division questioned the enforceability of at least collateral aspects of the *ketubah*. The court ruled that a husband could not be compelled to support a child taken into his home but not formally adopted by him on the grounds that a *ketubah* represents a general undertaking to be bound by Jewish law in all domestic matters. See *supra* note 85. In a later decision, *In re* Estate of White, 78 Misc.2d 157, 356 N.Y.S.2d 208 (Sur. Ct. 1974), the court addressed the nature of the *ketubah* and accepted the contention that the *ketubah* is "a matter of form and a ceremonial document rather than a legal obligation." 78 Misc.2d at 159, 356 N.Y.S.2d at 210 (citing George Horowitz, *The Spirit of Jewish Law* (New York, 1973) (1953), § 176). Accordingly, a widow who had signed an antenuptial agreement was denied recovery even of the sum expressly stipulated in the subsequently executed *ketubah*. In reaching this result, the court gave particular consideration to an affidavit of the officiating clergyman:

> The *Ketubah* in this case having been executed in today's times, must necessarily be interpreted under today's laws and applying the Jewish legal axiom "The Law of the land is the law", the Jewish Law says that the widow is entitled to that which the law of the land (New York State) allows her.

78 Misc.2d at 158, 356 N.Y.S.2d at 209. This is simply a mistaken interpretation of the "Jewish legal axiom" upon which it is unnecessary to dwell. The court cited George Horowitz, *The Spirit of Jewish Law* § 315, in assessing the value of the *ketubah* at approximately thirty dollars, a sum which in Horowitz' opinion "is not taken seriously as a burden or charge on the Husband's estate." 78 Misc.2d at 159, 356 N.Y.S.2d at 210. For a more accurate assessment of the value of the *ketubah*, see R. Abraham Chaim Noe, *Shi'urei Torah* 3:44 (1947). Differing values are assigned by R. Joseph E. Henkin, *Al Dvar Isur Shtei Nashim*, 32 *Ha-Pardes* (Tishri 1958), pp. 10, 11, and III R. Isaac Liebes, *Teshuvot Bet Avi* (1980), no. 137. See also Irving Agus, "*Shi'ur ha-Ketubah be-Tur Keneh Middah le-Emdatam ha-Kalkalit shel ha-Yehudim be-Germaniyah bi-Yemei ha-Beinayim*," Horeb, vol. 5 (1939), p. 143. For the various opinions regarding the quantity of silver in which the *ketubah* is denominated see R. Judah Kelemer, *Tosefet Ketubah* (Jerusalem, 1990), pp. 13–16.

Later, in *Stern*, a New York trial court held the *ketubah* to be a valid contract establishing a civilly enforceable obligation to execute a *get* when demanded by Jewish law. N.Y.L.J., Aug. 8, 1979, at 13, col. 5.

The validity of the *ketubah* as a binding contract was also an issue in an unpublished decision of the Oakland County Circuit Court, Roth v. Roth, no. 79–192709-DO (Mich. Cir. Jan. 23, 1980). The wife demanded a property settlement pursuant to the antenuptial agreement of the parties, namely, the *ketubah*. The court ruled: (1) property settlement provisions within antenuptial agreements made in contemplation of divorce are invalid in Michigan; (2) the *ketubah* does not make specific provision for a property settlement upon divorce; and hence

> Jewish law cannot be referred to in its totality as religious law only because Judaism denotes a nationality, a culture, and/or a comprehensive mode of existence that goes beyond the religious realm and therefore Jewish law can be divided as that which is strictly religious (defining the relationship between man and God) and one which is secular (governing the relationship between man and man). Further, the writing of a Get, its execution and delivery is not a religious act and although a rabbi is present to supervise and a scribe is utilized, this is only because the average Jewish man is not learned in Jewish law and he needs the rabbi and the scribe just as he needs his lawyer in a civil action.[98]

The court concluded that enforcement of a contract to execute a *get* does not pose a constitutional issue. Indeed, once the *get* is properly understood it becomes apparent that the principle of separation of Church and State does not bar enforcement of a promise to execute a *get*.[99]

(3) the disposition of property under the terms of the *ketubah* would require application of the underlying religious law. In declining to enforce the monetary terms of the *ketubah*, the court said that "[w]hile the division of property is a secular matter, the interpretation of ecclesiastic law is not... In the instant case, as an interpretation of ecclesiastical law would be necessary to derive a property division from the 'ketubah', this court cannot intervene." *Roth*, No. 79–192709-DO at 3. For a further discussion of *Roth*, see text accompanying notes 163–169 *infra*.

A similar issue was before an English court in Shahnez v. Rizwan, [1964] 2 All. E.R. 993, regarding enforcement of a Moslem marriage contract that provided for a deferred dower known as *mehar* or *mahr*. The court ruled the provisions enforceable. *Id.* at 998.

For a discussion of Avitzur v. Avitzur, 58 N.Y.2d 108, 446 N.E.2d 136, 459 N.Y.S.2d 572 (1983), see text accompanying notes 86–93 *supra*. In *Avitzur* the New York Court of Appeals affirmed a trial court's denial of a motion for summary judgment against a claim seeking specific performance of an arbitration clause in a *ketubah*.

98 N.Y.L.J., Aug. 8, 1979, at 13, col. 5. Stern v. Stern was cited by the New York Supreme Court in Rosenberg v. Rosenberg, N.Y.L.J., March 24, 1980, at 15, col. 5. In the course of divorce proceedings, the parties entered into a stipulation with regard to various property rights and agreed to the execution of a *get*. The wife proved to be less than fully cooperative but moved for specific performance of the remainder of the stipulations. Justice Rigler, citing both *Stern* and *Rubin*, directed the parties to secure a *get*. In doing so, the court followed the precedent established in *Rubin* that "[i]n the absence of following such a procedure, this court will not enforce the further rights and obligations of the parties under the stipulation." N.Y.L.J., March 24, 1980, at 15, col. 6. The question of compelling specific performance in the execution of the *get* in line with the decision in *Stern* was left in abeyance. The court did, however, state that "[i]f it is subsequently shown that the wife has deliberately refused to participate in the securing of a GET, the court will then consider whether specific performance will be against her." N.Y.L.J., March 24, 1980, at 15, col. 6.

99 The question whether execution of a *get* constitutes a religious act has been considered by a number of non-American courts as well. In Algeria, the *Decret Crémieux* of October 24, 1870 stripped Jewish ecclesiastical courts of jurisdiction they formerly enjoyed in matters of family law and provided that such matters be governed by French civil law. The question of compelling a religious divorce was raised almost immediately in the Dariente affair, which

The United States Supreme Court has interpreted the Establishment Clause as prohibiting state action that (1) lacks a secular purpose, (2) has a primary effect of advancing or inhibiting religion or (3) causes "excessive

was brought before the *Cour de Cassation* in 1876. 1877 S. Jur. I 27. Dariente had participated in a religious marriage ceremony in 1871 – but not a civil marriage – and later married another woman in a civil ceremony. He refused to deliver a *get* to his first wife. The Court of Appeal of Algiers sustained the first wife's action to compel Dariente to execute a *get*. The court found the religious marriage to be a "fact" that could give rise to prejudice but held that the plaintiff had suffered both an unjustifiable deprivation of her liberty to marry and an injury to her freedom of conscience. Most significantly, the court specifically found the act of the husband in executing the divorce to be non-religious and "above all an act of a civil and ordinary character." *Id.* The *Cour de Cassation* decision was based on principles of freedom of conscience and freedom to marry, principles that were held to override the provisions of the *Decret Crémieux*. It is significant to note that the husband was compelled to grant a religious divorce at a time when secular divorce did not exist in French civil law. See H. Patrick Glenn, "Where Heavens Meet: The Compelling of Religious Divorces," *American Journal of Comparative Law*, vol. 28 (1980), pp. 1, 14.

Courts in metropolitan France accepted this precedent as well. The earliest seems to be that of the Civil Tribunal of Metz, 1960 J.P.C. [*Juris-Classeur periodique, la semaine juridique*] 111632 (Trib. civ. Metz April 27, 1955). See also 1957 J.P.C. 11 9892 (Trib. Seine Feb. 22, 1957); 1960 J.P.C. 111632 (Trib. civ. Grenoble May 7, 1958); 1968 *Clunet* (Trib. Seine June 22, 1967); *Revue Critique* 474 (1969).

The Civil Tribunal of Metz compelled the husband to issue a *get* and assessed damages despite the wife's intervening remarriage. This factor served only to prompt the court to reject a day-to-day future accumulation of damages in the form of a lump sum assessment. In a decision of the Court of Appeal of Paris, 1960 J.P.C. 11 11632 (Feb. 4, 1959), a husband's claim that he had abandoned the Jewish faith and could not be forced to engage in the religious practices of Judaism was rejected. The court explicitly ruled that the act of delivering a *get* is, in Jewish law, not contingent upon the religious convictions of the husband and hence is devoid of religious significance. The granting of a *get* is described in that decision as a "purely civil formality" requiring neither attendance at synagogue nor the taking of oaths. More recently, in 1972, the French Court of Cassation, 1973 Cass. Civ. 493, 1973 G.P. 1.416 (Dec. 13, 1972), declared an order holding the husband responsible for refusing to deliver a *get* not to be in violation of the 1905 law of separation of Church and State. See Glenn, *supra*, at 15–16.

In Germany, although the cases are fewer and the precedent not as strong, courts have adopted the opposite position. A religious divorce first came to a German court in B. v. B., 57 R.G.Z. [Reichsgericht in Zivilsachen] 250 (1904) (German superior court). In connection with an agreement concerning alimony and property rights, the husband agreed to appear before a *bet din* to execute a *get*. Subsequently, he refused to fulfill his undertaking and was directed to do so by the trial court. The Imperial German *Reichsgericht* reversed this decision:

> [T]here do not exist, at the present time, any legal norms pertaining to marriage other than those promulgated by the State. Accordingly, we must dismiss the Appellate Court's idea that the declarations and the acts prescribed by the Jewish religion for the ritual divorce are "by and large" or "predominantly" or . . . even "exclusively" of a legal nature . . . They are, if still adhered to, acts of a purely religious nature. From that fact it immediately follows that the execution of such acts by way of legal coercion is not within the reach of the state. Now that the state has defined the borderline between its own sphere and that of religion, neither is to encroach upon the sphere of the other. In the realm of religion the binding force of obligations is a matter of conscience and spirit,

entanglement" with religion.[100] It is clear, for example, that a court could not order specific performance of a contract requiring a person to "go to confession or to say six Our Fathers and four Hail Marys."[101] The Establishment Clause forbids a court to become involved in such religious activity.[102]

In contrast, executing a *get* involves neither worship nor profession of faith. A *get* is nothing more than the rescission of a contract – a contract of marriage. It is an act of the parties themselves, not the decree of an ecclesiastic tribunal.[103]

> and the fulfillment of such obligations is a religious and ethical duty. In this sphere there does not and may not exist a legal binding of the will . . . Hence, in including in a contract of private law the husband's promise to consent to a religious divorce, the parties have, mistakenly, agreed upon a subject-matter which does not lend itself to a legal transaction; they have, therefore, entered into a contract legally impossible of performance.

Translation from Max Rheinstein, *Comparative Law of Contracts* (1944), pp. 6–7 (cited in Note, "Civil Enforceability of Religious Antenuptial Agreements," *University of Chicago Law Review*, vol. 23 (1955), pp. 122, 131–32).

In its decision the *Reichsgericht* specifically accepted the findings of the lower court that the granting of a *get* involves no profession of faith. Moreover, the court noted the possibility of the use of an agent by the husband if he desired not to be personally involved in the execution of a Jewish religious divorce. The husband's contention that compulsion could have violated his freedom of conscience was expressly rejected. 57 R.G.Z. at 254–55. These points, it may be remembered, were not to be appreciated by an American court until well over half a century later. The decision was predicated upon the principle of separation of Church and State, which, in the court's opinion, would have been compromised in enforcing the agreement. The decision makes no reference to the resultant impairment of the wife's freedom of religion that follows from non-enforcement of the parties' agreement.

Curiously, in the second German case in which this issue was raised, 9 *Monatschrift für Deutches Recht* 768 (1973) (OLGZ Köln), the Köln *Oberlandesgericht* failed to cite the earlier decision. The latter case is another one of the rare instances where a husband, rather than a wife, sought relief in a civil court. The court rejected the husband's petition to compel his wife to cooperate in the execution of a *get* on the grounds that to do so would be forcing the wife to participate in a religious ceremony in violation of the guarantees of religious freedom. In this case it was not the principle of strict separation of Church and State that was invoked, but rather the contention – rejected by the German superior court over half a century earlier – that execution of a *get* is a religious ceremony.

Although the decision of the Köln *Oberlandesgericht* rejected use of financial restraint in the form of *Zwangsgeld*, or financial penalty, as coercion to force participation in a religious ceremony, it left the door open for similar coercion in a different guise. In an aside the court stated that, although it could not command specific performance of a religious undertaking, compensatory damages for non-fulfillment were "certainly not excluded." See also Susan Maidment, *supra* note 14, at 626, n.71, who observes that an English court might refuse to grant specific performance but might award damages for breach of contractual obligation.

[100] See Committee for Pub. Educ. and Religious Liberty v. Nyquist, 413 U.S. 756, 772–73 (1973); Lemon v. Kurtzman, 403 U.S. 602, 612–13 (1971).

[101] See Margulies v. Margulies, 42 A.D.2d at 518, 344 N.Y.S.2d at 485 (Nunez, J., dissenting).

[102] See Walz v. Tax Comm'n of N.Y., 397 U.S. 664 (1970).

[103] See *supra* note 50. Noteworthy is the fact that it is precisely the absence of any religious element in the execution of a *get* that led to the abolition of the requirement for a *get* by the Reform Movement. See *Protokolle*, *supra* note 58, at 36, and Moses Mielziner, *supra* note 58,

The *get* itself "is theologically neutral, amounting to a formal release by the husband of his former spouse."[104] The proceedings are devoid of divine reference or religious formula. No blessings are uttered; no credos or professions of faith are pronounced.[105] Execution of a *get* does not require the participants to subscribe to any particular set of beliefs. Indeed, a *get* may (and, in order to enable the wife to remarry under Jewish law, must) be executed even if the husband has formally renounced Judaism.[106] Moreover, in ordering a husband to grant a *get* the court need not direct him to appear before an ecclesiastic tribunal. Since a *get* is not a judicial act, it may be drafted, witnessed and delivered under the supervision of qualified laymen.[107] Such

at 135. As stated by one Reform scholar: "[In Biblical and rabbinic law, divorce was a purely civil act which was never given religious sanctity. Hence divorce should be recognized as an act proceeding solely from the judiciary power of the state." Wolf Gunther Plaut, *The Growth of Reform Judaism* (New York, 1965), pp. 258–59. The refusal of traditional Judaism to accept this conclusion does not diminish the validity of the premise. See note 163 and accompanying text *infra*.

[104] Roth v. Roth, No. 79–192709-DO at 2 (Mich. Cir. Jan. 23, 1980). See note 164 and accompanying text *infra*.

[105] For a detailed, step-by-step description of the procedure followed in drafting and executing a *get*, see *Shulḥan Arukh, Even ha-Ezer* 154, *Seder ha-Get*. A literal translation of the text of the *get* reads as follows:

> On the . . . day of the week, the . . . day of the month of . . . , in the year . . . from the creation of the world according to the reckoning we count here, the city of . . . which is situated on the river . . . (and on the river . . .) (and situated near springs [or: wells] of water), I, . . . (also known as . . .), the son of . . . (also known as . . .), who stands this day in the city of . . . (also known as . . .), which is situated on the river . . . (and on the river. . .) (and situated near springs (or: wells] of water), have desired of my own will without being subject to duress and have abandoned and sent forth and dismissed thee to thyself, you, my wife, . . . (also known as . . .), daughter of . . . (also known as . . .), who stands this day in the city of . . . (also known as . . .), which is situated on the river . . . (and on the river . . .) (and situated near springs [or: wells] of water), who has been my wife from before. And now I have sent forth and abandoned and dismissed thee to thyself that thou be permitted and have authority over thyself to go and marry any man thou may desire, and no person shall protest against thee from this day and for ever more, and thou art permitted to every man (lit: and thou art unfettered with regard to every man). This shall be unto thee from me a bill of dismissal, and a letter of abandonment, and an instrument of divorce in accordance with the law of Moses and Israel.
>
> . . . the son of . . . , witness.
> . . . the son of . . . , witness.

[106] See *Shulḥan Arukh, Even ha-Ezer* 129:5.

[107] See generally *Shulḥan Arukh, Even ha-Ezer* 123, 130 & 133. Delivery of a properly drafted instrument by the husband to the wife in the presence of two qualified witnesses constitutes the essence of the divorce procedure. Customarily, the *bet din* issues a *petur*, i.e., a document declaring that a valid *get* has been executed and that the parties are free to remarry. The *petur*, however, is not an essential part of the divorce proceeding. The *petur* is issued solely for evidentiary purposes in order to obviate the necessity for the

matters are customarily supervised by rabbinic authorities only to assure that the *get* be executed in accordance with Jewish law and that its validity not be subject to challenge. Furthermore, if the husband finds personal participation repugnant, he may execute a *get* by appointing an agent to act on his behalf.[108]

The primary effect of judicial involvement in enforcing a promise to execute a *get* is neither to enhance nor inhibit religion; its purpose is to facilitate remarriage. The crucial question is whether religious divorce serves a secular purpose. The answer is that it does. In addition to furthering the religiously neutral state interest in ensuring that citizens perform their contracts, enforcement of a promise to execute a *get* completely dissolves the bonds binding partners in a "dead marriage"[109] and enables them to marry and rear families.

A Michigan court has found that failure to intervene not only denies the right to free exercise but also destroys the right to "liberty" guaranteed by the Fourteenth Amendment.[110] The latter "denotes not merely freedom from bodily restraint but also the right of the individual . . . to marry, establish a home and bring up children . . . "[111] Promoting marriage and encouraging the establishment of families furthers a secular purpose that permits judicial intervention.[112]

taking of testimony at some future time in order to establish eligibility for remarriage. Technically, even the *petur* may be issued by three competent laymen rather than by a *bet din* composed of ordained rabbis. See generally *Bet Shmu'el, Even ha-Ezer* 142:7; *Shulḥan Arukh, Even ha-Ezer* 154, *Seder ha-Get* § 26; *Kav Naki, Seder Get Rishon va-Sheni*, § 249.

108 See *Shulḥan Arukh, Even ha-Ezer* 140:1. The wife may similarly appoint an agent to receive the *get* on her behalf. See *Shulḥan Arukh, Even ha-Ezer* 140:30 and *supra* note 76.

109 Cf. Gleason v. Gleason, 26 N.Y.2d 28, 35, 256 N.E.2d 513, 516, 308 N.Y.S.2d 347, 351 (1970) (making a newly enacted grounds for divorce retroactive in order to end dead marriages).

110 Roth v. Roth, No. 79–192709-DO (Mich. Cir. Jan. 23, 1980). For further discussion of *Roth* see text accompanying notes 164–170 *infra*.

111 Meyer v. Nebraska, 262 U.S. 390, 399 (1923). See also Zablocki v. Redhail, 434 U.S. 374 (1977); Loving v. Virginia, 388 U.S. 1 (1967).

112 Moreover, it may be argued that enforcement of an agreement to execute a *get* does not fall within the ambit of the Establishment Clause altogether. Monrad Paulsen has argued that the "religious matching" provisions of adoption statutes are constitutional insofar as they reflect parental preference. The statutes usually provide that, in placing children for adoption, an attempt must be made, insofar as possible, to seek adoptive parents of the same faith as that of the natural parents. The underlying assumption is that such is the desire of the natural parents in surrendering their child for adoption. Paulsen argued that the principle of separation of Church and State does not prevent governmental enforcement of private preferences:

> The principle of separation cannot mean that religion is not to take benefit from state action. The state may see to it that the terms of a will which benefit the Roman Catholic Church are carried out. A trust providing income for the Methodist Church will be supported by the full complement of remedies available for such a purpose. In many instances the state gives scope to private choice.
>
> Religious-matching provisions are constitutional when they seek to uphold the right of a child to gain access to the religion of his choice, or, in the case of those too young to

In *Shapiro v. Shapiro*,[113] a New York trial judge issued a decision that, while not directly addressing the First Amendment, affirms that execution of a *get* is not "religious." The Rabbinical District Court of Tel Aviv issued an order directing a husband to execute a *get*. The husband then became a citizen of the United States and resident of Brooklyn. In a motion for summary judgment, the wife asked the New York court to treat the Israeli decree as a New York decree, citing the principle of comity. The judge ruled that the court must recognize the Israeli decree and enforce its directives. He ordered the husband to schedule "an appointment with the Rabbinical Council of America . . . to perform all the ritual acts of the 'get' ceremony in accordance with the direction of the Rabbinical Court."[114]

Noting that a finding that the order of a foreign court contravenes public policy would ban enforcement in American courts, the court ruled that the order to execute a *get* does not offend public policy. In contrast, an order of a foreign court requiring a person to perform an act of worship or the like would certainly offend public policy by violating First Amendment rights. This principle was clearly stated in *Machesky v. Bizzell*,[115] a decision dealing with the application of comity to the relationship between federal and state courts. In *Machesky* the court declared that "a federal court must yield to the important institutional interests in comity where only private rights are involved. Where, however, the institutional interests in comity collides [sic] with the paramount institutional interest protected by the First Amendment, comity must yield."[116] Similarly, in *Sheridan v. Garrison*[117] the court declared that "[t]here is a clear basis for the subordination of the comity principle to the protection of the first amendment rights in exceptional cases, and this basis is to be found in the nature of comity . . . and the cases that establish the overriding policy for vindicating first amendment rights immediately."[118] Thus, inherent in the application of comity is a finding that an order requiring the husband's execution of a *get* does not deprive him of liberties guaranteed

> possess a meaningful personal commitment, when they endeavor to maintain the right of a parent to select the religious education of his child. These laws are constitutional in these circumstances because *their purpose is to determine religious training with reference to a private rather than a governmental preference.*

Monrad G. Paulsen, "Constitutional Problems in Utilizing a Religious Factor in Adoptions and Placements of Children," in Dallin H. Oakes ed., *The Wall Between Church and State* (Chicago, IL, 1963), pp. 117, 141 (emphasis added).

[113] 110 Misc.2d 726, 442 N.Y.S.2d 928 (1981), *modified* 88 A.D.2d 592, 449 N.Y.S.2d 806 (1982).

[114] 110 Misc.2d at 731, 442 N.Y.S.2d at 931.

[115] 414 F.2d 283 (5th Cir. 1969).

[116] *Id.* at 291. See also Wallace v. Brewer, 315 F. Supp. 431, 450–51 (M.D. Ala. 1970).

[117] 415 F.2d 699 (5th Cir. 1969).

[118] *Id.* at 707.

by the First Amendment. *Shapiro*, then, must be understood as affirming the principle that execution of a *get* is not a religious act.

The findings of the trial judge in *Stern* resemble those of an earlier decision by a trial court in Manitoba, *Morris v. Morris*[119] (which *Stern* does not cite). There the trial court found the *ketubah* to be an enforceable contract, and directed the husband to appear before a *bet din*. On appeal, the Manitoba Court of Appeal reversed, over the dissent of its Chief Justice. While the Chief Justice agreed that the *ketubah* is an enforceable contract, he added one salient point:

> Since the wife is 37 years of age she is still within the child-bearing category. This aspect of Jewish law accordingly affects the civil rights of the wife, the man to whom she is presently united, and their potential offspring. To them the status of legality and legitimacy in the eyes of the orthodox Jewish community is a matter of real concern. To ignore the right to that status on the ground that it does not stem directly from the operation of the civil law is to blind oneself to realities. The common law of the twentieth century is not so rigid as to exclude such a right from the ambit of civil rights deserving protection.[120]

Recast in the language of American constitutional law, the argument is that refusal to permit litigation arising from a valid contract of this kind constitutes denial of basic civil rights and is a violation of an individual's right to free exercise of religion. Nevertheless, four justices voted to reverse in three concurring opinions.

Justice Guy (with Monnin) doubted whether the *ketubah* forms a contract at all.[121] He noted that the wife had remarried in a civil ceremony contrary to Jewish law without obtaining a religious divorce. In addition, in a misunderstanding of Jewish law, Justice Guy accused Mrs. Morris of violating Jewish law by petitioning the court for a civil decree:

> According to the statement as to the law of Moses and Israel, as agreed upon by the rabbis who signed the statement (which is included in the judgment of the learned trial Judge) the husband is the only one who can institute proceedings for a bill of divorcement. Yet, forsaking the law of Moses and Israel, the wife herself commenced divorce proceedings in the Canadian Civil Court.[122]

[119] 36 D.L.R.3d 447 (Manitoba Q.B.), *rev'd*, 42 D.L.R.3d 550 (Manitoba App. 1973).
[120] 42 D.L.R.3d at 558–59 (Freedman, C.J., dissenting).
[121] *Id.* at 565–67.
[122] *Id.* at 567–68.

Thus, even if it were correct to construe the *ketubah* as a contract providing for dissolution of the marriage through religious divorce, a divorce court, sitting as a court of equity, would not order a husband to give a *get* to a wife who has behaved inequitably by "forsaking the law of Moses and Israel" when suing for civil divorce: "But, it is argued, the Canadian law will uphold and enforce a contract. And it will. But one who comes to a court of equity must come with clean hands, and in the light of the facts we have in the present case, Mrs. Morris does not."[123]

Justice Guy's assumption that Jewish law forbids a wife to institute civil divorce proceedings is incorrect. Jewish law takes no cognizance of such proceedings. It does not forbid participation in them and a wife who commences them is not *ipso facto* guilty of "forsaking the law of Moses and Israel." The prescriptions of Jewish law governing issuance of a divorce apply solely to the bill of divorce in Jewish law, i.e., to the *get*. Moreover, although the husband or his agent must write the *get* and deliver it to the wife, it is simply not the case that Jewish law bars the wife from instituting divorce proceedings before a *bet din*. In certain cases, the court will accede to her demand and compel the husband to execute a *get*.[124] But even when her suit fails, the wife has not violated Jewish law by bringing a claim.

That the wife had entered into a second marriage by means of a civil ceremony should not bar equitable relief on the grounds of "unclean hands." Mrs. Morris has, after all, insofar as the secular state is concerned, not acted inequitably towards her former spouse. More sensitive to this issue is the trial court in *Koeppel*:[125] "It may well be that plaintiff has not lived up to the laws of her faith, but this should not forever bar her from rectifying the situation, if she so desires."[126]

Justice Hall concurred in setting aside the lower court's decision on the grounds that, since Mrs. Morris was free to remarry under Canadian law, her claim affected no civil right and hence could not be enforced.[127]

[123] *Id.* at 568.

[124] For specific causes for compelling a husband to grant a *get*, see *Shulḥan Arukh, Even ha-Ezer* 154.

[125] 138 N.YS.2d 366 (Sup. Ct. 1954), *aff'd*, 3 A.D.2d 853, 161 N.YS.2d 694 (1957). See *supra* notes 48–58 and accompanying text.

[126] 138 N.Y.S.2d at 373.

[127] 42 D.L.R.3d at 572 (Hall, J., concurring). The implication of this statement is that in a hypothetical situation in which absence of a religious divorce would effectively bar a valid marriage under secular law, a civil right does, in fact, exist and the court might compel a religious divorce in order to preserve the wife's freedom to contract a legally valid marriage. Such would be the case if the wife were to be a party to divorce proceedings in Canada but domiciled in Israel and subject to the laws of the State of Israel in any subsequent marriage.

Justice Matas concurred on two grounds: (1) Counsel for Mr. Morris referenced a published source claiming that a *get* issued at the direction of a non-Jewish court is invalid on the grounds of duress; and (2) Reform rabbis will officiate at a marriage ceremony notwithstanding the absence of a *get*. Justice Matas thus concluded that "[u]nder all the circumstances, it appears that allegations by applicant as to infringement of her civil rights are somewhat tenuous."[128]

Justice Matas' argument is surprising. Mrs. Morris represented herself as an adherent of Orthodox Judaism, hence concerned with the stigma upon herself and her future progeny within the community of Orthodox Jews. A marriage solemnized by a Reform clergyman would in no way mitigate that stigma. Also, four Winnipeg rabbis (including the chairman and a member of the Winnipeg *bet din*) testified that, in the case before the court, the *bet din* could supervise the Morrises' religious divorce pursuant to an order of the civil court. Indeed the lower court specifically found that the rabbis would welcome such an order. As emphasized by Chief Justice Freedman, "it is not lightly to be presumed that the rabbinical court would indulge in an exercise in futility by presiding over the grant of a divorce decree that it knew to be invalid."[129]

In *Minkin v. Minkin*[130] a judge of the Superior Court of New Jersey applied the approach of Justice Held in *Stern* and of the trial court in *Morris*, ruling that the *ketubah* constitutes a binding contract requiring a *get* when mandated by Jewish law and ordered specific performance. The court accepted expert

Such a case was heard by the Family Court of Australia in *In re* the Marriage of Shulsinger, 2 Fam. L. R. 11.611 (Fam. Ct. Australia 1977). The trial court sought and received an undertaking on the part of the husband that he would grant a *get*. On appeal, the propriety of exacting such an undertaking was questioned in light of the provisions of the Australian Constitution. The appeals court did not cite *Morris*, but in a decision consistent with the inference noted above declared:

> [W]hat his Honour was concerned with was the serious question of the injustice that would arise if the husband sought and obtained a divorce in Australia, but refused to relieve his wife of the obligations of the marriage. It is contrary to all notions of justice to allow such a possibility to arise in a court, and to say that the court can do nothing. Here the husband applied for divorce in Australia and, unless he takes steps to obtain a divorce in a Rabbinical Court the wife is effectively bound by marriage from the obligation of which he has been forever freed. Consistent with his duty under § 43(a) his Honour was bound to ensure, as far as he could, that the same freedom was made available to the wife, as would be available to the husband.

2 Fam. L. R. at 11.617.

[128] 42 D.L.R.2d at 575 (Matas, J., concurring).

[129] *Id.* at 558 (Freedman, C.J., dissenting).

[130] 180 N.J. Super. 260, 434 A.2d 665 (Ch. Div.1981).

testimony from four rabbis who testified that execution of a *get* involves no religious act.[131] Indeed, the court recognized that marriage is a contractual relationship and the *get* a rescission of the contract. Moreover, no one has considered statutes permitting clergymen to solemnize marriages as creating an excessive entanglement with religion: "The get procedure is a release document devoid of any religious connotation and cannot be construed as any more religious than the marriage ceremony itself." Accordingly, the court found "that the entry of an order compelling defendant to secure a get would have the clear secular purpose of completing dissolution of the marriage. Its primary effect neither advances nor inhibits religion since it does not require the husband to participate in a religious ceremony or to do acts contrary to his religious beliefs."[132]

[131] See *infra* note 166 and accompanying text. However, in Steinberg v. Steinberg, 1982 WL 2446, an Ohio appellate court considered the finding of a trial court that it had no authority to order performance of "what it considers a religious act." *Id.* at 1. The appellate court not only agreed that enforcement of a *get* would compel the recalcitrant wife to perform a religious act even though such an undertaking was incorporated in a separation agreement but also found that a court could not indirectly force cooperation by enforcing modification of alimony because of non-performance as provided in the separation agreement. *Id.* at 3. The latter finding represents a rejection of the ruling in Rubin v. Rubin, 75 Misc. 2d 776, 348 N.Y.S. 2d, 61 (Fam. Ct. 1973). *Rubin* involved a separation agreement that incorporated a settlement of financial claims against the husband and an agreement to cooperate in securing a religious divorce. The husband refused payment in the absence of such cooperation on the part of the wife. The husband's position was upheld on the grounds that, although the court must refrain from involvement in religious matters and hence could not direct specific performance with regard to a *get*, it did have the authority to enforce a financial agreement in which the religious act constituted a condition precedent. The court's involvement, it reasoned, was not with religious practice but with obligations made contingent thereupon. 75 Misc. 2d at 782.

[132] *Id.* at 266, 434 A.2d at 668. In Burns v. Burns, 223 N.J. Super. 219, 538 A.2d 438 (Ch. Div. 1987), the husband claimed that his religious beliefs had changed and he no longer believed in the necessity of executing a *get*. That, of course, is irrelevant. Not believing a *get* to be necessary is not an assertion that participation is precluded by religious belief. In *Burns* itself, the husband offered to give his wife a *get* if the wife would invest $25,000 in an irrevocable trust for the benefit of their daughter with the husband and another party of his choosing as joint trustees. Following *Minkin*'s treatment of the Establishment Clause, the court ordered the husband to submit to the jurisdiction of the *bet din* to initiate the proceedings for executing a *get*, or, in the alternative, to appoint an agent to act on his behalf. The husband also made a free exercise argument, claiming that ordering him to give a *get* would compromise his religious beliefs. The court rejected his argument, saying:

> A true religious belief is not compromised as the amount of money offered or demanded is increased. An offer to secure a "get" for $25,000 makes this a question of money not religious belief. This "offer," which is not denied by the plaintiff, takes this issue outside the First Amendment.

223 N.J. Super. at 223–224, 538 A.2d at 440. A Florida court found a waiver of First Amendment claims under similar circumstances, Fleischer v. Fleischer, 586 So.2d 1253 (Fla. App. 1991).

Fifteen years after *Minkin*, in *Aflalo v. Aflalo*,[133] a judge of the Superior Court of New Jersey rejected *Minkin*'s position that ordering a husband to give a *get* is consistent with the First Amendment. In *Aflalo* a wife refused to settle a divorce claim she brought against her husband unless the court ordered the husband to cooperate with her in obtaining a Jewish divorce. (The order was not to enforce a provision of the *ketubah*.) The husband refused to execute a *get* because he wanted to reconcile with his wife and asserted that he wished to appear with her before a *bet din* for that purpose. Unlike *Minkin*, *Aflalo* focused on the Free Exercise Clause, not on the Establishment Clause. Ordering the husband to give his wife a *get*, the court found, would violate his right to free exercise of religion. The judge rejected *Minkin*'s conclusion that executing a *get* is not a religious act. He argued, first of all, that a court would become entangled in religious affairs by becoming an arbiter of what is and is not "religious." But he also rejected *Minkin*'s conclusion that its order concerned purely civil issues. The order, he said, directly affected the religious beliefs of the parties. He characterized as unsound the argument that religion involves only one's relation to the Creator and not one's relation to other persons as may be obligated by religious traditions or teachings. Religion, he said, certainly does refer to the Creator, but it also refers to one's obedience to the will of the Creator.[134] Finally, the judge commented that "*Minkin* ultimately conjures the unsettling vision of future enforcement proceedings. Should a civil court fine a husband for every day he does not comply or imprison him for contempt for following his conscience? . . . The spectre of Henry being imprisoned or surrendering his religious freedoms because of action by a civil court is the very image which gave rise to the First Amendment."[135]

None of the arguments in *Aflalo* are persuasive. The first argument, that a court would become entangled in religious affairs by becoming an arbiter of what is "religious," ignores the obvious fact that courts cannot avoid determining what is and what is not religious; they must, after all, determine the boundaries of establishment and free exercise. The fact that practitioners of a religion disagree about what qualifies as "religious" does not obviate the necessity of making those determinations. The second argument, that the order in *Minkin* directly affected the religious beliefs of the parties, is simply untrue. To be sure, the order affected the parties' actions, but not their beliefs: it did not require either of the parties to hold or not to hold any particular belief. It did not compel an act precluded by belief. The contention that religion refers to one's obedience to the will of the Creator as the reason for performing a

[133] 295 N.J. Super. 527, 685 A.2d 523 (Ch. Div. 1996).
[134] 295 N.J. Super. at 539, 685 A.2d at 529.
[135] 295 N.J. Super. at 541–42, 685 A.2d at 530.

particular act would, if true, render "religious" any clearly mundane action that is motivated by religious belief.[136]

Even accepting the court's conflation of belief and practice, it is the wife's beliefs that prompt the *get*; the husband does not wish to remarry. Nor is the husband under any religious mandate requiring obedience to the will of the Creator. Most significantly, there is no violation of the husband's "religious freedom." Hence, there cannot be a "spectre of Henry being imprisoned or surrendering his religious freedoms." The Free Exercise Clause means that a court cannot (1) compel any religious act or (2) compel an act in violation of religious conscience. Insofar as the husband is concerned, the court in *Aflalo* is not directing him to obey the will of the Creator. Neither the husband nor the court believes that to be the case. The wife's motives in seeking a mundane act are irrelevant. Her free exercise is in no way compromised. Regarding (2), no claim of violation of conscience has been presented. The court is really saying that compelling a *get* is a violation of the Establishment Clause but has confused the Establishment Clause with the Free Exercise Clause and erroneously assumed that secular purpose is not enough for compatibility with the Establishment Clause, but that secular intent is required as well. That is manifestly incorrect. Consider the following hypothetical: Assume that A has stolen $100 from B. B is suing A for return of the $100, not because he wishes to recover his lawful property, but because he is concerned for the state of A's immortal soul. He subscribes to a religion in which the prayer uttered contains the formula, "Forgive us our debts even though we do not forgive our debtors," i.e., his religion does not provide for forgiveness in instances of theft. Although but for religious motives the plaintiff would not seek recovery, the act of recovering stolen property is utterly secular. The court does not and should not inquire into the victim's motives for pursuing the cause of action. The religious "motives" have no constitutional significance.

Finally, the judge's "spectre" of fining or imprisoning the husband for following his conscience sweeps far too broadly. The question posed by the Free Exercise Clause is more precise: whether the court is punishing someone for following the dictates of a specifically religious conscience. That is, is the state forbidding someone from believing in or practicing a religion or is it forcing someone to believe in or practice a religion? In *Aflalo* at no time did the husband object to giving his wife a *get* for reasons of religious conscience. Rather, he refused to execute a *get* because he wished to reconcile with his wife. Indeed, at the very same time he was refusing the *get* he was endeavoring

[136] The judge in *Aflalo* did get one point right: that forcing a husband to provide a *get* would nullify the efficaciousness of the *get* under Jewish law. 295 N.J. Super. at 539–40, 685 A.2d at 529–30. For an elaboration of this point, see text accompanying notes 202–14 *infra*.

to persuade his wife to appear before a *bet din* for the precise purpose of effecting a reconciliation – hardly the portrait of a conscientious objector.[137]

The *Stern* and *Minkin* decisions construe the *ketubah* as a contract providing, *inter alia,* that the husband will execute a *get* in favor of his wife when Jewish law requires it. In *Morris* the trial court construed the *ketubah* as obliging the husband to execute a *get* upon breakdown of the marriage as evidenced by a divorce decree issued by a civil court, even in the absence of specific grounds in Jewish law compelling a divorce. The *Stern*, *Minkin* and *Morris* courts do not appear to have been disturbed that the *ketubah* contains no such express undertaking. Indeed, the *ketubah* makes no explicit reference either to divorce or to the possible breakdown of the marriage. In none of these decisions is the absence of a specific undertaking to execute a *get* noted, much less acknowledged, as a problem to be overcome.

This omission reflects a lacuna in the argument. American courts say often that they do not make contracts for the parties. Yet these very courts are prepared to go beyond a literal reading of the words of a contract in construing its provisions in a manner consistent with the manifest intent of the parties.[138] The *ketubah* provides that the parties wish to be married "in accordance with the law of Moses and Israel" and recites that the husband assumes his obligations to his wife in "the manner of Jewish men." It is the announced intent of the parties that all matters pertaining to the matrimonial *res* be governed by Jewish law as evidenced by phrases such as "in accordance with the law of Moses and Israel,"[139] "to which you are entitled according

[137] In Mayer-Kolker v. Kolker, 359 N.J. Super. 98, 819 A.2d 17 (2003), an intermediate appellate court declined to reach the free exercise issue decided in *Aflalo*. Instead, it remanded for the development of a more complete record as to the parties' obligations under Mosaic law in their particular circumstances. A Pennsylvania trial court, in 1932, issued a flawed and laconic opinion refusing to order a husband to give a *get*, Price v. Price, 16 Pa. D. & C. 290 (Pa. Com. Pl. 1932). The judge refused to enforce an oral contract which he interpreted as requiring a husband to execute a *get* on two grounds: first, that the court has no right to order anyone to secure any kind of divorce, secular or religious, and second, that the court cannot mandate giving a *get* as a religious duty. 16 Pa. D. & C. at 291. See *supra* note 92 and accompanying text.

[138] See, e.g., Dittemore v. Dickey, 249 Mass. 95, 104–05, 144 N.E. 57, 60 (1924).

[139] Ze'ev Falk has contended that the phrase "according to the law of Moses and Israel" was used for the express purpose of stipulating that disputes be adjudicated in accordance with Jewish law. He argues that in multinational societies, such as the Persian and Greek empires, it was found necessary to stipulate at the time of the marriage which law was to govern. Ze'ev Wilhelm Falk, *Mevo le-Dinei Yisra'el bi-Yemei ha-Bayit ha-Sheni* (1971), vol. 2, p. 272. Historically that view is probably incorrect and certainly inconsequential. Certainly, expositors of Jewish law saw a different purpose reflected in the use of that formula. See, e.g., *Tosafot, Ketubot* 3a, which declares that those words are designed to condition the validity of the marriage upon exercise of rabbinic authority over annulment. There is no reason to assume that the instrument refers to any provisions of Jewish law other than those governing the inception of the marriage.

to the Torah" and "the manner of Jewish men" interspersed throughout the document.

In effect, these courts are construing the *ketubah* as incorporating Jewish matrimonial law in its entirety by reference. That law mandates the execution of a *get* in certain situations. Although not mentioned explicitly, the document contemplates dissolution of the marriage because a claim for payment of the monetary obligation recited in the *ketubah* may be made only upon termination of the marriage by the death of the husband or by divorce. In the case of a previously unmarried woman, the primary financial obligation in the *ketubah* is the payment of two hundred *zuzim* upon dissolution of the marriage. The parties doubtless want all matters concerning dissolution of the marriage to be in accordance with Jewish law. A bride concerned with collecting two hundred *zuzim*[140] is certainly also concerned with gaining the freedom to remarry and with keeping the onus of bastardy from future children. Indeed, given the realities of contemporary divorce settlements, the bride is unlikely to be concerned with the two hundred *zuzim* at all. Her real concern with the *zuzim* is fulfillment of a religious requirement that prior to marriage the husband undertake a formal obligation to pay the *zuzim* stipulated in the *ketubah*, because Jewish law forbids cohabitation in its absence. It must be assumed that, *a fortiori*, the bride is concerned with the protection of a religious requirement of far greater import: termination of the marriage in accordance with Jewish law by means of a *get*. Omission of explicit reference to a *get* may be understood as reluctance to dwell upon divorce at a time when the marriage has not yet been celebrated. It is for precisely this reason that even the events triggering the financial obligation imposed by the *ketubah* in the case of death or divorce are spelled out only with circumlocution.[141]

[140] The obligation of the *ketubah* is stated in silver coins known as *zuzim*. The value is determined by the weight of the coins. For the value of two hundred *zuzim*, see *supra* note 97.

[141] In Mayer-Kolker v. Kolker, 359 N.J. Super. 98, 819 A.2d 17 (2003), an intermediate appellate court declined to reach the free exercise issue decided in *Aflalo*. Instead, it remanded for the development of a more complete record as to the parties' obligations under Mosaic law in their particular circumstances. But cf. Victor v. Victor, 177 Ariz. 231, 866 P.2d 899 (1994), where the Arizona Court of Appeals held as a matter of law that the *ketubah* is insufficiently specific to include an unwritten mandate that a husband grant his wife a *get*, and therefore does not constitute an enforceable antenuptial agreement. The wife cited language that the parties will comply with the "laws of Moses and Israel." "Such a vague provision has no specific terms describing a mutual understanding that husband would secure a Jewish divorce." 177 Ariz. at 234, 866 P.2d 902. The court also reported that two rabbis had testified that the husband's refusal to give his wife a *get* "was not consistent with the proper exercise of his religion. This is, however, a decision which he must make and live with, and as the State should not seek to direct his religious practice, it should not interfere in that exercise, misguided though it may be." 177 Ariz. 232, 866 P.2d at 900.

2. Adultery Mandating a *Get* in Jewish Law

In *Morris*, the trial court found the *ketubah* to be a contract binding the parties to execute a "Jewish religious divorce" upon termination of the marriage. "[I]f there has been a civil divorce," wrote Chief Justice Freedman, "there must be a Jewish religious divorce."[142] Apparently, the court construed the *ketubah* as a contract mandating a *get* upon dissolution of the marriage without regard to the cause of its breakdown. In effect, the lower court and the dissenting opinions in *Morris* construed the *ketubah* as a contract requiring the parties to terminate their marriage in the manner it was solemnized, i.e., according to the law of Moses and Israel.

In *Stern*, the court construed the contract differently. It found that:

> [U]nder the Ketuba where a husband alleges infidelity on the part of the wife (as he did in his counterclaim herein) he may not resume cohabitation with her; that under the laws of Moses and Israel, the mere allegation alone by the husband of an act of adultery on the part of the plaintiff-wife obligated the defendant-husband to give the wife a Jewish divorce (a Get). For the husband to arbitrarily refuse to give the divorce in spite of the above, the wife would then be in "aguna" which is a state of limbo wherein she is neither married nor divorced since under Jewish law, she cannot re-marry nor can she divorce her husband.[143]

The court in *Stern* thus construed the contractual obligation more narrowly than the court in *Morris*. The *Stern* court did not interpret the *ketubah* as mandating a religious divorce for every breakdown of a marriage, nor did it find that Jewish law obligates the husband to execute a *get* in all cases of civil divorce. Rather, it found obligation only when a *get* is required by "the law of Moses and Israel." The *ketubah*, as construed in *Stern*, binds the parties to conduct the marital relationship according to "the law of Moses and Israel"[144] and hence to terminate the marriage with a *get* when Jewish law requires it. Logically, the obligation would exist whenever Jewish law requires a *get* whether or not the parties seek a civil divorce.

In *Stern*, the husband had counterclaimed for divorce on the grounds of adultery. The court accepted and relied upon expert testimony that the mere allegation by the husband of the wife's adultery under Jewish law obligates the husband to execute a *get*.[145] Similarly, in *Minkin* the court assumed that the

[142] 42 D.L.R.3d at 557 (Freedman, C.J., dissenting).
[143] N.Y.L.J., Aug. 8, 1979 at 13, col. 5.
[144] *Id.*
[145] *Id.*

laws of Moses and Israel "require the husband to give his wife a get when he alleges an act of adultery on his wife's part."[146]

Both courts misstate Jewish law. It is true that the husband may neither condone adultery nor resume cohabitation with an adulterous wife when adultery has been proven. Nevertheless, the prohibition against further cohabitation may not entail a concomitant obligation to execute a *get*; even less does it necessarily supply grounds for compelling the husband to grant a *get*.[147] In the absence of incontrovertible evidence of adultery, no rabbinic

[146] 180 N.J. Super. at 260, 434 A.2d at 666.

[147] Rambam does indeed declare, both in his *Mishneh Torah, Hilkhot Ishut* 24:18, and in the introduction to his *Commentary on the Mishnah*, that a husband must be compelled to divorce an adulterous wife. See *Piskei Din Shel Batei ha-Din ha-Rabbaniyim* (Rabbinical Court of Tel Aviv-Jaffa 1954), vol. 1, pp. 51, 54, and *Piskei Din Shel Batei ha-Din ha-Rabbanayim* (Rabbinical Court of Tel Aviv-Jaffa, 1974), vol. 9, pp. 172, 174. Rambam's position is followed by R. Menachem ha-Me'iri, *Bet ha-Beḥirah, Ketubot* 39a; *Teshuvot Radvaz*, vol. 2, no. 646; responsum of *Magen Avraham* appended to his commentary on *Tosefta, Nezikin*, reprinted in *Teshuvot Ge'onei Batra'i*, no. 62; *Bet Me'ir, Even ha-Ezer* 117:1, s.v. *ve-kol she-ken*; *Teshuvot Mahari Basan*, no. 8. See also *Piskei Din Shel Batei ha-Din ha-Rabbanayim* (Rabbinical Court of Tel Aviv-Jaffa, 1973), vol. 9, pp. 171, 174–76.

However, Rambam himself declares that this provision is applicable only when adultery has been established on the basis of the eyewitness testimony of two trustworthy witnesses. Cf. Rabbenu Asher, *Teshuvot ha-Rosh*, no. 32, § 19. It may be inferred from this responsum that coercive measures may be applied whenever intercourse is prohibited. See R. Ben-Zion Uziel, *Oẓar ha-Poskim*, vol. 2, addenda at 12. Similarly, Ritva, *Kiddushin* 81a, maintains that a husband who accuses his wife of adultery must be compelled to issue a *get*. See also R. Moses Sofer, Teshuvot *Ḥatam Sofer*, 1 *Even ha-Ezer*, no. 27; *Piskei Din shel Batei ha-Din ha-Rabbaniyim* (Rabbinical Court of Haifa, 1962), vol. 5, pp. 154, 157.

Although a husband who alleges infidelity on the part of his wife may not cohabit with her, and indeed will be constrained by the *bet din* from doing so even on the basis of his own uncorroborated statement, nevertheless, a *get* cannot be compelled in the absence of adequate evidence that adultery did, in fact, occur. Moreover, *Tosafot, Zevaḥim* 2a, rules explicitly that, even when it has been established beyond doubt that the wife has committed adultery, the husband cannot be compelled to grant a *get* in order to release his wife from the state of *igun* – a state in which she may neither cohabit with her spouse nor seek another. The position of *Tosafot* is espoused by *Teshuvot ha-Rashba*, vol. I, no. 840, and is codified as normative law by Rema, *Shulḥan Arukh, Even ha-Ezer* 117:1.

It has been suggested that the dispute between Rambam and *Tosafot* is limited to defining the obligation incumbent upon the *bet din* to prevent transgression of the statutory prohibition against cohabitation after adultery, i.e., to whether the *bet din* has the obligation, and hence the power, to compel a divorce under such circumstances in order to prevent further cohabitation. However, according to this analysis, both authorities maintain that the wife, at her option, has independent grounds to demand that the husband be compelled to execute a *get*. Hence, even *Tosafot* would agree that the wife, in enforcing her own rights, may initiate an action for divorce on the grounds of denial of consortium, despite the fact that continued consortium is biblically forbidden by reason of her misconduct. R. Akiva Eger, *Drush ve-Ḥiddush R. Akiva Eger*, addenda at 181 (New York, 1949); R. Moses Sofer, *Ḥiddushei Ḥatam Sofer, Nedarim*, addenda, s.v. *ba-rishonah* (New York, 1958); R. Pinhas Horowitz, *Netivot Lashevet, Even ha-Ezer*, no. 91; Abraham Isaiah Karelitz, *Ḥazon Ish, Even ha-Ezer* 109:2; R. Joseph E. Henkin,

authority has ruled that a husband may be compelled to execute a *get*, while many decline to sanction coercion of the husband even in the face of such evidence.[148]

Moreover, *Stern* and *Minkin* incorrectly formulate the relevant provisions of Jewish law as applied today. These were significantly vitiated as a direct result of the rabbinic ban against plural marriage. Rema, *Shulḥan Arukh, Even ha-Ezer* 178:9, rules that after Rabbenu Gershom's edict prohibiting polygamy a husband's claim of his wife's adultery does not bar continued marital relations, particularly when the charge is made in the context of domestic strife. Under such circumstances, the husband's claim is dismissed as self-serving because of suspicion that he is feigning belief in his wife's adultery in order

supra note 97, at 12. But see R. Ezekiel Landau, *Teshuvot Noda bi-Yehudah, Mahadurah Tinyana, Even ha-Ezer*, no. 66, who understands *Tosafot*'s comments as denying any such claim by the wife. See also *Noda bi-Yehudah, Mahadurah Kamma, Even ha-Ezer*, no. 42; *Teshuvot R. Akiva Eger*, no. 130, s.v. *u-be-ofan*; *Teshuvot R. Akiva Eger he- Ḥadashot*, no. 82 (Budapest, 1938).

According to this understanding of the controversy between Rambam and *Tosafot*, the wife may petition for an order compelling the husband to execute a *get* on grounds of denial of consortium whenever consortium is denied, including instances in which it is denied because of a prohibition of Jewish law. The same analysis would lead to an interpretation of Rambam's ruling requiring the testimony of two witnesses in order to cause the husband to execute a *get* as being applicable only when the *bet din* acts upon its own initiative. Rambam would then agree that, upon the petition of the wife, the husband may be compelled to issue a *get* even in situations in which cohabitation is forbidden solely on the basis of the husband's own uncorroborated statement. See R. Akiva Eger, *supra*; but see *Teshuvot Hemdat Shlomoh, Oraḥ Ḥayyim*, no. 18, §§ 42–43.

Other scholars argue that the wife forfeits any claim to a divorce on grounds of denial of consortium when such denial results from her own unlawful conduct. R. Akiva Eger, *Drush ve-Ḥiddush* (New York, 1949), addenda at 181, tentatively suggests that the ruling recorded in the *Mishneh Torah* may be construed as permitting coercion only to effect domiciliary separation but not to compel a *get*. Nevertheless, it is clear that, in his *Commentary on the Mishnah*, Rambam sanctions coercive measures to secure cooperation of the husband in issuing a *get* under such circumstances.

148 See the decision of the Tel Aviv *bet din, Piskei Din shel Batei ha-Din ha-Rabbaniyim* (Rabbinical Court of Tel Aviv-Jaffa, 1954), vol. 1, p. 51, mandating a *get* in such circumstances. But see the later decision of the Jerusalem *bet din, Piskei Din shel Batei ha-Din ha-Rabbaniyim* (Rabbinical Court of Jerusalem, 1955), vol. 1, p. 235, in which the *bet din* declared its unwillingness to compel a *get* even in such circumstances. See also R. Akiva Eger, *supra* note 147; *Teshuvot R. Akiva Eger*, no. 130, s.v. *u-be-ofan*; *Teshuvot R. Akiva Eger he-Ḥadashot* (Budapest, 1938), no. 82; *Oẓar ha-Poskim, Even ha-Ezer* 11:1. Nevertheless, the Jerusalem *bet din* did award the adulterous wife support and maintenance contingent upon the husband's refusal to grant a *get*. This award was made despite conflicting opinions regarding the wife's right to support and maintenance under such circumstances. See *Piskei Din shel Batei ha-Din ha-Rabbaniyim* (Rabbinical Court of Haifa, 1962), vol. 5, p. 172; *Piskei Din shel Batei ha-Din ha-Rabbaniyim* (Rabbinical Court of Tel Aviv-Jaffa, 1973), vol. 9, p. 172. See also *Oẓar ha-Poskim, Even ha-Ezer* 11:1 and the contributions of Rabbis Isaac ha-Levi Herzog, Ben-Zion Uziel and Jacob Moses Toledano in *Oẓar ha-Poskim*, vol. 2, addenda at 1–16.

to secure a divorce and freedom to marry another woman. Not only is cohabitation permitted, but the *bet din* also may compel the husband to fulfill his marital duties. In *Stern*, where the wife sought a *get* and posed no impediment to her husband's remarriage, thereby effectively waiving her right to consortium, his allegation of adultery may well have sufficed to prohibit continued cohabitation.[149] Nevertheless, on the facts of the case, in which the husband sued for divorce, the wife may, in fact, have at first desired reconciliation and pressed for a *get* only after the husband refused to continue the marital relationship. Moreover, in proceedings before a *bet din*, the husband might have sought to negate his charge of adultery on the plea that the allegation was made solely to gain certain advantages in civil proceedings. Under such circumstances consortium may indeed be permitted. The only proper forum for determining this issue in a particular case is a hearing before a *bet din*.

Furthermore, the husband's belief that adultery has occurred is meaningless unless predicated upon either (1) the wife's confession or (2) the testimony of at least one eyewitness.[150] The husband is prohibited from having intercourse with his wife only when he has substantial basis for his belief that she has committed adultery, not when his belief is mere conjecture. The court was misled in assuming that a mere allegation of adultery is sufficient either to compel a *get* or to preclude resumption of marital relations.

E. *Possible Remedy under Equitable Distribution Statutes*

In 1969, in *Brett v. Brett*,[151] a British court adopted a novel approach towards a husband who refused to grant his wife a *get*. The court assessed maintenance to be paid by the husband following a secular divorce, awarding £30,000 as a lump sum payment and alimony in the sum of £2000 per annum. The court declared that the lump sum payment would be reduced to £25,000 (with an increase of £250 in the annual payment) provided the husband obtained a religious divorce within fourteen days. The court justified the additional lump sum payment of £5000 as an increase in maintenance due to the inability of the wife to remarry and obtain other means of support. The rationale was that, when modification in the lump sum alimony award can be reasonably

[149] See R. Zevi Ashkenazi, *Teshuvot Ḥakham Ẓevi*, no. 30; *Piskei Din shel Batei ha-Din ha-Rabbaniyim* (Supreme Rabbinical Court, 1957), vol. 2, p. 197.

[150] See *Bet Shmu'el, Even ha-Ezer* 11:14; *Bi'ur ha-Gra, Even ha-Ezer* 11:17; *Teshuvot Maimuni, Hilkhot Ishut*, no. 5; *Va-Yomer Yitzḥak*, no. 131; *Piskei Din shel Batei ha-Din ha-Rabbaniyim* (Supreme Rabbinical Court, 1956), vol. 2, pp. 197, 200.

[151] [1969] 1 W.L.R. 487.

related to the financial need of a woman who has no prospect for remarriage, the enhanced award in the event a *get* is not granted does not constitute a penalty.[152]

An approach consonant with *Brett* has been embraced by at least one court in the United States in an equitable distribution of marital assets. In *Schwartz v. Schwartz*[153] a wife sued her husband for divorce, asking the court to postpone equitable distribution until the husband gave her a *get*. New York's Equitable Distribution Law requires that "[m]arital property be distributed equitably between the parties, considering the circumstances of the case and of the respective parties."[154] Her argument was that once a secular court granted equitable distribution the power of the husband to extract more from the wife in exchange for a *get* would persist and render any prior distribution inequitable. Thus it would be inherently inequitable for the court to grant the husband equitable distribution before he gives the *get*.

The court refused the wife's request, holding that a stay of trial on the economic issues in the divorce was beyond its power. However, in proceeding to trial the court was not prepared to ignore misuse of a power differential between the parties, such as withholding a *get* or appearance before a *bet din*. Equitable distribution requires a court to consider several factors. One of them concerns "any other factor which the court shall expressly find to be just and proper."[155] The court interpreted this factor to permit review of all the equities in the case, including the husband's behavior in granting or withholding a *get*.[156] Also, although the court did not mention it, equitable distribution requires the court to consider "the probable future financial circumstances of each party."[157] As in *Brett*, inability to remarry for religious reasons would often significantly affect probable future financial circumstances. The court would then be empowered to use the procedure in *Brett* and, in the absence of a *get*, order a distribution of property in favor of the wife reflecting her inability to remarry and the denial of support that ordinarily would be provided by a future husband. That consideration is even more explicit in the statute than the "just and proper" consideration that serves as grounds for determining equitable

[152] It should, however, be noted that since passage of the Matrimonial Proceedings and Property Act, 1970 Rich. 45 (U.K.), English courts have refused to consider the speculative prospects of remarriage as a relevant factor in establishing maintenance. See Wachtel v. Wachtel, 1973 Fam. 72.

[153] 153 Misc.2d 789, 583 N.Y.S.2d 716 (S.Ct. Kings Co. 1992).

[154] McKinney's DRL § 236(B)(5)(c).

[155] McKinney's DRL § 236(B)(5)(d)(14).

[156] 153 Misc.2d at 793, 583 N.Y.S.2d 719.

[157] McKinney's DRL § 236(B)(5)(d)(9).

distribution.[158] This procedure is possible even when the divorce is granted for fault, which is not an automatic bar to equitable distribution.[159]

Of course, such a procedure might invalidate the *get* under Jewish law. The higher award as a penalty for non-execution of the *get* is a form of coercion that may invalidate its execution. A crucial issue is whether Jewish law entitles the wife to the more generous distribution, because if it does not, then the more generous award becomes financial duress imposed upon the husband for the purpose of executing a *get*. This can be resolved only by a competent *bet din* upon examination of both the relevant provisions of Jewish law and the circumstances of each case.

F. *General Equitable Powers*

A Florida decision is the first in which an American court considered requiring cooperation in executing a Jewish divorce in the absence of a specific undertaking. In *Turner v. Turner*[160] a Florida trial court entered a divorce decree ordering, *inter alia*, the husband to cooperate with his wife in obtaining a Jewish divorce.[161] An appellate court struck down this portion of the decree on the grounds that the Florida statute provided solely for civil divorce and did not empower the court to require the parties to secure a religious divorce. The court thus avoided the constitutional issue arising from the question of whether requiring the husband to participate in a "religious ceremony" violates his "civil rights" and separation of Church and State.[162]

That the Florida divorce statute provided for civil divorce alone did not, however, mandate denying an order requiring the husband to cooperate in arranging a *get*. The wife appealed to the court in equity, not law. Since the Florida statute did not specifically preclude equitable relief, the court had the authority to examine the wife's argument on its merits.

Such an examination did occur in Michigan. The unreported decision in *Roth v. Roth*[163] is the most far-reaching decision calling for execution of a *get*. The Circuit Court had previously issued a decree annulling the Roths'

158 *Schwartz* was decided March 17, 1992. *Get* Law 2 came into effect six months later, on August 16. *Get* Law 2 gave explicit statutory authority to the reasoning advanced by the court in *Schwartz*. Had New York courts in general accepted the reasoning in *Schwartz*, the 1992 amendment to DRL § 236 would have been superfluous.

159 See, e.g., Kobylack v. Kobylack, 110 Misc.2d 402, 442 N.Y.S.2d 392 (Sup. Ct. Westchester Co. 1981); Giannola v. Giannola, 109 Misc.2d 985, 441 N.Y.S.2d 341 (Sup. Ct. Suffolk Co. 1981).

160 192 So. 2d 787 (Fla. Dist. Ct. App. 1966).

161 *Id.* at 788.

162 *Id.*

163 No. 79–192709-DO (Mich. Cir. Ct. Jan. 23, 1980). For a discussion of other aspects of *Roth*, see *supra* note 104 and accompanying text.

marriage. The wife then petitioned the court to order her husband to execute a Jewish divorce. The court upheld her demand, not because of a contract, but because

> [i]n matters of divorce and annulment the circuit court sits as a court of equity. Thus, it may order a husband to obtain a "Get" by virtue of its inherent power to advise an appropriate remedy for every wrong. This is necessary in the instant case for a civil divorce or annulment is ineffective without the religious divorce since if Plaintiff were to remarry she would be branded an adulteress.[164]

The court directed the granting of a *get*, even in the absence of contract, based on its inherent power to grant equitable relief.

In *Roth*, the court examined the constitutional issue, noting that the First Amendment prohibits judicial action that "lacks a secular purpose, has the primary effect of advancing or inhibiting religion, or which entangles the government excessively with religion."[165] The court found that directing the issuance of a *get* would involve none of these:

> In *S. S. & B. Live Poultry Corp v. Kashruth Association*, 158 Misc 358, 360; 285 NYS 879, 883 (1936), it was stated that Jewish law would be properly divisible into two parts; one strictly religious – the relationship of man to God, and the other secular – controlling the relationship of man to man. Such affairs as marriage and kinship obligations fall within the second categorization: the secular relation of man to his fellow man. This is not religious so as to bring it within the First Amendment definitions.
>
> It is without question that a state court cannot interpret ecclesiastical law. Such is not at issue in the case before this Court. This Court is persuaded that the bill of divorce itself is theologically neutral amounting to a formal release by the husband of his former spouse.[166]

Roth affirms the principles in *Rubin*[167] and *Pal*.[168] Marriage and divorce in Jewish law are matters of contract. They are "theologically neutral," involving no religious act.[169] Secular courts may become involved in them without violating separation of Church and State.[170]

[164] *Id.* at 2.

[165] No. 79–192709-DO at 2.

[166] *Id.* at 2–3.

[167] 75 Misc.2d 776, 348 N.Y.S.2d 61 (Fam. Ct. 1973). See *supra* notes 75–80 and accompanying text.

[168] N.Y.L.J., July 25, 1973 at 13, col. 5. See *supra* notes 68–74 and accompanying text.

[169] Cf., however, Steinberg v. Steinberg, *supra*, note 131.

[170] Jewish law does not consider execution of a *get* a religious act. Nevertheless, even were this to be a matter of doubt, such doubt should not bar judicial intervention. Professor Tribe asserts

V. RELIEF THROUGH NON-INTERVENTION

Even if it is unlikely that courts will adopt the remedy ordered in *Roth*, nevertheless *Roth* points the way towards securing the cooperation of divorcing parties without overt judicial involvement. Any attempt to involve secular courts must be tested against the Establishment Clause, in particular excessive entanglement. Nevertheless, cooperation may be achieved without compromising the Establishment Clause – and the Free Exercise Clause may indeed mandate the remedy.

In civil divorce it is neither petitioner nor respondent who dissolves the marriage; it is the state.[171] For centuries the secular law of all Western nations accepted the absolute indissolubility of marriage. This doctrine became part of common law. Civil divorce with the right to remarry did not arise until the middle of the sixteenth century. At first divorce was granted infrequently and only by grace of the sovereign or legislature. Thus, before 1857 no marriage could be dissolved in England other than by special act of Parliament. Recently, divorce by judicial decree has become statutory law in most Western nations. Divorce, then, should be viewed as a privilege rather than a right.[172]

that governmental involvement in any matter arguably non-religious is beyond the purview of the Establishment Clause:

> For the free exercise clause, a dichotomy can usefully be drawn between things "arguably religious" and things not even arguably having a religious character; all that is "*arguably religious*" should be considered religious in a free exercise analysis. For the establishment clause, an analogous dichotomy distinguishes all that is "arguably non-religious" from all that is clearly religious; anything "arguably non-religious" should not be considered religious in applying the establishment clause. Thus, when a government program has the effect of fostering, tolerating, or encouraging – but not mandating – an activity, the fact that the activity is only arguably religious is not enough to make the government program a violation of the establishment clause; as long as the activity is arguably not religious, the establishment clause has not been violated by its facilitation.

Laurence H. Tribe, *American Constitutional Law* (Mineola, NY, 1978), § 14-6, p. 828 (footnote omitted) (emphasis in original).

[171] See *supra* note 78.

[172] In one significant case, Boddie v. Connecticut, 401 U.S. 371 (1971), the United States Supreme Court described divorce as a right, albeit in a very limited context. In *Boddie*, Justice Harlan stated: "The State's refusal to admit these appellants to its courts . . . must be regarded as the equivalent of denying them an opportunity to be heard upon their claimed right to a dissolution of their marriages . . . " *Id.* at 380. However, this statement is made in the context of a holding that "due process does prohibit a State from denying, solely because of inability to pay, access to its courts to individuals who seek judicial dissolution of their marriages." *Id.* at 374. The focus of the decision in *Boddie* is an elucidation of the ambit of the due process clause and the right of access to the judicial process. The right to petition for redress of grievances does not imply that all petitions must be acted upon in an affirmative manner. Similarly, the right of access to the courts to be heard in a petition for divorce should not imply a concomitant right to receive a decree of divorce upon grounds provided by statute. Issuance of such decree

No citizen enjoys a right to divorce, but any may petition the state to confer a *privilege* and dissolve the marriage.[173]

Certainly the privilege may not be arbitrarily withheld. However, because the state is the active party in dissolving the marriage, and the petitioner cannot demand divorce by right, state action in granting a divorce should never interfere with or impede free exercise.

When a husband petitions for divorce without providing for a religious divorce, the court becomes a party to wreaking a gross inequity upon the wife. A divorce decree is designed to enable both parties to remarry. A woman who by reason of religious conscience is not free to remarry is deprived, by judicial decree, of the potential for consortium, the ability to establish a home and raise a family and, often, ongoing support and maintenance. The court, in issuing a divorce decree, establishes this inequity and, in effect, tells the divorced wife that she may herself remedy that inequity only by abandoning her conscience.

In *Roth*, the court held that dissolution of a marriage without a *get*, where the wife is effectively prevented from remarriage, would deprive her not only of her right to free exercise, but also of her right to liberty:

> Her right to "liberty" under the 14th Amendment would be destroyed. In defining the liberty guaranteed under the 14th Amendment, the United States Supreme Court stated:

ought to be a matter within the discretion of the courts. The "claimed right" is the right to be heard and the right to petition for the exercise of judicial discretion in an equitable manner. See also "Developments In the Law –The Constitution and the Family," *Harvard Law Review*, vol. 93 (1980), pp. 1156, 1310, n. 8.

173 See generally 27A C.J.S. Divorce § 25. Discretion of court, Database updated May 2010 ("Where a statutory ground of divorce is plainly shown to exist, the court has no discretionary right to deny a divorce, except where a proper defense is established. Generally, however, in furtherance of public policy, courts in divorce cases necessarily exercise judicial discretion to a large extent . . . ") and the cases cited in n. 5 therein. In Worthington v. District Court, 37 Nev. 212, 243, 142 p. 230, 241 (1914), the court declared:

> [D]ivorce is not among the inalienable rights of man or the ones granted by Magna Carta, the federal or state Constitution, or the common law, and, except at the will and subject to any restrictions imposed by the Legislature, has never been recognized as one of the guaranteed privileges of the citizen.

More recently, it has been argued that "[t]he Supreme Court has not recognized a substantive constitutional right to divorce." Developments in the Law, *supra* note 172, at 1309, citing the decision of in Sosna v. Iowa, 419 U.S. 393 (1975), in support. In *Sosna* the court used a rational basis test in rejecting a claim that a one-year residency requirement as a condition of instituting divorce proceedings unconstitutionally burdens the right to travel. 419 U.S. at 406. See also Note, "Jewish Divorce and the Civil Law," *De Paul Law Review*, vol. 12 (1963), pp. 295, 298–99, n. 19.

> "...the term has received much consideration... [W]ithout doubt, it denotes not merely freedom from bodily constraint but also the right of the individual... to marry, establish a home and bring up children, to worship God according to the dictates of his conscience..." *Meyer v. Nebraska*, 262 U.S. 390, 399 (1923).
>
> Plaintiff's Constitutional right to liberty as defined above must be protected. This Court finds that interest to be paramount to any possible intrusion upon Defendant in ordering him to obtain a religious divorce which is secular in nature.[174]

In acting upon a petition for a divorce in such circumstances, the court confronts a dilemma. A decree in the absence of a *get* impedes religious practice and interferes with liberty and free exercise; however, an order of specific performance may excessively entangle the court in religion and thus violate the Establishment Clause and, if a claim is made to the effect that participation is repugnant to recalcitrant party's religious scruples, the Free Exercise Clause as well. There is, however, at least one escape from the dilemma: recognition that the court's hands are tied and cannot grant the petition. In the face of competing but equally valid claims, the state must remain neutral. Although a divorce decree may not be denied arbitrarily, dissolution of a marriage is, in essence, an act of grace. The state may not act inequitably; nor dare it, through judicial action, interfere with other rights. Therefore, it should do nothing. The court need not order the husband to issue a *get*; but it should not grant his petition unless he has removed any impediment to his wife's remarriage. If the husband wants to divorce, he must create the circumstances in which the state may grant his petition without harming others.

The United States Supreme Court has recognized that Jefferson's "wall of separation between Church and State" is in reality a "blurred, indistinct, and variable barrier depending on all the circumstances of a particular relationship."[175] One authority has described a "zone of permissible accommodation" in which government actions "arguably compelled" by free exercise are not forbidden by the principle of separation of Church and State.[176] The First Amendment does not require courts to be oblivious to concerns born of religious conviction. In *Zorach v. Clauson*[177] the Supreme Court declared that there is "no constitutional requirement which makes it necessary for

[174] No. 79–192709-DO at 3.

[175] Lemon v. Kurtzman, 403 U.S. 602, 614 (1971) (Burger, C.J., for the Court). See also Joseph Tussman (ed.), *The Supreme Court on Church and State* (New York, 1962), pp. xv–xvi.

[176] Laurence H. Tribe, *supra* note 170, §§ 14-4 & 14-5 at 822–23.

[177] 343 U.S. 306 (1952).

government to be hostile to religion and to throw its weight against efforts to widen the effective scope of religious influence."[178] Surely religious scruples should be carefully weighed in determining whether equitable relief is appropriate.

The argument for a constitutional barrier against enforcing an express or implied promise to execute a *get* focuses upon three contentions: (1) An order directing execution of a *get* constitutes judicial entanglement in a religious act. (2) An order requiring cooperation of a recalcitrant party interferes with religious liberty and violates free exercise. (3) Whether or not the mandated act is religious, its function and purpose are religious and hence judicial enforcement violates the Establishment Clause. Even were these arguments sufficiently compelling to restrain a court from ordering specific performance, they fall short of forbidding refusal to grant a civil divorce in the absence of a *get*.

Concern that the judiciary would become entangled in religious practice is not apposite when the court is called upon to find only that dissolving the marriage would be inequitable. The court neither becomes involved in execution of the *get* nor commands execution. It is merely constrained by equity from action. Non-intervention is not entanglement.

Against the recalcitrant party's claim to free exercise in refusing to execute a *get* stands the claim of the opposing party that issuance of a divorce decree obstructs that party's free exercise by dissolving the marriage in a way that creates a religious barrier to any future marriage. Under such circumstances, and in light of the Court's long history of recognizing marriage as a fundamental liberty, a policy of non-intervention is appropriate.

The argument that even non-intervention constitutes establishment must be examined in light of conflicting analyses of the First Amendment. A rigid "strict separation theory" would indeed require a Jeffersonian "wall of separation between Church and State," which would preclude judicial cognizance of any religious concerns. Such a construction of the Establishment Clause, however, could only hamper free exercise. In *Abington School District v. Schempp*,[179] Justice Stewart remarked that "a lonely soldier stationed at some faraway outpost could surely complain that government which did not provide him the opportunity for pastoral guidance was affirmatively prohibiting the free exercise of his religion."[180] Professor Tribe has said that "[w]henever a free exercise claim conflicts with an absolute non-establishment

[178] *Id.* at 314.
[179] 374 US. 203 (1963).
[180] *Id.* at 309 (Stewart, J., dissenting).

theory, the support of the former would be more faithful to the consensus present at the time of the Constitutional Convention and of the First Congress."[181]

It is not necessary to adopt such an unequivocal position in order to defend a policy of not granting a divorce that would impose hardship upon one of the parties because of religious conviction. That end may be achieved by application of a "neutral principles" approach. Although such a policy may perhaps be incompatible with a "strict neutrality" theory, which would hold that "government cannot utilize religion as a standard for action or inaction because [the two religion clauses] prohibit classification in terms of religion either to confer a benefit or impose a burden,"[182] it is nevertheless clear that the Supreme Court has never adopted that theory.[183] Instead, as formulated in *Walz v. Tax Commission*,[184] the Court has sought "to find a neutral course between the two Religion Clauses, both of which are cast in absolute terms, and either of which, if expanded to a logical extreme, would tend to clash with the other."[185] In *Everson v. Board of Education*,[186] the Supreme Court declared that neither a state nor the federal government "can pass laws which aid one religion, aid all religions, or prefer one religion over another."[187] The "no-aid" rule enunciated in *Everson* is merely a rule of neutrality.

Non-intervention constitutes a particularly apt application of the "neutrality doctrine" expressed in *Walz*. Indeed, non-intervention is the most perfect expression of neutrality. It guarantees realization of the standard of religious liberty formulated by Justice Goldberg in *Abington*, that government "work deterrence of no religious belief."[188] Such neutrality should be required particularly in matters involving competing free exercise claims. As stated by Justice Black in *Everson*, "[The First] Amendment requires the state to be neutral in its relations with groups of religious believers and non-believers; it does not require the state to be their adversary. State power is no more to be used so

[181] Laurence Tribe, *supra* note 170, § 14-4, p. 819.

[182] Philip B. Kurland, *Religion and the Law of Church and State and the Supreme Court* 18 (Chicago, IL, 1962). It may, however, be contended that such a policy is consistent with the "strict neutrality" theory advocated by Kurland. Extension of the policy to recognize that a decree of divorce should be withheld in *any* situation in which an avoidable inequity would result would avoid "classification in terms of religion."

[183] Laurence Tribe, *supra* note 170, § 14-4, p. 821.

[184] 397 U.S. 664 (1970).

[185] *Id.* at 668–69.

[186] 330 U.S. 1 (1947).

[187] *Id.* at 15.

[188] 374 U.S. at 305 (Goldberg, J., concurring).

as to handicap religions than it is to favor them."[189] Surely, the state must be neutral in its relations with individuals no less than in its relations with groups; it should not become the adversary of one by conferring an inequitable benefit upon another.

Adoption of such a policy would require accommodation of religious belief and practice. However, it is well established that accommodation is consistent with a "neutral principles" understanding of the First Amendment. Surely accommodation through non-intervention is less sweeping than the accommodation sanctioned by the Court in *Zorach v. Clauson*,[190] in which released-time programs for religious study and prayer were upheld. As stated by Professor Tribe:

> This approach does, of course, entail a notion of accommodation – recognizing that there are necessary relationships between government and religion; that government cannot be indifferent to religion in American life; and that, far from being hostile or even truly indifferent, it may, and sometimes must, accommodate its institutions and programs to the religious interests of the people.[191]

VI. STATUTORY REMEDIES

An attempt to provide explicit statutory authority for withholding a civil decree of divorce in face of the husband's refusal to execute a religious divorce was embodied in a proposed addition to New York's Domestic Relations Law. A. 7980 was enacted by the legislature during the 1981–82 legislative session but subsequently withdrawn from the governor's desk by its sponsor. The proposal explicitly provided judicial discretion in the issuance of a divorce decree in cases where one of the parties to a divorce action refuses to cooperate in removing a barrier to remarriage by his or her spouse. The intent of the drafters was to formulate statutory language giving explicit recognition to the principle, articulated in *Roth*, that equitable relief in the form of a divorce decree ought not to be available to one party when the decree would result in a gross inequity to the other party, as would be the case if, for example, the other party would confront a barrier to remarriage that might readily be removed with the cooperation of the party seeking the decree. Enactment of this bill was an attempt to cloak with legislative authority a power that, as here argued, is already inherent in the prerogatives of a court of equity.

[189] 330 U.S. at 18.
[190] 343 U.S. 306 (1952).
[191] Laurence Tribe, *supra* note 170, § 14-4, p. 822.

Instead, in 1983, the New York legislature turned from affirming the equitable powers of the court to a mechanism predominantly in the hands of the parties. It enacted Section 253 of the Domestic Relations Law, which requires any plaintiff seeking the annulment of a marriage or a divorce to file with the court and serve on the defendant a sworn statement that he or she has taken "all steps solely within his or her power to remove all barriers to the defendant's remarriage . . . "[192] The statute requires both parties to file and serve the affidavit only when an action for divorce is based on living separate and apart pursuant to a judgment or a separation agreement and the defendant does not, as a consequence, contest the requested relief.[193] If the plaintiff in a contested action for divorce or annulment fails to file and serve the statement, or if the plaintiff or defendant in an uncontested action for divorce fails to file and serve the statement, in either case the court is not permitted to enter final judgment.[194]

The statute defines "barrier to remarriage" to include "any religious or conscientious restraint or inhibition, of which the party . . . is aware, that is imposed on a party to a marriage, under the principles held by the clergyman or minister who has solemnized the marriage, by reason of the other party's commission or withholding of any voluntary act."[195] The statute clarifies that the phrase "all steps solely within his or her power to remove any barrier to the defendant's remarriage" does not include "application to a marriage tribunal or other similar organization or agency of a religious denomination which has authority to annul or dissolve a marriage under the rules of such denomination."[196] The statute thus expressly excludes annulment by Catholic diocesan tribunals. Finally, the statute provides that, notwithstanding the filing of the prescribed verified statement, no judgment of annulment or divorce may be entered if the clergyman who has solemnized the marriage certifies that the plaintiff has failed to remove all barriers to the defendant's remarriage.[197]

Although the statute was drafted in general terms, in practice it applies only to Jewish divorce and to Islamic divorce (*talaq*). Like Jewish divorce, Islamic divorce requires the consent of the husband, but unlike Jewish divorce, Islamic divorce does not require the consent of the wife. Note that the statute requires only the *plaintiff* in a divorce action to file and serve the affidavit. It does not require the defendant to do so (unless the defendant is not contesting the plaintiff's request for relief). Yet Jewish divorce can be executed only if

[192] DRL § 253(3).
[193] DRL § 253(4).
[194] DRL § 253(3).
[195] DRL § 253(6).
[196] *Id.*
[197] DRL § 253(7).

both parties participate in the *get* proceedings. Suppose a husband files for civil divorce. The statute requires him to file and serve an affidavit but does not require his wife to file and serve an affidavit. But it may be the wife, not the husband, who refuses to participate in the Jewish divorce. If the wife is contesting the civil divorce (as she is apt to be doing if she is refusing to cooperate in a religious divorce), the statute provides the husband no recourse. The same problem cannot occur under Islamic law, which does not require consent of the wife. Thus DRL § 253 does not resolve all problems that may arise in instances of Jewish divorce.

The constitutional problems posed by a statute so ostensibly concerned with matters of religion are of greater magnitude than those attendant upon legislation predicated upon more general concerns of equity, as in the model act discussed below. The drafters of DRL § 253 presume that participation in a denominational religious ceremony, in effect, constitutes tacit assumption of an obligation to dissolve the marriage in accordance with the tenets of that denomination and that enforcement of such an undertaking is warranted on the basis of the "neutral principles" doctrine. Certainly, the statute serves to give notice that participation in a religious ceremony will constitute such an undertaking. The party who does not wish to enter into such an undertaking is perfectly free to seek out a clergyman whose religious beliefs do not require removal of a barrier to remarriage other than civil divorce or avail himself of the option of a civil marriage. He simply cannot choose to avail himself of marriage within a specific denomination without agreeing to terminate the marriage in accordance with the tenets of that denomination. Whatever the merits of that position, singling out ecclesiastical tribunals for exemption from the statute severely diminishes the force of the "neutral principles" argument. Furthermore, allowing the clergyman who has solemnized the marriage, and only that clergyman, to certify that the plaintiff has failed to remove all barriers to the defendant's remarriage constitutes an establishment of religion.

Furthermore, the phrase "barriers to remarriage" is vague. What is a "barrier to remarriage"? Is a husband's refusal to pay for his wife's rhinoplasty a "barrier to remarriage"? Is his refusal to pay for her psychotherapy a barrier? The law cannot mean to include such expenses in its charge to the parties to a divorce. Yet on a perfectly plausible reading of the statute, it does.

A statute of England and Wales, unburdened by the First Amendment, avoids the vagueness and indirection of the New York statute. It refers explicitly to "the usages of the Jews"[198] and also to "any other prescribed religious

[198] Divorce (Religious Marriages) Act, 2002, c. 27 (Eng.), 10A (1)(a)(i).

usages."[199] The statute provides that either party to a divorce may ask the court to order that a decree of divorce not be made absolute until a declaration is "made by both parties that they have taken such steps as are required to dissolve the marriage in accordance with those usages."[200] It provides that the court's order "may be made only if the court is satisfied that in all the circumstances of the case it is just and reasonable to do so."[201] Thus one knows precisely what it is that husband and wife must do, under Jewish law or under the "usages" of any other religion.

New York's Section 253 rapidly proved to be an insufficient remedy for the simple reason that the recalcitrant party, generally the husband, might choose to forego the benefits of a civil divorce. To be really effective some sanction would have to be applied for failure to cooperate in executing a *get*. Precisely for that reason some ten years after the enactment of DRL § 253 the New York legislature amended a different section of the Domestic Relations Law, DRL § 236, to provide that upon a failure to cooperate in the removal of a barrier to remarriage the court must take such failure into consideration when assessing both maintenance and the equitable distribution of matrimonial assets. Thus DRL § 253 is now commonly referred to as *Get* Law 1, and the amendment to DRL § 236 as *Get* Law 2.

Get Law 2 is certainly constitutionally more problematic than *Get* Law 1 because it involves not simply judicial non-intervention in the face of what are arguably equitable considerations, but instead applies pressure – and indeed duress – in the form of a financial penalty for non-cooperation. Levying a penalty courts establishment of a religion more obviously than does mere non-intervention. Moreover, *Get* Law 2 is also more problematic than *Get* Law 1 from the vantage of Jewish law. In Jewish law, as explained below, a threat by a judge to award enhanced maintenance or more favorable distribution of marital assets constitutes financial duress, which for many rabbinic authorities invalidates the execution of a *get* pursuant to that threat.

Thus *Get* Laws 1 and 2 are beset by a variety of problems. Within the American context, where statutes must conform to the First Amendment, both *Get* Laws, but especially *Get* Law 2, raise potentially confounding constitutional problems. The definition in *Get* Law 1 of "barriers to remarriage" is unworkably vague. And *Get* Law 2 threatens the validity of any Jewish divorce executed in any jurisdiction subject to its compulsion. Thus the New York legislature has found solutions to the problem of the "chained woman" – the *agunah* –

[199] Divorce (Religious Marriages) Act, 2002, c. 27 (Eng.), 10A (1)(a)(ii).
[200] Divorce (Religious Marriages) Act, 2002, c. 27 (Eng.), 10A (2).
[201] Divorce (Religious Marriages) Act, 2002, c. 27 (Eng.), 10A (3)(a).

that only create further problems. The seeds of the correct approach, however, were planted in the proposed 1982 New York statute that the legislature passed but that was, unfortunately, withdrawn at the last minute.

The following is a model statute patterned upon the proposed 1982 legislation but modified to make it clear that the provisions reflect broad equitable concerns rather than narrowly religious considerations:

> Section 1. The domestic relations law is amended by adding a new article to read as follows:
>
> SPECIAL PROCEDURE FOR PREVENTION OF INEQUITABLE CONSEQUENCES
>
> Article –
> § 1. Special procedure for prevention of inequitable consequences.
>
> 1. If, in an action for divorce, either the petitioner or respondent shall allege that when and if final judgment is rendered dissolving the marriage, said party shall suffer negative emotional, psychological or social consequences, including but not limited to consequences posing a potential barrier to prospective employment, choice of domicile, educational opportunities or remarriage as a result of the conduct of the other party, the court, unless it shall find the allegation to be devoid of merit, shall order the parties to submit the question to a fact-finding and mediation panel.
> 2. The panel shall consist of three members, one to be appointed by each party and the third to be appointed by the two members appointed by the parties. If the two members appointed by the parties fail to choose a third member within ten days, the court shall appoint a third member to the panel. If either party shall refuse or neglect to appoint a member to the panel within twenty days after the other shall have appointed a member and served written notice thereof upon the other requiring him to appoint a member, then the member so appointed by the first party shall have power to proceed as if he were appointed by both parties for that purpose.
> 3. The panel shall determine whether such inequitable consequences will indeed attend upon a judgment of divorce and if so, whether either party can prevent such consequences from occurring. The panel shall then mediate between the parties to prevent such consequences from occurring.
> 4. The panel shall have the power to issue subpoenas and administer oaths. The provisions of the civil practice law and rules in relation to enforcing obedience to a subpoena lawfully issued by a judge, arbitrator, referee or other person in a matter not arising in an action in

a court of record shall apply to a subpoena issued by a panel authorized by this section.

5. The panel shall report to the court its findings and the results of its mediation efforts.
6. If the mediation efforts of the panel have not brought about an equitable resolution of the problem the panel shall issue its recommendation for prevention of aforesaid consequences of a decree of divorce.
7. If either party fails to comply with the recommendation of the panel, the court, upon finding that a judgment of divorce would be inequitable under the prevailing circumstances, may withhold a final judgment of divorce until the recommendations of the panel have been implemented.

§ 2. This act shall take effect immediately.

The model statute in effect gives the parties the opportunity for recourse to resolve equitable issues between them. The mechanism involves an arbitration panel composed of three members. If the issue between them is the issuance of a religious divorce, the members will have to determine whether a religious divorce is required or advisable under the circumstances of the case. If the issue is a religious divorce the parties will presumably assure themselves that the members named to the panel are well versed in Jewish law. In effect, they are convening a *bet din* in accordance with the provisions of Jewish law, which, in the absence of a communal *bet din* – an institution that does not exist in the United States – entitles each litigant to name one member and the third to be named by the two members chosen by the litigants.

The statute, of course, does not refer to either Jewish divorce or a *bet din*. It is much broader in that it is designed for invocation in instances of any equitable consideration. If the concerns are entirely secular the parties are in effect creating an arbitration panel to make a determination with regard to whether equitable relief is appropriate. Constitutional issues are obviated by the model statute by virtue of the fact that it is designed not to mandate either state or judicial action, but to relieve the court of a duty to issue a decree of civil divorce when such a decree would be inequitable for any reason.

The effect of the statute and its legal and practical appeal is that, once enacted, actual convening of an arbitration panel or a *bet din* will occur rarely, if ever. The parties are on notice that there will be no civil decree if either of them attempts to perpetrate an inequity. When the inequity is obvious there is no rational reason for litigation. A panel would be convened in situations in which the recalcitrant party believes that considerations of equity that would mandate acquiescence do not exist. Such instances will assuredly be few and far between.

VII. DURESS IN EXECUTION OF A *GET*

Quite apart from considerations of American constitutional law, concern for the validity of the *get* in Jewish law would favor a procedure that does not directly involve civil courts in the execution of a Jewish divorce. Unlike a *get* executed by a husband in response to a judicial order, a *get* executed in order to secure a favorable response to a petition before the court is not subject to challenge in Jewish law on the grounds of duress.[202] The general rule is that if a non-Jew compels a Jew to execute a *get*, the *get* is invalid even if otherwise required by Jewish law. As noted earlier, in order for a *get* executed under duress to be valid in Jewish law two conditions must be met: (1) there must be sufficient grounds in Jewish law to compel the husband to divorce his wife; and (2) the coercion must be in the form of a directive – not to issue a *get* – but to obey the command of the *bet din*. The validity of the *get* in *Koeppel*,[203] *Stern*[204] and perhaps *Roth*,[205] where the court ordered the granting of a *get*,[206] is thus open to question.[207] When, as in *Margulies*,[208] the court

[202] Of course, a separation agreement or settlement is subject to challenge for duress under secular law should the husband use the threat of withholding the *get* to force the wife into making financial or other concessions. See, e.g., Segal v. Segal, 278 N.J. Super. 218 (1994); Perl v. Perl, 126 A.D.2d 91, 512 N.Y.S.2d 372 (1987); Golding v. Golding, 176 A.D.2d 20, 581 N.Y.S.2d 4 (1st Dep't 1992).

[203] 3 A.D.2d 853, 161 N.Y.S.2d 694 (1957). See *supra* notes 48–58 and accompanying text.

[204] N.Y.L.J., Aug. 8, 1979 at 13, col. 5. See *supra* notes 96–98 and accompanying text.

[205] No. 79-192709-DO (Mich. Cir. Jan. 23, 1980). See *supra* notes 164–170 and accompanying text. The language employed in *Roth* directs the husband "to apply for and obtain a Jewish divorce." No. 79-192709-DO at 3. Presumably, this language should be understood as directing the husband to execute a *get*. In each of these cases, the court would have been better advised simply to have ordered the parties to appear before a *bet din* for the purpose of adjudicating any controversy with regard to execution of a *get*. Such a judicial directive would be in the nature of: "Do that which the Jew[ish *bet din*] direct you." In *Morris*, Justice Wilson astutely ordered: "Allied with the declaratory order earlier pronounced, there will be an order that the respondent do present himself before the Beth Din to institute inquiry whether a bill of divorcement is necessary as between the parties, and to institute proceedings for the same should the Beth Din so determine." 36 D.L.R.3d 447, 458 (Manitoba Q.B. 1973).

[206] Whether an order was formally entered pursuant to the decision of the court and the husband actually threatened with sanctions for contempt of court appears to be of no material significance. Me'iri, *Gittin* 88b, in defining duress that serves to invalidate a *get*, declares: "[B]ut even if they confused and frightened him . . . it is absolute duress."

[207] See, e.g., the discussion of this issue by R. Moses Feinstein, *Iggerot Mosheh, Even ha-Ezer*, vol. III, no. 44.

[208] 42 A.D.2d 517, 344 N.Y.S.2d 482 (1973).

directs fulfillment of an undertaking on the part of the husband, the problem is more complex: (1) Is such an undertaking binding and enforceable in Jewish law?[209] (2) Even if the undertaking is otherwise enforceable in Jewish law, does a self-imposed obligation constitute duress?[210] Moreover, assuming that execution of a *get* pursuant to a self-imposed obligation is not regarded as an act performed under duress, such a *get* would be invalid when commanded by a secular court rather than a *bet din*.

The doubtful validity of a *get* executed under the threat of citation for contempt augurs against reliance upon such a threat for securing cooperation of the husband. However, a *get* executed in anticipation of some benefit or gain, not as the result of coercion or threat of penalty, certainly is valid.[211] Thus, Jewish law does not regard executing a *get* to gain the freedom to marry another woman as coercion. A *get* executed by a husband, not in response to a court order, but to get favorable consideration of a divorce petition, would be valid.[212]

Get Law 2 goes beyond *Get* Law 1 by mandating that the court take failure to cooperate in removing barriers to remarriage into account when awarding support and maintenance and in effecting equitable distribution of marital assets. This requirement in effect imposes a penalty upon the husband for non-cooperation. Even if the requirement were limited to taking failure to remove a barrier into consideration solely as a factor in determining the wife's financial needs due to her consequent inability to enter into a new marriage, Jewish law would characterize such an award as a penalty. The effect is a form of financial duress for failing to execute a *get*. *Get* Law 2 requires that the court "shall" take account of this factor. The term "shall" has the effect of commanding the judge to take that factor into consideration. Indeed *Get* Law 2 requires that, should the judge find reason not to take failing to cooperate into consideration, he must state his reason in writing.

209 According to the vast majority of rabbinic authorities such an undertaking is neither enforceable nor binding. See *Teshuvot Kol Aryeh, Even ha-Ezer*, no. 85, and *Teshuvot Imrei Yosher*, I, no. 6; cf. *Bet Shmu'el, Even ha-Ezer*, 134:7. In two reported cases, rabbinical courts in Israel have ruled that such an agreement on the part of the husband cannot be enforced. *Piskei Din shel Batei ha-Din ha-Rabbaniyim* (Rabbinical District Court of Tel Aviv-Jaffa, 1980), vol. 8, pp. 174, 179; *Piskei Din shel Batei ha-Din ha-Rabbaniyim* (Rabbinical District Court of Tel Aviv-Jaffa, 1969), vol. 7, pp. 353, 358–61. Regarding enforceability of such an undertaking on the part of the wife, see *Piskei Din shel Batei ha-Din ha-Rabbaniyim* (Supreme Rabbinical Court, 1956), vol. 4, pp. 353, 354.

210 E.g., an oath to execute a *get* or an undertaking to pay a penalty in the event that a *get* is not issued. See conflicting authorities cited by *Shulḥan Arukh, Even ha-Ezer* 154:5, and accompanying commentaries.

211 See generally Rema, *Shulḥan Arukh, Even ha-Ezer* 154:21, and accompanying commentaries.

212 See, e.g., R. Yitzchak Ya'akov Weisz, *Minḥat Yizhak*, vol. 8, no. 137.

The effect of *Get* Law 2 is to create what in Jewish law constitutes financial duress, whether or not the court informs the husband that he will find withholding a *get* to be to his financial disadvantage. The very existence of the statute poses a threat of a financial penalty for withholding a divorce. The question whether financial duress, and hence a credible threat of financial duress, constitutes duress in Jewish law has been a matter of significant controversy over the span of centuries. As codified by Rema, *Even ha-Ezer* 134:5, a religious divorce should not be executed under financial duress.

Jewish law regards offering a husband the choice between executing a *get* and suffering financial loss as a form of indirect coercion. The coercion is indirect because offering the husband a choice does not directly force him to execute the divorce; it gives him the opportunity of some other course of action, e.g., loss of a sum of money, in lieu of executing a divorce.

The earliest responsum dealing with indirect coercion in securing a *get* is found in a classic thirteenth-century work, *Teshuvot ha-Rashba*, IV, no. 40:

> Question: Reuben, the husband of Leah, and the relatives of Leah entered into an agreement requiring Reuben to divorce his wife, Leah. They agreed to a penalty of 1000 *dinari* [upon failure] to execute a divorce by a specified time. Subsequently, Reuben retracted and refused [to execute a divorce]; whereupon, the others warned him concerning the penalty . . . Because of this fear Reuben divorced [his wife] . . . Shall we rule this to be a coerced *get*? Answer: It appears to me that this *get* is coerced and is invalid.

Rashba maintains that any coercion in executing a *get*, even self-imposed as a voluntarily assumed penalty for non-execution, renders a *get* invalid. Rashba addressed his responsum to his student R. Menachem ha-Me'iri and Me'iri espouses the view expressed by Rashba in his own commentary on *Gittin* 88b. This view is disputed by R. Shimon ben Ẓemaḥ Duran, *Teshuvot ha-Rashbaẓ (Tashbaẓ)*, vol. II, no. 68, who declares: "One who says, 'I will give 100 gold pieces to the king if I do not divorce my wife' may divorce [his wife] and there is no question in the matter for since this obligation came of his own accord he divorces of his own will." This also appears to be the position of the thirteenth-century Tosafist, Rabbenu Peretz, as cited by *Tur Shulḥan Arukh, Even ha-Ezer* 154. A similar view is cited by R. Joseph Karo, *Bet Yosef, Even ha-Ezer* 134, in the name of R. Maimon Nagar, a late fourteenth-century Spanish authority. Rabbenu Peretz and R. Maimon Nagar distinguish between an oath to execute a *get* and a penalty assumed for non-performance. The former is regarded as a form of coercion that invalidates a *get* even if the oath is sworn voluntarily. Having bound himself by an oath to execute a *get*, the husband has no choice but to divorce his wife and hence the *get* is deemed involuntary. (See, however, *Bet Yosef, Even ha-Ezer* 154, who understands these authorities as declaring only that a *get* issued subsequent to an oath obliging the husband to divorce his wife is tainted by the appearance of coercion, but is not, properly speaking, invalid.) Assumption of a penalty for non-performance, in contrast, is not deemed coercion. Although the husband has undertaken to pay a penalty should he fail to execute a *get*, he nevertheless retains the option of satisfying the monetary obligation and not executing the divorce. Accordingly, these authorities regard execution of a *get* under such circumstances as a free expression of the husband's will.[213]

Rema, *Even ha-Ezer* 134:5, cites both conflicting opinions and rules that a *get* should not be executed in the absence of prior forgiveness of the penalty for non-execution, but adds that if a *get* has been executed under such circumstances it is valid even in the absence of prior forgiveness, provided that the penalty was assumed voluntarily.

The controversy between Rashba and other early authorities is limited to situations in which there is a direct relationship between the financial liability assumed by the husband and issuance of the *get*. Since imposition of the penalty is the direct result of failure to execute a divorce, the relationship is sufficient, in Rashba's opinion, to render the *get* the product of coercion. However, when the husband seeks to gain an extraneous benefit or escape from an unrelated obligation, the situation is different. Accordingly, R. Isaac ben Sheshet, *Teshuvot Rivash*, no. 127, finds no grounds to invalidate a *get* issued in order to escape penalties for non-payment of an unrelated debt. The case presented to Rivash involved a person cast into debtors' prison for non-payment of a debt. His wife's relatives offered to satisfy the debt and obtain his release on condition that he divorce his wife. Rivash finds no objection to executing a *get* under such circumstances "for he was not seized in order to [compel] him to divorce [his wife] but on account of his debt; the *get* is not coerced but [the product] of free will."

Teshuvot ha-Rashbaẓ, I, no. 1, modifies this decision by stating that such a *get* is valid only if the extraneous sanctions applied in order to secure the husband's compliance are legitimate, i.e., the debt which he is called upon to satisfy is legal and actionable. A divorce executed in order to escape payment of a debt that is not actionable is, in the opinion of *Tashbaẓ*, invalid. Since

[213] For a discussion of various attempts ro reconcile these apparently conflicting opinions see R. Mordecai Jaffe, *Levush, Even ha-Ezer* 134:8; R. Meir Posner, *Bet Me'ir, Even ha-Ezer* 134:4; *Mishkenot Ya'akov*, no. 38; *Arukh ha-Shulḥan, Even ha-Ezer* 134:23; *Ḥazon Ish, Even ha-Ezer* 99:6; and R. Elyakim Ellinson, *Sinai* (Tammuz–Sivan 5731), vol. LXXXIX, p. 144 ff.

it is invalid, *Tashbaẓ* regards such a claim as a disguised attempt to compel a *get*.

This interpretation of Rivash's position is rejected by the Sephardic authority, R. Elijah ben Ḥayyim, *Teshuvot Ra'anaḥ*, no. 43. In order to prevent precipitous marriages, the community had promulgated a *ḥerem* prohibiting any marriage ceremony in the absence of a quorum of ten. In violation of the ban, a man entered into marriage without a quorum and was incarcerated by communal officials, who made his release from prison contingent upon execution of a divorce. *Teshuvot Ra'anaḥ* finds that imprisonment was a penalty for violating the ban, but that a *get* issued in such circumstances would nonetheless be valid. The husband, argues this authority, was imprisoned not in order to compel divorce but for solemnizing a marriage in violation of the communal edict. *Teshuvot Ra'anaḥ* does not see release from prison in return for executing a *get* as coercion since the imprisonment is not the result of non-execution of a *get*.

The *bet din*, however, hesitated to rule in this manner because of the opinion of yet another authority. R. Moses ben Joseph di Trani, *Teshuvot Mabit*, vol. II, no. 138, rules that, even according to *Tashbaẓ*, measures may be taken to collect a legitimate unrelated debt and forgiveness of the debt may be offered as an inducement for a divorce only if the husband has a genuine choice and the measures taken will in reality serve to exact payment in the event that the husband declines to grant a divorce. In such cases the coercive action is indeed for a purpose extrinsic to the *get*; withdrawal of sanctions that would otherwise realistically be effective in compelling payment, in return for execution of a *get*, is thus not deemed to be coercion with regard to the *get*. However, when it is known that, despite the pressure brought to bear upon him, the husband cannot, or will not, pay the debt, the threat of compelling payment must, according to *Mabit*, be viewed as direct coercion of the *get*.

This restrictive view is contradicted by the same authority in another responsum, *Teshuvot Mabit*, vol. I, no. 22. A citizen of Safed was imprisoned by the civil authorities for "heretical" conduct and pleaded with the communal authorities to help secure his release. The authorities responded by offering to secure his release if, in turn, he would agree to divorce his wife and leave the jurisdiction. In this responsum, *Mabit* ruled that the *get* was valid despite the fact that the husband had no other means of securing his release from prison.

An attempt to resolve the apparent contradiction between these two responsa is undertaken in a latter-day work, *Simḥat Kohen*, *Even ha-Ezer*, III, no. 9. *Simḥat Kohen* distinguishes between coercion and forgiveness of punishment. This scholar argues that, even according to *Mabit*, the husband must be able to make a free choice only when coercive measures are applied in order to evoke a response. In such circumstances he must have a true choice between satisfying the debt or issuing a *get*. When no real choice exists, the *get*, according to *Mabit*, is invalid. However, declares *Simḥat Kohen*, when sanctions are applied as a punishment unrelated to the granting of a divorce, forgiveness or termination of the punishment in return for execution of a *get* is legitimate even according to *Mabit*. Accordingly, in *Teshuvot Mabit*, I, no. 22, the *get* is ruled to be valid since the civil authorities did not impose imprisonment upon the husband to compel a *get* but as a punishment for a completely unrelated matter. According to *Simḥat Kohen*'s analysis, a recommendation for commutation of a prison sentence imposed for other offences as a means of securing cooperation in execution of a *get* would have been valid even according to *Mabit*.

In light of the foregoing, duress may well exist even if a judge has not expressly indicated that he will, as prescribed by law, invoke *Get* Law 2 in determining maintenance and distribution of marital assets. A credible threat of coercion constitutes duress. The very existence of the statute constitutes duress. An attorney who fails to inform his client of the negative financial consequences of not cooperating in removal of a barrier to remarriage is guilty of malpractice. Hence, one must assume that a competent attorney will make the contents of *Get* Law 2 known to his/her client. The knowledge that the court has no choice but to enforce the provision of *Get* Law 2, it has been said, is *ipso facto* duress. The result is that the validity of every *get* executed by parties subject to the jurisdiction of a New York court is under a cloud. The irony is that a statute designed to ameliorate the *agunah* problem has had precisely the opposite effect. There are rabbis who have stated publicly that they will not perform marriages for women who have received a *get* subsequent to 1992. The remedy, of course, is either to delay execution of the *get* until there is no longer any outstanding issue before the court, i.e., after all financial matters have been adjudicated, or for the parties to execute a release having the effect of foregoing the advantages conferred by *Get* Law 2.[214]

VIII. A CONCLUDING OBSERVATION

It is over a century since matters pertaining to Jewish religious divorce first came before an American court. During this period numerous decisions have been flawed by an incorrect perception both of the nature of a *get* and of the

214 The Second Department has held that the provisions of *Get* Law 2 are subject to waiver. See Becher v. Becher, 245 A.D.2d 408, 667 N.Y.S.2d 50 (2nd Dep't 1997).

provisions of Jewish law regarding its execution. Although the constitutional issues involved in enforcing an agreement to effect a *get* have been examined in state courts, with conflicting results, they have not been directly examined by any federal court or by the highest court of any state. A proper understanding of the *get* as rescission of the contractual obligations and restrictions of matrimony effected by the parties themselves, rather than as a sacerdotal or religious act or as the decree of an ecclesiastic tribunal, should dispel the constitutional cloud that has made judicial enforcement of such undertakings uncertain.

Even absent an undertaking to execute a *get*, recognition of a divorce court as a court of equity, coupled with application of a neutral principles doctrine of First Amendment interpretation, would lead to a balancing of the competing claims, interests and constitutional rights of the opposing parties. Balancing such interests should yield, not necessarily an order to execute a *get*, but a policy of non-intervention expressed in withholding a decree of divorce in the absence of a *get*. The adoption of such a policy would prevent a gross inequity to one of the parties and preserve the fundamental right to marriage without compromising religious conviction.

COMMENT ON REASONING FROM PURPOSES

The practitioners of common law view the rules they are using and administering, be they judge-made rules or statutes or ordinances or even constitutional provisions, as containing purposes, the expression of which may be divined from the face of a rule, but need not be and most often is not, coincident with it. Moreover, these purposes give life to the rule, permit the rule to move forward through time and to evolve a series of cases. The assumption, of course, is that the bare statement of the rule is, most often, inadequate to the proper administration of the rule, that the bare statement of the rule, standing on its own, offers incomplete or misleading direction to the application of the rule. The doctrine of purposes is thus one of the central planks on which common law takes its stand as a distinctive system of legal reasoning.

Jewish law, in contrast, holds that mere finite human beings cannot know with certainty God's purposes in the law He revealed to Moses. One must be careful here. It does not necessarily hold that God does not have purposes or that those purposes are absent from His legal rules. Rather, it holds that while those purposes exist, human beings cannot know them, but can only speculate about them. Thus the discourse of purposes that so drives and informs the common law has entirely been missing from the literature of Jewish law over the millennia.

The corpus of Jewish law as contained in the Written Law is a series of rules and regulations. Only on rare occasions does the text provide a rationale for the rule that is stated dogmatically on the basis of revelation. The divine lawgiver chose not to reveal His purpose for reasons best known to Him. Man can speculate both with regard to what those reasons might be and why He chose not to reveal them. Indeed, there is a controversy between Rambam (the Latinate form is Moses Maimonides) and Sa'adia about whether there are reasons for many of the revealed laws. Sa'adia takes the position that the law ultimately is the product of divine will and in a fundamental sense is arbitrary. Sa'adia believes that the single most important purpose of any law is to compel disciplined obedience to the divine will. Rambam and those who follow in his philosophical footsteps maintain that the law is not arbitrary and that it is a function of divine reason rather than divine will. For Rambam, every law is predicated upon a cogent rationale; sometimes man can grasp the rationale, sometimes he cannot. Man's grasp may not be comprehensive in the sense that there may be multiple reasons underlying a given law, some of which are beyond human ken. But from the divine perspective there is always a purpose to the law even if to the human mind it appears arational (rather than irrational).

Since the rationale upon which any given law is predicated has not been revealed, one cannot really speak about the purpose of any given law. To speak of the purpose is to assert exhaustive knowledge of that purpose and such knowledge has not been revealed to man. In a system of law of that nature it is impossible for a jurist to engage in an analysis of purpose as a means of interpreting the law. Hence, the law acquires a life of its own which transcends any underlying purpose. The result is that even when the rationale is presumably understood, at least in part, the law in its applications does not necessarily express or further that purpose. The law becomes divorced from purpose. Quite frequently, the letter of the law does not coincide with the spirit of the law. The letter of the law must be observed even when such observance does not seem to further the purpose of the law and, indeed, even when it appears to be antithetical to the purpose of the law.

In every legal system a moral issue arises with regard to taking advantage of loopholes that enable an individual to circumvent the purpose of the law. In the present climate of opinion the popular press frequently reflects the notion that wealthy individuals are somehow behaving immorally when their net tax burden in terms of percentage of income is much less than the tax burden of ordinary wage earners. On the other hand, Judge Learned Hand famously wrote that one is entitled to arrange one's affairs to take advantage of any favorable provision of the tax code, that "there is not even a patriotic duty to increase one's taxes."[215] Plugging in to a neighbor's electric line and having the neighbor pay for the electric power siphoned off is certainly unethical. Yet in a German case in the early days of electricity, the court ruled that electricity is not a *Sache* and hence the siphoning does not constitute "theft" within the meaning of the applicable statute. As a matter of law the court was perhaps right; as a matter of ethics the court was undoubtedly wrong. But law and ethics do not necessarily coincide.

Judaism, however, is not only a religion of law; it is a religion of ethics as well, particularly if *imitatio Dei* is regarded as part of that ethical system. Man is therefore required to strive to achieve conformity with the "spirit of the law" in addition to the law itself. What then is one to do when obedience to the letter of the law thwarts the perceived spirit of the law?

Jewish law is quite familiar with arrangements designed to avoid the onus of applying the full force of the law. In rabbinic literature there is a term for such an arrangement; it is known as a "*ha'aramah*," a term that may best be translated literally as "a cleverness." The term "device" probably best captures the flavor of the term without connotation of a moral judgment. Such devices fall into three categories: (1) those disdained as inconsistent with the spirit of

[215] Helvering v. Gregory, 69F.2d 809, 810 (2d Cir. 1934), *aff'd*, 293 U.S. 465 (1935).

the law; (2) those regarded as commendable and actively encouraged; and (3) those regarded as neutral.

Perhaps the earliest example of a *ha'aramah* involves regulations over tithing. Talmudic exegesis establishes that biblical law requires tithing only of produce brought into an abode through the gates of the courtyard. The Gemara, *Berkakhot* 35b, bemoans the fact that "while earlier generations were wont to bring in their produce by way of the front door in order to make it liable to tithing, later generations bring in [the produce] by way of roofs, yards, or enclosures in order to exempt [the produce] from tithing." Clearly, that statement reflects a negative attitude towards the moral legitimacy of the "later generations." Indeed, some early authorities report that rabbinic legislation banned their subterfuge.

The reason for the negative view towards using such expedients is clear. The purpose of the tithe was to provide a livelihood for the Levites who served in the Temple and provided religious instruction to the entire populace. Without tithes, the Levites would have had to seek employment as artisans or laborers, making it impossible for them to discharge their sacred mission. The spirit of the law would have been thwarted. Thus, this is an example of a disdained *ha'aramah*.

The second category includes devices designed to promote conformity with the law. The first-born male offspring of a cow or a sheep belonging to a Jew is sanctified from birth to be a sacrificial offering in the Temple. With the destruction of the Temple, sacrifice is impossible. However, the first-born animal is still sanctified. One may not use it as a beast of burden or drink its milk or use its wool. The animal is a "sacred cow" that roams virtually at will – as is the case today in some Hindu communities – until the animal develops a blemish rendering it unfit for sacrifice. Unless and until that occurs, the animal is a halakhic nuisance in that it is of no benefit to God or man but creates an ongoing threat of inadvertent sin.

The remedy is to prevent the animal from becoming sanctified by transferring ownership of its pregnant mother to a non-Jew. After parturition both mother and first-born may be reconveyed to the original Jewish owner. Commandments concerning the first-born commemorate the sparing of Jewish first-born in Egypt while the first-born of the Egyptians perished in the last of the ten plagues. Hence, the first-born of an animal belonging to a non-Jew is not sanctified.

No one has ever suggested that it is improper to seek transfer of title on the grounds that it is a subterfuge designed to frustrate the purpose of the law. In this instance fulfilling the underlying purpose has become impossible: the animal cannot be brought as a sacrifice because the Temple no longer stands. Yet the law is not a dead letter; the restrictions governing sanctified animals remain in force. The only way to avoid transgression of both the letter and spirit of the law lies in obviating its provisions by vesting title in a non-Jew. This is so even if the original owner repurchases the first-born and its mother from the non-Jew. Employment of a "device" to accomplish that end is thus worthy of approbation.

The final category is best exemplified by the practice of selling *ḥameẓ* – foods forbidden during Passover – to a non-Jew. The sale takes place before the advent of the holiday and, typically, the original owner repurchases the same foodstuffs at the end of the holiday. To some, the transaction appears to be a charade since the parties are aware from the beginning that they will undo the sale at the earliest opportunity.

In fact, the arrangement is innocuous. Scripture forbids a Jew to retain any economic interest in *ḥameẓ* during the Passover week. A Jew in possession of forbidden foods on the eve of Passover may avoid transgression in one of three ways: (1) He may consume the foods in their entirety, an impossible feat if the quantity is large enough, or inadvisable in the case of a copious quantity of alcoholic beverages made from grain. (2) He may totally destroy such items by burning or the like, a procedure that may prove to be cumbersome and is wasteful but, nevertheless, is permissible. (3) He may transfer title to a non-Jew, who, since the 613 biblical commandments are binding only upon Jews, is in no way subject to the prohibition. Jewish law does not accord preference to any one of these options over the others. Accordingly, the expedient of sale to a non-Jew is regarded as both halakhically and morally neutral; it is neither encouraged nor discouraged. Choice of that option is generally dictated by considerations of practicality and conservation of wealth. There are no restrictions upon acquiring *ḥameẓ* after the holiday, even *ḥameẓ* owned by a Jew before Passover, provided that the sale to a non-Jew prior to the advent of the holiday has been properly consummated.[216]

Clearly before discussion of the rationale or spirit of the law can take place, it is necessary to determine what is demanded by the letter of the law. That enterprise is ordinarily not informed by purpose or policy considerations. It is a process that is conducted in accordance with analysis of text, application of canons of interpretation and human logic. There is certainly an interpretive process. But that process is carried on in what can best be described as a teleological vacuum, without reference to end or purpose. The process must go to wherever human intellect leads. "*Yikov ha-din et ha-har*" – "let the law

[216] See R. Moshe Sofer, *Teshuvot Ḥatam Sofer, Oraḥ Ḥayyim*, no. 102. See also R. Shlomoh Yosef Zevin, *Ha-Mo'adim be-Halakhah*, 7th ed. (Tel Aviv, 1960), pp. 245–55.

pierce the mountain."[217] As has been stated earlier, different individuals may arrive at different conclusions, each of which is equally valid. That too is part of divine intent. Every novel insight of a diligent student in any generation was revealed to Moses at Sinai. Man's charge is to recover the content of original revelation. Or, to phrase the same concept somewhat differently, giving those insights legal expression in the form of halakhic dialectic is, in effect, a process of ongoing revelation.

For purposes of categorization and for those purposes only, Jewish law distinguishes between a *ḥok* and a *mishpat* (plural, *ḥukkim* and *mishpatim*). *Ḥukkim*, generally speaking, are laws of religion and ritual. As such, they are idiosyncratic to religious law and are the product of revelation, binding solely because of revelation. In contrast, *mishpatim* are eminently rational, "had they not been recorded, it would be fitting to record them." Those rules, or some variation of those rules, are common to civilized societies. Since they are necessary for regulation of a well-ordered society, had they not been revealed, man would have had to "invent" them himself. That does not necessarily mean that *mishpatim* reflect the system of natural law. Natural law regards its propositions as dictated by reason and self-enforcing in the sense that moral reason not only dictates the substance of the law but also compels obedience to the law. From the perspective of Jewish tradition, such regulations are necessary for pragmatic considerations and, absent revelation, human society would be well advised to adopt such laws. Nevertheless, the *mishpatim*, rational and pragmatic as they may be, are binding solely because they are revealed dogmatically. It thus follows that even *mishpatim* are, in a fundamental sense, diverse from purpose. Certainly in application the Divine Lawgiver may have declared ramifications that are not immediately grasped by reason, whose effects are not necessarily pragmatic and which may appear to be divorced from social and interpersonal realia. As a result, there is no real distinction between interpretive processes applicable to both *ḥukkim* and *mishpatim*. In both cases interpretation is based upon explication of the legal text coupled with analytic dissection of the concepts reflected in those texts.

NOTES AND QUESTIONS

1. Sarah Kantor and Solomon Rubin, the wife and husband in *Kantor v. Rubin*, executed a religious divorce, but at no point did they seek a civil divorce. Why not? Does it help to know that the couple had been married in Russia in 1879 and lived there until they came to the United States in the

[217] *Sanhedrin* 6b.

late 1880's? Russia then had a version of the *millet* system developed in the Ottoman Empire. In the *millet* system each confession had its own court to administer the personal law belonging to that confession – its laws of divorce, adoption, charitable bequests, etc. Had Sarah and Solomon stayed in Russia and executed a religious divorce there, Russian law would have recognized the divorce and given it civil effect. (The dominant religious group in Russia, the Russian Orthodox Church, did not permit divorce.) Might they have assumed that American law would likewise give their religious divorce civil effect? Or were they reacting to the then extremely restrictive divorce law in New York, which limited the grounds of divorce to adultery? Note that both of them remarried religiously, but not civilly, and were therefore in the eyes of the state committing adultery.

2. Is it clear, after all, that Sarah abandoned Solomon? Certainly the court thought so. But in her own mind Sarah clearly had not. Sarah's argument, which the court rejected, was that she separated from her husband with mutual consent, and separation with mutual consent cannot constitute abandonment. Why did the court reject that argument? If Sarah and Solomon had decided not to execute a civil divorce by design and with full knowledge of the benefits Sarah could get as Solomon's civil widow, then is not depriving Sarah of her statutory share frustrating what in effect served as a "divorce" settlement?

A strong plurality of states has statutes that cut off a spouse guilty of various sorts of misbehavior from various benefits that might otherwise accrue upon the death of a spouse. See, e.g., N.Y. EPTL §§ 5-1.2(a)(5) and 5-1.2(a)(6). See also Linda Kelly-Hill, No-Fault Death: Wedding Inheritance Rights to Family Values, 94 Ky. L. J. 319 (2005). In other states courts rely on equitable powers to achieve some of the same ends. Professor Kelly-Hill has criticized using death as an occasion to make moral judgments of spousal behavior:

> [I]t may seem unduly harsh to impose the duty of securing divorce or legal separation upon an aggrieved party . . . [But r]equiring a legal termination of marriage or separation is the only nonintrusive measure that recognizes that marital privacy is to be protected both during life and at death. No exceptions should be made for the harmed individual who obtains a legal separation that does not terminate property rights, initiates a divorce action but dies before the divorce is finalized, or merely has sufficient grounds for legal separation or divorce. States that have adopted such lesser standards have created "black holes" that can make a surviving spouse ineligible for probate rights because sufficient grounds for divorce exist and, tragically, also ineligible for a property award pursuant to the divorce proceedings because the divorce was not decreed at the time of the decedent's death.

Linda Kelly-Hill, 94 Ky. L. J. 354–55.

3. Why not solve the *agunah* problem by means of an antenuptial agreement that would provide a financial penalty against a party who refuses to cooperate in the execution of a *get* after the marriage has been terminated by a civil decree of divorce? One problem is that penalty clauses are unenforceable in both Jewish and common law. Another is that self-imposed financial duress impedes the validity of a *get* in Jewish law. Consider that provisions for liquidated damages are enforceable in common law. Would a sum that could be construed as liquidated damages be acceptable when assumed for non-cooperation in the issuance or execution of a *get*? Remember that so long as a marriage recognized in the eyes of Jewish law continues the husband remains liable for support and maintenance.

4. Consider the following. A man subject to the jurisdiction of Israeli courts has obtained a *hetter me'ah rabbanim*[218] from an Israeli rabbinic court to enter into a second marriage to be solemnized in an American jurisdiction. In the absence of a valid divorce the second marriage is bigamous under secular law. Would an American court recognize the *hetter me'ah rabbanim* under the doctrine of comity? Remember, a *hetter me'ah rabbanim* does not terminate a marriage. It is a dispensation to commit polygamy. But remember also that it is granted only in circumstances in which any Western society would find grounds to issue a decree of divorce. In effect in Jewish law it is the functional equivalent of divorce. Would an American court look at form over substance?

5. Marriage in Jewish law is not a sacrament. It is a contract. The term "*kiddushin*," closely associated with "sanctity" or "holiness," is also the term for marriage. In neither of these usages does the Hebrew term mean "sacred" or "holy." The root meaning of the term is that which is separated from the physical, transcendental and off limits. "Holy, holy, holy is the Lord of Hosts" means nothing more than God is non-corporeal and transcendental, i.e., removed from the mundane physical world. When used as a term for marriage it means that the bride has become separated from, and off limits to, all other males; she has become exclusively reserved to her husband. She no longer has the capacity to enter into a similar relationship with any other male. In effect marriage is the conveyance by the bride of an exclusive conjugal servitude to the groom. All other aspects of the marital relationship – its privileges, prerogatives and duties – flow from the establishment of that contractual relationship. Divorce is simply the reconveyance of that servitude to the wife. Hence divorce in Jewish law requires an act of free will of the beneficiary of that servitude, i.e., the husband. After Rabbenu Gershom's prohibition of polygamy and his prohibition against divorcing a wife without

[218] See text following note 1 *supra*.

her consent, marriage constitutes an exclusive and reciprocal conjugal servitude requiring the consent of both parties. The *hetter me'ah rabbanim* is no more than rabbinic legislation (*takkanah*) creating an exception to a logically prior rabbinic ordinance permitting violation of the wife's exclusive servitude in limited circumstances. Rabbenu Gershom had the authority to limit his own edict; he did not have the authority to create exceptions to the biblical prohibition against polyandry.

6. Suppose that insurance contracts commonly contain a clause declaring that the contract shall be construed and enforced in accordance with the laws of the State of Delaware. Assume that Vatican City has enacted an insurance law and that the Bishop of Rome while seated upon his throne in the Basilica of St. Peter has announced that the law was divinely revealed to the founder of the Church. The legal experts who have previously drafted contracts with a clause incorporating the laws of the State of Delaware now find it advantageous to substitute incorporation of the laws of Vatican City. Would an American court enforce that clause? Is the clause "religious" for the purposes of the Establishment Clause just because it is supported by a claim of divine revelation or is religion a matter of substance rather than a claim of historical origin?

7. What, after all, is religion? Jewish law distinguishes between the obligations man has to God and the obligations man has to man. But, of course, the First Amendment must have its own definition of religion, and it is that definition, not any other, that controls whether a doctrine or practice or opinion or system of belief, when established by government, offends the First Amendment.

In the United States, the Founders' understanding of religion would have tracked the Jewish understanding – religion encompasses the obligations man owes to God – for the first two hundred years of the nation's history. But by the second half of the twentieth century the rise of religious pluralism had put in question the adequacy of the Judeo-Christian definition for deciding which doctrines or practices or opinions or systems of belief get the protections of the First Amendment.

The U.S. Supreme Court has had to define religion in a statutory context. See, e.g., *United States v. Seeger*, 380 U.S. 163 (1965) (provision protecting religious objectors to military service).

8. Would an American court enforce a judgment issued by a jurisdiction that has adopted *Sharia* (Islamic law)? Would it matter whether the judgment concerned a law that the First Amendment defines as religious?

Note that American courts have generally enforced defamation judgments rendered by foreign jurisdictions – such as England and Wales – whose defamation laws are less protective of free speech than the First Amendment. Thus a foreign judgment can be *executed* in the United States that could never be *issued* in the United States because it offends the First Amendment. In order to protect writers from such judgments the State of New York enacted the Libel Terrorism Protection Act in 2008. The Act permits New York courts to obtain jurisdiction over anyone who obtains a foreign libel judgment against a New York publisher or writer and to limit enforcement to judgments that satisfy "the freedom of speech and press protections guaranteed by both the United States and New York Constitutions." The Free Speech Protection Act, which performs a similar function, is currently before Congress.

9. Suppose applications for marriage licenses contained a clause declaring that if the parties choose to have the marriage celebrated by a clergyman they bond themselves to dissolve the marriage according to the tenets of the denomination in which the marriage was celebrated. Would that have an impact upon the First Amendment issues discussed above?

10. Suppose the application had a similar clause declaring that the parties agree to have all ancillary issues, including support and maintenance as well as custody of children, adjudicated by an ecclesiastic tribunal. Would such a clause be enforceable?

11. Can the argument be made that enforcing a contract to execute a religious divorce advances religion because it "has a primary effect of advancing . . . religion,"[219] in that it enables the spouse seeking the religious divorce to continue to live a faithful religious life? Would a contract to supply communion wafers have a primary effect of advancing religion because it enables those for whom communion is a religious requirement to continue to live a faithful religious life? Can the two cases be distinguished?

Our discussion takes the position that "[t]he primary effect of judicial involvement in enforcing a promise to execute a *get* is neither to enhance nor inhibit religion; its purpose is to facilitate remarriage." The Supreme Court in *Nyquist* spoke of "a primary effect," not "the primary effect." Could it be that enforcing a promise to execute a *get* offends the Establishment Clause even when it has more than one primary effect, so long as advancing religion is one of them? But suppose that *Nyquist* meant to require that advancing religion be the singular primary effect. Is it clear that facilitating marriage is the singular primary effect of enforcing a promise to execute a *get*? What if the spouse seeking to enforce the promise to execute a *get* would, in the absence of enforcement, abandon religion in order to remarry rather than abandon

[219] The second criterion in *Nyquist*. See note 100, *supra*, and accompanying text.

remarriage in order to continue practicing the religion? Would enforcement of a promise to execute a *get* then have facilitating remarriage as its singular primary effect?

12. Husbands frequently withhold the *get* because they are aggrieved as a result of an award of alimony or denial of child custody by a civil court. Jewish law mandates that all financial and interpersonal disputes between Jewish parties be litigated before a *bet din*. Does the husband have a moral right to demand that all such issues be submitted to the *bet din* hearing the wife's demand for a *get*?

13. Is refusal to enter into a religiously recognized matrimonial relationship a solution to the *agunah* problem? To rephrase the question, does Jewish law recognize common law marriage? (Remember that bastardy is not a barrier to inheritance in Jewish law and furthermore that bastardy does not result from extramarital liaisons but only from an incestuous relationship or a relationship with a woman married to another man.) There is a principle of Jewish law to the effect that a person does not engage in fornication when the same act could be an act of legitimate marital intercourse. Marriages can be contracted in three ways: (1) by transfer of an object of value (the wedding ring); (2) by means of a writing delivered by the groom to the bride; and (3) by an act of intercourse for the purpose of marriage. Is common law marriage intercourse for the purpose of marriage? Can you formulate the arguments that have been advanced by rabbinic scholars in debating both sides of this question?

14. Jewish law recognizes "shepherding prostitutes" as grounds for compelling the husband to execute a *get*. Assume that a husband has remarried on the strength of a civil divorce. Is duress designed to compel execution of a religious divorce by the husband legitimate on the grounds that his remarriage has the status of prostitution in the eyes of Jewish law?

15. Western law has created a hybrid. It reserves divorce to the state. It delegates solemnization of marriage, *inter alia*, to clergy who are restrained from performing marriages other than in conformity with state law. If separation of church and state precludes civil recognition of religious divorce why does it not also preclude recognition of civil marriage? If officiating at a religious divorce is not a penal offense, why is officiating at a religious marriage without prior issuance of a marriage license a penal offense?

16. Assume husband and wife genuinely wish to cooperate in the execution of a *get*. Subsequent to the enactment of *Get* Law 2 the parties are subject to duress that would force them to cooperate even had they not wished to do so. The situation is quite comparable to the same couple appearing freely before the *bet din* and wanting to execute a *get*. But a well-meaning friend

who has a handgun in his pocket accompanies them and announces that if the husband has a change of heart, he will not hesitate to use the weapon. Could a *bet din* accept the protestation of the husband that the "friend" is present uninvited and that his presence has no influence whatsoever upon his conduct?

Let us assume that the husband cooperates in the execution of the divorce, which is indeed invalid under Jewish law; if it is invalid then there is no barrier that the husband could remove. The barrier is certainly present; but the statute itself makes it impossible for him to remove it. Therefore the statute cannot ever be applied to Jewish divorce. The courts have refused to accept this argument, saying in effect to the husband, "You execute the divorce and let the rabbis figure it out afterwards." See *Schwartz v. Schwartz*, 235 A.D.2d 468, 652 N.Y.S.2d 616 (2nd Dep't 1997).

Suppose the husband returns to the *bet din* the next day and executes a second divorce, telling the *bet din* that of course he is doing it freely and that he freely executed the *get* the day before. Would the husband be correct in saying that the second *get* is certainly not executed under duress because the court could not conceivably order him to execute a second divorce? The first divorce, valid or invalid, was executed because of the threat of § 236, but if § 236 required him to do so, he did; if it didn't require him to do so, then there was no duress in the first place. Either way the second *get* is certainly free of any taint of duress.

3

Jewish Law and the State's Authority to Punish Crime

Judaism regards its system of law as transnational and transgeographic. All Jews, regardless of their place of domicile, are bound by the criminal and civil aspects of Jewish law no less than by its religious or ritual provisions.

Jewish law provides for the application of criminal sanctions only upon the testimony of two qualified eyewitnesses and a guilty verdict rendered by a court of competent jurisdiction – composed of adherents to Judaism and established in conformity with the relevant provisions of the statutes governing judicial bodies. Admonishing the accused, prior to his commission of a crime, that his contemplated behavior would indeed be criminal and of the punishment that would follow, as well as a court composed of twenty-three "ordained" judges, are necessary conditions for imposing either capital or corporal punishment. The "ordination" required is a form of licensure originating in the designation of elders by Moses as recorded in Numbers 11:24. These elders, in turn, transmitted this authority to their successors. The authority was then passed on from generation to generation in an unbroken chain of transmission over a span of centuries until it was forcibly interrupted during the period of Roman oppression subsequent to the destruction of the Second Commonwealth in 70 C.E. The result is that, at present, there are no individuals qualified to sit on such courts and hence, as a practical matter, existing rabbinic courts are not competent to impose either capital or corporal punishment.

Capital punishment is regarded as having been abrogated for another reason as well. On the basis of a well-recognized principle of scriptural exegesis, the Gemara, *Sanhedrin* 52b, establishes that capital punishment can be imposed only when the biblically prescribed sacrificial rituals continue to be performed in the Temple in Jerusalem. Hence lapse of the sacrificial order necessarily led to abrogation of capital punishment.

Jewish law also posits severe strictures against delivering either the person or property of a Jew to a gentile. Thus, *Shulḥan Arukh, Ḥoshen Mishpat* 388:9, declares that the person and property of even a "wicked person" and a "transgressor" remain inviolate even if the person is a source of "trouble" or "pain" to others. There is, however, an ambiguity inherent in this proscription. There may be reason to assume that the prohibition is limited to turning over a person or his property to the custody of an "oppressor" who inflicts bodily or financial harm in a malevolent or extralegal manner. Indeed, the terminology employed by *Tur Shulḥan Arukh, Ḥoshen Mishpat* 388, in codifying this provision, lends credence to such a restrictive interpretation, since *Tur* incorporates the term "*anas*" or "oppressor" in recording the prohibition. Nevertheless, it may be the case that employing this term does not serve to limit the scope of the prohibition but simply serves as an illustration. This view finds support in the omission of the term "*anas*" in the subsequent codification of the provision in the *Shulḥan Arukh*. The latter interpretation would, in the absence of other considerations, have the effect of banning physical delivery of a Jew to non-Jewish authorities as well as prohibiting conveyance of information that might be used against him in either a criminal or civil action. In accordance with that interpretation, such actions would not be countenanced even in situations involving a clear violation of a criminal statute and would apply even when the accused is assured the protection of due process of law.

I. THE KING'S JUSTICE

The crucial theoretical issue in determining the correct interpretation of this provision of Jewish law is the formulation of a legal principle that might provide for recognition of the jurisdiction of non-Jewish judicial authorities. Clearly, causing judicially cognizable harm to another person constitutes a tort in virtually every legal system unless justification for the harm is recognized by the system itself. It is equally clear that punishment meted out in accordance with the penal provisions of any given legal system is not regarded by that system as tortious. Accordingly, the question that must be addressed is whether Jewish law is prepared to recognize the authority and jurisdiction of another system of law in such matters.

Quite distinct from the corpus of law that it regards as incumbent upon its adherents, Judaism concurrently posits a parallel legal code that it regards as binding upon all of humanity, *viz.*, the "Seven Commandments of the Sons of Noah," or the Noahide Code. Standards of evidence and rules of procedure that form an integral part of the Noahide Code are far less restrictive than those adhered to by Jewish courts. Under the provisions of the Noahide Code, *inter alia*, testimony of a single witness is sufficient for conviction; no prior admonition is required; and the court may be composed of a single judge.

In the Jewish Commonwealth separate judiciaries were established: one exercised jurisdiction over the Jewish populace and administered Jewish law while the other sat in judgment upon non-Jewish nationals and rendered justice in accordance with the provisions of the Noahide Code.[1] The jurisdiction of non-Jewish courts and their authority to administer the Noahide Code was limited to gentiles.[2] Although the jurisdiction and authority of Noahide courts is not limited by either geographic area or historical epoch, Jewish law contains no explicit statutory provision that grants non-Jewish courts jurisdiction over Jewish malfeasors.

The earlier cited provisions regarding rules of evidence and judicial procedure apply only to the imposition of penal sanctions by Jewish courts as provided by statute. The monarch, however, was empowered to ignore the judiciary and its unique form of due process in imposing extrastatutory punishment when he deemed it necessary to do so to preserve law and order. Thus, Rambam, *Hilkhot Roẓeah* 2:4, writes: "Each of these murderers and their like who are not subject to death by verdict of the *bet din*, if a king of Israel wishes to put them to death by virtue of the law of the monarchy and the perfection of the world, he has the right to do so." It is not immediately clear whether the authority to impose "the King's justice" is limited to Jewish monarchs or whether it is the prerogative of every sovereign ruler.

A literal reading of I Samuel 8:5 seems to indicate that this power is shared by the kings of all nations. The elders of Israel demand of Samuel: "Appoint for us a king to judge us like all the nations," i.e., a monarch empowered to administer "the King's justice." In classic rabbinic sources, the phrase "to judge us" was certainly understood as having that connotation. Rabbenu Nissim Gerondi, *Derashot ha-Ran*, no. 11, seizes upon this phrase in explaining why the request for establishing a monarchy aroused Samuel's ire. Appointment of a monarch as the head of the Jewish Commonwealth constitutes one of the 613 biblical commandments and its fulfillment is regarded as having become incumbent upon the populace upon entry into the Promised Land.[3] Rabbenu Nissim explains that a monarch is required for two purposes: (1) to serve as commander-in-chief of the army; and (2) to serve as chief magistrate in administering extrastatutory punishment when it is necessary to do so to preserve the social fabric. A request for appointment of a king could not, in and of itself, have been a matter for censure. Rabbenu Nissim asserts that Samuel became angry because the request was couched in a manner that gave

1 See Rambam, *Hilkhot Melakhim* 10:11.

2 See *Hilkhot Melakhim* 9:14.

3 See Deuteronomy 17:15; *Sanhedrin* 20b; Rambam, *Hilkhot Melakhim* 1:1.

voice to a perceived need for imposition of "the King's justice." A well-ordered, law-abiding society has no need for the imposition of emergency *ad hoc* measures by the monarch; the punishments provided by statute and their imposition in accordance with the rigorous standards of due process prescribed by Jewish law should suffice to protect societal concerns. The request presented to Samuel reflected recognition by the petitioners that their society could not long endure on the basis of criminal procedure hobbled by a two-witness rule and a requirement for prior warning as well as a host of other impediments to actual imposition of penal sanctions. The anticipation by the petitioners of a breakdown of law and order, for which the sole remedy would have been imposition of "the King's justice," bespoke either an unacceptable lack of confidence in themselves or their peers or, even worse, a realistic assessment of moral degeneration.[4] Thus, explains Rabbenu Nissim, Samuel had ample cause for distress.[5]

Ostensibly, the phrase "like all the nations" indicates that this is a legitimate exercise of the royal prerogative among the nations of the world. It may however be that employment of the phrase does not reflect recognition of a normative, legal power vested in gentile sovereigns, but constitutes only a *de facto* statement of socio-political reality. In practice, in punishing evildoers, monarchs of antiquity certainly did not feel constrained by the limitations of the Noahide Code. Their customary practice may have been cited by the elders, not as an example of legitimate exercise of royal power, but simply as a paradigm for appointing a monarch over the Jewish populace in whom such power would be legitimately vested. If administration of "the King's justice" is a power limited to the monarch of a Jewish state, that legal institution cannot serve as the legitimating basis for imposition of penal sanctions by a non-Jewish government.

II. "THE KING'S JUSTICE" AND GENTILE SOVEREIGNS

Whether Halakhah regards non-Jewish sovereigns as endowed with the authority to impose "the King's justice" appears to be a matter of controversy among medieval authorities. The Gemara records the well-known dictum

4 See R. Abraham Benjamin Sofer, *Ketav Sofer, Parashat Shoftim*, s.v. *od nireh li*, and R. Yechiel Michel Epstein, *Arukh ha-Shulḥan he-Atid, Hilkhot Melakhim* 71:6–7. The thesis presented here incorporates elements elucidated by *Ketav Sofer* that are not explicitly formulated by *Derashot ha-Ran*.

5 Cf. *Sanhedrin* 20b, which declares that the elders of the generation couched their petition in appropriate language, as well as Rambam, *Hilkhot Melakhim* 1:2, who indicates that censure was occasioned by a disdain for the leadership of Samuel.

of Rabbi Samuel, one of the Amora'im of the Talmud, who declared: "*Dina de-malkhuta dina*" – "The law of the land is the law."[6] Justification of that principle is far from obvious. Numerous theories have been advanced in an attempt to explain why civil ordinances having no basis either in Scripture or in the Oral Law should be binding in Halakhah, the system of law regarded by Jewish teaching as binding upon Jews. Noteworthy are the remarks of Rabbi Samuel ben Meir (Rashbam) in his commentary on the Gemara, *Bava Batra* 54b:

> All the taxes, levies and customs of the kings that are customarily promulgated in their kingdoms are the law because all the members of the kingdom accept upon themselves the laws of the King and his statutes and therefore it is absolute law.

Rashbam's comments are problematic. They might well be interpreted as limiting Samuel's dictum to monetary obligations such as payment of taxes and levies. On the surface, such obligations might be explained on the basis of ordinary contract theory. Subjects who "accept upon themselves the laws of the King" voluntarily undertake to pay the taxes imposed by the monarch. A contractual obligation to pay an already announced levy is certainly enforceable. However, contract law, as posited by Halakhah, does not recognize the enforceability of an unspecified, open-ended obligation, the extent of which is to be unilaterally determined by another party. Yet it is clear that a subject does not have the right to reject a tax newly imposed by the king on a claim that he never previously accepted it. Moreover, Halakhah declines to recognize the validity of virtually any contract unless recorded in a properly drafted instrument or entered into by means of a formal act of *kinyan* – for example, formal delivery of a kerchief or other artifact, which serves a function analogous to that of symbolic delivery of consideration in common law.[7] An oral undertaking not accompanied by a formal act of *kinyan* is regarded as "mere words" and may be renounced at will.

Rashbam's thesis becomes entirely cogent if the "acceptance" of which he speaks is understood, not as contractual acceptance of a monetary obligation, but as acceptance of the sovereignty of the monarch. If so, Rashbam's comments serve to establish the principle that an obligation of obedience flows directly from voluntary acceptance of the authority of the monarch. The

[6] *Gittin* 10b; *Bava Kamma* 113a; *Bava Batra* 54b; and *Nedarim* 28a.

[7] The kerchief does not, however, represent a symbolic *quid pro quo* in a manner analogous to the peppercorn, but serves either to generate both firm intention and reliance, i.e., a meeting of the minds, or as evidence thereof. See R. Yecheskel Abramsky, *Dinei Mamonot*, 2nd ed. (1969), pp. 9–13, who argues that the requirement of *kinyan* is not absolute.

Gemara, *Sanhedrin* 20b, posits the actions of the king portended in I Samuel 8:5 as legitimate perquisites of his office. Rashbam, then, in essence, does no more than spell out the prescribed manner in which a monarch is vested with those prerogatives. Unlike kings of a Jewish commonwealth, who must be formally invested in office by the Great Sanhedrin and a prophet,[8] the authority of the monarch of a non-Jewish state is derived entirely from the consent of the governed, with such consent serving not only as a necessary condition, but also as the sufficient condition for exercise of royal powers. Accordingly, payment of taxes becomes a legitimate and legally binding obligation even in the absence of a specific undertaking with regard to such payment. The obligation is imposed by virtue of the authority of the sovereign, rather than freely assumed by the subject. It is only the sovereign's authority to act as sovereign that requires "acceptance" on the part of his subjects. Once such acceptance is forthcoming, no further legitimization is required for exercise of the prerogatives enumerated in I Samuel 8:5.

Of course, the premises implicit in this theory include: (1) the existence of a biblically recognized institution of "monarchy" as a legal category;[9] (2) extension of the halakhic institution of the monarchy to encompass non-Jewish sovereigns as well; and (3) recognition of the authority of the non-Jewish sovereign as binding upon Jewish subjects as well as upon non-Jewish nationals. Since, according to Rashbam, a gentile monarch is recognized as a "king" for purposes of Halakhah, it may well be assumed that a king enjoys all the perquisites of monarchy including the right to impose penal sanctions in administering "the King's justice."

This thesis is echoed in Rambam, *Hilkhot Gezeilah ve-Aveidah* 5:18. The preceding sections of chapter five are devoted to a full explication of Samuel's dictum "*Dina de-malkhuta dina.*" In the concluding section of that chapter Rambam writes:

> All of these matters are stated concerning a king whose coin circulates in those lands, for the inhabitants of that land have agreed upon him and rely that he is their master and they are his servants. But if his coin does not circulate he is [in the category] of a robber who uses force and like a group of armed bandits whose laws are not law. Similarly, such a king and all his servants are robbers in every respect.

8 See Rambam, *Hilkhot Melakhim* 1:3.

9 The monarch's power need not be unlimited, nor must it be vested in an individual rather than in a legislative or executive body. See Ramban, addenda to Rambam's *Sefer ha-Mizvot*, no. 17, who, in a different context, defines a monarch as "a king, a judge or whoever exercises jurisdiction over the populace."

Rambam clearly regards the halakhic status and authority of the king to be contingent upon the consent of the governed, which, in turn, may be ascertained by a determination of whether or not his coin is accepted *de facto* as legal tender. The right of coinage is not only a jealously safeguarded monarchial prerogative but constitutes a hallmark, indeed, the litmus test, of sovereignty. Acceptance of the king's currency bespeaks tacit acceptance of his authority and reliance upon his protection and rule. Thus, it is only a king who rules by virtue of the acceptance or acquiescence of his subjects who may legitimately exercise the royal prerogatives enumerated in I Samuel 8.

Rashbam and Rambam should be regarded as advancing an identical theory of *dina de-malkhuta dina* despite the fact that Rambam speaks of acceptance of the king's authority while Rashbam focuses upon acceptance of "the king's laws and statutes." Rashbam should not be understood as predicating the binding authority of the laws and ordinances of the kingdom upon explicit acceptance of each law individually. Rather, he should be understood as asserting that investiture of an individual in royal office *ipso facto* constitutes conferral of lawmaking authority. Hence "acceptance" of the king as monarch is tantamount to acceptance of his laws. The notion that acceptance of a monarch is at one and the same time the acceptance of his legislative authority is explicitly formulated by Ramban, in his commentary on *Yevamot* 46a, who equates the two concepts in stating, "since they accept his sovereignty and they accept his edicts."

It is evident that both Rambam and Rashbam regard *dina de-malkhuta dina* to be binding because promulgation of "the law of the kingdom" is a legitimate exercise of royal authority by the sovereign. Since the principle *dina de-malkhuta dina* is enunciated with regard to the laws of gentile nations it is clear that, for both Rambam and Rashbam, a non-Jewish ruler must enjoy the halakhic status of a monarch.[10] Since even a gentile monarch is entitled to exercise the prerogatives enumerated in I Samuel it may well be argued that such a monarch may legitimately punish disobedience of his decrees.[11]

10 See also Ramban, Rashba and Ritva, *Bava Batra* 55a; *Shitah Mekubbezet, Bava Kamma* 97b, s.v. *katav ha-Ramah*; Me'iri, *Bava Kamma* 113a and 113b; R. Joseph Karo, *Teshuvot Avkat Rokhel*, no. 47; and R. Moses di Trani, *Kiryat Sefer, Hilkhot Gezeilah*, ch. 5.

11 There are, of course, other theories of *dina de-malkhuta dina* that not only fail to provide a basis for penal authority but also seem to negate the view that gentile sovereigns enjoy the prerogatives enumerated in I Samuel 8. For example, Rabbenu Nissim, in his commentary on *Nedarim* 28a, declares that the principle of *dina de-malkhuta dina* is limited to a gentile ruler "because the land is his and he can say to [his Jewish subjects], 'If you do not fulfill my commands I will banish you from the land.'" According to Rabbenu Nissim's analysis, *dina de-malkhuta dina* establishes only the monarch's right to collect feudal duties or to collect "rent" in the form of taxes levied upon those granted a right of domicile. See also R. Dov Berish

That conclusion is reflected in the comments of Ritva, recorded in *Shitah Mekubbeẓet, Bava Meẓi'a* 83b, who declares that a gentile king may apprehend and execute thieves and that, accordingly, a Jew is permitted to turn over thieves to the king's officers. The talmudic discussion that serves as the basis for Ritva's comment is of seminal importance:

> R. Eleazar, son of R. Shimon, met an officer who was engaged in arresting thieves. [R. Eleazar] said to him, "How can you detect them . . . ? Perhaps you take the innocent and leave behind the wicked." [The officer said,] "And what shall I do? It is the king's command." [R. Eleazar] said to him, "Come, I will teach you what to do. Go into a tavern at the fourth hour of the day. If you see a man drinking wine, holding a cup in his hand and dozing, ask who he is. If he is a scholar, he has risen early to pursue his studies; if he is a laborer, he has risen early to do his work; if his work is at night, he may have been rolling thin metal. If he is none of these, he is a thief; arrest him." A report was heard in the royal court. They said, "Let the reader of the letter become the messenger." R. Eleazar, son of R. Shimon, was brought and he proceeded to apprehend thieves. R. Joshua, son of Karḥah, sent word to him, "Vinegar, son of wine! How long will you deliver the people of our God for slaughter?" [R. Eleazar] sent the reply, "I eradicate thorns from the vineyard." [R. Joshua] responded, "Let the owner of the vineyard come and eradicate his thorns." One day a laundryman met [R. Eleazar and] called him "Vinegar, son of wine." Said [R. Eleazar] to himself, "Since he is so insolent, he is certainly a wicked man." He exclaimed, "Seize him! Seize him!"[12]

Ritva questions how it was possible for Rabbi Eleazar ben Shimon to pass judgment without testimony of witnesses or prior warning and how it was possible for him to do so in a historical epoch in which the Sanhedrin no longer existed. Ritva explains that Rabbi Eleazar ben Shimon was the agent of the king and that the king may rightfully execute evildoers even in the absence of prior admonition and without the benefit of the testimony of two eyewitnesses.[13] Ritva further points to the extrajudicial execution of the Amalekite proselyte by King David, recorded in II Samuel 1:15, as an example of punishment on the basis of administration of "the King's justice." Thus Ritva explicitly states that, according to Rabbi Eleazar ben Shimon, even

Weidenfeld, *Teshuvot Dovev Meisharim*, vol. III, no. 89, and R. Shlomoh Zalman Auerbach, *Ma'adanei Ereẓ*, no. 20, sec. 12.

12 *Bava Meẓi'a* 83b.

13 See R. Benjamin Rabinowitz-Teumim, *Ha-Torah ve-ha-Medinah*, vol. IV, no. 80, who notes that R. Eleazar ben Shimon acted in an official capacity and contends that, even according to Ritva, only a person specifically delegated by the monarch to perform such functions may deliver a criminal into the hands of civil authorities.

non-Jewish monarchs are authorized to administer extrastatutory punishment in accordance with "the King's justice."

Nevertheless, examination of the talmudic discussion reveals that the matter is the subject of significant controversy. Rabbi Joshua ben Karḥah remonstrated with Rabbi Eleazar ben Shimon in exclaiming, "How long will you deliver the people of our God for slaughter?"[14] Moreover, the discussion concludes with a report that, when Rabbi Ishmael ben Yosi acted in a similar manner, the prophet Elijah appeared to him and voiced the identical complaint. When Rabbi Ishmael offered the same defense, "What shall I do? It is the king's command," Elijah responded, "Your father fled to Asia, you flee to Laodicea!"[15] Since the opposing position of Rabbi Joshua ben Karḥah is endorsed by none other than the prophet Elijah there is strong reason to assume that Rabbi Eleazar ben Shimon's position must be rejected as a normative legal position.

There is, however, a parallel narrative involving Elijah that may shed light upon this exchange as well. The Palestinian Talmud, *Terumot* 8:4, reports that a fugitive, a certain Ula bar Kushav, took refuge in Lod. The civil authorities surrounded the city and demanded that he be surrendered to them, threatening the entire populace with annihilation if the townspeople refused. Rabbi Shimon ben Lakish convinced the fugitive to allow himself to be turned over to the authorities. The Palestinian Talmud records that the prophet Elijah had been wont to reveal himself to Rabbi Shimon ben Lakish on a regular basis but that subsequent to that event Elijah failed to do so. Rabbi Shimon ben Lakish fasted repeatedly until Elijah again revealed himself. However, Elijah remonstrated that he was being forced to appear to an individual who had delivered a Jew to gentile authorities. Rabbi Shimon ben Lakish defended his actions, arguing that they were entirely in accordance with Jewish law. To this Elijah retorted, "Is this then the law of the pious?" The incident recounted in the Palestinian Talmud similarly involved deliverance of a fugitive to the hands of civil authorities for punishment in accordance with the law of the land, albeit in a situation in which the surrender of the individual in question was demanded by the authorities upon pain of death of all concerned, including the fugitive. Elijah did not protest that Jewish law does not sanction such action. Rather, he argued that, although entirely legitimate, such action does not behoove the pious. Similarly, the controversy between Rabbi Eleazar ben Shimon and Rabbi Joshua ben Karḥah may be understood, not as concerning a matter of normative law, but as pertaining to proper formulation of "the

[14] *Loc. cit.*

[15] *Loc. cit.*

law of the pious." Both agree that the king is empowered to execute those who flout his laws. Rabbi Joshua ben Karḥah, however, maintains that a pious person should not act in such a manner,[16] while Rabbi Eleazar ben Shimon maintains that, on the contrary, since the individual is clearly a wicked person, even "piety" demands that he be surrendered for punishment as a means of "eradicating the thorns from the vineyard."

Support for this analysis of the exchange between Rabbi Eleazar ben Shimon and Rabbi Joshua ben Karḥah may be found in the commentary of Ritva as recorded in his own novellae on that talmudic discussion. In stating the normative rule, Ritva offers the following comment: "Nevertheless, in a situation in which the king, in accordance with the laws of the kingdom, may not act in such a manner, his officer is similarly not permitted [to do so]; and if the king orders him to do so he must suffer death and not transgress."[17] The novel legal principle stated by Ritva is that the monarch may not act in an arbitrary and capricious manner, but must himself conform to the law promulgated in his kingdom. Concomitantly, illicit orders of the monarch must be resisted, even if such resistance entails martyrdom.

Ritva does, however, affirm that the monarch may impose punishment when it is in conformity with the laws of the kingdom.[18] Ritva's conclusion is remarkable in light of the fact that the prophet Elijah endorsed the view of Rabbi Joshua ben Karḥah, who maintains that a monarch may not legitimately impose "the King's justice" even under such circumstances. If so, whether the king's action is in accordance with the "laws of the kingdom" or is entirely capricious should be irrelevant. Ritva's comments are cogent only if Rabbi Joshua ben Karḥah's position, and Elijah's endorsement of that view, are regarded as based upon considerations of pious conduct rather than upon normative halakhic principles. Understood in that manner, Ritva asserts that,

[16] Cf. R. Samuel ha-Levi Woszner, *Teshuvot Shevet ha-Levi, Yoreh De'ah*, vol. I, no. 58, who regards Rabbi Joshua ben Karḥah's objection as limited to capital punishment because of considerations of piety, but then incongruously continues with a statement that "the law of the pious" applies to financial matters as well.

[17] *Shitah Mekubbeẓet, Bava Meẓi'a* 83b. See also Ritva, *Bava Batra* 55a. Ran, *Sanhedrin* 46a, expresses a similar view.

[18] See also Rashi, Deuteronomy 1:9, who states that if a judge of "other nations judges, executes, smites, suffocates, engages in perversion of justice or steals it is of no consequence." R. Meir Dan Plocki, *Ḥemdat Yisra'el, Kuntres Ner Miẓvah*, sec. 30, understands "perversion of justice" as a reference to rendering judgment in accordance with "the law of the land" rather than according to the law of the Torah. If so, reference to capital punishment should be interpreted in a similar vein. Understood in this manner, Rashi espouses a position identical to that of Ritva.

strictly as a matter of law, the king may order execution only in accordance with the laws of the land, but should he order execution in violation of established law one must suffer martyrdom rather than carry out an illicit directive. It nevertheless remains an act of piety to disregard the king's command to execute punishment in circumstances in which Jewish law does not provide for punishment to be imposed even though such punishment is in accordance with the law of the land.

Nevertheless, Ritva's caveat remains problematic. If the authority of a gentile sovereign to impose "the King's justice" is derived from I Samuel 8, it is difficult to fathom why his actions are legitimate only if they are predicated upon "the laws of the kingdom."[19] As has been shown earlier, acceptance of the authority of a monarch is not limited to contractual acceptance of already established legal norms. Indeed, acceptance of capital punishment cannot be made a matter of contractual stipulation. Accordingly, acceptance can only mean acceptance of the authority of the king. Pursuant to such acceptance on the part of his subjects, exercise by the monarch of the prerogatives recorded in I Samuel 8 becomes legitimate. There is no explicit statement in I Samuel requiring that the monarch act in accordance with a formally promulgated code of law rather than in accordance with his perception, on a case-by-case basis, of the need for punishment as a deterrent to antisocial behavior.

This limitation upon the king's power, denying him the right to punish transgressors other than in accordance with a formally promulgated code of law, can be explained on the basis of the position of Rabbi Shimon ben Ẓemaḥ Duran (*Tashbaẓ*).[20] While Ritva's statement is limited to crime, *Tashbaẓ* makes a much broader assertion:

> The king may not enact new laws other than those already enacted . . . for the laws of the monarchy are known to all and are already set down. Just as we have laws of the kingdom as declared by Samuel to Israel . . . similarly other nations have laws known to kings and it is with regard to [those laws] that [the Sages] declared *dina de-malkhuta dina*.[21]

Rashba similarly states:

> Just as we have laws of the kingdom as declared by Samuel to Israel similarly gentile kingdoms possess known laws and it is with regard to such laws that the

[19] Cf. the discussion of a similar problem in other sources by Dayan I. Grunfeld, *The Jewish Law of Inheritance* (Oak Park, MI, 1987), pp. 29–33.

[20] *Teshuvot Tashbaẓ*, vol. I, no. 158. See also *Teshuvot ha-Rashba*, vol. III, no. 29.

[21] *Tashbaẓ*, vol. I, no. 158. A similar view is expressed by Ramban, *Bava Batra* 55a.

> Sages declared that their laws are valid; but the laws on the basis of which the courts judge are not the law of the kingdom, rather the courts judge unto themselves on the basis of what they find in the works of [earlier] judges.[22]

Thus Rashba explicitly excludes "judge-made law" from the ambit of *dina de-malkhuta dina*.

These authorities apparently understand the phrase "like all the nations" that occurs in I Samuel 8:5 as indicating that the peoples of antiquity shared a common corpus of law firmly established and known to all. That corpus of law bestowed certain powers upon the monarch, but not necessarily the powers announced by Samuel as the prerogatives of the rulers of the Jewish commonwealth. Nevertheless, according to both Rashba and *Tashbaẓ*, gentile kings are limited to enforcement of statutes incorporated in that corpus of law just as Jewish kings could not exceed the authority vested in them by Samuel's declaration.

Ritva seems to adhere to this position in part and to deviate in part. Ritva presumably did not understand the phrase "like all the nations" as limiting the power of gentile kings to enforcement of the specific provisions of already enacted legislation handed down from antiquity; rather, he understood the phrase as curtailing a monarch's authority to criminalize an act *post factum* and restricting his penal authority to enforcement of the provisions of a previously announced system of law. According to Ritva, this is the salient point of the reference to the practice of the monarchs of "all the nations" whose penal systems merited endorsement and legitimization. The effect of incorporation of that phrase in the canon of Scripture is to deny non-Jewish monarchs the authority to act in an arbitrary or capricious manner. Thus Samuel's pronouncement serves to limit the authority of gentile sovereigns in a manner somewhat analogous, but not entirely parallel, to the manner in which the power of Jewish monarchs was limited. The power of Jewish kings was limited to the exercise of the prerogatives specifically delineated by Samuel whereas gentile kings were denied absolute dictatorial power on an *ad hoc* basis but were charged only with ruling and meting out justice in accordance with a formal system of law, the content of which was left to their discretion.

Support for this analysis of Ritva's position, that the talmudic controversy is limited to "the law of the pious," but that all agree that non-Jewish sovereigns may legitimately administer "the King's justice," is found in another medieval source. Rashba explicitly states that the controversy between Rabbi

22 *Teshuvot ha-Rashba*, vol. III, no. 29; see also *Bet Yosef, Tur Shulḥan Arukh, Ḥoshen Mishpat* 26 (end).

Eleazar ben Shimon and Rabbi Joshua ben Karḥah concerns solely how the pious should comport themselves but that, as a matter of law, both agree that it is permissible to assist the king in apprehending criminals.[23] Rashba writes:

> R. Eleazar ben Shimon apprehended thieves at the king's command and punished them as did R. Ishmael ben Yosi even though R. Joshua ben Karḥah called him "Vinegar, son of wine"... as did Elijah of R. Ishmael ben Yosi. Nevertheless, we should not deem them to be totally in error with regard to explicit legal provisions. Rather, because of their piety, they should have refrained from administering punishment not mandated by the Torah. That they were called "Vinegar, son of wine" was because they did not conduct themselves with piety as did their fathers... For anyone who is appointed by the king for this purpose may judge and act according to the sovereign decrees, for the king preserves the land by means of such judgments.[24]

However, the position that even a non-Jewish sovereign may legitimately impose "the King's justice" is contradicted by Rambam, *Hilkhot Rozeaḥ* 2:4, in his statement that "each of these murderers and their like who are not subject to death by verdict of the *bet din*, if a king of Israel wishes to put them to death by royal decree for the benefit of society he has the right to do so." In ascribing such authority only to "a king of Israel," Rambam appears to reject explicitly the notion that a gentile monarch is authorized to impose "the King's justice" and implies that even gentile subjects must be judged solely in accordance with the provisions of the Noahide Code.[25] Rambam's position is all the more remarkable in light of the fact that, as noted earlier, in another section of his *Mishneh Torah*, *Hilkhot Gezeilah ve-Aveidah* 5:18, Rambam limits the application of the principle of *dina de-malkhuta dina* to the edicts of a monarch whose sovereignty has been accepted by the populace. In so doing, Rambam implies that the authority of *dina de-malkhuta dina* is based upon the legitimate exercise of royal power, the monarchial prerogatives

[23] See *Bet Yosef*, *Tur Shulḥan Arukh*, *Ḥoshen Mishpat* 388.

[24] This analysis of the position espoused by Ritva and Rashba is reflected in a responsum of R. Moses Schick, *Teshuvot Maharam Shik*, *Ḥoshen Mishpat*, no. 50. The case involved a woman suspected of poisoning her husband. The question posed to Maharam Schick was whether or not she should be turned over to civil authorities in order to stand trial. After citing both Ritva and Rashba, Maharam Schick concludes that "sages of Israel" should not become actively involved, but should maintain a passive stance in the matter. Reflected in that position is the view that, although such acts would not be illicit, piety demands that "sages of Israel" not deliver the culprit for possible execution. See also *Sefer Ḥasidim*, no. 683, p. 3.

[25] Cf. *Teshuvot Maharam Shik*, *Ḥoshen Mishpat*, no. 50. For a discussion of Maharam Schick's interpretation of Rambam, see J. David Bleich, "Hasgarat Poshe'a Yehudi she-Baraḥ le-Ereẓ Yisra'el," *Or ha-Mizraḥ* (Nisan–Tammuz 5747), p. 254.

recorded in I Samuel 8. If so, Rambam's position is self-contradictory. If Rambam does indeed predicate *dina de-malkhuta dina* upon I Samuel 8, he must necessarily regard non-Jewish monarchs as vested with the prerogatives conferred by Scripture upon incumbents in royal office. If so, then, *mutatis mutandis*, a non-Jewish king must also be vested with the authority to impose "the King's justice."

Rambam's position may be understood on the basis of a responsum authored by Rabbi Moses Sofer, *Teshuvot Ḥatam Sofer, Likkutim*, no. 14. The primary question addressed by *Ḥatam Sofer* in that responsum is whether a non-Jewish judge may accept a bribe. His response is that, although the biblical injunction "Thou shalt not take a bribe"[26] is addressed to Jews and not to Noahides, nevertheless, a Noahide is commanded to render a true and just verdict and hence he dare not accept a bribe for purposes of subverting justice.[27] A judge who knowingly renders an unjust judgment, opines *Ḥatam Sofer*, is guilty of a capital crime under the Noahide Code. Accordingly, he rules that a Jew who presents a bribe to a non-Jewish judge, not only wrongs his adversary, but is also guilty of "placing a stumbling-block before the blind" in causing the judge to issue an unjust decision. *Ḥatam Sofer* then proceeds to distinguish between civil actions and criminal proceedings. Since bribery of a gentile is forbidden only if the bribe is designed to ensure a favorable judgment without regard to the merits of the case, a gift designed to ensure only impartial deliberation and expeditious disposition of the case is not prohibited.[28] Accordingly, rules *Ḥatam Sofer*, a bribe designed to ensure acquittal in a criminal proceeding cannot be forbidden since

> certainly there is no way that a Jew may [halakhically] incur the death penalty by operation of their laws [since they impose the death penalty] without witnesses, prior admonition and a court composed of twenty-three qualified Jewish judges and, accordingly, such execution is always contrary to the law of the Torah.[29]

[26] Deuteronomy 16:19.

[27] For further discussion of bribery under the Noahide Code see Ramban, *Commentary on the Bible*, Genesis 34:13; R. Joseph Saul Nathanson, *Teshuvot Sho'el u-Meshiv, Mahadura Kamma*, vol. I, no. 230; *Encyclopedia Talmudit*, vol. III, p. 355, n. 256; R. Bernard Chavel, *Peirush Ramban al ha-Torah*, vol. I, no. 192, s.v. *u-be-Yerushalmi*; R. Jonathan Eibeschutz, *Urim ve-Tumim* 9:1; R. Joshua Leib Diskin, *Teshuvot Maharil Diskin*, II, *Kuntres Aḥaron*, no. 5, sec. 223.

[28] In contradistinction to the law governing Noahide judges, a Jew may not accept a gift from a litigant even if it is only of trivial value, even if any attempt to influence the verdict is expressly disavowed and even if both parties present gifts of equal value. See Rambam, *Hilkhot Sanhedrin* 23:1 and 23:5.

[29] *Teshuvot Ḥatam Sofer, Likkutim*, no. 14.

Ḥatam Sofer's rejection of the authority of non-Jewish courts to impose the death penalty upon Jewish defendants would appear to apply with equal force to corporal punishment as well as to incarceration.[30]

Elsewhere, however, *Ḥatam Sofer* appears to espouse a different view. In another responsum, *Teshuvot Ḥatam Sofer, Oraḥ Ḥayyim*, no. 208, that authority poses a fundamental question. Granting that enumeration of specific actions in I Samuel 8 confers authority upon the monarch to engage in such practices, an examination of those verses reveals that they refer only to property rights and matters of personal service; they make no mention of either corporal or capital punishment. Where, then, is the source of authority for even a Jewish king to impose these sanctions other than in accordance with statute?

Ḥatam Sofer finds a source for the exercise of such power in Ramban's comments on Leviticus 27:29, "*Kol ḥerem asher yeḥeram min ha-adam lo yipadeh, mot yamut.*" The standard translation of the verse, "None devoted, that may be devoted of men, shall be ransomed; he shall surely be put to death," renders its meaning utterly incomprehensible. Little wonder, then, that medieval rabbinic exegetes and commentaries struggled to arrive at a proper interpretation of the verse. Ramban understands the term "*ḥerem*" (in this context) as connoting societal proscription of certain acts upon pain of death. Understood in this manner, the verse, by inference, serves to confer legislative power upon society for the purpose of achieving socially desirable goals and also to confer penal authority to enforce such decrees. According to Ramban, the verse must be understood as an elliptical reference to the violation of a *ḥerem* pronounced by society and serves to forbid substitution of a financial penalty for capital punishment incurred in violation of a communal edict. The verse then should be rendered as "No [violation] of a *ḥerem*, pronounced as a *ḥerem* by man, shall be ransomed; he [the violator of the *ḥerem*] shall surely be put to death." Ramban explains the biblical narrative, I Samuel 14:24–45, which recounts the actions of Jonathan and his incurring capital liability as predicated upon this scriptural provision. In eating honey Jonathan violated the communal edict pronounced by King Saul against partaking of food on the day of battle against the Philistines; hence Jonathan was subject to the death penalty. Ramban understands the verse "So the people rescued Jonathan, that he died not" (I Samuel 14:45) to mean that the community retroactively nullified its edict and, pursuant to that nullification, Jonathan was exonerated. Such edicts may be promulgated, asserts *Ḥatam Sofer*, either by the community as a whole or by the sovereign as the executive authority

30 See *Taz, Yoreh De'ah* 157:8.

of the community. It is apparently *Ḥatam Sofer*'s opinion that such authority is vested only in the Jewish community and hence only in a Jewish monarch. To be sure, the Jewish community in any country, using its power of *ḥerem*, could promulgate an edict making *lèse majesté* against the gentile sovereign a culpable offense as a violation of Jewish law. However, no such edict was ever promulgated. Accordingly, only the sovereign of a Jewish state may legitimately impose penal sanctions upon violators of his decrees.

Nevertheless, *Ḥatam Sofer* finds alternative grounds for asserting that non-Jewish monarchs may legitimately impose extrastatutory punishment. That authority, as well as authority for the principle of *dina de-malkhuta dina*, *Ḥatam Sofer* regards as being based, not upon I Samuel 8, but upon Song of Songs 8:12. The verse "My vineyard, which is mine, is before me; you, O Solomon shall have the thousand, and those that keep the fruit thereof two hundred" is cited by the Gemara, *Shevu'ot* 35b, in support of a statement to the effect that a king who causes the death of one-sixth of the world's population is not subject to punishment. The authors of *Tosafot, ad locum*, understand that verse as granting Solomon dispensation to cause the death of two hundred individuals to conquer and preserve the thousand. "Those that keep the fruit" may sacrifice two hundred so that Solomon shall "have the thousand." The king is granted authority to go to war for reasons of state even though casualties necessarily result, provided that casualties are limited to a ratio no greater than two hundred in twelve hundred, leaving a remainder of one thousand (a casualty ratio no greater than one-sixth). That dispensation, argues *Ḥatam Sofer*, is not limited to casualties incurred as a result of warfare but extends as well to infliction of loss of life among the king's own subjects in the course of actions designed to benefit the nation or to enhance the grandeur and honor of the sovereign.[31] The king, as "keeper of the fruit," may compromise the lives and welfare of some of his subjects to preserve the integrity of his "vineyard." *Tosafot*'s statement indicating that the king is empowered to sacrifice lives for national purposes is understood by *Ḥatam Sofer* as not limiting such authority to casualties incurred in the course of war but as empowering the king to execute citizens for any legitimate purpose involving "preservation of the vineyard," with warfare simply serving as a paradigm. *Ḥatam Sofer* draws a further inference in stating that the verse "and those that keep the fruit thereof two hundred" serves to establish not only the right of the monarch to take the lives of subjects in order to safeguard the State, but also authorizes him to take lesser measures, including expropriation of property, to provide for the needs of society. Accordingly, concludes *Ḥatam Sofer, dina de-malkhuta dina*,

[31] See also *Teshuvot Ḥatam Sofer, Ḥoshen Mishpat*, no. 44, which reiterates the same principle.

as a principle of jurisprudence expressive of the State's authority to disturb the rights of its citizens to the lawful enjoyment of property, is predicated upon Song of Songs 8:12.

In presenting the novel thesis that Song of Songs 8:12 serves as validation of the principle *dina de-malkhuta dina*, *Ḥatam Sofer* underscores the point that gentile monarchs are also vested with the power to impose penal sanctions upon miscreants. *Dina de-malkhuta dina*, as a normative principle of Jewish law, applies to the laws of non-Jewish states. If it is derived from Song of Songs 8:12 it follows that the verse must be regarded as delineating the authority of all monarchs, gentile as well as Jew. Accordingly, penal authority derived from that verse must also be vested in non-Jewish monarchs. There emerges, however, a contradiction between the position recorded in *Teshuvot Ḥatam Sofer, Oraḥ Ḥayyim*, no. 208, and his statement in *Teshuvot Ḥatam Sofer, Likkutim*, no. 14, denying the authority of a gentile king to impose capital punishment upon his Jewish subjects. Resolution of that problem requires a careful reading of the language employed in the latter responsum. *Ḥatam Sofer* declares such execution to be "*she-lo me-din Torah*," literally, that is "not *from* the law of the Torah"; he does not employ language categorizing capital punishment as imposed by civil authorities to be in violation of, or contradictory to, the law of the Torah. It would seem that in his careful choice of nomenclature, *Ḥatam Sofer* seeks to draw attention to the fundamental distinction between capital punishment as imposed by the *bet din* and capital punishment imposed by the king: the latter is viewed as discretionary whereas the former is mandatory. In his enumeration of the 613 commandments recorded in Scripture, Rambam, *Sefer ha-Miẓvot, miẓvot aseh*, nos. 226–29, declares that implementation of capital punishment by the *bet din*, when required by law, constitutes fulfillment of a mandatory biblical commandment. In fact, the *bet din* was required to impose four different forms of capital punishment in punishment of various transgressions of biblical law and Rambam posits a separate commandment mandating administration of each of those four modes of execution. When the requirements of law pertaining to evidence and judicial procedure have been satisfied, the *bet din* has no choice but to pronounce its verdict and to impose the appropriate punishment; the *bet din* does not enjoy discretion to suspend the sentence or to impose a lesser punishment. Not so with regard to "the King's justice." The king's power is *ad hoc* and intended to be exercised only in accordance with the needs of the hour. Hence the king may ignore the infraction, grant a pardon, commute or suspend a sentence. Thus, imposition of capital punishment by the king is categorized by *Ḥatam Sofer* as "not from the law of the Torah" in the sense that, since it is discretionary in nature, it is not mandated by Torah law. Since gentile courts may impose the death penalty upon Jews or incarcerate criminals only by virtue of their power to impose "the King's justice" and since, according to Jewish law, imposition of such sanctions by the sovereign cannot be mandatory, *Ḥatam Sofer* finds no impropriety in any attempt to avoid imposition of such a penalty.

Acceptance of *Ḥatam Sofer*'s thesis provides a basis for resolving the apparent contradiction in Rambam's codification. As noted earlier, I Samuel 8:5 does not contain any reference to either capital or corporal punishment. Rambam may well agree with *Ḥatam Sofer* in regarding that power as being derived from Leviticus 27:29. In any event, since it is not derived from I Samuel it is not among the royal prerogatives enjoyed by "all the nations that surround us" and hence Rambam, *Hilkhot Roẓeaḥ* 2:4, maintains that such power is limited to the ruler of a Jewish commonwealth. In adopting that view Rambam is nevertheless at variance with *Ḥatam Sofer* in maintaining that gentile kings are not authorized to impose capital punishment in administering "the King's justice." Presumably, Rambam understood the talmudic declaration exonerating a king who causes the death of one-sixth of the population as limited to casualties inflicted in the course of licitly undertaken warfare. Such a position is entirely compatible with a literal reading of *Tosafot*'s analysis of that dictum.

Accordingly, Rambam may be understood as maintaining that *dina de-malkhuta dina* is a derivative of royal authority conferred upon all monarchs on the basis of I Samuel and as maintaining that any sovereign "accepted" by the populace may exercise that authority. However, maintains Rambam, since penal sanctions are not enumerated in I Samuel, the sovereign has no authority to impose such sanctions other than in accordance with the statutory provisions of the Noahide Code. It therefore follows that, according to Rambam, it is forbidden to deliver a Jew to civil authorities for punishment; rather, the normative law, according to Rambam, is in accordance with the pronouncement of Rabbi Joshua ben Karḥah, "Let the owner of the vineyard come and eradicate his thorns."[32]

According to this analysis, Rambam regards Rabbi Joshua ben Karḥah as asserting a normative halakhic position rather than as asserting a standard of pious conduct, which, as has earlier been shown, is evidently the position of Ritva and Rashba. There then emerges somewhat of a problem about the nature of the controversy between Rabbi Joshua ben Karḥah and Rabbi Eleazar ben Shimon. If it is accepted that Rabbi Eleazar ben Shimon bases his position upon Song of Songs 8:12, as is the view of *Ḥatam Sofer*, it is extremely unlikely that Rabbi Joshua ben Karḥah would reject the halakhic principle derived from that verse without making it clear that the exegetical basis of the

[32] *Bava Meẓi'a* 83b.

principle is in dispute. It is similarly unlikely that Rabbi Eleazar ben Shimon regards the authority of a monarch derived from that verse to be limited to the infliction of casualties in the course of war, as may well be assumed on the basis of the comments of *Tosafot*, since that, too, should have been made clear in the words of the talmudic protagonists themselves.[33]

It should also be pointed out that a number of early authorities reject Ritva's analysis of the controversy between Rabbi Joshua ben Karḥah and Rabbi Eleazar ben Shimon and hence, even ignoring the difficulties with regard to that controversy posed by *Ḥatam Sofer*'s thesis, an alternate analysis of the controversy must be sought that will accommodate the position of the early authorities who do not accept Ritva's justification of Rabbi Joshua ben Karḥah's action. Ritva's contention that gentile rulers may exercise the monarchial prerogatives specified in I Samuel is clearly disputed by *Tosafot, Sanhedrin* 20b, in their comments upon another talmudic discussion. *Tosafot* are understandably troubled by the divine censure of the conduct of King Ahab as recorded in I Kings 21. Nabot refused to sell his vineyard to Ahab and, consequently, Ahab had him put to death and seized the vineyard. However, if I Samuel serves as a declaration of royal prerogatives, Ahab acted in a licit manner in expropriating Nabot's land and, since Nabot was culpable in not acceding to the king's demand, Ahab's punishment of Nabot did not warrant censure. *Tosafot* resolve the problem by declaring that the royal prerogatives described in I Samuel may legitimately be exercised only by a king who rules "over all of Israel and Judea by virtue of divine appointment." Since Ahab neither ruled over "all of Israel and Judea" nor ruled by virtue of divine appointment, he had no right to exercise the powers delineated in I Samuel. Since, according to *Tosafot*, even a Jewish king who does not rule by virtue of divine right as announced by a prophet or whose sovereignty is limited to only a portion of the Jewish populace enjoys none of the halakhic prerogatives of a monarch, it follows *a fortiori* that Jewish law does not recognize such powers as being vested in a gentile king whose reign does not satisfy those two necessary conditions. Thus, unlike Ritva, *Tosafot* certainly regard I Samuel as inapplicable to a non-Jewish sovereign.[34]

33 If, as is the position of both Ritva and Rashba, both R. Joshua ben Karḥah and R. Eleazar ben Shimon agree that the king enjoys the power to execute evildoers, there is no reason for them to present any further explanation of their conflicting views regarding the standard to be applied to the pious. That is the case even if such authority is derived from the Song of Songs rather than I Samuel 8, as is the view of *Ḥatam Sofer*. Presumably, the exegetical reference was omitted since it was well known and not at all a matter of controversy.

34 See R. Abraham Kahana-Shapiro, *Teshuvot Dvar Avraham*, vol. I, no. 1, note appended to *anaf* 2.

Accordingly, it may be suggested that Rabbi Eleazar ben Shimon's dictum "I am eradicating thorns from the vineyard"[35] can be understood in a manner other than as reliance upon the prerogatives associated with royal office.

Rema, *Ḥoshen Mishpat* 388:12 and 425:1, rules that in an age of collective punishment a person who engages in counterfeiting or the like may be turned over to civil authorities for punishment. As justification for that ruling, Rema cites the law of the "pursuer" (*rodef*), the provision of Jewish law that not only permits, but mandates, that a bystander come to the rescue of a putative victim whose life is threatened and that if there is no other way of preserving the life of the intended victim, rescue be effected by taking the life of the aggressor.[36] In the talmudic narrative that serves as the focus of the dispute between Rabbi Eleazar ben Shimon and Rabbi Joshua ben Karḥah, the criminals sought by the king were not only breaking the law but were, in actuality, jeopardizing the lives of innocent parties. Rabbi Eleazar ben Shimon came upon an official of the king who was apprehending individuals and delivering them for execution without at all endeavoring to distinguish between the innocent and the guilty.[37] Indeed, Rabbi Eleazar ben Shimon demonstrates that the thieves were avoiding detention because "they hide themselves as animals who secrete themselves by day" and hence only the innocent were being apprehended. The officer's response was, "What shall I do? It is the command of the king!" The officer clearly recognized that his actions were unjust but pleaded *force majeure*. In all probability, the king was well aware of the fact that arrests were being made indiscriminately but pursued such a policy because of a desire to instill fear in the hearts of thieves in an effort to cause them to desist from their nefarious conduct. Execution of the innocent was designed either to create a feeling of apprehension in those who were indeed criminals and had reason to fear that they too would be apprehended or to secure the cooperation of the citizenry, who as a result of the institution of that policy had reason to fear for their own lives, and bring pressure to bear upon the thieves to desist from their criminal activities. In any event, it is clear that the king was, in fact, executing the innocent because of the acts of some few malfeasors among the populace. It is, of course, possible that the king genuinely desired that only the guilty be apprehended but that the officer acted with misplaced zeal because he feared that were he to fail to report success in bringing the guilty to justice his own life would be forfeit. Either way, *de facto*, innocent persons were being put to death because of the activities of thieves. Thus, thieves were

35 *Bava Meẓi'a* 83b.

36 This rule is codified by Rambam, *Hilkhot Roẓeaḥ* 2:4.

37 *Bava Meẓi'a* 83b.

"pursuers" of the innocent no less so than the counterfeiters described by Rema on whose account the authorities were prepared to engage in collective punishment.[38] Since the thieves refused to abandon their criminal activities, they were branded "pursuers" by Rabbi Eleazar ben Shimon, who declared, "I am eradicating thorns from the vineyard." That statement may be taken to mean that the criminals were a threat to the innocent just as thorns are a threat to the grapes that would otherwise flourish in the vineyard. If so, Rabbi Eleazar ben Shimon was not merely defending his activities as not being in violation of Jewish law, as must be understood as having been the case according to Ritva's interpretation, but was declaring his actions to be obligatory. In branding the thieves "thorns" Rabbi Eleazar ben Shimon colorfully depicts them as persons engaged in destruction of the entire "vineyard" with the result that it was incumbent upon him to eliminate them to preserve innocent persons endangered by their activities.

If this analysis of the position of Rabbi Eleazar ben Shimon is correct, Rabbi Joshua ben Karḥah's response, "Let the owner of the vineyard come and destroy his thorns," becomes problematic. The retort does not seem to involve a denial of the facts of the case. If the facts were as described, Rabbi Eleazar ben Shimon's halakhic analysis is beyond cavil.

The controversy between Rabbi Eleazar ben Shimon and Rabbi Joshua ben Karḥah may well reflect disagreement over the level of certainty of impending loss of life that is required to trigger the law of pursuit. Even if Rabbi Joshua ben Karḥah did not himself appreciate the fact that the thieves were actually "pursuers" as well, once he heard Rabbi Eleazar ben Shimon declare, "I am destroying thorns in the vineyard," Rabbi Joshua ben Karḥah's retort, "Let the Master of the vineyard come and eradicate his Thorns," is entirely inappropriate. Rabbi Joshua ben Karḥah acquiesces in the assignment of the appellation "thorns" to the evildoers. If so, to refrain from taking action against them would constitute a violation of the biblical command, "And you shall cut off her hand, your eye shall not have pity" (Deuteronomy 25:12).[39]

The Gemara, *Sanhedrin* 72a, employing biblical exegesis, develops the principle that a burglar must also be presumed to be intent upon taking the life of the householder whose home he enters. It is to be presumed that if the householder discovers the intruder he will instinctively resist with all the means at his disposal in order to preserve hearth and home. The burglar, in

[38] Cf. R. Yitzchak Aharon of Vilkomir, *Einei Yizḥak, Bava Mezi'a* 83b, cited in the marginal notes "*Likkutim*," published in *Ein Ya'akov, Bava Mezi'a* 83b.

[39] Rambam, *Hilkhot Rozeaḥ* 1:7, records the law of the "pursuer" as being predicated upon this verse.

turn, recognizes the likelihood that lethal force will be used against him and hence it must be presumed that, if discovered by the householder in the course of breaking into his home, the burglar, fearing for his own life, will endeavour to strike first. Since the burglar is not only engaged in felonious activity but is also responsible for creating the danger to the householder, he is adjudged a "pursuer." The Gemara declares that an exception to this rule occurs in the case of a father engaged in burglarizing his son's home. In that case, the talmudic presumption is that a father will not attempt to kill his own son and, since this is known to the son as well, the son, if he should kill his burglarizing father, cannot seek exoneration by pleading that he was entitled to invoke the law of pursuit. In other cases, however, there exists a legal presumption that the burglar is a "pursuer." In their commentaries upon that discussion both Rashi and *Tosafot* indicate that, in the absence of a presumption of law, the "pursuer" may not be killed unless murderous intent on his part is known with certainty;[40] the "law of the pursuer" cannot be invoked on the basis of mere suspicion or in a case of doubt.[41]

A contemporary authority, the late Rabbi Moses Feinstein, *Iggerot Mosheh, Ḥoshen Mishpat*, II, no. 69, sec. 2, declares that the law of pursuit applies only in situations in which the murderous intent of the aggressor is known on the basis of an assessment "approaching certainty." However, a leading authority of the previous generation, Rabbi Chaim Ozer Grodzinski, *Teshuvot Aḥi'ezer*, I, no. 123, sec. 2, adopts a somewhat looser standard. In discussing the propriety of a therapeutic abortion, which, according to some, may be performed only when the life of the mother is threatened by the fetus as a "pursuer," *Aḥi'ezer* is prepared to rely upon the "assessment" of medical practitioners but does not indicate that their prognosis must be couched in terms indicating that, absent intervention, the likelihood that the mother will die "approaches certainty." The most elastic standard is apparently that of Rabbi Elijah of Vilna, *Bi'ur ha-Gra, Ḥoshen Mishpat* 388:74, who understands Rema as permitting summary execution of counterfeiters even when the danger to the community is not known with certainty but is only "feared" (*ḥeshasha*). In support of this view, *Bi'ur ha-Gra* comments that the principle is derived from the biblical provisions concerning a burglar and indicates that he regards the danger to the life of the householder in such a situation to be less than certain.

It may be the case that Ritva, in explaining the conduct of Rabbi Eleazar ben Shimon as based upon implementation of "the King's justice," declined to

[40] *Ḥiddushei ha-Ran, Sanhedrin* 73a, comments that the law of pursuit applies only to a person regarding whom "it is as clear as the sun that he intends to kill [the victim]."

[41] See also R. Isaac Schor, *Teshuvot Koaḥ Shor*, no. 20, s.v. *gedolah me-zu*.

explain the matter on the basis of the "law of the pursuer" because he did not regard it as being clear that the king would continue to apprehend and execute the innocent together with the guilty. Particularly with the king's appointment of Rabbi Eleazar ben Shimon as the official charged with bringing evildoers to justice as a result of the king having been impressed with that scholar's wisdom and sagacity, there may well have been reason to assume that the king's wrath was assuaged and that he would no longer pursue the matter so assiduously or that Rabbi Eleazar ben Shimon would be in a position to dissuade the king from imposing punishment indiscriminately upon innocent and guilty alike.

Tosafot and Rambam, however, certainly understood the talmudic narrative as reflecting a conviction on the part of all concerned that such practices would continue. Nevertheless, it may be postulated that Rabbi Eleazar ben Shimon did not know with certainty, or even in a manner "approaching certainty," that this would occur. The essence of the controversy between Rabbi Eleazar ben Shimon and Rabbi Joshua ben Karḥah may then have concerned whether the "law of the pursuer" may be invoked when the danger to the victim cannot be established with certainty or in a manner "approaching certainty." Accordingly, Rabbi Joshua ben Karḥah maintained that the "law of the pursuer" is applicable only in cases of virtual certainty while Rabbi Eleazar ben Shimon maintained that a significantly lesser degree of certainty is sufficient.

III. NATURAL LAW AND THE PENAL AUTHORITY OF THE STATE

Yet another theory explaining the principle *dina de-malkhuta dina* is advanced by Rashi in his commentary on *Gittin* 9b. The Mishnah declares that all civil instruments executed by non-Jewish courts are valid for the purposes of Jewish law even though the attesting witnesses are gentiles. Included in that category are deeds to real property that give legal effect to the transfer and that, ostensibly, must be signed by competent Jewish witnesses. Bills of divorce similarly executed are explicitly declared by the Mishnah to be invalid, presumably because of the absence of qualified attesting witnesses. Rashi endeavors to resolve the problem by indicating that, although gentiles are not subject to the provisions of biblical law concerning divorce, they are bound by the Noahide Code, which includes a commandment concerning "*dinin*." Rambam, *Hilkhot Melakhim* 9:14, defines "*dinin*" as an obligation to enforce the other provisions of the Noahide Code by appointing judges and other law enforcement officials, while Ramban, *Commentary on the Bible*, Genesis 34:13, defines "*dinin*" as commanding the establishment of an ordered system of jurisprudence for the governance of financial, commercial and interpersonal relationships.

Rashi's comments are remarkable because the Gemara itself, *Gittin* 10b, provides a different explanation for the validity of instruments drafted by gentile courts as posited by the Mishnah. The Gemara explains simply that the rule stipulated in the Mishnah is predicated upon the principle *dina de-malkhuta dina*. Accordingly, such instruments are regarded as valid in Jewish law because they are recognized as valid by "the law of the kingdom." Rashi's comment must then be understood, not simply as justification of the provision recorded in the Mishnah, but as an explication of the talmudic analysis of that position. Thus, in offering this comment, Rashi formulates a novel theory in justification of the principle *dina de-malkhuta dina*.

Rashi's thesis is compatible with Ramban's definition of *dinin* as understood by Rabbi Naphtali Zevi Judah Berlin, *Ha'amek She'elah, She'ilta* 2, sec. 3. Although Ramban clearly states that the commandment of *dinin* mandates establishment of a fully developed system of jurisprudence, he is silent on the contents of that corpus of law. Rema, *Teshuvot Rema*, no. 10,[42] and Rabbi Moses Sofer, *Teshuvot Ḥatam Sofer, Likkutim*, no. 14, assert that gentiles must govern their affairs by means of the applicable provisions of Jewish law as they pertain to civil matters and are not at liberty to reject or modify those provisions. According to this analysis of Ramban's position, *dinin* is simply the incorporation by reference into the Noahide Code of the jurisprudence of the Sinaitic Code. Rabbi Naphtali Zevi Judah Berlin expresses an opposing view in asserting that, according to Ramban, the Noahide Code is silent about specific provisions of law pertaining to matters of jurisprudence. The commandment mandates only that laws be propagated to preserve the social order; the content of those laws is left to be determined in accordance with the needs and discretion of each society.[43] According to that thesis, Rashi may be understood as declaring that *dina de-malkhuta dina* represents the exercise of the legislative authority sanctioned by the commandment concerning *dinin*. Hence, according to Rashi, the ultimate authority that renders "the law of the kingdom" binding upon the populace is the commandment concerning *dinin*.

However, one problem remains with regard to this analysis of Rashi's comment. Jews are bound by the 613 precepts of the Sinaitic Code rather than by the Noahide Code. Accordingly, the commandment concerning *dinin* is not part of the corpus of law binding upon Jews. Hence any novel aspect of

[42] See R. Jonathan Eibeschutz, *Urim ve-Tumim, Tumim* 110:3, who asserts that, for Rema, this includes rabbinic edicts as well.

[43] This is also the position of R. Iser Zalman Meltzer, *Even he-Azel, Hilkhot Malveh ve-Loveh* 27:1.

law predicated upon the principle of *dinin* should apply only to non-Jews but not to Jews.[44] Moreover, although *dinin* may confer authority upon gentiles to enact legislation as they see fit, as is the opinion of Rabbi Naphtali Zevi Judah Berlin, the jurisprudential aspects of Jewish law are established by biblical statute and are not subject to modification by society. Jews certainly do not have the right, for example, to abrogate the biblical obligation requiring an employer to pay a day laborer's hire immediately and to permit a 30-day grace period for payment. Similarly, Jews cannot vary the provisions governing qualifications of attesting witnesses. Rashi's comment might adequately explain why instruments drafted by gentile courts may be recognized and enforced among Noahides but fails to address the question of why they may properly be accepted and enforced by a *bet din* against a Jewish litigant.

Rashi's comment may be understood on the basis of a remarkable provision recorded by Rambam in the final section of his *Mishneh Torah*. Subsequent to a detailed codification of the provisions of the Noahide Code in general and of *dinin* in particular as well as of the provisions of law pertaining to the resident alien domiciled in the Jewish commonwealth who formally agrees to be bound by the Noahide Code, Rambam, *Hilkhot Melakhim* 10:11, writes:

> The *bet din* of Israel is obligated to establish judges for these resident aliens to judge them in accordance with these laws in order that the world not be destroyed. If the *bet din* sees fit to appoint judges from among them, they may do so; and if they see fit to appoint Jewish judges for them, they may do so.

However, Rambam himself, in an earlier ruling, *Hilkhot Melakhim* 9:14, states that establishing a judiciary for this purpose is an obligation incumbent upon gentiles. In keeping with the fact that *dinin* is a commandment addressed to Noahides rather than to Jews, there seems to be no basis in talmudic sources for positing the establishment of a Noahide judiciary as an obligation binding upon Jews as well as upon non-Jews. The Noahide Code requires gentiles to manage their own affairs without establishing a concomitant obligation in Jewish law requiring Jews to fill any lacunae resulting from non-feasance by Noahides. Rambam's justification of this ruling, "so that the world not be destroyed," is not culled from any prior rabbinic source and is not rooted in any particular commandment. It would appear that the obligation recorded by Rambam is not predicated upon any dogmatic precept but is the product of reason; the mandate is in the nature of what may be termed an obligation

[44] Cf. R. Betzalel Zolti, *Piskei ha-Din ha-Rabbaniyim*, vol. V, no. 268, who concludes that for this reason *dina de-malkhuta* is not applicable in the State of Israel.

of natural law. Society cannot exist long in a state of anarchy. Preservation of society – and of the world – is mandated by reason; hence reason dictates that the *bet din* must guarantee preservation of law and order by establishing a judicial system to administer the provisions of the Noahide Code.

Rashi's comment may be explained on the basis of a similar consideration. Although gentiles are explicitly subject to the commandment of *dinin*, the need to establish a system of jurisprudence is dictated by reason as well. Even if the Noahide Code were silent concerning such matters, reason dictates that laws be established and enforced. Normative principles discovered by reason are binding upon Jews and gentiles alike. Accordingly, it may be postulated that Rashi concludes that Jews living in societies in which they lack legal autonomy are bound to obey the law of the host country. Although, as a commandment, *dinin* addresses only Noahides, reason requires that Jews be bound by legislation authorized by that commandment.[45]

Rashi's comments elsewhere serve to indicate that reason further mandates that evildoers be punished as severely as necessary to deter others. The Gemara, *Niddah* 61a, records the following narrative:

> It was rumored concerning certain Galileans that they killed a person. They came to Rabbi Tarfon and said to him, "Sir, hide us!" [Rabbi Tarfon] replied, "What shall I do? If I do not hide you, you will be seen. Should I hide you? The Sages have said that rumors, even though they may not be accepted, nevertheless, should not be dismissed. Go and hide yourselves."

Tosafot comment that Rabbi Tarfon was concerned that the rumors might be true, the fugitives may indeed have committed an act of murder, and that, if so, Rabbi Tarfon's own life would be "forfeit to the king" as punishment for having harbored fugitives. Rashi, however, comments simply, "perhaps you have committed murder and it is forbidden to save you" without at all suggesting that Rabbi Tarfon was motivated by fear of punishment at the hands of the civil authorities. On the contrary, Rashi indicates that Rabbi Tarfon's concern was founded upon the illicit nature of the contemplated act of concealment rather than fear of retribution.[46] Rashi clearly assumes that, in terms of Jewish law, harboring a guilty fugitive constitutes an illicit act even though the guilty person is a fugitive from the justice of the civil state.

45 For a fuller discussion of reflections of natural law theory in rabbinic sources as well as of the positions of Rambam and Rashi see J. David Bleich, "Judaism and Natural Law," in *The Philosophical Quest: Of Philosophy, Ethics, Law and Halakhah* (2013), pp. 85–124.

46 This is certainly how Rashi was understood by Rosh, *Niddah* 61a. See also *Sefer Ḥasidim*, no. 683. But cf. R. Jacob Ettlinger, *Arukh la-Ner*, *Niddah* 61a, who understands Rashi's comment as referring to applicable secular law.

That position is cogent only if it is granted in advance that the prosecuting authorities may legitimately impose penal sanctions upon evildoers. Hence Rashi may readily be numbered among the authorities that maintain that a non-Jewish sovereign may legitimately impose penal sanctions in accordance with "the King's justice."[47]

Nevertheless, one point requires clarification. Punishment of wrongdoers may be a royal prerogative. That, however, does not establish an obligation to assist the king in exercising that prerogative. Surely this is true of the other royal prerogatives enunciated in I Samuel 8 and is equally true if the authority of the sovereign is derived from Song of Songs 8:12. Scripture merely grants license to the monarch to expropriate property, to exact personal services or to endanger the lives of the populace and also to punish those who disobey his edicts. However, Scripture does not require him to impose such punishments or demand that others assist him in doing so. By the same token, although the king may administer punishment on an *ad hoc* basis, there is no apparent statutory provision indicating that a person may not conceal an individual sought by the king. Rashi, then, must be understood as positing an obligation not to do so based solely upon the dictates of reason. Reason demands that a murderer be brought to justice and punished. Reason similarly demands that punishment be carried out only in accordance with legal procedures and only by duly constituted authorities because the alternative would similarly lead to a breakdown of the social order. Just as reason forbids a person to take the law into his own hands, it also mandates that there be no interference with the administration of justice by properly constituted authorities. Hence Rashi concludes that it is forbidden to shield a murderer and that Rabbi Tarfon could not allow himself to be in the position of doing so. A similar position attributed to Rashba is cited by Rabbi Joseph Karo in his commentary on *Tur Shulḥan Arukh, Bet Yosef, Ḥoshen Mishpat* 388. *Bet Yosef* quotes that authority as declaring, "for if everything is left to stand on the law of the Torah, as when the Sanhedrin imposes judgment, the world would be desolate." Rashba's comment is expressed in the context of a justification of the imposition of penal sanctions by civil authorities upon Jewish nationals and similarly reflects the position that such authority is derived on the basis of reason alone.[48]

[47] For justification of imposition of penal sanctions by secular authorities with consent of the governed on the basis of a theory of inherent powers of society, see R. Joseph Dov Cohen, *Ha-Torah ve-ha-Medinah*, vol. I, nos. 20–26.

[48] A similar theory is propounded by the nineteenth-century rabbinic scholar, R. Zevi Hirsch Chajes (*Maharaẓ Ḥayes*), in *Torat Nevi'im*, ch. 7, published in *Kol Sifrei Maharaẓ Ḥayes* (Jerusalem, 1958), vol. I, p. 48. *Maharaẓ Ḥayes* observes that disobedience of law leads to anarchy, but instead of asserting that there exists a natural law basis for enforcement of a

NOTES AND QUESTIONS

1. Central to an attempt to analyze the authority of the state is the issue of why one owes obedience to the law. The response of the theist would be that such is the will of God – with or without an attempt to explain why one must be obedient to the will of God. The theist's answer implies that dogmatic revelation of a legal corpus preempts the establishment of any other legal system unless enacted by divinely authorized subordinate legislators. The result is either fidelity solely to Jewish law or the introduction of other ideological justifications for supplementary systems of law. Those systems, to be binding, must be identified and rooted in authoritative sources. Hence the issue as to whether Jewish law does indeed recognize the legitimacy of any system of law outside its own confines.

2. The discussion takes the definition of a state as a given. We are confronted by a distinction between a "state" and illegitimate authority. What are the criteria or hallmarks of a "state" whose authority would be recognized by Jewish law?

That is, of course, an issue of serious concern to modern political theorists. The concept of the divine right of kings presumably accepts the notion that might makes right – a sort of *de facto* recognition of facts on the ground. That doctrine may, of course, include the notion that such facts come about by operation of divine providence. It is of more than passing interest to note that Rambam defined a "king" for purposes of "the law of the kingdom is the law" as a monarch whose coin is accepted by the populace. He proceeds to explain that acceptance of the monarch's coin constitutes contractual subservience to his authority.

Let us take as a hypothetical the situation in Kuwait during the first Gulf War. Did Iraqi law govern while Iraq was occupying Kuwait or did Kuwaiti law govern?

Does Rambam's definition imply that U.S. law is binding upon Jews residing in Panama (where U.S. paper money is the coin of the realm)?

3. As its title indicates, the issues addressed in this chapter concern the "secular" or "civil" state. The powers of a monarch in the Jewish commonwealth as well as the process of designating a monarch are beyond the scope of this discussion.

In the absence of a scion of the Davidic monarchy as the ruler of a modern-day Jewish state what is the Jewish law status of the State of Israel?

criminal code, he argues that the sovereign is empowered to punish transgressors by virtue of the "law of the pursuer." For a discussion of the difficulties inherent in *Maharaẓ Ḥayes'* position see the discussion in J. David Bleich, *Be-Netivot ha-Halakhah* (New York, 1996), vol. I, p. 105.

4. Could a person claim a free exercise privilege in refusing to testify in a criminal matter in state court, claiming that under Jewish law the state has no authority to punish crime? In *Smilow v. United States*, 465 F.2d 802 (2d Cir. 1972), the court rejected seventeen-year-old Jeffrey Smilow's First Amendment freedom-to-worship claim that he is privileged from testifying before a grand jury. He asserted that as an "observant and committed Jew" he must refuse to answer the grand jury questions or else suffer "Divine punishment and ostracism from the Jewish Community" as an "informer." In *Lieber v. Operman*, 473 F.Supp. 884 (E.D.N.Y. 1979), Nathan Lewin, who was negotiating for the disposition of possible charges against his clients, asked the prosecutors to use their discretion and decline prosecution. He argued that the traditional code, which forbade orthodox Jews from giving evidence against fellow Jews presented a formidable obstacle to a full investigation and might well present a First Amendment problem.

5. Jewish law recognizes not only a right but also an obligation to intervene in order to preserve the life of a victim of aggression. The aggressor (the pursuer) is known in Hebrew as a *rodef*. As applied to a third party potential victim, the law of the *rodef* goes beyond self-defense. Compare the law of the *rodef* with the status of an intervener in common law.

6. The focus of the discussion has been upon penal sanctions for violations of criminal statutes. Are there ways of compelling the payment of taxes other than criminalizing non-payment? Does a homeowners' association have the power to levy and compel the payment of assessments to improve the quality of life of residents of the neighborhood?

7. Authority has been cited above for the notion that the sovereign's authority is based upon some form of social contract. Is that notion compatible with the recognition by Jewish law that a person cannot consent to the taking of his life or to bodily harm?

8. Are there limits upon acts that may be criminalized? Are there some acts that may be legitimately criminalized under "the King's justice" but not under the Noahide commandment of *dinin*, or vice-versa? Would invocation of a theory of natural law lead to a more expansive power to criminalize or to a narrower one?

9. Many authorities maintain that the authority of a gentile monarch is rooted in I Samuel 8. The people clamor for a sovereign who shall "judge us in the manner of all the nations that surround us." Taken literally that is a descriptive statement. Other authorities regard it as prescriptive in the sense that in acquiescing to the demand of the people the Deity also endorsed the premise upon which it was based. In granting that authority to the Jewish king God prescriptively expressed endorsement of the exercise of such power

de jure by gentile sovereigns. Was that conferral of authority *carte blanche* or was it limited to what already existed *de facto*? As a practical matter insider trading was not prohibited in Mesopotamia. Does a modern state have the right to criminalize conduct of that kind under Jewish law?

10. It is certainly appropriate to relate the provisions of Jewish law to Jewish law's vision of the purpose and function of the state as well as to broad areas of political theory. However, caution is in order. In these matters, as in other areas of Jewish law, the law may be an expression of the theory and/or rationale but neither the theory nor the rationale can in themselves give rise to an extension of normative provisions to areas that are not addressed. Moreover, identification of theory and rationale is a human enterprise and as such is hardly infallible. It is therefore important not to confuse the spirit of the law, perceived or real, with binding provisions of the law.

4

The Sotheby Sale

During the latter part of June 1984, the prestigious auction firm, Sotheby Parke-Bernet, arranged the sale of sixty-one rare Hebrew books and manuscripts dating from the thirteenth to the nineteenth centuries. The two most valuable items – a hand-written Bible with the accompanying commentary of Rashi transcribed in Prague in 1489 and an illuminated Spanish High Holiday prayer book dating from the latter part of the fourteenth century – were sold privately for $900,000 to an anonymous purchaser, who presented them to the Jewish Theological Seminary. The remaining books were sold at public auction on June 26, 1984. The public sale realized a total of $1.45 million. The auctioned items are known to have belonged to *Die Hochschule für die Wissenschaft des Judenthums* (the College for the Study of Judaism), a Reform seminary in Berlin, which was closed by the Nazis in 1942. The books were therefore presumed to have been destroyed by the Nazis during World War II. The first indication that the books and manuscripts had indeed been preserved came in April 1984, when Sotheby's announced that an anonymous consignor would offer the items for sale on June 26. The auction took place despite protests by numerous Jewish groups and a last-minute effort by New York State Attorney General Robert Abrams to prevent the sale. Later it became known that the purported owner was Dr. Alexander Guttmann, a former faculty member of the *Hochschule*, who subsequently became a professor of rabbinics at Hebrew Union College in Cincinnati. Dr. Guttmann contends that shortly after the infamous *Kristallnacht* pillage in 1938, the President of the Board of Governors of the seminary presented the books to him as a gift so that he might smuggle them out of Germany. He maintains that he was approached to accept the volumes because he was in possession of an American visa, and that the books were conveyed to him gratuitously in order to induce him to spirit them out of Germany despite the great personal risk that such an undertaking entailed. The gift, claims Dr. Guttmann, was made in order that the books and manuscripts might be preserved for posterity.[1]

The Attorney General attempted to prevent the sale and, challenging Professor Guttman's ownership of the books and manuscripts, obtained an order from the New York State Supreme Court freezing all proceeds derived from the sale pending a trial to determine the rightful owner.[2] Ultimately, the dispute was resolved by court-approved settlement.[3]

Although the controversy has been quieted by the settlement, the case presents a number of intriguing issues of Jewish law relevant to the resolution of controversies over ownership of books rescued from the Nazis during the Holocaust. An analysis of the halakhic issues presented in the Sotheby case is, therefore, of practical, rather than merely theoretical, interest for those who conduct themselves in accordance with Jewish law. Moreover, although disputes regarding transfer of property are generally resolved in accordance with the law of the jurisdiction in which the property is situated at the time of transfer,[4] in this instance there are strong grounds for asserting that

1 See Defendant's Memorandum of Law in Opposition to Plaintiff's Motion for Preliminary Injunction at 9–10, Abrams v. Sotheby Parke-Bernet, No. 42255/84 (N.Y. Sup. Ct. Aug. 25, 1984).

2 Abrams v. Sotheby Parke-Bernet, No. 42255/84 (N.Y. Sup. Ct. Aug. 24, 1984) (order granting preliminary injunction).

3 Abrams v. Sotheby Parke-Bernet, No. 42255/84 (N.Y. Sup. Ct. Aug. 23, 1985) (stipulation and order of settlement). Under the terms of the settlement, Professor and Mrs. Guttmann received $900,000. The Prague Bible and the Spanish High Holiday prayer book were returned by the Jewish Theological Seminary and purchased for $900,000 by another anonymous benefactor, who presented the Prague Bible to Yeshiva University and the Spanish prayer book to the Hebrew University. Prior to delivery to these institutions, the books were made available for exhibition for three consecutive three-month periods at the Jewish Theological Seminary, the Hebrew Union College in Cincinnati and the New York Public Library.

According to the terms of the settlement, those items not duplicated in the library of any public institution were to be returned by the purchasers and allocated to various libraries upon the recommendation of the Jewish Restitution Successor Organization. The remaining funds realized from the sale were to be apportioned among various institutions for the acquisition of rare books.

4 See, e.g., Hutchison v. Ross, 262 N.Y. 381, 389–90, 187 N.E. 65, 68–69 (1933). (The validity and effect of a transfer of tangible personal property, as well as the capacity to effect such a transfer, are governed by the law of the state where the property is situated at the time of transfer.) Were this principle invoked in the Sotheby dispute, German law would apply. It is highly questionable, however, that any United States court would apply the law of Nazi Germany to such a case, since at the time that the events in dispute took place, Jews had been effectively denied access to German courts either as plaintiffs in suits involving non-Jews or for adjudication of disputes among themselves. Although Jews were not formally denied recourse to German courts until 1942, see R. Hilberg, *The Destruction of the European Jews* (rev. and definitive ed. 1985), vol. I, p. 11, as a practical matter, they were effectively barred from utilizing the legal institutions of the Third Reich in enforcing their rights even against fellow

New York courts should regard Jewish law as applicable in like cases both on grounds of comity[5] and because it is the law by which the parties felt

Jews at a much earlier date. See D. McKale, *The Nazi Party Courts* (Lawrence, KS, 1974), pp. 136–37. (Lawyers were threatened with expulsion from the Nazi party if they represented Jews in civil trials or in state courts). The only forum of law available to Jews for resolution of disputes was the rabbinic tribunal, whose decisions were predicated upon Jewish law. See *infra*, note 5.

5 Attention to the rationale underlying the principle of comity would augur in favor of a determination that the applicable law is Jewish law. Comity is founded upon the notion that parties who rely upon a recognized and established system of law ought to be accorded the protection offered by that corpus of law so long as the result is not offensive to public policy. See Lorenzen, *Huber's de Conflictu Legum, Illinois Law Review*, vol. 13 (1918), pp. 375, 403 (translation of Huber's classic treatise on comity). Jewish law, although not the law of any sovereign state, is recognized and established. Throughout the Middle Ages, and indeed until the period of the Emancipation, Jews were granted varying degrees of judicial autonomy in virtually all European jurisdictions. Although lacking geographic sovereignty, Jews constituted an *imperium in imperio* and their legal system was recognized by their countries of domicile. As stated by Israeli Supreme Court Justice Menachem Elon:

> In addition to its religious character, Jewish Law was also the national law of the Jewish people, because the entire chain of its evolution was the creative invention of that people. In this regard, Jewish Law differs from other religious legal systems, such as Canon Law or Moslem Law, which were not fashioned and developed by any single people but by the believers, Catholic or Moslem, among different peoples. Throughout its diaspora the Jewish people has regarded Jewish Law as its national law, the characteristic and essential part of its cultural possessions as a people and a nation.

Elon, "The Sources and Nature of Jewish Law and Its Application in the State of Israel," *Israel Law Review*, vol. II (1967), p. 518. Jewish law must be deemed, of necessity, to have been the national law of the Jews during the Nazi period. Jews had no option but to govern themselves by means of their own laws and their own communal institutions: the only alternative was lawlessness and anarchy.

In *Skornik v. Skornik, Piskei Din shel Bet ha-Mishpat ha-Elyon* (1954), vol. VIII, p. 151, Mr. Justice Agranot expressly affirmed that Jewish law should be accorded due standing by the secular courts of the State of Israel, a common law jurisdiction, on the basis of comity. The question addressed in that case was the validity of a marriage celebrated according to Jewish rites but which was not recognized in the country in which the marriage took place. Justice Agranot held that,

> with regard to a situation such as presented by counsel for the appellant in his stated question . . . for the limited purpose of giving validity to such a marriage, it is proper to defer to the foreign national law (lex patriae) of the parties at the time of their marriage, which only recognizes marriages celebrated in a special civil form, the other national law which the parties then had and which has continued to be their law up to the present, that is Jewish law.

Idem at 178. In explaining why this is so, Justice Agranot said:

> It is almost superfluous to explain today – what must now be plain to all – that the Jews, even after they were exiled from their country, never became, in their own eyes, a religious sect. According to their own assessment, they never ceased to be a nation whose place is among the other nations of the world. The absence [of the nation] from its own country, to which its sons continued to be faithful, was temporary and [the

bound.[6] The halakhic issues, therefore, are relevant to the judicial resolution of controversies concerning the ownership of books rescued from the Nazis

> nation] carried with it, through all its wanderings and during all periods of its exile, the enduring treasure of its culture and its national possessions; Jewish law is among those possessions.
>
> However, during the long period in which the Jews were compelled, in the lands of their dispersion, to confine themselves within the walls of the ghetto, Jewish law assumed more and more of a religious form. But at no time did it cease for this reason to be the national law of the Jews even after that wall had been breached and [the Jews] entered the broader world . . .
>
> . . . [T]he very moment that we admit – as we are obliged to admit – the continued existence of the Jews, in all generations and in all the lands of their dispersion, as a separate people, we must test the nature of Jewish law by the historic relationship of the Jewish people to this law. We are then compelled to conclude that the Jewish people indeed treated Jewish law throughout their historical epochs and throughout their dispersion as their unique property, as part of the enduring treasure of their culture. That is to say that this law served in the past as the national law of the Jews, and even today it bears this national character with regard to Jews wherever they may be.

Idem at 176–77.

The persuasiveness of this principle is exemplified by the following case: A man and a woman desire to enter into matrimony. They are domiciled in a jurisdiction that regards all marriage ceremonies as null and void unless celebrated pursuant to the issuance of a valid marriage license. The area is under Nazi occupation and all Jewish inhabitants have been killed in crematoria. The bride and groom are Jewish and have escaped deportation by going into hiding. For them to declare their identity in securing a marriage license would be tantamount to a self-pronounced sentence of death. They do, however, seek out an officiant well versed in Jewish law and scrupulously adhere to all aspects of relevant Jewish law governing the solemnization of marriage. Assuredly, the parties desire their actions to be governed by the only system of law realistically available to them – by Jewish law. Comity should accord the parties the protection and benefit of that corpus of law. This was clearly recognized and enunciated by Justice Agranot in *Skornik*. The facts pertaining to the transfer of books by the *Hochschule* to Professor Guttmann are analogous and Jewish law should apply for precisely the same reasons.

6 "The transfer of an interest in chattel is subject to the law of the situs of the tangible, personality . . . *in the absence of an indication by the parties that another law is to govern.*" Rosenbaum v. Consolidated Prods. Co., 81, N.Y.S. 2d 571, 572 (Sup. Ct. 1948) (emphasis added) (citations omitted), aff'd, 276 A.D. 1069, 96 N.Y.S.2d 490 (1950). Since such a transfer was illegal under German law, it is impossible to assume that Guttmann and Veit Simon wanted German law to apply to the transfer of property. Since unwillingness to abide by the offensive and discriminatory laws of Nazi Germany should certainly not be construed as refusing to be bound by any system of law, it is a cogent inference that the parties meant Jewish law – the only law relevant to the parties – to apply.

It is indeed the case that the parties were Reform Jews associated with a Reform academic institution and that the Reform movement has rejected the binding authority of Jewish law. However, Reform rejection of Jewish law is limited to laws concerning ritual and religious observance. The ethical and moral teachings of Judaism are resolutely affirmed by adherents of the Reform movement. See K. Kohler, *Jewish Theology* (1928), vol. 46 and ch. LIX. Jewish law governing matters of jurisprudence reflects those ethical and moral principles. This has been explicitly affirmed by exponents of Reform Judaism as evidenced by the statement of a noted Reform scholar: "The moral law is inscribed on practically

during the Holocaust era, and an analysis of the issues presented in the Sotheby case is of practical legal interest.

In an affidavit submitted to the court,[7] Professor Guttmann contends that in the spring of 1939, shortly after having been invited to teach at Hebrew Union College in Cincinnati, he was asked to meet with Dr. Heinrich Veit Simon, a prominent attorney and the president of the *Kuratorium*, or Board of Governors, of the *Hochschule*. At this meeting, Veit Simon, knowing that Guttmann was about to leave Germany with his wife and son, sought to ascertain whether Guttmann would risk taking some of the rare books and manuscripts belonging to the *Hochschule* library out of Germany. Both Veit Simon and Guttmann knew that Jews were prohibited from leaving Germany with valuables or with items of antiquarian interest and that, if caught, the punishment would be imprisonment in a concentration camp or immediate death. Guttmann alleges that, precisely because of the enormous risks involved, Veit Simon proposed that if he succeeded in removing the books and manuscripts from the country, they would become his personal property. Guttmann reports that, initially, he was reluctant to accept the offer. However, Veit Simon persisted and, after consulting with his wife, Guttmann agreed to smuggle the books out of Germany. For his own safety, as well as Veit Simon's, they agreed to conduct the affair in the utmost secrecy.

Veit Simon then instructed the Secretary and Chief Administrative Officer of the *Hochschule*, Hans Erich Fabian, and the Librarian, Jenny Wilde, to unlock certain bookcases so that Guttmann could select and remove the books and manuscripts in question from the bookshelves. Fearing, however, that the Gestapo might find the valuable books in his home, Guttmann temporarily hid them under some refuse in a basement shed.

In accordance with Gestapo requirements, the Guttmanns were obliged to prepare a list of the possessions they planned to take out of the country and to submit it to the Gestapo for approval. This was done to ensure that Jews took no

every page of rabbinical civil . . . law." Stephen M. Passamaneck, *A Motion for Discovery* (Los Angeles, 1977), p. 14. Although Reform Jews are likely to adjudicate commercial and personal disputes in civil courts, they do so, not because of their rejection of applicable Jewish law, but because, according to their interpretation, the talmudic dictum "The law of the land is the law" (*Nedarim* 28a; *Gittin* lob; *Bava Kamma* 113a; *Bava Batra* 54b) bestows precedence upon the civil law and judiciary established by the sovereign authority. All would concede that this is manifestly not the case with regard to the odious laws of the Third Reich; Jews during the Nazi era were effectively denied access to, and relief from, the German courts. See *supra*, note 4.

7 Professor Guttmann's narration of the circumstances surrounding his acquisition of the disputed books and manuscripts herein presented is culled from Defendant's Memorandum of Laws in Opposition to Plaintiff's Motion for Preliminary Injunction at 9–16, Abrams v. Sotheby Parke-Bernet, No. 42255/84 (N.Y. Sup. Ct. Aug. 24, 1984).

items of value with them when they fled. Knowing that the books would not be approved and that their inclusion on any list submitted to the Gestapo would jeopardize both his and Veit Simon's lives, Guttmann did not include them on the required list. He did, however, list a large number of unexceptional books from his personal library. After the list was approved, Gestapo agents came to the Guttmanns' home to supervise the packing of all their belongings and to make certain that only approved items would be removed. Working in Guttmann's study, the Gestapo checked the dates of publication of the various books being packed.

The packing of the books and other belongings could not be completed in a single day. At the end of the day, the Gestapo sealed the two doors of the study so that no one could reenter the room after they left. There was, however, a window-door that opened onto a small terrace. The Gestapo left the door unsealed because it was locked and appeared to offer no access from outside. Unknown to the Gestapo, the terrace onto which the door opened extended to a small adjoining bedroom. Guttmann had a key to the window-door and, after the Gestapo left, he climbed through the bedroom window onto the terrace, entered his study through the unsealed window-door carrying the books and manuscripts that had been hidden in the basement and replaced his own books with the rare books and manuscripts removed from the *Hochschule* library. Guttmann made certain that everything was packed as before and, in order not to leave evidence of the exchange, he painstakingly duplicated the knots tied around the books.

After making the exchange, Professor Guttmann hid the previously packed books in the shed where the rare books had been stored. The packing was completed the following day, and the books and manuscripts, together with all of the Guttmanns' other belongings, were put into two five-meter lift vans that were sealed by the Gestapo and shipped to Bremen where the ship on which they expected to sail to America was docked.

Consular officials unexpectedly delayed the Guttmanns' anticipated non-quota visa for almost a year. Meanwhile, war broke out in Europe and they could not take a German ship to the United States as planned. Instead, they had to travel via a neutral country and on a ship requiring payment in American dollars. Unable to borrow sufficient funds to take all their belongings with them, they had to consolidate their possessions into a single three-meter lift van.

Motivated principally by concern for the books and manuscripts, the Guttmanns left their baby with another family and went to Bremen to repack their belongings. In Bremen, however, they again had to operate under the watchful eyes of the Gestapo. Carefully, they discarded some items and repacked others, including the books and manuscripts. The Gestapo then spot-checked the items that had been repacked. In Professor Guttmann's own words, it was only "through the grace of God" that the packages containing the books and manuscripts were not inspected, and he was able to take them with him to the United States. Fortunately, the Guttmanns were saved from tragedy; the day after they returned to Berlin and reclaimed their son, the entire family with whom the child had been staying was arrested by the Gestapo.

For the next forty-five years, the books and manuscripts remained in Cincinnati, where Guttmann taught at Hebrew Union College. At the age of eighty-one, Guttmann, a man of little wealth, facing increasing medical costs, and wishing to leave his children a legacy, decided that the time had come to sell the books and manuscripts. Accordingly, he arranged for the Sotheby sale, the details of which have become public knowledge.

As noted, this incident has reawakened interest in the much broader question of the halakhic perspective concerning ownership of those books and religious artifacts seized by the Nazis during World War II that subsequently fell into Jewish hands as well as ownership of such items concealed from the Nazis and subsequently found by persons other than the original owners.

I. VESTING OF TITLE IN PERSONS SEIZED OF THE PROPERTY

The Gemara, *Gittin* 45b, states that it is proper to purchase sacred books from a non-Jew at a price that reflects their fair market value, so that they will not be desecrated or treated with disrespect. However, the Mishnah, *Gittin* 45a, declares that one should not pay an inflated price, lest non-Jews be prompted to seek out such items for theft in the anticipation that Jews will ransom them for extravagant sums. The sole question is whether one who purchases the items from the thief acquires valid title or is instead obligated to restore the stolen property to its original owner.[8]

There are a number of halakhic considerations, each of which may constitute sufficient grounds for title to be vested in persons who are in actual possession of the books. Each consideration warrants separate analysis.

A. Ye'ush *and a Successor in Due Course*

According to the law as formulated in the Talmud, the general rule is that one who receives stolen property may convey valid title to a successor in due course provided that the victim of the theft has experienced *ye'ush*, that is,

[8] R. Ya'akov Breisch, *Teshuvot Ḥelkat Ya'akov*, vol. I, no. 136, reports his impression that at some unspecified time, the Polish rabbinate issued a proclamation or ban (*ḥerem*) prohibiting the purchase of books "from the land of bloodshed" but expresses doubt about the continued binding force of that edict.

has despaired of recovery.[9] Whether or not *ye'ush* has occurred is ascertained either on the basis of the victim's statements or constructively by operation of law.

A purchaser of stolen property who is legally bound to return the purchased item to its rightful owner is ordinarily entitled to recover the purchase price paid for the item as well as any attendant expenses. This claim is vested in the purchaser by rabbinic enactment (*takkanah*).[10] Since the purpose of this legislation is to protect the innocent purchaser, some authorities maintain that the purchaser has no claim for reimbursement if the property was acquired from a notorious thief (*ganav mefursam*).[11]

The rule regarding sacred books is somewhat different. Since, as stated earlier, there is a duty to ransom sacred books from a non-Jewish thief in order to prevent sacrilege or disrespect, provided that they may be acquired at fair market value or less, and, moreover, since the purchaser is duty-bound to buy such items even from a notorious thief, the purchaser has recourse against the rightful owner for reimbursement of any expenses incurred to the extent of the fair market value of the books.[12]

As noted above, title vests in the purchaser only after *ye'ush* by the victim of the theft. *Shulḥan Arukh, Ḥoshen Mishpat* 361:3, and a number of leading authorities[13] rule that in cases of robbery (as distinct from theft), and absent evidence to the contrary, *ye'ush* is deemed not to have occurred because the victim anticipates that he will recover his property by instituting legal proceedings. However, the renowned rabbinic decisor, R. Ezekiel Landau, *Teshuvot Noda bi-Yehudah, Mahadura Tinyana, Even ha-Ezer*, no. 77, draws the logical conclusion in ruling that *ye'ush* is deemed to have occurred when legal remedies are unavailable for lack of judicial enforcement.[14] Ostensibly, this is the case when soldiers engage in looting in occupied territory.

9 Early authorities disagree whether a successor in due course acquires title only if *ye'ush* occurs before he comes into possession of the stolen goods or whether his possession ripens into title even if *ye'ush* occurs subsequent to his having come into possession. This controversy is reflected in a dispute between *Shulḥan Arukh* and Rema, *Ḥoshen Mishpat* 353:3.

10 See *Bava Kamma* 115a; *Shulḥan Arukh, Ḥoshen Mishpat* 356:2.

11 *Bava Kamma* 16a; *Shulḥan Arukh, Ḥoshen Mishpat* 356:2. See Rema, *Ḥoshen Mishpat* 356:3, who rules in accordance with the authorities who maintain that a purchaser from a notorious thief is entitled to reimbursement unless he had knowledge of the fact that the purchased chattel was stolen. Rema further declares that all agree that a purchaser from a notorious thief is entitled to reimbursement upon his declaration that he acted solely in order to protect the interests of the rightful owner.

12 See *Hagahot Asheri, Bava Kamma* 6:7; *Kezot ha-Ḥoshen* 356:3.

13 See *Sema, Ḥoshen Mishpat* 361:4; *Shakh, Ḥoshen Mishpat* 356:2; and *Bet Shmu'el, Even ha-Ezer* 28:1.

14 See also R. Meir Arak, *Teshuvot Imrei Yosher*, vol. II, no. 59.

Nevertheless, even under such circumstances, *ye'ush* may not occur for books printed in Hebrew for a different reason. *Tosafot, Bava Kamma* 114b, rules that a victim of theft does not ordinarily despair of the loss of books printed in Hebrew. This principle is codified as normative Halakhah by Rema, *Ḥoshen Mishpat* 236:8. The identical principle is recorded by Rema, *Ḥoshen Mishpat* 259:3, concerning lost property. The finder may acquire title to lost property only if there is reason to assume that the loser has despaired of its return. The presumption is that the original owner does not abandon hope of the recovery of Hebrew books because, realizing that the books are useless to non-Jews, he anticipates they will be sold to a Jew, who will endeavor to restore them to their rightful owner.

The question of whether it is proper to purchase books that have been plundered by marauding soldiers was first addressed by R. Meir Arak, author of the responsa collection *Imrei Yosher*, in conjunction with incidents that occurred during World War I.[15] In light of the foregoing discussion, it might be assumed that, absent *ye'ush*, a person acquiring Hebrew books from marauding soldiers would be required to restore them to their original owners. Nevertheless, in the case brought to his attention, *Imrei Yosher* ruled that the purchaser acquired valid title. It was reported to *Imrei Yosher* that Russian soldiers did not seize books in order to sell them. Rather, it appears that, at the time, paper was scarce and the looting soldiers seized books to use their paper as scrap. Accordingly, *Imrei Yosher* ruled that if, in the majority of cases, stolen books were converted into scrap or were seized simply for wanton destruction, *ye'ush* is to be construed. This ruling is based upon the principle that a person is presumed to despair, or not to despair, of the ultimate return of his stolen property depending upon the usual fate of such items in the majority of cases involving similar circumstances.

The application of these principles to the circumstances during World War II is the subject of controversy among contemporary writers. R. Pinchas Teitz, *Ha-Pardes*, Kislev 5711, applies the general rule concerning books printed in Hebrew and argues that *ye'ush* is not to be presumed for Hebrew books seized by the Nazis. An opposing view is espoused by R. Yitzchak Meir Rappaport, *Ha-Ma'or*, Adar 5715, and by R. Isaac Liebes, *Teshuvot Bet Avi*, I, no. 157. Their view is based upon a number of considerations:

1. Rabbi Rappaport declares that it was well known that the Nazis "destroyed and burned all Jewish books" and hence *ye'ush* must be presumed. R. Ephraim Oshry, *She'elot u-Teshuvot mi-Ma'amakim*, II,

[15] *Loc. cit.*

no. 8, states that "everyone knows" that the Germans seized books "to make paper" and therefore "the owners certainly despair" of ever recovering their books. R. Ya'akov Breisch, *Teshuvot Ḥelkat Ya'akov*, I, no. 137, also states *en passant*: "We know what was done to sacred books in the ... lands of bloodshed: that they were publicly burned with great ignominy."

These statements are, of course, not entirely correct. It is known that the Germans took pains to preserve certain libraries containing rare books and manuscripts with the intention of housing them together with Torah coverings, ark tapestries and other religious articles in the various synagogues of Prague, as a museum containing relics of a vanished people.[16] R. Yechiel Ya'akov Weinberg, who prior to World War II served as rector of the Rabbinical Seminary of Berlin (popularly known as the Hildesheimer Seminary), reported in his *Seridei Esh*, III, no. 71, that the Nazis preserved the books seized from libraries and added that "as is known, our library survived in its entirety and it reposes in Prague." Indeed, Rabbi Oshry reported that, in Kovno, the Germans transferred rare books to a library established by a collaborator named Rosenberg. To be sure, the Germans did not behave uniformly. It is likely that in some occupied areas they destroyed sacred books indiscriminately. Whether *ye'ush* is to be presumed would then turn upon the known or presumed comportment of the German army at a given time or place.

2. Another reason for assuming that, given the circumstances that prevailed during the Holocaust, *ye'ush* must be presumed even for sacred books is advanced by R. Isaac Liebes, *Teshuvot Bet Avi*, I, no. 157. Rabbi Liebes reasons that *ye'ush* does not normally occur for sacred books because the only way the thief may profit from stolen sacred books is by selling them to a Jew. Hence, the victim has no reason to despair of the return of his property. But, argues Rabbi Liebes, this consideration did not apply during World War II, because the Nazis were intent upon annihilating the entire Jewish people and it therefore did not enter their minds that the books would again come into the hands of Jews, since "from the day of the creation of the universe there never was a terrible edict such as this – to annihilate, to slay, and to destroy all Israel."

[16] The intention to preserve books as part of the holdings of the Central Jewish Museum that the Germans planned to establish in Prague is confirmed by historical sources. See Linda A. Altschuler & Anna R. Cohn, *The Precious Legacy* (New York, 1983), pp. 10 and 35. A photograph of a room containing books confiscated by the Nazis is reproduced on p. 35 of that volume.

Hence, the Nazis would find no Jewish purchasers for the books they pillaged.

Ascription of this intention to the Nazis is surely correct. However, the conclusion Rabbi Liebes draws is open to challenge. *Ye'ush* is a psychological phenomenon reflecting the victim's mental state and is not based on the intent of the perpetrator. Rabbi Liebes does indeed amplify his argument with an assessment of the victims' mental state: "In such a state, if they already despaired of their lives, did they not most certainly [despair] of their property? To whom would it occur to think thoughts of his house or fortune while under the nails of the angel of death, the impure foul oppressor, in the death camps and in the ghettos?" Despite its ringing eloquence, this argument is less than compelling. The diabolical designs of the Nazis are now a matter of historical record. But whether or not the intended victims recognized them at the time is a different matter. The historical record indicates that the Germans did everything possible to conceal their malevolent intentions from both the victims and the world at large. Moreover, there is every reason to assume that, even in the darkest hours of the Holocaust, the oppressed victims hoped and prayed for the defeat of the Germans at the hands of the Allies, and hence had reason to anticipate that they or their heirs would eventually reclaim their property.[17] Furthermore, even had the "final solution" been announced to the intended victims, *ye'ush* would not have ensued. It is unthinkable that Jews of the Holocaust generation would have been so lacking in faith as to believe that, in violation of His covenant with Israel, God would permit the annihilation of the entire Jewish community. Hence, the unfortunate victims would surely have clung to the belief that the plundered books would ultimately find their way into Jewish hands. Indeed, that belief has been confirmed by history. Accordingly, there appear to be no grounds for ascribing *ye'ush* to the owners of those books on the basis of Rabbi Liebes' argument.

3. A further reason for assuming that *ye'ush* occurred during the Holocaust even for Hebrew books is suggested by comments of R. Ya'akov Breisch in his *Ḥelkat Ya'akov*, I, no. 137, although he does not explicitly formulate the argument. The upheavals and deportations of World War II created situations in which, arguably, the Holocaust victims realized that there was scant chance that a person coming into possession of property stolen

[17] Cf. *Seridei Esh*, vol. III, no. 71, who comments that the victims of the Nazis never abandoned hope that the enemy would be vanquished and that evil would be eradicated.

from them, despite his best intentions and efforts, would ever be able to locate the rightful owners. At least for privately owned property it may be argued that, under such circumstances, *ye'ush* must be presumed to have occurred.

B. *Right of Conquest*

Apart from the principle of *ye'ush*, which vests title to stolen property in a successor in due course, but not in the thief, there exists another principle of Jewish law that, if applicable, would establish that the conquering armies had themselves acquired title to the looted property. *Ḥelkat Ya'akov* and Rabbi Teitz both suggest that purchasers of sacred books need not return them to their original owners because the Nazi conquerors acquired title to the spoils of war by virtue of the "right of conquest" (*kibush milḥamah*).

A responsum attributed to Rambam dealing with a virtually identical question appears in *Shitah Mekubbeẓet*, *Bava Meẓi'a* 24b. During a period of unrest, synagogues had been looted and Jews had purchased sacred books from the plunderers. Rambam was asked whether the purchasers had acquired valid title and hence might retain the books as their own, or whether they were obliged to return the stolen property to the original owners. Rambam responded that if the looting occurred at "the command of the king" the purchasers might retain the sacred books; otherwise, they were obliged to return the books upon reimbursement of the funds expended. Rambam based his ruling on a statement in the Gemara, *Avodah Zarah* 52b and 54b, that even the utensils of the Temple lost their sanctity when the Temple was pillaged by conquerors. *Ḥelkat Ya'akov*, however, maintains that this responsum does not serve as a compelling precedent. *Ḥelkat Ya'akov* contends that since subsequent rabbinic authorities do not cite Rambam's responsum, it cannot be deemed authoritative. In addition, both *Ḥelkat Ya'akov* and Rabbi Teitz express perplexity at Rambam's comparison of the theft of sacred books to the plunder of Temple vessels. They argue that the abrogation of the sanctity inherent in the appurtenances of the Temple is not relevant to the adjudication of mundane property rights.

The comments of these scholars notwithstanding, it appears that Rambam's position is not only clear but is supported by many other early authorities as well. The Gemara, *Gittin* 38a, declares that non-Jews acquire title, even against Jews, to property seized in the course of war, and that conquest in and of itself establishes title. Many commentators, including Rashi, maintain that, at least insofar as the property of Jews is concerned, the Gemara does not establish a novel mode of acquiring title; rather, title is incidentally acquired in the course of conquest by a standard mode, that is, by means of theft accompanied by *ye'ush*.[18] Under such circumstances, a successor in due course acquires valid title through the operation of the law of theft. According to these authorities, the import of the Gemara's statement concerning right of conquest is simply that *ye'ush* may be imputed whenever theft occurs in warfare since then no redress is available. This analysis of the concept of right of conquest is, however, disputed by Rashba in his commentary, *ad locum*. Rashba maintains that title is acquired by conquest in and of itself even when it is certain that the conquest is not accompanied by *ye'ush*.

Clearly the applicability of the principle of right of conquest regarding legal ownership of Hebrew books seized in the course of war is contingent upon the controversy between Rashi and Rashba. If, as Rashi maintains, title is acquired as a result of conquest only when the seizure is accompanied by *ye'ush*, right of conquest does not effect the alienation of title of Hebrew books since, as noted earlier, *ye'ush* does not ordinarily occur in conjunction with the theft of books printed in Hebrew. If, however, the right of conquest effects the transfer of title in and of itself, as Rashba maintains, there is no basis for an exception to that rule for sacred books.

It appears that, in distinguishing between looting "at the order of the king" and other forms of looting, Rambam espouses a view identical to Rashba's in maintaining that right of conquest establishes title, even absent *ye'ush*. In support of this thesis Rambam cites the rule that conquest can abrogate the sanctity inherent in Temple property. Rambam's citation of this principle should not be regarded as a mere metaphor. Extinguishment of title vested in the domain of the Temple is a necessary condition of the abrogation of the sanctity inherent in Temple property. Moreover, theft does not extinguish title vested in the Temple domain even if accompanied by conditions ordinarily associated with *ye'ush*. The thrust of Rambam's point seems to be that since, as to Temple property, ordinary theft even when accompanied by conditions of *ye'ush* does not extinguish title, the fact that "right of conquest" abrogates the sanctity associated with Temple property is evidence that conquest is a novel and independent mode of acquisition and is not merely an instance of acquisition of title by means of theft accompanied by *ye'ush*.

Rashba's thesis on the right of conquest is also espoused by R. Shimon ben Ẓemaḥ Duran, *Tashbaẓ*, II, nos. 126 and 127. A grandson of Rabbi Duran, R. Abraham ibn Tavah, *Ḥut ha-Meshulash, Tur ha-Shelishi*, no. 24, adds one significant qualification. The latter authority rules that if one purchases a

[18] See also the authorities cited by R. Abraham Dov Ber Kahane-Shapiro, *Dvar Avraham*, vol. I, no. 11, secs. 2 and 12.

"glass stone" from a non-Jew and resells it to a Jew and it is subsequently discovered that the object is actually a gem, the first purchaser has no recourse against the second because the first purchaser acquired property rights only to glass, not to a precious stone. Similarly, rules R. Abraham ibn Tavah, when the conqueror intends to use the seized books for scrap paper, he acquires title by conquest only to the extent of the scrap value of the items seized. Since the proprietary interest acquired by the plunderers is limited to the scrap value of the seized items, interest in any additional value remains vested in the original owner. Accordingly, since a Jew who acquires Hebrew books from plunderers cannot acquire better title than was vested in the seller, he must return the books to their original owners upon payment of their scrap value (or upon indemnification for expenses incurred in their purchase, whichever is greater).[19] Nevertheless, as pointed out by Rabbi Oshry, it seems obvious that if, as was at least sometimes the case during World War II, the looters, recognizing that books are inherently valuable (even if they did not know the full extent of their value), intended to preserve them rather than destroy them or use them as scrap, the plunderers acquired title to the full extent of their value by conquest and hence the purchaser need not restore the books to their original owners.[20]

R. Abraham Dov Ber Kahane-Shapiro, the venerable Chief Rabbi of Kovno, in his *Dvar Avraham*, I, no. 11, sec. 8, advances a novel thesis on the "right of conquest" that yields a modified application of this principle. He asserts that the right of conquest results in the vesting of title in a conqueror, and hence in a successor in due course, only so long as the object in question remains in the possession and control of the conqueror or his successor. The original owner, however, is not entirely divested of ownership but retains a residual title. Accordingly, if the conqueror loses possession and control of the captured property, the property does not become *res nullius*; rather, title is immediately restored to the original owner even without a formal act of acquisition on his part.

Thus, it appears that, according to *Dvar Avraham*, one who purchased or otherwise acquired sacred books from the Nazis may assert a right of ownership in some limited circumstances but not in others. A sharp distinction must be drawn between the situation in which a person purchased or seized property

[19] This analysis, of course, applies only to situations in which *ye'ush* has not occurred. The earlier-cited responsum of *Imrei Yosher* establishes that, absent evidence to the contrary, *ye'ush* may be assumed when it is known by the victims that the books are to be used as scrap. Under such circumstances, title is vested in the purchaser by operation of the law of theft.

[20] Contrary to Rabbi Teitz' comments, this conclusion in no way contradicts the ruling of *Ḥut ha-Meshulash* since it involves a materially different fact pattern.

still in German hands and the situation in which the property was acquired after the defeat of the Germans. If the purchaser acquired the books from the Germans while they still retained title by right of conquest, it follows that, according to Rashba, the purchaser is under no obligation to return the plundered items to their original owners. If, however, the purchaser came into possession of the books after the defeat of the Nazis, the situation is entirely different. According to *Dvar Avraham*'s analysis of the principle of right of conquest, the conqueror's title was extinguished upon loss of control and automatically reverted to the original owners prior to acquisition by the purchaser. Hence the purchaser is obliged to return the items to their original owners.

A significant limitation upon the operation of "right of conquest" as a mode of acquisition (*kinyan*) was stated in a 1954 decision of the Rabbinical Court of Jerusalem.[21] The case involved a dispute regarding ownership of a silver Torah crown, originally the property of a private party, a Hungarian Jew. During World War II, Hungarian fascists seized Torah ornaments together with all other valuables belonging to Jews. After the war, the Torah crown came into the possession of a communal institution in Jerusalem and was placed on display on Mount Zion. The original owner survived the war and immigrated to Israel. During the course of a visit to Mount Zion, he came upon the Torah crown, which he immediately recognized as his property because it was engraved with his parents' names. He was also able to produce a witness, the former sexton of the synagogue in his home community, who had personally delivered the Torah crown to the oppressors. The witness testified that he recognized the artifact and substantiated the plaintiff's claim of prior ownership. The respondent institution did not dispute these facts but contended that it had nevertheless acquired valid title. The claim was based in part upon an assertion that the claimant's title was extinguished by the right of conquest. The *bet din* rejected that contention. Pointing to the fact that the silver ornament had been seized by Hungarian Nazis rather than by German soldiers, the court asserted that title is acquired by conquest only in the course of war against a foreign country. Since a nation cannot engage in "war" against its own populace, reasoned the court, it cannot acquire title to the property of its own citizens by right of conquest.[22] Repressive acts committed by a

[21] *Piskei Din shel Batei ha-Din ha-Rabbaniyim*, vol. I, 169–73 (hereinafter *Piskei Din*). Among the members of the court were the noted scholars R. Yosef Shalom Eliashiv and the late R. Betzalel Zolti.

[22] It appears that this limitation upon the principle of *kibush milḥamah* is inconsistent with the thesis advanced by *Dvar Avraham*, vol. I, no. 1, sec. 5. *Dvar Avraham* asserts that *dina de-malkhuta dina* (the law of the land is the law) is not an independent principle of jurisprudence but is derived from *kibush milḥamah*. According to this thesis, the king is regarded as the

government or its armies against its own nationals were held to constitute acts of theft and robbery. Hence, the acts of the Hungarian fascists were, in the eyes of the law, indistinguishable from ordinary theft.[23]

The same distinction would apply to property seized by the Germans as well. *Mutatis mutandis*, no claim of title to property of German Jews seized

"conqueror" who acquires title to all property held by his subjects and therefore enjoys the authority to regulate its disposal. The view of the Jerusalem *bet din* also seems to be at variance with the analysis of *kibush milḥamah* expounded by R. Joseph E. Henkin, *Peirushei Ivra*, no. 3, secs. 10–12. Rabbi Henkin regards *kibush milḥamah* as belonging to a class of *kinyanim* which he regards as essentially ontological, rather than affective, in nature.

23 This analysis of the principle of "right of conquest" illuminates the cryptic comments of R. Israel Isserlein, *Terumat ha-Deshen, Pesakim u-Ketavim*, no. 69. A question was submitted to *Terumat ha-Deshen* concerning "books from Dresden" which had been seized by non-Jews under unexplained circumstances and which were subsequently purchased by Jews. *Terumat ha-Deshen* remarks that, under similar circumstances, his predecessors declined to rule unequivocally in favor of the purchasers. He reports that, at an earlier time, a similar question arose about purchasers of books from countries when "they took books by theft just as they took other property by way of theft." Earlier authorities had refused to rule that the rights of the heirs of the original owners had been extinguished. Hence, *Terumat ha-Deshen* declined to offer an advisory opinion but stated that if the litigants were to appear before him he would reflect further on the matter before reaching a decision.

Terumat ha-Deshen's comments are puzzling. He clearly did not deem *ye'ush* to have occurred since he speaks of the books as objects of theft that must be returned as a matter of law. Nevertheless, even in the absence of *ye'ush*, he was willing to take the purchaser's claim of title under advisement. Moreover, even had *ye'ush* occurred, the successors in due course would have been obligated to restore the books on principles of equity. See Section II of this chapter. If, however, it is posited that the books were seized as an act of war, *Terumat ha-Deshen*'s position can be explained in one of four possible ways:

1. *Terumat ha-Deshen* may be understood as agreeing with the view attributed to *Shakh* that spoils of war need not be returned to the original owner on the basis of equity. Assuming, as is evident from his comments, that *ye'ush* did not occur, *Terumat ha-Deshen*'s doubt may then have been whether the right of conquest secures title even in the absence of *ye'ush*, as is the opinion of Rashba, or whether the right of conquest is efficacious only when coupled with *ye'ush*.
2. Alternatively, *Terumat ha-Deshen* may have been fully in accord with the opinion of Rashba in maintaining that the right of conquest is effective even in the absence of *ye'ush* but was unsure whether the principles of equity in Jewish law apply to spoils of war as later announced by *Kezot ha-Ḥoshen* or whether they are not applicable as *Shakh* maintained.
3. *Terumat ha-Deshen* may have accepted the position of *Shakh* that equitable principles are limited to restoration of lost property but was in doubt as to whether the rabbinic decree concerning the return of stolen goods is limited and does not extend to spoils of war, as was maintained by the Rabbinical Court of Jerusalem, or whether the rabbinic decree applies to all seized property without exception.
4. It may be the case that the books in question were seized as an act of the host government against Jewish nationals. If so, *Terumat ha-Deshen*'s indecision may have involved precisely the novel point identified by the the Rabbinical Court of Jerusalem, i.e., whether the principle of "right of conquest" operates on actions of a government against its own nationals.

in Germany by the Nazis could be advanced under the principle of right of conquest. Although such a claim would be persuasive regarding the property of Jews seized by the Germans in other countries, no such claim could be entertained regarding property originally belonging to German Jews with whom Germany was technically not at war.[24]

It is self-evident that a claim of title based on the right of conquest can be entertained only for property that actually came into the possession of the Nazis but not for property seized in order to prevent it from falling into their hands. A claim of title to property seized in order to prevent its appropriation by the Nazis must be based on different principles of law.

C. Zuto shel Yam

Yet another, and perhaps more basic, argument can be made for assigning valid title to sacred books to individuals who took possession of the property during the Holocaust in order to prevent it from falling into the hands of the Nazis. The Gemara, *Bava Meẓia* 22b, states:

> Whence [do we learn] that an article lost through the flooding of a river may be retained [by the finder]? It is written, "And so shall you do with his ass; and so shall you do with his garment; and so shall you do with every lost thing of thy brother's, which he has lost and you have found" (Deuteronomy 22:3) [which means to say that only] if the object has been lost to him and may be found by any person [has it to be returned to him, and it follows that] a case like this is exempt [from the biblical law] since it is lost to him and cannot be found by any person.

On the basis of the principle that chattel "lost to all persons," that is, property facing imminent destruction, *ipso facto* becomes *res nullius*, the Gemara, *Bava Meẓi'a* 21b, declares that if a lost article is found in the intertidal space of the seashore (*zuto shel yam*) or on ground that is flooded by a river, the finder need not return the article even if it bears an identification mark. Rambam, *Hilkhot Gezelah ve-Avedah* 6:1, asserts that this provision concerning lost property is based on the general principle of *ye'ush*. Thus, according to Rambam, the Gemara simply declares that, absent evidence to the contrary, it must be

24 Nor can it be argued that, upon defeat of the Germans and seizure of Nazi-occupied territory by the allied forces, title became vested in the Allies – and hence in their successors – by the right of conquest since it is clear that the liberators did not seek to acquire title to booty previously seized by the enemy. On the contrary, the conquering powers made every effort to identify the rightful owners and to restore their plundered property. See *Seridei Esh*, vol. III, no. 71, and *Piskei Din*, vol. II, nos. 171–72.

assumed as an operative principle that an individual despairs of recovering any article that faces imminent destruction. Accordingly, Rambam declares that when *ye'ush* cannot be imputed with certainty or when the owner's conduct indicates that he does not despair of recovering his property, the rescuer cannot acquire title. However, Rosh, *Bava Meẓi'a* 2:2, adopts a position at variance with that of Rambam and asserts that one who rescues property from imminent destruction may always acquire title thereby. Rosh maintains that the rescuer may retain the property as his own, even if the original owner clearly indicates that he does not abandon hope of recovering his property. According to Rosh, protest and the assertion of a continuing property right is of no avail, just as a protest against "the falling of a wall or the sinking of a ship" would be of no avail. In effect, the proprietary interest of the original owner is extinguished in the face of imminent destruction.[25] *Shulḥan Arukh, Ḥoshen Mishpat* 259:7 and *Ḥoshen Mishpat* 368: 1, rules in accordance with the opinion of Rosh.

This *zuto shel yam* principle, however, may not be applicable to cases involving ownership of property acquired in time of war for a number of reasons:

1. As Rabbi Teitz points out, the relevance of the *zuto shel yam* argument to the circumstances of World War II would obviously depend upon varying local conditions. In some places, and at some times, it was known that the Nazis were intent upon destroying sacred books. In other places, and at other times, it was known that they wanted to preserve rare books and valuable artifacts for their own purposes.
2. Moreover, it is not entirely clear that destruction wrought by pillaging armies is comparable to a situation governed by *zuto shel yam*. In the matter brought to the attention of *Imrei Yosher*, the interlocutor argued that one who purchases Hebrew books subsequent to their seizure by marauding soldiers acquires valid title on the basis of *zuto shel yam*. Since the soldiers were about to destroy the books by reducing them to scrap paper, one who succeeds in purchasing the books from them has, in effect, rescued the books from the "intertidal space of the seashore" (*zuto shel yam*). In rescuing property destined for imminent destruction, the purchaser acquires valid title on his own behalf. *Imrei Yosher* dismisses that contention as applied to the situation brought to his attention with a cryptic statement: "The soldiers intended to cut them [but] since they had not as yet done [so] it is not comparable to *zuto shel*

[25] Cf. *Peirushei Ivra*, no. 3, sec. 10.

yam." *Imrei Yosher* apparently distinguishes between a natural disaster and an act requiring human volition. Since nature is governed by unvarying causal principles, an object that is about to be destroyed by a natural phenomenon and cannot be rescued by its owner is, for all intents and purposes, already destroyed insofar as the proprietor is concerned. However, when the object faces destruction at the hands of a human agent, its fate is not assured since the malefactor may undergo a change of heart. Hence, since destruction of the property is not already entailed as a necessity, the owner's proprietary interest does not become extinguished.[26]

3. The *zuto shel yam* argument can be cogently raised only in situations in which the property was spirited away by the claimant in order to prevent it from falling into the hands of the Germans or when the property had been seized from the Germans and the effect was to prevent its imminent destruction. This consideration does not apply in cases in which the items were hidden from the Germans by their owners and, having been spared from discovery and destruction, were found intact after the war. Of course, the argument based upon the general rule that *ye'ush* enables a successor in due course to acquire title applies even under such circumstances provided, however, that *ye'ush* has indeed occurred.
4. The *zuto shel yam* argument may not apply in circumstances in which the books were prevented from falling into the hands of the Nazis by non-Jews and were subsequently acquired by Jews. *Mordekhai, Bava Meẓi'a*, section 257, rules that a Jew cannot acquire title to property rescued from a sinking ship by purchasing the property from a non-Jewish rescuer since, under applicable civil law as reported by *Mordekhai*, the non-Jew is obligated to restore the property to its original owner.[27]

[26] The limitation placed by *Imrei Yosher* upon application of the principle of *zuto shel yam* is somewhat problematic. The talmudic foundation of this principle appears in both *Bava Meẓi'a* 24a and *Avodah Zarah* 43a. Although such reference is absent in *Bava Meẓi'a* 24a, the Gemara, *Avodah Zarah* 43a, discusses the rescue of property from armed legions and applies the same rule that governs the case of *zuto shel yam*. A similar rule is codified in *Shulḥan Arukh, Ḥoshen Mishpat* 181:1. Perhaps *Imrei Yosher* distinguished between situations in which the soldiers have actually begun to engage in wanton acts of destruction and situations in which they have merely seized booty with the intention of destroying their spoils but have not actually commenced acts of destruction. If so, *Imrei Yosher* would regard only the former situations, in which the intent has already been partially concretized, as being comparable to *zuto shel yam* and would view the rule expressed in *Avodah Zarah* 43a and *Shulḥan Arukh, Ḥoshen Mishpat* 181:1, as limited to situations of such nature.

[27] Contemporary maritime law recognizes a right of salvage in an endangered or derelict vessel and its cargo. The salvors are entitled to an award allowing them liberal compensation for

Mordekhai's ruling appears to be predicated upon this line of reasoning: An object located in *zuto shel yam* becomes abandoned property only when the owner himself cannot rescue it. Under such circumstances, the object is regarded as if it had already been destroyed. The presence of a potential rescuer does not preserve the property rights of the original owner because when property is about to be lost "to all men," a bystander is not obligated to act on behalf of the proprietor. The case is significantly altered upon the intervention of a non-Jewish rescuer who is bound by applicable provisions of civil law to restore the property to its original owner. The presence and action of the non-Jew effectively ensures that the property does not in fact face

their services rather than an award based simply upon *quantum meruit*. The amount of salvage compensation is in the discretion of the court. The amount of the award depends upon consideration of all the circumstances of each case and varies with the danger and difficulty of the salvage operation and the value of the property rescued. See Martin J. Norris, *The Law of Seamen*, 4th ed. (Rochester, 1985), vol. I, pp. 269–71 and 351–54. Medieval German law was, in some circumstances, even more favorable to the salvor. Founding itself upon the notion of "rightlessness" or outlawing of aliens, medieval law established the rule that, when a ship became stranded on the sea coast or in a river "that is touched the land" the dwellers on the shore had a so-called "strandage right" (*Strandrecht*) or, in the case of rivers, a "groundage right" (*Grundruhrrecht*), i.e., the right to appropriate the stranded chattel. Originally, this rule included the right to enslave any shipwrecked person.

This is, of course, at variance with the German "law of the land" reported by *Mordekhai*. The law applied in Germany during the lifetime of *Mordekhai* (1240(?)–1298) is somewhat unclear. At an early date, it was recognized that these provisions of maritime law served to restrain commerce. Accordingly, in 1220, Emperor Frederick II enacted a statute abrogating the rights of strandage or groundage. This edict was ignored by the Territorial rulers who regarded the seashore as their property and who continued to claim all wreckage washed upon the shore. However, the right of groundage did disappear at an early date on rivers other than the Rhine and the Main. In particular, the commercial cities sought to prevent the exercise of the right of wreck by the Territorial rulers and, in at least one incident which occurred in 1485, caused a Territorial bailiff who seized the goods of a stranded vessel to be hanged as a robber. In cities located on the banks of the Rhine and the Main and on the seacoast there occurred constant and violent disputes between the Territorial princes and the coast or riparian dwellers. See Rudolph Huebner, *A History of Germanic Private Law*, trans. Francis I. Philbrick (New York, 1968), p. 432.

Mordekhai was a disciple of Maharam of Rothenberg. Rothenberg is located near the Tauber River. There is some evidence that *Mordekhai* later lived in Goslar, which is located between the Mittellandkanal and the Elbe River. Subsequently, he resided in Nuremberg near the Pegnitz. See Israel Moses Ta-Shma, Mordecai ben Hillel ha-Kohen, *Encyclopedia Judaica* (Jerusalem, 1972), vol. XII, pp. 311–14 and *Rand McNally Atlas* (Chicago, IL, 1979), p. 30. It is unlikely that *Mordekhai* regarded the edict of Frederick II as binding in light of its rejection by local authorities. However, since he did reside in the vicinity of the Rhine or the Main, it is possible that groundage had already disappeared in the locale in which *Mordekhai* lived at the time that he issued his ruling. It is noteworthy that *Mordekhai* refers to a "river" rather than to a sea. It is certainly possible that, in order to facilitate trade, the municipalities of the area in which *Mordekhai* found himself had enacted legislation abrogating groundage and requiring the return of shipwrecked chattel to the original owner.

"imminent destruction." Nor, since the owner assumes that the non-Jew will discharge his legal obligations, is there reason for *ye'ush* to occur.[28]

II. OBLIGATIONS "BEYOND THE BOUNDARY OF THE LAW"

In the final analysis, none of the foregoing arguments may be dispositive. Rema, *Ḥoshen Mishpat* 259:7, 356:7 and 368:1, rules that both lost and stolen property must be returned to the original owner by a successor in due course, even though *ye'ush* has occurred, and even if the property has been rescued from imminent destruction. The obligation to restore lost or stolen property even under such conditions is in the nature of an obligation "beyond the boundary of the law" (*lifnim mishurat ha-din*). These obligations are duties imposed by equity rather than statute.[29] Nevertheless, the Gemara, *Bava Meẓi'a* 30b,

[28] *Mordekhai*'s ruling is normatively recorded by Rema, *Ḥoshen Mishpat* 259:7. However, Rema's citation of *Mordekhai*'s ruling is imprecise. In context, Rema's comments give the impression that the Jewish purchaser must return the property to the original owner because of civil law. *Mordekhai*, however, is careful to state that it was not the Jewish purchaser who had rescued the property. The clear implication is that, under the stated circumstances, the purchaser is obligated to restore the property by virtue of Jewish law irrespective of civil law considerations. *Mordekhai* is obviously asserting that the civil law provisions as they apply to non-Jews affect the *zuto shel yam* status of the property. Regarding whether a Jew would be bound by civil law under such circumstances, see Rema, *Ḥoshen Mishpat* 259:7 and 356:7, as well as *Shakh, Ḥoshen Mishpat* 356:10.

[29] Reflected in the parallel provisions of *din* and *lifnim mishurat ha-din* are principles roughly equivalent to the common law concepts of law and equity. In instances of *ye'ush, zuto shel yam* or *kibush milḥamah*, title becomes extinguished by operation of law, but the original owner may still recover his property for equitable reasons. In early common law, actions in law and actions in equity were brought before different judicial bodies and were adjudicated according to different principles. Although Jewish law never provided for separate tribunals, it contains a number of distinctions between adjudication in law and adjudication in equity. For example, as noted earlier, Rema, *Ḥoshen Mishpat* 259:3, states that when return of lost property is commanded by equity, but not by law, a poor man cannot be compelled to restore lost property to a wealthy individual.

Concerning lost or stolen property, another distinction arises. An award of chattel to the original owner by operation of law is, in effect, a decision that the title always remained vested in the original owner. The judicial verdict is merely a determination that the title vested in the original owner was never extinguished. On the other hand, an order commanding return of property for equitable reasons recognizes that title has indeed passed to the purchaser or finder but demands that the title be transferred back to the original owner. However, until transfer actually takes place, title remains in the finder or purchaser. For that reason, concludes Rabbi Teitz, one who is bound to return sacred books to their original owner by reason of an obligation that is "beyond the boundary of the law" may nevertheless enjoy the use of those volumes until the rightful owner is located. One who is obligated to return the volumes as a matter of law enjoys no such right.

Imrei Yosher permits use of such books by one who is in possession of them on other grounds. *Imrei Yosher* draws attention to the disagreement among halakhic authorities as to whether or

regards obligations of this kind as binding under biblical law. Elsewhere, the Gemara, *Bava Meẓi'a* 16b and 108a, bases certain similar obligations upon the verse, "And you shall do that which is right and good in the eyes of the Lord" (Deuteronomy 6:18). *Shakh, Ḥoshen Mishpat* 259:3, states that despite its extralegal source, fulfillment of this obligation as regards the restoration of lost or stolen property may be compelled by the court.

There is some question whether there exists a similar obligation to restore the spoils of war to their original owners. Rabbi Teitz assumes that no distinction can be drawn between property acquired by right of conquest and stolen property to which title has been acquired by a successor in due course after *ye'ush*. However, an entirely different view was expressed in the previously cited decision of the Rabbinical Court of Jerusalem.

Shakh, Ḥoshen Mishpat 356:10, distinguishes between the parallel obligations mandating the return of lost and stolen property even when acquired after *ye'ush*. According to *Shakh*, those obligations are separate and distinct. Rema, *Ḥoshen Mishpat* 356:10, predicates the obligation to redeem lost property subsequent to *ye'ush* upon the principle "that you shall do that which is right and good" but fails to cite that consideration with regard to stolen property. As understood by the Rabbinical Court of Jerusalem, Rema maintains that the obligation devolving upon the purchaser of stolen property to restore it to its rightful owner even though *ye'ush* has occurred is the product of rabbinic legislation as distinct from the parallel obligation concerning lost property, which Rema predicates upon the biblical admonition, "And you shall do that which is right and good." The latter obligation is not all encompassing and does not mandate the restoration of involuntarily alienated property to the original owner in all circumstances, e.g., when the loser is wealthy and the finder is impoverished. The obligation to act beyond the boundary of the law applies to lost property and requires its return even when *ye'ush* has occurred, but subject to the exclusions that exist regarding the obligation to do "that

not one may temporarily use lost property that bears no unique identification mark but that, nevertheless, does not automatically become the property of the finder. He declares that all would agree that a person may make use of plundered sacred books purchased from looters or their successors since "he has paid money and has performed a *mizvah*." Presumably, the consideration underlying this ruling is that the purchaser is entitled to reimbursement of the funds expended in retrieving the stolen property and retains a lien against the property for satisfying the claim. Since it is uncertain that the purchaser will ever be able to restore the property to its rightful owner and recover his expenses, he may, in effect, execute his lien by making use of the books. *Seridei Esh*, however, expresses reservations about this position, but nevertheless opines that a scholar who has custody of books belonging to the library of a rabbinical seminary may make use of them pending their return since "the administration of the library certainly would have lent them to him . . . "

which is right and good." Rabbinic law establishes a similar obligation with regard to stolen property. This rabbinic legislation requires a successor in due course to return stolen property to the original owner even though biblical law provides that when *ye'ush* has occurred, title is vested in the successor. As understood by the Rabbinical Court of Jerusalem, *Shakh* posits that obligation as absolute.

The Rabbinical Court of Jerusalem, however, declared that this rabbinic decree requiring return of stolen property even after *ye'ush* in all circumstances, even when the owner is wealthy and the present possessor is poor, is limited to stolen property in the conventional sense of the term. The *bet din* argued that there is no evidence indicating that the rabbinic decree concerning stolen property was intended to apply to the spoils of war as well. Policy considerations might well warrant a distinction between obligations imposed upon one who receives stolen goods and those imposed upon one who comes into possession of spoils of war. *Shakh*'s position is supported by the fact that Rema refers to the principle of "And you shall do that which is right and good" only in *Ḥoshen Mishpat* 259:7 respecting property threatened by imminent destruction in the form of *zuto shel yam* but fails to refer to this concept in *Ḥoshen Mishpat* 356:7 or 368:1 regarding the parallel obligation for stolen property.

Keẓot ha-Ḥoshen 259:3 expressed an opposing view. *Keẓot ha-Ḥoshen* regards the verse "And you shall do that which is right and good" as a general biblical principle mandating restoration of lost and stolen property to the original owner even after *ye'ush*. As a general principle designed to preserve property owners from undeserved loss, this provision, according to *Keẓot ha-Ḥoshen*, applies to spoils of war no less than to ordinary theft.[30]

[30] The comments of Rashi, *Ḥullin* 89a, tend to indicate that spoils of war should be restored to their original owner by a successor in due course at least on the basis of ethics. The Gemara declares, "As a reward for our father Abraham having said, 'I will not take a thread or a shoe-strap' (Genesis 14:23) his descendants were privileged to receive two commandments: the thread of blue [on the fringes of garments] and the strap of the phylacteries." Rashi remarks that Abraham was rewarded in this manner because "he did not wish to benefit from theft." Indeed, the Gemara itself subsequently employs the term "theft" in relation to this incident. The term "theft," as applied in this context, certainly cannot be understood in a literal sense. The verse cited by the Gemara was uttered by Abraham in declining the offer of the spoils of war proffered by the King of Sodom. Abraham apparently felt constrained to refuse, even though his status was that of a successor in due course, either because principles of equity recognized by the Jewish legal system apply to spoils of war as well as to stolen objects, or because of a general concern to act in accordance with an ethical standard "beyond the boundary of the law." Cf. *Shabbat* 120a, which characterizes refusal to profit from another's involuntary abandonment of property in the face of impending fire as an act of piety.

According to the analysis presented in the decision of the Rabbinical Court of Jerusalem, whether or not property alienated by the right of conquest must be restored to its original owner is a matter of controversy between *Shakh* and *Kezot ha-Ḥoshen*. Although the dispute was resolved on other grounds, in an obiter dictum, the Court declared that the opinion of *Shakh* should be regarded as normative, that is, a successor to property seized in the course of war need not restore the property to the original owners.[31]

Moreover, even according to *Kezot ha-Ḥoshen*, whose understanding of the principle of "And you shall do what is right and good" requires the return of spoils of war as well, the application of that principle to sacred books is unclear. Equity does not always compel return of lost property when title has become vested in the finder by operation of law. For example, Rema, *Ḥoshen Mishpat* 259:5, rules that Jewish law considerations of equity do not mandate the return of such property when the original owner is a wealthy person and the finder a pauper. Arguably then, were a like situation to occur concerning books, a poor man would not be required to return them to a wealthy person. Moreover, Rabbi Liebes, in his previously cited responsum, *Teshuvot Bet Avi*, I, no. 171, observes that "with regard to sacred books, all are poor." Presumably, the thrust of that statement is that wealth is of no avail for the acquisition or use of books if such books are not readily available. Therefore, even a wealthy person who has legitimately acquired title to lost or stolen books is entitled to the same equitable consideration as a poor person if he cannot readily replace the books whose return is demanded. Despite this consideration, Rabbi Liebes opines that the sentimental value attached by private owners to sacred books owned prior to the Holocaust always renders the original owner a "poor man" vis-à-vis his lost sacred books and that, regardless of their relative financial worth, the original owners must always be deemed "poorer" than a successor in due course.

Rabbi Liebes' argument compelling the return of books to Holocaust survivors under all circumstances, based as it is upon considerations of emotional attachment, would not apply when the original owner was a communal institution. Nevertheless, there may be strong reason to argue that, at least in some situations, equity should require the return of books to libraries and communal institutions. Despite the dictum "Nor is the entire community poor," recorded in the Palestinian Talmud, *Gittin* 3:7, the community may well be regarded

[31] The *bet din* also noted other distinctions that flow from the controversy between *Shakh* and *Kezot ha-Ḥoshen*. Duties stemming from equitable principles obligate individuals, but not communal entities. Moreover, as will be noted subsequently, such objections are extinguished if the original owner is wealthy and the finder or successor in due course is poor. In contradistinction, obligations generated by rabbinic edict are universal and binding upon all.

as "poor" vis-à-vis books and manuscripts not readily available to its members. Scholars within the community who are potential users of communally owned rare books are certainly "poorer" than unlettered but prosperous finders.

Curiously, Rabbi Oshry, in his responsum concerning the ownership of books rescued from the Germans during the Holocaust, fails to take note of considerations of equity in Jewish law. He reports that the Germans demanded that the inhabitants of the Kovno ghetto bring their valuables and books to certain designated collection points. A certain Yitzchak Greenberg collected a number of valuable books and, at considerable risk to his own life, placed them in a container, which he proceeded to bury in the ground. After the war, a number of former inhabitants of the ghetto returned to the site and commenced digging for the concealed valuables. In the course of the excavations, the container of books was uncovered. A former ghetto resident who was among the returnees recognized some of the volumes as his own and demanded that the finder of the container restore them to him.

It is not clear whether Greenberg rescued the volumes after they came into Nazi possession or whether he secreted them before they were delivered to the designated collection point. Elsewhere, *She'elot u-Teshuvot mi-Ma'amakim*, I, no. 14, Rabbi Oshry reports that the books collected from the ghetto residents were delivered to the deputy of Alfred Rosenberg, the German expert on Jewish culture. Since the Germans clearly intended to preserve those volumes, the *zuto shel yam* principle is not germane. Accordingly, if Greenberg acquired the books before they came into Nazi possession, title would have remained with the original owner (and hence, even after *ye'ush*, could not pass to the successor in due course, *viz.*, the finder). Since Greenberg certainly had no intention of stealing the books, he became, in effect, a gratuitous bailee when he assumed the obligation of preserving the books on behalf of the original owners. If, however, Greenberg acquired the books after their seizure by the Nazis, the result might be different. If the books were acquired under circumstances in which theft was followed by *ye'ush* (assuming that during the Holocaust *ye'ush* occurred even regarding Hebrew books), or if title became vested in the Nazis by right of conquest, Greenberg would have acquired title as a successor in due course. If he had acquired title and subsequently died without heirs, the books would have become the property of whoever happened to find them. If, however, Greenberg did not acquire title, the original owner would certainly have a claim against the finder of that property.

Unfortunately, this distinction does not emerge from Rabbi Oshry's discussion. Perhaps Rabbi Oshry omitted an analysis of the hypothetical alternative because, having been a witness to the events described, he may have known that, unlikely as it may seem, Greenberg had acquired the books after they had fallen into the possession of the Germans. Consistent with that presumed fact pattern, Rabbi Oshry ruled that the books were the rightful property of the finder. As noted earlier, if it were assumed that Greenberg secreted the books before they came into possession of the Nazis, it is doubtful that the property rights of the original owner were ever extinguished. More significantly, Rabbi Oshry fails to take note of the obligation enunciated by Rema mandating restoration of property to the original owner on the basis of equitable considerations. Thus, the first issue to be adjudicated is whether title to spoils of war vests in the captor even in the absence of *ye'ush*. The second, and more crucial, issue is identical to the issue identified by the Rabbinical Court of Jerusalem: whether or not obligations based on equity extend to property seized by the right of conquest.

Rabbi Rappaport, in his previously cited article, *Ha-Ma'or*, Adar 5715, rejects the contention that books preserved during the Holocaust must be returned to the original owners by reason of equity. He advances the curious argument that, since the original owners made no attempt to recover their property, they, in effect, engaged in "intentional *ye'ush*." He further asserts that Rema's ruling obligating the restoration of lost and stolen property as a matter of equity applies only when conventional *ye'ush* has occurred, but is inapplicable in situations involving intentional *ye'ush*, which is tantamount to voluntary abandonment of property. When property is intentionally abandoned, there is clearly no obligation to restore the property to its original owner even as a matter of equity.

However, this argument, as applied to the post-Holocaust situation, is rather tenuous. In the vast majority of instances, it is hardly the case that refugees voluntarily abandoned their property after the war. Most either had no opportunity to return to their former homes or would have found return to be too onerous. Rema's ruling, therefore, seems applicable to the return of property rescued during the Holocaust and recovered during the post-World War II period.[32]

III. PROFESSOR GUTTMANN'S CLAIM

The halakhic questions concerning the books in Professor Guttmann's possession are different from the foregoing cases in a number of ways. The Attorney General's action was based upon the contention that the books and

32 It may be noted that R. Yechiel Ya'akov Weinberg, *Seridei Esh*, vol. III, no. 71, peremptorily dismisses Rabbi Rappaport's conclusion as patently erroneous without offering a detailed critique of his position.

manuscripts were given to Guttmann for safekeeping. If that was so, Guttmann was a bailee and assumed the duty of safeguarding the materials on behalf of the rightful owner and, accordingly, cannot claim that he acquired title.

A remarkably similar question was presented to Rabbi Yechiel Ya'akov Weinberg and his reply is published in his collected responsa, *Seridei Esh*, III, no. 71. A faculty member of the Hildesheimer Seminary in Berlin selected a number of volumes from its library and concealed them from the Nazis. He survived the war and, taking the books with him, ultimately settled in Haifa. He then wrote to Rabbi Weinberg, the preeminent rabbinic scholar on the faculty of the seminary, and asked whether he might claim title to the books. Since he had acquired the books before they fell into Nazi hands, the sole basis for the claim was the *zuto shel yam* argument. Rabbi Weinberg responded by saying that, even if the argument were valid, there would nevertheless be an obligation to return the books on the basis of Rema's ruling that such property must be restored because of equitable considerations. Moreover, argued Rabbi Weinberg, the *zuto shel yam* argument is inappropriate in this case. Rabbi Weinberg reasoned that when his interlocutor came into possession of the books, he undoubtedly assumed that hostilities would soon end and that he would then return the books to the seminary library. In effect, he had no intention of acquiring title. Rather, he took possession of the books on behalf of their rightful owners and assumed the obligations of a bailee who accepts property for safekeeping. Rabbi Weinberg concludes his comments by stating that, in his opinion, it would be appropriate for the surviving directors and members of the faculty of the seminary to allocate a portion of the rescued volumes to the interlocutor as compensation for his efforts.

The facts in that case are similar to those in the Sotheby controversy, with the single exception that Guttmann maintains that the books were explicitly given to him as a gift. The controversy surrounding the Sotheby sale similarly involves a situation in which ownership of the books and manuscripts cannot be resolved on the basis of *ye'ush* or *zuto shel yam*. To the contrary, those claims are negated both by Guttmann's contention that the books were presented to him as a gift and by the Attorney General's contention that the materials were delivered to Guttmann for safekeeping as a bailment. If the books and manuscripts in question were indeed accepted as a bailment and subsequently smuggled out of Germany by Guttmann on behalf of the original owners, he cannot claim title by having acquired them on his own behalf on the basis of the *zuto shel yam* principle. A person rescuing such items from a flooding river upon the declaration that he is acting on behalf of the owner of such property could not later claim that he thereby acquired title for himself. A rescuer acting on behalf of the rightful owner cannot subsequently claim title on his own behalf. Nor can a finder of lost property claim title on the basis of *ye'ush* occurring after his assumption of the duties of a bailee. The finder, upon assuming the duties of a bailee, must preserve the bailment on behalf of the rightful owner.

Professor Guttmann's claim to title rests upon the contention that he received the books and manuscripts as a gift. That argument presents a new legal issue. Ordinarily, the burden of proof is upon the plaintiff. Since Guttmann is in possession of the disputed property, the general rule of *muḥzak* would ostensibly apply, that is, a person in possession of property who asserts a claim of title to the property is presumed to be its rightful owner.[33] The burden of proof lies with the litigant who seeks to defeat the *prima facie* evidence of possession. It follows that, since Guttmann is in possession of the disputed books and manuscripts, presumption of title lies with him and the plaintiff bears the burden of demonstrating that Guttmann's claim is specious.

However, if Guttman's claim to title can be rebutted, the fact that Guttmann is a *muḥzak*, that is, in actual possession of the disputed property, would not of itself establish title, particularly since the concept of a statute of limitations is alien to Jewish law. The fact that a litigant is a *muḥzak* merely confirms an otherwise cogent claim, but absent a cognizable claim, *muḥzak* alone is irrelevant. The Attorney General contended that, even granting that Veit Simon gave the books to Guttmann as a gift, Guttmann did not acquire valid title thereby because Veit Simon lacked legal authority to make a gift on behalf of the *Hochschule*. If so, Guttmann's claim is defective and his status as a *muḥzak* of no significance.

The bylaws of the *Hochschule* indeed provided that making a gift be subject to determination by the *Kuratorium* as a whole and were not to be within the domain of any single officer.[34] Nevertheless, this argument would not necessarily defeat Guttmann's claim of ownership. Guttmann candidly conceded that he had no knowledge of any action by the *Kuratorium* and was ignorant of any bylaw requiring it. Guttmann simply assumed that Veit Simon had the authority to act as he did. His assumption appears compatible with the provisions of Jewish law. The general presumption is that a person in possession of chattel lawfully enjoys the prerogatives he asserts over it. According to Guttmann, Veit Simon clearly asserted that he had the authority to dispose of

33 For a detailed discussion of the rule of *muḥzak*, see *Encyclopedia Talmudit*, vol. XIV, pp. 40–81.

34 *Statut der Lehr-Anstalt für die Wissenschaft des Judenthums*, §§ 6, 8 (1907) gives the board the power to act as agent for the institute in dealings with third parties and the obligation to oversee the financial affairs and property of the institute. This document is annexed to Defendants' Affidavits in Opposition to Plaintiffs' Motion for a Preliminary Injunction, Abrams v. Sotheby Parke-Bernet, No. 42255/84 (N.Y. Sup. Ct. Aug. 14, 1984).

the books and manuscripts. The fact that he delivered them to Guttmann with the knowledge and assistance of both the Secretary and the Librarian of the *Hochschule* lends credence to his assertion. Hence it must be assumed either that Veit Simon's colleagues on the *Kuratorium* specifically authorized his action or that, since formal meetings were forbidden by the German authorities and were extremely dangerous, the members of the *Kuratorium* delegated their responsibility to Veit Simon and authorized him to act on their behalf without prior consultation. The burden of proof in adjudicating a claim of the irregularity of an ostensibly legal action is upon the plaintiff.

Nevertheless, despite the distinct advantages enjoyed by the *muḥzak* in Jewish law, possession is not always *prima facie* evidence of ownership. At times, other principles are dispositive. When neither claimant is in actual possession of the disputed property, or when possession is not regarded as evidence of ownership, evidence of prior ownership generates a presumption of continued ownership.[35]

To be sure, the general rule regarding chattel is that when one litigant is in possession, his status as a *muḥzak* prevails against evidence of prior ownership. However, in certain situations that is not the case. One notable exception to the probative value of *muḥzak* is found in the claim of an artisan to ownership of artifacts in his custody. As recorded in *Shulḥan Arukh, Ḥoshen Mishpat* 134:1, the governing rule is that possession does not constitute *prima facie* evidence of ownership of items that an artisan customarily accepts for repair, since the artisan's possession can readily be explained on other grounds. The same principle would surely apply to raw materials customarily provided to a worker employed in a cottage industry. Presumably, the principle would also apply to a laborer who uses his employer's tools and who, in the course of his labor, customarily removes the tools from his employer's premises. Under such circumstances, physical possession of the tools would not support a claim of title. *Mutatis mutandis*, a scholar who is customarily entrusted by his employer with library materials to facilitate his research would not prevail as a *muḥzak* in a dispute over ownership.

Whether or not Guttmann enjoyed "artisan" status in relation to the disputed books and manuscripts depends largely upon (1) whether he was actively engaged in research, (2) whether those items were directly related to his research, and (3) whether the *Hochschule* ordinarily entrusted similar materials to members of the faculty for use in their homes or offices in conjunction with their research. It is, however, unlikely that all the items in dispute were

[35] This principle is known as *ḥezkat mara kamma*. For a general discussion of it, see *Encyclopedia Talmudit*, vol. XIV, pp. 147–74.

related to Guttmann's scholarly research. It is certainly unlikely – but not impossible – that the rarest items, *viz.* the Prague Bible and the illuminated Spanish High Holiday prayer book, were related to any academic project in which Guttmann, a professor of rabbinics, may have been engaged. To defeat Guttmann's reliance upon the principle of *muḥzak*, the plaintiff must prove that the books and manuscripts were related to Guttmann's research and that Guttmann was, in effect, an artisan.[36]

Another exception to the rule of *muḥzak* – and one that is more germane – is the category of "*devarim he-asuyin lehash'il u-le-haskir*" – "objects that are designed to be lent or leased." As recorded in *Shulḥan Arukh, Ḥoshen Mishpat* 133:5, possession of such property does not generate a presumption of title. The rationale underlying this provision is readily understandable. Ordinarily, possession combined with a claim of title places the burden of proof upon the opposing party because possession constitutes *prima facie* evidence of ownership. In the usual course of events, it may be assumed that an individual is in possession of an object precisely because he is the rightful

[36] There is a more fundamental reason why the claim that Guttmann is an artisan who cannot prevail as a *muḥzak* would fail to support the pleading submitted by the Attorney General. As recorded in *Shulḥan Arukh Ḥoshen Mishpat* 134:1, the original owner prevails over an artisan upon the claim that he delivered the property to the artisan for "repair." *Shakh, Shulḥan Arukh, Ḥoshen Mishpat* 134:2, points out that a prior owner would not prevail with a claim that he lent or leased the disputed item to the artisan. Nor, presumably, would the prior owner prevail with a claim that the artisan had stolen the object. Accordingly, in order to prevail against Professor Guttmann, the prior owner would have to claim explicitly that the books and manuscripts were delivered to him for use in his research, but a prior owner would not prevail with a claim that they were delivered to him merely for safekeeping. The underlying principle is that the claim must be that the chattel was delivered for a purpose associated with the artisan's craft. For an artisan, physical possession of the disputed property does not rebut such a claim. However, the fact that an artisan is a *muḥzak* does serve to rebut any other claim. Nor does the plaintiff enjoy the benefit of a *migo*, i.e., the contention that he might have pleaded that the item was delivered to the artisan for a purpose associated with his craft, thereby giving credence to his claim that it was delivered to the artisan for safekeeping. Such a plea is of no avail because *migo* cannot be invoked against a *muḥzak*. See Rema, *Shulḥan Arukh, Ḥoshen Mishpat* 82:12. For a discussion of the principle of *migo*, see Section IV of this chapter.

Nevertheless, in the present case, if it is ascertained that Guttmann had the status of an artisan vis-à-vis the books in question, he would not prevail on the basis of physical possession even though there is no actual claim that the items were lent to him for use in conjunction with his research. Indeed, since there are no survivors with actual knowledge of the circumstances surrounding the transfer, no one is in a position to refute Guttmann's contention. Nevertheless, as will be shown later, in such circumstances, the rabbinic court enters the appropriate pleading on behalf of the heirs on its own motion (*ta'aninan le-yatmi*). In acting on behalf of "orphans," the court enters whatever plea is in the best interest of the heirs who, lacking personal knowledge, are themselves unable to enter a plea. In this case, the rabbinic court would interpose the argument that the books might well have been lent to Guttmann for use in conjunction with his research.

owner. No such presumption exists for chattels that are customarily lent or leased since custody of the property can just as readily be attributed to loan or lease. Ordinarily, possession constitutes stronger evidence of title than does prior ownership. However, with objects designed to be lent or leased, evidence of prior ownership establishes a stronger presumption of title than does current possession.[37]

There is considerable disagreement among early authorities over the precise delineation of this category of chattel. According to some few authorities, most prominent of whom is Rambam, *Hilkhot To'en ve-Nit'an* 8:9, the category includes only objects that are manufactured or fashioned in order to be lent or leased. Rambam understands the talmudic term *asuyin le-hash'il u-le-haskir* quite literally as meaning "*made* for the purpose of lending or leasing." Accordingly, he understands this category as limited to objects such as "large copper pots that are used for cooking in banquet halls," ornaments used for the adornment of brides and similar objects produced or manufactured not for the use of a single consumer, but rather, designed to be leased to a succession of users. Excluded, according to Rambam, are all items designed for personal use including those that lend themselves to sharing with others, "for even a person's shirt and his bedclothes and bed may be lent." Nevertheless, Rambam freely concedes that some individuals habitually lend or lease ordinary chattels and hence, if there are witnesses to the fact that the item was lent or leased on a regular basis, the item is deemed to be included in the category of chattels, the possession of which does not constitute evidence of ownership. Thus, although books are not among the items that are produced specifically for the purpose of lending, nevertheless, books acquired by a lending library would certainly be included in that category, even according to Rambam.

However, most authorities, including Rif and Rabbenu Tam, define the category much more broadly and include in it any item customarily lent or leased to others provided that the object's owner is also known to lend or lease his chattel to others.[38] This view is cited by *Shulḥan Arukh*, *Ḥoshen Mishpat* 72:19. Excluded are expensive items and items of unique value that are not

[37] Whether or not proof of prior ownership prevails against a successor in due course who is a *muḥzak* with respect to items that are customarily lent or leased is the subject of a controversy between *Shulḥan Arukh* and Rema, *Ḥoshen Mishpat* 133:7. The rule is in accordance with Rema who maintained that a claim of prior ownership prevails even against a successor in due course.

[38] There is considerable disagreement among early authorities regarding whether the item must be one generally lent or leased, over whether the owner must be known to lend or lease chattel in general or the item in dispute in particular and regarding whether the owner must be known to lend or lease chattel to people in general or to the *muḥzak* in particular. See sources cited in *Encyclopedia Talmudit*, vol. VII, p. 150. The normative position adopted by Rema is cited in the text.

customarily shared with others. A number of authorities take note of the fact that individual sharing practices are highly subjective and accordingly rule that whether a specific item falls within this category must be determined by the judge on a case-by-case basis in accordance with his assessment of the personalities of the litigants and the relationship between them.[39] The determination, declares Rema, *Ḥoshen Mishpat* 72:19, is to be made "according to the perception of the judge in accordance with [his assessment of] the plaintiff and the defendant." Thus, unlike the application of most principles of Jewish law, the determination of this point is, in effect, subjective and lies with the judgment of the *bet din*.

There is certainly a strong basis for the argument that books that are customarily lent by libraries and academic institutions to faculty members and students must fall within this category. If so, evidence of prior ownership by the *Hochschule* might prevail against the evidentiary probity of Guttmann's present possession. The Gemara, *Bava Meẓi'a* 116a and *Shevuot* 46b, records that in a dispute over the ownership of a certain aggadic volume, Rava ruled that the book must be returned to its original owner.[40] Physical possession by the defendant, ruled Rava, was not dispositive because the book was characterized as a chattel customarily lent to others. Rashi, *Shevuot* 46b, maintains that Rava's ruling applies only to those aggadic volumes that a person "does not study constantly," but not to books in general because books are not customarily lent to others since they may become damaged through constant use. Most early authorities, however, follow the diametrically opposite position of *Tosafot, Avodah Zarah* 46b, which states that all sacred books must *a fortiori* be considered things customarily lent or leased because it is a religious duty to lend sacred books to others for the purpose of study. It may be assumed that Rashi would concede that reference works consulted only sporadically and for brief periods are in a category similar to aggadic works.

In rebuttal, it may be argued that rare books and manuscripts are not ordinarily lent to individuals for removal from the library. Rosh, *Shevu'ot* 7:5, and R. Menachem ha-Me'iri, cited by *Shitah Mekubbeẓet, Bava Kamma* 114b, *s.v. shema*, state that books that are "important" (*ḥashuvim*) or "desirable" (*neḥmadim*) are not included in the category of things customarily lent or leased. R. Meir of Rothenberg, *Teshuvot Maharam Rothenberg*, no. 480, issued a similar ruling regarding manuscripts. Thus it might appear that the rare books and manuscripts in the Sotheby collection are not to be considered books that are customarily lent or leased. Accordingly, since Guttmann was in possession,

39 See *Tur Shulḥan Arukh, Ḥoshen Mishpat* 72.

40 Aggadah is the non-halakhic component of the literature of the talmudic period. The tradition finds meritorious the intensive and ceaseless study of Halakhah as it is expressed in the Talmud.

the plaintiff would bear the burden of proof in refuting Guttmann's claim of ownership.

This conclusion, however, is open to question. It is indeed the case that libraries limit access to rare books and do not allow them to circulate. Nevertheless, it is not entirely unheard of for academic libraries to grant unusual privileges to certain scholars and faculty members. Consistent with Rema's ruling that whether or not an item is deemed a chattel designed to be lent or leased is to be determined on the basis of the court's assessment of the character and relationship of the litigants, a court might very well seek evidence concerning the *Hochschule*'s policy and particularly whether Guttmann enjoyed such privileges.[41] Moreover, given the unusual circumstances of the late 1930's, even rare volumes might have been "designed to be lent" since a prudent librarian might have become convinced that they would be safer in private hands. Rema's ruling that such a determination is to be made "according to the perception of the judge in accordance with [his assessment of] the plaintiff and the defendant" is certainly germane. Of particular relevance in reaching the determination is whether the *Hochschule* administration entered into, or sought to enter into, similar arrangements with other scholars in order to save at least a portion of the *Hochschule*'s collection of rare books and manuscripts from the Nazis. A rabbinic court would undoubtedly seek such evidence.[42]

It must also be stressed that, in accordance with Rema's ruling, in order for the plaintiff to prevail, a rabbinic court would have to find not only that the *Hochschule* would have lent the items in question under such circumstances, but also that Guttmann would have borrowed them. Rema stresses that the judge must assess the personalities of *both* plaintiff and defendant. Upon the facts of the case the *bet din* might well find it unlikely that a person would risk his life to preserve property belonging to others.

In an opinion accompanying his injunction restraining consummation of the sale, Justice Robert E. White observed that "it seems likely that Guttmann

[41] In a deposition submitted to the New York Supreme Court, Professor Guttmann declared that he was not permitted to remove rare books from the library premises. See Exhibits A & B to the Affidavit of Richard J. Davis submitted in Defendant's Memorandum of Law in Opposition to Plaintiff's Motion for a Preliminary Injunction at 14, Abrams v. Sotheby Parke-Bernet, No. 42255/84 (N.Y. Sup. Ct. Aug. 14, 1984).

[42] Such evidence may, of course, be difficult to obtain at this late date. In depositions submitted to the court, a number of persons associated with the *Hochschule* and Hebrew Union College testified that none of the other individuals associated with the *Hochschule* who succeeded in fleeing Germany brought similar rare books or manuscripts with them. See Findings & Conclusions of Law of Defendants at 16, Abrams v. Sotheby Parke-Bernet, No. 42255/85 (N.Y. Sup. Ct. June 14, 1985).

was one of many individuals who, in the Mosaic tradition, was [sic] charged with the safe transmission of the law and culture of the Jewish people."[43] That observation reflects an ideological assumption that, although common in other cultures, is foreign to Jewish tradition, at least in its application. To be sure, rabbinic literature dating from the talmudic period is replete with references to incidents in which individuals accepted martyrdom in order to disseminate Torah and transmit the Oral Law.[44] However, preservation of rare books and manuscripts, whose value is entirely historical and cultural, is in no way comparable to the preservation of the legacy of Sinai. The Torah is the patrimony of Israel and hence its preservation is synonymous with national self-preservation. Since preservation of life takes precedence over other values, including preservation of cultural legacies, Jewish law would disfavor endangerment to life to preserve even the most priceless historical treasure.

Quite to the contrary, self-endangerment that would not be sanctioned for the purpose of preserving cultural legacies might well be regarded as legitimate if assumed to secure a livelihood. In a responsum that has become classic in the annals of rabbinic law, R. Ezekiel Landau, *Teshuvot Noda bi-Yehudah, Mahadura Tinyana, Yoreh De'ah*, no. 10, ruled that hunting, when pursued as a sport, is forbidden because of the attendant danger but is nevertheless permitted to a person who earns his livelihood as a hunter "since everything which is for the purpose of one's sustenance and livelihood" is permitted by Jewish law. In support of this position, *Noda bi-Yehudah* cites the statement of the Gemara, *Bava Meẓi'a* 112a, exhorting the timely payment of a laborer's wages. The Gemara cites the verse "for he setteth his soul upon it" (Deuteronomy 24:15) and comments: "Why did he go up on a ladder, hang from the tree, deliver himself to death, if not for his wages?" It is clear, asserts *Noda bi-Yehudah*, that the Gemara recognizes an exemption from the general prohibition against exposing oneself to danger when the danger is assumed for the sake of earning a living.

There is little question that had a Jew approached a competent rabbinic authority in Berlin in 1939, informed him that he had the opportunity of smuggling rare books and manuscripts out of Germany in order to preserve them for posterity, apprised him of the attendant danger and requested a ruling regarding the propriety of smuggling the books, the rabbinic decisor would have ruled the action impermissible. Had the interlocutor, however, stated

43 Abrams v. Sotheby Parke-Bernet, No. 42255/84 at 9 (N.Y. Sup. Ct. Aug. 24, 1984) (order granting preliminary injunction).

44 See, e.g., *Berakhot* 60a and *Sanhedrin* 14a.

that he was departing for a distant land, that he was impoverished and that his prospects for being able to support a family were bleak, but that he had the opportunity to smuggle rare books out of Germany in order to sell them so that he might support himself and his family, the rabbinic authority's response might well have been positive.

Accordingly, even if it is determined that the books and manuscripts in dispute were designed to be lent insofar as the *Hochschule* was concerned, the court, in accordance with the dictum of Rema requiring an assessment of the character and disposition of both litigants, could not find for the plaintiff unless it were also to determine that Guttmann subscribed to a value system that would have permitted him to jeopardize his life solely for the sake of preserving historical and cultural treasures.

One further point must be made concerning the resolution of disputes regarding chattels customarily lent or leased. Evidence of prior ownership may be invoked against one who is in possession of chattel only when accompanied by a claim that the property was lent or leased to the *muḥzak*. In terms of normative law, evidence of prior ownership may not be invoked in support of a claim of theft other than against a notorious thief.[45] A claim that the property was delivered to the *muḥzak* simply for safekeeping would not prevail against a *muḥzak* except on the basis of *migo*,[46] that is, only when a claim that it was delivered to the *muḥzak* as a loan would have prevailed were such a claim to have been advanced. Accordingly, the argument against Guttmann is not that the books and manuscripts were delivered to him simply for safekeeping but that they were lent to him for his own use until such time as they might be restored to a relocated *Hochschule*. Hence, in determining whether a prior owner would prevail, a finding of whether the books and manuscripts were customarily lent under the prevailing circumstances becomes a matter of crucial significance.

The Attorney General did not claim that the *Hochschule* books were lent to Guttmann; rather, he claimed that they were entrusted to Guttmann for safekeeping. Jewish law ordinarily recognizes such a claim only on the basis of *migo*. Ordinarily the Attorney General's claim would not prevail against a person in possession. The only way it could prevail is if another foregone claim would have been available, in which case the present claim could be entertained on the basis of *migo*. In order to prevail on the basis of *migo*, the

45 See conflicting authorities cited in *Shulḥan Arukh, Ḥoshen Mishpat* 90:11, and the definitive ruling of *Shulḥan Arukh, Ḥoshen Mishpat* 133:6. See also *Shulḥan Arukh* and Rema, *Ḥoshen Mishpat* 357:1.

46 *Migo* is of no support for a claim of simple theft since there is a strong presumption in Jewish law that an individual will not commit theft. See *Shulḥan Arukh, Ḥoshen Mishpat* 133:6.

argument that chattel was lent to Guttmann would have to be of sufficient force to prevail had it been advanced on its own merit. Indeed, were an argument to prevail that the property was a simple bailment, the very concept of *muḥzak* would be rendered a nullity. Such a claim, were it to be entertained, would prevail regarding objects customarily deposited with bailees. That category – unlike the category of items customarily lent or leased – is virtually all-encompassing. In Guttman's case, however, the point is irrelevant. Under Jewish law, the court, acting on behalf of the heirs, would on its own motion advance the claim that the books had been lent to Guttmann; there would be no need to assert that they were delivered to him for safekeeping as the Attorney General concluded. If the books were designed to be lent or leased, a claim of prior ownership would ordinarily prevail, and the burden of proof would shift to Guttmann.

Despite the foregoing, the fact that the books and manuscripts were customarily lent is not in itself dispositive. The principle of *muḥzak* may yet apply even if the books and manuscripts are judged to fall within that category. *Shakh, Ḥoshen Mishpat* 72:91, raises a serious question: How can a person who has purchased an item of this nature ever establish proof of valid title? The original owner can always falsely claim that the item was not sold but merely lent or leased and recover it from the *muḥzak* on proof of prior possession. *Shakh* responds by asserting that a claim of purchase will prevail against a prior owner of chattels customarily lent or leased provided that the claim is asserted immediately upon discovery of the object in possession of the *muḥzak*.[47] Under such circumstances, the *muḥzak* enjoys the benefit of *migo*, that is, he might have concealed the object.[48] Had it been concealed there would have been no occasion for litigation. However, once an object that is customarily lent or leased is known to be in a person's possession, that person can no longer assert a claim to title based on purchase. Presumably, the same considerations apply to gratuitous transfers. Thus, even assuming that the items are customarily lent or leased, one might argue that Guttmann should prevail by operation of the *migo* of concealment. However, this argument is readily rebutted. Guttmann, it would appear, cannot rely upon the *migo* of concealment since, at this point, the value of the books and manuscripts to him lies solely in their salability. It would have been impossible for Guttmann to sell the books and manuscripts without both the sale itself and the fact that the books were originally part of the

[47] See also R. Yechiel Michel Epstein, *Arukh ha-Shulḥan, Ḥoshen Mishpat* 72:43.

[48] Cf., however, R. Jonathan Eibeschutz, *Urim ve-Tumim* 72:35 and *idem, Klalei Migo*, sec. 34, who disagrees with *Shakh* and rules that a claim of purchase regarding objects that are customarily lent or leased can never be asserted against a prior owner on the basis of current possession.

Hochschule library becoming public knowledge. Hence, it may be contended that Guttmann cannot rely upon a *migo* of concealment. Accordingly, were it established that the books fall within the category of things customarily lent or leased, the prior owner would prevail.[49]

IV. *ZUTO SHEL YAM* AS AN ALTERNATIVE PLEADING

As noted above, there is considerable question whether any person might have entered the library of a Jewish institution in Berlin in 1939, removed books and manuscripts, and thereby have acquired valid title on the basis of the *zuto shel yam* principle, that is, on the basis that property facing imminent destruction is already deemed *res nullius*. Ostensibly, however, resolution of this question is irrelevant insofar as Guttmann is concerned. Professor Guttmann is barred from establishing a claim to title on the basis of *zuto shel yam* because of his own contention that the disputed items were delivered to him in an attempt to prevent them from falling into Nazi hands. By Guttmann's own admission, destruction of the books was not imminent. The sole issue is whether these items were conveyed to him as a gift or accepted by him as a bailment. Had Guttmann taken possession of those items to preserve them for the bailor, he could not later claim to have acquired title to property that was *res nullius*.

Nevertheless, the question of whether Guttmann might prevail had he advanced the claim that he simply took the books, intending to keep them for himself in order to prevent them from falling into the hands of the Nazis, may well be dispositive even though Guttmann has conceded that this was not the case.

Jewish law incorporates the principle of *migo* in assessing the merits of certain pleadings. This principle has the effect of assigning a litigant the advantages of alternative pleadings that have not been advanced. Indeed, the litigant is granted not only the benefits of a foregone pleading, but also even the benefits of a pleading that is concededly false.[50] For example, a claim of

[49] See R. Jacob of Lissa, *Netivot ha-Mishpat* 72:34, who states that *Shakh* must be understood as ruling that a claim of purchase is sustained by *migo* only if the object is gratuitously displayed before the witnesses, but not if, for example, the person seized thereof dons a garment "for his own benefit" and only upon becoming aware of the presence of witnesses who recognize the garment as the presumed property of another does he declare that he has acquired title by virtue of purchase. Under such circumstances, asserts *Netivot ha-Mishpat*, there exists no *migo* of concealment. According to *Netivot ha-Mishpat*, adjudication of the question of whether or not a valid *migo* exists is in every case contingent upon "the assessment of the judges" with regard to whether the litigant might have concealed the object without prejudicing his own interests.

[50] The principle of *migo* is similar to pleadings in the alternative, which are a feature of other legal systems. The American legal system permits pleadings of two or more statements of claim or

prior repayment is not a good defense against the execution of a promissory note when a properly executed note is produced. The allegation of earlier repayment is deemed rebutted by the assumption that a debtor would not allow a creditor to retain possession of an instrument securing a loan which has been repaid; rather, the debtor would withhold payment until the note is delivered to him. However, unless the signatures of the attesting witnesses are authenticated, the defendant will ordinarily prevail if he claims the instrument was forged. A blameless defendant who, contrary to usual practice, has satisfied his indebtedness but has neglected to retrieve his promissory note is faced with a difficult choice: He may candidly concede the authenticity of the instrument and lose the case because his plea of prior payment cannot be accepted, or he may falsely claim the instrument to be a forgery in order to exonerate himself from payment of funds that he no longer owes. *Migo* effectively gives the debtor the advantage of pleadings he does not wish to advance for reasons of truthfulness. Since a pleading of forgery would have been sustained had it been made, a pleading of prior repayment will also be accepted and, by operation of law, given the same consideration as a pleading of forgery. The operative principle is that if the litigant was untruthful in advancing a claim of prior payment, he might have availed himself of a simpler and more direct falsehood by denying that a debt had ever existed and claiming that the instrument upon which the plaintiff relied was a forgery.

A similar principle may operate to the advantage of Guttmann. If Guttmann's claim of title by gratuitous conveyance does not prevail, it is because of a halakhic determination that the disputed books are things that

defense that are not only inconsistent, but mutually exclusive. The singleness requirement of the writ system that prevailed in early common law would have rendered the very notion of *migo* inconceivable. Under that system, a defendant might have several possibly non-contradictory defenses for a particular count and yet be forced to select one of them and abandon the others. If he chanced to lose on the defense selected, the fact that he might have succeeded on another defense would have been of no avail. This barrier was removed by statute in 1705, 4 Anne ch. 16, § 4 (1705). Subsequently, a defendant was permitted to interpose several pleas to the same court, with no requirement that they be consistent.

The famous Case of the Kettle, which is part of the folklore of the common law, probably best exemplifies the admissibility of inconsistent alternative pleading. The plaintiff claimed damages for a kettle, which he asserted the defendant had borrowed and had allowed to become cracked while in his possession. In answering that complaint, the defendant is reported to have pleaded: (1) that he did not borrow the kettle; (2) that the kettle was never cracked; and (3) that the kettle was cracked when he borrowed it. See C. Keigwin, *Precedents of Pleading at Common Law*, 270 (1910).

Whatever the sufficiency of alternative pleading in the past, under Rule 8(e)(2) of the Federal Rules of Civil Procedure and the provisions of other modern procedural codes, such pleading is perfectly proper although, for obvious reasons, inconsistent pleadings are seldom advised. In Jewish law the alternative pleading need not actually be advanced; the rabbinic court assigns the advantages of the foregone pleading by operation of law.

are customarily lent or leased. If so, physical possession is not sufficient to overcome a claim that the items were delivered as a bailment, since that claim is supported by evidence of prior possession.

However, prior possession would not defeat a claim to title by Guttmann predicated upon the principle of *zuto shel yam*. To be sure, as earlier indicated, the facts alleged by Guttmann negate any possible invocation of *zuto shel yam*. Nevertheless, Guttmann may yet avail himself of the advantages of counterfactual invocation of the *zuto shel yam* principle through *migo*. Were it to be established that a pleading of facts compatible with *zuto shel yam* would prevail, Guttmann would be entitled to whatever advantage he might have gained based on that pleading even though the pleading he advanced cannot prevail on its own merits.

The principle of *migo*, however, is not universally applicable. The advantages of foregone pleadings are available only to a defendant, not to a plaintiff. To put the same principle more precisely, the advantages of *migo* are available only to confirm possession of property but not to force a transfer of money or chattel (*migo le-hoẓi lo amrinan*).[51] At first glance, this constraint upon the application of *migo* should not bar its use to Guttmann's advantage since he is in actual possession of the disputed property. There is, however, some controversy among early authorities as to whether the advantages of *migo* may be employed against a claim of prior ownership. *Tosafot, Bava Batra* 32b, followed by a number of other talmudic commentators, asserts that the question of the efficacy of *migo* in the face of evidence of prior ownership is the subject of a disagreement between Rabbah and Rav Yosef concerning adjudication of a dispute involving conflicting claims to real property. The Gemara, *Bava Batra* 32b, rules in accordance with the opinion of Rabbah, who maintained that the principle of *migo* is applicable even in such circumstances. This rule has been codified by both Rambam, *Hilkhot To'en ve-Nit'an* 15:9, and *Shulḥan Arukh, Ḥoshen Mishpat* 146:25. *Tosafot, ad locum*, also maintains that the benefits of *migo* prevail against evidence of prior ownership, but only when the litigant seeking to prevail on the basis of *migo* is in possession of the disputed property.[52]

[51] See Rema, *Ḥoshen Mishpat* 82:12.

[52] See also R. Yom Tov Halperin, *Teshuvot Malbushei Tom Tov*, I, *Even ha-Ezer*, no. 15, *s.v. ha-yoẓeh*.

It may be noted that this qualification is disputed by the author of *Shev Shemateta* 4:24 and *Keẓot ha-Ḥoshen* 82:13, who maintains that *migo* may be invoked against a claim of prior ownership even when the pleading is not advanced by a person actually in possession of the disputed property. However, this issue is not relevant to the Sotheby sale since Guttmann was clearly in possession of the disputed property.

V. OWNERSHIP OF COMMUNAL PROPERTY

Finally, a basic question which must be answered is whether there exists a plaintiff who is in a position to advance a claim against Guttmann. Were the books in dispute property that had formerly belonged to a private party, according to Jewish law, only the original owner or his heirs would be entitled to sue Guttmann for recovery of the property. In the unlikely event that no living survivor could establish even a remote degree of kinship, the property would have become *res nullius* upon the demise of the original owner and his heirs and, at that point, Guttmann could have acquired title. The argument might be made that the *Hochschule* is defunct and its property rendered *res nullius*. Arguably, since there is no concept in Jewish law of a "successor institution," there exist no surviving heirs who can claim to have inherited the property of the *Hochschule*. Hence, Guttmann would be entitled to retain what, in effect, became ownerless property.

Jewish law, however, does not support such a contention. In Jewish law, corporations and organizations lack capacity to hold property as "legal persons." Property must be held by individuals, otherwise it is ownerless. Jewish law regards corporations, at least for the purposes of holding property, as partnerships.[53] Similarly, Jewish law deems communal property as property held in partnership by members of the community.

This principle and its application to the property of the *Hochschule* is illustrated by the provisions of law that apply to the sale of synagogue buildings. The Gemara, *Megillah* 26a, declares that synagogues located in metropolitan areas may not be sold. Rashi and Rashba in their respective commentaries explain that ownership of such property is not vested solely in the inhabitants of the city; rather, "everyone" has a proprietary interest in the synagogue property. Hence, since it is impossible to secure the acquiescence (either personally or through communal officers acting as agents) of each and every person who enjoys a

[53] See, for example, R. Ya'akov Breisch, *Teshuvot Helkat Ya'akov*, vol. III, no. 191. For a discussion of the status of corporations in Jewish law see Aaron Kirschenbaum, "Legal Person," *Encyclopedia Judaica*, vol. X, pp. 1567–70. See also R. Judah Aszod, *Teshuvot Mahari Asad*, no. 124; R. Moses Schick, *Teshuvot Maharam Shik, Yoreh De'ah*, no. 158; R. Shlomoh Kluger, *Ha-Elef Lekha Shlomoh, Oraḥ Ḥayyim*, no. 238; R. Eleazar Meir Preil *Sefer ha-Ma'or* (Jerusalem, 5713), no. 25; R. Saul Weingurt, *Yad Sha'ul* (Tel Aviv, 5713), pp. 35–49; R. Yitzchak Ya'akov Weisz, *Teshuvot Minḥat Yiẓḥak*, vol. III, no. 1; R. Moshe Sternbuch, *Mo'adim u-Zemanim*, III, no. 269, note 1; R. Menasheh Klein, *Mishneh Halakhot*, vol. VI, no. 277; R. Yitzchak Wasserman, *No'am* (5720), vol. III, pp. 195–203; R. Shlomoh Zalman Auerbach, *Ha-Ne'eman* (Tishri 5723), pp. 6–10 and 12; and R. Samuel Hibner, *Ha-Darom* (Tishri 5727), no. 24, pp. 108–16. Cf., however, R. Raphael Katzenellenbogen, *Yavneh*, vol. III, no. 7–12 (Nisan 5709), pp. 175–79, reprinted in *No'am* (5729), vol. XII, pp. 322–31, and subsequently reprinted in R. Raphael Katzenellenbogen, *Be'er Ro'i* (Jerusalem, 5742), no. 25.

proprietary interest, including those living in distant areas, the property cannot be alienated. *Tosafot*, Rashba and Rabbenu Nissim, *ad locum*, explain that all persons who contribute to the construction of a house of worship acquire a partnership interest therein. The synagogue of a village or hamlet is customarily erected solely with funds contributed by local inhabitants, and hence can only be sold with the acquiescence of the local population or their designated representatives. In large cities, funds for the construction of a synagogue are customarily solicited not only from local residents but also from travelers and others who are not residents of the city. Since, with the passage of time, those contributors can no longer be identified, the synagogue cannot be sold. In another formulation of the distinction between metropolitan synagogues and those located in other areas, *Tosafot, ad locum*, and Rosh, *Megillah* 4:1, explain the matter somewhat differently. These authorities explain that the benefactors intend title to be vested in all worshippers who use the edifice on a regular basis. A worshipper who relocates elsewhere does not automatically forfeit his proprietary interest. Thus, since in a large city it is impossible to locate each and every one of the vast number of people who at one time were regular worshippers, the synagogue of a metropolitan area cannot be sold.[54]

The various lines of reasoning advanced by each of these authorities appear to apply to the property of the *Hochschule*. The institution and its library were established and supported by the *Gemeindesteuer*, a communal tax levied upon all German Jews, and through the beneficence of Jews throughout the world. The benefactors certainly intended that the resources of the library be placed at the disposal of all scholars who might avail themselves of its facilities. Although authority to buy and sell property for the benefit of the institution may well have been vested by those benefactors in the officers and members of the board of the *Hochschule*, in Jewish law, title remains vested either in the benefactors or in the intended beneficiaries and their respective heirs. The property therefore remains a charitable trust to be used for the purposes intended by the benefactors.[55] At most, Guttmann might claim that, as the

[54] Other reasons for the restriction against the sale of synagogue buildings in metropolitan areas are advanced by Rambam, *Hilkhot Tefillah* 11:16, and by Rashba and Rabbenu Nissim, *Megillah* 26a. Those reasons have the effect of expanding the prohibition to preclude the sale of such edifices under all circumstances but do not negate the considerations advanced by the authorities who countenance sale in some limited and unlikely situations, *viz.*, in situations in which agreement to the sale by all benefactors and previous worshippers is forthcoming.

[55] This certainly appears to be the position adopted by *Seridei Esh*, vol. III, no. 71, concerning the property of the defunct Hildesheimer Seminary.

sole surviving member of the faculty of the *Hochschule*, and as the designated custodian of the books and manuscripts in his possession, he is entitled to the prerogatives of an *apotropus* or trustee and, in that capacity, he may claim the right to choose a successor, that is, he may designate the institution that is to be awarded custody of those items for the continued use of scholars.

Nevertheless, as shown earlier, absent a finding that Guttmann has the halakhic standing of an artisan or a finding that the books and manuscripts in dispute are in the category of "items customarily lent or leased," Guttmann's claim that the items in his possession were presented to him as a gift would prevail unless the claim were to be refuted by contradictory evidence.

NOTES AND QUESTIONS

1. Common law recognizes a distinction between lost property and abandoned property. But how would common law resolve a dispute between a finder, who claims the property was abandoned, and the original owner, who claims that it was merely lost? That is a matter of fact to be determined by the finder of fact – typically a jury – who would presumably decide on the basis of contextual circumstances applying a reasonable man standard. Since the finder makes no claim to ownership other than by finding the property, his possession would be meaningless unless he could prove actual abandonment, a burden that is virtually impossible to satisfy. However, Jewish law does not allow for the finding of fact on the basis of a subjective determination by a jury. Instead, it incorporates a notion of despair, *ye'ush*, which is much easier to prove than abandonment. Thus, Jewish law replaces the difficult issue of abandonment with the more tractable issue of despair.

It must also be noted that common law recognizes no duty to rescue human life and certainly not to rescue property. A person living in a common law jurisdiction who comes upon lost property is entitled to ignore it and refrain from taking custody in order to return it to its rightful owner. Jewish law, on the contrary, does impose an obligation to rescue human life and to take possession of lost property in order to restore it to its rightful owner.

Is the concept of *ye'ush* designed to encourage taking possession of lost property, or is it simply a substitute for the unwieldy notion of abandonment?

2. Assume that the Nazis had seized the library of the *Hochschule*, and gained title on the basis of *kibush milḥamah*. Subsequently, the Allies liberated Berlin. A platoon, one of whose members was a Jewish soldier who recognized the value of the rare books in the *Hochschule* library, secured the *Hochschule* building. Could the Jewish soldier gain title to the books simply by taking them? Does it make a difference whether the soldier was serving in the American army or in the Russian army?

3. There are two seemingly antithetical presumptions of law regarding claims of title. Possession is presumptive evidence that the property belongs to a person in possession who asserts a claim of title. Proof of prior possession is also presumptive evidence of ownership. These two forms of presumptive evidence are often in conflict: there may be proof of prior possession in support of the claim of one party, while the second party is presently in possession. When does present possession trump and when is the property assigned to the party in whom title is known to have been vested at an earlier point?

Present possession is not simply legal inertia. Present possession is evidence of ownership because, although people may lie, it is presumed that they do not generally commit theft. Prior possession is a procedural presumption rather than an evidentiary presumption. Therefore, the evidentiary presumption of possession trumps proof of prior possession, except in situations in which present possession can be explained on a basis other than theft, e.g., animals that wander from barnyard to barnyard, or items that are customarily entrusted to an artisan for repair. In common law possession simply means that the burden of proof is on the plaintiff when the plaintiff is the party who is not in possession. In Jewish law possession does not serve simply to define the counterparty as the plaintiff, but serves an evidentiary function as well.

4. In footnote 5 it was argued on the basis of *Skornik v. Skornik* that in the extraordinary circumstances of World War II Jewish law should govern the relationship between Guttmann and the *Hochschule*, because Jews were denied the protection of any other system of law. But Jewish law forbids its adherents from having recourse to secular courts that apply an alien system of law. Are there grounds to argue that the secular system should apply Jewish law in all property disputes arising out of transactions between observant Jewish litigants on the grounds that fidelity to Jewish law is an implied condition of all their agreements?

5. The concept of *lifnim mishurat ha-din*, or beyond the boundary of the law, is a rough equivalent of the notion of equity in common law. However, *lifnim mishurat ha-din* was not designed to be applied in an *ad hoc* manner. The doctrine was applied to smooth and soften rigid points of law taking into account particular facts of a situation and the relative positions of the parties. Thus, for example, there might be a requirement to return lost property even after *ye'ush* has occurred as reflecting general principles of fairness, but not when the finder has a particular need for the lost item and the rightful owner does not, e.g., an academic tome that comes into the possession of a scholar. The notion of equity can best be described as reflecting policy concerns that transcend the application of rigid rules of law. There is also the notion that action *lifnim mishurat ha-din* reflects a personal obligation in the form of "you shall do that which is right and good" (Deuteronomy 6:18), rather than adjudication of *in rem* property rights.

5

Torture and the Ticking Bomb

To say that the issue of torture, even in extremely limited circumstances, represents a moral dilemma is an understatement. One approaches the topic with extreme hesitation. Certainly, any thinking person, any human being possessing even rudimentary moral sensitivity abhors torture in all its forms. The international conventions banning torture are no more than the expression of the lowest common moral denominator of the human race.

Torture deprives the victim of the essence of humanity; it strips a person of dignity and renders him or her bereft of autonomy. Freedom of will, reflected in personal autonomy, is the essence of the human condition. The effect of torture is to humiliate and degrade the victim and to destroy the victim's volitional freedom.

I. THE LEGAL HISTORY AND THE CONTEMPORARY ATTITUDE

Historically, torture has been employed for a variety of purposes. At its most barbaric, torture has been used in a purely punitive or sadistic manner as, for example, when employed by victors against captives. At times, torture has been used in what may be described as a preventive or prophylactic manner as a means of intimidation. Thus, a ruler may seek to forestall future acts of treason by torturing political enemies. Similarly, an unstable regime may employ torture to terrorize political enemies. In such cases torture is used to intimidate. Those two types of torture – "punitive torture" and "intimidative torture" – are morally indefensible and repugnant.

Equally odious, albeit sanctioned in the past by some societies, is judicial torture, i.e., torture designed to elicit a confession from a criminal who is indeed guilty.[1] Until relatively recent times, European criminal procedure was

[1] For a comprehensive study of judicial torture see Priro Fiorelli, *La tortura guidigaria nel diritto commune*, 2 vols. (Milan, 1953–54).

heavily dependent on the use of torture. The European law of proof emerged in the city-states of northern Italy in the thirteenth century and spread throughout Europe as part of the reception of Roman law. The European law of proof replaced proof by ordeal conducted under the auspices of the Church. Trial by ordeal purported to achieve certainty by having judgment rendered by the unerring Deity. That mode of proof was effectively terminated by a decision of the Fourth Lateran Council in 1215. With abolition of divine determination of guilt, a standard of proof had to be devised that would eliminate the possibility of human error.[2]

For conviction of a crime punishable by death or maiming the European law of proof demanded testimony of two unimpeachable eyewitnesses. The parallel to the biblical two-witness rule is obvious. The practical problem that arises in applying this rule of proof is equally obvious: with such a high burden of proof conviction becomes virtually impossible. If the criminal justice system cannot punish perpetrators, crime is likely to become rampant. Jewish law recognizes that the two-witness rule is designed only for a society of righteous, law-abiding citizens for whom prescription of statutory punishment serves primarily as a pedagogic device. Jewish law provides that in an imperfect but real world criminals may be brought to justice either by application of the *ad hoc* emergency powers of the *bet din* or by imposition of the *mishpetei ha-melekh*, i.e., "the King's justice" designed to preserve the social fabric.[3] The procedures employed in such cases permitted relaxation of the rules

[2] For a further discussion of the law of torture as an adjunct of the European law of proof, see John H. Langbein, *Torture and the Law of Proof: Europe and England in the Ancien Régime* (Chicago, IL, 1979), pp. 3–7 and *idem*, "The European Law of Torture," *Torture*, ed. by Sanford Levinson (New York, 2004), pp. 93–103.

[3] In addition to establishing a two-witness rule as the standard of proof for conviction, Jewish law requires (1) that the culprit be warned in advance that his transgression carries with it capital punishment, (2) that the witnesses not contradict one another even about ancillary matters, (3) that the witnesses observe the act simultaneously and, finally, (4) that they be aware of each other's presence. In cases of homicide, and homicide only, there is a punishment available other than the biblically prescribed form of execution. The punishment consists of placing the convicted criminal in a cell (*kippah*), providing him with reduced rations of bread and water in order to shrink the digestive system and then feeding him barley in order to cause fatal distention. According to Rambam, that punishment was administered if any one of the first three conditions was not fulfilled; according to Rashi, it was administered if either of the first two or the fourth condition was not fulfilled. The punishment was not available in cases in which only a single witness observed the act and certainly not in cases in which the only evidence was circumstantial. See Rambam, *Hilkhot Roẓeaḥ* 4:8–9 and *Kesef Mishneh, ad locum*. In an otherwise thoroughly cogent discussion, Alan Dershowitz, *Why Terrorism Works* (New Haven, CT, 2002), p. 157, correctly identifies the problem created by the establishment of a two-witness rule but is simply in error in his explanation of how Jewish law remedied that problem.

of evidence in relying upon a single witness and even upon circumstantial evidence.[4]

In European criminal law the problem was mitigated by the fact that, in addition to the testimony of two eyewitnesses, confession by the defendant was accepted as proof of guilt. That law of proof could be effective only in cases of overt crime or repentant criminals. For the criminal law system to be effective, unrepentant criminals who committed clandestine crimes had to be forced to confess. The law of torture emerged as a means of regulating the process of coercing a confession.

A procedure emerged that provided for examination under torture. A standard of "probable cause" was established as a prerequisite for examination of the suspect under torture in order to ensure that only persons likely to be guilty would be subjected to the procedure. Probable cause consisted of either a single eyewitness or two items of circumstantial evidence, e.g., the suspect was seen departing the scene of the crime with a bloody dagger and the stolen loot. In theory at least, the confession was to contain details presumably known only to the perpetrator. In practice, leading questions as well as other devices provided the victim instruction regarding the statement required of him. There was also a requirement that the confession be confirmed subsequent to the cessation of physical duress. However, the hapless victim realized full well that failure to confirm freely would only occasion return to the torture chamber.

Thus, in effect, torture was designed to confirm conclusions previously reached through circumstantial evidence. To be sure, the law of torture was often abused in execution and when employed in instances of flimsy or nonexistent circumstantial evidence in extorting confessions from the innocent. At best, it was both superfluous and unreliable in confirming guilt already determined by other means.[5]

4 For a discussion of admissibility of circumstantial evidence in the Noahide Courts and in administration of "the King's justice" see J. David Bleich, "Capital Punishment in the Noahide Code," *Contemporary Halakhic Problems* (New York, 1983), vol. II, pp. 349–67.

5 British common law had no need for torture since it accepted circumstantial evidence in determining guilt. See Sir Frederick Pollack and Frederic W. Maitland, *The History of English Law*, 2nd ed. (Cambridge, 1898), vol. II, pp. 659–60. Prior to abolition of the ordeals, the defendant, in England, had the option of avoiding the ordeal by accepting a trial by jury. Consequently, it was possible to apply the same standard of proof to serious crime as had been applied to petty crime during the earlier period of trial by ordeal. The jury's verdict was not a divine judgment and hence did not require absolute proof. Accordingly, circumstantial evidence was accepted as sufficient. With abrogation of trial by ordeal, a jury trial became the only option. See *Torture and the Law of Proof*, p. 275.

However, torture by order of the Privy Council or the monarch was used in at least eighty-one cases during the Tudor-Stuart period between 1540 and 1640. See James Heath, *Torture and English Law: An Administrative History from the Plantagenets to the Stuarts* (Westport, CT,

It would be consistent with contemporary faith in the moral development of mankind during and after the age of the Enlightenment to believe that the great writers of that period, particularly Beccaria and Voltaire, shocked the conscience of Europe by exposing the inhumanity of torture and inspired the monarchs of Europe to abolish its practice. John Langbein, a legal historian, convincingly categorizes that view as a "fairy tale."[6] Langbein establishes a different causal nexus.

The rule of proof that gave rise to investigation under torture applied only to blood sanctions, i.e., death or maiming. The two-witness rule did not apply to sanctions imposed for lesser crimes that were punished by fines or minor corporal punishment. With the introduction of the galley sentence, the workhouse and incarceration as criminal sanctions it was possible to apply the same standard of proof to serious crime as had earlier been applied to petty crime with the result that torture became less significant for the administration of justice. Consequently, during the eighteenth century the system of judicial torture was gradually abolished in most European countries but nevertheless did survive in some few jurisdictions until early in the nineteenth century. By the beginning of the twentieth century, in a submission dated 1907, a contributor to the *Encyclopedia Britannica* was sufficiently confident that torture had been eradicated in Europe to write: "The whole subject is now one of only historical interest as far as Europe is concerned."[7]

Today, abhorrence of torture is emblematic of every civilized society. Jews, of all people, have profound historical cause to foster renunciation of torture in all its forms. From antiquity until the modern period Jews have repeatedly been singled out for all manner of cruelty at the hands of their oppressors. The forms of torture visited upon the *asarah harugei malkhut*, the ten renowned Sages of the mishnaic period who suffered martyrdom at the hands of the Romans, as so vividly described in both the *Yom Kippur* and *Tisha be-Av* liturgies, were replicated by crusaders, inquisitors and Cossacks. Jews continued to be prime victims of torture well beyond the Middle Ages.

Towards the middle of the nineteenth century, at a time when most people had come to believe that the practice of torture had been consigned to the

1982) and Langbein, *Torture*, pp. 81–128. Most of those cases involved real or suspected sedition or treason. See *Torture and the Law of Proof*, pp. 73–74. In the words of Sir Francis Bacon: "In the highest cases of treason, torture is used for discovery, and not for evidence." Hence, the coercive maneuvers employed in those cases can best be categorized as "intimidative torture" resorted to by a threatened monarch rather than as judicial torture. See J. Spendings, *The Letters and Life of Francis Bacon* (London, 1883), vol. III, p. 114.

6 *Torture and the Law of Proof*, pp. 10–12.

7 See James Williams, "Torture," *Encyclopedia Britannica*, 11th ed. (Cambridge, 1910–11), vol. XXVII, p. 72.

dustbin of history, Western society suffered a rude awakening as the result of an incident that profoundly affected the Jewish community: the Damascus affair of 1840.

A priest in Syria was found dead. Without a scintilla of evidence, Jews were accused of his murder. The political machinations that were contributing factors to the accusation are both complex and murky but the result was quite clear: a number of prominent members of the Jewish community were apprehended, held in prison and tortured until confessions were obtained. Reports of the affair reached Europe and civilized nations were appalled. They had assumed that the practice of eliciting confessions by means of torture had long since been abandoned. Torture might have been rampant in the Dark Ages but certainly could not endure in a modern enlightened age. Despite widespread acceptance of the ritual-murder myth, there was considerable agitation for the release of those hapless individuals. Prominent personages, including Sir Moses Montefiore in Britain and Adolphe Crémieux in France, became protagonists of the victims' cause. Ultimately, the innocent victims were released. Stories of unspeakable torture reaching Europe had been discounted as unbelievable but with the release of the victims the truth could no longer be suppressed. Eyes had been gouged and genitalia crushed. There had been multiple instances of children being tortured in order to force parents to confess.[8] Of course, in such circumstances victims will say anything demanded of them in the hope of avoiding further excruciating pain. As a result, the civilized world came to the stunning realization that not only is torture inconsistent with human sensibility but, moreover, confessions elicited under torture are meaningless and devoid of judicial probity.

Abhorrence of torture is certainly well grounded and leads to an understandable and, in a certain sense, correct result. The result has been the formulation by the family of nations of a principle couched in the form of a Kantian moral imperative: Abjure all torture, lest there be no setting of boundaries. The imperative is rational and persuasive, despite the fact that in extreme cases it may trigger application of the Latin maxim "*Fiat justitia et pereat mundus*" – "Let justice be done and let the world perish." Justice entails respect for human dignity, and human dignity requires preservation of the integrity of individual autonomy, which torture annihilates.

"Let justice be done" is axiomatic and requires no validation. It is the second clause – "and let the world perish" – that is problematic. The universality of this

[8] See Jonathan Frankel, *The Damascus Affair: "Ritual Murder," Politics, and the Jews in 1840* (Cambridge, 1997), especially pp. 37–43. For a description of a similar but less well known incident in Rhodes see *ibid.*, pp. 68–72. Ironically and sadly, as the nineteenth century progressed, ritual murder charges in Europe did not abate. See *ibid.*, pp. 438–40.

rule, its applicability in any and all circumstances regardless of consequence, requires examination. The most striking challenge to the universality of the ban on torture lies in the example of the ticking bomb.

II. THE TICKING BOMB: IS IT DIFFERENT?

The rationales against the other uses of torture have no significance in the dilemma of torture and the ticking bomb. Torture in the case of the ticking bomb is of an entirely different nature. It is neither punitive, nor intimidative, nor judicial. It is designed neither to give vent to sadistic instincts, nor to punish, nor to set an example. It is designed purely and simply to elicit information and circumstances will rapidly demonstrate whether or not the information elicited was accurate. Since it is designed to reveal information, it can perhaps best be termed "revelatory torture" to distinguish it from the other kinds of torture.[9] One writer has categorized this kind as "interrogational torture,"[10] and the term has been recast by another as "preventative interrogative torture."[11] The various forms of torture should not be confused. Arguments against, and sources decrying, other forms of torture cannot be applied *mutatis mutandis* to revelatory or preventative interrogative torture.

The most difficult moral dilemmas arise when moral imperatives come into conflict with one another. Judaism, unlike common law, posits a duty of rescue as a moral and halakhic imperative. "Do not stand idly by the blood of your fellow" (Leviticus 19:16), in its more obvious applications, requires rendering life-saving assistance in rescuing a potential drowning victim, helping a person escape from a fire, rendering medical assistance and even administering CPR. In such situations recognition of a duty of rescue is hardly exceptionable.

A particularly vexing conflict between discharging a duty of rescue and a conflicting moral obligation might well occur in the case of a "ticking bomb." Imagine a scenario in which a terrorist is known to have information regarding the location of a weapon of mass destruction, e.g., a chemical, biological or nuclear bomb, that has already been armed and is set to explode imminently. Explosion of the bomb will assuredly cause the deaths of countless thousands

9 A form of torture of this kind, known as "*torture préalable*," existed in France. According to this doctrine a duly convicted criminal awaiting execution could be examined under torture concerning other crimes and criminals, and particularly concerning accomplices. Voltaire defended *torture préalable* and, although Louis XVI abolished ordinary judicial torture in 1780, *torture préalable* was not banned until the reign of Louis XVI, in 1788. See *Torture and the Law of Proof*, pp. 16–17.

10 See Henry Shue, "Torture," *Torture*, p. 53.

11 See Oren Gross, "The Prohibition on Torture and the Limits of the Law," *Torture*, p. 232.

of innocent victims. Unspeakable tragedy can be averted only if the terrorist discloses where the bomb may be found so that it can be disarmed in a timely manner. But the terrorist refuses to cooperate. May one morally apply physical duress rising to the level of torture in order to elicit essential information that will save thousands of lives?

Some ethicists have taken the position that torture is a *malum per se* that can never be sanctioned regardless of consequences.[12] Absolutists assert that civilized people do not sanction torture and that a society that can be preserved only by resort to torture is not worth preserving. Their position is based upon deontological grounds rather than on assessment of consequences. For them, torture is inherently evil and can never be justified or excused.[13] Others present a slippery slope argument, contending that sanctioning torture in even the most egregious of circumstances would shatter the barrier posed by the moral and political taboo against torture, with the result that torture will no longer be perceived as noxious in less compelling circumstances.

Jurists typically point to the fact that torture is prohibited in international law by the Geneva Convention against Torture, the European Convention on Human Rights and the United Nations Convention against Torture and Other Cruel, Inhuman or Degrading Treatment or Punishment. The United Nations Convention entered into force in 1987 and has since been ratified by more than 130 countries,[14] as well as by statutes enacted in most democratic countries.

[12] Diverse views representative of a wide spectrum of contemporary thinkers, as well as discussions of treatment of torture in international law, are presented in a series of essays published in the previously cited work: *Torture*, edited by Sanford Levinson.

[13] See, for example, Elaine Scarry, *The Body in Pain: The Making and Unmaking of the World* (New York, 1985), pp. 27–59.

[14] Curiously, ratification by the United States may prove to have been more symbolic than substantive. In the resolution ratifying the treaty the Senate declared "... the United States considers itself bound by the obligation ... to prevent 'cruel, inhuman or degrading treatment or punishment,' only insofar as the term means the cruel, unusual and inhuman treatment or punishment prohibited by the Fifth, Eighth and/or Fourteenth Amendments to the Constitution of the United States." See Resolution of Advice and Consent to Ratification of the Convention against Torture and Other Forms of Cruel, Inhuman or Degrading Treatment or Punishment – Reservations, Declarations, and Understandings, part I (1), 136 Cong. Rec. § 17491 (daily ed., October 27, 1990). In effect, the Senate agreed to eschew only acts already prohibited by the Constitution. More significantly, linkage of the phrase "cruel, inhuman or degrading treatment or punishment" to conduct prohibited by the Fifth, Eighth and Fourteenth Amendments does not establish an unchanging definition. Terms and phrases employed in the Constitution are subject to interpretation by the courts. Accordingly, the meaning of the words "cruel, inhuman or degrading treatment or punishment" is restricted to the meaning assigned to them by United States courts in any judicial decision, including future decisions no less so than those handed down in the past. It then follows that a practice regarded as unconstitutional in the past may be ruled constitutional in the future and will not be independently banned by the Convention.

Other legal scholars adopt a variant posture, contending that the rule of law must indeed be upheld and that, as a matter of law, torture can never, and should never, be sanctioned but that, nevertheless, in exceptional circumstances society would be justified in failing to apply penal sanctions.[15] The underlying notion is akin to that of jury nullification. A defendant may be guilty beyond a shadow of a doubt and the jury may be absolutely convinced of his guilt and nevertheless return a verdict of not guilty so that the defendant will escape punishment. A jury may do so simply because its members have come to believe that the interests of justice are better served by withholding penal sanctions. A decision to employ torture might be ratified at any one of several stages in the judicial process: prosecutors might decline to press charges; the charge might be dismissed "in the interest of justice"; the jury might refuse to convict; the judge might mitigate or suspend punishment; and clemency always remains a final option.

A highly significant limitation of the constitutional rights in question was formulated by the U.S. Supreme Court in Chavez v. Martinez, 538 U.S. 760 (2003). In fragmented opinions the Court apparently accepted the notion that coercive interrogation is acceptable in situations in which eliciting information in a timely fashion is a matter of necessity. Earlier, in a kidnapping case, Leon v. Wainwright 734 F.2d 770 (11th Cir. 1984), in dicta having no direct bearing on the actual decision, a federal appellate court approved the conduct of Miami police who choked a suspect "until he revealed where [the victim] was being held." *Id.* at 770. The court unanimously categorized the conduct as that of "a group of concerned officers acting in a reasonable manner to obtain information they needed in order to protect another individual from bodily harm or death." *Id.* at 773. See John T. Parry, "Escalation and Necessity," *Torture*, pp. 150–52. The court's position, of course, may legitimate "revelatory" or "preventative interrogational torture" under United States law.

15 See, for example, Oren Gross, *Torture*, pp. 229–53.

Although couched in terms of a different legal doctrine, this is essentially the position of the Supreme Court of Israel in H. C. 5100/94 Public Committee against Torture in Israel v. The State of Israel, The General Security Services and Others, 553(4) PD 817 (1999). Translated excerpts from the decision are published in *Torture*, pp. 165–81. The Israeli court disallowed even moderate forms of physical pressure despite claims that such methods were necessary to save lives. Nevertheless, relying upon the conclusions of the 1987 report of the Landau Commission, the Israeli Supreme Court invoked the traditional common law defense of necessity and left open the possibility that an interrogator might avail himself of such a defense in a "ticking bomb" situation. See *infra*, note 33 and accompanying text.

A United States court might well recognize a necessity defense, particularly if American ratification of the Geneva Convention is not understood as an absolute and unequivocal acceptance of a ban against torture. See *supra*, note 14. If, however, the Geneva Convention is accepted unequivocally and without reservation, it is difficult to understand how a necessity defense could be entertained. The essence of a necessity defense is that the law is not designed for, and should not be applied to, situations in which its enforcement would create a greater harm than it seeks to eliminate. The defense requires that "the harm or evil sought to be avoided by such conduct [be] greater than that sought to be prevented by the law defining the offense charged." See Model Penal Code § 3.02(1)(a). Accordingly, the defense would not seem to be available when the law is expressly applicable to the circumstances giving rise to the claim of justification.

Post factum ratification excuses the act but does not provide legal justification. Extralegal action, even if subsequently ratified, does not establish legal precedent.

There is a striking precedent for such a moral stance in our contemporary judicial practice. For good reason, the various American jurisdictions have declined to legalize euthanasia. Yet in the few cases of mercy killing that have been brought to trial, by and large, juries have refused to convict or have found the defendant guilty of a lesser charge than homicide and, even when the defendant is found guilty, judges have mitigated the punishment.[16] The pristine moral value is preserved in theory while, when warranted, the harshness of its application is mitigated in practice.

This view does not really anticipate total proscription of torture. Instead, it leaves the decision in the hands of police interrogators, security officials or military commanders. In every particular case they would bear the responsibility of weighing the potential harm against violation of their duty to abide by the law, and of reaching an *ad hoc* determination. Such a policy anticipates that the powers that be will resort to torture only if they are convinced that their breach of legal norms is so obviously justified that no jury would impose criminal sanctions.

Inherent in that position is a measure of hypocrisy. The hypocrisy – and indeed unfairness to the moral agent – lies in an unwillingness to provide clear guidelines in advance. And that position also fails to take into account the very real element of subjectivity on the part of the jury. Some juries may be composed of legal purists who, enamored of the Roman law maxim or of what they perceive as an *a priori* equivalent, believe that obedience to law is the supreme moral value. Accordingly, they may well ignore any and all countervailing considerations and extenuating circumstances and conclude that justice requires that all breaches of the law be punished. On the other hand, an approach that does not sanction torture *ex ante* but allows for *post factum* ratification does have one positive aspect: It does not require the law to sanction the unsanctionable but in egregious cases permits society to tailor its response to the circumstances of the case.

There is, however, another possible moral response, one difficult to explain but nevertheless cogent. In a system that posits an obligation to rescue, the ticking bomb poses a palpable dilemma. The obligation to rescue is a reflection of the mandate to preserve human life. The talmudic aphorism that a person who preserves a single life is regarded as if he has preserved the entire world (*Sanhedrin* 37a) is not hyperbole; it is a succinct and eloquent reflection of the

[16] See American Law Institute, § 210.5, commentary at 106.

value of human life in the hierarchy of moral values. And precisely therein lies the essence of the dilemma. On the one hand, preservation of freedom is a fundamental value; torture designed to deprive an individual of freedom is a denial of that value. On the other hand, a moral agent is bound by an obligation to rescue. All thinking moral persons recognize that we ought to preserve both autonomy of will and human dignity; all thinking moral persons recognize a duty to preserve human life. Scrutiny of each of those principles separately raises no disagreement whatsoever. The moral value of each principle is crystal clear. That is why ethicists prefer to qualify moral observations with a *ceteris paribus* clause, i.e., all things being equal, X is good and Y is evil. All things being equal, we ought to strive not only for preservation but also for maximization of human dignity; all things being equal, we ought to respect individual autonomy; all things being equal, we ought to maximize preservation of human life. But in the real world all things are seldom, if ever, equal.

The case of the ticking bomb is a classic instance of the collision of two distinct and disparate moral values. In the classic example a fanatic has set a hidden nuclear device to explode in the heart of a major metropolis and only he knows where the bomb has been secreted. The device has been timed to explode imminently with the result that there is no time to evacuate the innocent populace. A variation of the same dilemma involves a scenario in which a bomb has been placed in one of several hundred school buildings. It is impossible to evacuate all of the schools but only the terrorist knows which school has been targeted. In a post September 11th scenario, an airplane has been hijacked and it has been determined that terrorists plan to strike an unidentified skyscraper or government building. Only by torturing one of the accomplices can the authorities determine the targeted building. In each of these examples torture is the only available means to elicit the information necessary to save innocent lives. Situations such as these require adjudication between competing values and a determination of which must be assigned priority. The sheer enormity of the stakes compels our attention.

But the case of the ticking bomb is by no means the first instance in our history in which these values have come into conflict. Patrick Henry was one of the heroes of the American Revolution. At the time when the colonies were in revolt against the British crown he proclaimed: "Give me liberty, or give me death!" To this day the motto "Live free or die" is engraved upon automobile license plates issued by the state of New Hampshire.

What was Patrick Henry's credo? He recognized that the preservation of human life is a moral desideratum and he also knew full well that if the revolution failed to achieve its goal the instigators would be hanged on the gallows as traitors to the Crown. But he also perceived the political institutions controlling his life and the lives of his fellow colonists as instruments for the effective denial of human freedom. The existing situation made it necessary to choose between two values; the choice was life versus freedom. In Patrick Henry's calculus, freedom was dominant and hence superior even to life itself.

Western society has, correctly or incorrectly, adopted the notion of human dignity as a paramount value and, at times, as even a greater value than life itself. It is that hierarchical ranking of values that constitutes the matrix against which many bioethical issues are adjudicated. "Death with dignity" has become a slogan employed not simply for the preservation of human dignity, even in death – a value that cannot be gainsaid – but for the sacrifice of longevity anticipation, whether brief and ephemeral or otherwise, i.e., the sacrifice of life itself for the sake of preservation of perceived dignity.

Little wonder, then, that when human dignity, personal autonomy and freedom of will come into conflict with preservation of life, even in situations in which there is a cognizable duty of rescue, Western society prefers the former over the latter. In the context of contemporary Western mores, the Geneva Convention's unequivocal and blanket ban on torture is not surprising. It is a global statement announcing that Western society stands firmly on the side of human dignity and personal autonomy as the encapsulation of the essence of the human condition. As such, those values are assigned priority over even life itself.

Moreover, in a strictly legal sense, arrival at that determination is not difficult because, even *ceteris paribus*, Western legal codes do not posit an obligation of rescue except in certain limited circumstances, e.g., an existing duty of care established on the basis of a contractual relationship.

Common law does not impose a duty to act as a Good Samaritan. A physician on his way to the golf course who comes upon the scene of a motor vehicle accident may refuse to stop without becoming subject to any penalty whatsoever. The duty of care is born of contract or of a special relationship; one does not, as a matter of course, owe a duty of rescue to a stranger. That remains the law in forty-eight of the fifty states. The sole exceptions are Vermont and Minnesota. In Vermont, if a person is capable of rendering life-saving assistance and does not, he is guilty of a misdemeanor and subject to a fine not in excess of $100. Minnesota has enacted a similar law, but in Minnesota human life is apparently viewed as twice as valuable since, in Minnesota, failure to render such assistance is punishable by a fine of up to $200.

We live in a society that accepts as part of its common cultural system of values the notion that there is no absolute legal obligation to rescue a person whose life is in danger, and in whose collective psyche is enshrined a concept of justice defined as a reflection of human dignity and personal autonomy. The various international conventions, which extend even to the case of the ticking bomb, do nothing more than record and apply the socio-moral norms commonly accepted by Western society.

Judaism has its own unique system of values and its own canons for resolving moral dilemmas. A Jew is referred to as an "*Ivri*," translated in the vernacular as a "Hebrew." Why are Jews termed Hebrews? The conventional explanation is that it is because their ancestor Abraham hailed from "*ever ha-nahar*" – the other side of the river [Euphrates]. The Midrash, *Bereshit Rabbah* 42:13, indicates that the appellation has a different connotation. Ideologically, the entire world stood on one side of the monotheism–polytheism conflict and Abraham stood alone on the opposing side. Inherent in that nugget of linguistic analysis is the proposition that, in moral controversies as well, it may be anticipated that the descendents of Abraham will be on "the other side." Thus, it is not at all surprising that in debates concerning contemporary moral issues Jewish law and tradition compel conclusions at variance from those espoused by society at large.

III. THE TICKING BOMB AND JEWISH LAW

A. *The Law of the Pursuer*

In confronting the moral dilemma posed by the ticking bomb it must be candidly acknowledged that the values reflected in Jewish teaching and the comparative weight assigned to those values are not congruent with the mores unhesitatingly accepted by the dominant culture. Judaism posits a duty of rescue that is virtually absolute. Not only does the duty of rescue compel intervention, it also reflects the paramount position Jewish law assigns to the preservation of life, with the result that, when preservation of life comes into conflict with other values, it is preservation of life that must triumph.

The value assigned to the preservation of innocent life is manifest in yet another provision of Jewish law applicable to resolution of the ticking bomb dilemma, that is, the law of the *rodef*. The term "*rodef*" is best translated as "pursuer" and refers to a would-be aggressor intent upon taking the life of his victim. In Jewish law, elimination of the *rodef* in order to save the life of the victim is not only permitted, but mandated. The rule is far broader than the principle of self-defense. A person whose life is threatened by another may exercise a right of self-defense; he may take the life of the aggressor to save his own life. However, although common law does allow for extension of the principle of self-defense in certain limited cases, e.g., a threat to the life of a spouse, self-defense is generally limited to the literal meaning of the term, to the defense of oneself. It does not apply to the rescue of a third party. Common law does not recognize a right, much less an obligation, to intervene in order to save the life of a stranger. Hence the claim that one was engaged in rescue is not a defense to a charge of homicide.

Refusing to justify intervention is consistent with the common law's failure to posit a duty of rescue. Since both the aggressor and the victim are strangers to whom no legal duties are owed, the common law stance is readily understandable. One life is pitted against another; one or the other will surely die. If one does not intervene the pursued will die, and if one does intervene the pursuer will perish. Absent an obligation to rescue the victim why should the blood of one be deemed "redder" than the blood of the other? If there are no grounds to choose between two lives there is no rationale that justifies the sacrifice of one person for the sake of the second. The result is legally mandated non-intervention.

Jewish law, on the contrary, mandates intervention. Not only is intervention to rescue the victim a defense against homicide but also failure to intervene violates a biblical commandment. The biblical provisions surrounding the law of the pursuer are clearly designed to protect the victim. Hence the law of the pursuer must be seen as an amplification of the obligation of rescue. Primacy of the obligation of rescue requires even forfeiture of the life of the perpetrator. Of course, invocation of the law of the pursuer in causing the pursuer's death is justified only if there is no other way to accomplish the necessary end and only if it can be established with the requisite degree of certainty that failure to intervene would result in loss of the victim's life.

Although such an element may well be present, the law of the pursuer should not be seen primarily as a vehicle for punishing the pursuer. The intervener does not act as a kangaroo court serving at one and the same time as prosecutor, judge, jury and executioner punishing a person who seeks to commit a crime. The law of pursuit is fully applicable even if the perpetrator is lacking in any measure of moral culpability. The pursuer may have gone berserk; he may be demented, a mental incompetent or a child having no halakhic or legal capacity and yet he is regarded as a *rodef* against whom the law of the pursuer is operative.

In American folklore there is an anecdote concerning pioneers traveling along the Wilderness Road. In the early days of American history, long before the United States extended from "sea to shining sea," there was a long period of westward migration. Settlers of the western territories were frequently attacked by Indians and were oft times forced to take refuge in hiding places in order to avoid discovery by Indian marauders. Apparently, in one such instance a baby began to wail. There was a distinct danger that the infant's cries would become audible to the enemy. In revealing the site in which the settlers were hiding, the infant would have compromised the safety of the entire group. In order to obviate the danger, the child's mother placed her hand over the baby's nose and mouth, causing him to suffocate. There was no other way to eliminate the threat caused by his cries.[17]

Moral theologians may debate the applicability of a double-effect doctrine; ethicists may quarrel over the justification of sacrificing a single person in order to save many; jurists may ponder the cogency of a necessity defense, but to rabbinic scholars the moral imperative in that situation was clear-cut and unequivocal.

A remarkably similar fact pattern is presented in a responsum published in a work devoted to halakhic problems that arose during the Holocaust.[18] The responsum also concerns a crying baby; the parents and others were hiding in a bunker somewhere in occupied Europe rather than in the Cumberland Trail; the enemy were not Indians, but Nazis. The choice was simple but heart-wrenching: Does one allow the baby to continue crying and thereby reveal the presence of Jews who will face certain and imminent death or does one eliminate the threat by suffocating the baby?

In Jewish law the baby has the status of a "pursuer," by virtue of the fact that it is engaged in conduct presenting a clear and certain danger to the lives of others. The infant intends no harm; no moral turpitude is entailed in the crying of a child; the child does not bear moral responsibility, nor does he possess legal capacity. The infant is innocence personified. Nevertheless, the child's acts, albeit unintentional, endanger others, and that factor, in and of itself, renders the law of the pursuer operative.

How is the operation of the law of the pursuer in such an instance to be understood? Certainly not in terms of the number of lives saved as balanced against the number of lives sacrificed. The ticking bomb example is generally presented as a hypothetical in which the lives of countless numbers of individuals are about to be extinguished. But the identical issues would be present even if but a single life were at stake. Judaism regards every life as endowed with infinite value. As schoolchildren we were taught that infinity added to infinity equals infinity. We now understand that in certain esoteric mathematical applications some infinities are greater than others, but in the moral realm all infinities remain equal. The rules and principles that apply to preserving countless lives apply with equal force to saving a single life.

[17] See Joseph Fletcher, *Situation Ethics* (Philadelphia, PA, 1966), p. 124.

[18] See R. Shimon Efrati, *Mi-Gei ha-Hareigah* (Jerusalem, 5761), no. I. R. Isaac Arieli, *Einayim la-Mishpat, Berakhot* 58a, describes a like situation, and similarly rules that the infant may be killed in order to eliminate the threat to the others in hiding.

But, if so, how can the taking of one life in order to save that of another be justified? Why must one prefer the life of the victim over the life of the aggressor, particularly when the aggressor is completely without guilt? The law of the pursuer reflects a simple principle, that society must take whatever measures may be necessary to eliminate violence. Whether or not the perpetrator has legal or even moral culpability is irrelevant. Violence is violence, and members of society are individually and collectively charged with eradicating violence. The law of the pursuer is most readily understood as the embodiment of a divinely announced policy principle. The reason or reasons that explain why the Torah enshrines elimination of violence in the law of the pursuer need not be belabored. The reasons are probably manifold and certainly subject to analysis and discussion, but are ultimately of little consequence since the moral values of Judaism are normative simply by virtue of the fact that they are declared as such by the Torah and enshrined in Halakhah as revealed at Sinai.

B. *Passive Pursuit*

The terrorist with knowledge of a ticking bomb might well be labeled a *rodef* but for one potentially salient point: A *rodef*, defined literally, is a person intent upon an overt act of violence. The terrorist in the ticking bomb scenario is not necessarily the person who armed the bomb or who was associated in any overt manner with preparing for the act of violence. He may be guilty only of failing to reveal information necessary to thwart the plotting; as such, his involvement is entirely passive. Is the law of the pursuer limited to persons engaged in overt acts or does it extend as well to persons causing harm, or who allow harm to take place, simply through non-feasance?

An answer to that question may be gleaned from analysis of a ruling recorded in the Palestinian Talmud, *Terumot* 8:10. The situation discussed involves a group of travelers surrounded by marauders who deliver an ultimatum: "Give us one of [your company] or we will kill all of you!" It is clear that the person to be delivered is marked for death. The ruling is unequivocal: "Even if they will all be killed let them not deliver a single Jewish life." The rule formulated by the Palestinian Talmud may otherwise be expressed as "Better two deaths than one murder." Better to allow everyone to be put to death rather than to become complicit in a single act of homicide. The rule precludes a person not only from serving as the proximate cause of the death of an innocent individual but also from remotely or indirectly contributing to his death. The number of lives to be lost as a result is irrelevant. In this case the law resonantly declares, "*Fiat justitia et pereat mundus.*" Justice requires that one not be complicit in a homicide even if the entire world will perish. That rule applies even if refusing to participate in homicide will contribute to even greater loss of life.

In the case discussed in the Palestinian Talmud the demand was for a single member of a group; failure to comply would result in extermination of the entire group, including the designated individual.

The Palestinian Talmud relates this rule to the seemingly contradictory narrative recorded in II Samuel 20:14–22. Sheba the son of Bichri was guilty of *lèse majesté* and King David ordered his execution. David's soldiers surrounded the city in which Sheba sought refuge and ordered the inhabitants to surrender the fugitive upon pain of themselves being collectively put to death. Delivery of Sheba the son of Bichri was regarded as acceptable and was found not to have violated the rule enunciated by the Palestinian Talmud. Two conflicting explanations are formulated in distinguishing the case of Sheba the son of Bichri. Resh Lakish maintains that the townsfolk acted correctly because the designated victim was indeed culpable of having committed a capital crime. In effect, his execution could not be considered culpable homicide. The conflicting opinion of R. Yoḥanon maintains that not only may a culpable individual be surrendered but that any other person might also be delivered to death in similar circumstances. According to the latter opinion the crucial factor in the case of Sheba the son of Bichri is that the choice of whom to deliver was not made by the townspeople but by those demanding his life. The crucial distinguishing factor, according to this view, is specification of the victim. In effect, the community cannot, of their own accord, select one of their number for death, because they have no right to prefer one person over another. But when relieved of that burden by virtue of the fact that others have made the selection, they may deliver the victim in order to spare the community.

The opinion of Resh Lakish requiring that the person delivered be criminally culpable is not difficult to understand. The victim is not only already a marked man, he is also deserving of his fate. Hence, what difference does it make how he meets his death? The second opinion, however, requires clarification. What rationale establishes specification by others as exculpation from homicide? Assuredly, specification by the perpetrator does not transform an innocent victim into a guilty party. If so, those who deliver the specified victim to death are abetting an act of homicide.

One incisive analysis is predicated upon recognition of the designated victim as having become, precisely by virtue of his designation for death, a *rodef*.[19]

[19] See R. Moses Feinstein, *Iggerot Mosheh, Yoreh De'ah*, vol. II, no. 60, *anaf* 2. See also R. Shalom Dov Wolpo, *Rodef u-Ba be-Mahteret* (Kiryat Gat, 5748), no. 25. Rabbi Wolpo's contention that the crying infant should not be considered a pursuer because "such is the nature of the world" (*kakh darko shel olam*) is unwarranted. The phrase occurs in Rambam's *Hilkhot Roẓeah* 9:6 with regard to a woman in childbirth whose life is threatened by the emerging fetus. The fetus is a pursuer and may be dismembered in order to preserve the life of the mother. However, once the head of the fetus has emerged and entered the birth canal that rule no longer applies

On first analysis, categorizing the designated victim as a *rodef* is difficult to comprehend. The designated victim is pursuing no one; he harbors no malevolent intent. He has done and is doing nothing at all. In truth, he himself is an entirely innocent victim. Through no fault of his own he happens to have fallen into the bad graces of a thoroughly evil person or persons who will not hesitate to kill others in order to take the life of the designated victim as well. The intended victim endangers others by being in a particular place at a particular time. It is his mere existence, the fact that he is living and breathing, that endangers others. Nevertheless, according to this opinion, he is categorized as a *rodef* and the law of the pursuer applies because his very presence in the group endangers the lives of others.

On this analysis it is apparent that the law of the pursuer applies even when the "pursuer" is not engaged in an overt act of aggression; the law of the pursuer applies equally when mere passive existence gives rise to danger to others.[20]

since one life cannot be sacrificed to save another. The Gemara, *Sanhedrin* 72b, explains the distinction by declaring that in the latter case "Heaven is pursuing her." Rambam rephrases that notion and interprets it as meaning "such is the nature of the world."

The limitation placed by the Gemara upon the definition of a pursuer excludes only situations in which the pursuit is at the hands of Heaven and any human involved is merely a passive instrument of providence. That is evident from the fact that a minor is considered bereft of *da'at* or rational capacity. Nevertheless, the law of the pursuer applies to a minor or a person who goes berserk and wields a gun or an infant that cries. Moreover, Rabbi Wolpo's conclusion is certainly precluded if R. Moses Feinstein's analysis of Rambam's statement as presented in his earlier-cited responsum is accepted.

20 The controversy recorded in the Palestinian Talmud persists in the writing of medieval codifiers. Rambam, *Hilkhot Yesodei ha-Torah* 5:5, rules that a designated victim may be delivered for execution in order to save the entire company only if he is culpable of the death penalty, while Rabbenu Nissim, *Yoma* 82b, rules that designation alone is sufficient. Rema, *Yoreh De'ah* 157:1, cites both views, but without a definitive resolution.

The controversy, however, is limited to situations in which the danger stems from the mere presence and existence of the "pursuer." Moreover, unlike other instances involving a pursuer, the Palestinian Talmud indicates that delivery of the designated victim is not consistent with "*mishnat ḥasidim*" – "the teaching of the pious" and that Elijah declined to continue to reveal himself to a person who had violated "the teaching of the pious" by acting in that manner. Rambam, *Hilkhot Yesodei ha-Torah* 5:5, qualifies the import of that categorization by ruling that, although the law permits such acts, "*ein morin ken le-khathilah*" – "one does not direct [action], in accordance with such [rule] *ex ante*." [Cf., however, R. Jacob Emden, *Even Boḥen* 1:73, who takes issue with Rambam's ruling and asserts that the rule is normative and should be relied upon as such. The incident involving Elijah and the concept of *mishnat ḥasidim*, asserts *Even Boḥen*, is limited to an *adam ḥashuv*, or prominent personage such as Resh Lakish, who should not involve himself even in such circumstances.] That rule stands in stark contradistinction to the rule of the pursuer codified by Rambam, *Hilkhot Roẓeaḥ* 1:9, 14 and 16, mandating elimination of the pursuer.

Rabbi Wolpo correctly states that the principle "*ein morin ken*" applies only to a purely passive individual whose "pursuit" arises simply from his existence. However, Rabbi Efrati opines that the principle applies to every pursuer who is an *ones*, i.e., who acts under duress. Accordingly, Rabbi Efrati regards refusal to suffocate an infant in a situation of the nature described earlier

To be sure, in the case of the ticking bomb it is not the physical existence of the recalcitrant terrorist that poses the danger but the terrorist's failure to speak. The passivity of non-feasance is even more pronounced then the passivity of existence. Nevertheless, the notion that passive non-intervention is encompassed within the law of the pursuer is assumed as a matter of course by R. Naphtali Zevi Judah Berlin in his commentary on *She'iltot de-Rav Aha'i Ga'on, Ha'amek She'elah, She'ilta* 142:9. Judges 21:5 records that any person who might fail to appear in order to participate in the action taken against the tribe of Benjamin would be put to death. *Ha'amek She'elah* asserts that the culpability of those individuals stemmed from the law of the pursuer. Failure to join in the disciplinary action of the community, he asserts, would expose fragmentation within the nation and strengthen the resolve of external enemies. Strengthening the hand of the enemy, even by purely passive non-feasance, according to *Ha'amek She'elah*, renders such an individual a pursuer.

Once it is recognized that a prospective act of commission is not required to trigger the law of the pursuer it may well be argued that refusal to divulge information necessary to countermand the lethal effect of an already committed act similarly constitutes an act, albeit a passive one, of pursuit. By failing to act the potential informant makes it possible for a calamity to occur. If so, he is a pursuer who may be eliminated in order to preserve the lives of potential victims.

as entirely commendable. That position, however, is untenable. The Gemara, *Yevamot* 33b and 61b, in the phrase "*pitui ketanah ones hu*" equates the freely willed, autonomous act of a minor with an act committed under duress. Rambam, *Hilkhot Rozeaḥ* 1:9, rules unequivocally that, not only a minor, but also a fetus must be killed when engaged in an act of pursuit. Indeed, it is in the context of a ruling with regard to a fetal pursuer that Rambam records the mandatory nature of the obligation to sacrifice the pursuer in order to preserve the victim.

[A possible contradiction to the principle of *pitui ketanah ones hu* in the discussion of the Gemara, *Sanhedrin* 55b, is dismissed by R. Elijah of Vilna, *Eliyahu Rabbah, Niddah* 5:5, and rendered compatible with that principle by R. Elchanan Wasserman, *Kovez He'arot*, no. 75, sec. 2. Rambam's disputed ruling, *Hilkhot Issurei Bi'ah* 3:2 and *Hilkhot Sotah* 2:4, to the effect that a minor who commits adultery is forbidden to her husband is based upon an extraneous consideration. See R. Meir Simchah ha-Kohen of Dvinsk, *Or Sameaḥ, Hilkhot Issurei Bi'ah* 3:2, s.v. *ulam.*]

The distinction between the case of an overt pursuer, in which intervention is mandated, and the situation of an entirely passive pursuer, in which intervention, although permitted, is not "the teaching of the pious," must lie in the fact that acts of violence or endangerment must be thwarted; in the case of a passive pursuer there is no potentially threatening act to prevent; hence, in the latter case, prevention of harm to the threatened innocent victim represents only fulfillment of a duty of rescue. In usual situations the life of one person may not be sacrificed in order to rescue another since "What makes you think (*ma'i ḥazit*) that one life is of greater value than another." That consideration is negated when the life to be sacrificed is that of even a passive pursuer. The element of "pursuit" compromises the value of the life of the pursuer. The net result is that the putative intervener may choose which life to preserve; he may choose to preserve the life of the victim by intervening or he may preserve the life of the passive pursuer by refusing to act. The "teaching of the pious" is that one not actively prefer one life over another when intervention is a matter of discretion.

Obviously, killing the very person who possesses crucial information necessary to save the lives of intended victims would defeat the very purpose of the law of pursuit. Dead people cannot talk and the information would be carried to the grave. Indeed, since the victims would not be rescued by eliminating the pursuer, the pursuer dare not be killed, because killing the pursuer cannot be justified in situations in which the victim is doomed in any event. But the law of the pursuer provides for far more than the elimination of the pursuer; the law of pursuit requires thwarting the nefarious intent of the pursuer by any means possible. Indeed, killing the pursuer is a capital offense if rescue can be accomplished in a less onerous manner, e.g., by maiming the pursuer and incapacitating him. The talmudic example is a situation in which the victim can be rescued by cutting off one of the limbs of the pursuer. In effect, the law of the pursuer allows only the force required to eliminate the threat. It is thus clear that the law of pursuit sanctions any form of bodily force, including mayhem, when necessary to preserve the life of the victim.

There is one significant limitation upon invoking the law of the pursuer in the context of a terrorist believed to be in possession of information, namely, the requirement for a threshold level of certainty that loss of innocent life will ensue if no intervention occurs. In the case of the ticking bomb the issue that is bound to arise is whether there exists the requisite degree of certainty that the suspect possesses information and that revealing such information will avert the impending calamity.[21]

C. *Intractable Pain*

It might be contended that, although the law of the pursuer warrants mayhem and even sacrifice of a limb, nevertheless torture inflicting insufferable pain is inhumane and more onerous than death and hence cannot be sanctioned

[21] For a discussion of the degree of certainty required by Jewish law for invocation of the law of the pursuer see *Contemporary Halakhic Problems* (New York, 1995), vol. IV, pp. 82–86.

Jeremy Bentham, who, as will be shown, *infra*, note 34, supported the use of torture in "a very few cases," addressed the issue of certainty by demanding the same degree of certainty as required for conviction of a crime:

> But now then how can it be ascertained whether it be in a man's power to give the information that is wanted of him? As well as it can be known whether he be guilty of any crime. Both of them matters of fact, equally open to enquiry. That it is now in his power is, it is true, a present matter of fact: that he did commit such or such a crime is a past matter of fact. Perfect certainty it must be confessed is an advantage scarce permitted to human kind; but a man may obtain as compleat a certainty respecting present facts as respecting past.

See *Northern Ireland Legal Quarterly*, vol. 24, no. 3 (Autumn 1973), p. 317.

under any circumstances. The argument would be that only measures up to and including death of the pursuer are sanctionable but torture is inhuman in the extreme and even worse than death. That argument is readily rebutted by reference to the law governing martyrdom as understood by virtually all early-day talmudic commentators. The Book of Daniel 3:12–23 recounts that Shadrach, Meshach and Abed-ne-go, identified by the Gemara as Hananiah, Mishael and Azariah, allowed themselves to be cast into a fiery cauldron rather than accede to the demand of Nebuchadnezzar that they worship an idol. The Gemara, *Ketubot* 33b, observes that, although those men accepted martyrdom with equanimity, "had they been tortured they would have worshipped the idol." Those commentators are uniform in assuming that the Gemara is not gratuitously and without evidence impugning the devotion of Hananiah, Mishael and Azariah or questioning their mettle in resisting duress. Instead, they understand the Gemara as declaring that, under the given circumstances, Hananiah, Mishael and Azariah would have been under no obligation to accept torture. But why not? The most obvious answer would be that, although Halakhah requires martyrdom on behalf of monotheism, it regards torture as even more onerous than martyrdom and does not require acceptance of torture as well. That is indeed the resolution offered by one anonymous early-day authority in order not to compromise adherence to the obligation of martyrdom in the face of idolatry.[22] However, that view is an individual opinion and is implicitly rejected by a host of other authorities who have addressed the problem and proposed other solutions.[23] It is clear that the consensus of halakhic opinion is that, when martyrdom is required, submitting to torture is required as well. Since there is no provision in Jewish law mandating the acceptance of any sanction more severe than death, it follows that Jewish law does not regard torture as more onerous than death.[24] By the same token, it follows that when preventative measures, including mayhem and death, may be imposed in order to restrain a pursuer, torture may be employed as well.

D. *Frustration of a Criminal Act*

In a ticking bomb scenario in which the terrorist was himself a participant in fashioning and arming the bomb, torture can be justified on other grounds as well. Jewish law provides for physical duress in order to secure compliance

[22] See *Shitah Mekubbezet, Ketubot* 33b, s.v. *u-be-kuntreisin piresh*.

[23] See, for example, the comments of *Tosafot, ad locum*, s.v. *ilmale*.

[24] See *Iggerot Mosheh, Yoreh De'ah*, vol. II, no. 174, *anaf* 4.

with biblical mandates. In constructing and arming the bomb the terrorist has completed the physical act that will render him culpable for homicide upon the death of his victims but the timing device delays the effect of the act with the result that there is a window of opportunity for canceling or rescinding the act.

Legal systems tend to treat equally those whose acts create harm and those whose acts create only the potential for harm but who later fail to intervene in order to prevent the actualization of such harm. A comparable halakhic example is the situation in which, on *Shabbat*, a person has placed dough in an oven or water on a stove. The physical act of Sabbath desecration is complete but there is no actual desecration until the bread becomes baked or the water becomes heated. In the interim period the dough or the water may be removed, rendering the earlier act innocuous. Just as duress may be applied *ab initio* in order to restrain a person from transgression,[25] a person may be compelled to perform an act necessary to thwart the effect of an earlier proscribed act and thereby retroactively render that act innocuous. Thus, a person who, on the Sabbath, has placed bread in an oven or water on a stove may be forcibly compelled to remove the bread before it becomes baked or the water before it becomes heated. Similarly, a person who has attached a timing device to a bomb may be compelled by force, even torture, to neutralize that act or to enable others to neutralize that act before it culminates in homicide.

E. *The Obligation of Rescue*

The same line of reasoning yields an identical result even in cases in which the terrorist was not complicit in constructing or arming the bomb but merely possesses detailed knowledge of the actions of others. To be sure, in such a situation the terrorist has performed no illicit act that he must be compelled to frustrate and thereby render innocuous. Although the terrorist may himself have done no harm and have caused no danger, he nevertheless has an

[25] Corporal force may be employed by any individual in order to prevent overt transgression by another. See *Bava Kamma* 28a, *Netivot ha-Mishpat* 3:1 and *Minḥat Ḥinnukh*, no. 8. Force may similarly be used to compel performance of positive obligations. However, *Yere'im*, no. 164, and *Mordekhai*, *Gittin* 4:384, maintain that duress may be applied to compel performance of a positive obligation only by a *bet din* whose members are recipients of the ordination conferred by Moses upon the judges appointed by him in the wilderness and subsequently transmitted from generation to generation. *Keẓot ha-Ḥoshen* 3:1 maintains that contemporary *batei din* are empowered to act as "agents" of earlier courts for this purpose. Disagreeing with those authorities, *Netivot ha-Mishpat* 3:1 asserts that a qualified *bet din* is not necessary for that purpose and hence even private parties may compel performance of *miẓvot*. See also *Meshovev Netivot* and *Netivot ha-Mishpat, Mahadurah Batra, ad locum*.

obligation to rescue. The terrorist, no less so than other persons, has a duty to save endangered lives. He, too, is commanded, "Thou shalt not stand idly by the blood of your fellow" (Leviticus 19:16). And Jewish law provides that people can be compelled to discharge biblically mandated duties.

Fulfilling positive obligations and avoiding negative transgressions frequently requires an expenditure of funds. A person is required – and may be compelled – to expend his entire fortune to avoid transgressing a negative commandment, for example, to obtain kosher food rather than resorting to eating forbidden food in order to sustain life.[26] According to some authorities, a person is required to expend no more than a tenth of his net worth,[27] and for others no more than a fifth of his assets[28] in order to fulfill a positive commandment, e.g., to acquire the four species for use on *Sukkot*.

The duty of rescue is couched in negative rather than positive terms: "Thou shalt not stand idly by the blood of your fellow." Jewish law requires expenditure of one's entire fortune if necessary in order to avoid transgressing a negative commandment. Ostensibly, expenditure of one's entire fortune should be required, if necessary, in order to avoid transgressing the negative commandment, "Though shalt not stand idly by." Such is indeed the position of many authorities. Others maintain that the disparity in the financial burden to be assumed is not dependent upon a negative versus a positive linguistic formulation of the obligation but upon whether the otherwise ensuing transgression is active or passive. According to that analysis, overt transgression of any commandment is to be eschewed, literally at all costs, even if the commandment is expressed in the passive voice, while avoiding a passive transgression requires expenditure of only one-tenth or one-fifth of one's resources even if the commandment is expressed negatively. An obvious example of the latter is the commandment, "Thou shall not stand idly by the blood of thy fellow." The injunction, in its formal sense, is a negative commandment yet it is transgressed by simple non-feasance.

Other than for the three cardinal transgressions, avoiding the violation of a commandment does not require sacrificing more than a person's entire fortune. Consequently, the duty of rescue certainly does not require expending more than a person's entire fortune. For that reason a person need not sacrifice

[26] See Rema, *Oraḥ Ḥayyim* 656:1.

[27] See *Bet Yosef*, *Oraḥ Ḥayyim* 656.

[28] See *Rema*, *Oraḥ Ḥayyim* 656:1. Cf. *Mishnah Berurah* 656:8, who regards expenditure of ten percent to be obligatory but the difference between ten and twenty percent to be discretionary. The issue is contingent upon interpretation of the statement of Rema, *Oraḥ Ḥayyim* 656:1. See R. Yechiel Michel Epstein, *Arukh ha-Shulḥan* 656:4. Cf. also *Bi'ur Halakhah* 656:1, s.v. *afilu* and R. Yo'av Yehoshu'a of Kintzk (Konskie), *Helkat Yo'av*, I, *Dinei Ones*, *anaf* 7.

a limb or an organ in order to rescue another, since the law presumes that a rational person would expend his entire fortune to avoid such loss. For the same reason a person need not accept physical pain or emotional anguish that he would willingly pay his entire fortune to avoid. However, infliction of physical pain below that threshold level is warranted as a means of compelling the obligation of rescue.[29] Accordingly, imposition of physical pain up to that magnitude would be justified in the case of the ticking bomb.

F. *Personal Autonomy*

Apart from the foregoing, in Jewish tradition and teaching torture in the case of the ticking bomb does not really present a moral dilemma arising from the collision of opposing moral values. According to Jewish teaching, the conflict between preserving life and preserving individual autonomy and human dignity in such a situation is apparent rather than real. There are a limited number of situations in which Jewish law demands freely willed acquiescence in the performance of an act but at the same time sanctions physical duress to secure assent. The primary example lies in compelling a recalcitrant husband to execute a bill of divorce in instances in which Jewish law recognizes the wife's right to demand a divorce. The fact that the *get* is halakhically mandated does not mitigate the halakhic requirement that the divorce be executed only pursuant to the free-will directive of the husband. Halakhah provides that a recalcitrant husband may be subjected to physical pain until he signifies acquiescence by saying, "I wish it." Rambam, *Hilkhot Geirushin* 2:20, in a departure from his usual wont in composing the *Mishneh Torah*, enters into a philosophical excursus in order to dispel the obvious paradox. If a *get* may be compelled in such cases, why the need for pronouncing the verbal formula, "I wish it"? And if an autonomous will is required in such circumstances, how can a declaration made under physical duress possibly be accepted as evidence of a freely willed act?

Rambam dispels the paradox by asserting that the human psyche is multi-layered. Every Jew wishes to fulfill his obligation to obey the commandments of the Torah as that obligation is accurately declared to him by competent rabbinic authorities. That is his innermost will. But it is not the only facet of his psyche. Man is also possessed of an "evil inclination," which is simply a cognomen for the corporeal nature of man, and hence subject to lust, desire, spite and a host of other emotions. Man's corporeal nature often causes him to desire what he is commanded to abjure and to shrink from performing

[29] For a fuller discussion, see *Contemporary Halakhic Problems*, vol. IV, pp. 282–85.

an act he is duty-bound to perform. A person's evil inclination may cause him to desire things that another part of his psyche, the good intention or spiritual component of his being, knows to be wrong and finds abhorrent. Quite often the two components of the psyche are at war with one another and not infrequently the evil inclination achieves dominance.

Halakhah, according to Rambam, recognizes that a person acts freely only when the "evil inclination" acquiesces in the desire of the deeper, more fundamental inner will. But the evil inclination is concerned solely with pleasure, sensual gratification and the like, all of which are forms of physical well-being. Pleasure and pain are antagonistic forces. The evil inclination lusts after pleasure but abhors pain. Pleasure may be desirable but not if accompanied by a commensurate degree of pain. Thus, the desire of the evil inclination for sensual gratification is readily cancelled by generating a situation in which the evil inclination rapidly determines that, on balance, there is no sensual profit in continuing pursuit of the particular gratification in question and, consequently, the evil inclination readily renounces the pursuit of that desire. The net result is that the evil inclination no longer presents an impediment to realization of the desire of the inner will. Cooption of the evil inclination results in realization of complete autonomy. Thus, in terms of Jewish teaching, physical duress designed to ensure compliance with divine law does not compromise individual autonomy. Quite the contrary, it eliminates impediments to expression of that autonomy.

IV. NON-JEWS AND THE TICKING BOMB

A. *The Law of the Pursuer*

The foregoing reflects the position of Jewish law and tradition as it pertains to Jews. Non-Jews, however, are not bound by the 613 precepts of the Sinaitic covenant; they are subject only to observance of the Seven Commandments of the Noahide Code. The Noahide Code does not contain a duty of rescue. Thus, common law and Western legal systems, which do not establish a legal requirement to act as a Good Samaritan, are consistent with Jewish teaching as addressed to non-Jews. It stands to reason that, if there is no duty of rescue, any attempt to elicit information, even potentially life-saving information, is nothing other than an illicit battery. Hence, international conventions banning torture would appear to be consistent with the universalistic aspect of Jewish teaching as it applies to the nations of the world.

Nevertheless, that conclusion would not be correct. The law of the pursuer is integral to the Noahide Code. Some authorities contend that a Noahide, no less so than a Jew, is duty-bound to intervene in order to eliminate a pursuer;[30] others assert that a Noahide is not obligated to eliminate the pursuer but that nevertheless a Noahide has full discretion to do so.[31] Unlike common law, the Noahide Code grants license to all persons to prevent acts of violence targeted against innocent victims even in the absence of a duty of care on the part of the intervener vis-à-vis the putative victim. Thus, although the Noahide Code does not require a physician to stop at the site of a motor vehicle accident for the purpose of rendering life-saving assistance, he may, and for some authorities, he must, intervene in order to prevent an act of violence. Reflected in those provisions is undoubtedly the consideration that eliminating violence constitutes a societal concern of a magnitude higher even than that of preserving human life.

Accordingly, a non-Jewish terrorist intent upon an act of aggression may be thwarted by any available means. Similarly, if he has armed a bomb he may be compelled by force to neutralize the threat or reveal the information needed to enable others to do so.

B. *Dinin*

Torture designed to compel disclosure of information about the location of a ticking bomb, when by happenstance such information comes into the possession of an innocent non-Jew, is an entirely different matter. Such an individual is not a pursuer; as a non-Jew he has no obligation of rescue. Hence there is no duty incumbent upon him that he may be compelled to discharge against his will. If so, ostensibly, torture of such a person should be regarded as an illicit battery.

Nevertheless, in the limited situation of an innocent non-Jew in possession of information regarding a ticking bomb there is license, and perhaps even an obligation, to apply torture, if necessary, in order to elicit the requisite information. Sanction for such a procedure may be derived from the last in the list of the seven Noahide commandments – *dinin* or "laws."

30 See R. Isaac Schorr, *Teshuvot Koaḥ Shor*, p. 32b; R. Isaac Shmelkes, *Teshuvot Bet Yiẓḥak, Yoreh De'ah*, vol. II, no. 162, sec. 4; and R. Meir Dan Plocki, *Ḥemdat Yisra'el* (New York, 5728), p. 178. Applicability of the law of the pursuer to Noahides seems to be indicated by the language of Rambam, *Hilkhot Melakhim* 5:4, and is assumed as a matter of course by R. Chaim Soloveitchik, *Ḥiddushei Rabbenu Ḥayyim ha-Levi, ad locum*. Cf. the gloss of *Ḥazon Ish* on *Ḥiddushei Rabbenu Ḥayyim ha-Levi, ad locum* and R. Eleazar Menachem Shach, *Avi Ezri, Mahadura Kamma, Hilkhot Roẓeaḥ* 9:6. An opposing view is adopted by *Teshuvot Ben Yehudah*, no. 12 and R. Chaim Chizkiyahu Medini, *Sedei Ḥemed, Kuntres ha-Kelalim, Ma'arekhet ha-Gimel*, no. 44.

31 See *Minḥat Ḥinnukh*, no. 296 and R. Shlomoh Zevin, *Le-Or ha-Halakhah*, 2nd ed. (Tel Aviv, 5717), p. 17. For a further discussion, see pp. 206–13, *infra*.

As formulated by Rambam, *Hilkhot Melakhim* 9:14, the essence of the commandment of *dinin* is an obligation to bring to justice violators of the first six of the Noahide commandments. Perpetrators must be punished; accordingly, Noahide societies have an obligation to establish a judicial system, to bring transgressors to justice and to impose capital punishment. Those obligations devolve upon society as a whole and upon each and every member of society. Rambam advances this analysis of *dinin* in conjunction with his elucidation of a particularly vexing biblical narrative. Genesis 34 records the abduction and violation of Dinah by Shechem the son of Hamor. Her brothers, Simeon and Levi, responded not simply by executing the perpetrator but by annihilating all the people of Shechem as well. Rambam asserts that the townspeople "saw and knew" what Shechem had done but failed to bring him to justice. Failure to punish the culprit, according to Rambam, is also a violation of the commandment of *dinin* and thus a capital offense. Failure to punish the perpetrator, according to Rambam, is as heinous a crime as the transgression.

According to Rambam, there is yet another duty imposed upon Noahides by the commandment of *dinin*. Rambam declares that courts must be established in order to judge violators and also "*le-hazhir et ha-am*" – to admonish the populace. The commandment of *dinin* not only establishes a duty to punish but also imposes another obligation as well, *viz.*, to prevent nefarious deeds before their inception. Rambam is clearly taking the position that Noahide courts are endowed with the power of injunctive relief, which they must exercise in order to prevent crime.

It must be remembered that the commandment of *dinin* imposes obligations not only upon society at large but upon individuals as well. Thus, there exist both a collective and an individual obligation to prevent crimes from being committed. Accordingly, in the ticking bomb scenario, although the potential informant may be innocent of any wrongdoing and not be bound by a duty of rescue, he nevertheless has an obligation to prevent a crime from taking place. Hence he can be compelled to divulge the information necessary to effect that end. Since society has the same obligation it may force him to divulge the information.

The commandment of *dinin* is a commandment to do justice and to ensure that the interests of justice are served. In order to establish a just society evildoers must be punished and crime prevented.

V. *HORA'AT SHA'AH* AND CONSTRUCTIVE TORTURE WARRANTS

The law of the pursuer justifies duress applied only to a person responsible in some sense for the impending calamity, even if the responsibility lies only in a failure to communicate information needed to avert a disaster. It cannot be invoked to justify torture of a totally uninvolved innocent individual as a means of indirectly bringing pressure to bear upon the person in possession of the requisite information. The most obvious example lies in torture of a terrorist's spouse, parent or child in anticipation that the terrorist, who might be willing himself to accept torture, will not allow a loved one to suffer a similar fate. Such an innocent and ignorant party simply cannot be characterized as a pursuer.

Miriam Gur-Aryeh[32] has pointed out that acceptance of a necessity defense – a possibility impliedly recognized in a 1999 decision of the Supreme Court of Israel[33] – would indeed serve *post factum* to justify torture even of totally innocent parties. It is precisely for that reason that she takes issue with employment of the doctrine of necessity by the Israeli court. The law of the pursuer, although not dependent upon moral or legal culpability, is predicated upon elimination of an evil; an innocent, uninvolved and ignorant bystander is neither actively nor passively engaged in an evil act. The notion of necessity involves acceptance of a lesser evil in order to avoid a greater evil. Application of the doctrine of necessity is not only consistent with the recognition of torture as a *malum per se* but is actually born of recognition and acceptance of the evil nature of the act. The aspect of necessity arises, misguidedly or otherwise, from an assessment that grievous harm done to one person will rescue a multitude. If so, the mechanism for averting the calamity is irrelevant; whether the person harmed is innocent or guilty is of no consequence; and whether the source of the threat is directly eliminated by means of the harm or whether the harm is only indirectly and tangentially related to the rescue has no bearing whatsoever upon the notion of necessity.

Absent a duty of rescue on the part of the potential torture victim, or if the torture under consideration is so onerous as to be equated with expenditure of more than the victim's entire fortune, there seems to be no way that Jewish law might recognize a principle analogous to the doctrine of necessity. Yet a parallel may be found in one source. The thesis is highly novel and probably not reflective of mainstream halakhic opinion and, although formally it involves a rather different principle, the thesis is indeed analogous to the doctrine of necessity.

Similarly, Alan Dershowitz's proposal that torture be sanctioned in certain limited circumstances such as the case of the ticking bomb but only pursuant to

[32] "Can the War against Terror Justify the Use of Force in Interrogations? Reflections in Light of the Israeli Experience," *Torture*, pp. 183–90.

[33] See *supra*, note 15.

obtaining advance judicial approval in the form of a "torture warrant" from an appropriate oversight body[34] is not without precedent in Jewish law. Indeed, the dual notions of "necessity" and "torture warrants" appear in the same source.

The Book of Esther records that, upon being informed of the decree issued by Ahasuerus for the annihilation of the entire Jewish people, Esther risked her own life in presuming to appear before the king without a royal summons. Putting aside the issue of self-endangerment, Esther's act was halakhicly problematic. According to rabbinic tradition, Esther presented herself for the purpose of a conjugal assignation in the course of which she presented her petition. However, according to the same rabbinic tradition, Esther was actually the wife of Mordecai. Her earlier liaisons with Ahasuerus were acts of adultery but permitted to her because of duress.[35] On this occasion she willingly and voluntarily made herself available to Ahasuerus for an adulterous act. Her conduct was sanctioned by Mordecai as a *hora'at sha'ah*, or *ad hoc* emergency measure, necessary for the salvation of the people of Israel. The biblical paradigm for a *hora'at sha'ah* is found in the narrative of Elijah and the sacrifices he offered on Mount Carmel in order to discredit the prophets of Baal. Mordecai and the Sanhedrin had the power to issue a *hora'at sha'ah* in order to prevent the annihilation of the entire Jewish people.

R. Abraham Isaac Kook, *Mishpat Kohen*, nos. 143 and 144, secs. 6–8, asserts that not only adultery, but even bloodshed is permitted on an emergency

34 See Alan Dershowitz, *Shouting Fire* (Boston, MA, 2002), pp. 476–77; *idem*, *Why Terrorism Works*, pp. 158–60 and 251, n. 6; and *idem*, "Tortured Reasoning," *Torture*, pp. 257–80.

The proposal for using torture pursuant to a judicial warrant was first formulated by the eighteenth-century utilitarian philosopher Jeremy Bentham in a manuscript published for the first time by W.L. and P.E. Twining, *Northern Ireland Legal Quarterly*, vol. 24, no. 3 (Autumn 1973), pp. 305–56. Bentham reports that despite his initial abhorrence of the very idea he has learned "to correct the first impressions of sentiment by the more extensive considerations of utility." As a result he writes that "I am inclined to think there are a very few cases in which for a very particular purpose, Torture might be made use of with advantage." *Ibid.*, p. 308. Bentham sanctions torture in situations in which "the thing which a Man is required to do" is "a thing which the public has an interest in his doing" and it is either certain that it is in his power to comply or in which probably though not certainly it is in his power to do; and for the not doing which it is possible that he may suffer, although he be innocent; but which the public has so great an interest in his doing that the danger of what may ensue from his not doing it is a greater danger than even that of an innocent person's suffering the greatest degree of pain that can be suffered by Torture, of the kind and in the quantity permitted to be employed. Bentham concludes this portion of his discussion with the observation: "Are there in practice any cases that can be ranked under this head? If there be any, it is plain there can be but very few." *Ibid.*, pp. 312–13.

35 See *Sanhedrin* 74b.

ad hoc basis for the purpose of preserving the entire Jewish people.[36] That power is inherent, he contends, in the authority to promulgate a *hora'at sha'ah*, or *ad hoc* emergency directive, in emergency situations. Rabbi Kook, however, acknowledges that authority for such action is limited to situations in which the entire Jewish people, or perhaps only the entire populace of the Land of Israel, is threatened but does not extend to the imminent destruction of a single community. If so, in practical terms, his thesis is applicable only when the threat is of the magnitude of a nuclear holocaust.

Of course, the question of which individual or group of individuals has the authority to promulgate a *hora'at sha'ah* of this nature is crucial. Needless to say, the power is not vested in a Noahide court or in administrative officials of a secular government. But Rabbi Kook broadens his thesis in a highly innovative maneuver, arguing that in such extreme circumstances an actual *hora'at sha'ah* is unnecessary. He argues that, in effect, there exists a "constructive" *hora'at sha'ah* sanctioning such practice. Were a duly qualified Sanhedrin in existence it would most certainly grant permission to take necessary action in such egregious circumstances; therefore, actual license is unnecessary.

The notion of *hora'at sha'ah* is similar to the doctrine of necessity in that it is an *ad hoc* acceptance of a lesser evil over a greater evil not incorporated in any statutory code. Necessity, however, is always an affirmative defense and can never be the subject of prior judicial license. In contradistinction, if Rabbi Kook's responsum is regarded as normative, guidance in determining what is encompassed in such a *hora'at sha'ah* is available before the fact to any student or reader pondering the options available to him. But, then, that is also the case with regard to any legal scholar who peruses the literature devoted to explication of the doctrine of necessity. In both cases the investigation is directed only to an assessment of what, after the fact, a jury would accept as necessity or what a *bet din* would regard as a legitimately construed *hora'at sha'ah*.

VI. AN AFTERWORD

In a certain sense the conclusions of this endeavor are counterintuitive. They certainly go against the grain of a sensitive contemporary moral conscience. We correctly abhor infliction of pain upon others; we correctly abhor anything akin to depriving a person of human dignity. We disdain depriving people of

[36] Rabbi Kook's interlocutor, R. Zalman Pines, however, contended that the power of *hora'at sha'ah* is limited to preventing transgression and does not extend to rescue of the community. Rabbi Kook vigorously contested that distinction.

autonomy; we certainly condemn the dehumanization of human beings. Yet, for Judaism, morality and ethics are not subjective. Morality is the product of the halakhic system, which itself is the embodiment of divine revelation.[37] Jewish law is the embodiment of a corpus of moral principles, not all of which are self-evident to the human mind.

The Roman law maxim is "Let justice be done even if the world is destroyed." The rabbinic maxim is "Let the law pierce the mountain." Let the law be enforced even if in the process it is necessary to bore through mountains; let justice be done even if the obstacles are deeply rooted human sensibilities. In the context of this discussion the appropriate maxim may well be "Let justice be done even if it must pierce the mountain of the human psyche."

37 See R. Ovadiah Bartenura, *Avot* 1:1.

NOTES AND QUESTIONS

1. The American Declaration of Independence speaks of humans as being "endowed by their Creator with certain unalienable Rights, that among these are Life, Liberty and the pursuit of Happiness." The notion of a divinely bestowed inalienable right reflects a natural law doctrine. Is society as a whole endowed with similar rights? If so, what is its moral imperative when societal rights come into conflict with individual rights? Is resolution of that issue relevant to the issue of torture and the ticking bomb?

2. Thomas Jefferson engaged in plagiarism in using an expression formulated by John Locke. Locke spoke of "lives, liberties and estates, which I call by the general name, property"[38] as natural rights. Perhaps like all good plagiarists Jefferson was simply trying to use somewhat different language. Or to the American mind is the pursuit of happiness simply a different way of expressing enjoyment of property?

3. Is conservation of societal resources also a natural right? Could torture ever be justified for the purpose of conserving natural resources?

4. Recognition of fundamental rights or values, either as *a priori* principles, or on some other grounds, is basic to any system of ethics. In Western culture there is little disagreement over what those values and rights are. Generally, problems arise only when rights or values come into conflict with one another, as in the real world they surely must. How does an ethical system deal with conflicts between values? Consider Robin Hood and the Sheriff of Nottingham. Does that narrative not reflect a different hierarchical ranking of values rather than the rejection of a value? Is that not the real issue in the dilemma of torture and the ticking bomb? What methodology is to be employed in resolving such conflicts?

5. Judaism clearly regards preserving human life as a cardinal value. Other religious traditions do not recognize an obligation to preserve life when preserving life requires "extraordinary means." Some ethical systems regard a violation of feminine modesty (say, submission to a gynecological examination by a male practitioner), or great inconvenience (say, relocation to a different locale), or inordinate expense as "extraordinary means." Can the different stances be explained as a reconciliation of conflict between competing values?

6. Historically torture was used in criminal cases to confirm guilt that had already been established by circumstantial or direct evidence. The criminal law systems that used torture were heirs to a legal tradition that had an extremely taxing evidentiary standard. Modern systems of criminal jurisprudence rely

[38] John Locke, *Second Treatise of Civil Government*, ch. 9, sec. 123.

upon the evidence that earlier societies sought to confirm by torture. We have, in effect, abandoned the confirmatory contribution of torture and are willing to rely upon other forms of evidence exclusively. In effect, there is a choice: the criminal law system must either "relax" the certainty of guilt or accept torture as a means of establishing guilt. How does one explain the adoption of one method of establishing near certainty over the other?

7. Consider mutual aggression, where each of two people is intent upon killing the other. Is there any justification for intervention by a third party?

A classic case involves a difficult birth in which non-intervention would result in the death of either mother or child. The Talmud imposes a rule of non-intervention in cases in which the forehead of the baby has emerged from the uterus, declaring that "it is Heaven that is the pursuer" (*Sanhedrin* 72b). The parallel discussion in the Palestinian Talmud has been understood as depicting the scenario as one of mutual aggression, to which the appropriate response is non-intervention.

8. Life and dignity are discrete values. Yet, there are times when the two cannot coexist. Death with dignity is a reflection of the stance that an undignified life is not worth living. Does that not imply that dignity is accorded higher value than life? If Judaism recognizes life as a paramount value, what would its position be on death with dignity?

9. How can the administration of capital punishment be reconciled with the infinite value of human life? Does the answer lie in an understanding of capital punishment as a deterrent and hence as a measure designed to prevent widespread abnegation of the values that have been compromised in an act of capital transgression? Or, has the capital transgression diminished the value of the life of the transgressor to the point that he has in effect dehumanized himself?

10. The supreme value of life in Jewish law is reflected in a variety of provisions, including the suspension of virtually all religious and ritual obligations in the face of threats to life as well as in the duty of rescue. The Noahide Code does not impose a duty of rescue. Is that a reflection of a diminished value attached to human life by the Noahide Code? If so, is transgression of other Noahide commandments justified in the face of an imminent danger to life? If there is an *a priori* justification for suspending prohibitions in the face of a danger to life, would a Noahide, who is not subject to a specific commandment demanding martyrdom in the face of idolatry, be justified in committing an act of idolatry in order to preserve his or her life?

6

War

PART ONE: WAR AND NON-JEWS

The prophet Habakkuk plaintively asks, "Why . . . art Thou silent when the wicked swallows up the man more righteous than he? For Thou makest men as the fish of the sea" (Habakkuk 1:13–14). Among the myriad species of the animal kingdom there are virtually none that prey upon their own kind. Carnivorous animals will devour other animals but not members of the same species. Preying upon members of the creature's own species is a phenomenon found only among the fish of the sea. Even a fish will swallow only a fellow creature smaller than itself. Man is unique among land animals in his propensity for attacking and destroying his fellow man. Man outdoes the fish not only in destroying others smaller and weaker than himself, but also in attempting to swallow up others equal to and better than himself.

"Pray for the welfare of the government, for without fear of [the government] men would swallow one another alive," advises the Mishnah, *Avot* 3:2. The base instincts of man are curbed only by fear. Individuals have reason to fear the power of the state. States, however, are subject to no higher temporal authority and hence have no reason for fear. Nations, as human institutions, give collective expression to the same base instincts that are inherent in the individuals of whom they are composed. As a result, nations, in their relationships with one another, behave precisely in the manner that the Mishnah ascribes to individuals: they "swallow one another alive."

The nations of the world have indeed attempted to regulate warfare, but its elimination remains a utopian ideal that eludes mankind. The Geneva Convention, the United Nations Charter and international treaties of friendship have certainly not effected a metamorphosis in the nature of man. There is a story told about a missionary who was sent on a mission into the wilds of Africa. When asked by his superiors to submit a report there was little of a positive nature for which he could claim credit. "Well," he was asked, "did you at least succeed in eradicating cannibalism in your area?" "No," he replied, "the natives are still cannibals, but at least they now eat with knives and forks." Renunciation of chemical and biological warfare, humane treatment of prisoners of war, etc., are certainly marks of "civilized" peoples, but on a more fundamental level these achievements are little different from a convention requiring cannibals to eat with knives and forks. "Civilized warfare" is inherently a self-contradiction.

Halakhah, as it applies to Jews, recognizes that man has no right to wage war against his fellow. War is sanctioned only when commanded by God, when divine wisdom dictates that such a course of action is necessary for fulfilling human destiny. Even a *milḥemet reshut*, or "discretionary war," is discretionary only in the sense that it is initiated by man and does not fulfill a divine commandment. But even a *milḥemet reshut* requires the acquiescence of the *urim ve-tumim* (as described, for example, in Numbers 27:21). The message transmitted via the breastplate of the High Priest is a form of revelation granting divine authority for an act of aggression. Judaism sanctions violence only at the specific behest of the Deity. Human reason is far too prone to error to be entrusted with a determination that war is justified in the service of a higher cause. Only God Himself can make that determination.

The teachings of Judaism regarding non-Jews are more complex. Non-Jews are not held to the same standards of behavior as Jews. Although the Noahide Code – the part of divine law binding upon non-Jews – prohibits murder, it does not necessarily prohibit the taking of human life under any and all circumstances. It is quite clear that when an individual's life is threatened, all persons, non-Jews as well as Jews, have an absolute right to eliminate the aggressor in self-defense.[1] "*Ha-ba le-horgekha hashkem le-horgo*" – "If one seeks to kill you, kill him first" (*Sanhedrin* 72a) is a principle that applies to Noahides as well as to Jews. Accordingly, a defensive war requires no further justification.

I. THE LAW OF PURSUIT

In situations in which an individual's own life is not directly threatened, but a threat exists with regard to the life of another human being, Jews are bound by the law of the "pursuer" (*rodef*). Jewish law not only permits, but demands, that anyone finding himself in the position of being able to save the life of an

[1] See *Sanhedrin* 57a; R. Yehudah Rosenbaum. *Teshuvot Ben Yehudah*, no. 21; *Minḥat Ḥinnukh*, no. 296.

intended victim must do so, even if such rescue necessitates sacrificing the life of the pursuer.

The question that requires examination is whether the law of pursuit, which mandates intervention by a third party in order to save the life of an intended victim, extends to Noahides as well. *Minḥat Ḥinnukh*, no. 296, concludes that Noahides have discretionary authority to intervene in such situations but do not have an absolute obligation to do so.

The Gemara, *Sanhedrin* 73a, attempts to derive the "law of the pursuer" from the commandment "Thou shalt not stand idly by the blood of your neighbor" (Leviticus 19:16). This commandment establishes a general obligation to come to the aid of a person whose life is endangered. Ultimately the Gemara derives an obligation to preserve the life of the victim even if it is necessary to sacrifice the life of the pursuer in order to accomplish this end from the verse, "For . . . the betrothed damsel cried and there was none to save her" (Deuteronomy 22:27). From this statement the Gemara infers that were a bystander present he would be obligated to preserve the betrothed damsel from violation by any means possible, including summary execution of the would-be rapist. By virtue of the juxtaposition (*hekesh*) of homicide and rape of a "betrothed damsel" in the immediately prior verse the Gemara derives a binding obligation requiring any and all bystanders to intervene and preserve the life of the intended homicide victim by any means possible.

Minḥat Ḥinnukh argues cogently that the commandments expressed in Leviticus 19:16 and Deuteronomy 22:27 are incumbent only upon Jews and hence cannot impose obligations upon non-Jews, who are bound only by the provisions of the Noahide Code. *Minḥat Ḥinnukh* does, however, adduce another source that serves as a basis for deriving the "law of the pursuer" and is applicable to Noahides as well. The Gemara, *Sanhedrin* 72b, cites the verse "Whosoever sheddeth the blood of man, by man shall his blood be shed" (Genesis 9:6) as granting dispensation to preserve the intended victim by eliminating the pursuer. The phrase "by man" is understood as calling for the shedding of blood "by any man," i.e., by persons witnessing the act, rather than as a reference to punitive measures to be undertaken subsequent to the act. Thus the Gemara understands the verse as referring, not to a homicide that has already been committed, but to the prevention of a would-be homicide. The verse, which was addressed to Noah, establishes a law not only for Jews, but for Noahides as well. The general principle is that any commandment given prior to Sinai is binding upon Noahides even subsequent to the Sinaitic revelation provided it has been reiterated at Sinai. The law of the pursuer is indeed repeated in Exodus 22:1. In the course of the same discussion, the Gemara, *Sanhedrin* 72b, states that the statute formulated in this passage, which provides that a thief who breaks into a dwelling during the night may be smitten without penalty, is based upon the assumption that the thief is not only intent upon larceny but will commit homicide as well if he meets resistance. Hence the thief is in effect a pursuer and may be put to death if necessary by virtue of the "law of the pursuer." *Tosafot, Sanhedrin* 72a, commenting on the redundancy of the multiple scriptural sources for the "law of pursuit," states that Exodus 22:1 serves only to establish a license for execution of the pursuer but does not make such a course of action obligatory. The obligation, according to *Tosafot*, is expressed solely in Deuteronomy 22:27. *Minḥat Ḥinnukh* assumes that *Tosafot* intend the comment to the effect that initial references to the law of pursuit grant only discretionary authority to be applicable to Genesis 9:6 as well. The phrase *ba-adam damo yishafekh*, according to *Minḥat Ḥinnukh*'s understanding, should thus be translated "by man *may* his blood be shed" and permits putting the aggressor to death when necessary to preserve the life of the victim, but does not mandate such action.[2] Accordingly, concludes *Minḥat Ḥinnukh*, Noahides are not only justified in acting in self-defense but may eliminate a threat to the lives of others as well, even though, unlike Jews, who are bound by Sinaitic revelation, they are under no obligation to do so.

Another authority, R. Meir Dan Plocki, *Ḥemdat Yisra'el*,[3] citing *Zekhuta de-Avraham*, argues that a non-Jew is not only permitted but, according to

[2] R. Shlomoh Zevin, *Le-Or ha-Halakhah* (Tel Aviv, 5717), p. 17, argues against *Minḥat Ḥinnukh*'s position and maintains that Noahides are not merely permitted, but are also obligated, to execute the pursuer in order to preserve the pursued. He argues that this is evident from the phrase "*domo yishafekh*," which he maintains must be translated as "by man shall his blood be spilled." It would appear, however, that the question raised by *Tosafot, Sanhedrin* 73a, under the word *af*, with regard to the earlier cited verse, which speaks of the *ba ba-maḥteret*, applies with equal validity to this verse. It would appear that *Tosafot*'s statement that the verse establishes permission rather than obligation applies to the subsequently cited verse "*ba-adam damo yishafekh*" as well.

Rabbi Zevin also cites the verses in Obadiah 1:11–13 addressed to Edom:

> In the day that thou didst stand aloof.
> In the day that strangers carried away his substance.
> And foreigners entered into his gates
> And cast lots upon Jerusalem,
> Even thou wast as one of them.
> But thou shouldst not have gazed on the day of thy brother,
> In the day of his disaster . . .
> Yea, thou shouldst not have gazed on their affliction.
> In the day of their calamity.

The prophet chastises Edom for standing by silently while aggression is committed against Israel. The implication, argues Rabbi Zevin, is that Noahides have an obligation to do battle against an aggressor.

[3] (New York, 1965), p. 178.

Rambam, is obligated to kill an aggressor in order to preserve the life of the intended victim. *Ḥemdat Yisra'el* bases his argument upon Rambam's understanding of the *mizvah* of *dinin*, the last of the seven commandments that constitute the Noahide Code. According to Rambam, the commandment of *dinin* establishes an obligation binding upon non-Jews to enforce the provisions of the Noahide Code and to punish Noahide transgressors. Accordingly, argues *Ḥemdat Yisra'el*, a non-Jew must kill the aggressor, not by virtue of the "law of the pursuer," but because of the *mizvah* of *dinin*, which obliges every Noahide to enforce the provisions of the Noahide Code, which, amongst other things, provides for the execution of murderers. *Ḥemdat Yisra'el* does express some reservation regarding the argument. He expresses uncertainty about whether the commandment of *dinin* mandates execution of transgressors only after the fact, or whether it requires intervention in the sense of "prior restraint" as well, in order to prevent an infraction of the Noahide Code. However, examination of Rambam's ruling in *Hilkhot Melakhim* 9:14 should dispel any doubt. Rambam rules that Noahides are required, by virtue of the *mizvah* of *dinin*, to establish a judicial system. The courts are required both to execute judgment and "to admonish the populace." The obligation "to admonish the populace" certainly establishes an obligation to exercise prior restraint. Although Rambam does not explicitly say that Noahides are empowered to use lethal force in preventing such infractions, it may well be argued that the Noahide court may use whatever coercive measures may be required in order to accomplish this end. Since the *mizvah* of *dinin* is incumbent not only upon an established judiciary, but also upon every individual Noahide, it follows that any Noahide may use lethal force, if necessary, to prevent the commission of a capital transgression by another Noahide.

Three other authorities, R. Isaac Schorr, *Teshuvot Tevu'ot Shor*, no. 20, p. 32b; R. Isaac Schmelkes, *Teshuvot Bet Yizḥak, Yoreh De'ah*, vol. II, no. 162, sec. 4; and R. Chaim Soloveitchik, *Ḥiddushei Rabbenu Ḥayyim ha-Levi al ha-Rambam, Hilkhot Rozeaḥ* 1:9, clearly say that Noahides no less than Jews are obligated to eliminate an aggressor in order to preserve the life of an intended victim. These authorities maintain that the law of pursuit constitutes an obligation binding upon Jew and non-Jew alike.

It may be inferred from Rambam's ruling, *Hilkhot Melakhim* 9:4, that a Noahide may execute a pursuer in order to preserve the victim. Jewish law specifies that if it is possible to preserve the life of the intended victim by merely maiming the pursuer it is forbidden to take the pursuer's life. However, should a Jew take the life of the pursuer when it is not absolutely necessary, Rambam, *Hilkhot Rozeaḥ* 1:13, rules that he is culpable only at the hands of Heaven but is not to be executed by a human court. In *Hilkhot Melakhim* 9:4, Rambam makes a distinction between a Jew and a Noahide regarding this provision, and rules that a Noahide who might have preserved the victim by merely maiming the aggressor is to be put to death for having taken a human life. The clear inference of this statement is that when it is necessary to take the life of the pursuer in order to preserve the victim, it is permissible, and perhaps even obligatory, for a Noahide to do so.[4]

The "law of pursuit" is certainly no less applicable when it is an entire community or nation that is pursued rather than an individual. Thus, military action is fully justified when undertaken either in self-defense or on behalf of a victim of aggression.

II. IS WAR SANCTIONED?

More fundamental is the question of whether there exists a general exclusion in the prohibition against homicide that justifies the taking of human life under conditions of war. Insofar as the Halakhah applicable to Jews is concerned there are obviously conditions, limited though they may be, under which this is the case. The various categories of obligatory war (*milḥemet mizvah*) and discretionary war (*milḥemet reshut*) encompass situations in which there is no immediate danger to the warring party. War is nevertheless permissible under at least certain restricted conditions even though the taking of human life is inevitable. These categories are, however, limited to Jews. The war against Amalek and the war for the conquest of *Erez Yisra'el* are wars that only Jews may undertake. A *milḥemet reshut*, or discretionary war, may be undertaken only upon the initiative of the monarch of the Jewish commonwealth with approval by the Sanhedrin and the *urim ve-tumim*. No analogous provision is found in Noahide law. It is therefore not surprising that virtually no discussion of whether a Noahide may legitimately engage in warfare is to be found in the writings of early authorities.

One latter-day authority does find grounds upon which to rule that non-Jews who engage in war are not guilty of murder. R. Naphtali Zevi Judah Berlin in his commentary on the Pentateuch, *Ha'amek Davar*, Genesis 9:5, finds dispensation for warfare in the very verse that prohibits homicide to the Sons of Noah: "And surely your blood of your lives will I require . . . and at the hand of man, at the hand of every man's brother, wilt I require the life of man." The phrase "at the hand of every man's brother" appears to be redundant, since it adds nothing to the preceding phrase "at the hand of

4 See, however. R. Yehudah Rosenbaum, *Teshuvot Ben Yehudah*, no. 21, cited by *Sedei Ḥemed, Klalim, ma'arekhet ha-gimel*, no. 44, who maintains that the "law of the pursuer" does not apply to Noahides. *Teshuvot Ben Yehudah* asserts that Rambam means to imply that only the pursued Noahide victim may kill his aggressor but that, under the Noahide Code, a third party has no right to intervene.

man." *Ha'amek Davar* understands this phrase as a limiting clause: "When is man punished? [If he commits homicide] when it is proper to behave in a brotherly manner." However, in a time of war, when animosity reigns among nations, the taking of life in the course of military activity is not punishable. Again, in *Ha'amek Davar,* Deuteronomy 20:8, this authority states that "even" a Jewish monarch may engage in battle, thereby implying that non-Jews are certainly not prohibited from doing so. Earlier, the Maharal of Prague, in his commentary on the Bible, *Gur Aryeh, Parashat Va-Yishlaḥ,* speaking of the action taken by the sons of Jacob against the inhabitants of Shechem, states that the family of Jacob constituted, in effect, a sovereign people and were permitted to do battle against another nation, since war is not forbidden under the Noahide Code. This position is, however, contradicted by a number of other authorities. R. Moses Sofer, *Teshuvot Ḥatam Sofer, Yoreh De'ah,* no. 19, declares wars of aggression to be forbidden to Noahides under all circumstances. In support of his position, *Ḥatam Sofer* cites the discussion found in *Sanhedrin* 59a. The Gemara declares that non-Jews do not enjoy the legal prerogatives of conquest (*lav benei kibush ninahu*). *Ḥatam Sofer* demonstrates that the Gemara, *Gittin* 38a, does indeed affirm that non-Jews, by virtue of the law of conquest, may acquire title to lands conquered in war. The phrase "*lav benei kibush*" must then be understood, argues *Ḥatam Sofer,* as meaning that non-Jews have no right to engage in wars of conquest even though *post factum* they may acquire title through conquest. R. Abraham Dov Ber Kahane, *Dvar Avraham,* vol. I, no. 11 and R. Menachem Ziemba, *Zera Avraham,* no. 24, advance the same argument. These authorities are in agreement with *Ḥatam Sofer* that non-Jews may not engage in wars of aggression under any circumstances.

III. JEWISH PARTICIPATION

Jewish participation in a war between non-Jews presents a complex problem. According to the authorities maintaining that Noahides are forbidden to wage wars of aggression, it follows that Jews are forbidden to participate in such wars. To aid and abet a non-Jew in transgressing the Noahide Code is a violation of the prohibition "Thou shall not place a stumbling block before the blind" (Leviticus 19:14). Moreover, it is clear that if the war is illicit for non-Jewish combatants there is no operative principle that conveys upon Jews the right to engage in battle. It is perhaps for this reason that *Tosafot, Avodah Zarah* 18b, cite the opinion of Rabbenu Elchanan, who rules that Jews may not participate in such wars.

R. Ze'ev Wolf Leiter, *Teshuvot Bet David,* no. 71, forbids voluntary enlistment in time of war because of the danger involved and describes the death of a soldier who does enlist as tantamount to suicide.[5] Rabbi Leiter also decries enlistment because the enlistee may take the lives of Jewish soldiers in the "enemy" army.[6] *Teshuvot Ḥatam Sofer*, vol. VI, no. 29, although also decrying voluntary enlistment, permits a conscript to hire a Jewish substitute. *Ḥatam Sofer* forbids enlistment because of the lack of kosher food in the armed forces and the necessity for violation of *Shabbat* restrictions, but fails to mention the intrinsic prohibition against military aggression, which he posits in the earlier cited responsum. This prohibition may have been omitted because *Ḥatam Sofer* intends his criticism to include peacetime enlistment and enlistment in armies engaged in wars of defense permitted to non-Jews. *Ḥatam Sofer* permits the hiring of a substitute only because the person hired would readily find others prepared to engage him as a mercenary and hence would in any event violate dietary and Sabbath restrictions![7]

Of particular import is the statement of *Mishnah Berurah* 329:17, who rules that Jews must allow themselves to be conscripted in accordance with the "law of the land."[8] The reason advanced is noteworthy: that the failure to do so will enrage the citizenry and may result in the loss of Jewish life. It is precisely this reason that Rema, *Oraḥ Ḥayyim* 334:25, gives in permitting a Jew to extinguish a fire on *Shabbat* even though the fire poses no danger to life. *Mishnah Berurah* does not discuss the legitimacy of war by non-Jews but permits Jews to participate simply as a matter of *pikuaḥ nefesh* (the overriding obligation to save a human life in jeopardy).

PART TWO: PREEMPTIVE WAR IN JEWISH LAW

I. COMMANDED WAR AND DISCRETIONARY WAR

The considerations of Jewish law and ethics as they apply to war in general, and Israel's incursion into Lebanon during the summer of 1982 in particular, are complex. Halakhah does recognize a category of war "to deliver Israel from the enemy." Such war is not only legitimate but also mandatory. Jewish

5 R. Meir Eisenstadt, *Teshuvot Imrei Esh, Yoreh De'ah*, no. 52, surprisingly permits voluntary enlistment despite the danger involved.

6 Rabbi Leiter also cites a narrative recorded by Josephus indicating that the inhabitants of Scythopolis forced the Jews among them to bear arms against fellow Jews in violation of Jewish law. See *The Life of Flavius Josephus*, sec. 6. See also *Or Zaru'a, Avodah Zarah*, ch. 1, no. 132.

7 Cf., however, *Mishneh le-Melekh, Hilkhot Malveh ve-Loveh* 4:2. It is of interest to note that in the same responsum *Ḥatam Sofer*, citing *Bava Batra* 8a, applauds the exemption of Yeshiva students from the draft. See also *Teshuvot Imrei Esh*, no. 52, who rules that "students of Torah" are exempt from conscription.

8 Cf. R. Samuel Turk, *Pri Malkah*, no. 64 and the response of R. Menasheh Klein, published in *Pri Malkah* as no. 65.

law also recognizes as a category of permissible war, wars undertaken in order "to diminish the heathens so that they shall not march against them." And, of course, Halakhah recognizes the legitimacy of self-defense, which need not be justified in terms of halakhically applicable categories of war. Any discussion of preemptive war in Halakhah must begin with an analysis of *Sotah* 44b, and of the exceedingly complex rabbinic commentaries thereto, as well as of the ruling of Rambam, *Hilkhot Melakhim* 5:1, which, as will be seen, lends itself to a variety of possible interpretations.

Jewish law recognizes two distinct types of war: *milḥemet miẓvah*, i.e., war commanded by the Torah and *milḥemet reshut*, i.e., war that is not commanded but that is permitted and hence "discretionary." The primary locus of the talmudic formulation of these two categories of war is the final Mishnah of the eighth chapter of *Sotah* and the accompanying discussion recorded in the Talmud, *Sotah* 44b. The Mishnah elucidates the scriptural verses that provide for a number of exemptions from military service. Deuteronomy 20:5–7 states:

> And the officers shall speak unto the people, saying: who is the man who has built a new house and has not begun living in it? Let him go and return to his house, lest he die in the battle and another man begin living in it. And who is the man who has planted a vineyard and has not redeemed [its fruit in the fourth year]? Let him go and return to his house, lest he die in the battle and another man redeem it. And who is the man who has betrothed a wife and has not taken her? Let him go and return to his house, lest he die in the battle and another man take her.[9]

The Mishnah concludes with the statement:

> To what does the foregoing apply? To discretionary wars, but in wars commanded by the Torah (*milḥamot miẓvah*) all go forth, even a bridegroom from his chamber and a bride from her canopy. R. Judah says: To what does the foregoing apply? To wars commanded by the Torah (*milḥamot miẓvah*), but in obligatory wars (*milḥamot ḥovah*) all go forth, even a bridegroom from his chamber and a bride from her canopy.[10]

[9] The immediately following verse, Deuteronomy 20:8, provides yet another exemption: "And the officers shall speak further unto the people and they shall say, who is the man who is fearful and faint-hearted? Let him go and return to his house, and let him not make the heart of his brethren faint as [is] his heart." This exclusion, however, applies to *milḥamot miẓvah* as well as to *milḥamot reshut*; see Radvaz, *Hilkhot Melakhim* 7:1, and commentaries *ad loc*.

[10] Regarding the apparent provision for conscription of women in obligatory wars see Radvaz, *Hilkhot Melakhim* 74:4, but cf. Rambam, *Sefer ha-Miẓvot*, introduction, concluding section of *shoresh* 14.

The Gemara, as understood both by Rashi and by Rambam in his *Commentary on the Mishnah*, establishes that no controversy exists between R. Judah and the Sages regarding the definition and scope of these basic categories. Insofar as the regulations specifically addressed by the Mishnah are concerned, the terms "*ḥovah*" ("obligatory") and "*mizvah*" ("commanded") are to all intents and purposes synonymous. All agree that wars waged by the House of David for the purpose of territorial expansion were discretionary and hence were governed by the provisions of Deuteronomy 20:5–7; similarly, all agree that the wars waged by Joshua for the conquest of the land of Canaan were obligatory and hence not governed by the provisions of Deuteronomy 20. Nevertheless, the Sages carefully employ the term "commanded" (*mizvah*) in speaking of the latter while R. Judah uses the term "obligatory" (*ḥovah*) with equal precision (rather than *mizvah*), even though both are in total agreement regarding the specific wars excluded from the provisions of Deuteronomy 20. The Gemara introduces a new category of war, *viz.*, wars "to diminish the heathens so that they shall not march against them," and posits a peripheral dispute between the Sages and R. Judah in order to explain their respective choice of nomenclature. The Gemara assumes that both the Sages and R. Judah agree that the provisions of Deuteronomy 20 apply not only to the wars of the House of David but also to preemptive strikes "to diminish the heathens so that they shall not march against them." The Sages regard such wars as "discretionary" because they are not undertaken in fulfillment of a biblical commandment and because such preemptive wars are conducted in the absence of any imminent danger. Accordingly, the Sages employ the terms "commanded" (*mizvah*) and "discretionary" (*reshut*) as antonyms. R. Judah, although he concedes that for statutory purposes such preemptive wars are included among the discretionary wars to which the provisions of Deuteronomy 20 apply, refuses to term them "discretionary"; R. Judah, despite the absence of an explicit biblical injunction, views the waging of such wars as constituting a *mizvah*. According to R. Judah, preventive war, although not obligatory, constitutes the fulfillment of a *mizvah* when necessary for purposes of security. Hence R. Judah finds it necessary to seek a different term to describe wars that are explicitly commanded by Scripture, e.g., the wars of Joshua for the conquest of Canaan. The latter are termed "mandatory" (*ḥovah*) by R. Judah. His use of the appellation "*mizvah*" in reference to preventive war notwithstanding, R. Judah concedes that only wars specifically mandated by Scripture are excluded from the provisions of Deuteronomy 20.

The Gemara seeks to discover a concrete halakhic application, as distinct from a purely semantic difference, of the issue that divides the Sages and R. Judah. A practical difference arising from their controversy is found by the

Gemara in the application of a general principle that provides that a person engaged in performing a *mizvah* is exempt from fulfilling other commandments. R. Judah considers the waging of preemptive war to constitute the fulfillment of a *mizvah*; hence, according to R. Judah, combatants are exempt from fulfilling other commandments while engaged in military duties associated with preemptive war. The Sages regard such incursions as discretionary and hence regard soldiers engaged in such battles as being fully obligated with regard to fulfillment of other commandments.[11]

[11] The text of the Gemara reads as follows:

> Said R. Yoḥanan: [A war that is designated as] permitted by the Sages is identical with [war that is designated as] commanded (*mizvah*) by R. Judah; [war that is designated as] commanded by the Sages is identical with [war that is designated as] obligatory (*ḥovah*) by R. Judah.
>
> Said Rava: All agree that the wars of Joshua to conquer [the land of Canaan] were obligatory [and] all agree that the wars of the House of David for territorial expansion were discretionary. They differ with regard to [wars for the purpose of] diminishing the heathens so that they shall not march against them. One [*viz.*, R. Judah] calls it commanded and one [*viz.*, the Sages] calls it permitted. The difference is with regard to [application of the principle that] one who is engaged in the performance of a commandment is exempt from the performance of [another] commandment.

The Gemara does not tell us explicitly whether it is R. Judah or the Sages who consider war "to diminish the heathens" to constitute a commanded war. Rashi and Rambam, in their respective commentaries, explain that R. Judah deems such war to be commanded while the Sages consider such war to be discretionary. (The interpretations of these authorities have been followed in the parenthetical interpretations within the translation above.) Indeed, Rashi's interpretation is taken directly from the words of R. Yoḥanan: "[A war that is designated as] permitted by the Sages is identical with [war that is designated as] commanded by R. Judah," i.e., there is a category of war that is deemed to be "commanded" by R. Judah while, according to the Sages, the identical war is merely "discretionary." The war in question is then identified by Rava as war "to diminish the heathens so that they shall not march against them." Thus there is no dispute between Rava and R. Yoḥanan; Rava merely amplifies the statement of R. Yoḥanan. According to both, the dispute between the Sages and R. Judah is with regard to whether participants in a war "to diminish the heathens" are exempt from fulfillment of other precepts. All are in agreement that the provisions of Deuteronomy 20:5–8 that apply to discretionary wars apply as well to war undertaken "to diminish the heathens."

This interpretation is contradicted by Me'iri in his commentary on *Sotah* 43a. Me'iri declares that it is the *Sages* who deem such war to be commanded while *R. Judah* regards it as merely "permitted." Of course, this understanding appears to be at variance with the statement recorded by the Gemara in the name of R. Yoḥanan.

R. Eliezer Waldenberg, *Hilkhot Medinah*, vol. II, *sha'ar* 4, ch. 1, secs. 2–3, explains that Me'iri must have posited a dispute between R. Yoḥanan and Rava: R. Yoḥanan declares the sole controversy between the Sages and R. Judah to be entirely a matter of nomenclature having no practical application; Rava contradicts this analysis and, referring directly to the Mishnah, declares that the Sages posit a "commanded" war that is governed by the selfsame regulation that applies to obligatory wars: the non-exclusion from military service of the individuals described in Deuteronomy 20. R. Judah, on the other hand, equates such war with "discretionary"

The question of whether a preemptive war is included in the category of *milḥemet mizvah* or *milḥemet reshut* is crucial for yet another aspect of

wars and maintains that those persons described in Deuteronomy 20 are conscripted only in obligatory wars but not for service in wars "to diminish the heathens." The phraseology employed by Rava, "The difference concerns [application of the principle that] one who is engaged in the performance of a commandment is exempt from the performance of [another] commandment" is understood by Me'iri as referring to exemption from an obligation associated with warfare itself, i.e., the obligation devolving upon those described in Deuteronomy 20 to recuse themselves from battle. That obligation is variously regarded as based upon the words expressed repeatedly in Deuteronomy 20, "let him go and return to his house," or the verse "he shall be free for his house one year" (Deuteronomy 24:5). See Rashi, Deuteronomy 20:7, *Sotah* 43a, and Rambam, *Hilkhot Melakhim* 7:10. The Sages regard participation in war "to diminish the heathens" as a *mizvah* and hence incumbent upon even those enumerated in Deuteronomy 20. Since participation in a war "to diminish the heathens" constitutes a *mizvah*, it exempts those enumerated in Deuteronomy 20 from the commandment to remove themselves from the battle arena.

[The Tosefta, *Sotah* 7:15, as apparently understood by Rashi, Deuteronomy 20:7, and Rambam, *Hilkhot Melakhim* 7:11, maintains that those exempt from conscription in *milḥamot reshut* may not serve even on a voluntary basis. See also the discussion in *Sotah* 44a concerning a prohibition against a bridegroom's participation in battle. Rabbi Waldenberg's analysis of Me'iri is apparently predicated upon this premise. One difficulty with this explanation lies in the fact that Rambam, on the basis of Sotah 44a, maintains that military service by such individuals involves, not a simple violation of a positive commandment, but transgression of two negative commandments: "When a man takes a wife he shall not go out in the army, nor shall he be charged with any matter" (Deuteronomy 24:5). The principle that one engaged in fulfillment of a *mizvah* is exempt from fulfillment of other precepts applies only to positive commandments but does not permit violation of negative precepts. (The usual explanation of why the exclusions from military service found in Deuteronomy 20 do not apply to commanded or obligatory wars is based upon rabbinic exegesis of the prefatory phrase in that section. "*Ki tezei la-milḥamah*" is understood to mean "*If* you go forth to war" rather than "*When* you go forth to war." The reference must then be to discretionary war since commanded war cannot be described in hypothetical terms.)]

See also *Sefer ha-Ḥinnukh*, no. 581, who apparently maintains that the exclusion of those enumerated in Deuteronomy 20 means simply that they cannot be compelled to perform military service but does not forbid voluntary enlistment. If so, the phrase "let him go and return to his house" cannot be understood as a *mizvah*. However, Rava's comment may be understood in an alternative manner. It may be understood to mean that the dispute between the Sages and R. Judah is *also* with regard to application of the principle that one who is engaged in fulfilling a commandment is exempt from fulfilling another commandment. It would be regarded as self-understood that exemption or non-exemption from participation in a war "to diminish the heathens" flows from its categorization as *mizvah* or *reshut*. See *Knesset ha-Gedolah, Hilkhot Melakhim*, ch. 5, appended to *Knesset ha-Gedolah*, vol. IV.]

Rabbi Waldenberg finds support for Me'iri's interpretation in the parallel discussion found in the Palestinian Talmud that reports that R. Yoḥanan declared that the dispute between the Sages and R. Judah is entirely one of nomenclature, while R. Ḥisda declared that there is a substantive dispute between them. The identical controversy, according to this analysis, is posited by the Babylonian Talmud as a dispute between R. Yoḥanan and Rava.

This analysis of Me'iri's comments yields a conclusion of crucial halakhic import. In this controversy the normative halakhah is decided in accordance with the majority position, i.e.,

Halakhah. The Mishnah, *Sanhedrin* 2a, stipulates that a discretionary war may be undertaken only upon the acquiescence of the Great Sanhedrin composed of seventy-one members. A subsequent Mishnah, *Sanhedrin* 20a, implies that only a monarch may undertake a discretionary war. Thus, a discretionary war cannot be justified unless undertaken by the king[12] with the permission of the Great Sanhedrin.[13] Moreover, in the context of a discussion of discretionary war, the Gemara, *Berakhot* 3b and *Sanhedrin* 16a, declares that the king may not undertake military action other than upon the approval of the *urim ve-tumim*.[14] Although in *Hilkhot Melakhim* Rambam fails to mention

that of the Sages. According to the interpretation of Me'iri, the Sages maintain that war to diminish the heathens is a *milḥemet miẓvah* rather than a *milḥemet reshut*.

It should, however, be noted that there is a distinct possibility that the text of the Me'iri's commentary contains a scribal error and that Me'iri actually wrote that war "to diminish the heathens" is a *milḥemet miẓvah* according to R. Judah but a *milḥemet reshut* for the Sages. In citing the text of Me'iri's remarks, R. Shlomoh Yosef Zevin, *Le-Or ha-Halakhah*, p. 13, makes precisely this correction without further comment.

Knesset ha-Gedolah, vol. IV, *Hilkhot Melakhim*, ch. 5, similarly explains that there is a dispute between R. Yoḥanan and Rava. According to *Knesset ha-Gedolah*, Rava declares that both the Sages and R. Judah maintain that war "to diminish the heathens" is a *milḥemet miẓvah* in the sense that the exemptions recorded in Deuteronomy 20 do *not* apply in its conduct. The sole dispute is whether combatants engaged in this warfare are exempt from fulfilling other precepts. According to the Sages they are exempt, while according to R. Judah they are not exempt. For that reason R. Judah terms such war *milḥemet reshut*, i.e., participants are not viewed as engaged in an activity exempting them from fulfilling other precepts. It is the view of *Knesset ha-Gedolah* that Rambam rules in accordance with the opinion of the Sages and includes preemptive war in the category of war "to deliver Israel from an enemy," which is classified by Rambam as a *milḥemet miẓvah*. This interpretation of Rambam is, however, contradicted by Rambam's own comments in his *Commentary on the Mishnah, Sotah* 8:7; see *infra*, note 22.

12 Ramban, addenda to Rambam's *Sefer ha-Miẓvot, miẓvot aseh*, no. 4, states that the requirement that war be undertaken only by a king must be understood as including not only a monarch but any sovereign authority. Thus he states that war may be undertaken by "a king, a judge or whosoever exercises jurisdiction over the people." For sources discussing Rambam's possible disagreement on this point, see *Contemporary Halakhic Problems*, vol. II, p. 207, note 27.

13 Rabbi Judah Gershuni, *Torah she-be-al Peh* (5731), vol. XIII, p. 150 f., advances the thesis that approval of the Sanhedrin is required only if the monarch finds it necessary to compel the populace to go to war and to conscript soldiers against their will, but that when the nation voluntarily agrees to go to battle approval of the Sanhedrin is not required. *Einayim la-Mishpat*, *Sanhedrin* 16a, advances a similar view. This view is supported by the comments of Me'iri, *Sanhedrin* 16a, who remarks that approval of the Sanhedrin is required in order to compel the populace to go out to battle. See also R. Abraham I. Kook, *Mishpat Kohen*, no. 145, and R. Saul Israeli, *Amud ha-Yemini*, no. 14 and no. 16, ch. 5, secs. 6–7. Cf. *Amud ha-Yemini*, no. 16, ch. 5, sec. 24.

14 Upon the twelve precious stones of the *urim ve-tumim* were engraved the names of the twelve tribes of Israel. In response to a specific query, various letters became illuminated. By means of the Divine Spirit the High Priest was enabled to combine the letters in order to discern the intended response.

consultation of the *urim ve-tumim* as a necessary precondition,[15] nevertheless, in the introduction to his *Sefer ha-Miẓvot, shoresh* 14, Rambam does state that a High Priest is required for the undertaking of war; i.e., the king and the Sanhedrin may not undertake military action other than upon acquiescence of the *urim ve-tumim* which is attached to the breastplate worn by the High Priest. Hence, absent a High Priest[16] who can consult the *urim ve-tumim*, offensive war in conformity with the stipulations of Jewish law is impossible. Ramban, in his addenda to Rambam's *Sefer ha-Miẓvot, miẓvot lo ta'aseh*, no. 17, declares that the requirement for consultation and approval of the *urim ve-tumim* is not limited to discretionary wars but applies with equal force to obligatory wars as well.[17]

Since no discretionary war could be undertaken other than upon approval of the *urim ve-tumim*, even discretionary war must be deemed to be undertaken with explicit divine approval and, conversely, no war could be undertaken other than with such divine sanction. Thus Abigail addresses King David and declares, "... for the Lord will certainly make such a sure house for my lord because my lord fights the battles of the Lord" (I Samuel 25:28). Rambam, *Hilkhot Melakhim* 7:15, cites this verse and applies it to discretionary wars in stating:

> And whosoever does battle with all his heart without fear and his intention is solely to sanctify the Name is assured that no harm will befall him and he will not meet with misfortune. He will build for himself a lasting house in Israel and he will acquire it for himself and for his children for eternity and he will merit life in the world to come as it is written, "For the Lord will surely make a sure house for my lord because my lord fights the battles of the Lord and evil is not found in you."

Moreover, many ritual prohibitions are suspended even when discretionary wars are fought. Thus, once a discretionary war has been undertaken, it is permissible to wage war on the Sabbath and combatants are permitted to partake of forbidden foods. The woman of "beautiful countenance" described in Deuteronomy 20:11 is permitted only to combatants engaged in discretionary wars but not to those engaged in commanded wars. It is thus clearly evident that even discretionary wars, when undertaken in accordance with the prescriptions of Halakhah, must be understood as undertaken by virtue of divine mandate. See *Hilkhot Medinah*, vol. II, *sha'ar* 4, ch. I, sec. 6. Indeed, *Mekom Shmu'el*, no. 8, suggests that the term "*reshut*" should be understood not as "permitted" or "discretionary" but as "licensed" or "sanctioned" in the sense that this kind of war requires *reshut Bet Din*, i.e., sanction of the Sanhedrin, as distinct from wars that are obligatory by reason of explicit scriptural mandate.

15 Cf. R. Yechiel Michel Epstein, *Arukh ha-Shulḥan he-Atid*, *Hilkhot Melakhim* 74:7, who suggests that even for discretionary wars consultation of the *urim ve-tumim*, although biblically mandated, is "perhaps" not a necessary condition of war. Although consultation of the *urim ve-tumim* constitutes a *miẓvah* and is required by virtue of biblical command, failure to engage in prior consultation, contends *Arukh ha-Shulḥan he-Atid*, does not affect the legitimacy of the war itself. See also *Le-Or ha-Halakhah*, p. 12, and cf. *Einayim la-Mishpat*, *Sanhedrin* 16a.

16 See, however, Rambam's reference to the function of the *urim ve-tumim* in *Hilkhot Klei ha-Mikdash* 10:11.

17 Rashi, in his commentary on the verse "and he shall stand before Eleazar the priest, who shall inquire for him by the decree of the Urim before the Lord" (Numbers 27:21), remarks that "even Joshua" was required to consult the *urim ve-tumim* "when he had need to go out to battle." Since the wars of Joshua were all commanded wars, i.e., for the conquest of the

Since both the Sages and R. Judah agree that war "to diminish the heathens" is discretionary rather than mandatory, it follows that preemptive war may be waged only by a sovereign with the approval of the Sanhedrin and permission of the *urim ve-tumim*. Rambam, *Sefer ha-Mizvot, shoresh* 14, expressly declares that "war and conquest of cities may not be other than by a king and upon the counsel of the Sanhedrin and a High Priest" and hence since *mizvot* associated with a "... king or a discretionary war ... are not incumbent other than during the existence of the Temple" it is self-understood that such *mizvot* cannot be fulfilled in our day. Thus, it would appear that, in our day, preemptive war "to diminish the heathens" cannot be sanctioned by Jewish law since, at present, there exists neither Sanhedrin nor *urim ve-tumim* to grant prior approval.

II. DEFENSIVE WAR

The concept of preemptive war and the situations in which such military action may be undertaken, even within the context of a *milḥemet reshut*, is the subject of considerable controversy among rabbinic commentators. A number of conflicting views center around the correct understanding of Rambam's formulation of this concept.

It might be anticipated that, in deciding between the conflicting views of R. Judah and the Sages, the normative halakhic ruling would be in accordance with the majority opinion, i.e., in accordance with the opinion of the Sages. Therefore, Rambam's formulation of the Halakhah is somewhat puzzling. In his *Mishneh Torah, Hilkhot Melakhim* 5:1, Rambam rules:

> The king may first wage only a *milḥemet mizvah*. What is a *milḥemet mizvah*? It is the war against the Seven Nations,[18] the war against Amalek and [a war]

territory inhabited by the Seven Nations, it must be inferred that Rashi agrees with Ramban in maintaining that consultation of the *urim ve-tumim* was necessary even in conjunction with commanded wars. See R. Judah Gershuni, *Mishpat ha-Melukhah, Hilkhot Melakhim* 5:2.

For a discussion of whether war against Amalek requires consultation of the *urim ve-tumim*, see R. Judah Gershuni, *Torah she-be-al Peh*, vol. XIII; cf. *Contemporary Halakhic Problems*, vol. I, pp. 16–18.

[18] The obligation to annihilate the Seven Nations assumes two distinct forms. A communal obligation to engage in war against those nations is here posited by Rambam, *Hilkhot Melakhim* 5:1, and by *Sefer ha-Ḥinnukh*, no. 425. A personal obligation to eliminate the members of those nations is formulated by Rambam, *Hilkhot Melakhim* 5:4, and by *Sefer ha-Ḥinnukh*, no. 425.

Various aspects of the commandment may be explained on the basis of this two-fold formulation. *Sefer ha-Ḥinnukh* declares that the obligation to annihilate the Seven Nations is incumbent upon both males and females equally and also expresses the view that the obligation is suspended when fulfillment would entail self-endangerment. *Minḥat Ḥinnukh* notes two apparent contradictions: (1) *Sefer ha-Ḥinnukh*, no. 525 and no. 603, in contradistinction to Rambam, *Sefer ha-Mizvot*, introduction, *shoresh* 14, rules that women are exempt from

(***Footnote 18 continued***)

participation in all wars including *milḥamot miẓvah*. (2) The waging of war, almost by definition, entails self-endangerment. Hence a commandment to wage war must be understood as explicitly requiring the placing of one's life at risk in fulfilling that obligation.

These problems are resolved if it is understood that the obligation is two-fold in nature: a communal obligation to wage war against the Seven Nations and a personal obligation to eliminate the members of those nations. Although women are exempt from conscription for purposes of engaging in communal warfare, they are required to eliminate members of the Seven Nations by virtue of their personal obligation. Conversely, in the absence of a state of war declared by the sovereign, no individual is obligated to endanger his life in an attempt to discharge his personal obligations with regard to eradication of the Seven Nations. See R. Moshe Sternbuch, *Mo'adim u-Zemanim*, vol. II, no. 164; R. Judah Gershuni, *Mishpat ha-Melukhah, Hilkhot Melakhim* 5:2; and R. Shlomoh Goren, *Torat ha-Mo'adim* (Tel Aviv, 5714), pp. 180 f.

One significant difficulty remains. The biblical source of the commandment to annihilate the Seven Nations is the injunction "you shall utterly destroy them" (Deuteronomy 7:2 and Deuteronomy 20:7). These biblical passages might well be interpreted as establishing either a communal or a personal obligation; it is difficult to deduce a two-fold obligation from a single phrase.

In order to resolve this difficulty, it should first be noted that in delineating a *millḥemet miẓvah* the Gemara, *Sotah* 44b, speaks of the "wars of Joshua to conquer," i.e., war for the conquest of the land of Canaan. Rambam, *Hilkhot Melakhim* 5:1, speaks, not of conquest of the land of Canaan, but of war against the Seven Nations. Of course, conquest of the land of Canaan involved war against the indigenous inhabitants, *viz.*, the Seven Nations. However, Rambam's substitution of his own terminology for that of the Gemara is significant in that it places negative emphasis upon such war as serving to destroy the Seven Nations rather than upon its positive aspect as a war for the conquest of the Land of Israel.

Conquest of the land of Canaan as an end in itself, as well as settlement in the Land of Israel, is deemed by Ramban to be mandated by the verse "And you shall drive out the inhabitants of the land and dwell therein" (Numbers 33:53). See Ramban, *Commentary on the Bible, ad loc.*, and *idem, Sefer ha-Miẓvot, miẓvot aseh*, addenda, no. 4. Rambam, as is well known, fails to record any positive commandment predicated upon that verse. Hence it may be assumed that, for Rambam, neither settlement in the Land of Israel nor conquest of the territory so designated constitutes a *miẓvah*. (See, however, *Megillat Esther, Sefer ha-Miẓvot, miẓvot aseh*, addenda, no. 4, who asserts that Rambam understands this passage as establishing a commandment to conquer the land, but that this commandment was binding only upon the generation of the original conquest rather than for posterity.) Indeed, Rashi understands the verse as constituting only prudent counsel, *viz.*, in order to assure permanence of settlement it is necessary first to drive out the inhabitants. See *Contemporary Halakhic Problems*, vol. II, pp. 193–99. It may be suggested that Rambam views the first clause of this passage as a commandment or, more precisely, as an amplification of the commandment recorded elsewhere, *viz.*, "you shall utterly destroy them." The latter passage establishes a personal obligation with regard to annihilation of the Seven Nations. That obligation is quite independent of considerations of settlement. *Sefer ha-Ḥinnukh* explains that eradication of paganism is the rationale underlying the commandment "you shall utterly destroy them." Indeed, the commandment is presented in precisely that context both in Deuteronomy 7 and in Deuteronomy 20. "You shall drive out the inhabitants of the land and dwell therein" may well have been understood by Rambam as a reiteration of the commandment recorded in Deuteronomy 7:2 and Deuteronomy 20:7 and hence this injunction is not enumerated by Rambam as a new commandment. However, in

> to deliver Israel from an enemy who has attacked them (*she-ba aleihem*). Thereafter he may wage a *milḥemet reshut*, which is a war against other people in order to enlarge the borders of Israel and to enhance his greatness and prestige.[19]

Rambam employs the terms *milḥemet mizvah* and *milḥemet reshut* in establishing dichotomous categories in accordance with the nomenclature adopted by the Sages. The Sages, it will be remembered, regarded a preemptive war "to diminish the heathens so that they shall not march against them" as being entirely in the nature of a discretionary war and hence had no need to introduce a third term, *viz.*, *milḥemet ḥovah*, in order to distinguish between preemptive war and war for the conquest of Canaan. The term "*milḥemet ḥovah*" is employed only by R. Judah in order to distinguish the various "commanded" wars from preemptive war.[20]

Rambam's formulation is puzzling on two counts: (1) Rambam fails to state that preemptive wars are discretionary and hence can be undertaken only by a monarch with the approval of the Sanhedrin. Indeed, Rambam completely fails to rule upon or to record the status of preemptive war.[21] (2) Among

Numbers 33:53 an entirely different *telos* is presented, *viz.*, "and dwell therein": Annihilation of the Seven Nations makes permanence of settlement a greater likelihood. Since, according to Rambam, residence in the Land of Israel is not a personal obligation, establishment of a permanent settlement must be a matter of communal concern. Hence "You shall drive out the inhabitants of the land" (in contradistinction to "you shall utterly destroy them") must also be addressed to the community in general rather than to individuals *qua* individuals. Thus the communal obligation to wage war against the Seven Nations is derived from Numbers 33:53 but is not deemed by Rambam to be a distinct *mizvah*. Rather, he regards it as merely supplementary to the general commandment formulated in Deuteronomy 7:2 and Deuteronomy 20:7 that establishes a personal obligation.

19 Rashi, *Sotah* 44b, describes the "wars of the House of David" as wars "which he fought in Aram Zoba in order to annex it to the Land of Israel and against others of his neighbors in order that they bring him tribute and servants to do taskwork." A literal reading of a narrative reported in *Berakhot* 3b and *Sanhedrin* 16a would yield the inference that a *milḥemet reshut* may be undertaken for economic reasons; see, however, *infra*, notes 50 and 59.

20 See *Leḥem Mishneh, ad loc.*

21 A novel view with regard to the purposes for which a *milḥemet reshut* may be undertaken is presented by R. Iser Zalman Meltzer, *Even ha-Azel, Hilkhot Melakhim* 5:1, on the basis of an inference from the phraseology employed by Rambam in his *Commentary on the Mishnah*. *Even ha-Azel* asserts that the Gemara focuses upon war "to diminish the heathens" only because of the need to categorize such warfare as *milḥemet mizvah* according to R. Judah. *Milḥamot reshut*, argues *Even ha-Azel*, are not circumscribed by specifically enumerated motives. Rather, since approval of the Sanhedrin is required for a *milḥemet reshut*, it is to be presumed that such permission will not be forthcoming unless there exists good and sufficient reason for waging war. Rambam, in his *Mishneh Torah*, omits all reference to war "to diminish the heathens," explains *Even ha-Azel*, because, according to the Sages who view hostilities undertaken for that purpose as a *milḥemet reshut*, such motivation is not of unique halakhic significance. However, this explanation does not really resolve the problem of Rambam's omission of this

milḥamot mizvah Rambam posits a category of war for which there is no apparent talmudic reference: "[a war] to deliver Israel from an enemy."

A facile solution to both problems might be found were it to be assumed that by "[a war] to deliver Israel from an enemy" Rambam intended simply to reformulate the Gemara's concept of a preemptive war.[22] However, that interpretation of Rambam's statement cannot be sustained for three reasons: (1) The appropriate canons of halakhic decision-making require a ruling in accordance with the majority opinion, i.e., in accordance with the opinion of the Sages. (2) If Rambam rules in accordance with R. Judah's opinion it would have been necessary for him to employ terminology distinguishing between *milḥemet mizvah* and *milḥemet ḥovah*. (3) Finally, according to R. Judah a preemptive war is analogous to war against the Seven Nations and against Amalek and, since it does fulfill a *mizvah*, participants in it are exempted from fulfilling other commandments. Nevertheless, even according to R. Judah, waging preemptive war requires a monarch and the consent of the Sanhedrin. Since, in the very next paragraph, *Hilkhot Melakhim* 5:2, Rambam states that the wars he has categorized as *milḥamot mizvah* do not require consent of the Sanhedrin, it is clear that war "to deliver Israel from an enemy" is not identical with the war depicted by the Gemara as undertaken "to diminish the heathens so that they shall not march against them."

Moreover, the phraseology employed by Rambam in this context – "*she-ba aleihem*" – although not unequivocal, is most readily understood as referring to defensive warfare in response to an armed attack rather than as referring to a preemptive strike. Thus *Ḥazon Ish, Oraḥ Ḥayyim-Mo'ed* 114:2, carefully defines the term "*she-ba aleihem*" as meaning "*she-kvar ba aleihem*" – "who has *already* attacked them."[23] This interpretation of Rambam is reflected in

category of *milḥemet reshut* since Rambam does find it necessary to refer specifically to other considerations for which a *milḥemet reshut* may be undertaken.

[22] Precisely such an interpretation is offered by *Knesset ha-Gedolah*, vol. IV, *Hilkhot Melakhim*, ch. 5. *Knesset ha-Gedolah* understands the phrase "the deliverance of Israel from an enemy *she-ba aleihem*" as meaning "the enemy who comes (i.e., who is about to come) upon them." *Knesset ha-Gedolah* suggests that this concept is synonymous with the category of war "to diminish the heathens so that they shall not march against them" discussed in *Sotah* 44b. Moreover, *Knesset ha-Gedolah* interprets the Gemara's discussion in a manner entirely at variance from that of Rashi and other commentaries with the result that a war "to diminish the heathens" is described as a *milḥemet mizvah* according to the Sages; see *supra*, note 11. *Knesset ha-Gedolah* himself concedes that this interpretation of the talmudic discussion is tortured and concludes by saying, "But what can I do, for the difficulty with the words of our master [Rambam] brought me to this."

[23] Cf., however, *Arukh ha-Shulḥan he-Atid*, *Hilkhot Melakhim* 74:4, who apparently understands the phrase "*she-ba aleihem*" as meaning "who is coming upon them" and declares that Rambam's ruling applies only in situations in which "there exists a suspicion that they will attack

the comments of an early authority, R. Menachem ha-Me'iri, in his *Bet ha-Beḥirah, Sotah* 43a. Me'iri indicates that the controversy between the Sages and R. Judah is limited to preemptive war against a potential aggressor. However, asserts Me'iri, in a situation in which an attack is already underway, all agree that military action in response constitutes an obligatory war. Me'iri writes, "[R. Judah and the Sages] disagree only when they go to war against their enemies because they fear lest [their enemies] attack or when it is known by them that the enemies are preparing themselves [for attack]," thereby implying that once the attack has commenced a defensive military response constitutes an obligatory war.

There is also a discrepancy between Rambam's definition of *milḥemet reshut* and the description of such war recorded by the Gemara. The Gemara, *Sotah* 44b, speaks of *milḥemet reshut* as "the wars of the House of David for territorial expansion (*le-revaḥah*)," while Rambam speaks of war, not only "to enlarge the borders of Israel," but also "to enhance [the monarch's] greatness and prestige."

Leḥem Mishneh endeavors to resolve these difficulties by interpreting Rambam's categorization of war "to enhance [the monarch's] greatness and prestige" as coextensive with war described by the Gemara as designed "to diminish the heathens so that they shall not march against them." The phrase "to enhance his greatness and prestige" is understood by *Leḥem Mishneh*, not as a reference to vainglorious considerations, but to war undertaken in order to instill fear in potential enemies so that they refrain from attack. War of this nature can, of course, be undertaken only with the approval of the Sanhedrin and the consent of the *urim ve-tumim*. Rambam, then, according to *Leḥem Mishneh*, rules in accordance with the opinion of the Sages and does not fail to include preemptive war in the category of *milḥemet reshut*.

Leḥem Mishneh's equation of Rambam's phrase "to enhance his greatness and prestige" with the Gemara's notion of a war "to diminish the heathens so that they shall not march against them" broadens the latter category so greatly

us." It is difficult to reconcile this statement of *Arukh ha-Shulḥan he-Atid* with *Arukh ha-Shulḥan he-Atid*'s own statement in the immediately preceding section, *Hilkhot Melakhim* 74:3, in which, in a different context, he categorizes preemptive action under the identical circumstances as a *milḥemet reshut* rather than as a *milḥemet mizvah*. *Arukh ha-Shulḥan he-Atid* declares that the categorization of such war in *Sotah* 44b as *milḥemet reshut* is solely for the purpose of excluding from military service those individuals described in Deuteronomy 20:5–8; however, in the case of military response to a potential aggressor, *Arukh ha-Shulḥan he-Atid* maintains that all agree that it is a *milḥemet mizvah*. Cf., also, *Amud ha-Yemini*, no. 16, ch. 5, sec. 25 and *infra*, note 31.

as to make it all-inclusive.[24] The Gemara's phrase certainly has the connotation that the heathens against whom the preemptive strike is undertaken constitute at least a potential danger. However, according to *Leḥem Mishneh*'s understanding, terrorizing even nations possessing no capacity for harm would be justified as a *milḥemet reshut* on the grounds that it is designed to instill fear in all and sundry.

Leḥem Mishneh's analysis of Rambam's views yields but one of a number of definitions of "war to diminish the heathens" and hence constitutes one of a number of positions on the permissibility of preemptive war. *Shiyurei Korban* (addenda to *Korban ha-Edah*, a standard commentary on the Palestinian Talmud) advances a more restrictive definition of war "to diminish the heathens so that they shall not march against them." *Shiyurei Korban*, Palestinian Talmud, *Sotah* 8:10, defines as a *milḥemet reshut* a war undertaken "against neighbors in the fear that with the passage of time they will wage war [against Israel]; therefore [the king] wages war against them at the present time in order to decimate them so that they not possess the might to attack Israel." According to *Shiyurei Korban*, preemptive war is warranted even in the absence of any fear of imminent attack, but is justified only when directed against a potential aggressor and designed to thwart the development of a capacity for attack.

The definitions of war "to diminish the heathens" presented both by *Leḥem Mishneh* and by *Shiyurei Korban* are contradicted by Rambam's statement in his *Commentary on the Mishnah*, *Sotah* 8:7. In explaining the controversy between R. Judah and the Sages, Rambam, according to the standard Ibn Tibbon translation of the *Commentary on the Mishnah*, declares, "But they disagree only about killing those who kill them in order to weaken them so that they will not kill [the people of] Israel and not do battle in their land." As depicted in this source, the war in question is hardly preemptive; it is directed against "those who kill them" and hence, in common parlance, would be termed a defensive war. If understood literally, Rambam here declares war against "those who kill them" to be a *milḥemet reshut* requiring for its conduct a king, Sanhedrin and *urim ve-tumim* and hence precluded in our day. According to this position, military action that is entirely preemptive does not qualify even as a *milḥemet reshut* and hence is never legitimate.

[24] See *Arukh ha-Shulḥan he-Atid, Hilkhot Melakhim* 74:3. *Arukh ha-Shulḥan he-Atid* states that the phrase "so that they shall not march against them" contradicts *Leḥem Mishneh*'s assumption and "clearly implies that they hear of this and have some indication that this is indeed the case"; absent such indication even a *milḥemet reshut* would not be warranted. See also *Ḥazon Ish, Oraḥ Ḥayyim-Mo'ed* 114:2.

Apart from the conceptual difficulties associated with a position that regards defensive action as subject to the restrictions placed upon a *milḥemet reshut*, a literal reading of the Ibn Tibbon text of the *Commentary on the Mishnah* is contradicted by Rambam's own earlier-cited statement in *Hilkhot Melakhim* 5:1 in which Rambam enumerates war "to deliver Israel from an enemy that has attacked them" as an instance of *milḥemet mizvah*.

These apparently contradictory statements may perhaps be reconciled if due consideration is given to the concluding phrase found in the *Commentary on the Mishnah*: ". . . so that they will not kill [the People of] Israel and not do battle in their land." Although the explanation is somewhat tenuous, the contradiction is resolved if we postulate that Rambam views such wars as discretionary only when required for defense at a time when the enemy has not yet penetrated the territory of the Land of Israel, as is evidenced by the words "and not do battle *in their land*." Rambam's statement in the *Mishneh Torah* describing war "to deliver Israel from an enemy" as a mandatory war would then be understood as restricted solely to defensive war conducted within the boundaries of the Land of Israel.[25] According to this analysis, military action designed only to defend the populace is categorized as discretionary; war for defense of the territorial integrity of the Land of Israel constitutes an obligatory war just as the original conquest of *Erez Yisra'el* is categorized a *milḥemet mizvah*.

This resolution of the apparent contradiction in Rambam's statements is far from incontrovertible.[26] The difficulty might well be resolved differently by reinterpreting Rambam's phraseology in the *Commentary on the Mishnah*. It is therefore not at all surprising to find that *Ḥazon Ish, Oraḥ Ḥayyim-Mo'ed* 114:2, understands the phrase "those who kill them," employed by Rambam in his *Commentary on the Mishnah*, to define war "to diminish the heathens" as referring, not to a situation in which Israel is under attack, but to one in which "they kill [people of] Israel intermittently but do not engage in battle . . . but

[25] Precisely such an interpretation of Rambam's statement in the *Mishneh Torah* is advanced by R. Ovadiah Hedaya, *Talpiyot*, vol. III, no. 3–4 (Nisan 5708), pp. 381–82, on entirely different grounds. See also R. Raphael Katzenellenbogen, *No'am*, vol. XVI (5733), p. 45 ff.

[26] This understanding of Rambam seems to be contradicted by *Eruvin* 45a. See our discussion in Section III and *infra*, note 39. Cf. R. Raphael Katzenellenbogen, *No'am*, vol. XVI, p. 45 ff. Moreover, as demonstrated in J. David Bleich, *Contemporary Halakhic Problems*, vol. II, pp. 193–99, there is strong reason to assume that Rambam maintains that conquest of the territory of the Land of Israel (as distinct from annihilation of the Seven Nations) either does not constitute a *mizvah* or, more likely, constituted a *mizvah* only during the period of the original conquest. See also *supra*, note 18. In addition, the term "*ezrat Yisra'el*" employed by Rambam appears to connote aid rendered to people rather than the defense of territory.

when they come upon an individual Jew or a group [of Jews] they kill him." The situation depicted by *Ḥazon Ish* is roughly analogous to a war of attrition. According to *Ḥazon Ish*, then, participation in military action in response to a war of attrition, although it does not constitute a *milḥemet ḥovah*, does, nevertheless, constitute fulfillment of a *mizvah* according to R. Judah, who, as will be remembered, describes war "to diminish the heathens" as a *milḥemet mizvah*. *Ḥazon Ish*, in his subsequent comments, seemingly has no difficulty in refusing to equate response to a war of attrition with defensive action against an enemy engaged in formal battle that is deemed obligatory. *Ḥazon Ish* does, however, express ignorance of any possible consideration that might explain the Sages' refusal to designate such action as constituting the fulfillment of a *mizvah*.

The Kapaḥ edition of Rambam's *Commentary on the Mishnah* contains an entirely different reading. According to that version, Rambam declares, "They disagree only about a war against nations that wage war against [Israel] in order to weaken [those nations]." The situation described cannot be understood as one involving actual hostilities against Israel because, as stated by Me'iri, a war of defense constitutes a *milḥemet mizvah* even according to the Sages. Such a defensive war is recognized by Rambam himself as a *milḥemet mizvah*, as indicated by his inclusion of war "to deliver Israel from an enemy who has attacked them" in the category of *milḥemet mizvah* in his codification of this concept in the *Mishneh Torah*. Hence the situation depicted as a *milḥemet reshut* undertaken "to diminish the heathens so that they shall not march upon them" must involve circumstances in which the heathens have as yet not engaged in actual hostilities but have announced their aggressive intentions or have made them readily apparent.[27] The circumstances depicted in the

27 Rema's ruling is, of course, entirely consistent with the position espoused by *Arukh ha-Shulḥan he-Atid*. However, as noted earlier, the preponderance of rabbinic authority is *contra* the position of *Arukh ha-Shulḥan he-Atid*. Thus, for example, *Ḥazon Ish*, as noted, declares that war "to deliver Israel from an enemy" constitutes a *milḥemet mizvah* only when the enemy has actually "come upon them" – terminology directly contradictory to that employed by Rema.

It should be noted that, in a statement dated Tammuz 9, 5742, the Chief Rabbinate Council of the State of Israel declared the war of *Shalom ha-Galil* to constitute a *milḥemet mizvah*. The war is described as necessary "to deliver Israel from an enemy" and Rema, *Oraḥ Ḥayyim* 330:6, is cited as broadening this category to encompass deliverance from a putative attack. It is, however, difficult to determine whether that proclamation is intended to be understood as halakhic or hortative in nature. The same statement continues with a discussion of the conduct of the Israeli Defense Forces and cites the verse "and your camp shall be holy" (Deuteronomy 23:15) in what can only be described as a homiletic vein. In its halakhic context, Deuteronomy 23:15 constitutes an exhortation to implement certain hygienic measures. This statement was published in its entirety in the *Algemeiner Journal*, July 16, 1982, p. 5. An English translation appeared in the *London Jewish Chronicle*, July 23, 1982, p. 35.

Kapaḥ version of the *Commentary on the Mishnah* are roughly the equivalent of a state of belligerence as distinct from a state of war.

Regardless of which text of Rambam's *Commentary on the Mishnah* is accepted as authentic, it is clear that, contrary to *Leḥem Mishneh*, war for the purpose of creating a climate of fear could not be sanctioned even as a *milḥemet reshut*; nor, contrary to the position of *Shiyurei Korban*, would Rambam sanction, even as a *milḥemet reshut*, military action undertaken simply to prevent a military build-up.

Me'iri, in his commentary on *Sotah* 43a, adopts a definition of war "to diminish the heathens" that is broader than that formulated by Rambam. Me'iri defines war "to diminish the heathens so that they shall not march against them" as an action undertaken by Israel "against their enemies because they fear lest [their enemies] attack or when it is known that the [enemies] are preparing themselves for attack." Me'iri's definition encompasses not only a declared state of belligerence but also a situation involving a military build-up or a situation in which it is known that the enemy is otherwise actively engaged in preparing for an attack. However, absent clear aggressive design on the part of the enemy, a military response does not qualify as a *milḥemet reshut* and is illegitimate even according to R. Judah.

In summary it may be stated that six diverse definitions of the category of war "to diminish the heathens so that they shall not march against them" may be gleaned from the writings of rabbinic commentators:

1. According to a literal reading of the *Ibn Tibbon* translation of Rambam's *Commentary on the Mishnah*, such military activity is sanctioned as a discretionary war against "those who kill them," i.e., if the enemy has actually been engaged in the taking of Jewish lives.
2. According to *Ḥazon Ish*, who understands Rambam to be referring to a situation in which "they kill [people of] Israel intermittently but do not engage in battle," only military response to a war of attrition is sanctioned as a discretionary war.
3. According to the Kapaḥ edition of the *Commentary on the Mishnah*, pre-emptive action is legitimate as a discretionary war only against "nations that wage war against [Israel]," i.e., against nations with whom a state of belligerence already exists.
4. According to Me'iri, such war is discretionary when there is cogent reason "to fear lest [their enemies] attack or when it is known that the [enemies] are preparing themselves for attack," i.e., in response to a military build-up or when it is known that the enemy is otherwise actively engaged in preparing to attack.

5. According to *Shiyurei Korban*, a preemptive strike is a legitimate form of discretionary war when directed against a potential aggressor in order to prevent the enemy from developing a military capability.
6. According to *Leḥem Mishneh*, military hostilities directed against any foreign power are justified as a form of discretionary war when designed to demonstrate military superiority in order to instill fear in potential aggressors.

In arriving at a normative halakhic ruling in light of these conflicting positions, consideration must be given to the fact that the last two definitions of war "to diminish the heathens," both of which are extremely broad, are opinions advanced by latter-day scholars that are not authoritative when contradicted by the statements of authoritative early decisors such as Rambam and Me'iri.

It must be reiterated that, even when sanctioned by Halakhah, preemptive war is a *milḥemet reshut*. Since a *milḥemet reshut* is precluded in our day, a resolution of the conflict between the various authorities who seek to define the concept of a war "to diminish the heathens" is not a matter that demands normative resolution, because, regardless of how the term is defined, no *milḥemet reshut* may be waged in the absence of a king, a Sanhedrin and the *urim ve-tumim*.[28] Military action in the guise of a *milḥemet reshut* requires a sovereign, at whose sole initiative such a war may be undertaken,[29] prior permission of a Sanhedrin[30] and acquiescence of the *urim ve-tumim*. Moreover, puzzling as his position may be, Rambam, in his codification of the law in the *Mishneh Torah*, neglects to enumerate preemptive war as a form of *milḥemet reshut*, thereby apparently rendering it illicit under all circumstances.

Accordingly, since discretionary war cannot be sanctioned in our day due to the absence of a Sanhedrin and the *urim ve-tumim*, it might appear that a definitive decision about the legitimate parameters of "war to diminish the heathens" is of no practical concern. This, however, is not entirely the case. We are confronted with two distinct categories of war: war "to diminish the heathens" and war designed to "deliver Israel from an enemy." Excluding wars of aggression, these categories appear to be dichotomous. Wars that are not to be categorized as designed "to diminish the heathens" would then be encompassed within the category of war "to deliver Israel from an enemy." Military action categorized as designed "to deliver Israel from an enemy" is a *milḥemet mizvah*. Thus, for example, according to *Kapaḥ*'s version of the

[28] See *Mishpat Kohen*, no. 145; *Le-Or ha-Halakhah*, p. 10; and *Amud ha-Yemini*, no. 16, ch. 5, sec. 4.

[29] See *supra*, note 12.

[30] See *supra*, note 13.

Commentary on the Mishnah, war against a professed enemy who poses no immediate danger is discretionary, but hostilities undertaken "when it is known that the [enemies] are preparing themselves for attack" would be a *milḥemet mizvah*, while according to Me'iri it would be in the nature of a *milḥemet reshut*.

This point is important in understanding what must be regarded as a seventh opinion on the distinction between war "to diminish the heathens" and war "to deliver Israel from an enemy." R. Yechiel Michel Epstein, *Arukh ha-Shulḥan he-Atid, Hilkhot Melakhim* 74:3–4, addresses Rambam's omission of any reference to war "to diminish the heathens" in his *Mishneh Torah* and resolves the question in a manner that yields a completely different understanding of the applicable Halakhah. *Arukh ha-Shulḥan he-Atid* asserts that the dispute between the Sages and R. Judah about the proper categorization of a war "to diminish the heathens" is limited solely to the issue of whether the bridegroom must go forth from his chamber and the bride from her canopy. But, asserts *Arukh ha-Shulḥan he-Atid*, all agree that, even according to the Sages, the king is obligated to engage in battle, not only to defend Israel against overt aggression, but also against potential aggressors "even when there is [only] a suspicion that they may attack us." Contrary to the interpretation of *Ḥazon Ish*, *Arukh ha-Shulḥan he-Atid* argues that Rambam's phraseology in the Mishneh Torah, "war . . . to deliver Israel from an enemy *she-ba aleihem*," refers not only to an enemy who has already attacked Israel but also to an enemy who is suspected of harboring aggressive intentions. Rambam describes war "to deliver Israel from an enemy *she-ba aleihem*" as commanded and, according to *Arukh ha-Shulḥan he-Atid*, that categorization includes war against a suspected enemy as well.

It must however be stated that *Arukh ha-Shulḥan he-Atid*'s analysis of Rambam's position is not paralleled in any other commentary. According to both Me'iri and *Ḥazon Ish*, war "to deliver Israel from an enemy" is legitimate only in response to an overt act of aggression.

III. RESPONSE TO DANGER

The conclusion that war "to deliver Israel from an enemy" is legitimate only in response to an overt act of aggression appears to be contradicted by Rema, *Oraḥ Ḥayyim* 229:6. *Shulḥan Arukh* codifies the ruling found in the Gemara, *Eruvin* 45a, that it is permissible, even on the Sabbath, to attack non-Jews who besiege Jewish cities when they threaten the lives of Jews and, in the case of a border city, even if they are intent only upon plunder or economic gain. Rema, in his gloss, appends a comment indicating that this ruling applies "even if they have as yet not come but they intend to come." The obvious import of Rema's comment is that a preemptive response is warranted, on the Sabbath no less than on weekdays, even if the enemy has not engaged in an overt hostile act. In light of the preceding discussion, such a situation could justify only a *milḥemet reshut*. But, since a *milḥemet reshut* is precluded in our day, it is difficult to explain the legitimacy of military action that is entirely preemptive in nature.[31]

However, if the source cited by Rema is examined carefully a different conclusion may be drawn. Rema's ruling is derived from *Or Zaru'a, Hilkhot Shabbat* 84:13. The phraseology employed by *Or Zaru'a* is extremely instructive:

> in a city close upon the border even if they come only for matters of hay and straw one goes out against them with arms and violates the Sabbath because of them . . . And no distinction should be made between a situation in which they have already besieged [the city] and [a situation in which] they say they intend to come and plunder; rather, when the news (*kol*, voice) goes forth that they intend to come to plunder, even though they have as yet not come, it is permissible to transport arms to safeguard [the city] and to generate a tumult in the city so that they shall not come, for it is not necessary to be cautious in [situations requiring] preservation of life.

A careful examination of the text shows that *Or Zaru'a* posits two distinct rulings. The first permits military hostilities even on the Sabbath. In that context the reference is solely to an enemy actively conducting a siege. The second contains a statement explicitly negating any distinction between an enemy actually engaged in a siege and one that merely contemplates hostile action. However, in the latter context, *Or Zaru'a* makes no mention of any military action. On the contrary, he refers only to bearing arms, i.e., transporting arms through a public thoroughfare, for the purpose of creating a tumult in order to frighten the enemy so that he will not act upon his malevolent designs. *Or Zaru'a* thus formulates two distinct rules: (1) An armed attack is warranted only when the enemy has actually commenced hostilities; only then is military action designed to take human life permitted as a *milḥemet miẓvah* "to deliver Israel from an enemy." This is a ruling that is encompassed within the rubric of *hilkhot milḥamah* – the laws of war: defensive war is proper and legitimate

[31] *Amud ha-Yemini*, no. 16, ch. 5, sec. 25, notes this contradiction and, in effect, rules in accordance with *Or Zaru'a* as against Me'iri. However, *Amud ha-Yemini* fails to analyze the various definitions of war "to diminish the heathens" that distinguish such undertakings from defensive war and hence serve to delineate the latter category as well.

in response to an attack.[32] (2) Preemptive action that does not entail the taking of life but only the violation of Sabbath restrictions is entirely permissible. Thus, arms may be donned and transported on the Sabbath, not for attack, but in order to frighten the enemy. This is a ruling encompassed within the rubric of *hilkhot Shabbat* – the laws of Sabbath: violation of Sabbath restrictions for preemptive purposes is permissible. The distinction is summed up in the final phrase: "for it is not necessary to be cautious (*ein medakdekin*) with regard to the preservation of life." Sabbath laws are suspended even upon a remote possibility of the loss of human life; however, the taking of life in the course of a war to "deliver Israel from an enemy" is warranted only in response to actual aggression.[33]

Rema's comment is culled from *Or Zaru'a*'s second ruling and presented in the context of *hilkhot Shabbat*. Rema appends his comment directly to the phrase "and one may violate the Sabbath because of them." The import of his gloss is that one may violate the Sabbath, not only in response to actual aggression, but also even in response to a presumed threat of aggression. However, Rema sanctions only the violation of Sabbath restrictions, e.g., transport of arms; nowhere does he sanction actual warfare in the absence of overt hostilities.

Accordingly, neither the statement of *Or Zaru'a* nor that of Rema serves to negate the conclusion that war is legitimate only in response to an overt act of aggression.[34]

IV. SELF-DEFENSE AS DISTINCT FROM WAR

Limiting the category of *milḥemet mizvah* to situations in which the enemy has already exhibited aggressive conduct (in the terminology of *Ḥazon Ish*: *she-kvar ba aleihem*) does not necessarily yield the conclusion that a potential aggressor must be permitted the advantage of the first strike. A limited form of preemptive action may be justified on much more elementary grounds than either *milḥemet mizvah* or *milḥemet reshut*. In order to elucidate this point, let us return to an earlier noted difficulty with Rambam's formulation of the various categories of *milḥemet mizvah*.

[32] Actually, *Or Zaru'a*'s first ruling need not be regarded as one bearing upon the conduct of a *milḥemet mizvah*. As will be shown later, response to actual attacks, at least to the extent necessary to repel the aggressor, is justified as self-defense.

[33] The statement of the Gemara, *Eruvin* 45a, permitting a military response in a situation in which a border settlement is besieged solely for plunder may be understood as limited to situations in which the enemy has already commenced hostilities.

[34] Cf., however, *Arukh ha-Shulḥan he-Atid* 74:3; R. Shlomoh Goren, *Maḥanayim*, no. 69 (Iyar 5722), p. 15, reprinted in *Torat ha-Shabbat ve-ha-Mo'ed* (Jerusalem, 5742), p. 356; *Amud ha-Yemini*, no. 16, ch. 5, sec. 25; and the statement of the Chief Rabbinate Council cited *supra*, note 27.

Rambam includes "[a war] to deliver Israel from an enemy who has attacked them" in his enumeration of *milḥamot miẓvah*. Although Rambam's categorization is entirely cogent, the Gemara does not specifically mention this type of war as an instance of *milḥemet miẓvah*. *Mareh Panim*, in a gloss on the Palestinian Talmud, *Sotah* 8:10, points to the following statement recorded in that section of the Palestinian Talmud as the source of Rambam's ruling:

> R. Judah used the term *milḥemet miẓvah* – e.g., when we attack them; *milḥemet ḥovah* – e.g., when they attack us.[35]

The Palestinian Talmud explicitly describes defensive wars as *milḥemet ḥovah* or obligatory wars. Although the Palestinian Talmud ascribes this view to R. Judah, *Mareh Panim* argues that there exists no dispute between the Sages and R. Judah on this point and hence Rambam incorporates "a war to deliver Israel from an enemy," i.e., a defensive war, in his list of *milḥamot miẓvah*.[36]

A more obvious source of Rambam's characterization of a defensive war as a *milḥemet miẓvah* may perhaps lie in a statement found in the Babylonian Talmud.[37] As noted earlier, the Gemara, *Eruvin* 45a, declares that it is permissible to resist aggression likely to result in loss of life by going to battle even on the Sabbath.[38] The Gemara must be understood as sanctioning such military activity in the guise of a *milḥemet miẓvah* rather than as a *milḥemet reshut* for two reasons: (1) A *milḥemet reshut* requires a monarch, a Sanhedrin and the *urim ve-tumim*, none of which were available during the period of the Amora'im. (2) A *milḥemet reshut* may not be initiated on the Sabbath. Indeed, the Gemara, *Shabbat* 19a, followed by Rambam, *Hilkhot Shabbat* 2:25, declares that a siege may not be commenced within a three-day period

35 The translation follows the reading of *Pnei Mosheh*. This opinion, as recorded in the Palestinian Talmud, posits a dispute between R. Judah and the Sages concerning the status of a purely defensive war in response to an enemy attack. According to *Pnei Mosheh*'s reading, R. Judah regards such a war as a *milḥemet ḥovah*, while the Sages regard it as a *milḥemet reshut*. *Pnei Mosheh*, in his *Mareh Panim*, states that the Babylonian Talmud accepts R. Judah's thesis since it views only preemptive war as the subject of dispute and maintains that the Sages agree with R. Judah's position. *Korban ha-Edah* records a variant textual reading according to which R. Judah views defensive war as a *milḥemet reshut* while the Sages categorize it as a *milḥemet miẓvah*. See R. Judah Gershuni, *Mishpat ha-Melukhah* 5:1; cf. *Arukh ha-Shulḥan he-Atid*, *Hilkhot Melakhim* 74:3.

36 See also *Keren Orah*, *Sotah* 44b. Cf. *Le-Or ha-Halakhah*, pp. 13–15; *Mishpat ha-Melukhah* 5:1; and R. Ovadiah Hedaya, *Talpiyot*, vol. III, nos. 3–4, pp. 380–84.

37 R. Aaron Soloveichik, *Or ha-Mizraḥ* (Tevet 5730), posits *Midrash Tanḥuma*, *Parshat Pinḥas*, sec. 3, as Rambam's source. Deuteronomy 26:17–18 states, "Harass the Midianites and smite them; for they harass you." *Tanḥuma* comments: "On the basis of this verse our Sages said, 'If [a person] comes to slay you, arise and slay him.'" In context, the mandated response is not merely individual self-defense but a defensive war.

38 See also *Arukh ha-Shulḥan he-Atid*, *Hilkhot Melakhim* 14:3. Cf., however, R. Shlomoh Goren, *Maḥanayim*, no. 69, p. 9, and *Torat ha-Shabbat ve-ha-Mo'ed*, p. 345; cf., also, *infra*, note 39.

prior to the Sabbath. Rashi, Deuteronomy 20:19, and *Leḥem Mishneh, Hilkhot Shabbat* 2:25, declare that this restriction applies only to discretionary wars but not to *milḥamot mizvah*.[39]

Parenthetically, it is evident that there is no requirement for acquiescence of the *urim ve-tumim* prior to initiating the type of warfare described in *Eruvin* 45a. No mention is made of such requirement either in the talmudic discussion or in the various expositions of this provision of normative Jewish law as recorded in *Shulḥan Arukh, Oraḥ Ḥayyim* 329:6. It is logical to assume that, although, as noted earlier, Ramban posits a requirement for acquiescence of the *urim ve-tumim* as a prior condition for waging a *milḥemet mizvah* as well as for waging a *milḥemet reshut*, permission is not required in the case of a defensive war. In light of the fact that R. Judah in the name of Rav expressed the dictum recorded in *Eruvin* 45a sanctioning defensive war in absolute terms at a time when the *urim ve-tumim* no longer existed, his statement may serve as a source for the conclusion that defensive war does not require prior dispensation of the *urim ve-tumim*.

It should not be assumed that inclusion among obligatory wars of a war "to deliver Israel from the enemy" is simply the application of the law of the "pursuer" (*rodef*).[40] Jewish law requires that a bystander must intervene in order to save the life of an intended victim.[41] This rule is subject to the qualification that the life of the aggressor is forfeit only if the intended victim cannot be saved other than by killing the aggressor.[42] Thus, the law of *rodef* would require that assistance be rendered to victims of military aggression. It is clear, however, that the category of *milḥemet mizvah* requires intervention even under circumstances in which the law of *rodef* would not mandate, or even permit, intervention.

According to virtually all authorities, a person need not jeopardize his own life in order to preserve the life of another.[43] Thus there is no obligation to

[39] Since the Gemara, *Eruvin* 45a, permits military action in defense of border settlements even when there is no certain threat to life, the response sanctioned cannot be understood as collective self-defense but as a halakhic category of war. This distinction will be elucidated below. See also *supra*, note 33.

[40] Cf. *Shiyurei Korban*, Palestinian Talmud, *Sotah* 8:10, who erroneously assumes that the law of pursuit incontrovertibly establishes an obligation to go to war to defend the victim of aggression.

[41] *Sanhedrin* 72b; Rambam, *Hilkhot Rozeaḥ* 1:6–7 and 1:9; *Shulḥan Arukh, Ḥoshen Mishpat* 425:1.

[42] *Sanhedrin* 49a, 56a and 74a; *Bava Kamma* 28a; Rambam, *Hilkhot Rozeaḥ* 1:7; and *Shulḥan Arukh, Ḥoshen Mishpat* 425:1.

[43] See *Teshuvot Radvaz*, vol. III, no. 1052; *Pri Megadim, Mishbezot Zahav* 328:7; *Shulḥan Arukh ha-Rav*, vol. VI, *Hilkhot Nizkei Guf va-Nefesh* 7; *Arukh ha- Shulḥan, Ḥoshen Mishpat* 426:4; and *Pitḥei Teshuvah, Ḥoshen Mishpat* 426:2. Cf., however, *Kesef Mishneh, Hilkhot Rozeaḥ* 1:14, and *Bet Yosef, Ḥoshen Mishpat* 426.

eliminate a *rodef* if it is necessary to risk one's own life in order to do so. Yet war, virtually by definition, constitutes a threat to the lives of all combatants. Hence any individual who might otherwise seek refuge and thereby protect his own life could not be obligated by virtue of the law of pursuit to engage in battle in order to "deliver Israel from an enemy."

Moreover, the law of pursuit can be invoked, and the life of the aggressor becomes forfeit, only when failure to intervene will certainly, or almost certainly, result in the death of the intended victim.[44] However, the Gemara, *Eruvin* 45a, sanctions defensive action, on the Sabbath as well as on weekdays, against heathens who besiege a border settlement even though the marauding forces seek only "straw and hay," i.e., they are intent only upon looting or exacting economic concessions. It is clear that in such situations there exists no imminent danger; it is not at all certain that any life will be endangered. There is, however, reason to fear that even if the aggressors' immediate pecuniary or economic goals are achieved without resistance, having penetrated border defenses, the enemy may engage in warfare at some future time and thereby endanger Jewish lives. The loss of fortified border settlements would leave the entire country exposed and defenseless. Hence defensive measures are warranted. These measures could not be justified by the law of pursuit since it is not certain, or even likely, that failure to respond militarily would result in loss of life. Nevertheless, Halakhah clearly justifies defensive war under these circumstances. Thus, while the law of pursuit may be invoked only in face of imminent danger to life, defensive war is justified in order to forestall even remote future danger.

Perhaps of even greater significance is the fact that war almost inevitably results in civilian casualties as well as the loss of combatants. The taking of innocent lives certainly cannot be justified on the basis of the law of pursuit. The life of the pursuer is forfeit in order that the life of the intended victim be preserved. However, should it be impossible to eliminate the pursuer other than by also causing the death of an innocent bystander, the law of pursuit could not be invoked even by the intended victim, much less by a third party who is himself not personally endangered. Since the law of pursuit is designed to preserve the life of the innocent victim, it is only logical that it is forbidden to cause the death of a bystander in the process, since to do so would only entail the loss of another innocent life. In such situations the talmudic principle

44 See Rashi, *Sanhedrin* 72a, s.v. *hakhi garsinan,* and Rashi, *Pesaḥim* 2b, s.v. *hakhi ka-amar; Teshuvot Koaḥ Shor,* no. 20; and *Iggerot Mosheh, Ḥoshen Mishpat,* vol. II, no. 69, sec. 2, s.v. *ve-la-khen.* Cf., however, *Bi'ur ha-Gra, Ḥoshen Mishpat* 388:74 and J. David Bleich, "Hasgarat Poshe'a Yehudi, she-Baraḥ le-Ereẓ Yisra'el," *Or ha-Mizraḥ* (Nisan–Tammuz 5747), pp. 260–61, reprinted in his *Be-Netivot ha-Halakhah* (New York, 1996), vol. I, pp. 97–98.

"How do you know that your blood is sweeter than the blood of your fellow?" (*Sanhedrin* 74a) is fully applicable.[45]

Were war to be sanctioned solely on the basis of the law of pursuit, military action would perforce be restricted to situations in which loss of life is inflicted only upon armed aggressors or active participants in the war effort; military action resulting in casualties among the civilian populace would constitute homicide, pure and simple. However, not only does one search in vain for a ruling prohibiting military activity likely to result in the death of civilians,[46] but there appears to be no discussion in classical rabbinic sources that takes cognizance of the likelihood of causing civilian casualties in the course of hostilities legitimately undertaken as posing a halakhic or moral problem.[47]

Thus specific sanction for a defensive war beyond application of the law of pursuit is required in order: (1) to justify conscription, i.e., coercion to endanger one's life in defending others; (2) to sanction defensive war to ward off aggression even when danger to life is remote; and (3) to sanction military activity that is likely to result in casualties among non-combatants. Nevertheless, a voluntary response posing no danger to civilians may be undertaken in face of imminent danger even preemptively. In halakhic terms, such resistance

45 *Amud ha-Yemini*, no. 16, ch. 4, discusses the applicability of this principle to the question of the sacrifice of non-Jewish lives for the preservation of Jewish lives. Notwithstanding terminology employed by Rashi, *Sanhedrin* 74a, s.v. *ma'i ḥazit*, Rabbi Israeli rules that it is forbidden to take the life of a non-Jew in order to save the life of a Jew. Cf. *Tiferet Yisra'el, Bo'az, Oholot* 7:10; *Noda bi-Yehuda, Mahadura Tinyana, Ḥoshen Mishpat*, no. 59; *Perashat Derakhim, Derush* 17; *Minḥat Ḥinnukh*, no. 296; and R. Eliezer Waldenberg, *Ẓiẓ Eli'ezer*, vol. X, no. 25, ch. 5, sec. 4. Cf., however, Palestinian Talmud, *Shabbat* 14:4, and R. Mordecai Halperin, *Assia* (Tammuz 5725), vol. X. no. 4, pp. 22–23. For an analysis of the problem posed by the Palestinian Talmud see the discussion in J. David Bleich, "Ḥashtalat Lev she-Nutal min ha-Torem she-lo ke-Din," *Or Ha-Mizraḥ* (Nisan–Tammuz 5748), pp. 293–95 and *Be-Netivot ha-Halakhah* (Hoboken, NJ, 2000), vol. III, pp. 157–58.

See Ra'avan, *Bava Kamma* 111b, and *Kesef Mishneh, Hilkhot Roẓeaḥ* 2:11, who declare that taking the life of a non-Jew is encompassed in the prohibition against homicide; see also *Mekhilta, Mishpatim* 4:58. The line of reasoning employed by *Ḥakham Zevi*, no. 26, and *Ḥut ha-Meshulash*, no. 17, with regard to theft of property belonging to a non-Jew would appear to apply, *mutatis mutandis*, to homicide as well. *Meshekh Ḥokhmah, Parshat Mishpatim*, s.v. *ve-yitakhen*, avers that the slaying of a non-Jew is a more severe transgression than taking the life of a Jew and that it is precisely for that reason that "punishment is reserved to Heaven." See also Ibn Ezra, *Commentary on the Bible*, Exodus 21:21. Cf. R. Simchah Shustal, *Koveẓ Nehora'i* (5740), vol. I, pp. 86–91.

46 *Amud ha-Yemini*, no. 16, ch. 5, sec. 1.

47 For a contemporary discussion of this issue see *Amud ha-Yemini*, no. 16, chs. 3–5. It may be noted that Scripture records that, prior to engaging in battle against Amalek, Saul said to the Kenites, "Go, depart, go down from among the Amalekites" (I Samuel 15:6). The clear implication is that, had the Kenites not heeded this admonition, Saul might have slain them with impunity in the course of the battle against Amalek.

is not encompassed within the rubric of war and does not require sanction as either *milḥemet miẓvah* or *milḥemet reshut*. Such response is essentially not an act of war but of simple self-defense. Individual self-defense is permitted by virtue of the principle "If [a person] comes to slay you, arise and slay him" (*Berakhot* 58a and 62b; *Sanhedrin* 72a). That response, which is legitimate on the part of any individual victim of putative aggression, is, *mutatis mutandis*, legitimate when undertaken by society as a whole as an aggregate of individual victims.

V. PREEMPTIVE WAR

Categorization of a preemptive attack as a *milḥemet reshut* is problematic regardless of the precise circumstances under which it is justified. Such action is not deemed mandatory but is nevertheless permitted as a *milḥemet reshut* despite the apparent absence of specific scriptural authorization.[48] *Korban ha-Edah*, Palestinian Talmud, *Sotah* 8:10, suggests that the legitimacy of preemptive war as a *milḥemet reshut* is derived by the Palestinian Talmud from the scriptural paradigm of King David's war against the Philistines.[49] Military action against the Philistines, asserts *Korban ha-Edah*, was not undertaken in order to conquer territory belonging to the Seven Nations indigenous to the land of Canaan or to expand the boundaries of the Land of Israel, but in order to prevent aggression.

It may well be that preemptive war undertaken in order to prevent future attack is justified as a *milḥemet reshut* analogous to a war for territorial aggrandizement or economic gain. The Gemara, *Berakhot* 3b and *Sanhedrin* 16a, seemingly indicates that discretionary war is warranted, not only when undertaken in order to enlarge the territory of the Land of Israel, but also when economically motivated.[50] Dispensation for such war is subject to approval of

48 Although not explicitly demanding participation in military activity designed to "deliver Israel from an enemy," Judges 5:23 pronounces a curse against Sisera: "'Curse ye Meroz,' said the angel of the Lord, 'curse ye bitterly the inhabitants thereof because they came not to the help of the Lord, to the help of the Lord against the mighty.'" Cf. R. Shlomoh Goren, *Maḥanayim* (*Erev Ḥanukkah*, 5714), no. 20, p. 7, reprinted in *Torat ha-Mo'adim*, p. 166; and *Maḥanayim* (5725), no. 97, p. 7, reprinted in *Torat ha-Shabbat ve-ha-Mo'ed*, p. 360.

49 See, however, *Panim Yafot, Parshat Shoftim, s.v. u-mi ha-ish*, who notes that the area inhabited by the Philistines, although not conquered by Joshua, was within the boundaries of *Ereẓ Yisra'el*. Hence King David's war against the Philistines constituted a *milḥemet miẓvah* since it served as a war of conquest for territory integral to the Land of Israel.

50 Cf., however, R. Reuben Margulies, *Margaliyot ha-Yam, Sanhedrin* 16a, secs. 22 and 23, and *idem, Niẓoẓie Or, Berakhot* 3b, who asserts that the hostilities in question were not undertaken for stark economic advantage but were directed against marauding bands who disrupted the economy.

the Sanhedrin and acquiescence of the *urim ve-tumim*. Acquiescence of the *urim ve-tumim* is tantamount to explicit divine sanction. Positing this requirement implies recognition that war may be undertaken only upon divine behest. Divine sanction for war in limited situations may be forthcoming even when there is no imminent threat. Accordingly, it may be understood that it is not economic gain *per se*, or territorial aggrandizement or enhancing the prestige of the monarch that justifies war; rather, any cogent benefit may serve as a justification, subject to divine approval as conveyed through the intermediacy of the *urim ve-tumim*.[51] Hence, prevention of a possible, albeit remote, danger is no less worthy a motive than economic gain. Therefore, according to the Sages, preemptive war is encompassed within the category of a *milḥemet reshut* but participation in such warfare fails to constitute a *mizvah*. However, R. Judah's view, which raises such participation to the level of fulfillment of a *mizvah*, but not to that of *ḥovah* or a mandatory undertaking, requires further clarification.

Quite apart from the foregoing, the nature of the dispute between R. Judah and the Sages is extremely difficult to explain. All agree that, as a discretionary war, an incursion "to diminish the heathens so that they shall not march against them" requires a monarch and a Sanhedrin; yet R. Judah and the Sages disagree regarding whether participation fulfills a *mizvah*.

R. Judah's position may perhaps be understood on the basis of another consideration. In matters not involving war, it is clear that society has an obligation to anticipate dangers and prevent possible loss of life even when the danger is remote. The Gemara, *Bava Batra* 7b, declares that the inhabitants of a city may compel one another to contribute the funds necessary for erecting fortifications, including the construction of a wall circumscribing the city, doors in the wall and bolts to secure the doors. The wall is designed to fortify the city in order to secure it against armed attack. Since the wall is constructed to preserve the lives of the inhabitants, all the townspeople may be compelled to contribute equally to defray the expenses, on the grounds that all derive equal benefit from the fortifications.

Fortifications represent more than a simple amenity; they are designed to protect against loss of life. Were construction of fortifications to be deemed necessary for eliminating an imminent danger to human life, each person would be required to do everything within his power to obviate or mitigate the danger. Were construction of the fortifications not feasible otherwise, each and every individual would be personally liable to bear the entire expense. At best, any individual who defrays such expenses would have a cause of action

[51] Cf. *Even ha-Azel, Hilkhot Melakhim* 5:1.

against his fellow townspeople for the reimbursement of funds spent on their behalf – but each person capable of doing so would be required to act on his own initiative and to act without delay.

This obligation does not exist for the construction of fortifications; no individual is liable for more than his proportionate share of the total expenditure. This is so because, in the circumstances described, there exists no imminent danger. Fortifications are commonly erected, not to protect against imminent danger, but in anticipation of future contingencies. Precaution against future danger is not an individual obligation but a societal one. Society as a whole must ensure that there are lifeguards, physicians and firemen trained to perform their functions and must provide facilities and incentives for their training, but no individual is obliged to enter these professions or to volunteer his services in performing such functions. Any member of society may demand that a wall be constructed and that locks and bolts be provided. An individual who expresses a legitimate concern about possible danger and proposes a realistic means for its alleviation must be heard and his demands fulfilled. The obligation to protect against danger of this nature rests upon society as a whole rather than upon any individual.[52]

A war "to diminish the heathens so that they shall not march against them" may be undertaken and the right forcibly to conscript soldiers for this purpose may be understood as flowing from the societal obligation to forestall future danger. Society has an obligation to prevent danger from arising. Granted that biblical sanction exists for undertaking preemptive war, and that such action constitutes a legitimate means of forestalling danger, society, through its sovereign, may be called upon to protect its members by engaging in military activity in order to forestall danger.

At the very minimum, prevention of possible future danger constitutes a matter of societal welfare. The Gemara, *Bava Batra* 8a, states that townspeople may levy taxes and compel one another to contribute the funds necessary to provide amenities such as a well from which to draw water. Rambam, *Hilkhot Shekhenim* 2:5, records a similar prerogative with regard to construction and maintenance of roads and streets. Nevertheless, participation in the provision of social amenities does not constitute fulfillment of a *mizvah*[53] even though

[52] See J. David Bleich, *Judaism and Healing* (New York, 1981), pp. 13–16.

[53] Persons engaged in providing social amenities should not be confused with those who "occupy themselves with the needs of the public" and who are therefore exempt from recitation of the *shema*. The latter category includes those engaged in preserving endangered property but not persons engaged in providing social amenities. See *Shulḥan Arukh, Oraḥ Ḥayyim* 70:4 and accompanying commentaries. Cf. *Teshuvot Imrei Esh, Yoreh De'ah*, no. 52.

members of society are entitled to institute legal proceedings to compel participation by their fellow citizens. Hence the position of the Sages may be understood by ascribing to them the view that prevention of future danger is regarded as entirely similar to providing other amenities, *viz.*, an actionable prerogative, but not a *mizvah*. Accordingly, preemptive war may, under certain conditions, be compelled but participation in such military activity does not constitute fulfillment of a *mizvah*. It therefore follows that a person participating in such military activity is not exempt from fulfillment of other *mizvot*.

R. Judah, on the other hand, may be understood as maintaining that forestalling future danger is qualitatively different from providing social amenities. Although, in the absence of imminent danger, no individual member of society is personally obligated to take such action, nevertheless, according to R. Judah, action that serves to eliminate future danger, when undertaken, *does* constitute fulfillment of a *mizvah* because it is designed to preserve life.[54]

If this analysis is correct, a similar dispute would exist with regard to the question of whether workmen engaged in erecting fortifications around the city are exempt from performance of other *mizvot*. According to the Sages, since no immediate danger exists, the status of laborers erecting fortifications is entirely similar to that of workmen engaged in providing social amenities and does not constitute fulfillment of a *mizvah*. According to R. Judah, such activity, although not obligatory upon any individual, nevertheless, when undertaken, does constitute a *mizvah kiyumit*, i.e., such activity does constitute fulfillment of a *mizvah*. Hence, workmen engaged in erection of fortifications, according to the position of R. Judah, would be exempt from performance of other precepts.

This analysis notwithstanding, preemptive war is not entirely analogous to the construction of fortifications. Every individual citizen has a right to demand the erection of fortifications and to compel his fellows to share the financial burden. Yet no individual enjoys the right to compel a preemptive strike even when the fear of future danger is cogent. Preemptive war as a form of *milhemet reshut* may be undertaken only upon the initiative of the sovereign with the consent of the Sanhedrin and acquiescence of the *urim ve-tumim*.

VI. KING, SANHEDRIN, AND *URIM VE-TUMIM*

The respective roles and functions of the king, the Sanhedrin and the *urim ve-tumim* require elucidation. It is unlikely that this tripartite requirement for

54 Cf. *Amud ha-Yemini*, no. 16, ch. 5, sec. 27.

declaration of war is designed to provide a system of checks and balances or simply to render actual warfare halakhically difficult. It is certainly reasonable to presume that each is designed to satisfy a separate and unique halakhic requirement and hence it is necessary to endeavor to discern each requirement's function.

The role of the monarch may be understood in light of a general difficulty associated with the obligation to engage in wars of defense in order "to deliver Israel from an enemy." The obligation to participate in war against the Seven Nations and in war against Amalek is, of course, rooted in specific biblical commandments. However, since the obligation to participate in a defensive war is not based on either the law of pursuit or the obligation to come to the aid of an endangered person, the precise reason why participation in a war "to deliver Israel from an enemy" is considered obligatory is not readily apparent. Since there exists no explicit biblical imperative to engage in such warfare, it is difficult to understand the basis for compelling self-endangerment.

It is precisely for this reason that a monarch is required for waging war. Jewish law recognizes that society has inherent power, albeit limited in nature, with regard to expropriation of the resources of its members. Thus society may levy taxes for the common welfare and compel payment. However, society lacks power to force individuals to place themselves in jeopardy even when endangerment of some is necessary to avert greater danger to the greater number. Jewish law endows the monarch with powers beyond those vested in society. The essence of monarchical power is the power of coercion. A monarch is empowered to force the populace to do his bidding. The king may expropriate property and may conscript soldiers to fight in his wars. Only the sovereign enjoys the power to compel his subjects to endanger their lives.[55] Rambam, *Hilkhot Melakhim* 5:2, defines the role of the king with regard to *milḥemet mizvah*: "He forces the people to go forth." Thus, Halakhah requires initiation by the king not only for a *milḥemet reshut* but also for a *milḥemet mizvah*. Since war requires conscription of soldiers whose lives are placed in jeopardy, war may be declared only by the king. Absent a monarch, there exists no power of conscription and each citizen may decline to participate in battle. Accordingly, despite the general obligation to preserve life and render

[55] See also *Mishpat Kohen*, no. 143 and R. Alexander Epstein, *Niv ha-Midrashiyah* (Winter–Spring 5728), pp. 72–80. The verse "Lest he die in the war" (Deuteronomy 20:5), as understood by *Sifrei, ad loc.*, and the earlier cited Mishnah, *Sotah* 44b, speaks of possible loss of life in the context of *milḥemet reshut*. Similarly, Rambam, *Sefer ha-Mizvot, mizvot aseh*, no. 191, in speaking of the function of the address delivered prior to battle by the *mashuaḥ milḥamah* (i.e., the "priest anointed for war" for the purpose of addressing the troops), describes the address as designed so that "their hearts be aroused to war and he bring them to endanger themselves."

assistance to one whose life is in jeopardy, a king is necessary for the proper conduct even of a war "to deliver Israel from an enemy" because, in the absence of a decree of the king committing the populace to war, no person is obligated to jeopardize his own life in order to save the life of his fellow.[56]

The role of the Sanhedrin in the declaration of war is somewhat less obvious but is discernible nonetheless.

The law of pursuit has two distinct formulations. When the pursuer is intent upon the death of his victim there is an absolute duty to eliminate the threat. Even a bystander must intervene and dare not plead that he declines to save one human life at the cost of another. Rambam, *Hilkhot Rozeaḥ* 1:9, writes, "This, too, is a negative commandment: not to spare the life of a pursuer." The positive obligation is cited by Rambam, *Hilkhot Rozeaḥ* 1:7, and predicated upon the verse "And you shall cut off her hand, your eye shall not pity her" (Deuteronomy 25:12). Yet another formulation of the law of pursuit is found in Exodus 22:1: "If a thief be found breaking in, and be smitten that he die, there shall be no blood shed for him." Scripture here provides that one who kills a thief incurs no punishment. The Gemara, *Sanhedrin* 72a, explains that it is to be assumed that a person will not permit his property to be seized unlawfully without offering resistance. The thief is deemed to be well aware of this instinctive psychological reaction and hence it is presumed that he is prepared to use lethal force should he meet with resistance. Accordingly, the thief is presumed to be a "pursuer" whose life is forfeit. However, in codifying this law, Rambam, *Hilkhot Geneivah* 9:7, states only that "All persons have permission to kill [the thief] whether on a weekday or on the Sabbath" but fails to posit an absolute obligation to kill him. It may be posited that the distinction between the thief who is the subject of this ruling and the aggressor described in *Hilkhot Rozeaḥ* whose life is always forfeit lies in the fact that the latter is actually intent upon an act of aggression while the former, although he may become an aggressor, is not yet engaged in an actual act of aggression. Elimination of the thief is a preemptive act. Such an act is permissible but not mandatory.

A similar distinction may be drawn for war. Defensive response to an attack is mandatory in order to save lives. Yet, although a preemptive strike is warranted when there is reason to anticipate danger, it is not mandatory in the absence of overt aggression. There are manifold considerations that may render preemptive war imprudent. Rambam, *Hilkhot Geneivah* 9:12, rules that a

[56] Cf. R. Raphael Katzenellenbogen, *No'am*, vol. XVI, p. 45 ff., who fails to recognize this salient point. Cf., also, the somewhat different analysis of R. Saul Israeli, *Torah she-be-al Peh* (5728), vol. X, p. 49 f.

householder who is certain that the thief will not kill him has no right to execute the burglar peremptorily in order to preserve his property. A householder who fully intends to offer no resistance when confronted with the threat of force has no right to take the life of the would-be thief preemptively simply in order to preserve his property.[57] Indeed, it would be highly prudent for the householder to comply with the demands of an armed intruder without offering resistance. Similarly, when it is anticipated that danger to the lives of the populace can be averted by other means, preemptive war may well be imprudent.

Moreover, as poignantly noted by *Minḥat Ḥinnukh*, no. 425, *milḥamot miẓvah* are obligatory even though all war, by its very nature, endangers the lives of combatants. Nevertheless, even the obligation of *milḥamot miẓvah* does not require undertaking suicide missions. War is obligatory only when there is sound military reason to assume that Israel will be victorious.[58] It would seem that the need to eliminate a potential aggressor is an imperative *causus belli* that renders even preemptive war permissible "in order to diminish the heathens so that they shall not march against them" only when the lives preserved are greater in number than the lives whose loss may be anticipated as a result of armed conflict. The justification of war in such circumstances is saving lives, not punishing the enemy.

Accordingly, the role of the Sanhedrin is readily discernible. The Sanhedrin is charged with assessing the military, political and economic realia and determining whether a proposed war is indeed necessary and whether it will be successful in achieving its objectives. Hence, the role of the Sanhedrin is limited to *milḥamot reshut*. Consent of the Sanhedrin is not required to sanction *milḥamot miẓvah* since the latter are commanded by God directly and must be carried out by virtue of divine fiat.[59]

57 The victim may, however, be entitled to willfully and consciously refuse to accede to theft of his property and, recognizing that his determination to offer resistance endangers his life, may then avail himself of the law of pursuit in defending himself against the oppressor. See R. Shlomoh Zalman Auerbach, *Moriah* (Sivan–Tammuz 5731), pp. 22–23, reprinted in his *Minḥat Shlomoh* (Jerusalem, 5746), no. 7, sec. 2.

58 Cf. R. Shlomoh Goren, *Torat ha-Mo'adim*, p. 179.

59 Rashi, *Berakhot* 3b, commenting on an incident related by the Gemara, states that the Sanhedrin was consulted "so that they might pray on their behalf." R. Reuben Margulies, *Margaliyot ha-Yam*, *Sanhedrin* 16a, sec. 23, and *Niẓoẓei Or*, *Berakhot* 3b, explains that the military action under discussion constituted a *milḥemet miẓvah* that did not require statutory consultation of the Sanhedrin. Alternatively, approval of the Sanhedrin may not have been required since, in the incident recorded, the war was undertaken upon the initiative of the populace. See *Einayim la-Mishpat*, *Sanhedrin* 16a and *supra*, note 13. Cf. *Amud ha-Yemini*, no. 16, ch. 5, sec. 6.

The role of the *urim ve-tumim* is much more difficult to elucidate. As noted earlier, Ramban maintains that acquiescence of the *urim ve-tumim* was required not only for *milḥamot reshut* but for *milḥamot miẓvah* as well. Yet war "to deliver Israel from an enemy" does not require consultation of the *urim ve-tumim*.

Although none of the commentators on the *Mishneh Torah* raise the question, it is difficult to explain why it is that war for "deliverance of Israel from an enemy" does not require consultation of the *urim ve-tumim*. As noted earlier, the absence of such a requirement may be inferred from the text of *Eruvin* 45a. Certainly, all who discuss the topic implicitly assume that war for this purpose requires no such consultation. The reference to consultation of the *urim ve-tumim* in the concluding section of the introduction to Rambam's *Sefer ha-Miẓvot* and in Ramban's addenda to that work may be understood as speaking of the requirement only in conjunction with wars of conquest. It is, of course, understandable that acts of violence undertaken by an individual in self-defense do not require permission of the *urim ve-tumim*. It is understandable that military action undertaken by a nation as a means of self-defense similarly require no specific *ad hoc* dispensation. However, as has been shown, military action undertaken in the guise of a *milḥemet miẓvah* "in order to deliver Israel from an enemy" goes beyond acts that an individual in similar straits might justify as a legitimate form of self-defense. Why, then, does this type of warfare not require the sanction of the *urim ve-tumim*?

Conversely, the requirement for acquiescence of the *urim ve-tumim* prior to engaging in war against the Seven Nations is particularly puzzling. Acquiescence of the *urim ve-tumim* is required, according to Ramban, not only for *milḥamot reshut* but also for *milḥamot miẓvah*, including war against the Seven Nations, despite the ongoing obligation to annihilate all members of the Seven Nations indigenous to the land of Canaan. This obligation is independent of the obligation to conquer the land of Canaan and to establish a Jewish homeland therein. The latter obligation may well be construed as contingent upon the advice and consent of the *urim ve-tumim* by virtue of its nature as a commandment whose fulfillment is the responsibility of the community as a whole. However, apart from a communal obligation to wage war against the Seven Nations, the commandment established a personal obligation as well and, so long as the members of the Seven Nations were identifiable, was binding at all times and in all places.[60] An individual was clearly not required to consult the *urim ve-tumim* prior to taking the life of a member of the Seven Nations. The obligation of society as an aggregate of its individual members is certainly

[60] See Rambam, *Hilkhot Melakhim* 5:4; and *Sefer ha-Ḥinnukh*, no. 525. See also *supra*, note 18.

not inferior to the obligation of an individual *qua* individual. Accordingly, the role of the *urim ve-tumim* in war against the Seven Nations is problematic.

In order properly to understand the consideration underlying the requirement for acquiescence of the *urim ve-tumim* as a necessary condition of halakhically sanctioned warfare, a somewhat extraneous matter that is nevertheless germane must be examined. The categories of *milḥemet miẓvah* and *milḥemet reshut* pertain only to wars fought by Jews. Other than in the context of war, self-defense or execution of transgressors convicted of capital offenses, the taking of human life is forbidden to both Jew and non-Jew alike. Since, insofar as non-Jews are concerned, there are no biblically sanctioned modes of war analogous to war for the conquest of the land of Canaan or the war against Amalek, it might well be presumed that non-Jews may not legitimately engage in warfare other than for the strictly limited purpose of self-defense. Indeed, a number of eminent authorities, including R. Moses Sofer, *Teshuvot Ḥatam Sofer, Yoreh De'ah*, no. 19, R. Abraham Dov Kahana-Shapiro, *Dvar Avraham*, vol. I, no. 11 and R. Menachem Ziemba, *Zera Avraham*, no. 24, adduce explicit talmudic authority in ruling that non-Jews are prohibited from engaging in war.[61] Nevertheless, an opposing view is found in the writings of one noted authority.[62] R. Naphtali Zevi Judah Berlin, in his commentary on the Bible, *Ha'amek Davar*, Genesis 9:5, finds justification for the view that the taking of human life in the course of war does not constitute culpable homicide.[63] The verse "But your blood of your lives will I require; from the hand of every beast will I require it; and from the hand of man, from the hand of a person's brother, will I require the life of man" (Genesis 9:5) contains one phrase that is an apparent redundancy. The phrase, "from the hand of man . . . will I require the life of man" pronounces man culpable for the murder of his fellow. To what point, then, is it necessary for Scripture to reiterate, "from the hand of a person's brother will I require the life of man?" Fratricide is certainly no less heinous a crime than ordinary homicide. *Ha'amek Davar* understands this phrase as placing a limitation upon the nature of homicide. The taking of human life constitutes homicide only when the relationship between the parties is like that between a man and his brother, i.e., during periods in which

[61] See *supra*, pp. 211–12.

[62] The Maharal of Prague espouses a similar view, albeit not based on the same line of reasoning, in his supercommentary on Rashi, *Gur Aryeh, Parashat Va-Yishlaḥ*, s.v. *she-ha-umot*. In explaining the action taken by the sons of Jacob against the inhabitants of Shechem, Maharal states that the family of Jacob constituted a sovereign people and was permitted to do battle against another nation since war is not forbidden under the Noahide Code.

[63] This view is also expressed in *Ha'amek Davar*, Deuteronomy 20:8. See also *Amud ha-Yemini*, no. 16, ch. 5, secs. 8–24.

harmony and brotherly love may be anticipated to reign between them. War, however, is the antithesis of brotherhood. Under conditions of war, maintains *Ha'amek Davar*, there is no punishment for taking human life. Since this verse occurs in the context of the prohibition against homicide for Noahides, *Ha'amek Davar* concludes that non-Jews are not culpable for taking human life in the context of warfare.

As noted earlier, numerous authorities contradict *Ha'amek Davar*'s position. Nevertheless, the verse cited by *Ha'amek Davar* might well be interpreted similarly even by the authorities who maintain that non-Jews have no dispensation to engage in wars of aggression under any circumstances. According to those authorities, the biblical categories of war are limited to Jews exclusively. However, it is not illogical to interpret Genesis 9:5 as excluding from the halakhic prohibition against homicide the shedding of blood in war provided that the war itself is legitimately undertaken, i.e., in situations in which the bonds of brotherhood have been severed. In theory, such exclusion is all-inclusive in nature and pertains to any legitimate military activity, whether undertaken by Jew or non-Jew. In practice, according to these authorities, the exclusion is applicable solely to Jews since it is established on other grounds that non-Jews may not legitimately engage in any war of aggression. The taking of any life when incidental to biblically sanctioned warfare is not homicide because at such times the relationship between the parties is not analogous to the relationship between man and his brother. It is, however, logical to assume that military action leading to civilian casualties may be regarded as legitimate on this basis only when the loss of civilian life is incidental to military purposes, but not when wantonly pursued as an end in itself.[64]

Accordingly, it may be argued that the function of the *urim ve-tumim* is to generate a state of war that is the antithesis of a state in which relationships between peoples are analogous to those between man and his brother. The latter relationship is the divinely mandated norm. Legitimate renunciation of that state requires divine sanction as manifest through the Divine Spirit utilizing the *urim ve-tumim* as a medium. Only in such a state may actions likely to produce civilian casualties be undertaken. In essence, the *urim ve-tumim* is required in order to legitimize military action that may cost the lives of innocent victims.

Each individual is indeed commanded to annihilate the members of the Seven Nations and the community as an aggregate of individuals is bound by a similar obligation. It is clearly not necessary to consult the *urim ve-tumim* prior to discharging that obligation in whole or in part. Permission of the *urim*

64 See *Amud ha-Yemini*, no. 16, ch. 5, sec. 32.

ve-tumim is required solely in order to establish a state of war legitimating military action that may result in the death of innocent victims.

However, since war "to deliver Israel from an enemy" is not preemptive but is undertaken only in response to hostile acts, the acquiescence of the *urim ve-tumim* is not required since such war is entirely defensive in nature. In such cases, the state of normalcy has already been shattered by the aggressor. The response, even if it involves the loss of innocent lives, is justified even without permission of the *urim ve-tumim* since it occurs in the absence of peaceful relations among nations. Hence, even though casualties among non-combatants may ensue, military activity is justified since the innocent victim's life is not taken by "the hand of his brother."

VII. CONCLUSION

As has been stated earlier, preemptive war is not sanctioned by Rambam as a form of *milḥemet mizvah*. Nor could preemptive war be sanctioned in our day as a *milḥemet reshut* since the necessary conditions for waging a *milḥemet reshut*, i.e., a monarch, a Sanhedrin and the *urim ve-tumim*, are absent. Nevertheless, limited types of preemptive incursion may well be justified under the law of pursuit. "If [a person] comes to slay you, arise and slay him," counsels the Gemara (*Berakhot* 58a and 62b; *Sanhedrin* 72a). Such action is not only justified but is mandatory under the law of pursuit. However, as has been shown earlier, the conditions under which self-defense may be carried out are quite different from the manner in which war may be conducted. The taking of human life in self-defense is justified only when necessary in order to eliminate a threat that is virtually certain to result in loss of life and only to the limited extent necessary to neutralize the danger. Moreover, in contradistinction to action justified by regulations governing warfare, innocent lives may not be taken when the sole justification for military action is the plea of self-defense.

Lest these conclusions be too hastily applied to events such as the 1982 Israeli incursion into Lebanon several further points must be emphasized:

1. Halakhah does not designate action in response to an armed attack as preemptive even if designed solely to prevent a future attack. Accordingly, aggression undertaken by the enemy renders any action taken in response a war "to deliver Israel from an enemy," which constitutes a *milḥemet mizvah*. There is no halakhic requirement that defensive war be limited to elimination of the immediate danger. The crucial issue, then, is whether an action is initiated as a deterrent or whether a given

action is undertaken in response to prior attack. Intermittent cessation of hostilities by the enemy does not signify termination of the aggression.[65] On the other hand, the purpose of such a war is not punishment of the enemy, but "to deliver Israel," i.e., to prevent Jewish casualties. Hence prudence would dictate that such action be undertaken only if casualties as a result of a military response are estimated as likely to be lower than anticipated losses in the absence of such response.

2. Preemptive military action undertaken according to the principle "If [a person] comes to slay you, arise and slay him" may well generate a counterattack. Response to the counterattack is a war "to deliver Israel from the enemy" even though the initial attack was not. The resistance is a response to "*kvar ba aleihem*" – "the enemy has already come upon them" – and thus is a war "to deliver Israel from an enemy." Hence, although the initial action must be limited to acts compatible with the law of pursuit and, for example, may not be directed against civilians, the enemy response justifies a *milḥemet miẓvah*. Once the enemy has actually "marched against them" further military action is war "to deliver Israel from an enemy" and may be carried out in accordance with the halakhic regulations governing the conduct of war.
3. It must also be noted that in some circumstances a *milḥemet reshut*, once undertaken, may be governed by the regulations applying to a *milḥemet miẓvah*. As noted earlier, Deuteronomy 20:5–7 provides for deferring military service for certain categories of men. These exclusions apply only to a *milḥemet reshut*. Hence, a king may not legitimately undertake a *milḥemet reshut* unless he is confident of victory without finding it necessary to conscript men in the deferred categories. However, once war is declared and the tide of battle threatens to overwhelm the Jewish forces, the legal situation changes. *Ḥazon Ish, Oraḥ Ḥayyim-Mo'ed* 114:2, logically asserts that once a battle starts and there is a danger of defeat, response to the danger is a *milḥemet miẓvah* and so even those exempt from military service are obligated to participate if their service is necessary for victory. The same consideration would logically apply even in the case of a war whose inception was illicit. The danger of defeat requires the "deliverance of Israel from an enemy," hence a *milḥemet miẓvah*.

Of course, application of these halakhic principles to any given situation requires determining the relevant facts.

65 See *Amud ha-Yemini*, no. 16, ch. 5, sec. 25.

NOTES AND QUESTIONS

1. In Jewish law war constitutes a legal category distinct from self-defense or even the elimination of a pursuer. The ramifications in Jewish law of establishing the existence of a state of war have been discussed in detail. Historically, Western societies have entered into formal declarations of war. Do legal consequences flow from the presence or absence of a formal declaration as is the case in Jewish law, or is the declaration simply a political gesture?

2. Prior to the United Nations Charter methods of conducting war were circumscribed by the Geneva Conventions. Even at that late date no attempt was made to regulate the declaration of war as distinct from the methods employed in conducting war. Jewish law, on the other hand, regulates the undertaking of war but says comparatively little about its methods. Can you account for the difference in emphasis?

3. In Jewish law a state of war renders collateral damage permissible. Is collateral damage involving a country's own nationals also permissible? Is there a difference whether the harm to them is active or passive? For example, did Great Britain have a right not to evacuate areas that the British knew were going to be attacked by V2's during World War II because they did not want the enemy to become aware of their intelligence capability? Was that concern sufficient to overcome a duty of rescue? Assume that there was an invasion of British territory. Would the British government have been justified in blowing up a bridge and causing loss of the lives of British subjects in order to prevent enemy forces from establishing a beachhead?

4. Absent warfare as a legal construct recognized by the Noahide Code, war can be sanctioned only as a form of collective self-defense or rescue of third party victims. How different is that from the provisions of the United Nations Charter? What degree of certainty concerning the threat of aggression is required under the Noahide Code? Under the United Nations Charter? In applying the Noahide Code how does one address the problem of collateral damage? How is collateral damage addressed under the United Nations Charter?

5. Article 1 of the United States Constitution effectively deprives the sovereign, i.e., the President, from declaring war and vests that power in Congress. We will leave it to constitutional scholars to formulate the distinction between "war" and "police action." Were the President to go to "war" without a declaration of war on the part of Congress it would presumably be an impeachable offense. Can the President morally interpose the Noahide Code as a defense? Is he indeed compelled to ignore Congress and embark on a war of self-defense and disregard the constitutional consequences?

6. Assuming, contrary to the weight of Jewish authority, that the Noahide Code allows for war, would a war entered into by a monarch against his own subjects be legitimate? Even in the absence of a moral right to wage war, non-Jewish states can acquire property interests by virtue of the right of conquest. Is there a right of conquest against the nationals of the sovereign's own country?

Such an issue arose in a case brought before the Supreme Rabbinical Court of Israel. The case involved ownership of religious artifacts that somehow came into the possession of an Israeli museum. The artifacts had been seized during World War II and were later identified by heirs of the original owner. The museum claimed that property rights of the original owner had been extinguished by virtue of the right of conquest. The case was complicated by the fact that the items were seized in Hungary, not by German forces but by members of the Hungarian Red Arrow organization. See "The Sotheby Sale" in Chapter Four of this volume.

7. Assume that the monarch enters into war without consulting the Sanhedrin or the *urim ve-tumim*. In the introduction to this chapter it has been pointed out that war is not an exception to the prohibition against taking a human life; Scripture commands, "Thou shalt not commit an act of homicide," rather than "Thou shalt not kill." Taking the life of a human being in the course of a legitimate war is, by definition, not homicide. Is killing a human being in the course of an unauthorized war simply an act of unauthorized warfare or is it also homicide?

COMMENT

A reading of the opening chapters of Genesis reveals that the anticipation of longevity in antiquity was much greater than in contemporary times. Longevity during the American colonial period was far shorter than today. Clearly longevity, a natural phenomenon, has fluctuated over the generations. There may be perfectly natural explanations for those fluctuations, although the rather lengthy lifetimes described in Genesis are difficult to explain in terms of the biological reality with which we are familiar. A student of talmudic literature could present a host of instances in which it is clear that biological and anatomical reality during the talmudic period was different from that of today. For example perforation of the intestine renders an animal non-kosher based on the halakhic presumption that death will follow within a twelve-month period. Today veterinary medicine can treat and cure that condition. Nevertheless, such an animal remains non-kosher because the law is engraved upon tablets of stone and reflects the empirical realia of the Sinaitic epoch.

The Hebrew phrase that describes the changed phenomenon is "*nishtaneh ha-teva*" – "the natural world has changed."

Until the eighteenth century in England stealing a loaf of bread was punishable by death upon the gallows. That punishment was accepted by society with moral equanimity. Today, we would regard that criminal sanction as "cruel and unusual punishment." Has there been a psychological change comparable to the changes that have occurred in the natural world? Are those changes the result of natural forces or of divine intervention?

Eradication of Amalek and of the Canaanite tribes was the subject of divine commandments. Today, we would categorize such activity as genocide. It should be noted that in our day neither Amalek nor the Canaanite tribes are identifiable ethnic groups. Hence those commandments are, to all intents and purposes, a dead letter. Is this also a case of moral sensitivity following changed reality?

7

Dead or Alive?

PART ONE: TIME OF DEATH

The conflict between authentic Jewish teaching and society's embrace of "brain death" as a criterion of death involves no scientific or factual controversy. It does involve disparate views about the sanctity of human life, regardless of quality, and conflicting perceptions of duties owed to the dying patient.

Judaism regards every life as being endowed with infinite value. It also regards every moment of life, regardless of quality, as endowed with infinite value. Until all vital forces ebb from the body, as evidenced by the total cessation of both respiratory and cardiac activity, human life must be treasured as a sacred gift. The adamancy of halakhic authorities in their refusal to accept "brain death" criteria is not at all an instance of otherworldly patriarchal figures refusing to acknowledge demonstrable scientific verities; it is entirely a matter of insistence upon the sanctity of every moment of human life.

Definitions, by their very nature, are tautologies. A definition of death cannot be derived from medical facts or scientific investigations alone. The physician is eminently qualified to describe the physiological state that he observes. But he can do no more than report his clinical observations. The physician may be called upon to determine whether medical science can, or cannot, be of further aid in maintaining or restoring vital functions. But, when such measures are potentially efficacious, the question whether a medical remedy or life support should actually be employed on behalf of a patient involves a value judgment rather than a scientific decision. Similarly, the question whether a human organism in any particular physiological state is to be regarded as a living person, and hence a deserving beneficiary of treatment, or as a corpse that may be abandoned with moral equanimity, is an ethical, religious and legal question, not a medical one. Accordingly, advances in medical diagnostic techniques, extremely valuable as they certainly are in determining the precise physiological state of the patient and in formulating a prognosis for cure, can have no bearing upon Jewish teaching on the duties owed a patient in a given physiological state.

The term "death" is descriptive rather than prescriptive; hence its use is a matter of convention. Were there a consensus to that effect, the term might be withheld until the onset of rigor mortis, or it might be extended to include a patient in a terminal coma or swoon.[1] Nevertheless, descriptive application of the term has come to portend extinction of duties of care and preservation of any remaining vital functions. Accordingly, for emotional and associative reasons, ascription of death to a human organism is, in common parlance, not simply a description of a particular physical state but also a principled judgment regarding how the organism is to be treated. Pronouncement of death signals, *inter alia*, a call to the undertaker, imminent commencement of mourning, notice to heirs that they may succeed to the decedent's estate and a declaration of spousal capacity to contract a new marriage. Those matters are moral, legal and halakhic in nature, not medical. It is perfectly possible to conceive of moral or legal systems in which they must abide decomposition of the body, the onset of putrefaction or rigor mortis. Rastafarians do demand the presence of these criteria before permitting interment of the corpse. The requirement imposed by statute in many European jurisdictions as recently as a century ago for the lapse of a seventy-two hour waiting period before burial effectively incorporated putrefaction among the criteria required for treating a person as a corpse. Common law, paralleling precisely the provisions of Halakhah, defined death as "total stoppage of the circulation of the blood and a cessation of the animal and vital functions consequent thereupon, such as respiration, pulsation, etc."[2] Absence of evidence of neurological activity in the brain is now the legal definition of death in most jurisdictions. Many physicians and ethicists advocate further reformulation of the definition of death so that a non-sapient patient in a permanent vegetative state may be pronounced dead. These conflicting positions involve no factual dispute whatsoever; the controversy is entirely over value judgments and/or received traditions.

I. HALAKHIC REJECTION OF BRAIN DEATH AS A CRITERION

A person unfamiliar with the extensive rabbinic literature concerning this topic may well ask whether Judaism cannot accommodate a neurological

[1] See Rambam, *Guide of the Perplexed*, book I, ch. 42, who does indeed assert that, in biblical usage, the word "*mavet*" is a homonym having precisely such connotations.

[2] *Black's Law Dictionary*, rev. 4th ed. (1968).

definition of death. Support for such a position might be adduced from a superficial reading of the Mishnah, *Oholot* 1:6: "And likewise cattle and wild beasts . . . if their heads have been severed, they are unclean [as carrion] even if they move convulsively like the tail of a newt (or lizard) that twitches spasmodically [after being severed from the body]."[3] Destruction of tissue as the result of liquefaction, it may be argued, is tantamount to severance or excision of such tissue. Consequently, there is indeed a measure of cogency in the argument that total liquefaction of brain tissue is tantamount to physiological decapitation.[4]

[3] See, however, the commentary of Rosh, *ad locum*, who differs from other commentators in asserting that, according to both Rashi and *Tosafot*, the definition of death recorded in the Mishnah is limited to death of animals but does not constitute a definition of death for human beings. Cf. *infra*, note 4 and R. Moses Feinstein, *Iggerot Mosheh, Yoreh De'ah*, vol. II, no. 174, sec. 1, who expresses doubt as to whether Rosh intends to exclude only the various other forms of "severance" of the head described *infra*, note 4, or actual decapitation as well.

[4] However, the argument is not conclusive. The Gemara, *Ḥullin* 21a, records three conflicting opinions regarding the connotation of the phrase "whose heads have been severed": (1) decapitation; (2) severance of the spinal column in the thoracic area together with severance of the trachea and the esophagus in their entirety; (3) severance of the spinal column in the thoracic area coupled with perforation of the major portion of both the trachea and the esophagus. *Tosafot* assert that there is a fourth opinion, *viz.*, severance of the spinal column and of the major portion of the muscle tissue surrounding the thoracic cavity. In a responsum written by the brother of *Taz*, appended to the commentary of *Taz, Yoreh De'ah* 26, the author asserts that severance of the spinal column in this context includes severance of the spinal cord as well. If "severance" of the head is to be understood as synonymous with death because of resultant dysfunction of the brain – or, more precisely, if dysfunction of the brain is tantamount to destruction of the brain and destruction of the brain is synonymous with death – the additional requirement for severance of the trachea and esophagus in whole or in part or of severance of muscle tissue is incomprehensible: severance of the spinal cord in the thoracic area effectively renders the brain dysfunctional. The requirement for severance of additional organs or tissue leaves no basis for a conclusion that even pithing of the brain is, in itself, synonymous with death. Death, then, appears to be defined, not as dysfunction or even destruction of the brain, but as removal or separation of the brain together with additional tissue from the body. Thus, even total lysis would not be categorized halakhically as decapitation because the trachea, esophagus and muscle tissue remain intact.

Moreover, Rambam, *Hilkhot Sheḥitah* 6:4, declares: "If the brain gushes out like water or flows like melted wax [the animal] is a *treifah*." A similar ruling is recorded in *Shulḥan Arukh, Yoreh De'ah* 31:2. Since, by definition, a *treifah* is alive, it follows that an animal or human being is regarded as yet alive even though the brain is entirely liquefied. See R. Yitzchak Zilberstein, *Yated Ne'eman* (Tevet 20, 5755), *Mosaf Shabbat*, p. 9.

It has been argued that severance of the head, as described in *Oholot* and defined in *Ḥullin*, is not a novel definition of death in terms of decapitation in the sense of destruction of the brain, but rather that the severe loss of blood as a result of decapitation renders all residual motion or movement of limbs or organs, including the heart, spasmodic. Thus, the essential and intrinsic criterion of life is vital motion; cardiac activity, which, as will be shown, is the primary indicator of life, is simply one form, and indeed the primary example, of vital motion.

Decapitation, however, involves physical severance of the entire brain from the body. Physiological decapitation, then, must also be defined as physiological destruction of the entire brain. That phenomenon has simply never been observed. To be sure, autopsies performed on patients pronounced dead on the basis of neurological criteria reveal that the brain has become a spongy, liquidy mass.[5] In colloquial medical parlance this phenomenon is categorized as "respirator brain" because the condition is found in patients sustained on a respirator for a lengthy period of time and is the result of lysis or liquefaction of the brain.[6] However, total lysis apparently does not occur in such patients; only a portion of the brain turns to liquid. It is indeed the case that tissue degeneration resulting in lysis is progressive in nature and consequently it might be assumed that at some point the entire brain will liquefy. Nevertheless, that phenomenon is not present at the time "brain death" criteria become manifest. There is no diagnostic method for determining when total lysis has occurred, nor has total lysis ever been observed upon autopsy. Although the neurological causes are obscure, there is strong reason to believe that cardiac activity ceases long before total lysis could possibly occur. Systemic death, including cardiac arrest, virtually always follows no later than two to ten days subsequent

Thus, *Oholot* 1:6 and *Yoma* 85a do not represent two disjunctive definitions of death, but reflect one unitary definition, *viz.*, vital motion in any organ or limb. *Yoma* 85a defines death as the total absence of motion in any organ of the body as manifested by cessation of both respiratory and cardiac activity; *Oholot* 1:6 defines death as the cessation of integrated, vital motion that attends the copious loss of blood accompanying decapitation. See J. David Bleich, *Ha-Pardes* (Tevet 5737), pp. 15–18; *Torah she-be-al Peh* (5744), vol. XXV, pp. 158–61; *Or ha-Mizraḥ* (Tishri 5748), p. 84; and *Be-Netivot ha-Halakhah* (Hoboken, NJ, 2000), vol. III, pp. 106–10.

The comments of R. Judah Aryeh of Modena in his commentary on *Ein Ya'akov*, *Amar ha-Boneh*, *Yoma* 85a, are readily understood on the basis of the foregoing analysis. R. Judah Aryeh of Modena sought to explain the criteria of death posited by the Gemara in light of Galen's proofs that it is the brain that is the source of sensation, respiration and movement. Accepting the notion that the brain is the "dwelling place of life" (*mishkan ha-ḥiyut*), he asserts that examination of the nostrils for absence of respiration and examination of the heart for absence of cardiac activity confirms that brain function – the source of all motion – has ceased as well. Hence, continued respiration or cardiac activity is conclusive evidence that brain function has not ceased; see *infra*, note 8. The comments of R. Judah Aryeh of Modena certainly do not serve as a basis for acceptance of neurological criteria of death. Cf. Fred Rosner and Moses D. Tendler, "Definition of Death in Judaism," *Journal of Halacha and Contemporary Society*, no. XVII (Spring 1989), p. 28, in which these comments are incompletely cited. It should also be noted that despite the inclusion of his aggadic commentary in standard editions of *Ein Ya'akov*, the views of R. Judah Aryeh of Modena are not generally cited in the annals of halakhic scholarship.

5 This is, however, not always the case. At times, particularly when the patient has been on a respirator for only a brief period of time before the diagnosis of brain death, changes in the brain may be minimal. See A. Earl Walker, *Cerebral Death*, 3rd ed. (Baltimore, MD, 1985), p. 123.

6 For a detailed description of "respirator death" see Walker, *Cerebral Death*, pp. 119–23.

to the manifestation of brain death criteria.[7] For reasons not fully understood by medical science, life, as conventionally defined, cannot long continue after brain function has been so seriously compromised.[8] Thus, "brain

[7] See President's Commission for the Study of Ethical Problems in Medicine and Biomedical and Biochemical Research, *Defining Death: A Report on the Medical, Legal and Ethical Issues in the Determination of Death* (July 1981), p. 17. The earliest study of the interval between manifestation of brain death criteria and systemic death reports that the heart can continue to function without any cerebral influence for one to seven days; see the discussion in "Colloque sur les états frontières entre la vie et la mort," ed. by Robert P. Vigorney, *Marseille Chirurgical* (January–February 1966), vol. 18, no. 1, pp. 1–194. Others have reported continued cardiac activity in brain dead patients for a period of between one and seven days, with an average of 2.5 days; see G.F. Ouakine, "Cardiac and Metabolic Alterations in Brain Death: Discussion Paper," *Brain Death: Interrelated Medical and Social Issues, Annals of the New York Academy of Sciences*, vol. 315 (1978), p. 252. Yet other early studies report that patients who manifest the Harvard Criteria will suffer somatic death within two to four weeks; see P.M. Black, "Brain Death," *New England Journal of Medicine*, vol. 299 (August 17, 1978), pp. 338–44 and vol. 299, no. 8 (August 24, 1978), pp. 393–401; and J. L. Bernat, "On the Definition and Criterion of Death," *Annals of Internal Medicine*, vol. 94, no. 3 (March 1981), pp. 389–94. A report of other studies conducted in three separate medical institutions during that period reveals that the median time between these two events was between 3.5 and 4.5 days; see Bryan Jennett *et al.*, "Brain Death in Three Neurological Units," *British Medical Journal*, vol. 282 (January 14, 1981), pp. 533–39. The same principal investigator reports that in none of those cases did cardiac activity persist longer than fourteen days; see Bryan Jennett and Catherine Hessett, "Brain Death in Britain as Reflected in Renal Donors," *British Medical Journal*, vol. 281 (August 1, 1981), p. 359. A more recent study reveals that, in the patients studied, spontaneous cardiac death occurred between eight hours and 10.4 days following brain death, with a mean of approximately 2.5 days; see Madeleine M. Grigg *et al.*, "Electroencephalographic Activity after Brain Death," *Archives of Neurology*, vol. 44, no. 9 (September 1987), p. 949. Another recent report concerning brain death in children reveals that the interval between clinical recognition of brain death and spontaneous cardiac death ranges between six hours and twelve days, with a mean of 3.7 days; see L. A. Alvarez *et al.*, "EEG and Brain Death Determination in Children," *Neurology*, vol. 38, no. 2 (February, 1988), p. 228. For reports of isolated instances of survival for longer periods see Joseph F. Parise *et al.*, "Brain Death with Prolonged Somatic Survival," *New England Journal of Medicine*, vol. 306, no. 1 (January 7, 1982), pp. 14–16 and subsequent letters to the editor published in vol. 306, no. 22 (June 3, 1982), pp. 1361–63. The longest reported period of survival subsequent to brain death occurred in a pregnant woman who delivered a baby by Caesarian section at 31 weeks' gestation, 63 days after a diagnosis of death was made on the basis of the Harvard criteria; see David R. Field, "Maternal Death During Pregnancy," *Journal of the American Medical Association*, vol. 260, no. 6 (August 12, 1988), pp. 816–22.

[8] Respiration is controlled by the vagus nerve, whose nucleus is located in the medulla; hence respiratory activity cannot continue after destruction of the brain stem or cessation of brain stem activity. The beating of the heart is autonomous, although the rate of the heartbeat is controlled by the sympathetic nervous system. Hence, in theory, cardiac activity may continue indefinitely even subsequent to destruction of the brain. Nevertheless, survival of the sympathetic nervous system is probably dependent upon cerebral influences. Hypothermia, which serves to counteract the stimulatory effect of the central system, has been reported in brain dead patients prior to cardiac arrest. Body temperature is regulated by the hypothalamus within the brain. It has been shown that hypothalamic activity persists, at least for a time, even in patients in whom "brain death" has been diagnosed. See *infra*, note 13. Thus it is quite

death," although not synonymous with death itself, is a harbinger of impending death.

The foregoing description of the physical state of the brain at the time of "brain death" is freely conceded by medical advocates of adoption of brain death criteria. Research scientists who support acceptance of neurological criteria for pronouncement of death argue, not that those neurological criteria establish that brain tissue has been destroyed, but that those criteria serve to establish that the brain has ceased to function and hence, although physically the brain remains intact, irreversible lack of functionality should be equated with excision or "death" of that organ. Thus it is not physical destruction of the brain but the physiological dysfunction of the organ that is equated with decapitation.

For halakhic purposes, dysfunction of an organ is not the equivalent of its destruction or excision. A male whose testes have been removed is forbidden to cohabit with a Jewish woman of legitimate birth; a person whose testes remain intact but have been rendered dysfunctional suffers no such liability. Similarly, an animal whose liver has been removed is a *treifah*[9] and its meat is forbidden; the meat of an animal whose liver performs no physiological function is permissible. Excision is defined as removal, either as a result of trauma or surgery. Alternatively, it is defined as degeneration of tissue,[10] either through necrosis to the degree that it becomes "tissue which crumbles in the finger" (*basar she-nifrakh be- ẓiporen*)[11] or through "decay" to the degree that it becomes "tissue which a physician scrapes away" (*basar she-ha-rofeh gorero*),[12] i.e., gangrenous tissue.[13] The brain tissue of a patient pronounced dead

possible that *total* cessation of all brain function, including hypothalamic functions, rapidly leads to cardiac death and, conversely, cardiac activity may persist for a relatively short period in brain dead patients only because the patients are as yet not truly "brain dead," i.e., some residual brain functions have not ceased. Cf. David Field, *supra*, note 7, p. 818.

9 For a definition of a *treifah* see Part Two of this chapter, Notes and Questions, no. 6.

10 It must be stressed that mere cessation of blood flow to the brain is not the halakhic equivalent of decapitation. Total curtailment of blood flow to an organ is not tantamount to excision of that organ for purposes of rendering the animal a *treifah*; only subsequent necrosis has that effect. Similarly, severance of the head from the body is not equated with death because of the absence of an integrated blood flow between the brain and the body but because of the physical severance of the brain from the body – or, arguably, its physiological equivalent in the form of total necrosis or total lysis of the brain – which is equated with disintegration of the organism and hence with death.

11 See *Ḥullin* 46b.

12 See *Ḥullin* 53b.

13 The Mishnah, *Bekhorot* 37a, and the Gemara, *Ḥullin* 46b, describe a "dry" (*yavesh*) or withered ear in a manner suggesting that a limb or organ in the state described is regarded as non-existent. The category of *yavesh* is defined by the Gemara, *Ḥullin* 46b, as the absence of even a "drop of blood" when the flesh is pierced. That level of degeneration is contrasted with that of *basar she-nifrakh be- ẓiporen* with the ensuing explanation that tissue of an internal organ that has

according to neurological criteria does not match, or even approximate, those levels of degeneration.[14]

Moreover, as a rejection of currently accepted criteria of "brain death," the foregoing is superfluous, indeed a form of "overkill." Currently accepted neurological criteria of death, singly or in combination, demonstrate only that specific neurological activities have ceased. For example, absence of elicitable reflexes confirms just that phenomenon and nothing more; absence of reflex activity does not demonstrate that all electrical activity has ceased. Even a flat EEG – which is not regarded as an absolute requirement for establishing brain death – demonstrates only the absence of elicitable brain waves; it does not rule out the possible presence of electrical activity below the sensitivity threshold of the apparatus. A British physician has candidly stated that "in the usual clinical context of brain death there is no certain way of ascertaining (other than by angiographic inference) that major areas of the brain such as the cerebellum, the basal ganglia, or the thalami, have irreversibly ceased to function."[15] Other medical researchers report that hypothalamic-pituitary function is maintained after the diagnosis of "brain stem death."[16] The hypothalamus, a structure that is part of the brain stem, regulates body temperature. It has been shown that hypothalamic activity persists, at least for a time, even in patients in whom "brain death" has been diagnosed.[17] There is also evidence that posterior pituitary function, specifically antidiuretic hormone secretion, persists in "brain dead" patients. Persons in whom the hypothalamus and neurohypophysis are non-functional should develop central diabetes insipidus because of the lack of antidiuretic hormone regulation. A number of studies have shown that many "brain dead" patients do not develop such a disorder.[18] One group of

not totally degenerated may possibly heal, but the tissue of an ear, once it has become "dry," can never heal because the ear is constantly exposed to the wind. Therefore, insofar as external organs are concerned, a lesser level of tissue degeneration is equated with destruction of the organ. Cf. *Iggerot Mosheh, Oraḥ Ḥayyim*, vol. I, nos. 8 and 9.

14 Walker, *Cerebral Death*, p. 122, comments: "The brains of persons suspected of brain death have minimal to severe necrotic changes. None of the brains are normal, but only 1 to 2% are completely mushy. The alterations found in brains from patients suffering from similar conditions and for essentially the same length of time are varied, which suggests that other factors are responsible for the changes."

15 Christopher Pallis, *British Medical Journal*, vol. 291 (September 7, 1985), p. 666.

16 G. M. Hall *et al.*, "Hypothalamic Pituitary Functions in the 'Brain-Dead' Patient," *Lancet* (December 6, 1980), p. 1259. See *supra*, note 6.

17 *Loc. cit.* See *supra*, note 6.

18 K. M. Outwater and M. A. Rockoff, "Diabetes Insipidus Accompanying Brain Death in Children," *Neurology*, vol. 34 (1984), pp. 1243–46; D. H. Fiser, J. F. Jimenez, V. Wrape and R. Woody, "Diabetes Insipidus in Children with Brain Death," *Critical Care Medicine*, vol. 15 (1987), pp. 551–53; M. Hohenegger, M. Vermes, W. Mauritz, G. Redl, P. Sporn and P.

researchers reported that only 8.5% of their patients showed clinical manifestations of diabetes insipidus.[19] Recent commentators have pointed out that the demonstrated phenomenon of residual neurological regulation represents not merely the presence of mere brain activity but brain function in the sense of "organized and directed cellular activity."[20]

Thus "brain death" criteria do not suffice for the diagnosis of permanent and irreversible cessation of all function of the brain stem. Certainly, total neurological dysfunction is compatible with continued cellular metabolism; unless metabolism has ceased the tissue perforce remains alive. Theoretically, blood flow studies and radioisotope scanning might be used to show that perfusion of the brain has ceased. Cellular decay of the neural tissue of the brain does indeed commence upon cessation of blood flow. Nevertheless, these techniques are inadequate for determining death in a manner consistent with halakhic requirements for a number of reasons:

(1) Although cellular decay of the brain does commence upon cessation of circulation of the blood, an indeterminate period of time is required for decay of the brain to become complete. Cessation of the flow of blood to the brain cannot in itself be equated with total cellular destruction of the brain. At present, there is no scientific method that serves to establish how much time must elapse following cessation of perfusion for total cellular decay to result. Moreover, as earlier indicated, it is likely that, physiologically, cardiac activity must cease well before this phenomenon could possibly occur.

(2) These techniques, in their current state of refinement, simply do not demonstrate that even perfusion of the brain has totally ceased. Investigators responsible for the development of these techniques claim only that such methods may be used to indicate cessation of circulation to the cerebrum, which is the seat of the so-called "higher functions" of the human organism. They are careful to describe the phenomena that they report as "cerebral death" rather than as "brain death."[21] These phenomena are compatible with some degree of continued circulation and perfusion of the medulla and the brain stem.

Eiselsberg, "P. Serum Vasopressin (AVP) Levels in Polyuric Brain-Dead Organ Donors," *European Archives of Psychiatry and Neurological Science*, vol. 239 (1990), pp. 267–69; and K. Arita, T. Uozumi, S. Old, M. Ohtani, H. Taguchi and M. Morio, "Hypothalamic Pituitary Function in Brain Dead Patients," *No Shinkei Geka*, vol. 16 (1988), pp. 1163–71.

19 A. Grenvik, D. J. Powner and J. V. Snyder, "Cessation of Therapy in Terminal Illness and Brain Death," *Critical Care Medicine*, vol. 6, no. 4 (July–August 1978), pp. 284–91.

20 Ami Halevy and Baruch Brody, "Brain Death: Reconsidering Definitions, Criteria, and Tests," *Annals of Internal Medicine*, vol. 119, no. 6 (September 15, 1993), p. 520.

21 See P. Braunstein *et al.*, "A Simple Bedside Evaluation For Cerebral Blood Flow in the Study of Cerebral Death," *American Journal of Roentgenology, Radium Therapy and Nuclear Medicine*, vol. 118, no. 4 (August 1973), pp. 757–67; and Julius Korein *et al.*, "Radioisotopic

In fact, in the original studies, radioisotope techniques did not demonstrate total cessation of circulation to the cerebrum, but only that affected circulation had decreased below the level necessary to retain its integrity. The scanning methods employed in those studies did not indicate that all circulation to even a part of the brain, i.e., the cerebrum, had been interrupted, but only that the rate of flow was below that necessary to maintain functional integrity. Thus, in a summary of findings that forms part of one of those studies, these techniques are described as "indicative of significant circulatory *deficit* to the cerebrum."[22] Those studies indicate the presence of up to approximately 24% of normal predicated blood flow.[23] More recently, another researcher has claimed that the isotope angiography that he employed is capable of showing termination of carotid circulation at the base of the skull,[24] but at the same time he frankly concedes that posterior circulation may continue with the result that "persistent perfusion and survival of the brain stem" remains a distinct possibility.[25] Another study involving a small number of pediatric patients used both the isotope bolus technique and cerebral angiography and somewhat surprisingly demonstrated persistent EEG activity despite negative blood flow studies.[26] The authors of that study candidly acknowledge that some circulation, either supplied by the external carotid system or in the form of limited cerebral perfusion, must have been present, albeit undetected by blood flow studies.[27] Yet another recent study reports that spontaneous respiration was observed in two patients in whom cerebral blood flow studies demonstrated no cerebral perfusion.[28] That finding is truly remarkable and demonstrates the inherent compatibility of negative blood flow studies with even the classic indicator of life.[29]

Bolus Technique as a Test to Detect Circulatory Deficits Associated with Cerebral Death," *Circulation*, vol. 51, no. 5 (May 1975), pp. 924–39.

22 Korein, "Radioisotopic Bolus Technique," p. 924.

23 See J. Korein, P. Braunstein *et al.*, "Brain Death: I. Angiographic Correlation with a Radioisotope Bolus Technique for Evaluation of a Critical Deficit of Cerebral Blood Flow," *Annals of Neurology*, vol. 2, no. 3 (September 1977), pp. 195–205. See also J. Pearson, J. Korein and P. Braunstein, "Morphology of Defectively Perfused Brains in Patients with Persistent Extracranial Circulation," *Annals of the New York Academy of Sciences*, vol. 315 (November 17, 1978), p. 267.

24 Julius M. Goodman *et al.*, "Confirmation of Brain Death with Portable Isotope Angiography: A Review of 204 Consecutive Cases," *Neurosurgery*, vol. 16, no. 4 (April 1985), p. 492.

25 *Loc. cit.*, p. 496.

26 See Stephen Ashwal and Sanford Schneider, "Failure of Electroencephalography to Diagnose Brain Death in Comatose Children," *Annals of Neurology*, vol. 6, no. 6 (December 1979), pp. 512–17.

27 *Loc. cit.*, p. 517.

28 See Madeleine Grigg *et al.*, "Electroencephalographic Activity after Brain Death," pp. 948f.

29 There have been at least two reported cases of the birth of live babies subsequent to the brain deaths of their mothers from natural causes. See William P. Dillon *et al.*, "Life Support

Moreover, it must be emphasized that blood flow studies are neither a legal requirement for pronouncing a patient dead on the basis of neurological standards nor are they routinely performed as a matter of medical practice.[30] Other neurological criteria are even less satisfactory than blood flow tests as halakhic criteria for establishing that cellular decay of the brain has occurred. Those criteria establish only irreversible cessation of neurological function in the lower regions of the brain; they do not constitute evidence that even a portion of the brain has been destroyed. *Oholot* 1:6 can, at most, be cited only to substantiate an argument that destruction of the entire brain is tantamount to death. Since radioisotope scanning techniques, even if employed, *do not* show termination of blood flow to the brain stem, any discussion of the validity of "brain death" in Jewish law is rendered theoretical by virtue of the fact that,

and Maternal Death During Pregnancy," *Journal of the American Medical Association*, vol. 248, no. 9 (September 3, 1982), pp. 1089–91; and David R. Field, *supra*, note 5. In a third case the patient satisfied generally accepted criteria of brain death although EEGs showed some slight, unspecific intermittent activity. However, the extensive brain damage evident upon post-mortem examination was compatible with clinical findings showing no detectable brain stem functions; see J. E. Heikkinen *et al.*, "Life Support for 10 Weeks with Successful Fetal Outcome after Fatal Maternal Brain Damage," *British Medical Journal*, vol. 290 (April 7, 1985), pp. 1237–38. *Tosafot, Ḥullin* 38b, *Bava Batra* 142b and *Niddah* 44a, maintain that, other than in cases of trauma, the fetus cannot survive the demise of its mother. Cf. *Magen Avraham, Oraḥ Ḥayyim* 330:10. Were "brain death" to be regarded by Halakhah as death, the reported phenomenon would constitute a post-mortem birth. This is, however, hardly a conclusive argument for rejecting neurological criteria since the principle that biological and physiological phenomena have undergone changes over a period of centuries (*nishtaneh ha-teva*) is well established; see *Tiferet Yisra'el, Bekhorot* 3:1. Nevertheless, the specter of a cadaver producing offspring does induce a measure of intuitive skepticism and should certainly give pause in accepting any novel theory that defines the mother as a cadaver. Despite the wide publicity given to a videotape presentation of the decapitation of a pregnant sheep and the subsequent birth of a live lamb, that experiment establishes nothing of halakhic import. The earlier cited comments of *Tosafot, Ḥullin* 38b, *Bava Batra* 142b and *Niddah* 44a, clearly indicate a recognition of the possibility of post-mortem birth when death results from trauma. See also *supra*, note 4.

In a similar vein, the need for, and the efficacy of, administration of pressor agents and antibiotics to patients declared "brain dead" but maintained on ventilators until organs can be harvested, although in itself of no halakhic import, is also a phenomenon that it is intuitively difficult to associate with a cadaver. See Christopher Pallis, "ABC of Brainstem Death: The Declaration of Death," *British Medical Journal*, vol. 286 (January 1, 1983), p. 39.

30 It should also be noted that, at least as applied by many physicians in clinical practice, recovery has occurred subsequent to manifestation of "brain death" criteria upon which the physician was prepared to rely. See William D. Goldie and Robert H. Price, "Recovery from 'Brain Death' with Absent Evoked Potentials," *Journal of Clinical Neurophysiology*, vol. 5, no. 4 (1988), p. 354; and A. Ogunyemi *et al.*, "Generalized Convulsive Seizure in a Patient with Clinical Features of Brain Death," *Epilepsia*, vol. 29, no. 5 (September–October 1988), p. 673. Amar S. N. Al-Din *et al.*, "Coma and Brain Stem Areflexia in Brain Stem Encephalitis (Fisher's Syndrome)," *British Medical Journal*, vol. 291 (August 24, 1985), pp. 535–36, report that three patients recovered from apneic coma accompanied by absent brain stem reflexes. The authors attribute the neurological phenomena manifested in those patients to brain stem encephalitis.

at present, the requisite criteria demanded by the advocates of that position are simply not demonstrable in a clinical setting.

A neurologist who accepts brain death criteria, Dr. James Bernat, has candidly conceded that:

> The bedside clinical examination is not sufficiently sensitive to exclude the possibility that small nests of brain cells may have survived . . . and that their continued functioning, although not contributing significantly to the functioning of the organism as a whole, can be measured by laboratory techniques.[31]

The Uniform Determination of Death Act does, however, specify that a person is dead only if he has sustained "irreversible cessation of *all functions of the entire brain*" (emphasis added). Quite apart from ongoing hypothalamic-pituitary function in patients manifesting clinically accepted criteria of "brain death," it is well established that clusters of brain cells may be perfused and continue to function on the cellular level. As Robert Veatch has noted, "The law does not grant a dispensation to ignore cellular function, no matter how plausible that may be."[32] Reliance upon neurological criteria of death in jurisdictions that have enacted a statute incorporating the language of the Uniform Determination of Death Act is in violation of the plain meaning of the statute.

(3) The performance of radioisotope scanning has no therapeutic benefit to the patient. In light of the halakhic prohibition against moving even the limb of a moribund patient, or *goses*, lest the patient's death be hastened it would be difficult, to say the least, to perform the procedure upon a moribund patient without violating applicable halakhic strictures.[33] The identical objection applies to at least some, if not most, of the various other neurological diagnostic procedures employed in pronouncing "brain death."[34]

The term "brain death" carries with it a certain emotional cachet and appeal. In point of fact, "brain death" is a misnomer: "Brain death" criteria establish irreversible neurological dysfunction, not cessation of metabolic functions; "brain death," when confirmed by blood flow studies, represents the onset

[31] James L. Bernat, "How much of the Brain Must Die in Brain Death?" *Journal of Clinical Ethics*, vol. 3, no. 1 (Spring 1992), p. 25.

[32] Robert Veatch, "The Impending Collapse of the Whole-Brain Definition of Death," *Hastings Center Report*, vol. 23, no. 4 (July–August 1993), p. 18.

[33] R. Shlomoh Zalman Auerbach is of the opinion that introducing a dye or other liquid, even in an already inserted intravenous line, constitutes a violation of this prohibition. See *Contemporary Halakhic Problems*, vol. IV, p. 347, note 56.

[34] Medically recognized danger posed by apnea testing has been documented by Joseph S. Jeret and Jeffrey L. Benjamin, "Risk of Hypotension During Apnea Testing," *Archives of Neurology*, vol. 51, no. 6 (June 1994), pp. 595–99.

of metabolic dysfunction, not necessarily "death" of the neural tissue; "brain death," even when supported by blood flow studies, represents confirmed metabolic dysfunction of only a portion of the brain, not of the brain in its entirety. "Brain death" criteria are not designed, properly speaking, to serve as clinical criteria for death but as proposed criteria for withholding further treatment and for withdrawing life-support systems. This is recognized and acknowledged by physicians who are sensitive to the ethical issues contingent upon this distinction. In a submission to the Working Party on Donor Organs of the Royal College of Physicians, dated January 23, 1987, two British physicians, Drs. D. Wainwright Evans and David J. Hill, correctly urge that a term such as "mortal brain damage" be substituted for "brain stem death."

None of this is at all novel. The chairman of the Ad Hoc Committee of the Harvard Medical School to Examine the Definition of Brain Death candidly acknowledged, "I was chairman of a recent *ad hoc* committee at Harvard composed of members of five faculties in the university who tried to define irreversible coma. We felt we could not define death. I suppose you will say that by implication we have defined it as brain death, but we do not make a point of that."[35] Consistent with that view the Harvard Committee's report setting forth clinical criteria of "brain death" was published under the title "A Definition of Irreversible Coma."[36] Other writers frankly conceded, "What we are attempting to define and establish beyond reasonable doubt is the state of irreversible damage to the brain stem. It is the point of no return."[37] Similarly, the statement concerning brain death issued in Great Britain by the Conference of Royal Medical Colleges in 1976 indicated that "brain stem death" is indicative of a hopeless outcome for the patient and recommended use of that criterion for removing the patient from a respirator in order to allow the patient to die.[38] Only in 1979 did that body declare that "brain stem death"

35 Henry K. Beecher, "Definitions of 'Life' and 'Death' for Medical Science and Practice," *Annals of the New York Academy of Sciences*, vol. 169, part 2 (January 21, 1970), p. 471.

36 *Journal of the American Medical Association*, vol. 205, no. 6 (August 5, 1968), pp. 337–40. Criticism on the grounds that use of this term "perpetuates confusion in the medical field between the state of being permanently unconscious, as are patients in a persistent vegetative state, and that of being dead" is unwarranted. See the report of the President's Commission for the Study of Ethical Problems in Medicine and Biomedical and Behavioral Research, *Deciding to Forego Life-Sustaining Treatment, A Report on the Ethical, Medical and Legal Issues in Treatment Decisions* (March 1983), p. 173. The distinction between irreversible coma and systemic death is clear and precise. Moreover, the persistent vegetative state is readily distinguishable from irreversible coma.

37 A. Mohandas and Shelley N. Chou, "Brain Death – A Clinical and Pathological Study," *Journal of Neurosurgery*, vol. 35, no. 2 (August 1971), p. 215.

38 This is the purpose for which neurological criteria are recognized in Sweden and Poland. In those countries manifestation of brain death criteria is not unequivocally equated with

may be equated with the death of a person. In a Supplementary Statement for the R.C.P. Working Party on Donor Organs, dated January 23, 1987, Dr. David J. Hill writes, "The motives for this change are ethically questionable, as is the logic upon which it is based, the assumption that 'all functions of the brain have permanently and irreversibly ceased.' This statement is, to say the least, doubtful."

Medical scientists employ the term "brain death" even though it is a misnomer because it is a term laymen can comprehend as denoting a physiological state in which any further treatment is not only contraindicated but would be regarded as ludicrous. Introducing the term "brain death" is a thinly veiled attempt to justify withholding treatment under the guise of a redefinition of terms. The purpose of this lexicographical exercise is to secure moral and emotional approbation for a policy that would otherwise be greeted with repugnance and even indignation. Withholding treatment has the effect of snuffing out human life. Any *ad hoc* decision to withhold treatment from a dying relative involves a great deal of soul-searching and frequently engenders feelings of guilt. On the other hand, no one advocates medical treatment or continuation of life-support for a corpse. Pronouncing a person dead has the emotional effect of removing any aura of further moral responsibility. In a less than fully informed world, semantic sleight of hand may affect popular perception, but it should not be permitted to affect the universe of moral discourse.

So-called brain death criteria simply have no basis in Halakhah both because the clinical conditions ostensibly posited by employment of the term simply do not exist and because, even if they did exist, they would not satisfy the halakhic criteria of death. In response to a question concerning one of the ramifications of employing "brain death" criteria, Rabbi Aaron Soloveichik has aptly and accurately stated, "In order to answer this question I have to have recourse to my imagination. Without recourse to imagination it is impossible

death but is accepted as warranting withdrawal of ventilating support. Consequently, in those countries, organs may not be removed for transplantation while the heart is still beating. See Christopher Pallis, "ABC of Brain Stem Death: The Position in the U.S.A. and Elsewhere," *British Medical Journal*, vol. 286 (January 15, 1983), p. 210.

In this country, recognition that "brain dead" persons are, in actuality, not dead is reflected in the ambivalence of some physicians engaged in medical research towards use of "neomorts" as experimental subjects. See Willard Gaylin, *Harvesting the Dead* (New York, 1974), pp. 23–30. See also Barry Collar, "The Newly Dead as Research Subjects," *Clinical Research*, vol. 37, no. 3 (September 1989), pp. 487–94. Dr. Collar reports that, since he regarded his experiments as having "elements common to both human experimentation on the living and organ donation," he sought to develop a protocol combining safeguards developed for each of those procedures. *Ibid.*, p. 489.

for me to assume even for a moment, for argument's sake, that the Harvard criteria conform to the halachah . . . "[39]

II. CESSATION OF RESPIRATION AS SOLE CRITERION

Although the halakhic inadmissibility of brain death criteria is obvious, there are alternative criteria, even more liberal in nature, for which a much stronger *prima facie* case can be made. A detailed analysis of those criteria is in order because of the erroneous perception, perhaps even in the eyes of some of their advocates, that those criteria are synonymous with a brain death standard without which transplant procedures could not be successfully performed. The criteria were formulated in conjunction with a decision of the Chief Rabbinate Council of the State of Israel endorsing liver transplants. In the fall of 1987, the Ministry of Health, after prolonged deliberation, granted permission to the Rambam Medical Center in Haifa to perform liver transplants. One of the issues given careful consideration in the course of the deliberations was acceptance of a brain death standard. Despite phenomenal advances in recent years in both medical science and technology, it is still not possible to perform liver or heart transplants if removal of the donor's organ is delayed until death has been pronounced on the basis of conventional criteria. Delay in removal of these organs results in tissue degeneration that renders the organ useless as a transplant. In the course of the deliberations the Minister of Health turned to the Chief Rabbinate Council to ascertain Jewish law on the question. The Chief Rabbinate Council pondered the issue for months but failed to arrive at a conclusion. In the interim a new Minister of Health was appointed and permission for proceeding with the liver transplant was granted. On 1 Ḥeshvan 5747, after the liver transplant had already been performed, the Chief Rabbinate Council announced its endorsement of so-called brain death criteria but stipulated a number of conditions to be followed in pronouncing death and in the removal of the organs. That position was formulated in response to a request by Hadassah Hospital in Jerusalem for permission to perform a heart transplant. The decision of the Chief Rabbinate Council was published in *Teḥumin*, VII (5746), pp. 187–92.[40] Pursuant to the announcement of that decision, many prominent and renowned rabbinic decisors issued

39 See *Journal of Halacha and Contemporary Society*, no. XVII (Spring 1989), p. 44.

40 This decision was later republished in *Barka'i*, no. 4 (Spring 5747), pp. 11–13, accompanied by discussions authored by R. Mordecai Eliyahu and R. Saul Israeli: *Assia*, vol. XI, no. 2–3 (Nisan 5747), pp. 70–83; *Sefer Assia*, vol. VI (5749), pp. 27–40; and *Sefer Assia*, vol. VII (5754), pp. 123–24. English translations of the statement of the Chief Rabbinate Council appear in

pronouncements declaring that reliance upon brain death criteria contravenes Jewish law.[41]

In addition to the decision of the Chief Rabbinate Council, dated 1 Ḥeshvan 5747, that appeared in *Teḥumin*, a further letter, dated 23 Adar 5747, together with appended clarifying comments, was subsequently circulated to rabbis in various communities. That letter has been published in *Or ha-Mizraḥ*, Tishri 5748. A paper prepared at the request of the Chief Rabbinate Council for use in their deliberations that addresses both the medical and halakhic aspects of this issue was prepared by Dr. Abraham Steinberg and was published in the same issue of *Or ha-Mizraḥ*.

Although reports in the media indicated that the Chief Rabbinate Council had endorsed brain death, a careful reading of the published materials reveals that the term "brain death" is not mentioned either in the original decision or in the subsequent explanatory comments drafted by that body.[42] The

Assia: Jewish Medical Ethics (English edition), vol. I, no. 2 (May 1989), pp. 2–10 and *Tradition*, vol. XXIV, no. 4 (Summer 1989), pp. 1–7.

[41] For a list of those authorities and the publications in which their statements appear see *Contemporary Halakhic Problems*, vol. IV, p. 332.

[42] The Chief Rabbinate Council apparently does not accept its own announced criteria as unequivocal indicators of death. Section 7 of its statement restricts their use to removal of organs from "accident victims for the purpose of transplantation." There is no reference in the statement to using the criteria in cases of terminal illness, nor to using them for accident victims, when transplantation of vital organs is not contemplated.

With publication of the text of this statement in the English-language edition of *Assia* the editor of that journal appended a footnote, p. 8, no. 26, indicating that restricting use of the criteria to "accident victims" is designed to limit application of the criteria to patients who are halakhically considered to be in the category of *treifah*, i.e., a person who, by virtue of either a congenital anomaly or a trauma, has suffered the loss or perforation of an organ and, as a result, will expire within twelve months.

There exists a minority view that sanctions the sacrifice of a *treifah* for the purpose of rescuing a non-*treifah*. The chief exponent of that view is *Minḥat Ḥinnukh*, no. 296. By implication, it may be attributed to some few other authorities as well. Such a position was advanced hypothetically by *Noda bi-Yehudah, Ḥoshen Mishpat, Mahadura Tinyana*, no. 59, only to be vigorously rejected by that authority as an absurdity. The permissive position was first advanced as a consideration in the removal of a donor's heart for transplant by R. Judah Gershuni, *Or ha-Mizraḥ* (Nisan 5729), reprinted in his *Kol Ẓofayikh* (Jerusalem, 5740), pp. 375–77. See also R. Mordecai Halperin, "Hashtalat Lev al Pi ha-Halakhah," *Emek Halakhah*, I (Jerusalem, 5746), pp. 96–104. The view of *Noda bi-Yehudah* is fully endorsed by R. Moses Feinstein, *Iggerot Mosheh, Yoreh De 'ah*, vol. II, no. 174; R. Yitzchak Ya'akov Weisz, *Minḥat Yiẓḥak*, vol. V, no. 7, secs. 6–9; R. Eliezer Waldenberg, *Ẓiẓ Eli'ezer*, vol. X, no. 25, ch. 5; and R. Shlomoh Zalman Auerbach, as cited by Dr. Abraham S. Abraham, *Nishmat Avraham, Yoreh De'ah* 252:8, n. 24. See also R. Simchah Bunim Lazerson, *Mishnat Ḥayyei Sha'ah: Hashtalat Evarim le-Or ha-Halakhah* (Jerusalem, 5754), pp. 41–46 and *idem*, *Assia*, vol. XIV, no. 3 (Tevet 5755), pp. 70–71.

Apparently the Chief Rabbinate Council was not prepared to accept the announced criteria unreservedly and was willing to rely upon them only when further supported by at least

reference in those documents is to "a person whose independent respiration has manifestly ceased and there is no anticipation whatsoever for its return," who, under such circumstances, is described as dead since "there is no life, nor is there a criterion of life." In their clarifying comments the Chief Rabbinate Council declared even more explicitly that "death is determined by cessation of respiration and not by destruction of the brain; destruction of the brain demonstrates that there is no independent respiration." In his article, Dr. Steinberg seeks to demonstrate that determination of death as formulated by the Sages of the Talmud is dependent solely upon lack of respiration but "since there are many situations in which it is possible to restore normal respiration it is necessary to support the determination of the Sages with proof that respiration has indeed ceased forever... This can be accomplished by means of demonstration of... destruction of the brain stem." The clear implication of that statement is that the determining factor in establishing that death has occurred is cessation of respiration. However, cessation of respiration as an absolute indicator of death must be total and irreversible. Accordingly, since as a result of contemporary advances in medical science there are clinical conditions in which respiration may be restored, it is therefore necessary to regard the patient as "possibly alive" until it has been demonstrated that the brain stem has been destroyed. Only then, according to Dr. Steinberg, is it absolutely certain that respiration cannot be restored. Thus, death is intrinsically defined as cessation of spontaneous respiration; neurological criteria serve only to substantiate and confirm the fact that respiratory death has indeed occurred. Accordingly, at the conclusion of his article, Dr. Steinberg entirely negates the opinion that "brain death" is itself an intrinsic criterion of death. Those who erroneously maintain that "brain death" constitutes a valid definition of death in Jewish law require blood flow studies in order to demonstrate that circulation to the brain has ceased, because they equate absence of blood circulation to the brain with physiological decapitation. Dr. Steinberg dismisses this requirement as superfluous because, he asserts, it is irreversible cessation of spontaneous respiratory activity that is the determining factor and that phenomenon can be established beyond doubt on the basis of other neurological criteria.

There is little question that if irreversible cessation of respiration were regarded as the sole criterion establishing that death has occurred, the theoretical possibility that, in some rare instances, respiration might be restored would be disregarded. The clinical symptoms of death delineated by the

the minority view that sanctions the sacrifice of a *treifah* in saving the life of a non-*treifah*. Consequently, the Chief Rabbinate Council restricted application of the criteria to "accident victims" and, even in the case of accident victims, for the express purpose of preserving life.

Sages of the Talmud were known by them not to be error-proof. *Masekhet Semaḥot*, ch. 8, reports that at a time when interment was carried out in hollow crypts in the side of a mountain it was customary to visit the burial site intermittently for a period of days after interment lest perchance some sign of life be evident. It is reported that on one occasion a person was found to be alive and survived for twenty-five years. *Teshuvot Ḥatam Sofer, Yoreh De'ah*, no. 338, dismisses the narrative as describing a highly improbable event that may occur "once in a thousand years." Cessation of respiration, declares Ḥatam Sofer, must be determined by "experts" and it is not only permissible, but also obligatory to rely upon such expert determination in order not to delay burial of the deceased. To be sure, when there is a persuasive medical possibility that respiratory arrest is reversible, e.g., when cardio-pulmonary resuscitation is medically indicated, mere absence of respiration cannot be assumed to be dispositive; otherwise, no further confirmatory indicators are required.

In many clinical situations, brain death criteria are no more necessary to determine that respiratory activity has irreversibly ceased than are blood flow studies. There are many end-stage illnesses in which an absolute determination that spontaneous respiration has irreversibly ceased can be made without benefit of neurological confirmation of "death" of the brain stem. The best examples of such medical conditions are amyotrophic lateral sclerosis (Lou Gehrig's disease) and anencephalus in newborns.

The position that irreversible cessation of respiration is the sole determining factor in pronouncing death leads to a conclusion that would be dismissed by everyone as absurd. Polio, fortunately, is not the scourge it was some years ago. But the memories of polio victims who were forced to breathe in iron lung machines for their survival are very vivid. If respiratory activity is regarded as the sole determining criterion of the presence of life, it would follow that a polio victim who is entirely dependent upon an iron lung machine or a similar device in order to breathe would be regarded as dead despite the fact that he is fully conscious and capable of engaging in intellectual activities requiring a high degree of cognition. Even if the polio victim's loss of respiratory activity cannot be positively diagnosed as irreversible, were respiratory activity to be accepted as the sole indicator of life, his subsequent demise would retroactively establish that death actually occurred upon loss of spontaneous respiration. The response, as might be anticipated, is that irreversible cessation of respiration is designed to be applied as the determining criterion of death only in cases in which the patient is no longer conscious. The problem, however, is not resolved thereby. Nowhere in rabbinic literature is there the slightest hint that consciousness is an indicator of life or that its absence is an indication that death has occurred. Moreover, even if that caveat is accepted, this position yields the conclusion that any non-sapient patient who has suffered irreversible respiratory arrest is dead regardless of the presence of other vital signs including cardiac activity and neurological functions as evidenced by a positive EEG.

III. THE TALMUDIC SOURCES

It therefore becomes necessary to examine the talmudic sources that serve as the basis for establishing a definition of death and to examine the criteria that are delineated for use in making that determination. The primary source of this definition is found in the Gemara, *Yoma* 85a, in connection with suspension of Sabbath regulations for the sake of preserving human life. The case in point concerns an individual trapped under the debris of a fallen building. Since desecration of the Sabbath is mandated even on the mere chance that human life may be preserved, the rubble must be cleared away, even if it is doubtful that a person might have survived under the debris. However, once it has been determined with certainty that the accident victim has expired, no further violation of Sabbath regulations may be sanctioned. The question that then arises is how much of the body must be uncovered in order to ascertain conclusively that death has in fact occurred. Two opinions are recorded. The first opinion cited by the Gemara maintains that the nose must be uncovered and the victim is to be pronounced dead only if, upon examination of the nostrils, no sign of respiration is detected. The second opinion maintains that death may be determined by examination of the chest for the absence of a heartbeat. Thereupon follows a statement of Rav Papa to the effect that there is no disagreement in instances in which the body is uncovered "from the top down." In such cases, absence of respiration is regarded by all as conclusive. The dispute, declares R. Papa, is limited to a situation in which the body is uncovered "from the bottom up" and thus the heart is uncovered first.

It is quite possible to read this statement of the Gemara as indicating that the controversy reflected in these two opinions is with regard to whether absence of a heartbeat is itself to be accepted as a sufficient condition in establishing that death has occurred. Accordingly, the first opinion insists upon examination of the nostrils in order to determine that respiration has ceased because respiration is the sole criterion of life. The second opinion maintains that, while if examination "from the top down" reveals that there is no respiration that in itself may be taken as a sufficient indication that death has occurred, nevertheless when the body is uncovered from "the bottom up" absence of cardiac activity is equally regarded as a sufficient indication that death has occurred. Since both Rambam, *Hilkhot Shabbat* 2:19, and *Shulḥan Arukh, Oraḥ Ḥayyim* 329:4, rule in accordance with the first opinion it might be concluded that respiration is indeed the sole determining factor and therefore irreversible cessation of respiration is both a necessary and sufficient criterion of death.

This analysis, attractive as it may be as a literal reading of the Gemara, is contradicted by Rashi in two separate comments. Rashi introduces the discussion in *Yoma* 85a with the remark that the controversy concerning examination of the nostrils or of the heart is limited to situations in which the victim is "comparable to a corpse in that he does not move his limbs." In those words, Rashi clearly negates any interpretation of the Gemara that would regard respiratory activity as the sole criterion of life. According to Rashi, the presence of any vital force, as evidenced by movement of an organ or limb is, by definition, a conclusive indication that death has not occurred.[43] The connotation of the term "*ever*" employed by Rashi is not limited to a limb but connotes any organ of the body.[44] Accordingly, ongoing cardiac activity is, in and of itself, an absolute criterion of life even in patients incapable of spontaneous respiration.

[43] The problem, however, is that there is no hint in the discussion recorded in *Yoma* 85a that absence of movement is a necessary criterion of death. It seems that Rashi bases himself upon the language employed in *Oholot* 1:6. The Mishnah incorporates the phrase "even though they convulse spasmodically" in postulating death as the necessary and immediate result of decapitation. Inclusion of this justificatory phrase seems superfluous in light of the definition of death formulated in *Yoma* 85a. Decapitation perforce terminates respiration. Since cessation of respiratory activity is itself equated with death, continued movement should be an irrelevancy undeserving of mention. Yet the Mishnah finds it necessary to take note of that phenomenon. Accordingly, deduces Rashi, the unstated underlying premise must be that movement of a limb is an indicator of life and its presence negates other criteria of death. If so, the presence of residual movement in a decapitated animal should negate its status as carrion. Confronting that objection to its equation of decapitation with death, the Mishnah distinguishes spasmodic motion, or *pirkus*, from normal, and hence vital, motion. Presence of the latter does indeed negate other criteria of death; the former is irrelevant. Hence the conclusion formulated by Rashi that other criteria of death become significant only if movement of limbs has totally ceased. For further development of this point see the discussion in *Torah she-be-al Peh* (5744), vol. XXV, pp. 158–59 and *Be-Netivot ha-Halakhah*, vol. III, p. 107.

Recognition of the fact that the Mishnah's sole reference to a criterion of death is to absence of movement leads to the concept that absence of a heartbeat and absence of respiratory activity do not constitute independent criteria which must also be satisfied; rather, respiratory and cardiac activity are simply vital forms of movement which must cease before the organism is regarded as dead. Accordingly, *Oholot* 1:6 and *Yoma* 85a do not represent two disjunctive definitions of death but reflect a single criterion, *viz.*, the absence of all vital motion. Acceptance of this analysis yields the conclusion set forth *supra*, note 4.

[44] The human body is described in *Bekhorot* 45a and by Rashi *ad locum* as composed of 248 "*evarim*."

Moreover, Rashi adds a further comment indicating that the dispute recorded in the Gemara is not a dispute over whether death can be pronounced disjunctively by determining the absence of either cardiac function or respiratory activity or whether it can be determined solely by the absence of respiration. Rather, declares Rashi, the controversy concerns the diagnostic reliability of external examination of the chest. Insistence upon examination of the nostrils, stresses Rashi, is not because presence or absence of cardiac symptoms is irrelevant but because "at times life is not recognizable at the heart but is recognizable at the nose." Rashi does not intend to suggest that spontaneous respiration may continue after cardiac arrest. He states simply that, for diagnostic purposes, it is necessary to examine the nostrils because inability to detect a heartbeat is inconclusive, as indeed it assuredly is, particularly in the case of a debilitated accident victim who may also be obese and, in addition, whose examination is performed without the aid of a stethoscope. In explaining the basis of the talmudic opinion that regards examination of the area surrounding the heart as sufficient, Rashi comments, "for it is there that the soul beats," i.e., the crucial indicator of life is the presence of a heartbeat. Rashi does not suggest that the opposing view rejects this fundamental verity; the opposing view rejects reliance upon examination of the heart, asserts Rashi, only because of the possibility of error in diagnosing the absence of a heartbeat. Rashi clearly understood that both opinions recognize cardiac activity as the primary indicator of the presence of life. Rashi's analysis leads inevitably to the finding that if, for whatever reason, cardiac activity persists after respiration has ceased the patient must be regarded as yet alive.

This analysis of Rashi's comments is expressly formulated by R. Zevi Ashkenazi, *Teshuvot Ḥakham Ẓevi*, no. 77. *Ḥakham Ẓevi* states explicitly that, in a situation in which "life" is not evident at the nose for whatever reason but is evident at the heart, the presence of cardiac activity is itself sufficient to negate any other presumptive evidence of death.[45] Ḥakham Ẓevi notes that in some cases a heartbeat may be imperceptible even though the individual is still alive. A weak beat may not be audible or otherwise perceptible since the rib cage and layers of muscle intervene between the heart itself and the outer skin. Respiration is more readily detectable, hence the insistence upon the examination of the nostrils. However, concludes *Ḥakham Ẓevi*, "It is most clear that

45 See R. Eliezer Waldenberg, *Ẓiẓ Eli'ezer*, vol. X, no. 25, ch. 4, sec. 7. Cf. also *Ẓiẓ Eli'ezer*, vol. IX, no. 46, sec. 5, who cites medieval writers on physiology – among them *Sha'ar ha-Shamayim*, a work attributed to the father of Gersonides – who declare that life is dependent upon nasal respiration because warm air from the heart is expelled from the nose and cold air, which cools the heart, enters through the nose. They thus clearly recognized that respiration without cardiac activity is impossible.

there can be no respiration unless there is life in the heart, for respiration is from the heart and for its benefit." According to *Ḥakham Ẓevi*, cessation of respiration constitutes the operative definition of death solely because lack of respiration, in usual circumstances, is also indicative of cessation of cardiac activity.[46] Similarly, R. Moses Sofer, *Teshuvot Ḥatam Sofer, Yoreh Deah*, no. 338, rules that absence of respiration is conclusive only if the patient "lies as an inanimate stone and there is no pulse whatsoever." In the same vein R. Joseph Saul Nathanson, *Yad Sha'ul, Yoreh De'ah*, no. 394, declares, "It is clear as the sun that the indicator of life is the beating of the heart or breathing of the nose." These sources indicate clearly that death occurs only upon cessation of both cardiac and respiratory functions.[47] Rabbenu Baḥya, in his commentary

[46] *Ḥakham Ẓevi*'s original ruling elicited the sharp disagreement of R. Jonathan Eibeschutz and sparked a controversy that has become classic in the annals of Halakhah. The dispute centered on a chicken that, upon evisceration, proved to have no discernible heart. The chicken was brought to *Ḥakham Ẓevi* for a determination as to whether the fowl was to be considered *treifah* because of the missing heart. *Ḥakham Ẓevi* ruled that the chicken was kosher because it is empirically impossible for a chicken to lack a heart since there can be no life whatsoever without a heart. The chicken clearly lived and matured; hence it must have had a heart that somehow became separated from the other internal organs upon the opening of the chicken and was inadvertently lost. The impossibility of life without a heart, in the opinion of *Ḥakham Ẓevi*, is so obvious a verity that even the testimony of witnesses attesting to the absence of the heart and the impossibility of error is to be dismissed as blatant perjury. R. Jonathan Eibeschutz, in a forceful contradictory opinion, argues that such a possibility cannot be dismissed out of hand. In his commentary on *Yoreh De'ah, Kereti u-Peleti* 40:4, R. Jonathan Eibeschutz contends that the functions of the heart, including the pumping of blood, might well be performed by an organ whose external form is quite unlike that of a normal heart and that may even be located in some other part of the body. This organ might be indistinguishable from other, more usual, tissue and hence the observer might have concluded that the animal or fowl lacked a "heart."

There is nothing in this opinion that contradicts the point made on the basis of *Ḥakham Ẓevi*'s responsum regarding determining the time of death. R. Jonathan Eibeschutz concedes that life cannot be sustained in the absence of some organ that performs cardiac functions. R. Jonathan Eibeschutz argues only that, in the apparent absence of a recognizable heart, some other organ may possibly perform these functions; he does not assert that life may continue following cessation of the functions normally performed by the heart.

[47] It must be emphasized that among both early-day and latter-day authorities there is not to be found a single commentator who contradicts Rashi's exposition in any way. Although some authorities, including *Teshuvot Radvaz*, vol. V, no. 108 and *Bet Yosef, Oraḥ Ḥayyim* 60, assert that Rashi's commentaries are not to be given the same weight as normative rulings of codifiers of the law, that principle of halakhic decision-making is not germane to the question at hand. *Ḥazon Ish* asserts that this principle is limited to comments that might reflect hypothetical positions or that might be construed as explaining an individual opinion recorded in the Gemara, but not to be applied to comments that are clearly intended as normative and definitive. Moreover, declares *Ḥazon Ish*, "All this could be discussed if there were some [authority] who disputed the matter and we would have need of deciding in accordance with the majority of opinions. But in the instant case in which we have not found a single early authority who disputes this matter, certainly the testimony of early authorities is accepted by

on Deuteronomy 6:5, describes the heart as the last of the organs of the body to die and remarks that the phrase "with all your heart" indicates that love of God must persist until the last moment of life, i.e., when death becomes complete upon cessation of the beating of the heart. The absence of other vital signs is not, insofar as Halakhah is concerned, sufficient to establish that death has occurred.

There is clear talmudic evidence establishing that cessation of respiration is itself not an absolute criterion of death. The Gemara, *Gittin* 70b, states that a person whose esophagus and trachea have been severed continues to enjoy legal capacity to execute a bill of divorce on behalf of his wife. Such an individual is described as "alive," albeit facing imminent death. He is regarded as living despite his obvious inability to breathe. Similarly, the Mishnah, *Ḥullin* 42a, enumerates perforation of the trachea as one of the forms of trauma that renders an animal a *treifah* and hence impermissible as food. It is noteworthy that apparently even perforation of the trachea in a manner resulting in termination of respiration renders the animal a *treifah* but not a *neveilah*, i.e., the animal is forbidden because it has suffered a trauma that will result in death but is not yet regarded as dead and hence is not forbidden as carrion. Certainly the individual described in *Gittin* 70b remains in full possession of his cognitive faculties, otherwise he could not signal his desire to execute a divorce; similarly, the condition of the animal described in *Ḥullin* 42a is compatible with a state of consciousness. However, as has been earlier noted, consciousness, while assuredly absent in an organism meeting halakhic criteria of death, is nowhere posited as a condition negating otherwise dispositive criteria of death.[48]

us as that which was spoken to Moses at Sinai." See letter of *Ḥazon Ish* included by R. Kalman Kahane in his article on the international dateline, *Ha-Ma'ayan* (Tammuz 5714), pp. 31–38 and reprinted in R. Menachem Kasher, *Kav ha-Ta'arikh ha-Yisra'eli* (Jerusalem, 5737), p. 195. See also *Ḥazon Ish, Kovez̧ Iggerot* (Bnei Brak, 5750), no. 15, as well as Me'iri, *Ḥullin* 32a. It should also be noted that the principle formulated by *Bet Yosef* and *Radvaz* is entirely negated by some authorities; see R. Chaim Joseph David Azulai, *Maḥazik Berakhah, Yoreh De'ah* 12:1 and *idem*, *Birkei Yosef, Ḥoshen Mishpat* 25:31. See also *Or ha-Mizraḥ* (Tishri 5749), pp. 86–88 and *Be-Netivot ha-Halakhah*, vol. III, pp. 148–50.

48 It has been argued that the statement of the Gemara, *Ḥullin* 21a, to the effect that severance of the vertebrae located in the neck together with severance of the major portion of the muscle tissue enveloping those vertebrae causes an individual to defile in the manner that a corpse defiles reflects a respiratory death standard since, presumably, cardiac activity is still present. This provision of Jewish law could not possibly be reflective of a respiratory death standard, for if it were the determining criterion for defilement there would be no reason for demanding the severance of surrounding muscle tissue in addition to the vertebrae located in the neck. In point of fact, Rambam, *Hilkhot Avot ha-Tum'ah* 2:1, describes that situation together with a situation in which the thigh has been removed, exposing the abdominal cavity, as among the

The position reflected in Rashi's comments does eliminate any objection raised on the basis of the statements found in *Gittin* 70b and *Ḥullin* 42a. Rashi stipulates that the criteria enumerated in *Yoma* 85a presuppose absence of any movement.[49] Hence movement of any kind negates any other indication of death. In an unpublished letter to the editor of *Or ha-Mizraḥ*, R. Saul Israeli, a member of the Chief Rabbinate Council, indicates that the Chief Rabbinate Council endorsed cessation of respiration, when confirmed by brain death criteria, as an absolute indicator of death only because, in such situations, muscular movement is absent. This qualification goes beyond the position formulated in the statements issued by the Chief Rabbinate Council, neither of which stipulates any such condition. Quite apart from the fact that Rashi clearly states that it is irreversible cessation of both respiratory and cardiac activities that is required in order to establish that death has occurred, this modification of the notion of respiratory death is unsatisfactory for a number of reasons.

(1) Movement of extremities is not incompatible with cessation of respiration or with so-called brain death criteria. There are cases reported in the medical literature of patients manifesting accepted neurological criteria of brain death in whom movement has been observed.[50] There is no obvious reason to presume that this movement is a form of non-vital spasmodic movement or *pirkus* described in *Oholot* 1:6, since the movement both appears to be indistinguishable from ordinary muscular movement and can continue over a comparatively long period of time.

(2) A person afflicted by an illness or illnesses causing irreversible cessation of respiration plus total paralysis, e.g., a patient suffering from a severe form

situations in which an animal is regarded as carrion for purposes of defilement and adds the words "even though [the animal] is still alive." Rambam is clearly stating that a person may be alive for all legal purposes but nevertheless be capable of defiling like a corpse. Even more explicit is Rambam's statement in *Hilkhot Sheḥitah* 3:19: "An animal whose thigh has been removed . . . similarly if the spinal column has been broken together with the major portion of the flesh . . . or the major portion of the trachea has been severed or the esophagus has been pierced even minutely in the area in which ritual slaughter may be performed this is *neveilah me-ḥayyim* and ritual slaughter is of no avail." An animal that has suffered a trauma resulting in a perforated esophagus is clearly alive but nevertheless defiles as a *neveilah me-ḥayyim*. The same is true for an animal whose neck vertebrae have been severed.

49 Hence, as indicated earlier, *Ḥatam Sofer* declares that death cannot be pronounced unless the patient lies "as an inanimate stone." The principle that absence of motion is a necessary condition of death is confirmed by R. Shalom Mordecai Schwadron, *Teshuvot Maharsham*, vol. VI, no. 124.

50 See Leslie P. Ivan, "Spinal Reflexes in Cerebral Death," *Neurology*, vol. 23, no. 6 (June 1973), pp. 650–52; S. Mandel, A. Arenas and D. Seasta, "Spinal Automatism in Cerebral Death," *New England Journal of Medicine*, vol. 307, no. 8 (August 19, 1982), p. 501; and Allen H. Ropper, "Unusual Spontaneous Movements in Brain-Dead Patients," *Neurology*, vol. 34, no. 8 (August 1984), pp. 1089–92.

of polio, would perforce be regarded as dead on the basis of the criteria set forth by the Chief Rabbinate Council and Rabbi Israeli. It must again be emphasized that absence of consciousness is not posited in talmudic sources as a necessary criterion of death.

(3) If it is granted that movement of a limb is incompatible with death and hence in itself establishes that the patient is alive, presence of a heartbeat establishes, *mutatis mutandis*, that the patient is yet alive. Surely, the motion of the cardiac muscle is no less the manifestation of a vital force than is muscular movement in an extremity.

It must be emphasized that the heartbeat of a patient sustained on a respirator is in no sense artificial. A patient in such a state is incapable of spontaneous respiration and will certainly die if removed from the respirator. The reason is very simple: a normally functioning heart cannot sustain life if the blood it pumps is deprived of oxygen. A perfectly healthy person cannot survive in a vacuum chamber for more than a matter of minutes. A respirator assists only in the delivery of oxygen; it does not artificially pump blood through the body, as is the case when a patient is placed on a heart-lung machine. Typically, the heart of a "brain dead" patient is entirely healthy and performs all cardiac functions in a normal and spontaneous manner. Were this not the case the heart would be useless for transplantation purposes since it would not be capable of sustaining life in a recipient.

R. Moses Feinstein, *Iggerot Mosheh, Yoreh De'ah*, vol. II, no. 146, explicitly and unequivocally rejects brain death criteria as incompatible with Halakhah "since it is not mentioned in the Gemara or the Codes that there is an indicator of life in the brain." It is precisely for this reason that Rabbi Feinstein, *Iggerot Mosheh, Yoreh De'ah*, vol. II, no. 174, categorizes excision of the heart from a donor for transplantation as homicide.

Nevertheless, the Chief Rabbinate Council reports in its statement that in later years Rabbi Feinstein reversed his earlier position and accepted neurological criteria of death as valid for purposes of Jewish law. Any such report is contrafactual and not borne out by the record.[51] Rabbi Feinstein's opposition

[51] The context of the alleged reversal is not made clear in that statement. If it is inferred from a report cited in footnote 2 of the statement to the effect that Rabbi Feinstein permitted an organ recipient to undergo transplant surgery, it is unwarranted since such a ruling does not entail the endorsement of brain death criteria in pronouncing the death of the donor. Removal of an organ in contravention of Halakhah does not render implantation of the organ impermissible. See J. David Bleich, *Or ha-Mizraḥ* (Nisan–Tammuz 5748); R. Aaron Soloveichik, *Journal of Halacha and Contemporary Society*, pp. 45–47; idem, Or ha-Mizraḥ (Nisan–Tammuz 5748), pp. 301 f.; and R. Eleazar Kahanow, *Ha-Metifta* (5747), pp. 64 f.

For a detailed analysis of Rabbi Feinstein's position as well as the view of R. Shlomoh Zalman Auerbach see *Contemporary Halakhic Problems*, vol. IV, pp. 343–50 and accompanying notes.

to heart transplantation on the grounds that it entails murder of the donor is reiterated in *Iggerot Mosheh, Ḥoshen Mishpat*, vol. II, no. 72. That volume was published in late 1985, some eight months before Rabbi Feinstein's death.

Rabbi Feinstein's position is most clearly enunciated in concluding remarks in his earlier published responsum, *Iggerot Mosheh, Yoreh De'ah*, vol. II, no. 146:

> However, it is certain and elementary that the nose is not the organ which gives life to men . . . Rather the brain and the heart are those [organs] that give life to men . . . We have the indicator of life only through the nose even though [the nose] does not cause respiration because we cannot properly recognize [life] in the heart or in the navel *and certainly we cannot recognize [life] in the brain* [emphasis added]. The connotation of the verse ". . . all in whose nostrils is the breath of the spirit of life" (Genesis 7:22) does not [refer to] the intrinsic spirit of life for that is certainly not in the nose; rather, the spirit of life which we see is [perceived] in the nostrils even though it is not seen in the large limbs, the limbs of motion, and [it is perceived in the nostrils] even after it is no longer perceived either in the beating of the heart or the navel.

Those comments certainly reflect a clear recognition that the primary vital force in the human organism is the beating of the heart. Other criteria must be sought and their absence is accepted as evidence of cessation of life only because, in some circumstances, absence of a detectable heartbeat is an unreliable indicator that death has actually occurred. Clearly, the presence of a spontaneous heartbeat is itself an absolute indication of the presence of life in the organism. The matter is perhaps best summed up in the words of R. Eliezer Waldenberg, *Ẓiẓ Eli'ezer*, vol. X, no. 25, ch. 4, sec. 7:

> There are those who err in thinking that examination of the nose is indicative of cessation of brain activity and, on the basis of this, wish to establish that life is contingent upon the brain . . . In truth this is an absolute error and contradicts that which our Sages, of blessed memory, have established on our behalf . . . "And there is nothing new under the sun" (Ecclesiastes 1:9). There have already been many among those who are great in wisdom who were inclined to think that way, i.e., that life is contingent upon the brain, but greater persons came and disproved these notions as is recorded in *Teshuvot Ḥakham Ẓevi* . . .

A comprehensive discussion of neurological criteria of death and Jewish law, including the positions of Rabbis Feinstein and Auerbach, is presented in the recently published work of David Shabtai, *Defining the Moment: Understanding Brain Death in Halakhah* (New York, 2012).

NOTES AND QUESTIONS

1. The discussion describes human life as "sacred" in stating, "Human life must be treasured as a sacred gift... it is entirely a matter of insistence upon the sanctity of human life." The word "sacred" in rabbinic tradition and biblical usage has a precise, and somewhat unfamiliar, meaning. To be "sacred" is to be on the other side of, or beyond, a boundary. It is to be "out of bounds," "off limits." It is to be inaccessible in the ordinary way, to the ordinary person, at ordinary moments in time. Thus, in the wedding ceremony the groom addresses the bride, "Be thou sanctified unto me according to the laws of Moses and Israel." The bride does not become a "sanctified" entity in the sense in which the term is used in common parlance. The phrase has a purely legal connotation, viz., the bride in accepting the ring from the groom becomes "off limits" to all men other than the groom, and loses the capacity to contract another marriage unless the marriage is terminated by divorce or by death of the groom.

"Sacred" also takes on what is, in effect, the opposite of its primary meaning. "Holy, holy, holy is the Lord of Hosts..." (Isaiah 6:3), a phrase that figures prominently in the synagogue prayer service, means that the Deity is a transcendental incorporeal being. This meaning would probably best be captured by translating the term "holy" as *ousia*, the Greek word for "pure being" or a "simple substance." To be "sacred" is to be *without* bounds, to have no boundary. To be "sacred" is to be infinite, in the sense of not finite, that which cannot be counted or measured or encompassed within metes and bounds.

When the discussion refers to human life as "sacred," it is in the second sense of the word: human life is described as "endowed with infinite value." The word "infinite" in this context does not mean "countably infinite"; it does not mean "countable and larger than any finite quantity." Instead, it means "uncountable," "not subject to being measured or counted." To say that human life has "infinite value" is not to say that its value is greater than any other possible value. There are other values that are also infinite. Indeed, Judaism teaches that a person must accept martyrdom rather than commit an act of idolatry. Rather, it is to say that its value cannot be traded off or measured against other mundane values, that its value cannot enter into a calculus of relative values.

Of course, we do end up putting a value on human life in many contexts. We decide to build a road one way rather than another way because it is cheaper. Yet we know, often with some precision, that the cheaper road will "cost" more lives and the more expensive "cost" fewer. Society places a value upon human life in decisions not to provide medical care for all of its citizens in all cases. We value human life in damage awards, in establishing minimum safety standards in the workplace and for consumer products, and in setting speed limits for automobiles.

Are such decisions compatible with the "infinite value" of human life as understood by Halakhah? Would a society run according to Halakhah make different policy decisions? Can these various issues be distinguished from the considerations involved in determining time of death?

A meaningful response would involve a philosophical and halakhic analysis of the doctrine "the Lord preserves the simple" (Psalm 116:6), which forms the basis of the justified risk-taking that is necessary in virtually all facets of human life. For a discussion of this doctrine and the definition of acceptable dangers, see J. David Bleich, *Bioethical Dilemmas: A Jewish Perspective*, vol. II (Southfield, MI, 2006), pp. 239–46.

Our society frequently places a dollar value upon human life in determining which medical procedures to make available and which to deny. The most egregious example is the Oregon Medicaid program, which began in 1994. Oregon each year decides how much money it is willing to provide for its Medicaid program. It then rank-orders procedures according to lives saved per unit cost. ORS § 414.720. For example, pregnancy, neonatal care and vaccination are highest on the list of priorities because they save a great number of lives for very little cost per life saved. Heart transplants save more lives than liver transplants. Since enough money remained in the Medicaid budget, heart transplants were always covered. But in early years after providing for heart transplants there was no money left over for liver transplants, which cost more than heart transplants per life saved. A recent list enumerates 680 potentially beneficial therapeutic procedures for specifically defined medical conditions, and funds only the first 503 on the list. As a result, in 2008 most liver transplants were funded, but liver transplants for treatment of cancer of the liver and the intrahepatic bile ducts (#575) did not make the cut. Oregon Health Services Commission, "Prioritized List of Health Services," January 1, 2008.

Oregon might well increase funding of Medicaid and cover all 680 potentially beneficial modes of treatment. But then it would either have to raise taxes or curtail its highway beautification program or diminish other state-funded amenities. Such public policy decisions reflect value judgments. Would a society governed by the values reflected in Halakhah make different policy decisions?

Is there a halakhic obligation to spend all available resources in preserving even a single life? If not, what are the limits of the financial obligation of rescue and what is the rationale upon which such limits are based? Is the financial obligation a personal obligation, a societal obligation or an obligation to be borne "jointly and severally" by all members of society? To begin answering these questions, consider Abraham S. Abraham, *Nishmat Avraham III: Ḥoshen Mishpat* 426:1, note 1 (Brooklyn, NY, 2004).

2. Our discussion of time of death is derived from the two (and only two) passages in the Talmud that address the question: When does Jewish law consider a living creature to be dead?

The first passage is recorded in the first chapter of *Oholot*, one of the tractates in the Talmud devoted to the subject of ritual impurity (*tum'ah*). (A person or vessel that contracts *tum'ah* becomes *tamei*, ritually impure.) *Oholot* (or "tents") concerns the ritual impurity conveyed by a dead body to persons or vessels coming into tactile contact with sources of impurity or to persons and vessels under the same tent or roof as a corpse. The primary consequence of becoming ritually impure is that the person or vessel is not permitted entry into the Temple Mount and a person who is ritually impure may not partake of sacred foods such as sacrificial offerings, the portion of the produce presented to the priest (*terumah*) or tithes.

The second passage appears in the Gemara, *Yoma* 85a. "*Yoma*" means "day" (in Aramaic), referring to the Day of Atonement, *Yom Kippur*. *Yom Kippur* is the "Sabbath of Sabbaths" in the Jewish calendar. Discussion of some regulations pertaining to even ordinary Sabbaths thus finds its way into *Yoma*. On the ordinary Sabbath one must not cook, but one may eat uncooked food or food that has been cooked prior to the Sabbath; on *Yom Kippur* one may not eat or drink at all. Nor may one engage in any activity prohibited on the Sabbath. Movement of rubble under normal circumstances is a forbidden activity. However, Sabbath restrictions are suspended for the purpose of saving human life.

3. Is there room for a distinction between death as applied to animals and a determination of the time of death of human beings? Is there room for a distinction between definition of the concept of death for purposes of ritual impurity and for purposes of the rescue of human life? Review the interpretation of *Oholot* espoused by Rosh as cited in note 3. The majority view regards death or the criteria of death as an empirical phenomenon shared in common by all members of the animal kingdom.

A question that is not addressed in this material is whether the criteria of death are synonymous with death itself or whether death is a metaphysical and hence unobservable event such as the departure of the soul from the body, of which we are aware only because of its physical correlates. Would resolution of that issue have a bearing upon applicability of *Oholot* to criteria for determination of human death?

It is generally accepted in rabbinic Judaism that only human beings have immortal souls. However, Sa'adia Ga'on (882–942) as well as others among the post-talmudic heads of the Babylonian academies accepted the view of the *Mu'tazila*, a school of medieval Islamic philosophers, that divine justice requires that animals be rewarded for suffering in the world-to-come. Rambam rejects that view in his *Guide for the Perplexed*, book III, ch. 17. Can the controversy between Rosh and other early-day authorities cited in note 3 be explained on the basis of those conflicting views?

4. Does the discussion take the position that the passage in *Oholot* precludes a criterion for time of death that is less restrictive than some equivalent of severing the head, or that the passage simply cannot provide evidence for the proposition that Jewish law tolerates a less stringent criterion? On what basis does the discussion derive its criterion for time of death?

Remember, as pointed out in Chapter One, definitions of biblical terms are part of the Oral Law tradition. Even when the law itself is inherently rational, matters of definition and application may appear to the human mind to be arbitrary and divorced from any identifiable rationale. Hence, formulation of halakhic rules must be derived from authoritative rabbinic proof texts.

5. The Uniform Determination of Death Act provides that a person is dead only if he has sustained "irreversible cessation of *all functions of the entire brain*." Bearing in mind that (1) there is ongoing hypothalamic-pituitary function in patients manifesting clinically accepted criteria of brain death[52] and (2) clusters of brain cells may be perfused and continue to function on the cellular level, is contemporary medical practice in conformity with the statute? A prominent bioethicist has noted, "The law does not grant a dispensation to ignore cellular function . . . " Robert Veatch, "The Impending Collapse of the Whole-Brain Definition of Death," *Hastings Center Report*, vol. 22, no. 4 (July–August 1993), p. 18. If so, should the focus of discussion be whether the Uniform Determination of Death Act is halakhically acceptable or should discussion focus on the fact that in the absence of any patient who actually meets the criteria of the act, the question is moot?

6. Most states have adopted statutes updating the common law definition of time of death (irreversible respiratory and cardiac failure) in order to reflect a neurological criterion. New York is one state that has not. Its courts have therefore had to face the issue of whether to continue to follow the common law definition or to update it. Harvesting organs, which was a focus of the

[52] The hypothalamus, which is located just above the brain stem, is a gland linking the nervous system to the endocrine system via the pituitary gland. The pituitary is located at the base of the brain.

discussion, is only one interest at stake. In *People v. Eulo*, 63 N.Y.2d 341 (1984), the New York Court of Appeals faced another.

Eulo shot his girlfriend in the head. The hospital put her on a respirator in order to keep her alive. Neurological evaluation revealed that her "entire brain had irreversibly ceased to function." Physicians pronounced her dead, removed her kidneys for transplant and disconnected her from the respirator. A grand jury indicted Eulo for second-degree murder. Although the trial judge had not expressly instructed the jury about the criteria to be applied in determining time of death, he did tell them that they might consider removal of the victim's organs as a superseding cause of death. Upon conviction, Eulo appealed, arguing that, in the absence of a clear instruction about time of death, the jury may have wrongly used neurological criteria to convict him of homicide.

Writing for a unanimous court, Chief Judge Cook rejected the argument. He agreed that it would have been "better practice" for the judge to have expressly instructed the jury about the criteria for death. Nevertheless, he disagreed that the instruction should have been strictly confined to the traditional common law criterion of irreversible cessation of cardio-respiratory functions:

> Ordinarily death will be determined according to the traditional criteria of irreversible cardiorespiratory repose. When, however, the respiratory and circulatory functions are maintained by mechanical means, their significance, as signs of life, is at best ambiguous. Under such circumstances, death may nevertheless be deemed to occur when, according to accepted medical practice, it is determined that the entire brain's function has irreversibly ceased.
>
> Death remains the single phenomenon identified at common law; the supplemental criteria are merely adapted to account for the "changed conditions" that a dead body may be attached to a machine so as to exhibit demonstrably false indicia of life. It reflects an improved understanding that in the complete and irreversible absence of a functioning brain, the traditional loci of life – the heart and the lungs – function as part of an integrated organism.

63 N.Y.2d 355–356.

Although the trial judge had failed to instruct the jury on neurological criteria, the Court of Appeals affirmed:

> [T]he brain-based criteria are supplemental to the traditional criteria, each describing the same phenomenon of death. In the context of a criminal case for homicide, there is no theoretical or practical impediment to the People's proceeding under a theory that the defendant "cause[d] the death" of a person, with death determined by either criteria.

63 N.Y.2d 359.

Do you agree that "brain-based criteria are supplemental to the traditional criteria, each describing the same phenomenon of death"?

7. Suppose a comatose woman is sustained on life-support systems. Her husband has contracted a second marriage that, on the surface, is bigamous. Shortly after the marriage, neurological tests are administered which demonstrate that the patient is brain dead. The husband is charged by the district attorney with bigamy. His defense is that the neurological tests demonstrate that brain death has occurred. If so, brain death presumably occurred some time before the tests were administered. The husband contends that his wife was already brain dead before the marriage ceremony took place, and that the burden of proof to show the contrary rests upon the district attorney. Will the husband prevail?

Does society really want a husband to contract a second marriage while his wife is still occupying a bed in an ICU?

It has been suggested that the law might establish different criteria of death for different purposes. For example, a more liberal set of criteria might be established for permitting removal of organs and a more stringent set of criteria for purposes of summoning an undertaker. See Amir Halevy and Baruch Brody, "Brain Death: Reconciling Definitions, Criteria, and Tests," *Annals of Internal Medicine*, vol. 199, no. 6 (September 15, 1993), pp. 519–25.

The *Eulo* court certainly did not want to see the perpetrator released on the plea that there was a supervening cause. Could the matter have been resolved legislatively by enacting a statute defining homicide as "the infliction of a mortal wound"?

Are different definitions of death for different purposes a cogent legal response to the different perceived societal desiderata present in the wide variety of cases in which definition of time of death is crucial? Would such a solution be available in Jewish law?

8. In Catholic doctrine death is the separation of the soul from the body. The Church itself takes no doctrinal position on "the biological signs that indicate with moral certainty that this event has already occurred." National Catholic Bioethics Center (NCBC).[53] But the Church itself takes the position that life need not be prolonged when it is possible to prolong life only for a period of time that is "morally meaningless." Juan de Lugo, *De Justitia et Jure*, Disp. 10, anno. 30. So one Catholic position on time of death is that neurological death is not death, but that neurological death is sufficient warrant to terminate treatment.

[53] http://www.ncbcenter.org/page.aspx?pid=1285#whyAccept, website accessed August 5, 2013.

But precisely because the Church itself cannot take a position on the biological basis of death, the NCBC's position remains controversial. In an interview on ZENIT, E. Christian Brugger, a Professor of Moral Theology at St. John Vianney Theological Seminary, pointed out that although Pope John Paul II stated that, when "rigorously applied," the neurological criterion "does not seem to conflict with the essential elements of a sound anthropology," the Church's doctrine is a moral doctrine and not a biological doctrine, and so the Pope's position is not, "properly speaking, an authoritative teaching of the Magisterium."[54]

Nevertheless, the NCBC asserts that "medical research has indicated that the irreversible loss of brain function provides a firm indicator that death has already occurred."[55] Is not the NCBC's position identical to the position advocated by the Harvard Ad Hoc Committee?[56] Did not the Harvard Committee seek to define death as "irreversible coma"? Why does the medical profession insist on describing a person manifesting the defined neurological criteria as "dead" rather than as being in a state of terminal coma? Is this a semantic sleight of hand?

9. Would Halakhah consider a patient whose body has been cryogenically frozen to be dead? If the answer is yes, and if it were possible to revive the body, would Jewish law permit its destruction? Has a prophet with the power to resurrect the dead committed homicide if he kills a person in contemplation of resurrecting him?[57] Does a married woman have capacity to contract a second marriage between the death of her husband and his resurrection by a prophet? Even after resurrection by the prophet? Has a surgeon committed homicide when he removes a diseased heart from a living patient for the purpose of implanting an artificial heart in its stead? If a person suffers cardiopulmonary arrest and is resuscitated, was he dead in the interim? Or, for that matter, has a surgeon committed homicide when he stops the beating of the heart in order to perform open-heart surgery? If death is defined as irreversible cessation of certain physical functions, is "irreversible" to be understood as naturally irreversible, irreversible barring human intervention or irreversible

54 http://www.zenit.org/en/articles/transplants-from-murder-victims, website accessed August 5, 2013.

55 National Catholic Bioethics Center, http://www.ncbcenter.org/page.aspx?pid=1285#why Accept, website accessed August 5, 2013.

56 See *supra*, text accompanying notes 35 and 36.

57 Proof text for the phenomenon of prophetic resurrection may be found in 2 Kings 4:18–27, which reports that the prophet Elisha resurrected the son of the Shunammite woman, and in Ezekiel 37:1–14. Cf. the discussion in J. David Bleich, *The Philosophical Quest: Of Philosophy, Ethics, Law and Halakhah* (2013), pp. 305–23.

as retroactively determined by all relevant empirical events? Many of these issues are discussed in Part Two of this chapter.

10. May a state impose a neurological criterion of death on a person who conscientiously objects to it?

In 1990, in *Employment Div., Dept. of Human Resources of Oregon v. Smith*, 494 U.S. 872 (1990), the Supreme Court held that the Free Exercise Clause of the United States Constitution does not prohibit burdens on the exercise of religion imposed by neutral laws of general applicability. The Court thus declined to subject free exercise claims to strict scrutiny, the balancing test set forth in *Sherbert v. Verner*, 374 U.S. 398 (1963), which requires states to demonstrate that laws substantially burdening free exercise be justified by a compelling governmental interest. After *Smith* only laws that fail to meet the related requirements of neutrality and general applicability are subject to strict scrutiny. See *Church of Lukumi Babalu Aye v. City of Hialeah*, 508 U.S. 520, at 531–32 (1993).

Three years after *Smith*, Congress enacted the Religious Freedom Restoration Act, 42 U.S.C.A. § 2000bb et seq., which reversed the result in *Smith* and restored strict scrutiny to free exercise claims. However, in 1997, in *City of Boerne v. Flores*, 521 U.S. 507 (1997), the Supreme Court held RFRA unconstitutional as applied to the states, because it was an improper exercise of Congress' enforcement power under Section 5 of the Fourteenth Amendment. RFRA remained constitutional as applied to the federal government. See, e.g., *Hankins v. Lyght*, 441 F.3d 96 (2d Cir. 2006) ("RFRA is constitutional as applied to federal law under the Necessary and Proper Clause of the Constitution"). *Flores* thus restored *Smith*'s neutrality standard to the states, while maintaining RFRA's strict scrutiny test for the federal government.

Suppose Congress were to reenact RFRA under its power to regulate interstate commerce. Could its provisions then constitutionally apply to the states? If so, would imposition of a neurological criterion for death substantially burden the free exercise of the Jewish religion, and could it be justified by a compelling state interest?

Some state constitutions employ a test that may be more accommodating than the test in *Smith*. New York's constitution provides an example. Where the First Amendment protects the "free exercise" of religion, New York's Free Exercise Clause, N.Y. Constitution, article I, § 3, protects the "free exercise and enjoyment of religious profession and worship," while declaring that "the liberty of conscience hereby secured shall not be so construed as to excuse acts of licentiousness, or justify practices inconsistent with the peace or safety of this state." The New York Court of Appeals has thus applied a test balancing "the interest of the individual right of religious worship against the interest of the [s]tate which is sought to be enforced," *People ex rel. DeMauro v. Gavin*, 92 N.Y.2d 963, 964 (1998) (internal quotations omitted).

PART TWO: ARTIFICIAL HEART IMPLANTATION

Implantation of a mechanical heart presents society with a wide array of ethical questions. These questions notwithstanding, one can only applaud the advances in medical technology that have made implantation of an artificial heart a reality. From the Jewish point of view the development is all the more welcome because, in the past, rabbinic decisors have been constrained to decry cadaver heart transplants. Their position was based primarily upon the consideration that it is medically feasible to accomplish a successful heart transplant only by relying upon neurological criteria of death in salvaging the donor's heart.

At the time of the performance of the first successful heart transplants, a number of leading halakhic authorities pronounced the procedures to be in violation of Jewish law. Some claimed that each heart transplant entails two homicides, *viz*., the immediate demise of the terminally ill donor from whom the healthy heart is removed and the premature death of the recipient.[58] In order to salvage the heart of the donor for transplant, the heart must be removed before the onset of tissue degeneration. Were the physician to wait until the patient could be pronounced dead on the basis of the halakhic, and heretofore commonly accepted, criteria of death, use of the heart for transplantation would be precluded. Hence, physicians contemplating removal of the heart must perforce rely upon brain death criteria in pronouncing the death of the donor. However, brain death criteria are halakhically unacceptable. The overwhelming consensus of authoritative rabbinic opinion is that, for all legal and moral purposes, death occurs only upon cessation of both the cardiac and respiratory function.[59] Jewish law forbids any act, either direct or indirect, that has the effect of hastening death, including withdrawal of life-support systems as well as actual removal of the heart itself. The situation with regard to the criteria used to pronounce the death of the donor in order to facilitate procurement of hearts for transplant procedures remains unchanged. Therefore,

58 See R. Moses Feinstein, *Ha-Pardes*, Adar-Nisan 5729, p. 4; and *idem*, *Iggerot Mosheh*, *Yoreh De'ah*, vol. II, no. 174.

59 See sources cited in *Contemporary Halakhic Problems*, vol. I, pp. 377–93; J. David Bleich, "Neurological Criteria of Death and Time of Death Statutes," *Jewish Bioethics*, pp. 303–16; and R. Aaron Soloveichik, "The Halakhic Definition of Death," *Jewish Bioethics*, pp. 296–302. See also *supra*, pp. 252–76.

such procedures violate Jewish law insofar as they require the removal of the heart from a donor who, in the eyes of Jewish law, is yet alive.

The question of whether the transplant procedure constitutes homicide of the recipient is another matter. During the initial period of heart transplant surgery, when these procedures were essentially experimental, it may perhaps have been the case that statistically anticipated longevity was decreased, rather than enhanced, as a result of the procedure. Following the early transplant operations there was indeed a long hiatus during which few transplants were performed because of the unacceptably high incidence of rejection of transplanted hearts by recipients. However, with the development of immunosuppressive drugs, the facts have changed radically. By 1980 the twelve-month survival rate for recipients of heart transplants was approximately 65%.[60] Between 45% and 50% of all recipients survive for a period of at least five years following implantation.[61] In contrast, in one study it was found that more than 90% of patients who presented clinical profiles identical to those of individuals chosen to receive cadaver transplants, but who did not receive heart transplants because appropriate donor organs could not be found, succumbed to death from heart disease within a three-month period.[62] For transplants that occurred between 1997 and 2004 the one-year survival rate was 88% for males and 86.2% for females. The five-year survival rate for males was 73.2% and for females 69%.[63]

Obviously, since artificial heart implantation does not involve a human donor, the problem of foreshortening the donor's life is not germane. As to the prospect of enhanced longevity for the recipient, it is too early for any meaningful judgment to be made. Since, at the time of this writing, only a small number of artificial heart implantations have been attempted in human subjects, assessment of the success rate and evaluation of the potential for enhanced or diminished longevity are premature. It is nevertheless clear, at

60 See P. E. Over, E. B. Stinson *et al.*, "Cardiac Transplantations: 1980," *Transplantation Proceedings*, vol. 13, no. I (March 1981), p. 203. Some medical centers have, in several recent years, achieved a one-year survival rate of 75%. See Jack G. Copeland, Robert B. Mammana *et al.*, "Heart Transplantation: Four Years' Experience with Conventional Immunosuppression," *Journal of the American Medical Association*, vol. 251, no. 12 (March 23–30, 1984), p. 1563.

61 Over, "Cardiac Transplantation," p. 203; Bruce A. Reitz and Edward B. Stinson, "Cardiac Transplantation – 1982," *Journal of the American Medical Association*, vol. 248, no. 10 (September 10, 1982), p. 1225; and Arthur L. Caplan, "Ethical and Policy Issues in the Procurement of Cadaver Organs for Transplantation," *New England Journal of Medicine*, vol. 311, no. 15 (October 11, 1984), p. 981.

62 Over, "Cardiac Transplantation," p. 203.

63 "Heart Disease and Stroke Statistics – 2012 Update: A Report from the American Heart Association," *Circulation*, vol. 125, no. 1 (January, 2012), p. e205.

least after the fact, that the implantation of an artificial heart in the first instance in which it was undertaken was entirely warranted in terms of enhanced longevity. Given Dr. Barney Clark's clinical profile, the decision to replace his diseased heart with a mechanical device was entirely prudent. Without the operation, Dr. Clark faced imminent death as evidenced by the fact that his physicians performed the operation a day earlier than scheduled because they were convinced that he would otherwise not survive the night. Since the patient did survive for a period of 112 days subsequent to the implantation there is no question that the procedure did succeed in prolonging his life.[64]

This is not to say that implantation surgery does not pose a significant philosophical question regarding the essential characteristics of humanhood. Indeed, some have questioned whether the recipient of a mechanical heart may, properly speaking, be termed a human being.

Whether the recipient of an artificial heart is or is not a human being in the legal sense of the term is probably of greater moment to Jews than to others. To be sure, were a recipient subsequently to become a victim of homicide, the perpetrator might formulate a defense based on the plea that human life came to an end with the surgical removal of the natural heart. But there is nothing to prevent society from conceding the semantic argument while recognizing that the recipient should not be regarded as a mere robot. Society might then, through appropriate legislation and otherwise, proceed to treat the recipient of a mechanical heart as a human being for all legal and moral purposes.

Jewish law, however, is much more formalistic. Since Halakhah does not enjoy the luxury of formulating new categories it cannot beg the question. There are a number of practical corollaries to the theoretical question of whether the recipient of a mechanical heart is deemed to be a human being: (1) May the recipient's wife remarry without benefit of a *get* (religious divorce)? (2) Do his heirs immediately succeed to his estate? (3) If the recipient is not a human being, is he then a corpse requiring immediate burial? (4) Must the family immediately observe *shiv'ah* and recite *kaddish*? To be sure, these questions constitute a *reductio ad absurdum* and evoke the intuitive reaction that the recipient is indeed a human being. Nevertheless, our intuitive response requires reasoned analysis and substantiation.

In the early days of transplant surgery, theologians and moralists raised the question in only a slightly different guise. Subsequent to receiving a transplanted heart, does the patient retain his previous identity or does he acquire the persona of the donor? If it is assumed that the heart is the *sine qua non* of personal identity, *a fortiori*, it must be presumed to constitute a necessary

64 See *New York Times*, March 24, 1983, p. 1, col. 5.

condition of humanhood. This, it seems, is not a view espoused by Judaism. Although cardiac activity is the crucial indicator of the presence of life, the heart is not the hallmark of personhood.

An attempt has been made to demonstrate, on the basis of halakhic dialectic, that the significance of cardiac activity lies, not in the ontological status of the heart itself, but rather in its function in causing blood to course through the body.[65] Hence, a patient whose circulatory system is sustained by a mechanical heart is deemed to be endowed with life. Since cardiac activity, even minus the *kardia*, is a sufficient condition of life, it follows that cardiac activity within a human organism equals a living human being. The various halakhic issues attendant upon artificial heart implantation have been discussed in J. David Bleich, *Be-Netivot ha-Halakhah*, vol. III, pp. 111–25.

I. REMOVAL OF A RECIPIENT'S HEART AS MURDER, TRANSPLANTATION AS RESURRECTION

Prior to undertaking an analysis of the status of the recipient of a mechanical heart, attention should be drawn to a significant problem that applies with equal force to the implantation of both cadaver and artificial hearts. At the time that the early cadaver transplants were undertaken, some scholars contended that the transplant procedure constitutes an act of homicide insofar as the recipient is concerned, not because of an attendant diminution of life expectancy, but because the removal of the diseased heart, in and of itself, is homicide.[66] The identical question arises concerning the removal of a diseased heart for the purpose of facilitating the implantation of an artificial one.

Assuming, *arguendo*, that in the eyes of Jewish law, the patient is deemed to be dead upon removal of the natural heart, it would follow logically that a patient who successfully undergoes an implant and becomes reanimated would be categorized as a person who has risen from the dead. Thus, a successful implant would constitute a form of resurrection. The question that must be posed is, then, whether removal of the patient's heart, when performed by one who has the intent and ability to restore his "victim" to life, constitutes a homicide in the event that the victim is indeed actually resurrected. For example, may a prophet, who is certain that he possesses the power to resurrect the dead, kill another person and then restore him to life? Or is

[65] See *Be-Netivot ha-Halakhah*, vol. III, pp. 106–10.

[66] See R. Judah Gershuni, *Or ha-Mizraḥ* (Nisan 5729), p. 133, reprinted in *idem*, *Kol Ẓofayikh* (Jerusalem, 5740), p. 373; and R. Menachem Kasher, *Teshuvot Divrei Menaḥem*, *Ḥoshen Mishpat*, no. 27.

the prophet forbidden to kill a person even under such circumstances, since the act of killing constitutes murder? To transpose the question to its medical context: Assuming that the removal of a diseased heart constitutes homicide, may a physician remove the heart of his patient if he is confident that the patient will be reanimated after implantation of an artificial heart? Or is the surgeon forbidden to perform an act that is technically murder even though he does so for the purpose of restoring the patient to life and healing him?

The Gemara, *Megillah* 7b, relates:

> Rabbah and R. Zeira celebrated a Purim repast together. They became intoxicated. Rabbah arose and slit R. Zeira's throat. On the next day he prayed on his behalf and restored him to life. Next year he said, "Come and we will conduct the Purim repast together." He [R. Zeira] replied, "A miracle does not occur at every moment."

As related in this narrative, R. Zeira expressed the fear that the miracle of the previous year would not be repeated and that Rabbah might not succeed in restoring him to life. R. Zeira does not appear to be concerned that, even if Rabbah were successful in performing an identical miracle a second time, he would yet have transgressed the prohibition against murder. Hence, it might be inferred that, when restoration of the victim to life is indeed a certainty, the act of killing does not entail transgression of the prohibition against homicide.

However, some commentators interpret the incident reported in *Megillah* 7b in a manner that renders this conclusion nugatory. Maharsha explains that Rabbah did not actually slit R. Zeira's throat; rather, explains Maharsha, Rabbah forced R. Zeira to drink an excessive amount of wine so that he became deathly ill and later Rabbah "restored him to life," i.e., Rabbah cured him by means of prayer. Similarly, Me'iri explains that Rabbah did not slaughter R. Zeira but "forced wine down his gullet." Moreover, Rabbah could not have been deemed culpable for his act since he had clearly reached the stage of the "drunkenness of Lot" and hence, by reason of mental incompetence, could not be held responsible for his actions.[67]

[67] See *Eruvin* 65a. It should be noted that numerous rabbinic authorities rule that it is forbidden to place oneself in a situation in which one will be exempt from the fulfillment of commandments and exonerated from liability for transgression by reason of drunkenness or the like. Nevertheless, there may be no prohibition in circumstances such as are recorded in *Megillah* 7b in which there is no intention to transgress, and indeed in which it is far from certain that transgression will occur, particularly when the person is intent upon fulfilling a *mizvah*. R. Zevi Yecheskel Michelson, *Teshuvot Tirosh ve-Yizhar*, no. 127, citing Rashi, *Kiddushin* 33a, declares that inducing a state in which a person is exempt from fulfillment of commandments is forbidden only when accompanied by specific intent to secure such exemption. R. Malkiel Zevi

II. DOES RESURRECTION REVERSE DEATH?

It may, however, be argued that the question regarding the permissibility of homicide in anticipation of subsequent restoration to life is based upon a contra-halakhic assumption. The question, as formulated, assumes that death and reanimation are two separate and discrete events. It may, however, be the case that, from the vantage point of Jewish law, when death is followed by resurrection, reanimation effectively nullifies the antecedent death and, for purposes of Halakhah, the individual is deemed never to have died. The litmus test is whether or not a marital relationship survives the decease of one of the marriage partners and his or her restoration to life. Or, to phrase the same question somewhat differently, is a person who has died and been resurrected required to enter into a new marriage ceremony with his or her own "widow" or "widower" in order that they may be permitted to live together as man and wife? This question is posed by R. Chaim Joseph David Azulai in his commentary on *Shulḥan Arukh, Birkei Yosef, Even ha-Ezer* 17:1, regarding the marital status of the wife of R. Zeira. *Birkei Yosef* writes:

> With regard to the wife of R. Zeira [it is the case that] when her husband was slain and died her marriage was certainly dissolved and she became permitted to all others. And when R. Zeira was restored to life the next day it was necessary to contract a marriage with his wife anew for she was an unmarried woman, as is the case with regard to one who is reconciled with his divorced wife in which case a new marriage is required since the original marriage is no longer extant, having been dissolved by means of a *get* [bill of divorce], and a new entity is now created. Similarly, in this case, in which the husband has died, his death renders her permissible [to others] and nullifies his matrimonial relationship, and when he comes alive it is a new matter. Or perhaps the provision that "a woman acquires herself with the death of the husband" (*Kiddushin* 2a) applies only when he dies and remains deceased, but if he is not buried and is restored to life by a prophet or a pious man it becomes manifest that such death was not death in the manner of the death of all men. And the original marriage is not nullified [with the result that she remains] a married woman and lacks legal capacity to contract a marriage with any other man while her husband, when he is restored in life, is permitted to her immediately as was the case prior to his death.

In resolving this question, *Birkei Yosef* cites a discussion presented in the Palestinian Talmud, *Gittin* 7:3. The Mishnah, *Gittin* 76b, declares, "[If a man says,] 'This is your *get* if I do not return within twelve months,' and he dies

Tennenbaum, *Teshuvot Divrei Malki'el*, vol. V, no. 148, rules that the conduct is permissible in pursuit of a *mizvah*.

within twelve months, it is no *get*." In the course of the discussion in the Babylonian Talmud focusing upon this Mishnah, the Gemara, *Gittin* 76b, poses the following query:

> R. Eleazar asked a certain elder: "When you permitted her to marry, did you permit her to do so immediately or after twelve months? Did you permit her to marry immediately since he cannot come, or did you permit her to marry after twelve months when his condition was fulfilled?"

The consideration that gives rise to this question is not immediately clear. Granted that the retroactive validity of the divorce is questionable, logically, the wife should nevertheless be permitted to marry immediately: If the *get* is valid retroactively she is a divorcee; if not, she is a widow. In either contingency she attains halakhic capacity to contract a marriage immediately following the death of her husband. Rashi, in his commentary, *ad locum*, concedes that this is, in fact, the case. Determination of a woman's status as a divorcee rather than as a widow is significant, comments Rashi, only if the husband dies without issue. If the divorce is effective retroactively she is free to remarry as a divorcee; if not, as a childless widow, she is subject to the obligation of levirate marriage, the obligation of a widow and her deceased husband's brother to marry.

The parallel discussion in the Palestinian Talmud, *Gittin* 7:3, places the matter in an entirely different perspective:

> Is she permitted to marry [immediately]? R. Ḥaggi said, "She is permitted." R. Jose said, "She is forbidden to marry; I say perhaps miracles befell him and he was restored to life."

The Palestinian Talmud clearly not only considers the possibility of a levirate obligation but also questions the woman's right to remarry as a widow.[68] To be sure, none of the codifiers of Jewish law adopts the position of R. Jose in forbidding the immediate remarriage of the widow. *Birkei Yosef* observes that R. Jose's fear that "perhaps miracles befell him and he was restored to life" is set aside on the basis of empirical considerations but is not dismissed on substantive grounds. The probability of miraculous resurrection is so unlikely, asserts *Birkei Yosef*, that it need not be of any concern. *Birkei Yosef* observes that the discussion in the Palestinian Talmud does nevertheless demonstrate that,

[68] Cf., however, R. Chaim Kanievsky, *Siaḥ ha-Sadeh, Kuntres ha-Likkutim*, no. 4, who endeavors to rebut *Birkei Yosef*'s argument by contending that the Palestinian Talmud is concerned solely with the question of levirate marriage, and who maintains that, although the marital relationship is irrevocably severed upon the death of the husband, the conditional divorce is void under such circumstances because the stipulated condition voiding the divorce was fulfilled.

were such a miracle to occur, the matrimonial relationship would be viewed as having survived the death of the husband and his subsequent restoration to life. *Birkei Yosef* asserts that there is no reason to assume that the Babylonian Talmud disputes this view; rather, it ignores the contingency on empirical grounds.[69]

According to *Birkei Yosef*'s analysis, it necessarily follows that removal of a diseased heart, followed by implantation of either a cadaver organ or an artificial heart, does not constitute homicide since, in his view, death is retroactively nullified by subsequent animation.

It is apparent that the question left unresolved in the Babylonian Talmud is not resolved, nor is it the subject of controversy in the Palestinian Talmud. In permitting immediate remarriage, R. Ḥaggi does so only when her status either as a widow or as a divorcee entails a capacity to remarry. He is silent regarding a situation in which an impediment to remarriage may exist by virtue of a possible levirate obligation and hence in which a determination of status as a divorcee rather than as a widow is crucial. R. Jose, of course, forbids remarriage in all instances because of the possibility that the husband may be restored to life. Rambam, *Hilkhot Gerushin* 9:11, takes note of the problem concerning remarriage in the face of a possible levirate obligation as formulated in the Babylonian Talmud and indicates that the question remains unresolved. In failing to indicate a barrier to remarriage in the absence of a possible levirate obligation, Rambam inferentially rejects the view of R. Jose. In rejecting the opinion of R. Jose, Rambam is consistent with his view that resurrection of the dead will occur only at the culmination of the messianic era.[70]

69 Similarly, when the halakhically posited criteria of death, including cessation of cardiac activity, are manifest but the patient is subsequently resuscitated it must be assumed that the patient was not dead during the intervening interval. See R. Moshe Sternbuch, *Kuntres Ba'ayot ha-Zeman be-Hashkafat ha-Torah* (Jerusalem, 5729), ch. 1, p. 9, and R. Shlomoh Zalman Auerbach, cited by R. Gavriel Kraus, *Ha-Ma'ayan* (Tishri 5729), p. 20. Thus, it is only *irreversible* criteria of death that establish that death has indeed occurred.

70 R. Jose's refusal to permit remarriage because of the possibility that "miracles befell him" and that the husband was restored to life appears to contradict the halakhic principle that notice need not be taken of improbable and unlikely contingencies.

The controversy between R. Jose and R. Ḥaggi can perhaps best be understood in light of the controversy between early rabbinic authorities over the sequence of events that will unfold in the eschatological era. Rambam, in his *Ma'amar Teḥiyat ha-Metim*, and Ramban, in his *Sha'ar ha-Gemul*, maintain that resurrection will take place subsequent to the advent of the Messiah and will usher in the period of the world-to-come. Sa'adia Ga'on, in the seventh treatise of his *Emunot ve-De'ot*, maintains that there will be two periods of resurrection: the righteous will be restored to life in the days of the Messiah; others will be resurrected subsequent to the Day of Judgment, marking the commencement of the period of the world-to-come. This is also the view of R. David ibn Zimra, *Teshuvot Radvaz*, no. 1069 (vol. III, no. 644), and appears to be the position of *Tosafot*, *Pesaḥim* 114b, s.v. *eḥad*, as well. Cf., also, the position espoused by R. Abraham ibn Ezra in his commentary on Daniel 12:2.

There are, however, latter-day authorities who disagree with the principle formulated by *Birkei Yosef*. The Gemara, *Niddah* 6lb, declares, "Commandments will be abrogated in the eschatological era," i.e., subsequent to the resurrection of the dead. Rabbi Elchanan Wasserman, *Kovez̧ Shi'urim*, vol. II, no. 29, formulates two possible analyses of that dictum: (1) The underlying principle may be that fulfillment of *miz̧vot* is contingent upon a specific time period or historical epoch. Just as ritual obligations were not incumbent in the pre-Sinaitic era so, also, will those obligations lapse in the post-resurrection era. (2) Alternatively, the principle enunciated in *Niddah* 61b may simply be that the resurrected dead are not required to perform *miz̧vot*. The principle that "the dead are free" of all obligations, derived from Psalms 88:6, entails irrevocable abrogation of all further responsibility for fulfillment of commandments. Hence, the dead are relieved of all ritual obligations even subsequent to their resurrection. According to the latter analysis, release from obligation is not limited to any particular epoch. Accordingly, the principle would apply even in contemporary times in the unlikely event that a particular corpse would miraculously be restored to life prior to the general resurrection. Whether or not the dead who were restored to life by the prophet Ezekiel were required to observe the commandments is contingent upon which of these two analyses is accepted. Similarly, according to the authorities who maintain that the righteous will be restored to life during the messianic era, the question of their obligation to fulfill *miz̧vot* in the interim between their resurrection and the advent of the world-to-come is contingent upon which of these two analyses is regarded as correct. R. Elchanan Wasserman asserts that *miz̧vot* are eternally valid and binding, at least in theory, even in the period of the world-to-come. He advances arguments demonstrating that the second analysis is correct and that, in reality, there will be no obligation to fulfill commandments in the world-to-come only because death, in and of itself, irrevocably terminates the

Categorization of resurrection at the hands of a prophet as improbable, insofar as halakhic determinations contingent thereupon are concerned, appears to be incontestable and hence it may be assumed that even R. Jose assigns no halakhic import to that contingency. However, the advent of the Messiah is not only probable but also certain. Accordingly, it appears that R. Jose espouses a view similar to that of Sa'adia Ga'on in maintaining that resurrection of at least a portion of Israel will occur at the time of the Messiah. Hence, he must consider the possibility that the Messiah may appear within the twelve-month period stipulated by the husband and the further possibility that the husband may be among those privileged to be restored to life during that period. R. Ḥaggi, in disagreeing with R. Jose, may well have adopted a position similar to that of Rambam and Ramban, *viz.*, that resurrection will take place only in conjunction with the ushering in of the period of the world-to-come, a period in which corporeal and sensual activity will not occur. In rejecting R. Jose's view, Rambam is consistent with the view regarding the time of resurrection expressed in his *Ma'amar Teḥiyat ha-Metim*.

obligation to perform *mizvot*.[71] Accordingly, termination of obligation is not rescinded by subsequent restoration to life. This position entails negation of the notion that resurrection nullifies, or reverses, an earlier demise.[72] Since resurrection is not tantamount to a reversal of death, there is no logical manner in which a prior marital relationship can be regarded as having been reestablished by resurrection.

III. CAN AN ANIMAL SURVIVE REMOVAL OF ITS HEART?

However, even rejection of *Birkei Yosef*'s position does not necessarily entail acceptance of the view that removal of a diseased heart constitutes an act of homicide. During the early period of cadaver heart transplants some rabbinic scholars argued that the question is reducible to the subject of a celebrated controversy between two eminent eighteenth-century authorities, R. Zevi Ashkenazi (*Ḥakham Ẓevi*) and R. Jonathan Eibeschutz. A young woman eviscerated, soaked and salted a chicken, but failed to find a heart. She consulted R. Zevi Ashkenazi who, as recorded in *Teshuvot Ḥakham Ẓevi*, nos. 74, 76 and 77, ruled that the animal was kosher. *Ḥakham Ẓevi* reasoned that, since it is impossible for any creature to survive without a heart for even a brief period of time, it must be assumed that the chicken, which had thrived and developed normally, must indeed have been endowed with a heart.[73] The absence of a heart, declared *Ḥakham Ẓevi*, must assuredly be attributed to a predatory cat that must have been in close proximity. Not content with simply ruling regarding the case presented to him, *Ḥakham Ẓevi* further announced that "even if witnesses will come and testify that they saw with open eyes that nothing was removed from the body of the chicken, it is certain that their testimony is false for it is contrary to reality." In sharp disagreement, R. Jonathan Eibeschutz, *Kereti u-Peleti* 40:4, declared that the testimony of credible witnesses cannot be dismissed peremptorily but rather "it must be assumed that there was some piece [of tissue] which does not appear as a heart but which is designed to fulfill the functions of the heart, but yet the chicken is *treifah* since it is not a normal heart."[74] It has been argued that, since according to *Ḥakham Ẓevi*

71 See also Rambam, *Sefer ha-Mizvot, shoresh* 3; cf., however, *Sifra, Parashat Ẓav* (Leviticus 7:35), sec. 158.

72 R. Chaim Kanievsky, *Siaḥ ha-Sadeh, Kuntres ha-Likkutim*, no. 4, espouses an opposing view.

73 See *supra*, pp. 271 ff.

74 Cf., however, R. Abraham Isaiah Karelitz, *Ḥazon Ish, Yoreh De'ah* 4:14, who takes issue with *Kereti u-Peleti*, arguing that the chicken thus described is indeed kosher. *Ḥazon Ish* argues that, although removal of the heart does indeed render the animal a *treifah*, there is no source for a ruling that an anomaly of the heart similarly renders the animal a *treifah*.

it is impossible for any creature to survive without a heart, removal of a diseased heart *ipso facto* causes the death of the patient and hence constitutes homicide. Reanimation by subsequently implanting a cadaver heart would thus be viewed either as a form of *pirkus*[75] (convulsive movement) or as the generation of a new life.

Actually, the same argument can be formulated in a manner consistent with the position of *Kereti u-Peleti*. As already noted, this authority accepts the basic premise that, absent a heart, a living creature cannot survive. *Kereti u-Peleti* merely posits the possibility that cardiac functions may be assumed by an organ that does not at all resemble a normal heart. Hence *Kereti u-Peleti* might well concede that removal of the heart from a living creature would lead to its immediate demise.

However, according to the conflicting view of R. Ya'akov Friedman of Karlin, *Mishkenot Ya'akov, Yoreh De'ah*, no. 10, removal of a diseased heart would not constitute homicide. According to *Mishkenot Ya'akov*, some residual vital force remains even subsequent to removal of the heart.[76] Hence, since according to *Mishkenot Ya'akov* removal of the heart does not *ipso facto* entail death, a diseased heart might be removed in order to implant a cadaver heart without violation of the prohibition against homicide.

In point of fact, the identical question arises regarding all forms of open-heart surgery. Although the heart is not removed in the course of such procedures, the heartbeat is stopped in order to prevent pulsation of the heart from causing a continuously moving surgical field. Life is sustained by a heart-lung machine that oxygenates the blood and circulates it. If *Ḥakham Ẓevi* is to be understood as declaring that under no circumstances can life persist in the absence of a heart, it follows that, by the same token, life cannot persist in the absence of a functioning heart. It is clear that life is not contingent upon the mere physical presence of a heart but upon the continued pulsing of the heart that causes blood to course through the circulatory system. Nevertheless, no rabbinic authority has argued that causing the temporary cessation of cardiac function in the course of open-heart surgery, in and of itself, constitutes homicide. Even in

75 See *Oholot* 1:6: ". . . and likewise cattle and wild beasts . . . if their heads have been severed they are unclean (as carrion) even if they move convulsively after being cut off." Movement that is not the product of vital forces is not indicative of life; hence, if removal of the heart is *ipso facto* identified with the occurrence of death, subsequent implantation of a heart must be regarded either as prolonging "convulsive" movement, i.e., as "artificial life," or as a form of resurrection.

76 See also R. Chaim Benveniste, *Knesset ha-Gedolah, Yoreh De'ah* 40; R. Joseph Saul Nathanson, *Sho'el u-Meshiv, Mahadura Tinyana*, vol. IV, no. 108; and R. Shalom Mordecai Schwadron, *Da'at Torah, Yoreh De'ah* 40:8.

accordance with the view expressed by *Ḥakham Ẓevi*, it is only the irreversible cessation of cardiac activity that constitutes death. When, however, cardiac activity is interrupted and subsequently restored it is retroactively established that the original cessation was not associated with the death of the person.[77] Were this not so, it would follow that successful resuscitation following cardiac arrest is a form of resurrection of the dead.

The same line of reasoning may be applied to transplant surgery involving use of a cadaver heart. *Ḥakham Ẓevi* does indeed declare that life cannot exist without a heart, but he does not assert that life cannot exist other than with the original heart with which the living being was endowed. Hence, removal of the original diseased organ and its replacement with a cadaver heart may be viewed as merely a temporary cessation of cardiac activity that does not constitute death even according to *Ḥakham Ẓevi*.

However, implantation of an artificial heart differs significantly from a cardiac transplant. The recipient of a cadaver transplant is endowed with a functioning heart; the recipient of an artificial heart possesses an artificial organ. In the latter case, normal cardiac function has irreversibly ceased. Arguably, the artificial organ produces only artificial life. If so, removal of the diseased heart under such circumstances might constitute homicide since removal of the heart effectively terminates natural life in an irreversible manner.

Yet it would appear more logical to assume that *Ḥakham Ẓevi* would concede the validity of *Kereti u-Peleti*'s basic point, *viz.*, that although no creature can survive without a heart, nevertheless, life does not require an organ possessing the form and characteristics associated with a normal, natural heart, but may be sustained by any organ which performs the functions associated with the heart. *Ḥakham Ẓevi* would then disagree with *Kereti u-Peleti* only to the extent that, absent the perceived presence of a normal heart, he finds no reason to posit the existence of an unrecognizable organ that performs the functions of a heart. Since apparently *Ḥakham Ẓevi* deemed it so unlikely that the chicken in question might possess some unrecognizable organ that assumed the functions of the heart, he asserted that it must be presumed that a normal heart was indeed present and hence the animal is to be declared kosher.[78] Nevertheless, although *Ḥakham Ẓevi* forcefully asserts that life cannot persist in the absence of a heart, there is no reason to presume that he would fail to concede that life might indeed be sustained by means of some other organ which performs the functions usually associated with the heart or even by means of a mechanical device designed to perform those functions. Accordingly, *Ḥakham Ẓevi*'s position does not yield the conclusion that a

[77] See *supra*, note 69.

[78] See *supra*, note 74.

patient whose life is sustained by means of a heart-lung machine or by means of an artificial heart must be regarded as deceased. Hence, even according to *Ḥakham Ẓevi*, removal of the diseased heart need not be regarded as an act of homicide.

However, *Ḥakham Ẓevi*, *Teshuvot Ḥakham Ẓevi*, no. 77, does acknowledge that, although life cannot exist without a heart, lifelike movement may persist subsequent to the removal of the heart. Such movement of a creature subsequent to removal of its heart is described by *Ḥakham Ẓevi* as merely convulsive in nature (*pirkus*):

> Similarly, when the heart has been removed, even though [the creature] is dead, and, in the case of a human, defiles in a tent and, in the case of an animal, [defiles as] carrion, it is possible for [the creature] to run and to move. This is the *pirkus* described in *Oholot*. But, all this notwithstanding, [the creature] is dead and not alive.

Nevertheless it is clear that, even according to *Ḥakham Ẓevi*, the vitality manifested by the recipient of an artificial heart is not in the category of *pirkus*. This may be demonstrated on the basis of a number of talmudic sources that, absent such conclusion, would contradict the thesis enunciated by *Ḥakham Ẓevi*. The Gemara, *Ḥullin* 33a, states:

> R. Aḥa bar Jacob said: One may infer from the ruling of R. Simeon ben Lakish that a Jew may be invited to partake of internal organs, but a gentile may not be invited to partake of internal organs. What is the reason? For a Jew, the matter is contingent upon the act of slaughter; since the animal has been properly slaughtered, it is permitted [to Jews]. For gentiles stabbing is sufficient and the matter is contingent upon death [of the animal]. [Therefore] these [internal organs] are comparable to a limb [cut off] from a living animal.

This dictum is predicated upon the previously announced opinion of R. Simeon ben Lakish, who declared that, upon severance of the trachea and esophagus, the internal organs which are suspended from these structures are, for purposes of halakhic categorization, regarded as having been separated from the animal and "placed in a basket" (*ke-manḥa be-dikula damya*), i.e., they are no longer regarded as integral to the animal but merely as reposing in the body cavity which serves them as a "basket." Since these organs are regarded as having been "removed" from the animal before it expired, the organs are forbidden to gentiles as "a limb cut off from the living animal."[79]

[79] For a detailed exposition of this halakhic concept, see Rashba, *Torat ha-Bayit he-Arukh*, *Bayit Sheni*, *sha'ar shelishi*.

The heart, which is suspended from the trachea by means of the bronchial tubes, is among the internal organs regarded as being placed in a basket as a result of the act of slaughter that entails severance of the trachea. This categorization involves acceptance of the principle that the animal remains alive even though the heart has been removed. Consideration of the heart as having been "placed in a basket" implies that the heart is no longer regarded as part of the animal. Yet, the internal organs are deemed to be "cut off from the living animal" despite the simultaneous "excision" of the heart. This can only mean that, despite the "removal" of the heart, the animal is regarded as still living since, were the animal regarded as already dead, the prohibition against partaking of "a limb cut off from the living animal" would not apply.

Thus, the position reflected in *Ḥullin* 33a appears to conflict with the view espoused by *Ḥakham Ẓevi*. According to the Gemara, upon slaughter of the animal, the heart is deemed to have been separated from the body and to have been "placed in a basket," but the animal is nevertheless regarded as yet living. However, for *Ḥakham Ẓevi*, life can no longer be present subsequent to the removal of the heart. According to *Ḥakham Ẓevi*, the prohibition against "a limb cut off from the living animal" should not apply. In declaring the prohibition applicable to internal organs subsequent to severance of the trachea, the Gemara seems, in effect, to adopt the position that life persists subsequent to the removal of the heart.

A similar apparent contradiction to *Ḥakham Ẓevi*'s thesis emerges from the discussion of the Gemara, *Ḥullin* 121b:

> R. Oshaia taught: If a Jew slaughtered an unclean animal on behalf of a gentile, upon cutting both [the trachea and the esophagus] or the greater part of both, even though [the animal] still convulses, it conveys the uncleanliness of a foodstuff but not the uncleanliness of carrion. A limb severed from it is regarded as severed from the living animal and is forbidden to Noahides even after life has departed [from the animal].

Here, again, it is evident that the Gemara assumes that life persists subsequent to the slaughter of the animal even though the heart is deemed to have been excised and "placed in a basket" by virtue of the act of slaughter. Similarly, the Mishnah, *Gittin* 70b, declares:

> If both [the trachea and the esophagus] or the major portion of both were cut and he declared, "Write a bill of divorce for my wife," they may write and deliver [the bill of divorce].

Again, we are confronted by the identical problem. If the trachea and the esophagus have been severed, the heart must be deemed to have been "placed in a basket." If, as is the opinion of *Ḥaḥam Ẓevi*, there is no possibility of life in the absence of a heart, and, as is evident from *Ḥullin* 33a, severance of the trachea and the esophagus is tantamount to excision of the heart, how is it possible to execute a valid *get* on behalf of a person who has the halakhic status of a corpse?

The matter may, however, be placed in proper perspective upon examination of the comments of Rabbenu Nissim and R. Menachem ha-Me'iri in their respective commentaries on *Ḥullin* 32b. The Gemara, *Ḥullin* 32b, states: "R. Simeon ben Lakish said, 'If he severed the trachea and afterwards pierced the lung (before he cut the esophagus) the slaughter is valid.'" This dictum demonstrates that, subsequent to severance of the trachea, the lung is regarded as though it has been "placed in a basket." Ordinarily, piercing the lung of an animal renders the animal a *treifah* and its meat unfit for consumption. In the case described by R. Simeon ben Lakish, the esophagus had not been severed and the act of slaughter remained incomplete. Nevertheless, the perforation of the lung is of no import. Rashi explains that, since the lung is suspended from the trachea, upon severance of the trachea, the lung is regarded as having been removed in its entirety from the animal and "placed in a basket." Hence, since the lung is no longer an integral part of the animal, perforation of the lung cannot render the animal a *treifah*. The lung, in effect, is regarded as having been completely removed and its disposition no longer has any effect upon the animal. Rabbenu Nissim, *Ḥiddushei ha-Ran, ad locum*, cites the comment of an anonymous early authority to the effect that, similarly, perforation of the heart or of the liver subsequent to the severance of the trachea does not render the animal a *treifah* "for all that is suspended from the trachea derives its vitality from it." Rabbenu Nissim himself disagrees with this position and states that the heart cannot be deemed to have been "placed in a basket." Rabbenu Nissim reasons that severance of the trachea cannot be regarded as tantamount to removal of the heart "for if the animal is completely dead how would the severance of the esophagus render the animal permissible?" The thrust of Rabbenu Nissim's argument is that, were the animal to be deemed dead by virtue of the severance of the trachea (which, on the basis of the principle *ke-manḥa be dikula damya* is tantamount to excision of the heart), no act of slaughter could possibly be valid unless both the trachea and the esophagus were severed simultaneously. Slaughter of an animal requires the severing of both the trachea and the esophagus, but they need not necessarily be severed simultaneously. In the case described in *Ḥullin* 32b, the lung was perforated subsequent to severance of the trachea but prior to cutting the esophagus. But since severing the trachea, which is tantamount to excision of the heart, has the effect of "killing" the animal, the subsequent severing of the esophagus is performed on an already "dead" animal and, logically, should be of no effect.

A twentieth-century scholar, R. Menachem Kasher, *Teshuvot Divrei Menaḥem*, I, *Ḥoshen Mishpat*, no. 27,[80] suggests that the disagreement between the two positions recorded by *Ḥiddushei ha-Ran* lies in acceptance or rejection of *Ḥakham Zevi*'s thesis. According to the first opinion recorded by Rabbenu Nissim, life continues to be present even subsequent to "removal" of the heart by means of severance of the trachea and, hence, completion of the act of slaughter by severing the esophagus renders the animal permissible. The second opinion, i.e., the position espoused by Rabbenu Nissim himself, also recognizes that slaughter can be performed only on a living animal. For this reason, the second opinion maintains that, since the act of slaughter obviously cannot be performed on a dead animal, it follows that severance of the trachea cannot cause the heart to be deemed to have been "placed in a basket." If that were indeed the case severance of the esophagus would be of no avail. Accordingly, Rabbi Kasher asserts that, in expressing his view with regard to the impossibility of survival in the absence of a heart, *Ḥakham Zevi* follows the second opinion recorded by Rabbenu Nissim.

This analysis is most unlikely. It is highly improbable that *Ḥakham Ẓevi*, who maintained that his thesis was empirical in nature, would concede that these early authorities are in disagreement with regard to what he perceived to be a matter of objective reality rather than with regard to a point of law. This objection acquires enhanced cogency in light of *Ḥakham Ẓevi*'s statement in *Teshuvot Ḥakham Ẓevi*, no. 77, to the effect that, not only is life contingent upon the heart, but that "with regard to this no person has ever disagreed." Moreover, according to this analysis of the second position advanced by Rabbenu Nissim, it follows that, although it is forbidden to invite a gentile to partake of internal organs of a non-kosher animal, it is nevertheless permitted to invite a gentile to partake of the heart of such an animal. A position of this nature is not found in the writings of any rabbinic decisor, i.e., there exists no statement to the effect that the heart is not included among the internal organs that may not be presented to a gentile. Moreover, the previously cited statements of the Gemara, *Ḥullin* 33a and *Gittin* 70b, appear to contradict the first position recorded by Rabbenu Nissim.

In order properly to understand *Ḥakham Ẓevi*'s thesis it would appear that a sharp distinction must be drawn between actual, physical excision of the heart

80 This material originally appeared in *No'am*, vol. XIII (5730), pp. 10–20.

and a situation in which the heart is not physically separated from the body, but, for purposes of establishing the relevant halakhah, is regarded as having been "placed in a basket." Indeed, it is undeniable that, even subsequent to severance of the trachea, the heart not only remains physically attached to the body but also continues to pump blood through the circulatory system. In this regard, the heart is distinguishable from the lung, whose primary attachment to the body is by means of the trachea and which cannot continue to perform respiratory functions subsequent to severance of the trachea.

Bearing this point in mind, it is possible to explain the controversy between Rabbenu Nissim and the anonymous author of the first opinion cited by him with regard to whether the heart must be deemed to have been "placed in a basket." The anonymous first authority cited by Rabbenu Nissim maintains that the heart is deemed to have been "placed in a basket" upon severance of the trachea, even though it is still attached to the body by means of a yet functioning circulatory system. Rabbenu Nissim himself maintains that, in light of the continued attachment of the heart to the body, by means of the circulatory system and by virtue of its continued functionality, the heart cannot be deemed to have been "placed in a basket" simply because the trachea has been severed. Nevertheless, even the anonymous authority who espouses the first opinion would concede that, since the heart continues to function, life remains present in the animal. Therefore, even though the heart is regarded as having been "placed in a basket," the animal is nevertheless not regarded as dead. Accordingly, the Gemara, *Ḥullin* 33a, regards a limb severed from the animal as having been severed from a living animal. Similarly, a human being whose trachea has been severed is still regarded as alive and retains capacity to execute a *get*, as is evident from the statement of the Gemara, *Gittin* 70b. According to *Ḥakham Ẓevi*, this would not be the case in a situation in which the heart has been physically excised. In the latter case, since the heart has been totally separated from the body and has entirely ceased to function, it is impossible, according to *Ḥakham Ẓevi*, for any residual vitality to remain. Thus, *Ḥakham Ẓevi*'s comments must be understood as applying only to situations in which the heart has been physically removed, but not to situations in which, only as a halakhic construct, is the heart deemed to have been "placed in a basket."

This distinction finds support in the comments of Me'iri, *Ḥullin* 33a:

> Since we have explained that, whenever the trachea is severed, the lung is regarded as if it is placed in a basket, some are of the opinion that even if one were to come and remove it totally before the esophagus is severed [the slaughter] is valid. But this is not at all correct... The principle is stated

> only with regard to perforation [of the lung, *viz.*,] that [the animal] is not rendered a *treifah* in that manner since perforation and other *treifot* do not kill immediately; but whenever [the lung] is totally removed [the animal] dies before slaughter and there is no doubt that it is carrion.

In these comments, Me'iri distinguishes, even with regard to the lung, between mere perforation of the lung subsequent to severance of the trachea and actual removal of the lung. In the case of the former, the animal is not a *treifah* because, as indicated by the Gemara, the lung is regarded as having already been "placed in a basket." Nor is the animal regarded as already dead on the basis of what is only "constructive" placement in a basket. However, declares Me'iri, if the lung is removed subsequent to severance of the trachea, but before severance of the esophagus, the animal is *neveilah*, or carrion. The animal is regarded as having died immediately upon removal of the lung prior to severance of the esophagus since the animal cannot survive the physical removal of the lung. Indeed, Me'iri's position parallels that of *Ḥakham Ẓevi*: *Ḥakham Ẓevi* asserts that survival without a heart is impossible; Me'iri, in effect, declares that, similarly, survival without a lung is impossible.

It should also be noted that there is no evidence that the author of the first opinion cited by Me'iri disagrees with *Ḥakham Ẓevi*. The anonymous author of the first opinion asserts only that the animal may survive for at least a brief period subsequent to removal of the lung and, accordingly, the animal is rendered permissible for food if the esophagus is severed during that period. A similar statement is not made with regard to removal of the heart; the authority who espouses that opinion may well agree that removal of the heart results in instantaneous death so that severance of the esophagus is of no avail.

IV. MOVEMENT AS THE INDICATOR OF LIFE

Me'iri's comments certainly support a distinction between actual physical removal of an organ and what may be termed "constructive" removal of the organ. Constructive removal denotes a situation in which a halakhic status of removal is posited on the basis of interpretation and analysis of attendant circumstances. In a situation of constructive removal of the heart, the heart remains *in situ* but, for purposes of Halakhah, is regarded "as if" it were placed in a basket. Thus *Ḥakham Zevi*'s statement regarding the impossibility of life in the absence of a heart may be viewed as applying only to physical removal of the heart but not to situations in which the heart is only regarded "as if" it were placed in a basket.

However, merely to draw a distinction between actual and constructive removal of the heart is not to present a conceptual basis for that distinction. *Ḥakham Zevi* recognizes that it is entirely possible that movement may be manifest in various organs and limbs of the body even subsequent to physical removal of the heart. Such motion is dismissed by *Ḥakham Zevi* as "the convulsive movement referred to in *Oholot*, but nevertheless [the animal] is dead and not alive." Although severance of the trachea renders the heart "as if" it were placed in a basket, it would be possible similarly to characterize the residual motion manifest after severance of the trachea as "convulsive movement," which is not at all an indicator of the presence of life. Yet, as has been shown earlier, in situations in which the heart remains *in situ*, but is regarded "as if" it were already placed in a basket, the animal is regarded as still living.

The Mishnah, *Oholot* 1:6, states, "And likewise cattle and wild beasts . . . if the heads have been severed, they are unclean [as carrion] even if they move convulsively like the tail of a newt (or a lizard) that twitches spasmodically after being cut off." Decapitation is here depicted as a definitive indication that death has occurred. But decapitation is hardly the only recognized symptom of death. The Gemara, *Yoma* 85a, posits other indicators of death as well. The case in point concerns an individual trapped under a fallen building. Since desecration of the Sabbath is mandated even on the mere chance that a human life may be preserved, the debris of a collapsed building must be cleared away even if it is doubtful that the person under the rubble is still alive.

However, once it has been determined with certainty that the person has expired, no further violation of Sabbath regulations may be sanctioned. The question that then arises is how much of the body must be uncovered in order to ascertain that death has in fact occurred? The Gemara cites two opinions with regard to that question. The first opinion cited by the Gemara maintains that the nose must be uncovered and the victim of the accident pronounced dead only if no sign of respiration is found at the nostrils. A second opinion maintains that examination of the chest for the absence of a heartbeat is sufficient to determine that death has occurred. It is evident that both opinions regard respiration as the crucial symptom indicating the existence of life. Hence both opinions agree that absence of respiration at the site of the nostrils is a sufficient criterion of death. The second opinion merely adds that absence of a heartbeat is also to be deemed sufficient evidence that death has actually occurred. This is evident from the statement of R. Papa quoted by the Gemara in clarification of this controversy. R. Papa states that there is no disagreement between the two opinions in instances in which the body is uncovered "from the top down." In such cases all regard the absence of respiration as conclusive. The dispute, declares R. Papa, is limited to situations in which the body is uncovered "from the bottom up" and thus the heart is uncovered first. The controversy in such cases is whether the absence of a heartbeat is sufficient evidence, in and of itself, to establish that death has occurred, or whether further evidence is required, namely, the uncovering of the nostrils. The necessity for examining the nostrils is based upon the assumption that it is possible for life to exist even though such life may be undetectable by means of examination of the chest for the presence of a heartbeat. Rashi succinctly comments that the first opinion maintains that examination of the chest is insufficient to determine whether or not life is present "for at times life is not evident at the heart but is evident at the nose."

It would appear that reflected in these two sources, *Oholot* 1:6 and *Yoma* 85a, are two independent criteria, either of which is sufficient to establish that death has occurred: (1) decapitation; and (2) cessation of cardiac activity as manifest by absence of respiration.

R. Moses Sofer, *Teshuvot Ḥatam Sofer, Yoreh De'ah*, no. 338, posits a tripartite test to be utilized in determining whether or not death has occurred. *Ḥatam Sofer* declares, "But in any case, once [the patient] lies as an inanimate stone and there is no pulsation whatsoever, and if subsequently respiration ceases we have only the words of our holy Torah that he is dead." *Ḥatam Sofer* adds a further criterion in addition to those found in *Yoma* 85a, *viz.*, absence of all bodily movement with the result that the patient lies "as an inanimate stone." The other criteria posited by *Ḥatam Sofer* are based upon the discussion in *Yoma* 85a. The absence of pulsation required by *Ḥatam Sofer* is clearly synonymous with cessation of cardiac activity. *Ḥatam Sofer* requires that the absence of detectable cardiac activity must be accompanied by cessation of respiration in accordance with the opinion recorded in *Yoma* 85a which maintains that examination of the area surrounding the heart is not to be relied upon since, at times, a heartbeat may indeed be present but not be discernible. In this ruling *Ḥatam Sofer* follows the position of Rambam, *Hilkhot Shabbat* 2:19, *Shulḥan Arukh, Oraḥ Ḥayyim* 329:4, and other codifiers who rule in accordance with the opinion that examination of the nostrils is an absolute requirement. Thus, according to *Ḥatam Sofer*, death may be pronounced only upon manifestation of three criteria: (1) cessation of all bodily movement; (2) absence of pulsation; and (3) total absence of respiration.

Although *Yoma* 85a fails to specify absence of bodily motion as a necessary criterion of death, it is certain that the source of *Ḥatam Sofer*'s position is Rashi's elucidation of that text. Commenting on the Gemara's query, "How far must he examine?" Rashi remarks, "If [the victim] appears as dead, [i.e.,] he does not move his limbs." The clear inference to be drawn from Rashi's comment is that, if animation is manifest in muscular movement, the victim is perforce known to be alive. Further examination is pointless since an individual in such a state cannot be pronounced dead on the basis of the absence of detectable signs of cardiac or respiratory activity. This, however, does not resolve the problem; it merely pushes the problem back one step. *Ḥatam Sofer* may well have relied upon Rashi's statement, but on what basis did Rashi determine that absence of bodily movement is a necessary condition of death?

Careful examination of the words of the Mishnah, *Oholot* 1:6, yields a ready source for Rashi's position. The Mishnah states, "If their heads are severed they defile [as carrion] even though they move convulsively in a manner similar to the tail of a newt which convulses." The Mishnah carefully distinguishes between convulsive movement (*pirkus*) and movement which is indicative of animation produced by vital forces. This distinction is evidenced by the Mishnah's categorization of convulsive movement as comparable to the reflexive, twitching motion of the severed tail of a newt. The necessity for such a distinction can only reflect the antecedent premise that bodily movement is ordinarily a sufficient criterion of the continued presence of life. Thus, there arises a need for a distinction between motion that is a veridical criterion of life and mere *pirkus*, or convulsive movement, which is not a sign of vital animation. Accordingly, Rashi comments that other criteria of death assume significance only if the victim or patient appears to be dead as evidenced by the fact that "he does not move his limbs" because, in the case of a person who has not been decapitated, bodily movement, in and of itself, is an absolute sign of vitality.

Indeed, of necessity, the Mishnah must be construed as serving to establish the principle that motion constitutes a sufficient indicator of life. Were this not the primary thrust of the Mishnah, the explanatory phrase "even though they convulse . . . " would be entirely superfluous. Assuming, as we must, that, in accordance with *Yoma* 85a, the Mishnah recognizes that absence of respiration constitutes a necessary criterion of death, a decapitated animal would perforce be deemed to be dead were absence of respiration, in and of itself, a sufficient criterion of death since, obviously, a decapitated animal cannot breathe. Hence, a formulation of a distinction between vital and non-vital movement would be entirely superfluous. At most, the Mishnah might have incorporated an explanatory phrase to the effect that "even though they convulse they defile [as carrion] for respiration has ceased" without finding it necessary to stress that convulsive movement is not indicative of the presence of residual life forces.

It may further be argued that *Yoma* 85a does not serve to establish criteria of death independent of the criterion of death recorded in *Oholot* 1:6 with the effect that death is defined as either cessation of cardiac activity, as evidenced by absence of respiration, or as decapitation. Rather, it may be postulated that the essential criterion of death is cessation of all bodily movement. Thus, decapitation may be viewed as constituting death, not merely by reason of severance of the head from the body, but because decapitation causes cessation of all vital motion. As is evident from the explanatory phrase of the Mishnah in *Oholot*, were subsequent convulsive movements to be regarded as vital movement, decapitation, in and of itself, would not constitute death. Thus, the essential distinction between a living creature and a corpse is that the latter lies as an "inanimate stone." Accordingly, neither respiration nor cardiac activity need be viewed as a unique activity indicating the presence of life; rather, respiration and cardiac activity should be regarded merely as specific forms of bodily movement. Hence, whenever either cardiac or respiratory activity is present, the organism must be regarded as yet animate on the basis of bodily movement that is indicative of the presence of vital forces.

Placed in this context, Rashi's comment declaring that examination for signs of cardiac and respiratory activity is required only when the victim shows no evidence of movement and appears as an "inanimate stone" serves not only to qualify the discussion in *Yoma* 85a but also to provide the framework for a conceptual understanding of the criteria posited by *Yoma* 85a. Rashi's comment underscores the notion that bodily movement is the essential symptom of life and that whenever such motion is present the patient is *ipso facto* alive. *Yoma* 85a serves to establish that movement as an indicator of life is not restricted to gross motion of limbs, but includes the more subtle and spontaneous motion of the pulsating heart and respiring lungs as well.

This understanding of the absence of motion as the essential criterion of death yields an obvious distinction between physical removal of the heart and severance of the trachea. According to *Ḥakham Zevi*, life cannot persist subsequent to actual removal of the heart for the simple reason that continued vital motion becomes impossible. Although severance of the trachea results in a situation in which the heart is deemed to have been "placed in a basket," such determination is a halakhic construct and, as such, is germane only to matters of purely halakhic concern, *viz.*, whether the heart is deemed to be integrated within the body or is deemed to be disassociated from the body. The question of whether an organism is alive or dead is not at all contingent upon a determination of whether the heart is deemed to be an integral part of the body. It is not removal of the heart *qua* removal that causes death, but the cessation of motion following closely in the wake of such removal that is the criterion of death. Hence, severance of the trachea may serve also to separate the heart from the body (rendering it as if "placed in a basket") for all matters pertaining to contiguity of the various organs; but severance of the trachea is irrelevant to a determination of the occurrence of death because the heart, although it may be deemed to have been "removed," nevertheless continues to perform all cardiac functions. Since the heart continues to beat normally, continued cardiac "movement" serves as an indicator that life is yet present. *Ḥakham Zevi*'s thesis to the effect that no creature can survive without a heart must be understood as applying only to situations in which the heart is physically detached and removed from the body in a manner that prevents the heart from animating the body with the result that all bodily motion ebbs. Were the detached heart somehow capable of causing motion to persist in the body, there would be no reason to reach a determination that death has occurred. Precisely such a situation arises upon severance of the trachea. Halakhically, the heart may be viewed as detached, but, empirically, the organism remains capable of motion and hence the individual is deemed to be alive. Thus a gentile may not be invited to partake of the organs of a non-kosher animal which has been slaughtered, but which has not yet died, because the animal remains alive despite severance of the trachea.

This, then, is precisely the position espoused by the anonymous exponent of the first opinion cited by Rabbenu Nissim who maintains that perforation of the heart subsequent to severance of the trachea does not render the animal a *treifah*. According to that view, since the trachea has already been severed by the act of slaughter, perforation of a heart is tantamount to perforation of a heart already "placed in a basket" and no longer an integral part of the animal. Hence, perforation of the heart does not render the animal a *treifah*. Nevertheless, the animal is not deemed to have expired since the heart continues to function. Therefore, the animal is not regarded as carrion and the act of slaughter may be completed. If, however, the heart were to be completely severed from the body and physically removed prior to completion of the act of slaughter, i.e., prior to the severing of both the trachea and the esophagus, the animal would indeed be deemed to be carrion. This is so since, by virtue of removal of the heart, the animal has, according to *Ḥakham Zevi*, been put to death prior to the completion of the act of slaughter.

Rabbenu Nissim himself disagrees with this position and asserts that the heart is never to be regarded "as if it had been placed in a basket." Rabbenu Nissim apparently reasons that recognition that the animal has, in fact, not died, as evidenced by the fact that the heart continues to pump blood through the circulatory system, logically entails acceptance of the position that the heart is not already "in a basket" but continues to function as an integral part of the organism. Hence, in the opinion of Rabbenu Nissim, so long as the heart remains attached to the body and functions as the animating force of the circulatory system, it is deemed to be an integral part of the body even though it is no longer attached to the body by means of the trachea. According to Rabbenu Nissim, the heart cannot be deemed to have been "placed in a basket" so long as the circulatory system is operative. Hence, according to Rabbenu Nissim, perforation of the heart in such circumstances renders the animal a *treifah*.

This consideration obviously does not pertain in situations in which the heart has been completely detached and removed from the body cavity subsequent to severance of the trachea. According to the opinion cited by Me'iri, the identical considerations apply to the lungs as well and the animal is deemed to have succumbed immediately upon physical removal of the lungs. Thus, both positions recorded by Rabbenu Nissim, as well as the opinion cited by Me'iri, are entirely compatible with the thesis advanced by *Ḥakham Ẓevi*.

Acceptance of the explanation that the presence of cardiac activity is not a unique indicator of the presence of life, but rather that it is simply a form of movement indicative of the presence of vital forces, yields a significant point with regard to the status of a patient during surgery undertaken for implantation of an artificial heart. It has previously been established that only irreversible cessation of vital functions – as distinct from transitory, reversible cessation of such functions – is indicative of death. Since cardiac activity occupies no privileged position in the determination of death, and since it is not the mere presence of the heart or the function of the heart as a unique organ which is the essential indicator of life, but rather the "movement" of the heart as a form of integrated, vital movement of the organism which indicates that life is present, it follows that temporary cessation of cardiac activity during the course of a surgical procedure is neither cause nor evidence of death. In such procedures the integrated vital movements of the body are not permanently halted; they are merely temporarily interrupted. Since "movement" is indeed restored to the body and it is precisely integrated, vital movement, which is the essence of life, whether such movement is produced by a natural heart or by an artificial organ is of no moment. So long as animation can be restored, life has not yet ebbed. Implantation of an artificial heart has the effect of restoring animation; the movement restored by means of implantation of an artificial heart is not mere convulsive motion but is vital in nature.

The conclusion that such motion is not mere *pirkus*, or convulsive movement, is evident from the comments of Rambam in his *Commentary on the Mishnah, Oholot* 1:6. Rambam distinguishes vital movement from convulsive movement by postulating that vital movement is "the motor force which diffuses throughout the limbs from a single root and source." It is clear that such integrated motion is manifested by the recipient of an artificial heart.

To be sure, *Ḥakham Ẓevi* does declare that in the absence of a heart it is impossible for any creature to survive. However, it is certain that *Ḥakham Ẓevi's* comments must be understood as asserting only that it is impossible for any creature to live without an organ, or apparatus, which performs the functions normally associated with a heart. Hence, absent any indication of the existence of some other organ or device, the presence of a normal biological heart must be inferred and conclusively assumed. Accordingly, *Ḥakham Ẓevi* rules that there existed no basis for a conclusion that the chicken brought before him was a *treifah*. However, there is no reason to assume that *Ḥakham Ẓevi* would deny the possibility that life might be sustained by means of a transplanted heart or by means of an artificial apparatus. Certainly, if it is "movement" in general, rather than cardiac movement specifically, which is the primary indicator of life, whether the source of that "movement" is natural or artificial is immaterial. The crucial point established by *Ḥakham Ẓevi* is that there is no life in the absence of integrated vital movement, and, conversely, whenever such "movement" is present, life exists.

V. IS THE RECIPIENT OF AN ARTIFICIAL OR CADAVER HEART A *TREIFAH*?

The question that remains is whether or not the recipient of either an artificial heart or a cadaver transplant is to be regarded as a *treifah*. A *treifah* is an animal or human being suffering the loss or perforation of certain organs. The condition may be the product of congenital anomaly or the result of trauma. Animals in the category of *treifah* are *ipso facto* non-kosher and their meat may not be consumed. In the case of a human being this question is of significance solely with regard to whether the murder of such a person is a capital crime since, in Jewish law, the murder of a *treifah* is a form of non-capital homicide. The Gemara, *Sanhedrin* 78a, declares:

> Our Sages taught: If ten men struck a man with ten staves, whether simultaneously or one after the other, and he died, they are not liable. R. Judah ben Beteira said, if one after the other, the last is culpable because he hastened [the victim's] death. R. Yoḥanan said: Both engaged in exegetical interpretation of the same verse, "and he that killeth *kol nefesh* [lit., 'all life'] of man shall surely be put to death" (Leviticus 24:17). The Sages maintain that *kol nefesh* limits [culpability] to [the taking of] the whole life; R. Judah ben Beteira maintains that *kol nefesh* [implies] whatever there is of life.
>
> Rava said: All agree that one who kills a *treifah* is not liable: [and that] if he slew a person who is moribund (*goses*) by virtue of an act of God [lit., at the

> hands of Heaven] he is culpable. They disagree only with regard to a person who is moribund as a result of a human act [lit., at the hands of man]: One likens him to a *treifah* and [hence] his slayer is exempt, the other likens him to a person who is moribund by virtue of an act of God [lit., at the hands of Heaven] and [hence] his slayer is culpable.

In a three-part article that appeared in *Ha-Tzofeh* (Tevet 8, Tevet 15 and Tevet 22, 5743), Rabbi Shlomoh Goren attempts to define the phrase "at the hands of Heaven" in a rather novel manner. Rabbi Goren argues that the term "at the hands of Heaven" as employed in *Sanhedrin* 78a is to be understood in precisely the same manner as it is understood in the context of an entirely unrelated discussion recorded in *Yevamot* 75b. The Gemara, *Yevamot* 75b, states that, although Scripture declares that a person who has "wounded testicles" is forbidden to engage in sexual intercourse (Deuteronomy 23:2), the prohibition is limited to wounds suffered "at the hands of man." However, one who has been wounded "at the hands of Heaven" is not subject to this restriction. Rashi and Rosh define the term "at the hands of Heaven" as connoting injuries suffered as a result of "thunder or hail" or a condition that results from a congenital anomaly. However, Rambam, *Hilkhot Issurei Bi'ah* 16:9, states that the concept of an injury sustained "at the hands of Heaven" also encompasses damage sustained as a result of any illness or physiological disorder. *Shulḥan Arukh, Even ha-Ezer* 5:10, accepts this position. Rabbi Goren states:

> According to the opinion of Rambam and those who follow his position, in every instance the severance of an organ as a result of disease in that organ is deemed to be a wound at the hands of Heaven and [the individual] is fit [to engage in intercourse]. But, according to the opinion of Rashi, since the surgical procedure and severance of the organ is performed at the hands of man, even though the removal is necessary by virtue of an illness at the hands of Heaven, the matter is considered as if it had occurred at the hands of man. The same is true with regard to our case, [*viz.,*] one who kills a person possessing an artificial heart. It has been demonstrated that one who kills a *treifah* at the hands of man is liable to capital punishment at the hands of the *Bet Din*, but the slayer of a *treifah* at the hands of Heaven is exempt from punishment by man but liable at the hands of Heaven. The same is true with regard to one who slays a person who possesses an artificial heart since the implantation is the result of a grave cardiac illness which arises in a natural manner at the hands of Heaven. According to the opinion of Rambam, one who slays [such an individual] is liable to the death penalty even at the hands of the Sanhedrin and is judged as an outright murderer. But, according to Rashi and Rosh and those who follow their opinion, one who slays a person possessing an artificial heart will be exonerated from the death penalty at the hands of the *Bet Din*.

The view expressed by Rabbi Goren is obviously predicated upon the interpretation of Rambam's position advanced by *Teshuvot Ḥatam Sofer, Even ha-Ezer*, vol. I, no. 17. According to *Ḥatam Sofer*, Rambam maintains that a surgeon's removal of the testes for therapeutic reasons is considered to be "wounding at the hands of Heaven." However, other authorities assert that, even according to Rambam, whenever removal of the testes is accomplished surgically, the "wounding" is deemed to be "at the hands of man" even if performed for therapeutic purposes.[81]

However, Rabbi Goren's position is subject to challenge on more fundamental grounds. The distinction drawn by the Gemara, *Yevamot* 75b, between a wound sustained "at the hands of man" and a wound sustained "at the hands of Heaven" is limited in application. That distinction serves to delineate the prohibition against sexual intercourse on the part of an individual who has sustained an injury to the genital organs but is of absolutely no import with regard to the distinction drawn in *Sanhedrin* 78a between a person rendered moribund "at the hands of man" and one rendered moribund "at the hands of Heaven." The distinction is entirely understandable with regard to the halakhic disabilities associated with wounds to the genitalia but lacks cogency with regard to culpability for the slaying of a moribund person.

Sefer ha-Ḥinnukh, no. 559, states that the prohibition against intercourse by a person wounded in the genital organs is designed to impose sanctions against those who would cause intentional damage to their sexual organs. It was the wont of monarchs in antiquity to emasculate servants in order to create eunuchs, who were then placed in charge of the royal harems. Persons contemplating such a procedure would not be prepared to accept the onus of a stricture prohibiting intercourse and hence the effect of the prohibition is to prevent intentional damage to sexual organs. *Sefer ha-Ḥinnukh* concludes his comments with the statement that this explanation serves to illuminate the halakhic distinction between an individual who is wounded "at the hands of man" and one who is wounded "at the hands of Heaven." Since the purpose is to prevent intentional emasculation, no purpose would be served in extending the prohibition to persons wounded "at the hands of Heaven."

In light of *Sefer ha-Ḥinnukh*'s exposition, Rambam's extension of the concept of wounding "at the hands of Heaven" to encompass injury to the genital organs sustained as a result of illness or disease (and, as understood by *Ḥatam Sofer*, even to surgical removal of the genital organs for therapeutic purposes) is readily understandable. Thus, according to this position, the primary distinction between a wound sustained "at the hands of man" and a wound

[81] For a fuller discussion of Rambam's position, see J. David Bleich, *Contemporary Halakhic Problems* (New York, 1989), vol. III, pp. 151–53.

sustained at "at the hands of Heaven" is a distinction between intentional injury designed to destroy reproductive capacity and unintentional, undesired injury born of illness or disease. Such considerations are entirely irrelevant to the definition of a "*goses* at the hands of man" as distinct from a "*goses* at the hands of Heaven."

Moreover, the essence of the distinction between a "*goses* at the hands of man" and a "*goses* at the hands of Heaven" is expressly formulated by the Gemara, *Sanhedrin* 78a. In the discussion of the dispute between the Sages and R. Judah ben Beteira regarding ten men who struck a man with ten staves, the Gemara states:

> One likens him to a *treifah*, the other likens him to a person who is rendered moribund at the hands of Heaven. He who likens him to a *treifah*, why does he not liken him to a person rendered a *goses* at the hands of Heaven? – [Because] a *goses* at the hands of Heaven has not sustained an [injurious] act; but an [injurious] act has been done to this one. And he who likens him to a *goses* at the hands of Heaven, why does he not liken him to a *treifah*? – A *treifah* has his vital organs cut, but this one has not had his vital organs cut.

It is evident that the murderer of a "*goses* at the hands of Heaven" is liable to the death penalty because the *goses* is deemed to be fully alive even though moribund. In every case in which a life is destroyed by means of an act of murder it is only residual longevity that is extinguished. In every instance the residual longevity constitutes the entire life-complement of the victim. Destruction of such life-complement by a single aggressor constitutes homicide. Thus the murderer of a newly born child and the murderer of an octogenarian are equally liable despite the disparate life expectancies of the respective victims. Homicide is defined as the termination of human life through an act of man regardless of the life expectancy of the victim. The murderer of a "*goses* at the hands of Heaven" is culpable because the moribund individual is yet alive and the brief life span available to him constitutes an entire life-complement insofar as the victim is concerned. Hence the murderer has deprived the victim of the latter's full longevity anticipation, brief as it may be. The murder of a "*goses* at the hands of man" is readily distinguishable. The culpability of the murderer of such an individual is a matter of dispute precisely because the perpetrator is not solely responsible for extinguishing the victim's full life-complement. Since the victim had already been smitten by another aggressor, the last aggressor has not single-handedly deprived the victim of his natural life expectancy because "an act has been done to him." In such a case the life-complement has been destroyed as the result of the acts of multiple individuals. None of the perpetrators is liable to the death penalty since, according to the Sages, capital culpability exists only when a single aggressor destroys the entire life-complement of the victim.

It follows, therefore, that a gravely ill patient who is rendered moribund by a surgical procedure must be deemed a "*goses* at the hands of man," despite the therapeutic purpose of the procedure and the entirely laudable design of the surgeon. The murderer of such a patient has not deprived the victim of the latter's full life-complement since, in point of fact, an antecedent human act, *viz.*, the surgical procedure, has contributed to the destruction of the patient's life-complement. The surgical procedure clearly constitutes a human act as a result of which the residual life is not deemed to be a "whole life." Hence it is absolutely clear that the culpability of the murderer of a person already rendered moribund (albeit unintentionally) by virtue of an unsuccessful medical procedure would fall within the ambit of the controversy between the Sages and R. Judah ben Beteira.

This point may also be established on the basis of the comments of Rosh, *Nazir* 4b. The Gemara declares that a Nazarite is not only forbidden to defile himself through tactile contact with a corpse but is also forbidden to touch a *goses*. Rosh declares that this prohibition is limited to contact with a "*goses* at the hands of Heaven" but does not include the touching of a "*goses* at the hands of man." *Teshuvot Ḥatam Sofer, Yoreh De'ah*, no. 338, explains that, according to Rosh, contact with a "*goses* at the hands of man" is not deemed to constitute defilement since a "*goses* at the hands of man" is not as close to death as is a "*goses* at the hands of Heaven." *Ḥatam Sofer* expresses amazement because this distinction, as drawn by Rosh, is the antithesis of the distinction drawn by the Gemara, *Sanhedrin* 78a, with regard to culpability for homicidal acts. Similarly, the author of the published marginal glosses on Rosh's commentary writes that the rationale underlying Rosh's distinction is that a "*goses* at the hands of man" is deemed to be endowed with a higher degree of vitality than is a "*goses* at the hands of Heaven." He then proceeds to question the cogency of Rosh's assessment since "according to the Sages, whose opinion is normative, a '*goses* at the hands of man' is deemed to be 'a dead person,' which is not the case with a '*goses* at the hands of Heaven.'"

In an attempt to resolve this difficulty, R. Zevi Hirsch Chajes, in his commentary on *Nazir* 4a, states:

> A distinction must be made: With regard to capital punishment there is a statutory requirement as it is written, "*kol nefesh*, whatever there is of life," and hence [absence of culpability] is contingent upon an act, as Rashi explains *ad locum*. In the case of a "*goses* at the hands of man" an act was done to him antecedently and therefore one who kills him has killed a "dead person."

> This is not the case with regard to defilement, since it is predicated essentially upon death. Therefore, [with regard to a "*goses* at the hands of man"] there is the consideration that [the victim] may have swooned and does not yet defile. Whereas [with regard to a "*goses*] at the hands of Heaven," since there is no external causative act, therefore, once the illness has become so severe that [the patient] is moribund there is no longer any doubt that criteria of death are present.

It is clear from these comments that a greater degree of vitality is present in a "*goses* at the hands of man" than is present in a "*goses* at the hands of Heaven." This consideration notwithstanding, all are in agreement that one who slays a "*goses* at the hands of Heaven" commits a capital crime, whereas the Sages maintain that one who slays a "*goses* at the hands of man" is not liable to capital punishment. The reason for regarding a "*goses* at the hands of man" as lacking in "vitality" is that he has been the victim of an antecedent act of aggression that has resulted in diminished vitality. Since intent obviously plays no role in determination of the presence or absence of vitality, a victim rendered moribund as a result of a surgical trauma cannot be deemed to be a "*goses* at the hands of Heaven" and hence is not in the halakhic category of "*kol nefesh*" – "a whole life."

Rabbi Goren's comments are even more puzzling in view of the fact that, although the Sages and R. Judah ben Bateira disagree with regard to the culpability of one who kills a "*goses* at the hands of man," with regard to the halakhic status of a *treifah* there is no distinction between one who is rendered a *treifah* "at the hands of man" and one who is rendered a *treifah* "at the hands of Heaven." As is reflected in the rulings of *Rambam*, *Hilkhot Evel* 4:5, and *Shulḥan Arukh*, *Yoreh De'ah* 339:1, a moribund person may acquire the status of a *goses* even though no organ is removed or perforated. A *treifah*, however, is defined not simply as one suffering from a terminal malady but as one suffering the loss or perforation of specific organs. The slayer of a *treifah* is exempt from capital punishment by virtue of statutory law that makes no distinction with regard to the source of such anomaly.

By definition, the recipient of a successful artificial heart implantation is not moribund and hence is not a *goses*. Nevertheless, such a person may be a *treifah*. Perforation of the heart renders the victim a *treifah* and, *a fortiori*, removal of the heart would render the patient a *treifah*. However, according to Rambam's definition of *treifah*, demonstrative success of artificial heart implantations coupled with anticipated survival for a significant period of time would serve to remove the recipients from the category of *treifah*. Rambam, *Hilkhot Sheḥitah* 10:12–13, rules that, with regard to animals, the criteria established by the Gemara delineating the various forms of *treifah* are immutable. However, with regard to capital homicide, Rambam, *Hilkhot Roẓeaḥ* 2:8, rules:

> Every person is presumed to be complete and his murderer must be put to death unless it is known with certainty that he is a *treifah* and the physicians declare that this trauma has no cure by human agency and that he would die of it if he were not killed in some other way.

Thus, according to Rambam, with regard to human beings, determination that the individual is a *treifah* is a matter of medical diagnosis.

There is little question that, at present, the recipient of an artificial heart must be considered a *treifah* even according to the opinion of Rambam. It is, however, entirely possible that, with the passage of time and accompanying advances in medical technology, the recipient of an artificial heart may no longer be considered a *treifah*. Under such circumstances Rambam would maintain that the murderer of the recipient of an artificial heart would be liable to the death penalty.

COMMENT ON HALAKHIC CONSTRUCTS

The discussion at times uses terms such as "deemed" or "regarded as" to describe certain halakhic categorizations. For example, the discussion notes that the internal organs suspended from the trachea and the esophagus are "regarded as having been separated from the animal and 'placed in a basket'" immediately upon severance of the trachea and esophagus in the course of kosher slaughter (p. 297). The internal organs are described as "deemed to be 'cut off from the living animal' despite the simultaneous 'excision' of the heart" (p. 298). The discussion gives a special name to the operations of "regarding as" or "deeming": It calls them "halakhic constructs." Just what is a "halakhic construct"? On the surface, it resembles what we commonly call a "legal fiction." The heart is not really being "placed in a basket"; the law only "regards" it as having been "placed in a basket." But is it a legal fiction? Can Halakhah, which understands itself as a legal system of divine origin and authority, tolerate the manipulation implicit in the use of "legal fictions"?

Every legal system has its fictions.[82] Only many of those fictions are not fictitious at all. It may be useful to describe various categories of so-called legal fiction in the common law and American legal system, and then to explore similar devices in Halakhah.

Corporations were unknown in common law. They are the product of legislation. The purpose, or purposes, of creating the concept of a corporation are manifold. At the least, it makes it possible for a society to fashion an efficient and complex financial structure.

Corporations are legal persons. But, of course, corporations are not persons in any non-legal sense of the term. They have, as Lord Coke famously said, "No soul to damn, no body to kick." To call a corporation a legal person is simply to say that just as natural persons have the right to sue, to be sued, to redress in court, so also has the state granted this right to a legal construct.

But assigning these rights to a corporation does not create a fiction. It is simply a legal expedient for recognizing certain rights and prerogatives that shareholders in the corporation exercise in a particular formal legal manner.

Law often recognizes certain categories and then proceeds to speak of them in a "constructive" fashion. For example, in matrimonial law abandonment is fairly straightforward and readily determined. A spouse has either left the marital abode or not. The law attaches certain consequences to having left the marital abode. It attaches those consequences because in leaving the

[82] Indeed, Hans Vaihinger argues that every *science* has its fictions as well. For an exposition of Vaihinger's "philosophy as if" as it affects law, see Lon L. Fuller, *Legal Fictions* (Stanford, CA, 1967).

spouse has to all intents and purposes destroyed the marital relationship. But a spouse can destroy the marital relationship without physically leaving. A spouse who conducts himself or herself in a manner that effectively destroys the relationship without physically leaving the marital domicile has nonetheless "constructively abandoned" the marriage. Or, consider the doctrine of "constructive discharge." An employer wants to get rid of an employee. The ordinary way of doing that is to discharge the employee. But let us say that, for some reason, the employer wants to get rid of the employee without discharging him, perhaps because the employer does not want his unemployment insurance premiums to go up. So instead of openly discharging the employee, the employer makes life perfectly miserable for him at work, hoping he will quit on his own. The employer is accomplishing the same result as discharge – the employee is gone – but without having to incur its costs. The employer has discharged the employee in all but name. He has "constructively discharged" the employee.

In neither case has the law created a fiction. It is essentially a matter of definition. The law defines abandonment or discharge in a non-literal way. It looks to the empirical and/or legal effect of abandonment or discharge and then recognizes that the same effect may result without literal abandonment or discharge and proceeds to treat those conditions in the same way that it treats actual abandonment or discharge. As such, the concepts can hardly be called fictions.

At times, the law explicitly defines common terms in a manner at variance with ordinary usage. Chapter One gave one example: the New York State Health Code contains a prologue in which it defines a hospital. Lo and behold, nursing homes are defined as hospitals. Blue Cross and other insurance carriers do not recognize nursing homes as hospitals and therefore insist that at certain points in recovery the patient be transferred from a hospital to a nursing home. Everyone recognizes that the two types of institutions are vastly different. Nevertheless, the applicable New York statute declares that nursing homes are hospitals. The purpose of such definition in the preamble of a statute is verbal economy. Instead of spelling out multiple times in the same statute that the rule and regulations are applicable to nursing homes and hospitals the statute states simply that wherever the term "hospital" occurs it has the additional connotation of "nursing home." In such cases the nursing home has not been "fictitiously" transformed into a hospital. Applying the term "hospital" to a nursing home is not fictitious; it is simply a form of shorthand.

Sometimes, however, a legal fiction is indeed a fiction. Common law, for example, once considered all actions to be local, meaning that an action could be tried only before a jury of the vicinage in which the events underlying the action took place. This was a perfectly sensible restriction in an era when juries were presumed to be in a position to judge the truth or falsity of the facts parties were contesting on the basis of their own knowledge and observations and when events were confined to a single place. But when jurors ceased to be witnesses and became dispassionate arbiters of a record and when far-flung commercial transactions rendered obsolete the assumption that events must necessarily be local, then the right of appearing before a jury of the vicinage ceased making universal sense: it was appropriate for some claims, but not for others. But courts were unwilling to abandon the formal requirement that an action be brought in the place where the facts underlying the action took place. So actions that courts allowed to be brought elsewhere – transitory actions as opposed to local – required a fiction. Courts permitted the plaintiff in an appropriate case to plead satisfaction of a venue requirement that had not in fact been satisfied. Suppose parties entered into a contract in New Orleans and performed it there. But the party accused of breach could only be found in Richmond, Virginia. The plaintiff was permitted to bring the lawsuit in Richmond simply by alleging that the events underlying the breach of contract claim took place in "New Orleans, Louisiana, to wit, Richmond, Virginia." Cf. *Livingston v. Jefferson*, 15 F. Cas. 660 (C.C. D. Va. 1811). The pleading is a falsehood that lays bare and displays the fact of its falsehood. It is a fiction pure and simple.

This latter category of legal fiction is alien to Halakhah and the halakhic process. One might question the validity of judicial activism in creating such a fiction without explicit authorization by the legislature. Nevertheless, in the common law system judges have arrogated such powers to themselves and *sui generis* have created precedent and hence authority for such procedures. Such a process would be incompatible with the halakhic system. In Halakhah courts do not have the power to "make law" in any sense of the term; their power is entirely interpretive. Rabbinic synods – rabbinic bodies having legislative authority – do have the power, in certain carefully delineated areas, to promulgate rules of general applicability. Thus, they might conceivably enact an ordinance defining New Orleans as Richmond, or, better, declaring that any act performed in New Orleans shall have the same effect as an act performed in Richmond (just as Parliament certainly has the authority to do so without causing anyone to raise a legal eyebrow). But a rabbinic court, adjudicating a particular case, has no *ad hoc* authority.

Halakhah does not recognize corporations as legal entities. Precisely what effect the establishment of a corporation would have in Halakhah is beyond the scope of this discussion. The simplest answer is that Halakhah would regard it as a partnership while recognizing that the provisions of any civil statute governing corporations would be incorporated by reference into any contract to which the "corporation" is a party. It is not inconceivable that a properly constituted rabbinic synod might provide for corporations by promulgating a *takkanah* (an ordinance by legislative fiat). But, as in common law, there is no judicial authority to do so.

The legal fictions of Halakhah are in the nature of either constructs or specialized definitions. For the most part they are definitional in nature. In ordinary language a "wall" is a solid structure designed to provide privacy and protection against the elements. For purposes of Sabbath regulations two poles connected by a wire placed upon the top of their flat surfaces constitute a "wall." That "wall" is a wall for purposes of Sabbath regulation, but not necessarily a wall for other halakhic purposes, e.g., a *sukkah* or booth used in celebrating the festival of *Sukkot*. In that case it is the statute promulgated by the divine legislator and transmitted through the Oral Law that provides the definition of a "wall." The accompanying glossary is incorporated in the Sabbath statute but not in the *Sukkot* statute.

The concept of "placing in a basket" is analogous to the legal concept of a constructive category. For example, constructive abandonment is a situation in which the effect of abandonment has been accomplished even though abandonment has not occurred in the literal sense of the word. In the case of abandonment we clearly recognize the effect of abandonment and it is the effect, rather than the fact, that is of legal import. Hence, we regard constructive abandonment no differently than actual abandonment.

It is fundamental to the halakhic process to recognize that man cannot presume to fathom exhaustively the purposes of the divine lawgiver. Although, to be sure, halakhisists and philosophers from time immemorial have tried to decipher the underlying purposes of the *mizvot*, they have unfailingly recognized that any comprehensive elucidation is impossible. The system itself recognizes that the minutiae of the *mizvot* as well as their application in various situations are independent of any humanly perceived rationale. Thus the concept of a "limb cut off from a living animal" is an ontological concept subject to definition of the concept "cut off" that is not necessarily coextensive with the purpose of the prohibition as fathomed by the human intellect. See R. Joseph Ber Soloveitchik of Brisk, *Bet ha-Levi, Parashat Bo*.

The underlying purpose and rationale of the prohibition against eating "a limb cut off from a living animal" cannot be exhaustively comprehended by the human mind. The prohibition against eating a "limb cut off from a living animal" does not depend upon usual moral notions such as anti-vivisection or the prevention of cruelty to animals. Although these moral concerns may be the ultimate rationale upon which the commandment is predicated, the commandment is formulated and applied in a manner independent of its rationale. Halakhah informs us that "placing in a basket" is tantamount to being "cut off from a living animal" without disclosing the purpose of the categorization. That is to say that the effect of "placing in a basket" is the same as the effect of being "cut off," although in the nature of things we may not fully appreciate what that effect is. Thus within the halakhic system "placing in a basket" is the constructive equivalent of "cutting off."

The notion of "cut off from a living animal" requires a definition of the term "cut off." If a foreleg is attached to the body only by a tendon, is it "cut off" from that body? If only 51% of the diameter of the leg has been cut, is the leg "cut off" from the body? These issues are addressed and resolved in Halakhah. Organs attached to the body by the trachea or esophagus are regarded as "cut off" from the body, because attachment through the tenuous adhesion of the esophagus or trachea is not regarded as "attachment" within the halakhic definition of the concept. An organ attached by means of a flimsy structure such as the trachea or esophagus is constructively detached. For purposes of Halakhah those organs have been constructively removed and placed within the shell of the body, which is described as a "basket."

NOTES AND QUESTIONS

1. As demonstrated in the discussion, Halakhah contains explicit criteria of life. However, to say that a person is alive does not address the question of who the person is. A mature adult is the same person as the toddler or the infant that emerged from his mother's womb. Yet at the same time, the individual in different stages of life is different. Nevertheless, we regard the infant, the toddler, the adolescent, the mature adult and the geriatric as one and the same person. That categorization rests upon a concept of personal identity that has long troubled philosophers. What are the criteria of personal identity and at what point is an individual no longer the same person?

Our discussion demonstrates that a person in whom an artificial heart has been implanted is alive. But is he still the same person? It is certainly possible to transplant multiple organs and ultimately it may become possible to construct multiple artificial organs. At what point, if any, does an individual lose his original identity?

A visceral reaction would be that a person is defined in terms of his mental processes, so that he is one and the same person as long as he retains his own brain. That is akin to the philosophical position that makes personal identity contingent upon memory. Definition of a person in terms of his or her mental processes is likewise subject to the Prince and the Pauper objection that was raised against the thesis that it is memory that explains personal identity. See John Locke, *An Essay Concerning Human Understanding*, book 2, ch. 27. See also Thomas Reid, *Essays on the Intellectual Power of Man*, essay III, ch. 4, and John Butler, "Personal Identity," in Joseph Butler, W. E. Gladstone, and Samuel Clarke, *The Analogy of Religion: Natural and Revealed to the Constitution and Course of Nature. To Which Are Added Two Brief Dissertations: I. Of Personal Identity; II. Of the Nature of Virtue; and a Correspondence with Dr. Samuel Clarke* (Oxford, 1897).

The theologian might argue that it is the presence of the soul that accounts for personal identity and that as long as the soul remains in the body the individual retains his identity no matter how many organs are replaced. But then, if we were to accept transplantation of multiple organs or implantation of multiple artificial organs, how would we ascertain that the same soul resides in that body? Most Jewish philosophers reject the notion of transmigration. However, the Kabbalists accepted it. If the soul departs from the human body and enters that of a dog, is the result the identical persona? Certainly no one would accept the position that a brute animal in which a human soul has entered has the halakhic status of a human being, much less the legal or halakhic status of the person whose soul has been incarnated in an animal. If the soul has entered a machine, i.e., a body composed of artificial parts, even if that entity is alive, is it still the same person? It is undoubtedly the case that the recipient of an artificial heart is not only alive but also has the identity of the person whose heart has been replaced. That would probably be true even if both an artificial heart and an artificial brain were to be implanted. What has not been addressed and remains puzzling is a theory of identity that would justify that conclusion.

2. Suppose the recipient of an artificial heart were to become a victim of homicide in a jurisdiction governed by American law. Suppose also that the killer were to defend on the grounds that he could not have killed the recipient because the recipient was already dead: *human* life came to an end with surgical removal of the victim's heart. There is nothing to prevent an American jurisdiction from conceding the defense while at the same time recognizing that the recipient should not be regarded as a mere robot. What in the nature of Halakhah precludes the approach that is so eminently possible in American law?

Homicide by definition means the killing of a human being. If the recipient is not "alive" then the taking of his life cannot be homicide. Of course, an American jurisdiction could promulgate legislation making "roboticide" a capital crime akin to homicide. Or, it could redefine homicide as the killing of a human or of an animated robot capable of cognition. An American jurisdiction has this ability because civil legislation is man-made and the legislature is all-powerful within the boundaries of constitutional restraint. The legislature would be creating a legal fiction by redefining a commonly used and understood term for the specific purpose of a criminal statute. Halakhah does not grant rabbinic legislators such broad power. To be sure, the sovereign and/or the courts do have authority to impose sanctions that are *ultra vires*. But those are always in the form of *ad hoc* emergency measures necessary to preserve the fabric of society rather than in the form of broad legislation applicable in all circumstances. Halakhah recognizes the Deity as the lawgiver. Although rabbinic synods enjoy subordinate legislative authority, that power is significantly limited, particularly in the area of criminal law.

3. The book of Ezekiel reports the resurrection of dead persons by the prophet. Suppose that the wife of one of those resurrected by Ezekiel contracted a marriage subsequent to the death of her husband but prior to his resurrection. What would be the legal status of her second marriage? The status of children born during the interim? The status of the woman and her second spouse after the resurrection of her first husband? Similarly, what is the legal status of a woman who contracts a second marriage while her husband, who is undergoing open-heart surgery, is connected to a heart/lung machine? Are the situations different?

4. The problem addressed by this reading is a problem that Halakhah creates for itself. In its insistence upon a definition of death focused upon cardiac activity, it gives rise to the problem of the status of an individual possessing an artificial rather than a natural heart. But at the same time, the law, in accepting neurological criteria for death, creates a similar problem. If life is defined in terms of cerebral activity, what will be the status of the recipient of an artificial brain? When and if artificial, implantable brains are perfected will the American legal system have to address precisely this question? Will this halakhic analysis have anything to offer in resolving that issue within the context of the American legal system?

5. Rabbinic scholars considered the status of a woman whose husband died and was resurrected because (1) such miracles are recorded in Scripture, and (2) they recognized that a divine legal system must be comprehensive and hence applicable in all conceivable contingencies. The problem addressed in our discussion does not focus upon either a miraculous event or a bizarre hypothetical. If removal of the heart is legally and halakhically synonymous with death, "biological resurrection" is an apt description of successful heart implantation (natural or artificial). Rabbinic scholars recognized full well that reality is subject to change (and even that today's science fiction is tomorrow's reality).

Neither common law nor the statutes of any American jurisdiction explicitly address the status of a wife whose husband has died and been resurrected, if for no other reason than that from the advent of the era of the common law until the present no one has presented a contemporaneous claim of miraculous resurrection.

American jurisdictions – both by legislation and in common law – have faced and resolved a set of comparable questions. Common law accepts absence of a spouse for a period of seven years as evidence of death and permits the spouse to remarry. In the event that the first spouse returns, however, the second marriage becomes void. Some states have enacted statutes modifying the common law rule. Article 12 of New York's Domestic Relations Law, for example, reduces the required period of absence from seven years to five. The statute also provides for dissolution of the prior marriage – if the absent spouse resurfaces, the subsequent marriage remains valid. DRL §§220 and 221.[83] Is the common law rule applicable to "resurrection" after death or are the two situations distinguishable?

6. A *treifah* is an animal or human being suffering the loss or perforation of certain organs. The condition may be the product of congenital anomaly or the result of trauma. Animals in the category of *treifah*, even those that are otherwise kosher, *ipso facto* become non-kosher and their meat may not be consumed. In the case of a human being the status of *treifah* has only a single legal effect: in Halakhah the murder of a *treifah*, unlike the murder of persons who do not suffer this disability, is a form of non-capital homicide. (Non-capital homicide is punishable at the hands of Heaven and on an *ad hoc* basis by means of application of "the King's justice.")

The Talmud, Tractate *Ḥullin*, carefully defines the various categories of *treifah*. The rule of thumb is that a *treifah* is an animal or person who, even with appropriate veterinary or medical treatment, will not survive for more than 12 months. Advances in veterinary science have no effect upon the definition of a *treifah* for purposes of the dietary code. However, for the purpose of capital punishment, Rambam, *Mishneh Torah, Hilkhot Rozeaḥ* 2:8, rules that categories of *treifah* are to be defined in light of the medical knowledge and technology of the day.

7. Cryogenics will probably never be successful because of damage caused cells by crystals formed in the freezing process. Assume, however, that short-term freezing is perfected with the result that maintaining blood flow during

[83] Article 12 is known as the "Enoch Arden" law, after a poem by Tennyson. The eponymous character in Tennyson's poem, returning to his old home many years after a shipwreck to find his wife and children happily ensconced with another man, resolved not to destroy the second marriage. Instead, he "paced back toward his solitary home again."

open heart surgery by means of a heart-lung machine is no longer necessary. We have already established that only irreversible cessation of cardiac activity and blood flow constitutes death. If at some time in the future it does become possible to thaw the patient, does that establish that today, even though the procedure has not yet been perfected, the patient, frozen for a brief period of time, is alive because cessation of cardiac activity and blood flow will eventually become reversible in fact? Or, to phrase the question somewhat differently, is "irreversibility" defined in the here-and-now and hence subject to change, or is it a concept to be defined in terms of absolute knowledge and perfection of technology? Is it not precisely this issue that plays the determining role in Rambam's distinction between the definition of a *treifah* for purposes of capital punishment and the definition of a *treifah* for purposes of the dietary code?

Lest this hypothetical seem bizarre, consider a situation in which an attacker causes cardiac arrest that is reversible by use of a defibrillator. Is the victim "dead" if the defibrillator is available but located a ten-minute journey from the victim, as a result of which the defibrillator can be of no effect? Is "irreversibility" to be defined contextually or as an objective physiological state? Is the perpetrator's guilt as a murderer dependent on the resolution of this question? Suppose another person shoots the victim in the head in this ten-minute interim: Which person is guilty of homicide?

8

Rabbinic Confidentiality

I. THE 1998 PROCEEDING

"Can you trust your rabbi?" is the question raised in the minds of many in the wake of a high profile New York law case. A late 1998 decision of a Justice of the New York Supreme Court holding one rabbi liable for damages resulting from the violation of the confidence of a congregant and ordering an evidentiary hearing for clarification of certain disputed facts in the case of a second rabbi has caused consternation in diverse quarters.

Inaccurate and provocative media reports further heightened interest in the case. Many, including the judge, were shocked not so much at the breach of confidence itself but at the argument of the defense that Jewish law mandated the defendants' actions, in the case in question. Those more familiar with the applicable provisions of Jewish law were equally shocked not so much at the court's headlong thrust into a quagmire of factual, legal and constitutional issues as by its wholly improper and injudicious excoriation of the defendants' invocation of "the protection of the Torah" in defense of their conduct. That conduct, which the defendants unquestionably believe to be not only permitted but also mandated by Jewish law, is described by the Court as conduct that "so transcends the bounds of decency as to be regarded as both intolerable and atrocious." Remarkably, not a scintilla of proof was adduced either charging the defendants with misrepresentation of Jewish law or challenging their good faith in its application.

In substituting its own unqualified (mis)understanding of Jewish law for that of two erudite and respected rabbis, whose stature within their community was acknowledged by the Court itself, the Court has engaged in as blatant an example of judicial *chutzpah*[1] as has been seen in recent years. In allowing

[1] With the occurrence of the term "*chutzpah*" in a U.S. Supreme Court decision, National Endowment of the Arts v. Finley, 118 S. Ct. 2168 (1998), the term has become firmly ensconced

such a determination to color its decision the Court exposes itself to a charge of breaching the wall of separation between Church and State. Moreover, in interpreting the statute in question as requiring clergymen to govern their professional conduct in a manner they find to be religiously offensive the Court has probably violated the right of free exercise of religion guaranteed by the First Amendment.[2]

in legal parlance. For an interesting survey of earlier judicial decisions in which the term has appeared as well as of its connotations see Jack Achiezer Guggenheim, "The Evolution of *Chutzpah* as a Legal Term: The *Chutzpah* Championship, *Chutzpah* Award, *Chutzpah* Doctrine, and Now, the Supreme Court," *Kentucky Law Journal*, vol. 87, no. 2 (1998–99), pp. 417–38.

[2] In an earlier period of constitutional law jurisprudence it would have been obvious that the defendants might have asserted a free exercise claim in support of an exemption to an obligation of confidentiality arising from the statute. Whether or not they would prevail would have depended upon a demonstration of a countervailing compelling state interest in barring their testimony. Although in New York as well as in many other states the privilege is vested in the communicant, an analysis of the history of the clergy–penitent privilege indicates that it arose from a perceived need to protect from citation for criminal contempt Catholic priests, who are barred by canon law from violating the sanctity of the confessional regardless of the consequence to themselves. See Edward M. Cleary, *McCormick on Evidence*, 4th ed. (St. Paul, MN, 1992) § 76.2. Indeed, although of dubious constitutional validity, the statutes of some states, including Idaho (Idaho Code § 9–20 3) (Michie 1948), Illinois (Ill. Comp. Stat. 5/8–803) (West 1992), Montana (Mont. Code Ann. § 26-l-804) (1997), Utah (Utah Code Ann. § 78–24) (1996), Washington (Wash. Rev. Code Ann. § 60.060) (West 1995) and Wyoming (Wyo. Stat. § 1–12–101) (1977), still restrict the privilege to penitential communications in the course of discipline "enjoined by the church," i.e., by a religious denomination requiring confession. Michigan (Mich. Comp. Laws Ann. § 600.2156) (West 1986) similarly limits the privilege to confessions made "in the course of discipline enjoined by the rules or practice of such denomination." The applicable Vermont statute (Vt. Stat. Ann. 12, § 1607) (1947) provides even more explicitly that "A priest or minister of the gospel shall not be permitted to testify in Court to statements made to him by a person under the sanctity of a religious confessional." Oregon (Or. Rev. Stat § 40.260) (1981) extends the privilege to communications made to a clergyman "authorized or accustomed to hearing confidential communications" but *only* if "under the discipline or tenets of that church" the clergyman "has a duty to keep such communications secret." See, however, *infra*, note 54. Moreover, despite its historical origin, other justifications have been advanced for recognition of the privilege. See *infra*, section IV. However, regardless of any particular rationale adopted in defense of the privilege, it would be difficult to argue that the state has the same compelling interest in encouraging free and open communication between a clergyman and a congregant as it has between a physician and a patient or even between an attorney and a client. However, the decision of the U.S. Supreme Court in Employment Division, Oregon Department of Human Resources v. Smith, 494 U.S. 872 (1990), 110 S. Ct. 1595, 108 L.Ed2d 876, had the unfortunate effect of emasculating the freedom of religious practice previously regarded as guaranteed by the Free Exercise Clause of the First Amendment. The court ruled that general laws that are religion-neutral and generally applicable, but have the incidental effect of burdening religious practice, are not unconstitutional.

It should, however, be noted that in at least one case a New York court has held that the decision of the U.S. Supreme Court in *Employment Division v. Smith*

Together with those of many other states, the laws of the State of New York provide that communications to a clergyman are privileged in the sense that

does not curtail the right to free exercise of religion guaranteed by article I, § 3 of the New York State Constitution. Despite the similarity of the state and federal provisions, the New York court declared:

> [T]his Court cannot ignore the New York Court of Appeals' long history and commitment to the protection of individual rights and liberties beyond those afforded by the U.S. Constitution, and federal constitutional law. Given this history and commitment . . . and the importance of this free exercise right, it is hard to imagine that New York would not continue to apply a "strict scrutiny" standard of review, and a balancing of the state's competing interests and the fundamental rights of the individual.

See *In re* Rourke, 159 Misc.2d 324, 327, 328 603 N.Y.S.2d 647, 650. Cf., however, *In re* Miller, 252 A.D.2d 156, 158, 684 N.Y.S.2d 368, 370 (A.D. 4th Dept. 1998), in which the Court noted that the Court of Appeals "has not definitively stated whether the scope of [N.Y. Const. art I. § 3] is coextensive with the Free Exercise Clause of the First Amendment of the U.S. Constitution, nor has it decided whether the analytical approach adopted by the United States Supreme Court in Employment Div., Ore. Dept. of Human Resources v. Smith, *supra*, should be applied in resolving claims that N.Y. Constitution article I, § 3, has been violated." Such a balancing test with regard to the clergyman–penitent privilege was earlier applied in *In re* Fuhrer, 100 Misc.2d 315. 318, 419 N.Y.S.2d 426, 429 (1979). See *infra*, note 41.

There are two reported cases in other states in which tort actions were brought against clergymen who revealed confidential communications. In each of those cases the court acknowledged that if the breach of confidence occurred pursuant to religious doctrine the clergyman might indeed be immune from tort liability.

In Snyder v. Evangelical Orthodox Church (1989), 216 Cal. App.3d. 217, 264 Cal. Rptr. 640, the plaintiffs confessed their adulterous relationship to members of the church hierarchy. Despite a promise of confidentiality, those confidences were divulged to the assembled congregation in the course of Sunday services as well as to a "gathering of local priests, ministers, pastors and guests." The plaintiffs asserted claims, *inter alia*, for breach of a fiduciary duty of confidentiality and infliction of emotional distress. The California Court of Appeals for the Sixth District noted that the record did not show whether it is a canon of respondents' belief that confessions (penitential or not) are revealed to the congregation unless the offender repents; whether it is a church practice for the substance of a confession to be shared among the church officials; or whether it is consistent with church doctrine to reveal the substance of a confession to anyone outside the church, and if so, under what circumstances.

If so, declared the court, "The court must next consider whether the interests which are invaded by respondents' religious practices are of sufficiently significant interest to the state to warrant the application of tort liability." The Court of Appeal then proceeded to spell out in detail the balancing test to be applied.

More recently, Alexander v. Culp, 124 Ohio App.3d 13, 705 N.E.2d 78, addressed the case of a plaintiff who met with a clergyman for marital counseling in the course of which he disclosed that he engaged in a number of extramarital liaisons and was currently involved in an adulterous relationship. The clergyman revealed that information to the plaintiff's wife. In addition, the clergyman advised the wife that her husband was unworthy of trust and counseled her to obtain a restraining order against the husband, to change the locks on the doors of the marital home and to initiate divorce proceedings. The Ohio appellate court found the factual allegations sufficient to state a viable claim for common law negligence. In *Alexander*, the defendant did not assert a free exercise claim based upon a religious obligation to inform the wife of her husband's adultery. The Court explicitly noted, "Whether a particular case interferes with First Amendment freedoms can be determined on a case by case basis."

the clergyman cannot be required to "disclose a confession or confidence made to him in his professional character as spiritual advisor unless authorized to do so by the communicant." This provision, incorporated in §4505 of New York's Civil Practice Law and Rules, is included among statutes regulating admissibility of evidence in legal proceedings, thereby making communications to a clergyman privileged much in the same manner that interspousal communications and communications by a client to his or her attorney and by a patient to his or her physician are privileged. The purpose of granting legal privilege to such communications is to encourage free and open discourse between the individuals to whom the privilege is extended. The New York statute provides that only the person confiding in the clergyman can waive the privilege.

On its surface the statute does no more than restrict the admissibility of testimony of the clergyman in a court of law. Nevertheless, in a decision issued on November 18, 1998 in *C. L.*[3] *v. Rabbi Tzvi Flaum and Rabbi David Weinberger*[4] and reissued with revisions on March 4, 1999,[5] Justice David Goldstein, sitting in the New York Supreme Court in Queens County, ruled that a woman whose confidence had allegedly been breached by the named clergymen was entitled to sue for damages.

Apart from the foregoing, it would appear that even in the post-*Smith* era Justice Goldstein's interpretation of CPLR 4505 renders it unconstitutional in its application as a vehicle to prevent clergymen from disclosing information when they feel that they are required to do so by the tenets of their faith. *Smith* limits the restriction imposed by the Free Exercise Clause to legislation specifically designed to impede or regulate religious practices. CPLR 4505, bearing the title "Confidential Communication to clergy privileged," targets religious functionaries exclusively. The burden that, in Justice Goldstein's opinion, it places upon clergymen is not at all incidental to general and neutral enforcement of a statute but, since it singles out clergy for imposition of the burden flowing from the privilege, is a direct regulation of religious conduct.

Moreover, although it is less obvious, the statute as interpreted by Justice Goldstein may offend the Establishment Clause. Previously, rabbis were receptive to congregants seeking to unburden themselves in the belief that they were free to act in accordance with the obligations imposed upon them by Jewish law in dealing with information revealed in confidence. However, unlike Catholic priests, rabbis do not have an absolute obligation to bear "confession" or to allow themselves to become privy to a confidential communication. In the wake of the decision in C. L. v. Flaum, a rabbi may very well decide that, in order to avoid conflicting halakhic and legal obligations as well as possible legal sanctions, he will decline to receive confidential communications. As a direct result, the congregant will be deprived of the advice, guidance, solace and comfort of his clergyman. Since such ministration is readily available from clergy of other faiths, the effect is to grant preference to those faiths over Judaism and even to motivate penitents to seek out clergy of those religions rather than rabbis of the Jewish faith. Arguably, a statute having that effect is in violation of the Establishment Clause.

3 The full name of the plaintiff has been omitted for obvious reasons. The role of the defendants redounds to their credit rather than to their embarrassment.

4 *New York Law Journal* (November 24, 1998), p. 29, col. 4.

5 179 Misc.2d 1007, 687 N.Y.S.2d 562 (Sup. 1999).

The woman, who had been separated from her husband, was involved in a dispute over which parent should be awarded custody of the couple's four daughters. The husband submitted separate affidavits signed by the two rabbis in which they expressed the opinion that the spiritual welfare and general well-being of the children would best be preserved by awarding custody to the father. In support of that conclusion the rabbis cited various facts concerning the mother's religious behavior and comportment that she had disclosed to them, allegedly in confidence. This information was incorporated in a sealed matrimonial file and disclosed only to the Court having jurisdiction over the custody proceeding. Despite those facts, Justice Goldstein, in a separate action, found that, in submitting their affidavits and in discussing the matter with her husband, the rabbis had breached a fiduciary duty of confidentiality owed to the plaintiff.[6]

[6] The reason underlying Justice Goldstein's ruling that the plaintiff is entitled to compensation for damages sustained as a result of the rabbis' breach of confidence is less than clear. The statute in question establishes a rule of evidence and, at least on its surface, nothing more. The statute does not command a clergyman to respect confidences, does not brand disclosure on the part of the clergyman a breach of contract and does not declare such breach to constitute an actionable tort. In a recent case, Alexander v. Culp, 124 Ohio App.3d 13, 18, 705 N.E.2d 378, 381, the Court of Appeals of Ohio ruled explicitly that a statute prohibiting a clergyman from testifying with regard to a confidential communication does not protect the communicant from disclosure outside legal proceedings. [The sole jurisdiction to impose sanctions for violation of the privilege is Tennessee. Tenn. Code Ann. § 24-1-206 (1989) makes violation of the statute a misdemeanor punishable by imprisonment for a period not greater than thirty days and/or a fine not to exceed fifty dollars. The penal sanction is apparently imposed only for disclosure "in giving testimony as a witness in any litigation" but does not apply to breach of confidence in other contexts.] Of course, one might argue that it is an evident condition of the contract between a patient and his physician, a client and his attorney and a congregant and his clergyman that confidences be held inviolate. Alternatively, one might argue that the duty arising from the professional relationship is fiduciary in nature and hence its breach constitutes a tort. [Some courts have found that individuals have a constitutionally protected interest in maintaining the privacy of medical information. See, for example, Doe v. City of New York, 15 F.3d 204 (2d Cir. 1994). The constitutionally protected right of privacy would arguably extend to other types of personal information as well. See, however, Paul v. Davis, 424 U.S. 693 (1976), in which the Supreme Court held that the constitutional right of privacy does not include the right to keep private information confidential. In any event, a constitutional right of privacy can be asserted only against government officials or when there is some form of government involvement, e.g., funding provided to a hospital.] Moreover, those arguments might be made even in the absence of a statute establishing an evidentiary privilege. Were this the Court's reasoning, an appeal to the statute would serve only as evidence of the underlying contractual obligation or fiduciary relationship. The statute, then, serves as evidence of liability but not as the source of such liability. Nevertheless, in ordering a hearing in the case against one of the rabbis for the purpose of determining whether or not a third party was present when the conversation took place, the Court seems to assume that liability can exist only if it is generated by the statute. The presence or absence of a third party is crucial with regard to the privileged nature of the communication insofar as its exclusion from evidence is concerned; contractual

The latter point, i.e., the determination that discussion of the matter with the husband, as distinct from submission of an affidavit in connection with the custody proceedings, constitutes a breach of a duty of confidentiality, is puzzling since the only confidential information disclosed to the rabbis by Mrs. L. was that she had ceased the practice of monthly immersion in a ritualarium (*mikveh*) in order to deny her husband consortium. (Jewish law forbids a woman from having intercourse if she has not immersed herself in a ritual bath following a period of separation after menstruation.) Obviously, that goal, as announced by Mrs. L. herself, could not be achieved without the husband's awareness of his wife's failure to attend the ritualarium. It is difficult to understand how disclosure of information to an individual to whom the confider had already divulged the selfsame information constitutes a breach of confidence. It is even more difficult to understand how such disclosure could cause further damage that might give rise to a cause of action.

With regard to the alleged breach of a fiduciary duty in submitting the affidavits, the Court ruled not only that the plaintiff was entitled to recover damages but that the action of the rabbis

> was not only improper, it was outrageous and most offensive, especially considering the status and stature of these defendants within the community, a standard which they readily abdicated here. From what was done, it is palpably clear why this determination is one of the apparent first impression – no member of the clergy . . . would dare breach the sanctity of his or her office to make public the type of confidential, private disclosures at issue in this case . . .
>
> Moreover, to violate such basic rights under the guise of religious necessity, conviction or the protection of the Torah, is not only wrong, it is outrageous . . . [7]
>
> Bearing in mind the sanctity to be accorded such communications between clergy and penitent, and the necessity for confidentiality in conjunction with such spiritual counseling, without the fear of any reprisal or disclosure, it is both outrageous and intolerable that such communications would be revealed, even where, as here, this occurs in part in the context of a judicial proceeding. In my view, the conduct so transcends the bounds of decency as to be regarded as both intolerable and atrocious.[8]

The Court's deprecatory reference to "the guise of religious necessity, conviction" and "the protection of the Torah" betrays a profound ignorance of Jewish law. Far from being wrong, much less outrageous, the action of the

and fiduciary responsibilities, however, are generally not affected by the presence or absence of third parties.

7 179 Misc.2d at 1016, 687 N.Y.S.2d at 569–70.

8 179 Misc.2d at 1019, 687 N.Y.S.2d at 571.

rabbis (who together with the husband's attorney believed both that their affidavits were admissible as evidence[9] and that their testimony was likely to be persuasive) was both laudable and halakhically mandated.

[9] There is indeed strong support for the argument that, despite the unqualified privilege expressed in CPLR 4505, the testimony of a clergyman with regard to a privileged communication should be regarded as admissible in a custody proceeding. Although there is no case law dealing with the clergyman–penitent privilege within the context of a child custody proceeding, New York courts have repeatedly held that the physician–patient, attorney–client and psychotherapist–patient privileges cannot be invoked in such proceedings.

Over fifty years ago, in People ex rel. Fields v. Kaufman, 9 A.D.2d 375, 377, 193 N.Y.S.2d 789, 791 (1st Dep't 1959), the Supreme Court, Appellate Division, First Department, ruled that confidential psychiatric, psychological and social welfare reports concerning rehabilitation of a mother following paralytic poliomyelitis must be made available to the opposing party. In refusing to recognize the privileged nature of that information the Court declared:

> Where the welfare of children is concerned and in furtherance of the duty of the State as *parens patriae*, courts are not so hidebound or limited that they may not depart from strict adversary concepts. By analogy, it appears that so important is the duty of the State deemed to be in its role as *parens patriae*, so vital is its concern for its infant wards, that from birth to maturity their welfare is paramount even when compared with the rights of the natural parents.

That position was affirmed by the Court of Appeals in Kessler v. Kessler, 10 N.Y.2d 445, 452, 225, N.Y.S.2d 1,5 (1962). In People ex rel. Chitty v. Fitzgerald, 40 Misc.2d 966, 967,244 N.Y.S.2d 441, 442 (Sup. Ct. Kings Co. 1963), the Court followed that principle in disregarding the patient–physician privilege on the grounds that "the right of the petitioner to invoke the patient–physician privilege must yield to the paramount rights of the infant."

In Baecher v. Baecher, 58 A.D.2d 821, 396 N.Y.S.2d 447, 448 (2d Dep't 1997), *appeal denied* 43 N.Y.2d 645, 402 N.Y.S.2d 1026 (1978), in addition to invoking the *parens patriae* doctrine, the Appellate Division found yet additional grounds for admitting an otherwise privileged communication: The Court ruled that "the defendant waived his right to the privilege by actively contesting custody, thereby putting his mental and emotional well-being into issue." The notion of automatic waiver in custody proceedings was also employed by the Supreme Court in an unreported case, Conderre v. Conderre, 1990 WL 312774, 1 (Sup. Ct. Suffolk Co. 1990). In that case, however, the court required that the medical records be reviewed by the court and that only those portions deemed to be relevant and material be disclosed. Again in McDonald v. McDonald, 196 A.D.2d 7, 13, 608 N.Y.S.2d 477, 481 (2d Dep't 1954), the Second Department, citing *Baecher* and *Chitty*, declared that "it is well settled that in a matrimonial action, a party waives the physician–patient privilege concerning his or her physical condition (see CPLR 4504) by actively contesting custody." See also Proschold v. Proschold, 114 Misc.2d 568, 451 N.Y.S.2d 956 (Sup. Ct. Suffolk Co. 1982).

The question of an attorney–client privilege in custody cases was first addressed in New York by the Court of Appeals in Jacqueline v. Segal, 41 N.Y.2d 215, 222, 417 N.Y.S.2d 884, 888 (1979), at about the same time as the issue of psychotherapist privilege was being discussed by the Second Department in Baecher v. Baecher. The Court of Appeals cited precedents establishing that, insofar as the attorney–client privilege is concerned, "such right ought to depend on the circumstances of each case" in ruling that an attorney may be compelled to disclose the address of his client in order to prevent the unsuccessful litigant from frustrating the court's judgment rendered in the best interests of the child.

The public policy considerations upon which the clergyman–penitent privilege is based are surely no weightier than the physician–patient or attorney–client privilege. As is the case with

II. CONFIDENTIALITY IN JEWISH LAW

A. *The Sources and Nature of the Obligation*

Judaism does not recognize a particular fiduciary obligation of confidentiality in association with any professional relationship. Thus, for Judaism, there is no specific physician–patient, attorney–client or clergyman–penitent "privilege." But, at the same time, Judaism binds each and every one of its adherents, laymen as well as professionals, by an obligation of confidentiality far broader than that posited by any other legal, religious or moral system. Nevertheless, the privilege is neither all-encompassing in scope nor, when it does exist, is it absolute in nature.

1. Leviticus 19:16

Jewish law prohibits divulging personal information concerning another person even when the information is not received in confidence. The prohibition is derived from the biblical verse "You shall not go as a bearer of tales among your people" (Leviticus 19:16). As formulated by Rambam, *Mishneh Torah, Hilkhot De'ot* 7:2: "Who is a talebearer? One who carries reports and goes from one person to another and says, 'So-and-so said this' or 'Such and such have I heard about so-and-so.' Even if he tells the truth, [the talebearer] destroys the world." Talebearing is forbidden even when unaccompanied by malicious intent and even if the information is not derogatory. That even non-malicious and non-derogatory talebearing is encompassed within the ambit of the prohibition is evident from the immediately following statement of Rambam: "There is a much more grievous sin than this that is included in their negative prohibition and that is 'evil speech' (*lashon ha-ra*), i.e., speaking derogatorily of one's fellow even though one speaks the truth." It is clear that the phrase "such and such have I heard about so-and-so" does not refer to information divulged by "so-and-so" about himself whether in confidence or otherwise; the phrase connotes information communicated by a third party. Although disclosure of information revealed by a person concerning himself is certainly subsumed within the prohibition, Rambam's ruling makes it quite clear that disclosure is prohibited even though no breach of confidence is involved.

regard to those privileges, the best interests of minor children should take precedence over the policy considerations underlying the statutory clergyman–penitent privilege. Moreover, as with other statutory privileges, initiation of custody proceedings should be regarded as an automatic waiver of the clergyman–penitent privilege as it pertains to determining which parent is better qualified to be entrusted with the care of minor children.

Judaism also prohibits disclosure of a communication of non-personal information not within the public domain unless prior permission for such disclosure has explicitly been granted. Thus, in effect, all communications are deemed confidential and hence privileged unless the privilege is waived. Moreover, with regard to derogatory personal information, a waiver does not constitute *carte blanche* for indiscriminate dissemination of such information.[10] The privilege, it should be noted, even if not subject to waiver, is in the nature of a general right of privacy rather than an exclusion from admissible evidence in legal proceedings. Privacy does not serve as a barrier to judicial inquiry. Nevertheless, in most circumstances, such communications would not be admissible as evidence on the basis of the hearsay rule, which in Jewish law is far broader in its exclusions than in other legal systems.

2. Leviticus 1:1

The prohibition against divulging a non-personal confidential communication is formulated by the Gemara, *Yoma* 4b: "Whence is it derived that [if] one relates something to one's fellow [the latter is Commanded], 'Thou shalt not

[10] See *Ḥafeẓ Ḥayyim, Be'er Mayim Ḥayyim, Hilkhot Lashon ha-Ra* 2:3 and 2:28 as well as the commentary of R. Binyamin Cohen on *Ḥafeẓ Ḥayyim, Ḥelkat Binyamin* (Brooklyn, NY, 1993), *Bi'urim, Hilkhot Lashon ha-Ra* 2:21 and 2:61. Of interest also is a brief note by R. Chaim Saul Kaufman of Gateshead that appeared in a European Torah journal, *Kol ha-Torah*, no. 60 (Nisan 5756), p. 118. R. Kaufman expresses uncertainty with regard to whether *lashon ha-ra* is permitted with the express permission of the subject of the talebearing. R. Kaufman then refers to the above-cited remarks of *Ḥafeẓ Ḥayyim* with the comment that it may be inferred from *Ḥafeẓ Ḥayyim*'s remarks that communication of *lashon ha-ra* is prohibited even under such circumstances.

Cf., however, R. Ya'ir Chaim Bacharach, *Teshuvot Ḥavvot Ya'ir*, no. 62, who appears to assert that it is permitted to make demeaning comments about a person with that person's permission. See also *Ḥelkat Binyamin, loc. cit.*, who makes much the same point on the basis of *Ḥafeẓ Ḥayyim*'s remarks in *Be'er Mayim Ḥayyim, Hilkhot Lashon ha-Ra* 2:28.

A differing position is ascribed to *Ḥafeẓ Ḥayyim* by R. Issachar Tamar, in his commentary on the Palestinian Talmud, *Alei Tamar* (Alon Shevut, 1992), vol. II, *Ta'anit* 3:4. Rabbi Tamar recounts a narrative concerning *Ḥafeẓ Ḥayyim*. *Ḥafeẓ Ḥayyim*, in an expression of modesty, is reported to have made a self-deprecatory comment but later to have had reason to regret his words. *Ḥafeẓ Ḥayyim* is reported to have remarked that the incident, which occurred after publication of his classic work on *lashon ha-ra*, taught him that it is forbidden to speak *lashon ha-ra* even with regard to oneself. Rabbi Tamar finds support for that position in a comment of the Palestinian Talmud, *ad locum*. Cf., however, R. Yehudah Herzl Henkin, *Teshuvot Bnei Banim* (Jerusalem, 1998), vol. III, no. 18, who rejects the validity of the inference drawn from the anecdote concerning *Ḥafeẓ Ḥayyim* and rebuts the argument made on the basis of the comment of the Palestinian Talmud. R. Herschel Schachter, *Nefesh ha-Rav* (Jerusalem, 1994), p. 150, cites a cryptic comment of R. Joseph B. Soloveitchik declaring that a person is forbidden to utter a statement that would impugn his own reputation. The position that a person may not make derogatory statements regarding himself seems to be contradicted by the previously cited comments of *Teshuvot Ḥavvot Ya'ir*, no. 62.

tell' until [the former] tells him 'Go tell'? For it is said, 'And the Lord spoke to him from the tent of meeting *l'emor*'" (Leviticus 1:1). Rashi understands the prohibition to be based upon talmudic exegesis interpreting the word "*l'emor*," which is spelled *lamed, alef, mem, resh*, as a contraction of two words: "*lo emor*" – "do not say."[11] Thus, the written word vocalized in two alternative ways literally constitutes a double entendre: "to say" and "do not say." As explained by *Or ha-Ḥayyim*, Exodus 25:2, the initial phrase of the immediately following sentence beginning "Speak to the children of Israel" clearly places upon Moses an affirmative obligation to repeat what he has been told. Taken together, the two sentences declare, in effect, that Moses may not speak other than when expressly directed or granted permission to speak. As formulated by the Gemara, Moses is admonished "Do not tell!" unless and until he is told, "Go tell!" Prior to their communication to Moses, the contents of revelation were reserved to the Deity and, accordingly, the contents of revelation would have been held inviolate by Moses on the basis of the injunction "Do not say" had he not been commanded explicitly "*l'emor*," to speak and disclose that information to Israel. Interpreting the statement of the Gemara in a manner consistent with that of Rashi, *Sefer Mizvot Gadol, lo ta'aseh*, no. 9, regards violation of this injunction as transgression of a biblical commandment.[12] This talmudic statement is cited as normative by *Magen Avraham, Oraḥ Ḥayyim* 156:2, and serves to establish a formal obligation to regard the communication of any personal or proprietary information as confidential unless permission for disclosure is explicitly granted.

Both Maharsha, *ad locum*, and R. Baruch ha-Levi Epstein, *Torah Temimmah*, Leviticus 1:1, offer an interpretation of the derivation that is less elegant but far simpler than that advanced by Rashi.[13] According to those scholars the prohibition is predicated upon the plain meaning of the word "*l'emor*." The term "*l'emor*" is rendered in English translations as "saying." That translation portrays the entire sentence, "And God spoke to Moses saying," as a prefatory comment conveying the notion that the ensuing passages constitute

[11] See Maharsha, *ad locum*.

[12] However, *Sefer Mizvot Gadol*'s interpretation of the word "*l'emor*" is somewhat different from that of Rashi. *Sefer Mizvot Gadol* also interprets that word as a contraction, but as the assimilated contraction of the words "*lav amur*," i.e., "a negative commandment has been stated [with regard to this matter]."

R. Baruch ha-Levi Epstein, *Torah Temimmah*, Leviticus 1:1, regards the statement of the Gemara, *Yoma* 4b, as establishing a rabbinic prohibition. Cf., however, *Bet ha-Beḥirah, Yoma* 4b, who describes the stricture against disclosure of a non-personal communication, imparted in a confidential manner, as merely a matter of *derekh erez*, or unseemly behavior.

[13] This interpretation of *Yoma* 4b is inherent in the comments of *Or ha-Ḥayyim*, Exodus 25:2. See *infra*, note 15.

the content of what was "said" to Moses. In effect, the sentence is rendered as a declaration indicating that what follows constitutes the content of God's communication to Moses. The translation of "*l'emor*" as "saying," although it serves to make the sentence read smoothly in the vernacular, is contrary to the plain meaning of the text and is probably incorrect. The initial letter *lamed* is a prefix meaning "to" and hence the word "*l'emor*" should properly be understood as a contraction of "*le-emor*" and translated as "to say," i.e., God commanded Moses "to say" the words of the verses that follow. Accordingly, the import of the text is not a declaration to the effect that the subsequently recorded verses were communicated to Moses, but an indication that Moses was commanded to declare those verses to the children of Israel. The appropriate, albeit infelicitous, translation would be: "And God spoke to Moses to say."[14] However, although linguistically accurate, this rendition of the passage seems to render the entire verse redundant. The very next verse begins with the phrase "Speak to the children of Israel and say to them." That phrase is synonymous in meaning with "*l'emor*" and renders "*l'emor*" superfluous. The plain inference, comments Maharsha, is that Moses would not have had the right to transmit the divine communication unless given express permission by God to do so.[15] Hence that directive is recorded in order to teach that, absent such a waiver, all communications are to be regarded as confidential.

Other early-day scholars find the obligation to regard all personal or proprietary communications as privileged to be reflected in yet another verse. R. Menachem ha-Me'iri, in his commentary on *Yoma* 4b, and R. Levi ben Gershon (Ralbag), in his commentary on the scriptural passage, understand Proverbs 11:13 as reflecting the principle enunciated by the Gemara, *Yoma* 4b. Proverbs 11:13 is usually translated as "He that goes about as a talebearer reveals secrets, but he who is of faithful spirit conceals a matter." Me'iri, however, renders the first half of the verse as "He who reveals a secret is a talebearer" while both Me'iri and Ralbag understand the second part of the verse as referring to a person who "conceals a matter" even though it has not been divulged to him as a secret.

14 This nuance of meaning is accurately captured in the standard Yiddish translation published in the *Bet Yehudah* edition of the Pentateuch, which renders the "*l'emor*" as "*ẓu zogen*" rather than as "*zogendig*."

15 *Torah Temimmah* differs from Maharsha only in understanding that the principle is derived from the plain meaning of "*l'emor*" and is not based upon its redundancy in light of the immediately following "Speak to the children of Israel." *Or ha-Ḥayyim*, Exodus 25:2, understands the Gemara's comment much in the same manner as *Torah Temimmah* but comments that "*l'emor*" alone would have served only to give Moses discretionary license to divulge the prophetic message he received; the phrase "speak to the children of Israel" is in the imperative voice and serves to make it incumbent upon Moses to do so.

B. *Limitations upon the Obligation*

It should be noted that there is no "statute of limitations" or time period subsequent to which the obligation of confidentiality expires. The Gemara, *Sanhedrin* 31a, reports an incident involving a student who revealed a matter he had heard in the House of Study twenty-two years after receiving the information. R. Ammi expelled the student from the Academy declaring, "This student reveals secrets!"[16]

However, the privileged nature of a private communication is by no means absolute. Respect for privacy and the inviolability of a confidential communication certainly do not take precedence over preservation and protection of the lives and safety of others. The overriding obligation to protect the lives of others is of sufficient weight to oblige the confidant to take whatever measures may be necessary to eliminate the danger. An oath not to divulge such information when required by Halakhah to do so is regarded as an oath to transgress a commandment and is invalid.[17] Thus, for example, a physician must inform the motor vehicle bureau that his patient is an epileptic and should be denied a driver's license. The obligation to violate the confidential information entrusted to the physician in such situations is included within the "law of the pursuer." A person engaged in an act that will lead to the death of another must be prevented from causing such death even if the consequences of the act are entirely unintended. R. Elijah of Vilna, *Bi'ur ha-Gra, Ḥoshen Mishpat* 425:10, states explicitly that the "law of the pursuer" applies even in the absence of intention to do harm.

The obligation to divulge information that may preserve a life is not limited to situations involving a "pursuer" but extends to all situations in which lack

[16] *Sefer Mizvot Gadol*'s citation of this narrative seems to indicate that he regarded the matter divulged to have been subject to the privilege established by *Yoma* 4b. Rashi, *Sanhedrin* 31a, describes the incident as involving *lashon ha-ra*. If that comment is understood literally the infraction was far more severe than revealing a secret. It may well be that Rashi did not employ the phrase literally but intended only to dispel the notion that the matter revealed was a scholarly insight heard in the course of discussion in the House of Study. If so, Rashi's comments serve to establish that such information is not privileged although, to be sure, there is an obligation to attribute any novel insight to its proper source. See *Avot* 6:6.

Yoma 4b should be understood as establishing that the contents of the Torah are within the proprietary domain of the Deity and could not legitimately have been disclosed by Moses other than upon explicit dispensation. The same principle is applicable to mortals. However, once God, as the proprietor of that information, has made it available to mankind through Moses it is within the public domain. Since, as stated by the Palestinian Talmud, *Pe'ah* 2:4, the subsequent Torah insights of all scholars were revealed to Moses at Mt. Sinai, no person may assert a privilege of confidentiality. Cf., however, R. Saul Israeli, *Teḥumin* (5743), vol. IV, pp. 354–60.

[17] See Rema, *Shulḥan Arukh, Yoreh De'ah* 239:7 and R. Eliezer Waldenberg, *Ẓiẓ Eli'ezer*, vol. XIII, no. 81, sec. 2.

of the information would lead to a possible loss of life. Apart from the general principle that preservation of life takes precedence over other religious and personal obligations, failure to disclose such information would constitute a violation of "You shall not stand idly by the blood of your fellow" (Leviticus 19:16).

Concern for preservation of life is by no means the sole legitimate motive for violating confidentiality. Even information that is derogatory and personal, and hence subsumed within the prohibition against gossip-mongering, must be disclosed if it is necessary to prevent serious harm. Rambam, *Mishneh Torah, Hilkhot Rozeaḥ* 1:14, followed by *Shulḥan Arukh, Ḥoshen Mishpat* 426:1, rules that if an individual "hears that gentiles or apostates are plotting misfortune" for another person, he must bring the matter to that person's attention. Failure to do so, declares Rambam, constitutes a violation of the commandment "You shall not stand idly by the blood of your fellow." The "misfortune" of which Rambam speaks includes financial loss as well as bodily harm. This is evident from Rambam's comments in his *Sefer ha-Mizvot, lo ta'aseh*, no. 297, in which he indicates that the commandment applies in all situations in which an individual is "in danger of death or loss." The "loss" to which Rambam refers is loss of money or profit, as reflected in the ensuing discussion, in which Rambam cites a statement of the *Sifra*, Leviticus 19:16, declaring that withholding testimony in a financial dispute constitutes a violation of the commandment "You shall not stand idly by the blood of your fellow."

It is instructive to note that the prohibition against talemongering and the obligation to rescue one's fellow from physical or financial harm are joined in a single biblical verse: "You shall not go as a talebearer among your people; nor shall you stand idly by the blood of your fellow." The verse should be understood as prohibiting dissemination of derogatory information but not at the cost of standing idly by while one's fellow suffers harm.

Ḥafez Ḥayyim, Be'er Mayim Ḥayyim, Hilkhot Rekhilut 9:1, cites additional sources that reflect the same principle. Jewish law provides that adverse possession of land for a period of three years is *prima facie* evidence of purchase. A person who has openly and notoriously occupied a field for that period of time need no longer preserve a deed of purchase in order to validate a claim of title. However, protest by the person previously in possession of the property that the occupancy is an unlawful trespass is sufficient to negate the claim of the occupant with the result that, unless the occupant can produce a deed, title is awarded to the prior owner. The protest must be registered in the presence of witnesses but need not necessarily be expressed in the presence of the occupant. Rashbam and *Tosafot, Bava Batra* 39b, indicate that individuals hearing such a protest are duty bound to inform the occupant of what they have heard. They are clearly "talebearing" in reporting to the person in possession that he has been branded a trespasser and a thief by the person lodging a protest. The witnesses, as well as others to whom they reveal the incident, are nevertheless required to convey that information so that the person in possession, if he is indeed the rightful owner, will exercise vigilance in preserving his deed. It is the concern for averting financial loss that serves as sanction for an otherwise impermissible disclosure of information. *Sefer ha-Ḥinnukh*, no. 247, makes a more general statement in declaring that when the intent is to "remove harm and to still the quarrel" the prohibition against gossip-mongering does not apply.

The classic work dealing with Jewish law as it applies to slander, defamation of character and talebearing is *Ḥafeẓ Ḥayyim*, authored by R. Israel Meir Kagan. In *Hilkhot Rekhilut, klal* 9, *Ḥafeẓ Ḥayyim* emphasizes that disclosure of derogatory information, even when the information is not received in confidence, dare not be lightly undertaken. *Ḥafeẓ Ḥayyim* rules that, even when designed to prevent harm or loss, disclosure is justified only when a series of conditions are met: (1) Disclosure may be made only after careful deliberation establishes that potential for harm really exists. (2) The information disclosed should be presented accurately without embellishment or exaggeration. (3) The sole motivation prompting disclosure must be the desire to prevent harm; no disclosure may be made when prompted, even in part, by personal animosity.[18] (4) The benefit of the disclosure cannot be achieved in any other way. (5) The disclosure will not lead to any harm or loss to the person who is the subject of the information disclosed other than the liability that would be imposed upon that person by a *bet din* on the basis of the facts and the available evidence.

R. Ya'akov Breisch, *Teshuvot Ḥelkat Ya'akov*, vol. III, no, 136, argues that, under such circumstances, disclosure is mandated, at least according to some authorities, by another commandment as well. "Thou shalt not place a stumbling block before the blind" (Leviticus 19:14) is understood in rabbinic sources

[18] When these conditions are fulfilled disclosure is warranted not as an exception to the prohibition against talebearing, but because the act does not fall within the definition of "talebearing." Animosity is sufficient to bring the disclosure within the ambit of the prohibition. Accordingly, in *Be'er Mayim Ḥayyim*, *Hilkhot Rekhilut* 9:3, *Ḥafeẓ Ḥayyim* recognizes that a person who does experience such animus is caught on the horns of a dilemma: He is forbidden to disclose because of the prohibition against talebearing. But in withholding the information he transgresses the command "You shall not stand idly by the blood of your fellow." Accordingly, *Ḥafeẓ Ḥayyim* declares, "It is my intention [to say] that at the time of disclosure he [must] force himself to intend benefit and not [disclose] because of animosity." See also R. Moshe Bleich, "Appointing Students as Monitors," *Ten Da'at*, vol. XII (Summer 1999), pp. 76–77.

as prohibiting an individual from causing another person to "stumble" by committing a transgression and also as an admonition against giving detrimental advice in mundane matters. Rambam, *Mishneh Torah*, *Hilkhot Roẓeaḥ* 12:4, extends the concept not only to providing direct aid in committing a sin but also to "strengthening the hands of transgressors." R. Judah Rozanes, *Mishneh le-Melekh*, *Hilkhot Kelayim* 1:6, maintains that even a passive stance may constitute "strengthening the hands of transgressors" and hence is forbidden by Rambam as placing a "stumbling block before the blind." *Mishneh le-Melekh* employs this thesis in explaining an otherwise difficult ruling of Rambam. Rambam rules that a Jew may not permit a gentile to make use of a tree belonging to a Jew for purposes of grafting a branch of one species upon a tree of another species. Even passive acquiescence constitutes a violation of the prohibition against "placing a stumbling block." *Ḥelkat Ya'akov* argues that since not only assistance in transgression but also offering poor counsel is prohibited by this commandment, "passive" counsel that is deleterious in nature is also forbidden. Advice designed to cause unhappiness or financial loss is clearly forbidden. Hence, according to *Mishneh le-Melekh*, failure to provide information and advice for the purpose of averting such unfortunate results is also a form of "placing a stumbling block before the blind." Accordingly, concludes *Ḥelkat Ya'akov*, a person is not justified in maintaining his own counsel in circumstances in which circumspection would result in grief or financial loss to others.

Obligations arising from the commandment not to stand idly by the blood of one's fellow and the prohibition against placing a stumbling block before the blind obligate a person to prevent harm or loss; they do not give rise to an affirmative obligation to maximize the profit or enhance the material well-being of one's fellow. Accordingly, *Ḥafeẓ Ḥayyim* rules that disclosure of derogatory personal information is mandatory if necessary to prevent loss but makes no such statement with regard to disclosure for the purpose of financial advantage.

Violation of a confidence that does not involve talebearing but is protected by the prohibition of *bal tomar* [i.e., *lo emor* – do not say] may well be a different matter. In an article published in *Teḥumin*, vol. IV (5743), the late R. Saul Israeli declares that such a confidence may be breached even in order to achieve a financial benefit provided, however, that there will be no resultant harm to the person who has imparted the information. Rabbi Israeli observes that the Sages decried refusing to allow another person to derive benefit from one's property when there is no harm or loss to oneself as the "trait of Sodom." Accordingly, in the absence of evidence to the contrary, there is no reason to assume that the party whose confidence is violated would act wickedly in withholding such information. On the contrary, argues Rabbi Israeli, the halakhic principle "A person is pleased that a *mizvah* be performed with his property" serves to establish a constructive waiver of confidentiality.

It seems that Rabbi Israeli is correct in stating that non-personal communications may be divulged in such circumstances without prior permission. Moreover, there appears to be talmudic evidence that serves to establish that such information may be divulged for the benefit of another party even over the express objection of the person from whom the information was obtained.

The Gemara, *Avodah Zarah* 28a, in recounting a problematic anecdote, reports that R. Yoḥanan once suffered a severe toothache. He received treatment at the hands of a prominent gentile woman on a Thursday and a Friday. R. Yoḥanan declined to visit her on *Shabbat* because he was occupied with his students and therefore requested instructions so that he might administer the therapy to himself. The woman was reluctant to divulge that information lest it became available to others as well. Accordingly, she demanded that R. Yoḥanan swear an oath not to reveal the information. R. Yoḥanan swore that "to the God of Israel he would not reveal" the information and then promptly imparted the information in his Sabbath lecture on the excuse that he did indeed swear not to reveal the information "to the God of Israel" but that he reserved the prerogative of revealing the information "to the people of Israel." Addressing the concern raised on account of profanation of the Divine Name involved in this subterfuge, the Gemara responds that immediately upon receiving the information R. Yoḥanan revealed his intention to discuss the matter publicly.[19] Presumably, R. Yoḥanan did so in the context of reproving the woman for attempting to reserve such beneficial therapeutic information for her own exclusive use.

The Gemara limits its discussion to the problems posed by the oath sworn by R. Yoḥanan not to reveal the information. But, putting aside the strictures imposed by the oath, it is manifestly clear that the woman in question imparted the requisite pharmacological information to R. Yoḥanan in confidence and that she expressly informed him of her desire that this esoteric information remain her secret. The information, to be sure, was not personal and certainly was not pejorative. It was, however, information within the exclusive possession of the woman–not unlike the information conveyed to Moses by God that would perforce have remained a divine secret if not for God's express permission to transmit the information to the people of Israel. The sole but

[19] See *Teshuvot Ḥavvot Ya'ir*, no. 69, who comments that R. Yoḥanan's conduct in this matter was appropriate only because the health issue involved was a matter of public need.

crucial distinction is that the medical information in question was of direct and tangible benefit to R. Yoḥanan's audience and its divulgence did no harm to the woman who entrusted the information to R. Yoḥanan. On the basis of the narrative as it is reported there is every reason to assume that the woman in question did not charge a fee for her medical ministrations and hence suffered no adverse financial effect.[20] Indeed, *Leḥem Setarim*, one of the classic commentaries on *Avodah Zarah*, resolves another difficulty unrelated to this discussion with the observation that no compensation was involved because "since [the woman] was a courtesan she had no need to accept a fee and moreover if [her services were rendered in return] for a fee how is it that she did not wish to disclose what [R. Yoḥanan] must do on *Shabbat* until he swore?"[21] Presumably, her motive in refusing to share the information with toothache sufferers was a desire for power or self-aggrandizement, or sheer pettiness. It would seem that this talmudic narrative serves to teach that the proprietary interest with regard to non-personal confidences established by the prohibition of *bal tomar* need not be respected by a confidant when it is exercised as a "trait of Sodom."[22]

[20] See R. Yitzchak Glick, *Ḥinnukh Bet Yiẓḥak* (Brooklyn, NY, 5759), no. 34, who cites a narrative recorded in the Gemara, *Shabbat* 133b, in declaring that a professional secret may not be divulged even if failure to do so will cause a loss of income to the physician.

[21] Cf. R. Yitzchak Zilberstein, *Ẓohar* (Jerusalem, 5759), vol. IV, ed. R. Eliyakim Dworkes, pp. 190–92, who discusses only the issue of interference with earning a livelihood and, in distinguishing between competition with a gentile and competition with a fellow Jew, notes that the courtesan was a non-Jew.

[22] This thesis also resolves a puzzling aspect of the midrashic explanation of Jacob's statement recorded in Genesis 49:1. On his deathbed, Jacob addresses his sons saying: "Gather yourselves together that I may tell you that which should befall you in the end of days." Jacob then proceeds to tell them nothing of the sort; he criticizes some and blesses others but does not at all engage in prognostication. Rashi, basing himself on a midrashic comment, explains that Jacob did indeed intend to reveal when the redemption would occur but God, not wishing the information to be revealed prematurely, caused the *Shekhinah* to depart from Jacob with the result that he no longer possessed the information.

The Sages of the Midrash resolved the problem of textual interpretation but they have left us with an even graver problem. Whatever information Jacob possessed by virtue of the resting of the *Shekhinah* upon him was in the nature of a divine communication. If God desired His communication to Jacob of the date of the Redemption to be privileged, by what right did Jacob attempt to reveal it to his children? The prohibition of *bal tomar* should apply to the prophecy received by Jacob no less so than to the prophecy received by Moses. If, however, it is understood that there are no proprietary rights or rights of confidentiality that can be asserted when such information is of potential benefit to others and its disclosure entails no loss to the holder of the privilege, the problem is readily resolved. Jacob believed the information to be of significant psychological and emotional benefit to his progeny and since, virtually by definition, there could be no "harm" to God in its disclosure, he felt fully justified in imparting the information to his sons.

III. RABBIS AND THE CLERGYMAN–PENITENT PRIVILEGE

The information governed by the prohibition of *bal tomar* as posited by the Gemara, *Yoma* 4b, is not coextensive with the information governed by the clergyman–penitent privilege. Accordingly, disclosure of such information as required by Jewish law when necessary for the material benefit of a third party presents no conflict with the requirements of civil law. Communications for which a clergy–penitent privilege may be claimed are virtually always of a kind to which the much more stringent prohibition against talebearing applies. Circumstances in which Jewish law requires a breach of confidence involving such information are quite rare. In general, Jewish law mandates disclosure of confidential information only when necessary to avert significant harm. Even secular law recognizes an exception to the rule of confidentiality when a threat to life or serious physical harm exists.[23] It is little wonder that Jewish law recognizes the same exception when a threat to spiritual welfare exists, as was the case in the matter before the New York court.

[23] Although there is no case law with regard to the clergyman–penitent privilege (cf., however, *infra*, note 60, regarding the New Jersey statute), many courts have held not only that the physician–patient privilege is suspended in face of danger to another person but that, at least in some circumstances, the physician has an affirmative duty to disclose a foreseeable harm to an identifiable third party who is at risk. Probably the most widely cited case applying that principle is Tarasoff v. Regents of University of California, 17 Cal.3d 425 (1976). In *Tarasoff* the California Supreme Court held that when a psychotherapist determines or, pursuant to the standards of his profession, should determine that his patient presents a serious danger of violence to another, the therapist has an affirmative duty to use reasonable care to protect the intended victim against such danger, and that the duty may require the physician to warn the intended victim of the danger. See generally John C. Williams, Annotation, "Liability of One Treating Mentally Afflicted Patient for Failure to Warn or Protect Third Persons Threatened by Patient," 83 A.L.R.3d 1201 (1978 and Supp. 1992). For a discussion of *Tarasoff* and its progeny, see Timothy E. Gammon and John K. Hulston, "The Duty of Mental Health Care Providers to Restrain Their Patients or Warn Third Parties," *Missouri Law Review*, vol. 60, no. 4 (Fall 1995), pp. 749–97; Peter Lake, "Revisiting *Tarasoff*," *Albany Law Review*, vol. 58, no. 1 (1994), pp. 97–173; Michael L. Perlin, "*Tarasoff* and the Dilemma of the Dangerous Patient: New Directions for the 1990s," *Law & Psychology Review*, vol. 16 (Spring 1992), pp. 29–63. See also John C. Williams, Annotation, "Liability of One Treating Mentally Afflicted Patient for Failure to Warn or Protect Third Persons Threatened by Patient," 83 A.L.R.3d 1201 (1978 and supp. 1992).

Physicians have also been held liable for failing to warn others about the risk of transmission of communicable disease. See, for example, Skillings v. Allen, 173 N.W. 663 (Minn., 1919) (negligent failure to disclose risk of transmission of scarlet fever). See also Gammill v. United States, 727 F.2d 950,954 (10th Cir. 1984) (physician may be found liable for failing to warn person at risk for exposure of the danger) and Bradshaw v. Daniel, 854 S.W.2d 865 (Tenn., 1993) (extending liability to include failure to disclose to patient's wife that she was at risk for contracting Rocky Mountain Spotted Fever, a non-contagious disease but one which appears in clusters). See generally Tracy A. Bateman, Annotation, "Liability of Doctor or Other Health Practitioner to Third Party Contracting Contagious Disease from Doctor's Patient," 3 A.L.R. 5th 370 (1992).

The very fact that the plaintiff instituted proceedings in a civil court for recovery of damages by itself vindicates the rabbis' judgment. Seeking redress against a fellow Jew in a civil court rather than in a *bet din* is itself a serious breach of Halakhah and departure from the lifestyle of an observant Jew. As such, the plaintiff's motion betrays a fundamental lack of religious probity.

The applicable New York statute and the laws of other jurisdictions may well exclude from evidence the testimony of a clergyman even in situations in which Jewish law permits breach of confidentiality. But, even assuming that Justice Goldstein is correct in his view that the statute also creates a fiduciary relationship, the fiduciary relationship of a rabbi to his congregant must, by its very nature, be circumscribed by the provisions of Jewish law. A member of the Jewish faith who seeks the counsel of a rabbi rather than that of a psychologist, social worker or marriage counselor understands quite well that the rabbi's actions will be governed by Jewish law and tradition. The congregant places his faith and trust in the rabbi in anticipation that the rabbi will act in precisely that manner. The uniqueness of a fiduciary relationship under the secular legal system is based upon the concept that it is a relationship predicated upon trust and hence violation of that trust is actionable. If a rabbi is trusted to relate to his congregant on the basis of Jewish law, the rabbi's recognition of the limits that Jewish law places upon confidentiality can hardly be deemed a violation of the fiduciary relationship arising from that confidence. To put the matter quite simply, in situations in which Jewish law requires the rabbi to divulge information, the congregant does not, and should not, have a "reasonable" expectation of confidentiality. Accordingly, the courts should recognize an implied waiver of statutory confidentiality in those cases in which disclosure is required by the faith of the confidant.

Moreover, if a rabbi is bound by a fiduciary duty, his duty is not to his congregant but to a higher authority. The Internal Revenue Service and the Social Security Administration seem to have an intuitive understanding of this point. Although, typically, rabbis are hired by congregations and compensated in the form of a salary, the I.R.S. does not demand that congregations withhold income tax from the salaries of their clergy or file W2 forms on their behalf. Clergymen serving congregations make contributions to the Social Security system as self-employed individuals. In a very real sense, the members of a synagogue may pay the rabbi's salary but he is not their employee; the rabbi is the employee of the Almighty. Certainly, the rabbi's fiduciary obligation is to God, and only through God to the congregant.

Let it be noted that, as will be discussed later in greater detail, clergyman–penitent statutes are directly attributable to the burden placed upon a priest by canon law. The Church requires its priests to hold the sanctity of a confession inviolate even upon pain of incarceration or death. In states in which the priest–penitent privilege is not recognized, were a judge to threaten a priest with citation for contempt for refusing to divulge information revealed to him in the confessional, the priest would feel bound to accept imprisonment despite the requirements of a secular legal system. A rabbi, in some limited circumstances, may be equally obligated by his religious convictions to violate a confidence. His recognition of a religious obligation to do so should not give rise to puzzlement any more so than does the priest's refusal to violate the same confidence.

At the same time a rabbi is under no automatic obligation to reveal that a crime has been committed even if the crime was revealed to him in a context not encompassed within the clergyman–penitent privilege. The obligation to disclose, on the infrequent occasions in which it may exist, is based entirely upon the need to prevent harm and is totally unrelated to society's desire to punish crime. Accordingly, only a well-founded fear of repetition of the criminal act that might be prevented by disclosure of past misdeeds would make disclosure mandatory.

An absolute clergyman–penitent privilege, if applied to rabbis, would yield results that no Jew could accept in good conscience. Assume, for example, that a butcher afflicted by pangs of conscience, but not yet willing to mend his ways, confesses to a rabbi that the meat he offers for sale is not kosher. For the rabbi to act as if he has no such knowledge is to make a mockery of his fiduciary responsibilities to his other congregants, not to speak of his own religious duties. The rabbi's position – and responsibilities – are analogous to those of a psychiatrist who discovers that a patient is planning to commit mayhem. The rabbi's obligation to prevent sin is no different from the physician's responsibility to prevent bodily harm.

In this regard the obligations of a rabbi and a physician are, from a Jewish law perspective, quite similar, and the perspective of Jewish law is at variance with that of the American legal system with regard to the obligations of both. For Judaism, a physician's obligation does not flow from a contractual or fiduciary obligation to his patient; the physician's duty flows from an obligation to heal imposed upon him by the Deity. The selfsame obligation to seek healing and prolong life is imposed upon the patient as well. The patient in seeking medical care and the physician in providing such ministration are together fulfilling an obligation imposed upon them jointly by the Creator of all life. Accordingly, the physician dare not accede to the wishes, or even to the directives, of a patient when they conflict with his duty to God, for it is to the Deity that he owes an overriding fiduciary duty. A person seeking the services of a religiously observant physician, psychologist, attorney or rabbi should know and respect the moral and professional values of his confidant. Which thief would entrust a policeman with details of a contemplated bank robbery? If a person is so foolhardy as to plan harm to another individual he only compounds such foolhardiness in divulging his intention to any other human being, all the more so to one whose own moral and professional values require disclosure of the confidence. The congregant in seeking counsel and the rabbi in providing guidance are both engaged in the sacred task of discovering and carrying out the will of God. Each owes a duty to God rather than to the other; to the extent that one owes a duty to the other it is because that duty flows from a duty to God.

It is not at all correct to conclude that rabbis are bound by the decision in *C. L. v. Flaum*[24] or by §4505 of the CPLR on the grounds of *dina de-malkhuta dina* (the law of the land is the law). The finding of the Court in *C.L. v. Flaum* that the rabbis were in breach of a fiduciary obligation does not mean they are in violation of either a criminal or civil statute; it means only that the aggrieved party can sue for damages in a civil court.

Moreover, not every civil law is binding in religious law as *dina de-malkhuta dina*. Assuredly, a law requiring violation of a religious precept, even if its purpose is not anti-religious and it is non-discriminatory in nature, e.g., a law requiring all citizens to cast ballots in an election held on *Shabbat*, is not binding in Halakhah and would require an act of civil disobedience on the part of citizens of the Jewish faith.[25] Similarly, a law requiring a Jew to stand idly by while his fellow goes to his death is, from a religious perspective, null and void. A law that requires a person to remain silent in face of spiritual danger to an innocent victim is entirely unworthy of religious respect, much less of enforcement under pain of religious sanction. The only issue that is

[24] More generally, there is strong support for the thesis that the principle *dina de-malkhuta dina* is limited to laws promulgated by a sovereign or by a legislature. According to some authorities, common law, "judge-made law" or even judicial interpretation of an ambiguous statute is not endowed with the authority of *dina de-malkhuta*. Thus *Teshuvot ha-Rashba*, vol. III, no. 109, writes, "But the judgments issued by courts are not the law of the realm; rather, courts judge independently in accordance with what they find in judicial works." See also *Teshuvot ha-Rashba*, vol. VI, nos. 149 and 154, as well as *Me'iri*, *Bava Kamma* 113b, s.v. *kol mah she-amarnu*.

[25] Delineation of the parameters of *dina de-malkhuta dina* is far beyond the scope of this undertaking. Suffice it to say that among early-day authorities there are over half a dozen conflicting theories designed to explain why *dina de-malkhuta* is binding in Jewish law. The ramifications and application of *dina de-malkhuta* vary directly with those theories. According to all authorities, there are areas of *dina de-malkhuta* with regard to which Jewish law is neutral, i.e., it neither requires disobedience nor reinforces the bindingness of that law by elevating it to a religious duty. With regard to such laws the Jewish national is no different from his non-Jewish fellow countryman who accepts and obeys the law for reasons entirely divorced from religious duty.

germane is the severity of the burden that a Jew is obligated to accept in fulfilling a particular religious obligation. Discussion of the threshold level of civil or criminal sanctions that would excuse a Jew from fulfillment of such an obligation is beyond the scope of this endeavor.

As one might have expected, Justice Goldstein's decision in *Flaum* was reversed on appeal.[26] In a brief decision the appellate court ordered summary judgment for the defendants on the narrow grounds that the plaintiff's privilege had been waived by the presence of a third person during conversations with the clergymen. By reversing on grounds of waiver of the privilege the appellate court avoided, and hence left unresolved, the serious substantive issues raised in this case.

IV. LEGAL ACCOMMODATION OF RABBINIC DUTY

It is clear that situations will arise in which, for reasons of conscience, a rabbi will find it impossible to obey the law as announced by the trial court in *Flaum*. If that interpretation of the clergyman–penitent privilege prevails, a solution must be found that will render the statute inapplicable in situations in which it creates a conflict between the law and religious conscience. In assessing the policy considerations auguring for or against a "religious exemption" from the clergyman–penitent privilege it is necessary to identify the rationale underlying the privilege and the purpose it is designed to serve.

The most commonly offered rationale is that the privilege is designed to foster the clergy–penitent relationship much in the same manner as the physician–patient, attorney–client and spousal privileges are designed to foster particular relationships by shielding communications within those relationships.[27] However, although society has a legitimate interest in fostering each of the latter relationships, societal actions designed to foster a clergy–penitent relationship may constitute a violation of the Establishment Clause of the First Amendment. Nevertheless, the underlying rationale can be reformulated in terms of religious accommodation, i.e., not that the privilege has been established to further a societal interest in fostering the clergy–penitent relationship, but that the privilege has been established as a permissible

[26] See C L. v. *Tzvi Flaum*, 278 A.D.2d 373; 717 N.Y.S.2d 617 (2000).

[27] See Mary Harter Mitchell, "Must Clergy Tell? Child Abuse Reporting Requirements versus the Clergy Privilege and Free Exercise of Religion," *Minnesota Law Review*, vol. 71, no. 3 (February 1987), pp. 760–77 and J. Michael Kiel, "Law and Religion Collide Again: The Priest-Penitent Privilege in Child Abuse Reporting Cases," *Cumberland Law Review*, vol. 28, no. 2 (1997–98), pp. 682–83.

accommodation of the desire of religionists freely to enter into such relationships. As stated by the New York Court of Appeals:

> It is clear that the Legislature by enacting CPLR 4505 and its predecessors responded to the urgent need of people to confide in, without fear of reprisal, those entrusted with the pressing task of offering spiritual guidance so that harmony with one's self and others can be realized.[28]

Similarly, the U.S. Supreme Court has recognized that "the priest–penitent privilege recognizes the human need to disclose to a spiritual counselor, in total and absolute confidence, what are believed to be flawed acts or thoughts and to receive priestly consolation and guidance in return."[29]

Some commentators have sought to justify evidentiary privileges, including the clergy–penitent privilege, in terms of privacy interests.[30] Although, on the basis of existing case law, it is difficult to argue that the constitutionally protected right of privacy includes the right to confidentiality of private information,[31] the concern for privacy is certainly a legitimate rationale for statutory protection of communications for which secrecy is generally anticipated. The intimacy of the interaction between clergyman and congregant reflects a highly personal and private relationship. If privacy is itself an end, rather than an instrumental means to certain goals, and is also worthy of protection as an end, the clergyman–penitent relationship certainly qualifies as a private relationship.

A third rationale is accommodation of a need that is intrinsically human rather than religious. Human beings have a psychological need to unburden themselves of flaws and deficiencies of conduct. Reassurance that their behavior is not an aberrant deviation from the norm and/or advice designed

[28] 47 N.Y.2d 160, 166, 390 N.E.2d 1151, 1154, 417 N.Y.S.2d 226, 229 (1979).

[29] Trammel v. United States, 445 U.S. 40, 51 (1980).

[30] See, for example, Richard O. Lempert and Stephen A. Saltzburg, *A Modern Approach to Evidence* (St. Paul, MN, 1977), pp. 614–15; McCormick, § 72; Charles L. Black, Jr., "The Marital and Physician Privileges – A Reprint of a Letter to a Congressman," *Duke Law Journal*, vol. 1975, no. 1 (March 1975), pp. 48–49; Thomas A. Krattenmaker, "Testimonial Privileges in Federal Courts: An Alternative to the Proposed Federal Rules of Evidence," *Georgetown Law Journal*, vol. 62, no. 1 (October 1973), pp. 85–94; David W. Louisell, "Confidentiality, Conformity and Confusion: Privilege in Federal Court Today," *Tulane Law Review*, vol. 31, no. 1 (December 1956), pp. 110–11; Reese, p. 60; Stephen A. Saltzburg, "Privileges and Professionals: Lawyers and Psychiatrists," *Virginia Law Review*, vol. 66, no. 3 (April 1980), pp. 614–15 and 618–21; and Robert Weisburg and Michael Wald, "Confidentiality Laws and State Efforts to Protect Abused or Neglected Children: The Need for Statutory Reform," *Family Law Quarterly*, vol. 18, no. 2 (Summer 1984), pp. 191–93.

[31] See Paul v. Davis, 424 U.S. 693 (1976), in which the Supreme Court held that the right of privacy does not serve to protect the confidentiality of private information. Cf., however, *supra*, note 6.

to prevent future lapses serve to promote psychological well-being. Accordingly, the religious practice of confession, whether formal or informal, serves a cathartic function as part of the process of dealing with feelings of guilt. This rationale for the privilege is reflected in the words of the Supreme Court in *Trammel v. United States*: "The priest–penitent privilege recognizes the *human need* (emphasis added) to disclose to a spiritual counselor, in total and absolute confidence, what are believed to be flawed acts or thoughts and to receive priestly consolation and guidance in return."[32]

There can, however, be little question that, historically, the privilege was originally designed as an accommodation not of the religious practice of the confiders, but of the clergy's religious objection to disclosure. The legal basis of the priest–penitent privilege is rooted in the Code of Canon Law. Canon 1318 states: "A confessor who directly violates the Seal of Confession incurs an automatic (*latae sententiae*) excommunication . . . " There is strong evidence that English law recognized and respected the Seal of Confession from the time of the Norman Conquest in 1066 until the English Reformation in the sixteenth century.[33] In the sixteenth century, the Anglican Church replaced the Roman Catholic Church as the established Church of England. With the passage of time many changes in church practice were introduced, including a dwindling of emphasis upon, and ultimately elimination of, confession.[34] Since confession was no longer necessary and since the Anglican Church did not have a requirement of secrecy, clerics were no longer in need of legal protection. Some contemporary historians are of the opinion that the privilege terminated at the time of the Reformation.[35] However, Wigmore, in his classic treatise on evidence, asserts that it survived until the Restoration.[36] In either event it is clear that during the seventeenth century the privilege was no longer recognized.[37] Thus, the historical record lends support to the view that the

[32] Trammel v. United States, 445 U.S. 40, 51 (1980).

[33] See Scott N. Stone and Ronald S. Liebmann, *Testimonial Privileges* (Colorado Springs, CO, 1983), § 1.01; John C. Bush and William H. Tiemann, *The Right to Silence: Privileged Clergy Communication and the Law* (Nashville, TN, 1983), pp. 39–41; and Jacob M. Yellin, "The History and Current Status of the Clergy-Penitent Privilege," *Santa Clara Law Review*, vol. 23, no. 1 (Winter 1983), pp. 96–101.

It is likely that, even in that early period, English law recognized an exception to the privilege in cases of treason. See Bush and Tiemann, p. 47. *Garnet's Case*, 2 Howell's State Trials 218, 242 (1606), should probably be understood as an example of the exception. Father Garnet was found guilty, probably of misprision or treason, for refusing to reveal information concerning the Gunpowder Plot, a failed plot to assassinate King James I. Cf. Yellin, pp. 99–101.

[34] See Bush and Tiemann, pp. 49–53; and Yellin, p. 102.

[35] Bush and Tiemann, pp. 53–54; Stone and Liebmann, § 6.01; and Yellin, p. 103.

[36] James H. Chadbourn, *Wigmore on Evidence* (Boston, MA, 1976), vol. VIII, § 2394.

[37] Bush and Tiemann, pp. 120–122; and Yellin, p. 103.

privilege was designed as an accommodation of religious practice and was designed for the protection of the cleric.

The history of the privilege in the United States lends even more support to this understanding of the rationale underlying the privilege. Since the privilege was no longer recognized in England, it was not part of the common law imported to the New World. The first known case involving clergy privilege is *People v. Phillips*, decided by the New York Court of General Sessions in 1813.[38] The case involved Father Kohlmann, a Roman Catholic priest who, after returning stolen goods to their owner, refused, in the course of grand jury proceedings, to identify the person who had delivered the goods to him. In the confessional, the defendant, Daniel Phillips, revealed to his parish priest that he had knowingly received stolen goods. The priest insisted that Phillips return the stolen items. Phillips then brought the stolen goods to Father Kohlmann under cover of confidentiality of the Seal of Confession and the priest returned the items to the rightful owner.[39] Father Kohlmann was subpoenaed to appear before a grand jury to identify those responsible for the crime. In refusing, Father Kohlmann testified:

> if called upon to testify in quality of a minister of a sacrament, in which my God himself has enjoined on me a perpetual and inviolable secrecy, I must declare to this honorable Court, that I cannot, I must not answer any question that has a bearing upon the restitution in question; and that it would be my duty to prefer instantaneous death or any temporal misfortune, rather than disclose the name of the penitent in question. For, were I to act otherwise, I should become a traitor to my church, to my sacred ministry and to my God. In fine, I should render myself guilty of eternal damnation.[40]

The court upheld the priest's right not to testify under the right of "free exercise of religious profession and worship" guaranteed by the New York constitution adopted in 1777.[41]

38 The case is abstracted in *Western Law Journal*, vol. 1, no. 3 (December, 1843), pp. 109–14. The records of an attorney who participated in the case are published in Note, "Privileged Communications to Clergymen," *Catholic Lawyer*, vol. 1, no. 1 (January 1955), pp. 199–209. That material originally appeared in William Sampson, *The Catholic Question in America* (New York, 1813; offset ed., New York, 1974), a work devoted entirely to the *Phillips* case. In addition to the decision of the court, the work includes the arguments presented by both sides as well as a lengthy appendix regarding the sanctity of the confessional.

39 See documentation supplied by Michael W. McConnell, "The Origins and Historical Understanding of Free Exercise of Religion," *Harvard Law Review*, vol. 103, no. 7 (May 1990), pp. 1410–11; and Sampson, p. 5.

40 See McConnell, p. 1411.

41 Subsequently, however, with the development of an extensive body of case law limiting free exercise rights in the face of a compelling state interest, courts were no longer willing to

However, four years later in another unreported case, *People v. Smith*,[42] a different New York court ruled that no such privilege existed for a Protestant minister. The court did not clarify the grounds for the distinction. To be sure, unlike Protestant denominations, the Catholic Church requires its adherents to confess sins and binds its priests to secrecy. It would, however, be an error to ignore the impact that Father Kohlmann's impassioned testimony must have had upon the Court. There is every reason to assume that the Court did indeed believe that the priest would have accepted "instantaneous death or any temporal misfortune" rather than violate the sanctity of the confessional.[43]

The specter of a priest languishing in jail because he has been sentenced for criminal contempt is not very pleasant. There is always public sympathy for civil disobedience entered into for ideological reasons rather then for personal profit or benefit. Sympathy for civil disobedience in the name of religious liberty is even greater.[44]

In seeking to compel the testimony of a Roman Catholic priest, the law faces a no-win situation. The law must recognize that the testimony will simply not be forthcoming.[45] The law then has the option of holding itself up to ignominy in a futile attempt to enforce its dictates or of pretending that no infraction has occurred and allowing the priest to flout the law. Either way the law will not be obeyed and will be held in disrespect. Far wiser to carve out a religious exemption that the public perceives as principled, libertarian and respectful of religion. Recognition of a priest–penitent privilege allows the law to escape from between the horns of the dilemma and to preserve both religious freedom and respect for the law.

Indeed, although often overlooked, the Free Exercise Clause of the First Amendment was rooted, at least in part, on precisely that consideration. The Framers of the Constitution of the United States made extensive use of the writings of John Locke and his influence upon the First Amendment was

recognize the clergyman–penitent privilege as a constitutionally protected right. Thus, for example, when in *In re* Fuhrer a rabbi contended that both the freedom of religion guaranteed by the constitution of the State of New York as well as the Free Exercise Clause of the First Amendment protected him against a forced disclosure, the Court applied a balancing test in declaring that "where it is asserted that governmental action impermissibly treads on one's right to freely exercise one's religion, a balance must be struck weighing the governmental interest to be served against the claimed infringement of one's First Amendment rights." 100 Misc.2d 315, 318, 419 N.Y.S.2d 426, 429 (1979). See *supra*, note 2.

42 2 City Hall Rec. (Rogers) 77 (N.Y. 1817). See Note, "Privileged Communications," p. 209.

43 See Seward Reese, "Confidential Communication to the Clergy," *Ohio State Law Journal*, vol. 21, no. 1 (Winter 1963), p. 81.

44 Cf. Yellin, pp. 111–12.

45 Cf. Yellin, p. 110.

most direct.[46] Locke recognized that religious intolerance was inconsistent with both public peace and good government and viewed religious rivalry and intolerance as among the most severe political problems of his day. Locke regarded civil strife and lawlessness, not to speak of war amongst nations, as the product of religious turmoil. In an essay written in 1689, Locke states: "It is not diversity of opinion, which cannot be avoided; but the refusal of toleration to those that are of a different opinion, which might have been granted, that have produced all the bustles and wars, that have been in the Christian world, upon account of religion."[47] Elsewhere, decrying the futility of religious coercion, Locke writes, "... let divines preach duty as long as they will, 'twas never known that men lay down quietly under the oppression and submitted their backs to the blows of others, when they thought they had strength enough to defend themselves."[48] The way to avoid such strife is by assuring toleration and liberty of religious practice for all. Freedom of religious practice also enables a government to govern effectively. A populace that perceives its religious principles to be thwarted by the government will harbor deep resentment and disrespect for the ruling authority. The government will be delegitimized in the eyes of those whose religious liberties are denied; respect for the government and its laws will be compromised.

Thus, there might be strong reason to craft a priest–penitent privilege to be granted to Catholic priests but not to other clergy for whom confidentiality does not rise to the level of inviolability. That distinction was intuitively recognized by the New York court. However, the principle of equality in the eyes of the law demands that a privilege granted to some be granted to all. And so, in 1828, the New York legislature enacted the nation's first statute recognizing the clergy privilege.[49] Arguably, the Anti-Establishment and Equal Protection clauses of the U.S. Constitution, which are now binding upon the states, demand no less. In any event, most clergy will not testify concerning confidential communications regardless of whether there is a statutory privilege.[50] Moreover, as one commentator has noted:

> If the clergyman believes that he has a duty of confidence that is unwaivable by religious doctrine ... The clergyman will be guided by the tenets of his faith rather than the rules of evidence, and he will risk contempt of court rather than compromise the protection of his ecclesiastic integrity. To compel

46 See McConnell, pp. 1430–31.

47 John Locke, *Letter on Toleration, The Works of John Locke*, vol. VI (London, 1823), p. 53.

48 See H. R. Fox Bourne, *The Life of John Locke*, vol. I (London, 1876), p. 190.

49 See N.Y. Rev. Stat. pt. 3, ch. 7, tit. 3, § 72 (1828).

50 See Seward Reese, "Confidential Communication to the Clergy," *Ohio State Law Journal*, vol. 21, no. 1 (Winter 1963), p. 81.

> disclosure would force the clergyman to choose between his religion and the court's wrath. The clergyman will probably be more willing to suffer at the hands of a human judge than at the hand of the Judge of Judges.[51]

It would be paradoxical in the extreme to apply a privilege designed to accommodate religious conscience and practice in a situation in which it would have precisely the opposite effect. Forcing a clergyman to remain silent when his religious conscience demands that he speak out is no less a violation of religious liberty than is coercion in forcing him to violate the Seal of Confession.

If the clergy privilege is designed to prevent the disrespect for law that would flow from inevitable disobedience to the demand for testimony, it would be anomalous to generate the identical disrespect for law that would arise from religiously mandated disobedience of a demand for non-disclosure. An attempt to seal the clergyman's lips upon threat of either criminal or civil sanctions when he believes that the tenets of his faith require that he disclose information imparted to him in confidence is likely to be frustrated by the clergyman's perceived duty to a higher authority. The inevitable result will be lessening of respect for temporal law.

Memories of religious oppression of Jews by government officials under color of law have not yet receded from the collective memory of the Jewish community. Lack of respect, not only for discriminatory laws and oppressive regimes, but also for government and civil law in general, persists in the psyche of many of those who experienced discrimination and religious persecution in the past. Scandalous events, of which we have witnessed far too many, serve to underscore how pernicious and infectious such attitudes can be. Forcing rabbis to become lawbreakers in violating the clergyman–penitent privilege when Jewish law demands that they do so is inimical both to the interests of the Jewish community and to the interests of society at large. Prudence demands that citizens not be subjected to crises of conscience that will inevitably result in erosion of respect for the law.

V. A PROPOSED REMEDY

There is, however, a relatively simple legislative solution that would both preserve the benefits of the privilege and accommodate free exercise concerns. The clergy privilege is currently recognized in each of the states, the District of

[51] Jeffery H. Miller, "Silence is Golden: Clergy Confidence and the Interaction between Statute and Case Law," *American Journal of Trial Advocacy*, vol. 22, no. 1 (Summer 1998), p. 64.

Columbia and in federal courts.[52] At present, in New York, the communicant holds the privilege, i.e., only the congregant[53] can waive the privilege and authorize testimony by the clergyman.[54] In other states, e.g., Illinois,[55] Ohio,[56] Maryland[57] and Virginia,[58] the privilege is held by the clergyman.[59] In those

[52] This is true for the federal rules of evidence as well. The clergy privilege was first recognized in federal common law in Totten v. United States, 92 U.S. 165, 107 (1875), and was reaffirmed in Mullen v. United States, 263 F.2d 275, 276 (D.C. Cir. 1958) (Faby, J. concurring), and is now embodied in Rule 505 of the Federal Rules of Evidence. However, Rule 501 provides that in federal civil actions, when an element of a claim or defense is determined by state law, the existence and scope of a privilege shall be determined by applicable state law. In Eckmann v. Board of Education of Hawthorn School District No. 17, 106 F.R.D. 70, 73 (E.D. Mo. 1985), the court ruled that the privilege recognized by federal common law belongs to the cleric.

[53] The corollary to this rule is that when the privilege is waived by the congregant the clergyman may be compelled to testify. See, however, Pennsylvania v. Musolina, 467 A.2d 605, 611 (Pa. 1983), in which the Court ruled that a priest was not required to testify even though the defendant had disclosed the religious communication in his confession to the state.

[54] Ohio's statute, Ohio Rev. Code Ann. § 2317.02 (Banks-Baldwin 1996), provides that the clergyman "may testify by express consent of the person making the communication except when the disclosure of the information is in violation of the clergyman's, rabbi's, priest's, or minister's sacred trust."

[55] Ill. Comp. Stat. 5/8–803 (West 1992).

[56] Ohio Rev. Code Ann. § 2317.02.

[57] Md. Code Ann., Cts. & Jud. Proc. § 9–11 (1978).

[58] Va. Code Ann., § 8.01–400 (Michie 1994). See Seidman v. Fishburne-Hudgin Foundation, Inc., 724F.2d 413 (4th Cir. 1984).

[59] Many of these statutes, including a number of those vesting the privilege in the communicant, contain language apparently limiting the privilege of confessions made in the course of discipline enjoined by the rules or practices of the denomination. See Reese, pp. 67–73 and *supra*, note 2.

Thus, in Magar v. Arkansas, 826 S.W.2d 221, 222 (Ark. 1992), the privilege was denied to a minister of the New Life Christian Fellowship who testified that "confession is not a tenet of his church and keeping evidence of a crime confidential is within the discretion of the pastor"; in Illinois v. Diercks, 411 N.E.2d 97, 101 (Ill. App. Ct. 1980), the court found that the defendant failed to establish that disclosure of the confession "would be enjoined by the rules or practices of the Baptist Church"; and in Kansas v. Andrews, 357 P.2d 739, 743 (Kan. 1960) cert. denied, 368 U.S. 868 (1961), the court denied the privilege to a Baptist minister under the then governing state statute on the grounds "that there was no course of discipline in the Baptist church by which a member thereof was enjoined to confess his sins to a minister of the church." See also Johnson v. Commonwealth, 310 Ky. 557, 221 S.W.2d 87, 89 (1949); Radecki v. Schuckardt, 50 Ohio App.2d 92, 4 Ohio Op.3d 60, 361 N.E.2d 543, 546 (1976); and Annotation, Matters to Which the Privilege Covering Communications to Clergyman or Spiritual Adviser Extends, 71 A.L.R.3d 794, 807–08 (1976).

In effect, in these decisions the courts understand the statutes involved as reserving the privilege to Catholics and any others who may require confession to a clergyman by virtue of church discipline. See, however, Scott v. Hammock, 133 F.R.D. 610 (Dist. Ct. Utah 1990), in which a federal magistrate interpreted the relevant language of the Utah statute in a much broader manner. The Federal District Court certified the question to the Supreme Court of Utah, which accepted a broad interpretation of the statute. See Scott v. Hammock, 870 P.2d 947 (Utah 1994). It should be noted that the Michigan statute (Mich. Comp. Law

states, although the clergyman cannot be compelled to testify, he may choose to voluntarily disclose the content of the communication.[60] Accordingly, the religious concerns of the Jewish community would best be served if states in which the privilege is held by the penitent, including, *inter alia*, Connecticut, Massachusetts, Michigan and Ohio, as well as New York, were to amend their codification of the privilege and stipulate that it may be waived by the clergyman.[61] The result would also conform with the original intent and purpose of the privilege, which was designed not so much to encourage free and open communication between clergyman and congregant as it was to protect the religious liberty of priests and penitents.

Ann. § 600.2156) (West 1986) refers specifically to a "minister of the gospel, or priest of any denomination whatsoever, or duly accredited Christian Science practitioner" in prohibiting disclosure of "any confession" made "in the course of discipline enjoined by the rules or practice of such denomination." Since Christian Science does not require confession to a clergyman or practitioner, inclusion of Christian Science practitioners among the clergy upon whom the privilege is conferred presumably indicates that the terms "confession" and "discipline" must be construed broadly.

60 A number of states, including Georgia (Ga. Code Ann. § 24–9–22) (1982), Michigan (Mich. Comp. Law Ann. § 600.2156) (West 1986), Missouri (Mo. Ann. Stat § 491.060) (West 1996), Vermont (Vt. Stat: Ann. Tit 12, § 1607) (1947) and Wyoming (Wyo. Stat. § 1–12–01) (1977), also vest the privilege in the clergyman but, if read literally, either declare the clergyman to be incompetent to testify or otherwise employ absolute language negating the possibility of a waiver. Cf., however, Alpharetta First United Methodist Church v. Stewart, 221 Ga. App. 748,472 S.E. 532 (1996), which includes dicta in which the Court assumes *en passant*, without discussion or reference to the language of the statute ("... nor shall such minister, priest, or rabbi be competent or compellable to testify ... "), that the privilege may be waived by the clergyman. See also Eckmann v. Board of Education of Hawthorn School District, *supra*, note 52, in which a federal court interpreted the Missouri statute as giving the clergyman the right to claim or waive the privilege.

61 Many states, California (Cal. Evid. Code § 1030–1034 (West 1995)) and New Jersey (N.J. Stat. Ann. § 2A:84A-23 (West 1994); N.J. R. Evid. 511) among them, provide that the privilege may be claimed either by the communicant or by the clergyman. Those statutes would also require modification to permit disclosure by the clergyman when compelled to do so by reason of religious conscience much as the New Jersey statute presently permits (but does not require) the clergyman to waive the privilege if the communication "pertains to a future criminal act."

NOTES AND QUESTIONS

1. Common law recognizes a person's proprietary interest in his body. The law thus protects him against battery and his person is inviolate. Hence, the need for informed consent even for medical treatment. Jewish law, on the other hand, recognizes a duty of rescue, including an obligation to treat when life is threatened, even against the wishes of the patient. Jewish law vests proprietary interest in man's body in the Creator who made it; or, to use Plato's phrase, man is the chattel of the gods. Paradoxically, in Jewish law, each person enjoys a quasi-proprietary interest in information concerning him. The law thus requires a waiver for divulging any information about a person other than in circumstances in which the person would have an obligation to divulge the information under Jewish law. Common law, on the other hand, recognizes no such personal proprietary interest. Privileged communications are privileged only because a statute imposes a duty of confidentiality and imposes it for policy reasons rather than because of proprietorship.

This framework serves to illuminate the manner in which obligations of confidentiality play themselves out in these diverse legal systems. For policy purposes, which approach is preferable?

2. Allegations of sexual or other kinds of molestation of students by a teacher have come to the attention of the principal. Upon investigation, the allegations remain just that – allegations – neither proven nor refuted. The laws of the state require, under pain of penal sanction, that school officials report such matters to the appropriate authorities. In light of the material in this chapter and in Chapter Three, how should the principal comport himself?

3. The school has reached an agreement involving the resignation of the teacher. (1) The teacher has applied for a position in another school. Officials in the other school ask the principal for information concerning the prospective new hire. How should the principal respond? (2) The principal has become aware of the teacher's pending application at another school. What, if any, are his obligations?

4. Would divulging unsubstantiated allegations by the principal to a third party, i.e., a prospective employer, subject the principal and/or his school to a suit for defamation and/or financial damages?

5. Rabbenu Gershom of Mainz, circa 1000 C.E., promulgated an ordinance forbidding reading another person's mail. Why was that activity not already forbidden as a breach of confidentiality?

6. Are there any grounds in Jewish law for prohibiting the gathering of data, either general or personal, by means of electronic devices (as in wiretapping, for example)? Remarkably, one scholar contends that the biblical prohibition

against talebearing includes bearing tales to oneself. See *supra*, note 10. Subsequent to acquiring information by means of an electronic device, for what use, if any, may the information be employed?

7. A physician has diagnosed an incurable, life-threatening malady in one of his patients. In the society pages of the local newspaper, he reads a report of the patient's engagement to be married. What, if any, are the physician's obligations to divulge this information to the espoused?

8. Same fact pattern as in the immediately preceding question, but instead of a life-threatening malady, the physician diagnoses infertility.

9. A pediatrician has been treating a brown-eyed infant. He has noticed that the infant's mother is blue-eyed. Recently the father has brought the infant to a physician for a routine examination. The physician notices that the father also has blue eyes. What are the implications for paternity? What, if anything, should the physician divulge to the father?

10. Many if not most jurisdictions require a physician to report a diagnosis of a sexually transmitted disease to state authorities. Is that consistent with a Jewish law mandate of confidentiality? In New York neonates are routinely tested anonymously for AIDS. A neonate cannot be infected with AIDS unless the disease was transmitted by its mother. The law forbids the physician who may come into possession of such information to transmit that diagnosis to the mother without her specific authorization. Would Jewish law sanction or demand civil disobedience?

9

Cloning

> In the year six hundred of the sixth millennium the gates of wisdom will open on high and the fountains of wisdom [will open] below and the world will be readied to enter the seventh millennium. As a person who readies himself to enter the Sabbath on the sixth day, from the time the sun [begins to] decline, so with this as well. An allusion: "In the six hundredth year of the life of Noah . . . all the fountains of the great deep were split and the windows of the heavens were opened." (Genesis 7:11)
>
> ZOHAR, BERESHIT 117a

The world has witnessed quantum leaps in scientific and technological advances since the mid-nineteenth century or, according to Jewish reckoning, since 5600, i.e., the year six hundred in the sixth millennium. As foretold by the *Zohar*, the benefits are not merely pragmatic; the explosion of human knowledge is attributed by the *Zohar* to heavenly inspiration and heralds the advent of the eschatological era of the seventh millennium.

God reveals Himself in the processes of nature with the result that insightful understanding of the laws of nature is, in at least some minuscule way, tantamount to apprehension of the Deity. Thus Rambam, *Hilkhot Yesodei ha-Torah* 2:2, writes that love of God is acquired by reflection upon His wondrous created works in which His wisdom can be discerned and, in *Hilkhot Yesodei ha-Torah* 4:12, Rambam declares that increased understanding of the nature of created entities carries with it enhanced love of God. Accordingly, the *tikkun*, or perfection, of which the *Zohar* speaks in describing the burgeoning of knowledge as the harbinger of the eschatological era is at one and the same time both preparation in the physical sense and preparation in the intellectual sense. In the physical sense it is comparable to Sabbath preparations carried out on the preceding day, so that, with the coming of the Messiah, man may enjoy undisturbed leisure to engage in spiritual pursuits; it is also perfection in the sense of intellectual preparation and development in the form of appreciation of the grandeur of creation, and hence of the Creator, so that man will be equipped for the more profound understanding of the nature of God that will be attainable in the eschatological era.

There can be no doubt that unraveling the mysteries of procreation and the genesis of human life are integral to this process. Attempts to fathom those mysteries are entirely laudable. Whether or not those endeavors yield any licit practical benefit is secondary; their major value, as that of all aspects of theoretical science, lies in qualitatively enhanced fulfillment of the commandment "And you shall love the Lord, your God" (Deuteronomy 6:5). The legitimacy of *acting* upon such scientific information is another matter. Not everything that can be done should be done; that which is possible is not for that reason moral.[1]

I. SCIENTIFIC BREAKTHROUGH AND POTENTIAL

Not everything that *can* be done *should* be done. But it is a truism that, in the usual course of human events, that which *can* be done *will* be done.

Since the early 1970s ethicists have grappled with the implications of human cloning.[2] What was then a vague specter now looms as an imminent reality. With the most recent breakthrough in the cloning of fetal mice in Hawaii it is evident that "advances in science are coming faster than even the most confident scientists had imagined."[3] Dr. Lee Silver, a mouse geneticist and reproductive biologist at Princeton University, described the speed at which cloning has progressed as "breathtaking" and added, "Absolutely, we are going to have cloning of humans."[4] Notwithstanding the protestation of scientists such as Dr. Ryuzo Yanagimachi, whose cloning experiments have electrified the scientific world, that "we should stick to reproduction the way that Mother Nature did for us,"[5] it is now conjectured that in vitro fertilization clinics will soon add human cloning to their repertoires.[6]

[1] Cf. the statement ". . . what is technically possible is not for that reason morally admissible," Congregation for the Doctrine of the Faith, *Instruction on Respect for Human Life in Its Origin and on the Dignity of Procreation* (*Donum Vitae*) (February 22, 1987), introduction, sec. 3.

[2] See Willard Gaylin, "The Frankenstein Myth Becomes a Reality: We Have the Awful Knowledge to Make Exact Copies of Human Beings," *The New York Times Magazine* (March 5, 1972), pp. 12–13, 41–49.

[3] *New York Times* (July 23, 1998), p. A1.

[4] *Ibid.*, p. A20.

[5] *New York Times*, July 24, 1998, p. A12.

[6] *New York Times*, July 23, 1998, p. A20. In an editorial accompanying the report of the cloning of Dolly, the editors of *Nature* voiced the opinion that "Cloning humans from adults' tissues is likely to be achievable any time from one to ten years from now." See *Nature*, vol. 385, no. 6619 (February 27, 1997), p. 753.

The new era of reproductive technology was ushered in with the birth of Dolly on July 5, 1996, at the Roslin Institute in Roslin, Scotland.[7] The birth of a cloned sheep was the culmination of research undertaken by Dr. Ian Wilmut on behalf of PPL Therapeutics Ltd., a small biotechnology company with headquarters in Edinburgh. The purpose was to use sheep to generate drugs for treating human diseases such as hemophilia and cystic fibrosis. Genetic engineering had already been employed to produce sheep whose milk contains a drug, alpha-1 antitrypsin, that is used to treat cystic fibrosis. The purpose of cloning sheep was to avoid the laborious and expensive process of genetically engineering large numbers of animals individually. With cloning, once an animal has been genetically adapted, the process need not be repeated; the animal can simply be cloned and, since all its clones will have identical genetic characteristics, the clones will also produce the same drug.[8]

The research was certainly not conducted in a vacuum. Scientists have long been able to use skin cells from a frog to clone embryos that grow to the tadpole stage before dying. Much more successful is a process known as twin splitting. In 1993 Dr. Jerry Hall and Dr. Robert Stillman of George Washington University separated as yet undifferentiated fetal cells of embryos to the two, four and eight cell stages of development and allowed each cell to develop as a separate embryo. The immediate precursor of the Roslin experiment was the work of Dr. Steen Willadsen, who was the first to clone a sheep[9] successfully from an embryo cell. Willadsen took cell nuclei, which contain the genetic blueprint encoded in DNA, and added them to animal ova whose own nuclei he had removed.[10]

However, cells derived from early embryos are not suitable for genetic engineering. Manipulation of embryo cells leads to their death, with the result that they cannot be grown in a laboratory so that genes can be added in order to cause the organism to produce pharmaceutical agents. Moreover, vast numbers of cells must be grown in order to ensure that at least a few will become genetically modified. Wilmut and his associate, Dr. Keith Campbell, successfully took the nucleus of a cell removed from the udder of a mature

7 A full report of the methods employed in causing that event to occur was published by I. Wilmut *et al.*, "Viable Offspring Derived from Fetal and Adult Mammalian Cells," *Nature*, vol. 385, no. 6619 (February 27, 1997), pp. 810–13.

8 See Gina Kalata, *Clone: The Road to Dolly and the Path Ahead* (New York, 1998), p. 25.

9 Much earlier, in 1981, to the excitement of the scientific community, a prominent German researcher, Dr. Karl Illmensee, and a younger colleague, Dr. Peter Hoppe, reported the successful cloning of three mice from early embryo cells. However, a formal investigation of charges of scientific fraud culminated in a somewhat equivocal report and Illmensee's reported results were not duplicated. For an intriguing survey of the entire episode see *Clone*, pp. 120–56.

10 *New York Times*, June 3, 1997, p. C1; *Clone*, p. 129.

sheep and inserted it into the ovum of a ewe from which they had previously removed the existing nucleus. The egg was then jolted with a burst of electricity, causing it to behave as if it were newly fertilized. The difficulty of the procedure is evidenced by the fact that it successfully culminated in the birth of a lamb only after 277 attempts.

Some time after the birth of Dolly, ABS Global Inc., a company in De Forest, Wisconsin, announced the birth of Gene, a calf that was cloned from a genetically altered fetal cell.[11] Less than two years after the cloning of a sheep from an adult cell, Dr. James Robl of the University of Massachusetts at Amherst and Dr. Steven L. Stice, a scientist employed by Advanced Cell Technology, a commercial firm, reported the cloning of Holstein calves from genetically engineered fetal cells taken from a fifty-five-day-old male Holstein embryo.[12] Two hundred seventy-six fetal cells were inserted into an equal number of unfertilized cow eggs whose own genetic material had been removed. At the end of a week only thirty-three embryos remained alive. Twenty-eight of those were transferred to eleven cows that served as surrogate mothers. Four calves survived to parturition, but one of the calves died five days after birth as the result of a congenital heart defect. Robl and Stice had previously attempted to clone calves from adult cells but none of the fetuses survived. There have been other unpublished reports of cows pregnant with fetuses cloned from adult cells[13] but there have been no reports of the birth of other cows or sheep cloned from adult cells.

More recently and more dramatically, biologists at the University of Hawaii have reported the cloning of over fifty mice, including clones of clones, from the cells of adult mice.[14]

These experiments have implications far beyond the goal of facilitating the manufacture of pharmaceutical products from genetically altered cells, which itself is potentially of far-reaching benefit in the treatment of numerous diseases and disorders. Cells of mature organs are capable of reproducing themselves but cannot be altered to form the cells of different organs. In effect, the DNA of differentiated cells is programmed to reproduce cells of one specialized type and of no other. Thus, for example, if a pancreas is destroyed, other cells in the body cannot generate a new pancreas. Successful cloning of adult cells demonstrates that, when inserted into an ovum, the program of a cell's

[11] *New York Times*, December 2, 1997, p. A24.

[12] See Jose B. Cibelli *et al.*, "Cloned Transgenic Calves Produced from Nonquiescent Fetal Fibroblasts," *Science*, vol. 280, no. 5367 (May 22, 1998), pp. 1256–58.

[13] *New York Times*, May 23, 1998, p. A11, col. 1.

[14] See T. Wakayama *et al.*, "Full-Term Development of Mice from Enucleated Ocytes Injected with Cumulus Cell Nuclei," *Nature*, vol. 394, no. 6691 (July 23, 1998), pp. 369–74.

DNA can be reversed, thereby allowing the cell to reproduce and develop into cells of other bodily organs. When the process is more fully understood, it may become possible to create particular organs to replace those that become diseased or destroyed.

As noted, subsequent to the successful cloning of Dolly, the prospect of human cloning became much more than a theoretical conjecture. The initial reaction of both ethicists and scientists was that human cloning is morally unacceptable. President Clinton, following the recommendation of the National Bioethics Advisory Commission, banned the use of federal money to conduct human cloning experiments and requested that privately funded enterprises adhere to a voluntary ban on human cloning. Nevertheless, at present, other than in California,[15] the cloning of a human being is legal in the United States, although prohibited by law in Britain, Spain, Denmark, Germany and Australia.[16]

Despite the generally negative view of cloning humans, G. Richard Seed, a Chicago physicist who has been involved in various forms of fertility research since the early 1970's, has announced that he has assembled a team of scientists for the purpose of cloning a human being before the procedure is banned and is seeking venture capital for the project.[17] Moreover, the climate of opinion has changed rapidly. Decades ago, two fertility experts, Sophia J. Kleegman and Sherwin A. Kaufman, wrote that reproductive breakthroughs pass through several predictable stages. Reactions proceed from "horrified negation" to "negation without horror" to "slow and gradual curiosity, study, evaluation" and, finally, to "a very slow but steady acceptance."[18] The volte-face about the prospect of human cloning is best expressed in a headline that appeared in the *New York Times*: "On Cloning Humans, 'Never' Turns Swiftly into 'Why Not.'"[19] In that article Dr. Steen Willadsen, the cloning pioneer who developed the fundamental methods for cloning animals, is quoted as saying that it is just a matter of time before the first human is cloned. Earlier, John Paris, a Jesuit ethicist, remarked that he was certain that humans would be cloned: "I can't imagine a world in which someone won't try it. There are

[15] *New York Times*, December 2, 1997, p. A24.

[16] *Clone*, p. 32.

[17] *Washington Post*, January 7, 1998, pp. A2–A3. A company named Clonaid has already been established in the Bahamas in contemplation of offering cloning for fees of $200,000 and higher. At the time the *Washington Post* article was written, the firm's scientific director stated that "Before the year 2000, there will be a human cloned on this planet." See John Carey, "Human Clones: It's Decision Time," *Business Week*, August 10, 1998, p. 37.

[18] Sophia J. Kleegman and Sherwin A. Kaufman, *Infertility in Women: Diagnosis and Treatment* (Philadelphia, PA, 1966), p. 178.

[19] December 2, 1997, p. A1.

two things that drive man – power and money. And fame leads to fortune. Someone will try it."[20]

The present climate of opinion makes analysis of the moral and ethical issues involved in cloning imperative. But the enterprise must be undertaken honestly and objectively. To quote the late Professor Paul Ramsey, it is imperative that we

> raise the ethical questions with a serious and not a frivolous conscience. A man of frivolous conscience announces that there are ethical quandaries ahead that we must urgently consider before the future catches up with us. By this he often means that we need to devise a new ethics that will provide the rationalization for doing in the future what men are bound to do because of the new actions and interventions science will have made possible. In contrast, a man of serious conscience means to say in raising urgent ethical questions that there may be some things that men should never do. The good things that men do can be made complete only by the things they refuse to do.[21]

II. HUMAN INTERVENTION IN THE NATURAL ORDER

Faith communities that base their moral teaching upon natural law regard various forms of artificial procreation as immoral. The immorality of such acts lies not in their artificiality *per se* but in the fact that they thwart the natural character of the transmission of human life. In its Thomistic formulation, the essence of natural law is a divinely ordained teleological system and the notion that divine wisdom, in guiding all creatures to their proper ends, imparts moral law to man through the medium of his intellect. As a rational creature, man's intellect inclines him towards the actions and goals proper to his nature. Thus, according to natural law theorists, among other things, lying, gluttony, drunkenness and contraception are all immoral for essentially the same reason. Such acts are performed by a human faculty created for a readily discernible purpose. The evil in the immoral conduct lies in the abuse of a natural faculty by its use in an unnatural manner.

These natural law theorists further assert that it is in the nature of man to transmit life through conjugal union. Use of body fluids or tissue for generation of life in some other manner, they contend, constitutes a subversion of man's teleological function and purpose. They maintain that it is the conjugal act by which the spouses become one flesh, and only the conjugal act, that is designed

[20] *Clone*, p. 39.

[21] Paul Ramsey, *Fabricated Man: The Ethics of Genetic Control* (New Haven, CT, 1970), p. 122.

for the purpose of generating human life. In effect, the phrase "... and they shall be one flesh" (Genesis 2:24) is understood by these theorists as having a double meaning: (1) A man "shall cleave to his wife" in order that they "shall be one flesh," i.e., that they may jointly produce a single flesh, namely, a child. Hence the announced *telos* of the conjugal act is procreation. (2) The generation of a child reflexively causes the parents themselves to become "one flesh." Thus generation of new life has as its *telos* solidification of the marital bonds.[22] Generation of a human life in some other manner and for some other purpose violates the divinely ordained *telos* for which the human body was created. On that analysis, homologous artificial fertilization is unacceptable because it separates the unitive and procreative aspects of propagation of the human species. Thus it has been stated that:

> By comparison with the transmission of other forms of life in the universe, the transmission of human life has a special character of its own, which derives from the special nature of the human person. "The transmission of human life is entrusted by nature to a personal and conscious act and as such is subject to the all-holy laws of God: immutable and inviolable laws which must be recognized and observed. For this reason one cannot use means and follow methods which could be licit in the transmission of the life of plants and animals.[23]

With regard to cloning specifically, the same source declares:

> attempts or hypotheses for obtaining a human being without any connection with sexuality through "twin fission," cloning or parthenogenesis are to be considered contrary to the moral law, since they are in opposition to the dignity both of human procreation and of the conjugal union.[24]

There is no reflection in the Jewish tradition of a doctrine establishing a global prohibition that forbids man to tamper with known or presumed *teloi* of creation. There are indeed individual thinkers who have explained the rationale underlying particular *miẓvot* in a manner echoing such a concept. Biblical commandments prohibiting the interbreeding of species and the mingling of diverse agricultural species certainly lend themselves to such an interpretation. Although Rashi, in his commentary to Leviticus 19:19, regards those

[22] Cf. the Yiddish folk saying, "A *shidekh vert nisht geschlossen biz s'iz geboren a kind*" – "A match is not sealed until a child is born."

[23] Congregation for the Doctrine of the Faith, *Instruction on Respect for Human Life in its Origin and on the Dignity of Procreation: Replies to Certain Questions of the Day*, introduction, sec. 4, http://www.vatican.va/roman_curia/congregations/cfaith/documents/rc_con_cfaith_doc_19870222_respect-for-human-life_en.html.

[24] *Ibid.*, ch. 1, sec. 6.

restrictions as *ḥukkim*, i.e., arational statutes not subject to human inquiry, Ramban, *loc. cit.*, takes sharp issue with Rashi and opines that interbreeding and prohibited mingling of species are forbidden as constituting illicit tampering with creation. Ramban states that God endows every creature and every plant with cosmically arranged distinctive features and qualities, each designed to reproduce itself so long as the universe endures. Crossbreeding and crossfertilization produce a reconfiguration of those distinctive qualities and also compromise reproductive potential. By engaging in such activities man usurps the divine prerogative in producing a new species or entity with its own novel set of attributes and, presumably, less than optimally suited to fulfill the divinely ordained *telos* associated with the original species.

Ibn Ezra has been understood as presenting the matter in a somewhat different light. He has been understood as declaring that the Torah prohibits crossbreeding of species because it thwarts propagation of the species and hence represents an injustice to the animals who are prevented from fulfilling the divine purpose of propagating their respective species,[25] and as explaining the prohibitions against the mixture of agricultural species as well as against the combination of linen and wool in the cloth of a garment as violating the natural order decreed by the Creator.[26] R. Samson Raphael Hirsch had no difficulty explaining the prohibition against *sha'atnez* (the mixing of linen and wool) in similar terms. Indeed, R. Hirsch understood all *ḥukkim* as reflecting the principle that man should not interfere with the order and harmony – and hence the *telos* – of creation.[27] According to R. Hirsch, such laws are distinguished from *mishpatim*, or so-called rational commandments, only because our duties towards fellow men are more intelligible to us by virtue of our recognition of our own needs and aspirations. That particular purposes are similarly assigned to animals and even to inanimate objects is not immediately grasped by the human intellect and hence *ḥukkim* are depicted as arational. It is noteworthy that, although R. Hirsch regards these commandments as designed to prevent

[25] See R. Abraham Ibn Ezra, *Commentary on the Bible*, Leviticus 19:19, and R. Judah Leib Krinsky, *Karnei Or*, *loc. cit.* See also R. Abraham Chill, *The Mitzvot: The Commandments and Their Rationale* (Jerusalem, 1974), p. 236.

[26] See the supercommentary to Ibn Ezra of R. Shlomo Zalman Netter, Leviticus 19:19, published in the *Horeb* edition of the Pentateuch (Jerusalem, London, New York, 5711). A similar interpretation was earlier advanced by *Ohel Yosef* and *Mekor Ḥayyim* in their respective works on Ibn Ezra published in *Margaliyot Tovah* (Stanislav, 5687). *Mekor Ḥayyim* also understands Ibn Ezra's comments regarding interbreeding of animal species in a like manner. However, these scholars' understanding of the passage in question is less than compelling. Cf. R. Abraham Chill, *The Mitzvot*, p. 236.

[27] See R. Samson Raphael Hirsch, *The Nineteen Letters of Ben Uziel*, Eleventh Letter; *idem*, *Horeb*, sec. 327.

interference with divinely ordained *teloi*, unlike natural law theologians, he regards the *teloi* themselves as not being immediately available to human reason. That is certainly confirmed by the fact that no natural law philosopher has ever asserted that the manufacture of linsey-woolsey or even agricultural hybridization is intuitively perceived as violating the divine plan for creation.

If tampering with the ostensive or presumed nature of animal species were always forbidden, most forms of genetic engineering would be illicit. No bacterium is designed by nature to clean up oil spills by metabolizing petroleum or to excrete human insulin for use by diabetics. In the absence of evidence in rabbinic sources to the contrary, it must be assumed that, even accepting Ramban's explanation of the prohibition against interbreeding or R. Hirsch's broader analysis of the rationale underlying *ḥukkim* in general, such strictures must be understood as limited to those matters explicitly prohibited.[28]

Indeed, there is a perceptible tension between the concepts enunciated by Ramban and R. Samson Raphael Hirsch and the many midrashic sources indicating that man is an active partner in the process of creation and, as such, is charged with bringing creative processes to completion. The biblical charge to Adam exhorting him to "fill the earth and conquer it" (Genesis 1:28) seems to give Adam *carte blanche* to engage in any form of conduct that is not specifically proscribed. The problem is readily resolved if it is understood that, in general, the functions and *teloi* of the products of creation are not immutable; that the Creator did not intend to bar man from applying his ingenuity in finding new uses and purposes for the objects of creation;[29] and that there is no injustice to animal species or inanimate objects in doing so. Immutability of function and *telos* is the exception, not the rule. Thus, for example, it has never been suggested that manufacturing and using synthetic fibers in the making of clothes is in any way a contravention of either the letter or spirit of the law.[30] The exceptions were announced by the Creator as

[28] Rambam, *Guide for the Perplexed*, book III, ch. 37, regards the *ḥukkim* as prohibitions designed to stem idolatrous conduct. The actions in question, he asserts, were cultic practices associated with pagan worship and sacrifice. According to Rambam's understanding of these commandments, there is no hint of a negative attitude with regard to intervention by man in the natural order.

[29] Cf. R. Joseph B. Soloveitchik, "Confrontation," *Tradition*, vol. VI, no. 2 (Spring–Summer, 1964), p. 20.

[30] It is indeed the case that one finds occasional comments in rabbinic writings representing those prohibitions in phraseology that is general and unqualified; see, for example, the sources cited *supra*, note 26. Nevertheless, it seems that those comments must be understood in the manner herein indicated.

formal prohibitions.[31] It is precisely because human reason cannot intuit, or even comprehend, when and under what circumstances contravention of the natural order is inappropriate that these commandments are in the nature of *ḥukkim*.

More generally, man's creative power, at least to the extent that it does not involve the creation of novel species, is extolled in rabbinic sources. Rabbinic exegesis understands "*Shaddai*" as an acronym: *she-amarti le-olami "dai"* – "Who said to My universe, 'Enough!'" Thus *Midrash Rabbah* 46:2 renders the verse, "I, the Lord *Shaddai*" (Genesis 17:1), "I am the Lord who said to the universe 'Enough!'"[32] R. Jonathan Eibeschutz, *Tiferet Yonatan, ad locum*, followed by R. Joseph Dov Soloveitchik, *Bet ha-Levi, ad locum*, explains that, in His creation of various artifacts, God arrested their development before completion. Man plants a seed, the seed germinates, a stalk grows and kernels of wheat develop. The Creator could well have made it possible for the kernels to crumble into flour, for the flour to absorb rain or moisture from the atmosphere, for the wind to churn the water-drenched flour so that dough be formed and for the heat of the sun to bake the mixture in order to yield a product that might literally be termed a "breadfruit." Instead, the Creator arrested the process long before its completion and ordained that grinding the wheat, mixing the flour with water, kneading the dough and baking the bread be performed by man. Similarly, the flax plant could have been endowed with

[31] Maharal of Prague speaks about natural objects created during the six days of creation in juxtaposition to matters that are "above," or transcend, nature. The latter were created only in potential but are actualized by man. The prime example of that phenomenon is the fire that was produced by Adam. Thus man's role is "completion" (*hashlamah*) of the process of Creation. It is the divine plan that such a "completion" of Creation occur. Maharal asserts that it is the divine will that even interspecies such as the mule come into being, although not in circumstances that involve violation of Torah law. Thus crossbreeding was permitted to Adam because the emergence of interspecies is integral to the "completion" of the universe. According to Maharal, crossbreeding by a person who is not commanded otherwise (or in situations in which the prohibition does not apply) does not constitute a violation of the divine will or of the divinely ordained *telos* because "the way of Torah is one thing and the way of completion is another matter entirely." See R. Judah Loew, *Be'er ha-Golah*, ch. 2, s.v. *be-Masekhet Pesaḥim*.

[32] The Midrash includes "heaven" and "earth" as well as well as "universe" in this reference. A somewhat different version is presented by the Gemara, *Ḥaggigah* 12a. In *Ḥaggigah* the reference is to containment of the portion of the earth covered by the waters of the sea. The comment "Enough!" with regard to the "earth" and "heaven" (despite contemporary theories of an expanding universe) should also be understood as connoting a similar concept. However, if so, the term "universe" appears to be redundant. Moreover, understood in this manner, the comment seems inappropriate in the context in which it appears, *viz.*, in conjunction with the commandment to Abraham concerning circumcision. It is that problem that led *Tiferet Yonatan* to understand the comment as having an additional connotation.

properties causing strands of flax to separate and intertwine themselves in a cloth which might grow in the shape of a cloak. Instead, the process is arrested and then brought to completion by man. Indeed, the Gemara, *Shabbat* 30b, declares that in the eschatological era the Land of Israel will yield "cakes" and "linen garments." *Bet ha-Levi* explains that the import of that statement is simply that, in the end of days, God will allow the processes of creation to be culminated by modifying the natural order in a manner that will permit the creative process to become complete and thus spare man any travail. In the interim, however, He has declared, "Enough!" i.e., He has precipitously interrupted the process of creation and coopted man, who must complete the process, as a collaborator in fashioning the universe.

The concept of man as an active partner in bringing the process of creation to completion as portrayed in the aggadic statement of the Gemara reappears much later in rabbinic writings as an explanation of the nature of the forms of "labor" that are prohibited on the Sabbath. In the nineteenth century, R. Jacob Zevi Mecklenberg, *Ha-Ketav ve-ha-Kabbalah*, Exodus 20:10, and R. Samson Raphael Hirsch,[33] each writing independently, took note of the fact that the "labor" prohibited on Shabbat is not a correlative of physical exertion. For example, carrying or stacking heavy objects, so long as it is performed within the confines of a private domain, entails no violation of any biblical prohibition, while placing even a small quantity of food over an already existing flame constitutes a capital transgression. These scholars develop the thesis that on the Sabbath the Jew is commanded to emulate God, who desisted from creative endeavors on the seventh day. The notion of exertion or expenditure of physical energy in association with the Deity is entirely noncognitive. God "rested" on the seventh day "from all His work that He created" (Genesis 2:2) solely in the sense that He ceased bringing novel entities into being. Man, too, assert these writers, is commanded to rest on the seventh day, not from physical labor, but from activities that complete the creative process and bring it to fruition. Thus God created foodstuffs, but many are inedible until cooked; man initiates the process of cooking that renders the foodstuffs edible and in doing so completes the creation of food. God arrested the creative process by saying "Enough!" and left it for man to bring the process to final culmination. It is precisely this activity – completion of the creative process – that is prohibited to man on the Sabbath regardless of how effortless and physically undemanding the task may be. To rephrase the concept, six days a

33 *Commentary on the Bible*, Genesis 2:2 and Exodus 20:10; *Horeb*, sec. 144; and *The Nineteen Letters*, Thirteenth Letter.

week man engages in completing the tasks left uncompleted by the Creator and by doing so becomes an active partner in the process of creation; on the seventh, the Jew emulates the Creator by ceasing and desisting from all such creative endeavors.

It is abundantly clear that human intervention in the natural order is normatively interdicted only to the extent that there are explicit prohibitions limiting such intervention. Moreover, there is no evidence either from Scripture or from rabbinic writings that forms of intervention or manipulation not expressly banned are contrary to the spirit of the law. To the contrary, Jewish tradition, although it certainly recognizes divine proprietorship of the universe, nevertheless gratefully acknowledges that while "The heavens are the heavens of God" yet "the earth has He given to the sons of man" (Psalms 115:16). In bestowing that gift upon mankind, the Creator granted man dominion over the world in which he lives and over the living species that are coinhabitants of that world. Man has been given license to apply his intellect, ingenuity and physical prowess in developing the world in which he has been placed subject only to limitations imposed by the laws of the Torah, including the general admonition not to do harm to others, as well as by the constraints imposed by good sense and considerations of prudence.

There is ample reason to assume that Jewish teaching would not frown upon cloning either animals or humans simply because it is a form of asexual, and hence "unnatural," reproduction. The Gemara, *Sanhedrin* 65b, relates that R. Ḥanina and R. Oshia met every Friday for the purpose of perusing *Sefer Yeẓirah*, an early kabbalistic work, in order to create a calf for their Sabbath meal. The Gemara recounts this anecdote without the slightest hint of censure. The text incontrovertibly yields two principles: (1) asexual husbandry, at least of animal species, is morally innocuous; and (2) harnessing metaphysical forces, or "white magic," at least when practiced by masters of the Kabbalah, is acceptable. Although there is nothing in this narrative that may be cited as providing an explicit basis for extending such sanction to creation of a hybrid, interbreed or genetically engineered animal, the report certainly reflects acceptance of the legitimacy of asexual, and hence homologous, reproduction of animals.

Me'iri, *Sanhedrin* 67b, finds asexual reproduction, at least of animals, to be not only permissible but even empirically possible. He asserts that creation of "beautiful creatures other than from a sexual union" is known "from scientific books" to be a phenomenon that is "not in the realm of the impossible." Me'iri declares that employment of natural causes for purposes of asexual reproduction is not to be regarded as a form of magic or sorcery and hence is entirely permissible.

III. MAN AS CREATOR OF MAN

The notion that man is an active partner of the Deity in the process of creation extends to the creation of members of the human species as well. This is poignantly reflected in the words of the Sages recorded in *Kiddushin* 30b: "There are three partners in [the conception of] a person: his father, his mother and God." Thus man, in engaging in procreation in order to promulgate the human species, is depicted as an active participant in the ongoing process of creation. The question is whether procreative license is limited to sexual reproduction or whether it encompasses asexual or homologous reproduction as well.

There may well be cogent reason to distinguish between various forms of asexual reproduction, so that approbation of a particular mode of reproduction may not necessarily be approbation of all. Thus, for example, parthenogenesis, although homologous, is more closely akin to natural reproduction, with the result that it is less likely than cloning to be found objectionable. Similarly, artificial splitting of an embryo in the earliest stages of cell division represents a relatively minimal level of human intervention. Cloning involves a much higher degree of manipulation and interference with the natural order. Least natural is the creation of a *golem* or anthropoid in whom replication of already existing human genetic material is completely lacking. For reasons requiring no elaboration, creation of a *golem* is the only form of asexual reproduction heretofore addressed in rabbinic literature. Although cloning may present an array of halakhic and moral issues significantly different from those posed in the fashioning of a *golem*, examination of extant *golem* literature is instructive for the purpose of establishing a framework in which the contemporary problem can be examined.

The most significant source by far is the narrative recorded by the Gemara, *Sanhedrin* 65b. According to Rashi's understanding, the Gemara cites the verse "Your iniquities have been a barrier between you and your God" (Isaiah 59:2) as establishing that, but for their supposedly minor transgressions, the righteous would find it within their power to emulate God and create a universe.[34] Presumably in illustration of that point, the Gemara reports that Rava created a man and sent him to R. Zeira. R. Zeira spoke to the man but he did not

34 Cf. *Midrash Tehillim*, Psalm 3. *Midrash Tehillim* states: R. Eleazar said, "The sections of the Torah were not given in order for, had they been given in order, anyone who would read them would be able to create a universe, to resurrect the dead and to perform wonders. Therefore the order of the Torah was concealed."

answer. Thereupon R. Zeira said to him, "You stem from [our] colleagues.[35] Return to your dust."

R. Zeira must have been aware that the creature appearing before him was an anthropoid before he attempted to engage him in conversation; otherwise, it would have been impossible for R. Zeira to have known that he was not simply confronting a mute person. R. Zeira then proceeded to destroy the creature because as an artificial creature he regarded it as defective or undesirable.[36] Had the anthropoid been capable of speech R. Zeira would presumably have had no problem with its continued existence.

Maharsha's comments *ad locum* are most revealing in this regard. Maharsha comments that speech is the "power of the soul." The anthropoid could not speak, declares Maharsha, because Rava lacked the ability to create a soul and R. Zeira proceeded to destroy it precisely because it was not endowed with a human soul. It follows from Maharsha's analysis that had Rava, either by harnessing the teachings of *Sefer Yeẓirah* or otherwise, been capable of creating an anthropoid endowed with a soul, R. Zeira would have had no objection.[37]

Maharsha's analysis underscores the import of the Gemara's original statement declaring that, in the total absence of transgression, the righteous are capable of creating not merely an anthropoid but even an entire universe and resolves the tension between that statement and R. Zeira's destruction of the anthropoid actually created by Rava. The Gemara ascribes the power of

35 Maharsha cites anonymous sources who regard the term "*ḥavrayya*" used in this context as the plural form of the Aramaic equivalent of the Hebrew "*ḥaver*" that appears in Deuteronomy 18:11. If so, the term refers to animal charmers or magicians and is indeed employed in that manner by the Gemara, *Shabbat* 45a. See parallel occurrences cited by Marcus Jastrow, *Dictionary of Talmud Babli, Yerushalmi, Midrashic Literature and Targum*. See also Moshe Baer, "On the *Ḥavrayya*," *Bar Ilan: Annual of Bar Ilan University* (Ramat Gan, 1983), vol. XX–XXI, pp. 83–86 and Moshe Idel, *Golem* (Albany, 1990), pp. 27–28.

36 It should be noted that a fourteenth-century commentator on the *aggadot* of the Talmud, R. Shem Tov ibn Shaprut, *Pardes Rimmonim* (Sabionetta, 5314), p. 13a, asserts that the anthropoid was not veridical but an *aḥizat einayim*, i.e., an illusion in the form of man. According to *Pardes Rimmonim*, Rava produced an illusion in order to test R. Zeira; the latter perceived its real nature and, accordingly, commanded it to return to dust. See also Gershom G. Scholem, "The Idea of the *Golem*," *On the Kabbalah and Its Symbolism*, trans. Ralph Manheim (New York, 1965), p. 188.

37 For the relationship between speech and reason see J. David Bleich, *Contemporary Halakhic Problems* (New York, 1983), vol. II, pp. 368–70. See also R. Baḥya ben Asher, *Commentary on the Bible*, Genesis 2:7, and *idem*, *Kad ha-Kemaḥ*, vol. II (Lvov, 5698), 103b. For other kabbalistic sources disassociating speech from reason see Scholem, *On the Kabbalah*, pp. 193–94. The human soul is an ontological entity and is either identical with, or the source of, man's rational faculty. The vital or animating force in living creatures, including man, is not uniquely human and hence even in man is referred to as the animal or animating soul.

creation to the righteous in terminology that is entirely matter of fact. There is no hint that such power should not be utilized, just as there is no censure of R. Ḥanina and R. Oshia for having created a calf. R. Zeira did not destroy the *golem* created by Rava because he disapproved of Rava's attempt to engage in the enterprise, but because the result was unsatisfactory. Rava, presumably because of the "inequities" that constitute a barrier between man and God, was incapable of creating a man endowed with a soul. Had it indeed been within Rava's power to do so, R. Zeira would not have interfered. However, upon discovering the inherent deficiency of the anthropoid, R. Zeira destroyed the creature.[38] Although the considerations that prompted R. Zeira to act in that manner are not spelled out, R. Zeira undoubtedly had reason to fear that the imperfect anthropoid arising from a failed attempt to create a human would prove to be a source of grief. Indeed, as will be noted later,[39] this indeed proved to be so in the case of the *golem* purportedly created by R. Elijah of Helm.

Nevertheless, even if man has the power to create a clone endowed with a human soul, there may well be reason to question whether that power should be used. Lurking beneath the surface of theological opposition to cloning is not simply that artificial creation of human beings represents an illicit mode of *imitatio Dei* but that success in such an endeavour would have a profound psychological effect upon the perceiver, *viz.*, perception of the uniqueness of the Deity as compromised by human emulation of the creative function would lead to denial of divine creation of the universe and even to denial of the existence of God.

That concern is indeed echoed in one kabbalistic source. One of the earliest medieval references to the creation of a *golem* is found in a thirteenth-century work, *Seifer ha-Gematri'ot*, authored by disciples of R. Judah the Pious.[40] That source reports:

> Ben Sira wanted to study *Sefer Yeẓirah*. A voice [*bat kol*] came out and said, "You cannot do it alone." He went to Jeremiah his father. Ben Sira is [numerically equivalent to] Ben Yermiyahu [the son of Jeremiah], and they studied it and after three years, a man was created to them, upon whose forehead it was written *EMeT*, as on the forehead of Adam. And the created one said to them: "If the Unique One, the Holy One, Blessed be He, [who] created Adam, when He wanted to kill [*le-hamit*] Adam, He erased a letter from *emet* and what remained is *MeT* [dead], even more so I would like to do it

[38] See *infra*, note 54.

[39] See *infra*, note 53 as well as notes 58–59 and accompanying text.

[40] This work is published in Abraham Epstein, *Beiträge zur jüdischen Altertumskunde* (Vienna, 1887), pp. 122–23.

> and you shall no longer create a man, so that people shall not err concerning him, as it happened in the generation of Enosh."[41] This is why Jeremiah said: "Cursed is the man who relies on Adam." The created man said to them: "Reverse the combination of the letters backwards." And they erased the *alef* from his forehead and he immediately turned into ashes.[42]

As expressed in *Seifer ha-Gematri'ot* the concern to which the *golem* gives voice is that he might be deified as, according to the midrashic tradition cited in this narrative, had previously occurred in the generation of Enosh when people prostrated themselves before Adam, believing that he was God because of his gargantuan height.

However, the same narrative is presented in a somewhat different manner by the anonymous author of a manuscript treatise titled *The Secret of the Name of 42 Letters*:

> We found in *Sefer ha-Bitaḥon* written by R. Yehudah (ben Bateirah) that Jeremiah, of blessed memory, was studying *Sefer Yeẓirah* alone. A voice came out and said to him: "Take a companion." He went to Sira his son and they studied [together] for three years in order to accomplish what was written. Then they that feared the Lord spoke one with the other. At the end of three years, when they wanted to combine the alphabets, according to the *Ẓeruf* [combination], the *Mikhlol* and the *Ma'amar*, a man was created, and on his forehead it was written, *YHVH Elohim Emet*. In the hand of that man there was a knife, and he was erasing the *alef* of the word *emet* and there remained *met*. Jeremiah rent his garment and said to him, "Why did you erase the *alef* of *emet?*" He answered him, "I will tell you a parable . . . Thus is God, when He created you in the image, likeness and form. Now, when you created a man like Him, the people will say that there is no God in the world but you." Jeremiah told him, "If so, how can we repair it [*mai takanteh*]?" He answered them, "Write the letters backwards on the dust that was thrown, by the intention of your heart, and do not think about the way of [its] honor or of its order [*tikkuno*] but do all this backwards." And they also did so and that man became before their eyes dust and ashes. Then Jeremiah said, "Indeed it is worthwhile to study these matters for the sake of knowing the power and dynamics of the creator of the world, but not in order to do [them]. You shall study them in order to comprehend and teach."[43]

[41] Cf. Rambam, *Hilkhot Avodah Zarah* 1:1. For an even more precise comparison with the generation of Enosh see Scholem, *On the Kabbalah*, p. 181.

[42] Translated by Idel, *Golem*, p. 64. See also the translation published in Scholem, *On the Kabbalah*, p. 179. The Hebrew text appears in the Hebrew version of Scholem's work, *Pirkei Yesod be-Havanat ha-Kabbalah ve-Samalehah*, trans. Joseph Ben-Shlomoh (Jerusalem, 1976), p. 400.

[43] Translated by Idel, *Golem*, p. 67. See also the translation published in Scholem, *On the Kabbalah*, p. 180. The Hebrew text appears in *Pirkei Yesod*, p. 401. The text of this work was

Whether or not successful cloning of a human being in the early years of the twenty-first century would have the same profound psychological impact as the creation of an awesome anthropoid in the days of Jeremiah or even in the thirteenth century is speculative. Neither polytheistic confusion nor deification of man appears to be likely in our day, although belief in the Deity's role as Creator of the universe, and of man in particular, may be weakened in the minds of some. Moreover, the concern voiced in this anonymous kabbalistic treatise is not reflected in authoritative halakhic sources. Nevertheless, there is a widespread perception that any attempt at human cloning would constitute extreme hubris on the part of man.

IV. IMPORT OF THE *GOLEM* LITERATURE

The rabbinic literature devoted to the *golem* is of importance to cloning with regard to another matter pertaining to cloning as well, *viz.*, in the halakhic status of a clone. In its broadest terms, the question is whether an anthropoid enjoys the halakhic status of a human being. Particular issues that have been addressed explicitly are whether destruction of an anthropoid is homicide, whether an anthropoid can be counted in a *minyan* and whether its corpse defiles in the manner of a human cadaver. Analogous questions have also been raised about animals created in a similar manner, e.g., may the meat of such an animal be cooked in milk and may the animal be offered as a sacrifice. The discussion of these questions with regard to anthropoids is only the first step in an analysis of the relevant halakhic issues since generation from human gametes, gestation in vitro as well as normal parturition, as will be shown, may significantly alter the conclusions. These discussions are, however, relevant to the analogous situation of a cloned embryo or an embryo fertilized in vitro that is also subsequently artificially incubated outside the mother's womb, as described by Aldous Huxley in his *Brave New World*.

In the course of Jewish history there have been numerous reports concerning the creation of a *golem* by various individuals.[44] In the annals of Halakhah,

published by David de Gunzburg, "La Cabale à la veille de l'apparition du Zohar," *Ha-Kedem*, vol. I (1907), p. 115.

See also Joseph Dan, *The Early Kabbalah* (New York, 1986), pp. 54–55 and Idel, *Golem*, p. 67. Cf. Gershom Scholem, "The *Golem* of Prague and the *Golem* of Rehovoth," *Commentary* (January 1966), p. 64.

44 See the various reports cited by Scholem, *On the Kabbalah*, pp. 158–204, and by Idel in his work, *Golem*. See also Byron L. Sherwin, *The Golem Legend: Origins and Implications* (New York, 1985). For accounts of the most widely known *golem* story, that of R. Judah Loew of Prague, see Yudl Rosenberg, *Nifla'ot Maharal* (Warsaw, 1909), trans. J. Neugroschel, *Yenne Velt: The Great Works of Jewish Fantasy and the Occult* (New York, 1976); Chaim Bloch, *Der Prager Golem* (Berlin, 1920), trans. H. Schneiderman, *The Golem of Prague* (Vienna, 1925); and Gershon Winkler, *The Golem of Prague* (New York, 1980).

most significant by far is the narrative of R. Zevi Ashkenazi. R. Zevi Ashkenazi, *Teshuvot Ḥakham Ẓevi*, no. 93, reports that his grandfather,[45] R. Elijah Ba'al Shem of Helm, had created a *golem*.[46] *Ḥakham Ẓevi*'s son, R. Jacob Emden, *She'ilat Ya'aveẓ*, vol. II, no. 82, adds that when the *golem* "grew stronger and greater because of the Divine Name written on a paper attached to his forehead," R. Elijah became afraid that the *golem* would wax harmful and destructive. R. Elijah therefore destroyed the creature by tearing the paper from the *golem*'s forehead, whereupon the *golem* fell to the ground as a lump of dust.[47]

Although the discussion is directed to an entirely different issue, *Ḥakham Ẓevi*, perhaps prompted by the fact that his grandfather subsequently destroyed the *golem* that he himself had created, remarks, *en passant*, that even if the *golem* is deemed human for other purposes, its destruction is not a violation of the prohibition against homicide. The basic assumption, that there is no attendant prohibition, is amply evidenced by R. Zeira's conduct with regard to the anthropoid created by Rava. The simplest explanation for R. Zeira's lack of concern in taking the life of the anthropoid is that such a creature is not deemed to be human – and perhaps not even an animal[48] – and hence can be destroyed with impunity. As will be noted later, this is indeed the position of the sixteenth-century kabbalist, R. Moses Cordovero, *Pardes Rimmonim*, ch. 24, sec. 10, as well as of the early seventeenth-century authority (and ancestor of *Ḥida*), R. Abraham Azulai, *Ḥesed le-Avraham, Ma'ayan Revi'i, nahar* 30. *Ḥesed le-Avraham* asserts that the vitality of a creature created by means of *Sefer Yeẓirah* is comparable to the "vitality of an animal" and that, since anthropoids do not enjoy the status of human beings,[49] their destruction

45 Idel, *Golem*, p. 229, note 22, observes that it is unlikely that R. Elijah was the grandfather of *Ḥakham Ẓevi* since the latter was born in 1660 while R. Elijah died in 1583. Idel assumes that the reference is to a great-grandfather.

46 A similar report regarding the same figure appears in late seventeenth-century Christian sources. See Scholem, *On the Kabbalah*, pp. 200–03. See also Idel, *Golem*, pp. 207–11.

47 See also R. Jacob Emden's account of the *golem* created by R. Elijah as presented in his *Megillat Sefer* (Warsaw, 5656), p. 4 and in his *Mitpaḥat Sefarim* (Altona, 5529), p. 45a.

48 If an anthropoid is not deemed to be human solely because it lacks a human soul it might nevertheless have the status of an animal. If, however, it is not a human because it does not have human progenitors it should, for the same reason, not be considered to be an animal. For a discussion of whether painless, but purposeless, killing of an animal involves the prohibition of cruelty to animals (*ẓa'ar ba'alei ḥayyim*), see *Contemporary Halakhic Problems*, vol. III, pp. 205–17.

49 R. Joseph Rosen, *Teshuvot Ẓofnat Pa'aneaḥ*, vol. II, no. 7 (Jerusalem, 5728), goes further in remarking that, for purposes of Halakhah, a creature produced by means of *Sefer Yeẓirah* has no cognizable existence and for that reason the anthropoid in question was commanded by R. Zeira to return to dust. If those comments are taken literally, it would follow, for example, that it would be permissible to cut the hair or pare the nails of a *golem* on *Shabbat*. Regarding creation of a *golem* on *Shabbat* see *infra*, note 65.

entails no transgression. *Ḥesed le-Avraham* was followed in this position by his descendant, R. Chaim Joseph David Azulai (*Ḥida*), *Maḥazik Berakhah*, *Oraḥ Ḥayyim* 55:1, and later in his *Mar'it he-Ayin*, *Sanhedrin* 65b.

However, *Ḥakham Ẓevi*, at least for the purpose of his initial discussion, assumes that an anthropoid does enjoy the status of a human being and hence was constrained to find an alternative justification for R. Zeira's conduct. *Ḥakham Ẓevi* cites the discussion of the Gemara, *Sanhedrin* 57b, with regard to feticide. The Gemara adduces Genesis 9:6, which is conventionally rendered "Whosoever sheds the blood of a man, by man shall his blood be shed." The Hebrew phrase "*ba-adam damo yishafekh*" in the verse "*shofekh dam ha-adam ba-adam damo yishafekh*" is readily translated in that manner, i.e., "by man shall his blood be shed." However, since the biblical text contains no commas and the word "*ba-adam*" can equally well be understood as meaning "within man," the verse can also be rendered "Whosoever sheds the blood of a man within a man, his blood shall be shed." For purposes of talmudic exegesis the verse is indeed understood as having the latter meaning. Hence the ensuing talmudic query: "Who is a 'man within a man'?" And the immediate response: "One must say this is a fetus in the mother's womb." That interpretation forms the basis for the Gemara's determination that feticide is a capital offense in the Noahide Code. *Ḥakham Ẓevi* alludes to that discussion in declaring that since an anthropoid is not formed in a woman's womb its destruction cannot constitute homicide.

Ḥakham Ẓevi's opinion regarding the destruction of an anthropoid was challenged by R. Gershon Leiner, popularly known as the *Radzyner Rebbe*, in his *Sidrei Taharot*, *Oholot* 5a. Acceptance of *Ḥakham Ẓevi*'s thesis would logically lead to the conclusion that, since Adam was not born of a human mother, Adam might have been murdered with impunity – a conclusion *Sidrei Taharot* regards as absurd, particularly since Adam was created by God as a human *par excellence*.

The major problem, however, is that the talmudic interpretation is not at all intended to be a literal reading of the scriptural passage but expresses an additional level of meaning reflecting the notion that the particular language in which the commandment is couched is designed to incorporate feticide within the parameters of the prohibition against homicide. The rabbinic interpretation may well be understood as inclusive rather than exclusive. As such, the rabbinic interpretation of the verse should be understood as having the effect of rendering its meaning: "Whosoever shall shed the blood of *even* a man within a man, his blood shall be shed." Or to put it differently, the exegetical interpretation is designed to expand the ambit of the prohibition to include "a man within a man," but does not ordain that characteristic as a necessary condition of applicability.

More significantly, the verse in question was addressed to Noah and forms part of the Noahide Code. The verse serves to elucidate the crime of homicide as integral to the Seven Commandments of the Sons of Noah. Murder as one of the 613 commandments of the Sinaitic Code binding upon Jews is prohibited on the basis of entirely different verses. Indeed, albeit with a number of highly significant exceptions, there is a plethora of authorities who maintain that, for Jews, feticide, although forbidden on other grounds, is not a form of homicide.[50] Those authorities clearly regard extension of the prohibition to encompass feticide as limited solely to the prohibitions that form part of the Noahide Code. Similarly, even if the verse is regarded as limiting the prohibition to the killing of a person born of a woman's womb, the limitation should also be regarded as applicable only to the Noahide Code.

The particular issue addressed by *Ḥakham Ẓevi* is whether the *golem* may be counted as one of the ten men necessary to constitute a *minyan*, i.e., a quorum for public prayer. In effect, the issue addressed by *Ḥakham Ẓevi* is not the anthropoid's status as a human being but his status as a Jew.[51] Indeed, although *Ḥakham Ẓevi*'s final position is somewhat ambiguous, the anthropoid's status as a human is taken for granted, as evidenced by the argument presented. *Ḥakham Ẓevi* cites the dictum recorded in *Sanhedrin* 19a: "He who rears an orphan in his home, Scripture considers it as if he had begotten him" and, without further elaboration, astonishingly concludes, "Likewise since [the *golem*] is the handiwork of the righteous he is included among the sons of Israel for the handiwork[52] of the righteous are their progeny." However, *Ḥakham Ẓevi* dismisses his own argument on the grounds that, were the anthropoid capable of providing any benefit (*to'elet*), e.g., were he qualified to serve as a member of a *minyan*, R. Zeira would not have been justified in destroying him.[53] The implication is that the *golem* was ineligible to serve as a member of a *minyan* because the *golem* shares neither the responsibilities nor the prerogatives of members of the Jewish community and hence that *Ḥakham Ẓevi* does not

[50] For a discussion of those sources see *Contemporary Halakhic Problems*, vol. I, pp. 326–39.

[51] *Ḥazon Ish, Yoreh De'ah* 116:1, accepts the possibility that a *golem* may be human, but denies that it can have the status of a Jew.

[52] The phrase "*ma'aseh yedeihem*" is employed by *Ḥakham Ẓevi* in the sense of "handiwork" or "artifacts." The source for this comment is apparently *Bereshit Rabbah* 30:6 and is cited by Rashi, Genesis 6:9. However, in that source the phrase is "*ma'asim tovim*," meaning "good deeds."

[53] R. Chaim Joseph David Azulai, *Mar'it ha-Ayin, Sanhedrin* 65b, dismisses this argument with the observation that R. Zeira would have been entirely justified in destroying the anthropoid because of a fear that he might wreak havoc. See also *infra*, notes 58–59.

regard a *golem* as Jewish.[54] Whether or not his concluding comment indicates that the *golem* is also not to be regarded as human is unclear.[55]

In his earlier cited responsum, *Ḥakham Ẓevi*'s son, R. Jacob Emden, questions his father's conclusion regarding the anthropoid's eligibility to be counted as a member of a *minyan*. *She'ilat Ya'avez* sees no reason why a *golem* endowed with auditory perception and capable of understanding words addressed to him should not be capable of speech as well and hence assumes that the anthropoid created by Rava was not only incapable of speech but was deaf as well. But, notes *She'ilat Ya'avez*, a deaf-mute cannot be included in a *minyan*. Accordingly, argues *She'ilat Ya'avez*, adjudication of the status of an anthropoid in that context is superfluous. The identical observation is made by R. Chaim Joseph David Azulai, *Birkei Yosef, Oraḥ Ḥayyim* 55:4. It would follow from these comments that there is no evidence to rebut *Ḥakham Ẓevi*'s original argument – assuming it is regarded as cogent in the first place – establishing the *golem*'s status as a Jew. *She'ilat Ya'avez*, however, concludes his responsum by citing an earlier authority, *Hesed le-Avraham, Ein Ya'akov, Ma'ayan Revi'i, nahar* 30, who comments that the vitality of a *golem* is that of an animal and hence the *golem* must be regarded as "an animal in the form of man" whose destruction

[54] R. Chaim Joseph David Azulai, *Birkei Yosef, Oraḥ Ḥayyim* 55:4, cites a letter of R. Judah Leib Katz, a son of the *Sha'ar Efrayim*, who finds support for the view that an anthropoid cannot be included in a *minyan* in the talmudic report that R. Eliezer chose to emancipate his slave in order to complete a quorum. Why did R. Eliezer not simply create a *golem*, queries this scholar. Since he did not do so, Rabbi Katz infers that a *golem* would have been ineligible to serve in that capacity. *Birkei Yosef* dismisses that argument for three reasons: (1) R. Eliezer may have refrained from creating an anthropoid as an act of piety; (2) creation of a *golem* requires extensive preparation and cannot be undertaken at will; (3) emancipation of a slave is simpler and preferable because it involves no transgression when undertaken for a valid purpose. *Birkei Yosef* notes conflicting authority with regard to the latter point. R. Chaim Pelaggi, *Ruaḥ Ḥayyim, Yoreh De'ah* 1:18, cites an earlier authority who asserts that a newly created anthropoid may have the status of a minor. Cf. *infra*, note 61 and accompanying text. *Ruaḥ Ḥayyim* observes that, according to that view, it follows that an animal created in a similar manner may not be offered as a sacrifice until the statutory eight-day period following birth has elapsed and cites an authority to whom that question was a matter of doubt.

[55] R. Chaim Eleazar Shapira, *Darkei Teshuvah, Yorah De'ah* 7:11, raises the question of whether an animal slaughtered by a properly supervised anthropoid may be eaten and cogently relates that issue to the question of whether a *golem* is deemed to be a human being. *Darkei Teshuvah* asserts that, according to *Ḥakham Ẓevi*, the anthropoid is human and hence an act of slaughter performed by an anthropoid renders the meat of the animal permissible. It is thus clear that *Darkei Teshuvah* assumes that *Ḥakham Ẓevi* regarded the anthropoid both as a human being and as a Jew. If so, it is unclear why the anthropoid cannot be counted in a *minyan*. If the reason is, as stated by R. Ẓadok haKohen of Lublin, because the anthropoid is not included in "speak to the children of Israel" as cited later in the text, the anthropoid should for the same reason be excluded from the category of individuals competent to perform ritual slaughter.

entails no transgression.[56] *Hesed le-Avraham*, and apparently *She'ilat Ya'avez* as well, maintain that a *golem* is not human.

Writing in the latter part of the nineteenth century, R. Judah Aszod, *Teshuvot Maharya*, vol. I, no. 26, asserts that *Hakham Zevi*'s original quandary regarding including an anthropoid as a member of a *minyan* must be understood as a question according to only one school of rabbinic thought. *Shulhan Arukh, Orah Hayyim* 55:6, rules that a person who is asleep may be counted as a member of the quorum of ten. *Bet Yosef*, in his commentary on the *Tur*, *ad locum*, attributes that view to his teacher, Mahari bei Rav. *Taz, Orah Hayyim* 55:4, takes sharp issue with that view and argues that the status of a sleeping person is inferior even to that of a minor. Referring to *Bet Yosef*'s own citation of a comment of the *Zohar*, *Taz* declares that the soul departs from a person during sleep with the result that a sleeping person is in a state of quasi-death and devoid of sanctity. In defense of the ruling of *Shulhan Arukh*, *Mahari Asad* declares that the comment of the *Zohar* must be understood as applying only to a person sleeping alone. When, however, there is a group of ten and the *Shekhinah* rests upon them the *Shekhinah* does not depart simply because one member of the group has fallen asleep. Under such circumstances, declares *Mahari Asad*, the soul of the sleeping person remains in his body.

Mahari Asad observes that, if a sleeping person cannot be counted as a member of a *minyan* because his soul has temporarily taken leave of his body as maintained by *Taz*, *a fortiori*, an anthropoid "in whom there is no soul at all, only an animating spirit" cannot be counted towards a *minyan*. Thus, he observes, *Hakham Zevi*, in formulating his question, must have assumed with conviction that the normative view is that of *Shulhan Arukh*, i.e., that a person may be counted towards a *minyan* even while asleep.

The ruling of *Hakham Zevi* and *She'ilat Ya'avez* disqualifying an anthropoid from being counted in a *minyan* and *She'ilat Ya'avez*' view that an anthropoid is not deemed to be a human being for purposes of Halakhah was challenged by R. Zadok ha-Kohen of Lublin, *Kuntres Divrei Halomot*, sec. 6.[57] As reflected in the title of the work, R. Zadok reports that the argument in its entirety occurred to him in a dream. The position espoused by *Hakham Zevi* and *She'ilat Ya'avez* is based upon the fact that R. Zeira destroyed the *golem* sent to him by Rava,

[56] *Hesed le-Avraham*'s view is followed by his descendant R. Chaim Joseph David Azulai, *Mahazik Berakhah, Orah Hayyim* 55:1, and *idem*, *Mar'it he-Ayin*, *Sanhedrin* 65b. See also R. Daniel Trani, *Ikkarei Dinim* (also cited as *Ikkarei ha-Dat*), *Orah Hayyim* 3:15. It is of interest to note that with reference to counting a *golem* in a *minyan*, *Mishnah Berurah* 55:4 cites *Ikkarei Dinim* together with *Hakham Zevi*.

[57] Published as an addendum to R. Zadok's *Resisei Lailah*. A translation of this material is provided by Idel, *Golem*, pp. 220–23.

an action those authorities deemed unthinkable were the *golem* to have been able to serve a worthwhile purpose such as being included in a *minyan*. R. Ẓadok, however, notes that it is in the nature of a *golem* continuously to grow and expand, as *She'ilat Ya'aveẓ* reports was the case with regard to the *golem* created by R. Elijah of Helm.[58] Interestingly, R. Ẓadok notes that the Gemara reports that R. Ḥanina and R. Oshia created their calf only on the eve of the Sabbath. Had they created it earlier in the week, conjectures R. Ẓadok, by *Shabbat* it would have grown much too large.[59] R. Ẓadok maintains that the *golem* created by Rava must have been created for some specific purpose not disclosed by the Gemara and was destroyed by R. Zeira because of the fear that as it continued to grow it would wreak havoc. It will be remembered that it was for that reason that R. Elijah of Helm destroyed the *golem* that he had created. Hence, argues R. Ẓadok, there is no evidence that an anthropoid should not be considered human.

Curiously, R. Ẓadok seems to accept *Ḥakham Ẓevi*'s original contention that the anthropoid is not only human but also a Jew because the anthropoid was created by a righteous Jew. Nevertheless, R. Ẓadok maintains the anthropoid is not endowed with a soul and hence is neither rewarded nor punished in the afterlife. Accordingly, he argues, when Moses is directed to transmit a commandment and addressed in the words "speak to the children of Israel," the admonition does not include an anthropoid.

It is remarkable that R. Ẓadok adopts this position while simultaneously asserting that we must assume that a *golem* is endowed with reason.[60]

58 Cf. *Bereshit Rabbah* 34:2, in which Adam is depicted as a *golem* "stretched out from one end of the world to the other," and *Bereshit Rabbah* 14:10, in which Adam is described as a *golem* extending in height from earth to heaven. It was only after Adam sinned that he was reduced to human proportions, although, according to the earlier cited *Sefer ha-Gematri'ot*, he remained enormous in height.

59 Cf. *Teshuvot ha-Rashba*, vol. 1, no. 413, who opines that the feat can be performed only on the sixth day of the week, the day on which animals were created.

60 Cf., however, R. Chaim Joseph David Azulai, *Maḥazik Berakhah, Oraḥ Ḥayyim* 55:1 and *idem, Mar'it he-Ayin, Sanhedrin* 65b, who declares that under no circumstances is it possible for man to create an anthropoid who is endowed with reason and ascribes that position to Maharsha, *Sanhedrin* 65b, as well. In *Mar'it he-Ayin* he declares that only God has the power to breathe "into his nostrils the breath of life," i.e., of reason, as described in Genesis 2:7. This is actually the earlier cited view of *Ḥesed le-Avraham*, although *Ḥesed le-Avraham* less categorically confines his statement to a depiction of an anthropoid created on the basis of *Sefer Yeẓirah*. Scholem, *On the Kabbalah*, pp. 198–99, and Idel, *Golem*, p. 55, cite sources that attribute this position to the early-day scholar, R. Shmuel he-Ḥasid, the father of R. Judah he-Ḥasid. Those sources associate that view with a hymnal phrase in the High Holy Day liturgy, namely, "Intelligence and speech are [the prerogative] of the Life of the Worlds."*Maḥazik Berakhah*'s categorical declaration that "the Sages have no power to endow [the anthropoid] with reason" makes it more difficult to understand R. Zeira's attempt to converse with the

Consistent with that view, he disputes *She'ilat Ya'avez*'s contention that an anthropoid cannot be considered for inclusion in a *minyan* by virtue of the fact that he is a deaf-mute. Developing a thesis that is more fully articulated in other sources,[61] R. Ẓadok declares that disqualification of a deaf-mute is not absolute. R Ẓadok adopts the view that a deaf-mute lacks legal capacity solely because, since he is deprived of the ability to communicate, he cannot develop intellectually. The anthropoid, however, contends R. Ẓadok, is created "as a mature man," and therefore it should be assumed that he is endowed with reason in a manner comparable to an adult.[62] In the case of an anthropoid, lack of speech, asserts R. Ẓadok, is to be attributed to the fact that it lacks "a portion of God from above." R. Ẓadok attributes the source of speech to the divine power breathed into Adam as recounted in the verse "and He breathed into his nostrils the breath of life" (Genesis 2:7) in accordance with Targum Onkelos' translation of "the breath of life" as "the speaking spirit (*ruaḥ memallela*)." But, according to R. Ẓadok, since the anthropoid is fully developed in every other way there is no reason to assume that his rational faculty is defective.

anthropoid as described in *Sanhedrin* 65b. According to *Maḥazik Berakhah*'s view, it must be assumed that R. Zeira did not immediately perceive that man cannot create a rational anthropoid and hence he could not conclude that the anthropoid did not have the status of a human until it became clear that the anthropoid lacked the power of speech.

R. Moses Cordovero, *Pardes Rimmonim*, ch. 34, sec. 10, ascribes a vitality to the *golem* higher than that of the animal soul but nevertheless not human. According to *Pardes Rimmonim*, the parts of which the creature is formed strive upward toward their source in the upper world and come closer to their source in that world than does an animal. According to *Pardes Rimmonim*, the *golem* does not die as an animal does but simply returns to its element, the earth. Accordingly, causing a *golem* to return to dust is not an act of murder. See Scholem, *On the Kabbalah*, pp. 194–95. *Pardes Rimmonim*'s position seems to be similar to, but not identical with, that of *Ḥesed le-Avraham*, who seems to equate the vitality of the *golem* with that of an animal. Cf., however, Scholem, *On the Kabbalah*, p. 194, note 4.

R. Judah Loew, *Ḥiddushei Aggadot Maharal me-Prague*, *Sanhedrin* 65b, similarly states that man cannot create an anthropoid capable of speech. Maharal makes this assertion on the basis of the curious argument that man cannot create his equal any more than God can create His equal.

On the other hand, a commentary on *Sefer Yeẓirah* of uncertain provenance but attributed to R. Sa'adia Ga'on speaks of the power to produce an anthropoid endowed with a soul. See Scholem, *On the Kabbalah*, p. 192. Probably of greater significance are the earlier cited sources that depict the *golem* created by Jeremiah and Ben Sira as endowed with speech. See *supra*, notes 40–43 and accompanying text. *Sefer ha-Bahir*, sec. 136, also indicates that, were it not for sins, man might create an anthropoid capable of speech.

61 For an analysis of the various views concerning this matter see *Contemporary Halakhic Problems*, vol. II, pp. 365–75.

62 With the exception of the source adduced by *Ruaḥ Ḥayyim*, as cited *supra*, note 54, no rabbinic writer has suggested that the anthropoid, upon creation, has the status of a newly born infant and must wait thirteen years before attaining legal capacity as an adult. See, however, *Likkutei Ḥever ben Ḥayyim*, cited in *Likkutei He'arot*, appended to *Teshuvot Ḥakham Ẓevi*, no. 93.

Rabbinic writers discuss various other halakhic aspects of the status of an artificial animal created by means of *Sefer Yeẓirah*. *Shelah, Parashat Va-Yeshev*, declares that an animal created in such a manner does not require ritual slaughter and, moreover, its *ḥelev* (fat from certain portions of the body, which in the case of sacrificial animals is offered on the altar) and blood are permissible.[63] R. Meir Leibush Malbim, in his commentary on Genesis 18:8, indicates that the meat of such a creature may be cooked and eaten with milk. Malbim employs that halakhic observation in explaining how it was possible for Abraham to serve the angels who visited him dairy foods together with the meat of a calf. According to Malbim, the calf that was served was created by Abraham by means of *Sefer Yeẓirah*, with the result that eating its meat together with milk was entirely permissible.[64] R. Ẓadok asserts that such an animal cannot be offered as a sacrifice since the biblical section defining the suitability of animals for sacrificial purposes begins with the phrase "When a bull or a sheep or a goat will be born" (Leviticus 22:27).[65]

It is evident that there are four[66] distinct views with regard to the status of a *golem*: *Ḥesed le-Avraham*, *She'ilat Ya'aveẓ* and possibly *Ḥakham Ẓevi* maintain that its status is that of a brute animal; R. Ẓadok ha-Kohen maintains that it is

63 This is also the position of *Teshuvot Sedei ha-Areẓ*, *Yoreh De'ah*, no. 1, and of *Ruaḥ Ḥayyim*, *Yoreh De'ah* 1:18. Cf., however, the anonymous interlocutor in *Teshuvot Sedei ha-Areẓ* and *Darkei Teshuvah*, *Yoreh De'ah* 7:11, who suggest that such an animal may require slaughter and its *ḥelev* and blood may be forbidden because of *mar'it ayin*, i.e., because an onlooker may suspect that a transgression is taking place. This is also the position of the author of *Darkei Teshuvah*, R. Chaim Eleazar Shapira, as expressed in his *Divrei Torah*, *mahadura revia'ah*, sec. 75. *Ikkarei Dinim*, *Yoreh De'ah* 1:22, remarks that "perhaps" the creature requires ritual slaughter because of *mar'it ayin*. See also *infra*, note 64.

64 Interestingly, Malbim observes that the onlooker would not have suspected a violation of the prohibition against milk and meat because it was commonly known that Abraham created animals in this manner. It should be remembered that the final section of *Sefer Yeẓirah* reports that Abraham mastered the methods therein described and succeeded in performing acts of creation. See Scholem, *On the Kabbalah*, pp. 169–72.

65 Rosh, *Pesaḥim* 10:13, and *Shelah*, *Vavei ha-Amudim*, ch. 20, sec. 16, assume as a matter of course that it is forbidden to write a Torah scroll on *Shabbat* by means of invocation of the Divine Name. *Teshuvot Ḥatam Sofer*, vol. VI, no. 29, regards such an act as constituting a rabbinic infraction. See also *Teshuvot Yad Yiẓḥak*, vol. I, no.35.

A Sephardic authority, R. Abraham Anakava, *Teshuvot Kerem Ḥemed*, vol. I, *Oraḥ Ḥayyim*, no. 3, discusses in great detail the question of whether it is permissible to create a *golem* on *Shabbat*.

See also R. Moshe Sternbuch, *Mo'adim u-Zemanim* (Jerusalem, 5431), vol. IV, no. 319, as well as sources attributed to R. Yosef Shalom Eliashiv, *Moriah* (Elul 5758), p. 65. See also *supra*, note 49.

66 As noted *supra*, note 60, *Pardes Rimmonim* actually represents a fifth view since he regards the *golem* as a loftier being than a brute animal. Nevertheless, insofar as the halakhic status of such a creature is concerned, there is no difference between his position and that of *Ḥesed le-Avraham*.

human in every sense; Maharsha and R. Gershon Leiner maintain that only an anthropoid endowed with speech is human; *Ẓofnat Pa'aneaḥ* maintains that an anthropoid does not at all have the status of a living creature.

V. CLONING AND SPECIES IDENTITY

As stated at the outset, discussion of the halakhic status of a *golem* may appear to be esoteric and irrelevant to the status of a cloned animal or person. That presumption, however, is incorrect. The *golem* literature demonstrates the unassailability of the status of a cloned human as a human being according to the view of Maharsha, R. Ẓadok ha-Kohen and R. Gershon Leiner.[67] In order to establish the humanity of a human clone according to the authorities who espouse a conflicting view of the status of an anthropoid it is necessary to distinguish between a clone and a *golem*.[68]

The crucial distinction between a *golem* and a clone is that a *golem* is created, if not *ex nihilo*, then from mere dust, but clearly lacks a human progenitor. A human clone, although the product of asexual reproduction, does have a human progenitor. There is no evidence that Halakhah assigns a living creature membership in a particular species solely on the basis of sexual reproduction or on the basis of the identity of both parents as members of a common species. On the contrary, Halakhah is cognizant of the existence of interspecies and attributes to the progeny the identity of the species of the mother. Whether the identity of the father, and with it membership in the father's species as well, is to be attributed to offspring produced by interbreeding is a matter of talmudic controversy.

Identification as a member of a species is best summed up in a pithy comment attributed to R. Chaim Soleveitchik. It is reported that R. Chaim explained a certain halakhic concept by posing the following query: Why is a horse a horse? Is it a horse because it manifests certain characteristics that are necessary conditions of being a horse, or is a horse a horse because its mother was a horse? The answer is that a horse is a horse because its mother

[67] This seems to be true for R. Chaim Joseph David Azulai as well. *Ḥida* declares that a *golem* is not human because it is impossible under any circumstances for man to create an anthropoid endowed with reason. A product of homologous reproduction would undoubtedly be endowed with reason. As such, it must be regarded as created by God – albeit with human cooperation, as is the case with sexual reproduction – and hence, according to *Ḥida*, such a being would be entirely human in nature.

[68] Since they make no specific mention of an anthropoid endowed with reason, it is possible, but not demonstrable, that those scholars would concede that a *golem* created by man and possessing reason is human.

was of that species. For that reason the Mishnah, *Bekhorot* 5b, declares that the offspring of a kosher animal is kosher even if it has the appearance and physical attributes of a non-kosher animal and, conversely, the offspring of a non-kosher animal is non-kosher even if it has the appearance and physical attributes of a kosher animal. Thus identity as a member of a particular species is determined not by distinguishing characteristics, but by birth.

Applied to the human species, it may well be that humans differ from other members of the animal kingdom by virtue of defining characteristics such as being featherless bipeds or being endowed with reason, yet the progeny of beings categorized as human by virtue of having been endowed with those attributes at the time of Creation are also human even if the progeny lack those characteristics.

Similarly, R. Elchanan Wasserman remarks several times in his writings that, although the concept of *yoẓei* (outgrowth) is generally associated with the status of food products, it does not represent a novel rule limited to determining the permitted or prohibited nature of a foodstuff for purposes of the dietary code. Rather, asserts R. Elchanan, any thing emitted by, or proceeding from, a particular entity has the status of the entity that created it. Thus, the concept of *yoẓei* serves as the principle for determining identity as a member of a species, with such determination of identity having consequences for the resolution of issues of religious law.[69]

The term *yoẓei* used in the foregoing is not to be understood in its narrow halakhic sense according to which, for example, the milk of a non-kosher animal is forbidden as *yoẓei*. Halakhah distinguishes between the prohibition against eating the meat of a non-kosher animal and its milk, which is prohibited on the basis of an independent and less severe prohibition. The concept as employed herein is best reflected in a comment of Rashi, *Ḥullin* 90a, s.v. *alma*, in which Rashi notes that a prohibition attendant upon an embryo in an early stage of gestation is temporally prior to the actualization of the prohibition against eating the sciatic sinew that is triggered only during a later stage of gestation (*viz.*, upon development of the sciatic sinew) and explains that the first prohibition is regarded as having temporal priority even with regard to fetal tissue produced later in the gestational period. Thus Rashi asserts that the prohibition against partaking of the flesh of sacrificial animals devolves upon an embryo within the womb of a sacrificial animal and is regarded as preempting the further prohibition attendant upon the subsequently developing sciatic sinew. That priority carries over even to tissue that clearly develops

[69] See *Koveẓ He'arot*, no. 33, sec. 8 and no. 59, sec. 12; *Koveẓ Inyanim*, *Ḥullin* 17a; and *Koveẓ Shi'urim*, vol. I, *Pesaḥim*, sec. 120.

subsequently.[70] Rashi's comment reflects the notion that, for the purposes of halakhic status, tissue produced as a result of natural growth and maturation is regarded as having the same identity as the tissue from which it is generated.

The concept underlying Rashi's comment is readily discernible in the very nature of the prohibition against eating the flesh of forbidden species. An adult animal is much larger and heavier than it was at the time of birth. Yet a person who consumes any part of the flesh of the adult animal is subject to the penalty of lashes. Were the additional weight acquired by the animal regarded as mere *yoẓei* comparable to its milk the penalty of lashes would be inappropriate. The conclusion to be deduced is that any part of the animal resulting from natural growth and development of the animal itself is endowed with the same halakhic identity as the nascent animal from which it developed.[71] The same principle explains why the progeny of an animal is endowed with the halakhic status of its progenitor rather than as mere *yoẓei*.[72]

Thus, there can be no question that, for example, a sheep cloned from a cell of another sheep and gestated within the womb of a ewe has the halakhic status of a sheep. Similarly, a human cloned from the cell of another human and gestated within the womb of a human female is a human being. It would appear that the same conclusions with regard to species identity would apply to a cloned animal or to a person who develops artificially in a laboratory incubator, with a possible exception in the latter case for the punishment of the perpetrator of an act of homicide directed against such a person.[73]

The question that must be addressed is the status of an animal cloned from a cell of an animal of one species but nurtured in the womb of a female of another species. For example, what is the status of an animal cloned from the cell of a pig but gestated in the womb of a cow or a ewe? Is the offspring, in effect, a kosher pig?

70 *Tosafot*'s disagreement with Rashi should be regarded as limited in nature by virtue of the fact that the sinew, according to *Tosafot*, is regarded, not as another stage in the development of the flesh of the embryo, but as a totally novel structure arising, as it were, *sui generis*.

71 Philosophers have long struggled with the problem of identity reflected in the phenomenon of an infant who becomes a mature adult but is regarded as one and the same person despite the fact that the physical components of the adult are clearly not present in the infant. For a discussion of theories advanced to resolve this problem see "Personal Identity," *Encyclopedia of Philosophy* (New York, 1972), vol. VI, pp. 95–107. See also J. David Bleich, "The Problem of Identity in Rashi, Rambam and the Tosafists," *The Philosophical Quest: Of Philosophy, Ethics, Law and Halakhah* (2013), pp. 273–303.

72 The comments of *Avnei Nezer, Yoreh De'ah*, no. 75, secs. 7–8, in connection with the classification of a bird as a member of a particular species despite the fact that the egg from which it develops is halakhically considered to have become putrid are helpful in illuminating this concept.

73 See *supra*, note 50 and accompanying text and *Contemporary Halakhic Problems*, vol. IV, p. 240, note 10.

Elsewhere,[74] it has been argued that Halakhah recognizes parturition as generating a maternal relationship. Presumably, that is the case not only for an individual maternal–filial relationship but for species identification as well since, as has been shown, species identity is a concomitant of maternal identity.

Nevertheless, if the position that *ḥosheshin le-zera ha-av* – that consideration is given to the seed of the father – be accepted, the offspring must be regarded as a member of the two separate species – in the example given, part pig, part cow or part sheep. Thus, *Shulḥan Arukh, Yoreh De'ah* 28:3, as amplified by *Shakh, Yoreh De'ah* 28:7, rules that the progeny of a stag and a ewe has doubtful status as a "part deer" because the question *ḥosheshin le-zera ha-av* is an unresolved halakhic issue.

It would appear that the principle of *ḥosheshin le-zera ha-av* is not founded on the fact that the father literally contributes *zera* (or sperm in a literal sense), but upon whether the father's donation of chromosomes or perhaps even of cytoplasm is of sufficient halakhic significance to cause the developing embryo to be regarded as the "*yoẓei*" or "outgrowth" of the father. If so, the principle of *ḥosheshin le-zera ha-av* is applicable to any and all sources of genetic material that contribute to the development of an animal. Accordingly, from the viewpoint of Halakhah, the animal, male or female, from which the cloned cell is taken is regarded as the "father" regardless of the organ from which the cell is taken.[75] In the case of human cloning, *ḥosheshin le-zera ha-av* would render the person from whom the nucleus is taken a "parent"[76] whether the individual is a male or a female.

74 For a discussion of the sources upon which this conclusion is predicated see *Contemporary Halakhic Problems*, vol. II, pp. 91–93.

75 More problematic is the status of a clone produced by removing the nucleus of a cell derived from an animal of one species, inserted in the cytoplasm of a cell of an animal of a second species and gestated by an animal of a third species. The halakhic issue is whether the principle of *ḥosheshin le-zera ha-av* extends to a "father" who contributes non-genetic material.

76 If the individual from whom the cell is taken is a male, his status is clearly that of a "father." If the individual is a female, it would be reasonable to assume that her status is that of a "mother" and that the clone, in effect, has two mothers. This assumption is based upon the premise that *ḥosheshin le-zera ha-av* is a principle concerning parenthood rather than with regard to paternity specifically.

There are numerous halakhic differences attendant upon status as a "father" or "mother." The most obvious and also the most theoretical is whether the admonition required for capital punishment for "wounding" must be couched in language warning against wounding a father or wounding a mother. Even were it possible to impose capital punishment subsequent to the lapse of the Great Sanhedrin, the question would remain theoretical since *ḥosheshin le-zera ha-av* remains an unresolved halakhic issue.

The issue is more actual with regard to whether a paternal or a maternal sibling relationship exists between the clone and other progeny of the clonor. Levirate obligations and the effectiveness of *ḥaliẓah* as a means of nullifying the levirate links are limited to brothers sharing a single father but not to brothers sharing a single mother. Thus, if a female donor of a nucleus

Although at present the matter is in the realm of science fiction, it must be freely conceded that this analysis yields a number of conclusions that may be counterintuitive. Offspring produced from a cloned cell of a monkey or chimpanzee implanted in a human womb, although having both the genotype and phenotype of an animal, would be regarded as human for purposes of Jewish law. It is indeed evident from the discussion of the Gemara, *Niddah* 23b, that an animal-like creature born of a human mother is regarded as a human being.[77] Conversely, a cell cloned from a human and gestated within the womb

were to be regarded as a "father" rather than a mother, levirate obligations would exist if two such male clones were produced and one of them died without issue.

There are also differences regarding consanguineous relationships. For example, a marital relationship with the mother of one's maternal grandfather is rabbinically forbidden but such a relationship with the grandmother of a maternal grandfather is permitted. However, maternal grandmothers in the female line are prohibited no matter how many generations they are removed. See *Shulḥan Arukh, Even ha-Ezer* 15:2–3. Hence the son of a woman cloned from the nucleus of a female would be permitted to marry the donor's grandmother if the donor is deemed to be a "father" but not if the donor is deemed to be a "mother."

R. Joseph Babad, *Minḥat Ḥinnukh*, no. 189, tentatively suggests that, if a hermaphrodite sires a male child and then has a sexual relationship with the child involving the father's female organs, the parties may be liable for incest between a son and his "mother" and also suggests that if the hermaphrodite father engages in a male homosexual relationship with the child they may be liable for incest as well as for homosexual activity. *Minḥat Ḥinnukh* certainly suggests that gender itself, rather than the male or female sexual act, may determine motherhood or fatherhood. However, in applying the principle of *ḥosheshin le-zera ha-av* it is not necessary to resort to *Minḥat Ḥinnukh*'s hypothesis. *Ḥosheshin le-zera ha-av* simply results in recognition of the non-gestational parent as a parent by virtue of application of the more general principle of *yoẓei*. It then seems reasonable to assume that, if the "parent" is a female, her status is that of a "mother" even if the result is that the child has two mothers. Unlike the case of the androgynous father who sires a child, there is no apparent reason to convey the status of a "father" upon the female donor. On the other hand, one might insist that a non-gestational parent is, by definition, a "father" rather than a "mother." That hypothesis is certainly contradicted by *Minḥat Ḥinnukh*'s speculative comments.

77 The Gemara clearly recognizes the theoretical possibility of the converse, of a human-like creature being born to an animal. If born to a member of a kosher species, the Gemara questions whether or not the offspring may be slaughtered for food since, although it possesses a "hoof," it does not have the characteristic split hoof of a kosher species. From the very formulation of the question it is evident that the Gemara did not regard a creature of this sort as enjoying the status of a human being.

The principle that identity of the mother as a human determines the status of her progeny regardless of the physical characteristics of the offspring might appear to be contradicted by a discussion of the Palestinian Talmud, *Niddah* 3:2. Describing hypothetical human offspring, the Palestinian Talmud states:

> Suppose it is entirely human but its face is animal-like and it reads from the Torah. Can one say to it, "Come and be slaughtered"? Suppose it is entirely animal-like but its face is human and it plows the field. Can we say to it "Come and perform *ḥaliẓah* or levirate marriage"?

On the surface, the Palestinian Talmud seems to declare that the human status, or absence thereof, of a creature having mixed physical characteristics should be determined on the basis

of a primate, despite being endowed with both the genotype and phenotype of a human, would, on the basis of the halakhic principle of *ḥosheshin le-zera ha-av*, have the halakhic status of a doubtful human being.

One additional point should be made about the status of a cloned human being. A clone acquires human status by virtue of the fact that it is a *yoẓei* of a human being, i.e., by virtue of its generation from human tissue. Nevertheless, it seems quite evident that, if a clone is produced from a cell of a male, the male does not thereby fulfill the biblical commandment to procreate. Stated differently, a male cannot fulfill his obligation to procreate by siring a clone. The birth of a child *sine concubito* as exempting the father from further biblical obligation to procreate has been discussed elsewhere.[78] Although some authorities disagree, the majority of rabbinic decisors rule that a male is discharged from further obligation even if the child is not conceived as a result of intercourse. Nevertheless, it would seem quite strange to extend that notion to the case of a childless person who creates an anthropoid by means of metaphysical methods gleaned from *Sefer Yeẓirah*.[79] It seems cogent to assume that, even if a sexual act is not required, nevertheless, the children whose birth is the subject of the commandment are those produced from male semen.[80] In context, the command "be fruitful and multiply" is formulated in

of the creature's rational capacity. However, *Pnei Mosheh*, in his commentary *ad locum*, points out that the statement is made in an *ad absurdum* vein, and its import is to assert that such questions could not arise because such a creature cannot survive for any period of time. The creature's lack of viability is directly relevant to the purely technical question of whether the mother is subject to the impurity associated with childbirth. That issue is a matter of controversy between the Sages and R. Meir, as is recorded in the Mishnah that serves as the focus of the discussion.

Notice must also be taken of the controversy recorded in the Mishnah, *Kelayim* 8:5, regarding whether creatures known as *adnei ha-sadeh* defile as humans. It may be suggested that the crux of the controversy is whether the creatures in question are anomalous descendants of humans, presumably as a result of genetic mutation, or an independent animal species. However, Rabbenu Shimshon, in his commentary *ad locum*, cites a comment of the Palestinian Talmud that *adnei ha-sadeh* are creatures tied to the ground by a structure resembling an umbilical cord and that, on the basis of rabbinic exegesis, R. Jose, whose opinion is recorded in the Mishnah, regards them as grouped together with humans solely for purposes of ritual defilement.

78 *Contemporary Halakhic Problems*, vol. IV, p. 240, note 9 and *Bioethical Dilemmas: A Jewish Perspective* (New York, 1998), vol. I, pp. 251–53. Exemption from further obligation to procreate is a concomitant of recognition of a paternal relationship with regard to a child born *sine concubito*.

79 If, contrary to what is here stated, it is to be assumed that even creation of an anthropoid by means of *Sefer Yeẓirah* satisfies this requirement it should then follow that in cloning it is the physician or technician who performs the cloning procedure who fulfills the obligation of procreation rather than the passive donor of the cell.

80 R. Eliezer Waldenberg, *Ẓiẓ Eli'ezer*, vol. XV, no. 45, has advanced a similar position with regard to in vitro fertilization. It is his contention that the many authorities who maintain that a sexual act is not necessary for fulfillment of the commandment with regard to procreation maintain that position only because both production of the gametes and fertilization of the

the plural in the Hebrew even though it is binding only upon the male and is also immediately preceded by the phrase "male and female did He create them."[81] It would thus seem that, even if actual cohabitation is not required, the commandment is nevertheless fulfilled only if the child is the product of gametes contributed by both the male and the female.[82] If so, for example, birth of a child cloned from a cell taken from the cheek would not release the donor from further biblical obligation.

VI. POTENTIAL HARM TO THE CLONE

Although, from the vantage of Jewish tradition, animal cloning presents no ideological or halakhic problem, the same cannot be said about the cloning of a human being. The ethical implications of fetal experimentation, which, by its very nature, may result in the birth of a defective neonate, were analyzed some time ago by Professor Paul Ramsey.[83] In the early days of in vitro fertilization Professor Ramsey argued that it represented an immoral experiment upon a possible future life, since no researcher can exclude the possibility that he may do irreparable damage to the child-to-be. In the words of Professor Ramsey: "We ought not to choose for another the hazards he must bear, while choosing at the same time to give him life in which to bear them and to suffer our chosen experimentations."[84]

This argument is no less applicable to homologous reproduction than to artificial conception and is consistent with the norms of Torah ethics. Jewish

ovum are entirely natural. *Ẓiẓ Eli'ezer* contends that in vitro fertilization, which he describes as effecting a change "in the order of creation," is entirely different and that as an "unnatural" form of procreation it cannot lead to fulfillment of the *miẓvah*. That position is challenged by R. Avigdor Nebenzahl, *Assia*, no. 34 (Tishri 5743), cited by Abraham S. Abraham, *Nishmat Avraham, Even ha-Ezer* 1:6, note 5, sec. 3, on the grounds that, despite the "unnatural" externality of in vitro fertilization, the intrinsic physiological processes involved in fertilization and conception are entirely natural. That certainly is not the case with regard to cloning.

81 In his tentative assertion that a *golem* may be counted towards a *minyan* because "He who receives an orphan in his home, Scripture considers it as if he had begotten him" and because "the deeds of the righteous are their progeny," *Ḥakham Ẓevi* certainly did not intend to intimate that the commandment of *peru u-revu* can be fulfilled by performing good deeds or even by raising an orphan in one's home.

82 An intriguing problem is presented in the hypothetical case in which the cloned cell is a male sperm. In such a situation the genetic material of the sperm would replace the nucleus of the ovum, but the remaining cytoplasm of the female gamete would enter into the reproduction process. If such a procedure ever becomes possible, the child will not really be a clone since it will possess only half of a full complement of genes, but that is not a matter of halakhic relevance.

83 Paul Ramsey, "Shall We 'Reproduce'?", *Journal of the American Medical Association*, vol. 220, no. 10 (June 5, 1972), pp. 1346–50, and vol. 220, no. 11 (June 12, 1972), pp. 1480–85; and *idem*, *The Ethics of Fetal Research* (New Haven, CT, 1975).

84 Paul Ramsey, *Journal of the American Medical Association*, vol. 220, no. 11, p. 135.

law does not sanction abortion motivated solely by a desire to eliminate a defective fetus, nor does it sanction sterile marriage as a means of preventing transmission of hereditary disorders. However, it does discourage marriages that would lead to the conception of such children. The Gemara, *Yevamot* 64b, states that a man should not marry into an epileptic or leprous family, i.e., a family in which three members have suffered from those diseases. This declaration obviously represents a eugenic measure designed to prevent the birth of defective children. It follows, *a fortiori*, that Judaism would view with opprobrium overt intervention in natural processes that might cause defects in the fetus.

There is some question whether the Gemara's negative statement with regard to entering into a marital relationship with a woman whose family has a history of leprosy or epilepsy represents a formal interdiction or simply constitutes sound eugenic advice. The talmudic dictum is presented in the ambiguous form "*lo yisa adam*," which may be understood either as an imperative, "a person dare not," or as having a much weaker prudential meaning, "a person ought not." The dictum is recorded in the same language by Rambam, *Hilkhot Isurei Bi'ah* 21:30, and by *Shulḥan Arukh, Even ha-Ezer* 2:7. Unfortunately, there is scant discussion of this statement either in the talmudic commentaries or in commentaries upon Rambam or *Shulḥan Arukh*. However, the formulation employed by *Tur Shulḥan Arukh, ad locum*, may be instructive. The Gemara defines a family of epileptics or of lepers as a family in which there have been three occurrences of the disease. In recording that provision *Tur* adds that if there have been only two such occurrences "it is permissible [to marry]." Employment in this context of the term "*shari*" or "it is permissible" would seem to indicate that in a situation involving a family in which there have been three such occurrences the marriage is not merely imprudent but impermissible.[85]

It should also be noted that the Gemara, on the very same page on which this statement is presented, employs almost identical language in declaring that a twice-widowed woman should not marry a third time for fear that her third husband will meet an untimely death as well. The consensus among early-day authorities is that such a marriage is not merely ill advised, but is prohibited.[86] It would be cogent to assume that the Gemara has herein recorded two separate but parallel rabbinic edicts, one based upon concern for the life of the prospective husband, the other based upon concern for the well-being of

85 This also appears to be the understanding of R. Samuel Ehrenfeld, *Teshuvot Ḥatan Sofer*, no. 137.

86 See *Shulḥan Arukh, Even ha-Ezer* 9:1 and commentaries thereto; cf., however, *Oẓar ha-Poskim, Even ha-Ezer* 9:1, sec. 1.

prospective issue of the marriage. R. Isaac Schmelkes, *Teshuvot Bet Yiẓḥak, Even ha-Ezer*, vol. I, no. 46, sec. 3, strives to show that the prohibition against marrying a woman who has buried two husbands is rabbinic in nature. That is also the position of *Besamim Rosh*, no. 276.[87] However, numerous authorities, including *Teshuvot Ketav Sofer, Even ha-Ezer*, no. 13 and *Teshuvot Bet Shlomoh, Even ha-Ezer*, no. 18, maintain that, in light of the danger involved, the prohibition is biblical in nature.[88] Moreover, Ritva, in his commentary on the talmudic discussion, indicates that the prohibition against marrying a twice-widowed woman is subsumed under the prohibition against suicide. Since marrying a woman who stems from a family of epileptics or a family of lepers, even if formally prohibited, is presumably banned only by rabbinic decree,[89] no comparison can be drawn between the negative statement regarding such marriages and the statement decrying marriage to a twice-widowed woman if it is accepted that the latter prohibition is biblical in nature.

On the other hand, Rambam, *Teshuvot Pe'er ha-Dor*, no. 156, cited by *Kesef Mishneh, Hilkhot Isurei Bi'ah* 21:31, maintains not only that there is no prohibition against entering into marriage with a twice-widowed woman but that such a union does not even pose an intrinsic danger. Rambam understands the Gemara's negative attitude as based entirely upon the fear that people experience in such situations and the resultant harm that can be engendered even by psychological causes. Hence, if the parties are sanguine with regard to the matter, Rambam sees no reason to discourage, much less prohibit, the marriage. Nevertheless, Rambam does take the genetic danger of epilepsy and leprosy seriously as evidenced by his unqualified statement in *Hilkhot Isurei Bi'ah* 21:30. Accordingly, for Rambam, as well, there is no theoretical parallel between the Gemara's statement concerning twice-widowed women and women from families with a history of epilepsy or leprosy.

Be this as it may, as noted earlier, the sole rabbinic source to offer a concrete basis for even an inferential conclusion is *Tur Shulḥan Arukh* and that conclusion is not challenged by evidence from any other source. Nevertheless, acceptance of the fact that the Sages promulgated a eugenic ordinance in order to prevent occurrences of epilepsy and leprosy does not entail the conclusion

87 For additional sources that subscribe to this view see *Oẓar ha-Poskim, Even ha-Ezer* 9:1, sec. 1.

88 For additional sources maintaining that the prohibition is biblical in nature see *Oẓar ha-Poskim, Even ha-Ezer* 9:1, sec. 1.

89 Although "wounding" or causing harm to another person even indirectly must be regarded as biblically forbidden, it is unlikely that causing such harm to an unborn child who would otherwise not be born is included in the prohibition against harming a fellow man. Were that to be the case it would necessarily follow that all unions likely to result in progeny suffering from any genetic defect would be forbidden.

that they prohibited any and every marriage carrying a greater than normal risk of hereditary defects in potential progeny,[90] much less that they established a prohibition against artificial forms of reproduction that carry with them such risks. On the contrary, rabbinic ordinances in general are not paradigmatic; their ambit is limited to that which is explicitly proscribed.

Nevertheless, such prohibitions are reflective of underlying policy considerations. The concern in this case was clearly the prevention of congenital anomalies. There is little question that were the Sages legislating in response to contemporary circumstances and in possession of scientific information available to us they would have targeted other genetic anomalies. Given the values they so clearly espoused there is strong reason to suppose that they would have decried fetal experimentation and human cloning because of the inherent danger of producing congenital defects. It must also be recognized that birth outside of a family unit carries with it the potential for psychological burden. Clones are likely to suffer even greater psychological problems. Since serious psychological problems are as real and as burdensome as physical defects it is likely that the Sages would have viewed their imposition upon as yet unborn children with disfavor.

This consideration notwithstanding, the prohibition against causing harm to a fellow human being admits of some exceptions. Accordingly, there are conceivable situations in which an unborn life may be burdened with potential defects in order to achieve an overriding purpose.

It must be emphasized that, despite its tragic nature, overcoming infertility does not warrant causing harm to another. It has been contended that the therapeutic exemption to the prohibition against "wounding" is not limited to "wounding" oneself or allowing a physician to perform a surgical procedure in order to benefit the subject of the procedure but includes even an act of "wounding" performed upon an individual who himself or herself derives no personal benefit from the assault.[91] Nevertheless, in no way does that line of reasoning justify the potential harm to a fetus that may occur in the course of cloning. Cloning is not restorative in nature. The process neither cures a malady nor restores a dysfunctional organ to its intended purpose. The effect of cloning is to provide a child for a couple to raise and thereby satisfy a deeply felt human need. Cloning, particularly since it does not fulfill the commandment to "be fruitful and multiply," is, from the vantage of Jewish law, analogous

90 Cf. *Teshuvot Ḥatan Sofer*, no. 137, who appears to assert that such marriages are prohibited in all situations in which there have been three occurrences of any serious disease deemed to be hereditary.

91 See *Contemporary Halakhic Problems*, vol. IV, pp. 302–09.

to adoption. Adoption ameliorates the pain arising from infertility, but does not remedy the underlying physical cause. An adopted child may be loved and cherished, but adoption is not a "cure" for infertility. Neither adoption nor cloning can be accorded the halakhic status of a "cure." Hence it must be concluded that, if cloning is otherwise regarded by Jewish teaching as immoral, it cannot be sanctioned as a means of alleviating the effects of infertility. It is almost superfluous to add that this is so even if cloning is contemplated in order to preserve the family line of a Holocaust survivor who has no other living relatives.[92]

It has also been suggested in some quarters that cloning may be morally acceptable in situations in which the sole child of parents who have become infertile develops a terminal disease. By means of cloning, the parents could use a cell obtained from the child to create another child who would be an exact replica of the child they are about to lose. However, tragic as such cases may be, there is nothing in those circumstances halakhically to distinguish them from more usual situations of infertility.

VII. MORAL AND LAUDABLE PROCEDURES

Nevertheless, there are some rare situations in which cloning, despite the risks, may be regarded as moral and even laudable. Despite the contrary view of some early-day authorities, the overwhelming consensus of rabbinic opinion is that restrictions governing interpersonal relationships, including the prohibitions against theft and "wounding," are treated no differently from purely religious prohibitions and are suspended in the face of danger to human life.[93]

There have been unfortunate cases of children afflicted with leukemia whose only chance of survival is a bone marrow transplant. To be successful, a donor must be genetically compatible, otherwise the transplant will be rejected. When bone marrow of family members is incompatible, finding a suitable match is exceedingly difficult. There have been cases of the mother of such a child becoming pregnant in the hope that the newly born child will be a suitable donor. However, the statistical probability that the child will be a compatible donor is only twenty-five percent. If cloning were available, parents, in these rare situations, could clone the ill child. The newly born

92 Cf. *Clone*, p. 17.

93 The most frequent discussion of this issue in a medical context is in conjunction with post-mortem dissection of a corpse. For a survey of the conflicting positions regarding this matter see J. David Bleich, *Judaism and Healing: Halakhic Perspectives*, augmented edition (Jersey City, NJ, 2002), pp. 202–08.

infant would be disease-free but would be genetically identical to its afflicted sibling. Medically, the child would be an ideal donor.

There may well be other forms of research requiring cloning designed to find a cure for disease that may benefit individuals who are in the category of a *holeḥ le-faneinu*, an individual for whom the danger and potential benefit is regarded as actual rather than merely hypothetical. Under such limited circumstances – and only in such circumstances – human cloning, when scientifically prudent and undertaken with appropriate safeguards, may be deemed appropriate and halakhically sound.

More significantly, cloning technology may prove to be extremely beneficial in cell and tissue therapy. Embryonic stem cells have the ability to differentiate into any cell type and, in theory, could be produced from human blastocysts. Perfection of cloning procedures would make it possible for a person to provide the nucleus of his own cell to replace the nucleus of a donor egg. Stem cells could then be taken from the developing blastocyst and induced to differentiate in culture.[94] Those cells would be genetically identical to those of the person from whom the nucleus was taken with the result that cell and tissue replacement would be possible without the problems of rejection currently attendant upon transplantation. Rejection of transplants occurs because the body's immune system recognizes the transplanted tissue as foreign. Cloned tissue is genetically identical to the tissue from which it is cloned and hence will not be rejected. The goal of such technology would be the cloning of human tissues and organs rather than of human beings. Although the cloning of human beings is highly problematic, the cloning of tissues and organs for therapeutic purposes is entirely salutary.

There is one final lesson to be learned from the *golem* literature. Absence of a prohibition against creating an anthropoid does not mean that rabbinic scholars encouraged such endeavors. Thus, to cite but one source, R. Chaim Joseph David Azulai, *Birkei Yosef*, *Oraḥ Ḥayyim* 55:4, notes that, in order to complete a *minyan*, R. Eliezer chose to emancipate his slave rather than to create a *golem*. *Birkei Yosef* regards R. Eliezer as having been quite capable of that feat but comments that R. Eliezer refrained from creating a *golem* as an act of piety. Many scholars frowned upon engaging in *kabbalah ma'asit* or "white magic" because of fear that the procedure might go awry, because of fear of misuse for less than noble purposes or because of fear that this

94 For a discussion of the propriety of destroying nascent human life generated in this manner and at this very early stage of development see *Contemporary Halakhic Problems*, vol. IV, p. 24, n. 10 and *Bioethical Dilemmas*, vol. I, pp. 209–11.

esoteric knowledge might fall into the hands of unworthy persons.[95] The identical concerns surround creation of the modern-day *golem* in the form of the product of homologous reproduction and similar restraint is in order.

Society certainly has reason to regard the development of cloning technology with concern. Such concern is by no means limited to the exaggerated fear of the specter of mad scientists engaging in cloning for nefarious purposes *à la The Boys from Brazil*. Quite apart from the earlier discussion regarding concern for potential defects in the clonee, society has reason to fear that untrammeled cloning may result in a disproportionate number of clones of one gender, that a multiplicity of persons identical to one another may spell confusion and give rise to an assortment of social problems and that idiosyncratic preferences may create an imbalance in the distribution of physical attributes and human talents. These and other demographic concerns are quite real. Tampering with natural processes in a manner that would lead to social upheaval is not included in man's mandate "to fill the earth and conquer it" (Genesis 1:28). Assuredly, society is justified in preventing such a situation from arising. Accordingly, society has both the right and the obligation to regulate experimental endeavors designed to perfect techniques necessary for the successful cloning of humans. The goal of such regulation should be assurance that those skills be utilized only for purposes beneficial to society.

95 For a series of quotations from the writing of kabbalists inveighing against actual implementation of practical Kabbalah see R. Moshe Hillel's introduction to his edition of R. Elijah Ba'al Shem Tov's *Toldot Adam* (Jerusalem, 5754), pp. 38–39. See also Joshua Trachtenberg, *Jewish Magic and Superstition* (New York, 1939), p. 22.

NOTES AND QUESTIONS

1. A cloned embryo allowed to develop in the laboratory certainly does not have a "mother." If the cloned blastocyst is inserted in the uterus of a woman and carried to term, is that woman the "mother" of the newborn infant? Is the maternal relationship genetic, in which case the woman carrying the fetus is simply a human incubator, or is the maternal relationship established on the basis of "labor pains," i.e., parturition, in which case the gestational mother is the halakhic mother as well?

Does the same question arise in cases of surrogate motherhood? What are the implications with regard to possible conflicts over custody of the child? Are "best interests" simply an additional factor in awarding custody to a progenitor or are "best interests" an independent factor trumping all others?

2. Does a clone have an identity distinct from that of the person from whom he or she has been cloned? Is the identity of a child different from the identity of a parent? Consider the Roman law notion of representation as applied to inheritance, as a result of which the heir is also liable for the debts of his progenitor. A theologian would probably say that the identity of a child is not that of a parent, because each is endowed with a separate and discrete soul. Is that true of cloning as well, and if so, how would one ascertain that clonor and clonee possess separate souls?

The adult is regarded as one and the same person as the infant whose image has been captured on a photograph. Some philosophers have explained identity on the basis of spatio-temporal contiguity. If so, does not the clonee share a single identity with the clonor?

If the clonor and clonee are one person, are they entitled to vote twice? To collect separate Social Security checks? To marry different women without committing bigamy? Is sexual intercourse between the clonor and the clonee's wife adultery? Is it incest?

3. Any attempts at cloning humans involve a risk that the cloning will be successful but result in a congenital abnormality. Is that risk morally acceptable? Failure to clone means that there is no life to be burdened by an abnormality. But cloning that results in such an anomaly represents a burden that has been imposed by the scientist who undertakes the cloning. Is it moral to create a life with a burden when the life would otherwise not exist?

Is it moral for a man and a wife who are both Tay-Sachs carriers to allow themselves to become parents of a Tay-Sachs child? Is there a moral difference between natural reproduction and procreation by means of cloning? With each pregnancy two carriers of Tay-Sachs have a one in four chance of producing a

Tay-Sachs baby. Is the degree of probability of producing a child with a defect germane?

4. The first hamburger using cloned beef has already been produced and consumed. Since the cloned burger had no natural fat, it was fried in butter. Assuming that the stem cells that were used in the production of the meat came from a kosher animal, was the hamburger non-kosher because of the admixture of milk and meat? Does this provide an opportunity for a kosher cheeseburger? Assume the stem cells were derived from a non-kosher animal. Is the meat kosher? Assuming that the stem cells were removed from a living animal, is that tantamount to a limb torn from a living creature and would it render the meat subsequently produced non-kosher? If it is prohibited because the cell is removed from a living animal, is this product, then, forbidden to Noahides as well?

5. Does reproduction by means of cloning fulfill the commandment to "be fruitful and multiply"? Is the commandment fulfilled by artificial insemination? Jewish tradition teaches that the commandment is incumbent only upon the male of the species. Certainly, Scripture does not command the type of procreation fictionalized in the motion picture *Junior*. Does that not suggest that the commandment mandates the sexual act rather than the teleological result of the act? Is a male who has sired children other than by sexual intercourse still bound by the commandment?

6. Assume that Albert Einstein is on his deathbed. One of his physicians removes a number of cells from inside his cheek and proceeds to clone a number of Albert Einsteins. Does he have a moral right to do so without permission? Does the estate of Albert Einstein have a financial claim against the physician who engaged in this endeavor?

7. Assume a society that would like to reduce its birth rate because of demographic concerns. Most people would regard limiting a couple to one child, as has been done in China, as morally abhorrent. Would it be morally acceptable to limit the number of clones produced because of demographic concerns? Is it morally acceptable to limit the number of children born as a result of assisted procreation? As a result of artificial insemination?

A Note on Halakhic Sources

To aid those unfamiliar with halakhic scholarship, we offer a brief chronological survey of basic rabbinic texts cited in this work.

The oral interpretation of biblical law, passed down from Moses through the sages of each generation, was first codified and redacted by R. Judah ha-Nasi (d. 219 C.E.) in the topical compendium known as the Mishnah. The Mishnah is subdivided into six Orders, each of which deals with a broad self-contained area of the law (e.g., *Nezikin* (Torts)). The six Orders are further subdivided into a total of sixty-three tractates, each of which explores a circumscribed topic (e.g., *Sanhedrin* (Courts)) within the more general Order. Scholars of the Mishnahic era are known as *Tanna'im*. The Gemara, a large body of commentary to and expansion upon the *Mishnah*, developed over the next four centuries. There are two Gemarot (plural of Gemara), one that was composed in the Babylonian academies and another that represented the contributions of Palestinian scholars. The former is the more exhaustive of the two Gemarot; citations to any of the tractates refer to the Babylonian Gemara unless otherwise indicated. Scholars cited in the Gemara are known as *Amora'im*. The Mishnah and the Gemara form the component parts of the Talmud, the basic text of rabbinic learning. Citation to the Talmud is made to the tractate and the page (e.g., *Sanhedrin* 3a).

The post-talmudic history of Jewish scholarship is divided into three eras: the era of *Ge'onim* (roughly 500–1050 C.E.), the era of *Rishonim* (early scholars – roughly 1050–1550), and the era of the *Aḥaronim* (latter-day scholars – roughly 1550 to the present). Outstanding among the *Ge'onim* is Saadia Gaon, whose philosophical works are considered classics to this very day. Prominent among the *Rishonim* whose works are cited in this book is Rambam (R. Moses ben Maimon, Maimonides; 1135–1204), author of the *Mishneh Torah*, a formal code of Jewish law. This code is divided into a number of books, each book being subdivided into sections, chapters, and laws. Citations to the *Mishneh Torah* are to the work itself, the section, chapter, and law (e.g., *Mishneh Torah, Hilkhot Tefillah* 11:16). *Tur Shulḥan Arukh*, also known simply as *Tur*, was authored by R. Jacob ben Asher (1280–1314), who was a son of Rosh. *Tur* introduced the division of Jewish law applicable after the destruction of the Temple into four parts: *Oraḥ Ḥayyim, Yoreh De'ah, Even ha-Ezer*, and *Ḥoshen Mishpat*. *Tur Shulḥan Arukh* served as the precursor of R. Joseph Karo's *Shulḥan Arukh*, in which that division is preserved. R. Joseph Karo's *Shulḥan Arukh*, composed during the middle of the sixteenth century, together with the contemporaneous glosses of Rema (R. Moses Isserles), serves as the authoritative Code of Jewish Law. Citations to the *Shulḥan Arukh* are to the work itself, the subdivision, chapter, and law (e.g., *Shulḥan Arukh, Ḥoshen Mishpat* 356:2). Commentaries on the *Shulḥan Arukh*, which appear on the same page as the text in the standard version of the code, are cited by author, the work itself, subdivision, chapter, and law (e.g., *Shakh, Shulḥan Arukh, Ḥoshen Mishpat* 256:7). Other *Rishonim* cited in this work include:

Rif (R. Isaac Alfasi; 1013–1103), a Moroccan scholar who lived in the city of Fez. He presents a *précis* of the halakhic portions of the Talmud and adjudicates between conflicting talmudic views. His work served as a basis for later compendia of Jewish law.

Rashi (R. Solomon ben Isaac; 1040–1105), a French scholar and the foremost commentator on the Bible and the Talmud. Rashi's commentary is an explanation of the text, often colorful and replete with realistic concrete description. It is indispensible to the study of the Talmud. Rashi's commentary is found on the same page as the text on which he is explicating and cites the author, the tractate of the Talmud under discussion, and the page (e.g., Rashi, *Sanhedrin* 3a).

Ramban (R. Moses ben Nahman, Nahmanides; 1194–1270), a Spanish authority known for his commentary on the Written Torah, talmudic novellae, and philosophical writings.

Rashba (R. Solomon ben Abraham Adret; 1235–1310), a Spanish rabbi and scholar best known for his commentary on numerous tractates of the Talmud. Like the Rashi commentary, Rashba's comments follow the pagination of the Talmud and are cited in similar style.

Tosafot are collections of comments on the Talmud arranged according to the order of talmudic tractates. These comments were written by the students of Rashi and their descendants and are found on the actual page of the text being explicated. They are cited in a manner similar to that of Rashi's commentary.

Rabbenu Nissim (R. Nissim ben Reuben Gerondi; 1310(?)–1375(?)), a Spanish talmudist best known for his commentary on the Talmud. His commentary is cited in a manner similar to that of the Rashi commentary.

Mordekhai (Mordekhai ben Hillel ha-Kohen; 1240(?)–1298), an author and rabbinic authority in Germany. Mordekhai's fame rests on his *Sefer Mordekhai*. This gigantic compendium consists of elaborations on talmudic problems.

R Menaḥem ben Solomon ha-Me'iri (1249–1316), a scholar from Provence whose *Beit ha-Beḥirah*, a commentary on the Talmud, summarizes the subject matter of that work, giving both the meaning and the rule of law derived therefrom.

Rosh (R. Asher ben Jehiel; 1250–1327), a talmudist whose major work sums up the decisions of earlier codifiers and commentators. His work is cited by author, tractate, chapter, and comment (e.g., Rosh, *Shevu'ot*, 7:4).

Aside from the commentaries and codes, rabbinic writings include a vast number of works from the responsa literature that provide great insight into the decision-making process of the Jewish judge. Prominent among the works cited are: R. Israel Isserlein (1390(?)–1460), *Terumat ha-Deshen*; R. Zevi Ashkenazi (1656–1718), *Ḥakham Ẓevi*; R. Ezekiel Landau (1713–1793), *Noda bi-Yehudah*; R. Akiva Eger (1761–1837), *Teshuvot R. Akiva Eger*; R. Moses Sofer (1763–1839), *Ḥatam Sofer*; R. Meir Arak (1855–1926), *Imrei Yosher*; R. Chaim Ozer Grodzinski (1863–1940), *Aḥi'ezer*; R. Abraham Kahana-Shapiro (1870–1943), *Dvar Avraham*; R. Abraham Isaiah Karelitz (1878–1953), *Ḥazon Ish*; R. Joseph Elijah Henkin (1881–1973), *Edut le-Yisra'el*; R. Yechiel Ya'akov Weinberg (1884–1966), *Seridei Esh*; R. Ya'akov Breisch (1895–1976), *Ḥelkat Ya'akov*; R. Moses Feinstein (1895–1986), *Iggerot Mosheh*; and R. Eliezer Waldenberg (1917–2006), *Ẓiẓ Eli'ezer*. Such works cite the author, the work, and the responsum number.

The foregoing is based in part upon N. Lamm and A. Kirschenbaum, "Freedom and Constraint in the Jewish Judicial Process," editor's note, *Cardozo Law Review*, vol. 1 (1979), p. 99.

Transliteration Style

The transliterations in this volume conform to the standard system used in academic works.

Two letters in particular require explanation. One is the Hebrew ח (*chet*), which is transliterated as *ḥ*. The other is the Hebrew צ (*tsadi*), which is transliterated as *ẓ*. Though Hebrew does not employ upper- and lower-case letters, English does. The transliterations reflect that distinction.

Index of Passages Cited

1. Bible

Genesis, 5, 250
- 1:28, 365, 394
- 14:23, 152
- 17:1, 366
- 18:8, 381
- 2:2, 367
- 2:24, 363
- 2:7, 370, 379, 380
- 34, 199
- 34:13, 113, 122
- 49:1, 341
- 6:9, 376
- 7:11, 357
- 7:22, 276
- 9:5, 211, 245, 246
- 9:6, 208, 209, 375

Exodus, 5
- 12, 5
- 20:10, 367
- 20:13, 5, 6
- 21:21, 236
- 22:1, 208, 209, 242
- 23:2, 10
- 25:2, 334, 335
- 35:1, 11

Leviticus
- 1:1, 333, 334
- 19:14, 212, 338
- 19:16, 179, 195, 208, 332, 337
- 19:19, 363, 364
- 22:27, 381
- 24:17, 309
- 27:29, 114, 117
- 7:35, 309

Numbers
- 11:24, 100
- 27:21, 207, 219
- 33:53, 221, 222

Deuteronomy
- 1:9, 109
- 16:18, 13
- 16:19, 113
- 17:15, 102
- 18:11, 370
- 20, 215, 216, 217, 218, 221
- 20:11, 219
- 20:19, 234
- 20:5, 241
- 20:5–7, 214, 215, 248
- 20:5–8, 216, 224
- 20:7, 217, 221, 222
- 20:8, 212, 214, 245
- 22:27, 208, 209
- 22:3, 146
- 23:15, 227
- 23:2, 310
- 24:1–4, 25
- 24:15, 163
- 24:3, 18
- 24:5, 217
- 25:12, 120, 242
- 26:17–18, 233
- 30:12, 15
- 30:12–14, 15
- 6:18, 151, 173
- 6:5, 273, 358
- 6:8, 7
- 7, 221
- 7:2, 221, 222

Judges
- 21:5, 191
- 5:23, 237

I Samuel, 106, 110, 117, 118
14:24–45, 114
14:45, 114
15:6, 236
25:28, 219
8, 106, 110, 113, 114, 115, 118, 126, 128
8:5, 102, 105, 111, 117
II Samuel
1:15, 107
20:14–22, 189
I Kings
21, 118
II Kings
4:18–27, 283
Isaiah
59:2, 369
6:3, 277
Ezekiel, 322
37:1–14, 283
Obadiah
1:11–13, 209
Habakkuk
1:13–14, 206
Psalms
115:16, 368
116:6, 278
3, 369
88:6, 293
Proverbs
11:13, 335
Song of Songs
8:12, 115
Ecclesiastes
1:9, 276
Daniel
12:2, 292
3:12–23, 193

2. Babylonian Talmud

Berakhot
3b, 218, 222, 237, 243
58a, 187, 237, 247
60a, 163
62b, 237, 247
9:5, 8
74b, 201
Shabbat
120a, 152
130a, 12
133b, 341
19a, 233
30b, 367
45a, 370
60b, 10
Eruvin
13b, 7, 12
45a, 226, 230, 232, 233, 234, 235, 244
65a, 289
Pesaḥim
10:13, 381
114b, 292
2b, 235
Yoma, 279
4b, 333, 334, 335, 336, 342
82b, 190
85a, 255, 269, 270, 274, 279, 303, 304, 305, 306
Megillah
26a, 169, 170
4:1, 170
7b, 289
Ḥaggigah
12a, 366
Yevamot
33b, 191
46a, 106
61b, 191
64b, 389
65a, 39
75b, 310, 311
92a, 14
Ketubot
33b, 193
39a, 65
3a, 62
64a, 40
Nedarim
28a, 104, 106, 134
Nazir
4a, 313
4b, 313
Sotah, 214
43a, 216, 217, 224, 228
44a, 217
44b, 214, 221, 222, 223, 224, 233, 241
7:15, 217
8:10, 225, 233, 234, 237
8:7, 218, 225
Gittin
10b, 104, 123, 134
3:7, 153
38a, 141, 212
4:384, 194
45a, 136
45b, 136
6b, 7
7:3, 290, 291
70b, 273, 274, 298, 300, 301

76b, 290, 291
88b, 82, 84
9b, 122
Kiddushin
2a, 290
30b, 369
33a, 289
41b, 35
81a, 65
Bava Kamma
113a, 104, 106, 134
113b, 106, 345
114b, 138, 161
16a, 137
28a, 194, 234
6:7, 137
97b, 106
Bava Meẓi'a
108a, 151
112a, 163
16b, 151
2:2, 147
24a, 148
24b, 141
257, 148
30b, 150
83b, 106, 107, 117, 119, 120
Bava Batra
142b, 261
32b, 168
39b, 337
48a, 40
54b, 104, 134
55a, 106, 109, 110
7b, 238
8a, 213, 239
Sanhedrin
16a, 218, 219, 222, 237, 243
20a, 218
20b, 105, 118
2a, 218
31a, 336
37a, 182
49a, 234
52b, 100
56a, 234
57a, 207
59a, 212
5a, 14
65b, 376, 378, 379, 380
72a, 120, 207, 209, 235
72b, 205, 208, 234
73a, 208, 209
74a, 234, 236
Shevu'ot
35b, 115
46b, 161
7:5, 161
Avodah Zarah 341
18b, 212
28a, 340
43a, 148
46b, 161
52b, 141
54b, 141
Avot
1:1, 203
3:2, 206
6:6, 336
Ḥullin, 254, 323
121b, 298
17a, 383
21a, 254, 273
32a, 273
32b, 299
33a, 297, 298, 299, 300, 301
38b, 261
42a, 273, 274
46b, 257
53b, 257
89a, 152
90a, 383
Bekhorot
3:1, 261
Niddah
23b, 386
3:2, 386
44a, 261
5:5, 191
61a, 125
61b, 293
37a, 257
45a, 270
5b, 383
Oholot
1:6, 255, 270, 304, 305

3. Palestinian Talmud

Pe'ah
2:4, 336
Terumot
8:10, 188
8:4, 108

Index of Names and Subjects

Abbot, Thomas Kingsmill, 1
Abington School District v. Schempp, 74, 75
Abortion, 121, 389
Abraham, 152, 185, 366, 381
Abraham, Dr. Abraham S., 266, 279, 388
Abrams v. Sotheby Parke-Bernet, 130, 131, 134, 136, 156, 157, 162, 163, 168, 250
Ad Hoc Committee of the Harvard Medical School to Examine the Definition of Brain Death, 263
Adam, 11, 365, 366, 371, 372, 375, 379, 380
Adam ḥashuv, 190
Adnei ha-Sadeh, 387
Adoption, 44, 49, 54, 94, 392
Adultery, 20, 23, 24, 25, 36, 40, 64, 65, 66, 67, 70, 94, 191, 201, 327, 395
Aflalo v. Aflalo, 47, 60, 61, 62, 63
Agunah, 20, 64, 65, 79, 87, 95, 98
Aha, R. bar Jacob, 297
Ahab, 118
Ahasuerus, 201
Aḥizat einayim, 370
Akiva, R., 12
Al-Din, Amar S.N., 261
Alei Tamar, 333
Alexander v. Culp, 327, 329
Alimony, 51, 59, 67, 98
Alpharetta First United Methodist Church v. Stewart, 354
Altschuler, Linda A., 139
Alvarez, L.A., 256
Amalek, 220, 223, 236, 241, 245, 251
American Revolution, 183
Ammi, R., 336
Amran, David Werner, 30
Amud ha-Yemini, 218, 224, 229, 231, 232, 236, 240, 243, 245, 246, 248
Anakava, R. Abraham, 381
Anas, 101
Annulment, 21, 28, 35, 62, 69, 77
Antenuptial agreement, 34, 45, 46, 49, 63, 95
Anthropoid, 369, 370, 371, 373, 374, 375, 376, 377, 378, 379, 380, 382, 387, 393
Apotropus, 171
Arak, R. Meir, 137, 138
Arbitration, 45, 46, 47, 48, 50, 81
Arenas, A., 274
Arita, K., 259
Arukh ha-Shulḥan, 39, 85, 165, 195, 234
Arukh ha-Shulḥan he-Atid, 103, 219, 223, 224, 225, 227, 230, 232, 233
Arukh la-Ner, 125
Asarah harugei malkhut, 177
Asexual reproduction, 368, 369, 382
Asher, Rabbenu, 65
Ashwal, Stephen, 260
Asuyin le-hash'il u-le-haskir, 160
Aszod, R. Judah, 169, 378
Avi Ezri, 198
Avitzur v. Avitzur, 45, 47, 48, 50
Avnei Nezer, 384
Azulai, R. Abraham, 374
Azulai, R. Chaim Joseph David, 273, 290, 375, 376, 377, 378, 379, 382, 393

B. v. B. (Germany), 51
B. v. B. (New York), 48
Ba ba-maḥteret, 209
Ba-adam damo yishafekh, 209, 375
Babad, Joseph R., 386
Bacharach, R. Ya'ir Chaim, 333

Bacon, Sir Francis, 177
Baecher v. Baecher, 331
Baer, Moshe, 370
Baḥya ben Asher, R., 272, 370
Baḥya Ibn Pakuda, 4
Bal tomar, 339, 341, 342
Bartenura, R. Ovadiah, 203
Basar she-ha-rofeh gorero, 257
Basar she-nifrakh be- ẓiporen, 257
Bastardy, 20, 36, 63, 98
Bat kol, 371
Bateman, Tracy A., 342
Be'er ha-Golah, 366
Be'er Mayim Ḥayyim, 333, 338
Be'er Ro'i, 169
Becher v. Becher, 87
Beecher, Henry K., 263
Ben Sira, 371
Be-Netivot ha-Halakhah, 127, 235, 236, 255, 270, 273, 288
Benjamin, Jeffrey L., 262
Ben–Shlomoh, Joseph, 372
Bentham, Jeremy, 192, 201
Benveniste, R. Chaim, 295
Bereshit Rabbah, 376, 379
Berlin, R. Naphtali Zevi Judah, 123, 124, 191, 211, 245
Bernat, Dr. James L., 256, 262
Besamim Rosh, 390
Bet ha-Beḥirah, 65, 224, 334
Bet ha-Levi, 11, 319, 366, 367
Bet Me'ir, 65, 85
Bet Shmu'el, 54, 67, 83, 137
Bet Yehudah, 335
Bet Yosef, 84, 85, 111, 112, 195, 234, 272, 273, 378
Bi'ur ha-Gra, 67, 121, 235, 336
Bi'ur Halakhah, 195
Bioethical Dilemmas, 278, 387, 393
Birkei Yosef, 273, 290, 291, 292, 293, 294, 377, 393
Black, Jr., Charles L., 347
Black, P.M., 256
Bleich, J. David, 47, 112, 125, 127, 176, 226, 235, 236, 239, 255, 275, 278, 283, 285, 288, 311, 370, 374, 384, 392
Bleich, R. Moshe, 338
Bloch, Chaim, 373
Blood flow, 257, 259, 260, 261, 267, 268, 323, 324
Blood letting, 13
Blood loss, 254, 255
Board of Education v. Cracovia, 47
Boddie v. Connecticut, 71
Boerger v. Boerger, 45
Bourne, H.R. Fox, 351
Boys from Brazil, The, 394
Bradshaw v. Daniel, 342
Braunstein, P., 259, 260
Brave New World, 373
Breisch, R. Ya'akov, 136, 139, 140, 169, 338
Brett v. Brett, 67, 68
Brewer v. Cary, 45
Bribery, 113
Brody, Baruch, 259, 282
Brown v. Board of Education, 9
Brugger, E. Christian, 283
Burglary, 120, 121
Burial, 253, 268, 287
Burns v. Burns, 59
Bush, John C., 348
Butler, John, 321
Butler, Joseph, 321

C. L. v. Rabbi Tzvi Flaum and Rabbi David Weinberger, 328, 345, 346
Caesarian section, 256
Campbell, Dr. Keith, 359
Canaan, 215, 216, 221, 222, 237, 244, 245, 251
Capital punishment, 100, 109, 110, 112, 114, 116, 117, 175, 176, 199, 205, 310, 313, 314, 323, 324, 385
Capital transgression, 6, 16, 113, 189, 205, 210, 309, 314, 321, 367
Caplan, Arthur L., 286
Carey, John, 361
Case of the Kettle, 167
Catholicism, 36, 77, 282, 326, 328, 348, 350
Chadbourn, James H., 348
Chajes, R. Zevi Hirsch, 126, 313
Chavel, R. Bernard, 113
Chavez v. Martinez, 181
Chertok v. Chertok, 28, 29, 30, 31, 32
Chief Rabbinate Council, 232, 265, 266, 267, 274, 275
Child support, 44, 49
Chill, R. Abraham, 364
Chou, Shelley N., 263
Church of Lukumi Babalu Aye v. City of Hialeah, 284
Chutzpah, 325
Cibelli, Jose B., 360
Circumcision, 13

Circumstantial evidence, 175, 176, 204
City of Boerne v. Flores, 284
Civil disobedience, 345, 350, 356
Clark, Dr. Barney, 287
Clarke, Samuel, 321
Cleary, Edward M., 326
Clergyman–penitent privilege. *See Chapter Eight*
Clinton, Bill, 361
Cloning. *See Chapter Nine*
Code of Canon Law, 348
Cohen, R. Binyamin, 333
Cohen, R. Joseph Dov, 126
Cohn, Anna R., 139
Collar, Barry, 264
Comity, 21, 29, 31, 55, 95, 132, 133
Committee for Pub. Educ. and Religious Liberty v. Nyquist, 52, 97
Commonwealth v. McClelland, 45
Conderre v. Conderre, 331
Confession, 39, 67, 176, 178, 326, 327, 328, 348
Confidentiality. *See Chapter Eight*
Conscription, 213, 214, 217, 218, 221, 236, 239, 241, 248
Consortium, 20, 26, 39, 40, 65, 66, 67, 72, 330
Constitution of the United States, 4, 7, 8, 9, 11, 20, 33, 34, 35, 36, 38, 42, 43, 46, 54, 56, 72, 73, 75, 78, 79, 81, 88, 180, 249, 284, 322, 325, 326, 327, 347, 350, 351
Contemporary Halakhic Problems, 176, 192, 196, 198, 218, 220, 221, 226, 245, 266, 275, 285, 311, 370, 374, 376, 380, 384, 385, 387, 391, 393
Contract, 34, 35, 37, 38, 42, 45, 47, 49, 62, 104
  acceptance of, 29, 104, 110
  breach, 52
  enforcement of, 33, 35, 44, 62, 95, 104
  rescission of, 20, 21, 52, 59, 88
  terms of, 95
  validity of, 56
Copeland, Jack G., 286
Corbett v. Corbett, 25
Cordovero, R. Moses, 374, 380
Corporal punishment, 39, 100, 114, 117, 177
Corporations, 169, 316, 318, 319
Crémieux, Adolphe, 178

Da'at Torah, 295
Daiches, Samuel, 30
Damascus affair of 1840, 178
Dan, Joseph, 373
Dariente affair, 50
Darkei Teshuvah, 377, 381
De Justitia et Jure, 282
De Lugo, Juan, 282
Death penalty, 5, 113, 114, 117, 190, 310, 312, 315
Death, time of. *See Chapter Seven*
Debt, 85, 86, 87
Decapitation, 254, 255, 257, 261, 267, 270, 303, 304, 305, 306
Declaration of Independence, 204
Denton v. James, 45
Der Prager Golem, 373
Derashot ha-Ran, 102, 103
Dershowitz, Alan, 175, 200, 201
Devarim he-asuyin lehash'il u-le-haskir, 159
Di Trani, R. Moses ben Joseph, 86, 106
Dillon, William P., 260
Dina de-malkhuta dina, 104, 105, 106, 110, 111, 112, 113, 115, 116, 117, 122, 123, 124, 144, 345
Dinah, 199
Dinei Mamonot, 104
Dinin, 122, 123, 124, 125, 128, 198, 199, 210
Diskin, R. Joshua Leib, 113
Dittemore v. Dickey, 62
Divorce. *See Chapter Two*
Doe v. City of New York, 329
Doppelt, Frederic Aubrey, 37
Dower rights, 26, 32
Drush ve-Ḥiddush R. Akiva Eger, 65, 66
Duran, Rabbi Shimon ben Ẓemaḥ, 84, 110, 142
Duress, 58, 79, 82, 83, 84, 87, 95, 98, 99, 176, 180, 190, 191, 193, 194, 196, 197, 201
Duty of rescue, 179, 182, 183, 184, 185, 186, 191, 195, 197, 198, 199, 200, 205, 249, 355
Dvar Avraham, 142, 143, 144, 212, 245
Dworkes, R. Eliyakim, 341

Eckmann v. Board of Education of Hawthorn School District, 353, 354
Edom, 209
Efrati, R. Shimon, 187, 190
Eger, R. Akiva, 65, 66
Ehrenfeld, R. Samuel, 389
Eibeschutz, R. Jonathan, 113, 123, 165, 272, 294, 366
Ein Ya'akov, 120, 255
Einayim la-Mishpat, 187, 218, 219, 243
Einei Yiẓḥak, 120
Eiselsberg, P., 259
Eisenstadt, R. Meir, 213

Elchanan, R., 383
Eleazar ben Shimon, R., 107, 108, 109, 111, 112, 117, 118, 119, 120, 121, 122, 291, 369
Eliashiv, R. Yosef Shalom, 144, 381
Eliezer, R., 12, 13, 377, 393
Elijah, 108, 109, 112, 190, 201
Elijah Ba'al Shem of Helm, R., 371, 374, 379
Elijah ben Ḥayyim, R., 86
Elijah of Vilna, R., 121, 191, 336
Elisha, 283
Eliyahu Rabbah, 191
Eliyahu, R. Mordecai, 265
Ellinson, R. Elyakim, 85
Ellman, Ira Mark, 33, 34
Elman, Peter, 30
Elon, Menachem, 30, 132
Emden, R. Jacob, 190, 374, 377
Emek Halakhah, 266
Employment Division, Oregon Department of Human Resources v. Smith, 284, 326, 327, 328
Emunot ve-De'ot, 292
Encyclopedia Britannica, 177
Encyclopedia Judaica, 169
Encyclopedia of Philosophy, 384
Encyclopedia Talmudit, 157, 158, 160
Enoch Arden, 323
Epstein, Abraham, 371
Epstein, Louis M., 30
Epstein, R. Alexander, 241
Epstein, R. Baruch ha-Levi, 334
Epstein, R. Yechiel Michel, 39, 103, 165, 195, 219, 230
Equal Protection Clause, 9, 44, 351
Equitable distribution, 68, 69, 83
Equity, 24, 26, 27, 57, 67, 69, 70, 72, 74, 76, 78, 79, 80, 81, 94, 145, 150, 152, 153, 154, 155, 156, 173
Erev Ḥanukkah, 237
Ereẓ Yisra'el, 211, 226, 237
Establishment Clause, 47, 51, 52, 54, 59, 60, 61, 71, 73, 74, 75, 78, 96, 97, 328, 346, 351
Esther, 201
Ettlinger, R. Jacob, 125
Eugenics, 389, 390
European Convention on Human Rights, 180
Evans, Dr. D. Wainwright, 263
Even Boḥen, 190
Even ha-Azel, 123, 222, 238
Ever ha-nahar, 185
Everson v. Board of Education, 75
Ezrachi, Rabbi B.N., 44
Ezrat Yisra'el, 226

Fabian, Hans Erich, 134
Falk, Ze'ev Wilhelm, 30, 62
Falkoff v. Sugerman, 32
Feinstein, R. Moses, 82, 121, 189, 190, 254, 266, 275, 276, 285. *See also Iggerot Mosheh*
Feticide, 375, 376
Fetus, 121, 189, 191, 261, 375, 389, 391, 395
Field, David R., 256, 257, 261
Fifth Amendment, 180
Findling, R. Moshe, 44
Fiorelli, Priro, 174
First Amendment, 20, 33, 42, 43, 49, 55, 56, 59, 60, 70, 73, 74, 75, 76, 78, 79, 88, 96, 97, 128, 284, 326, 327, 346, 350
Fiser, D.H., 258
Fisher v. Congregation B'nai Yitzhok, 34
Fleischer v. Fleischer, 59
Fletcher, Joseph, 187
Fourteenth Amendment, 9, 54, 72, 180, 284
Fourth Lateran Council, 175
Frankel, Jonathan, 178
Frankena, William, 3
Franklin v. Franklin, 23
Frederick II, 149
Free Exercise Clause, 33, 34, 45, 47, 54, 56, 59, 60, 61, 62, 71, 72, 73, 74, 75, 128, 284, 326, 327, 328, 349, 350, 352
Friedman, R. Ya'akov of Karlin, 295
Fuller, Lon L., 316

Galen, 255
Gammill v. United States, 342
Gammon, Timothy E., 342
Garnet's Case, 348
Gaylin, Willard, 264, 358
Gemeindesteuer, 170
Geneva Convention, 180, 181, 184, 206, 249
Gerondi, Rabbenu Nissim, 102, 103
Gershom of Mainz, Rabbenu, 19, 66, 95, 96, 355
Gershuni, R. Judah, 218, 220, 221, 233, 266, 288
Gersonides, 271
Get. See Chapter Two
Gevurot Anashim, 39, 40
Giannella, Donald A., 33
Giannola v. Giannola, 69
Gladstone, W.E., 321
Gleason v. Gleason, 54

Glenn, H. Patrick, 51
Glick, R. Yitzchak, 341
Goldie, William D., 261
Golding v. Golding, 82
Goldstein v. Goldstein, 49
Golem, 369, 370, 371, 372, 373, 374, 376, 377, 378, 379, 380, 381, 382, 388, 393, 394
Goodman, Julius M., 260
Goren, R. Shlomoh, 221, 232, 233, 237, 243, 310, 311, 314
Goses, 262, 309, 312, 313, 314
Gottlieb v. Gottlieb, 34
Greenberg, Yitzchak, 154, 155
Grenvik, A., 259
Grigg, Madeleine M., 256, 260
Grodzinski, R. Chaim Ozer, 121
Gross, Oren, 179, 181
Grunfeld, Dayan I., 110
Guggenheim, Jack Achiezer, 326
Guide for the Perplexed, 253, 280, 365
Gunzburg, David de, 373
Gur Aryeh, 245
Gur-Aryeh, Miriam, 200
Guttmann, Dr. Alexander, 130, 131, 133, 134, 135, 136, 155, 156, 157, 158, 159, 161, 162, 164, 165, 166, 167, 168, 169, 170, 171, 173

Ha'amek Davar, 211, 212, 245, 246
Ha'amek She'elah, 123, 191
Ha'aramah, 90, 91
Hackett v. Hackett, 45
Ha-Darom, 169
Ha-Elef Lekha Shlomoh, 169
Ḥafeẓ Ḥayyim, 333, 337, 338, 339
Hagahot Asheri, 137
Ḥaggi, R., 291, 292, 293
Ha-Kedem, 373
Ha-Ketav ve-ha-Kabbalah, 11, 367
Ḥakham Ẓevi, 236, 271, 272, 294, 295, 296, 297, 298, 299, 300, 301, 302, 303, 306, 307, 308, 309, 374, 375, 376, 377, 378, 379, 381, 388
Ha-Kohen, R. Mordecai, 44
Halevy, Amir, 259, 282
Ḥaliẓah, 385, 386
Hall, Dr. Jerry, 359
Hall, G.M., 258
Halperin, R. Mordecai, 236, 266
Halperin, R. Yom Tov, 168
Ha-Ma'ayan, 273, 292
Ha-Ma'or, 138, 155
Ḥameẓ, 92
Ha-Mo'adim be-Halakhah, 92
Ha-Ne'eman, 169
Ḥanina, R., 368, 371, 379
Hankins v. Lyght, 284
Ha-Pardes, 138, 255, 285
Ḥatam Sofer, 117, 118, 212, 213, 268, 274, 304, 305, 311, 313
Ha-Torah ve-ha-Medinah, 107, 126
Ha-Tzofeh, 310
Ḥazon Ish, 65, 85, 198, 223, 225, 226, 227, 228, 230, 232, 248, 272, 273, 294, 376
Heart, artificial, 285, 286, 287, 292, 296, 297, 308, 309, 310, 314, 315, 320
Heartbeat, 256, 269, 270, 271, 273, 275, 276, 295, 303, 304
Heath, James, 176
Hedaya, R. Ovadiah, 226, 233
He-Ḥasid, R. Judah, 379
He-Ḥasid, R. Shmuel, 379
Heikkinen, J.E., 261
Ḥelev, 381
Ḥelkat Binyamin, 333
Ḥelkat Ya'akov, 140, 141, 339
Helkat Yo'av, 195
Helvering v. Gregory, 90
Ḥemdat Yisra'el, 109, 198, 209, 210
Henkin, R. Joseph E., 49, 65, 145
Henkin, R. Yehudah Herzl, 333
Henry, Patrick, 183, 184
Ḥerem, 86, 114, 115, 136
Herzog, Rabbi Isaac ha-Levi, 66
Ḥesed le-Avraham, 374, 375, 377, 378, 379, 380, 381
Hessett, Catherine, 256
Hetter iska, 15
Hetter me'ah rabbanim, 20, 95, 96
Hibner, R. Samuel, 169
Ḥida, 374, 382
Ḥiddushei ha-Ran, 121, 299, 300
Ḥiddushei Rabbenu Ḥayyim ha-Levi, 198, 210
High Priest, 218, 219, 220
Hilberg, R., 131
Hill, Dr. David J., 263, 264
Hillel, R. Moshe, 394
Hinduism, 91
Ḥinnukh Bet Yiẓḥak, 341
Hirsch, R. Samson Raphael, 364, 365, 367
Ḥisda, R., 217
Hochschule für die Wissenschaft des Judenthums, 130, 133, 134, 135, 157, 158, 161, 162, 164, 166, 169, 170, 171, 172, 173

Hohenegger, M., 258
Holeḥ le-faneinu, 393
Holocaust, 131, 134, 139, 140, 146, 153, 154, 155, 187, 392
Homicide, 6, 175, 182, 186, 188, 189, 194, 208, 209, 211, 212, 236, 245, 246, 250, 275, 282, 283, 285, 286, 287, 288, 289, 290, 292, 294, 295, 296, 297, 309, 312, 313, 315, 321, 323, 324, 373, 374, 375, 376, 384
Homosexuality, 386
Hoppe, Dr. Peter, 359
Hora'at sha'ah, 199, 201, 202
Horowitz, George, 49
Horowitz, R. Pinhas, 65
Ḥovah, 216
Huebner, Rudolph, 149
Ḥukkim, 93, 364, 365, 366
Hulston, John K., 342
Hurwitz v. Hurwitz, 45, 49
Ḥut ha-Meshulash, 142, 143, 236
Hutchison v. Ross, 131
Huxley, Aldous, 373

Ibn Ezra, R. Abraham, 236, 292, 364
Ibn Pakuda, Bahya, 4
Ibn Shaprut, R. Shem Tov, 370
Ibn Tavah, R. Abraham, 142, 143
Ibn Tibbon, 225, 226, 228
Idel, Moshe, 370, 372, 373, 374, 378, 379
Idolatry, 193, 205, 277, 365
Iggerot Mosheh, 82, 121, 189, 193, 235, 254, 258, 266, 275, 276, 285. *See also* Feinstein, R. Moses
Illinois v. Diercks, 353
Illmensee, Dr. Karl, 359
Imitatio Dei, 371
Imrei Yosher, 138, 143, 147, 148, 150
In re Estate of Goldman, 31
In re Estate of White, 49
In re Fuhrer, 327, 350
In re Luck, 45
In re Miller, 327
In re Rourke, 327
In re Spondre, 21
In re the Marriage of Kenneth I. Goldman v. Annette C. Goldman, 42
In re the Marriage of Shulsinger, 58
In vitro, 358, 373, 387, 388
Inheritance, 98
Interbreeding, 363, 364, 382
Isaac Arieli, R., 187
Ishmael ben Yosi, R., 108, 112
Islam, 33, 77, 78, 96, 280
Israel v. The State of Israel, The General Security Services and Others, 181
Israeli, R. Saul, 218, 236, 242, 265, 274, 275, 336, 339, 340
Isserlein, R. Israel, 145
Isserles, R. Moses, 85
Ivan, Leslie P., 274

Jacob, 341
Jacob of Lissa, R., 166
Jacqueline v. Segal, 331
Jaffe, R. Mordecai, 85
Jastrow, Marcus, 370
Jefferson, Thomas, 73, 74, 204
Jennett, Bryan, 256
Jeret, Joseph S., 262
Jerusalem, 13
Jimenez, J.F., 258
Johnson v. Commonwealth, 353
Jose, R., 291, 292, 293, 387
Joseph v. Joseph, 25, 26
Josephus, 213
Joshua, 215, 216, 219, 221
Joshua ben Karḥah, R., 108, 109, 112, 117, 118, 119, 120, 122
Judah Aryeh of Modena, R., 255
Judah ben Beteira, R., 309, 312, 313, 314, 372
Judah the Pious, R., 371
Judah, R., 214, 215, 216, 217, 218, 220, 222, 223, 224, 225, 227, 228, 230, 233, 234, 238, 240
Judaism and Healing, 239, 392
Judicial intervention, 20, 32, 33, 34, 43, 47, 52, 54, 59, 60, 70, 71, 73, 74, 79, 97, 137
Jurisprudence, 116, 122, 123, 124, 125, 133, 144, 204, 326

Kabbalah ma'asit, 393
Kad ha-Kemaḥ, 370
Kaddish, 287
Kagan, R. Israel Meir, 338
Kahana-Shapiro, R. Abraham Dov Ber, 118, 142, 143, 212, 245
Kahane, R. Kalman, 273
Kahanow, R. Eleazar, 275
Kalata, Gina, 359
Kanievsky, R. Chaim, 291, 294
Kansas v. Andrews, 353
Kant, Immanuel, 1, 178
Kantor v. Bloom, 22, 23, 24, 25

Kantor v. Cohn, 26
Kantor v. Rubin, 93
Kaplan v. Kaplan, 49
Kardia, 288
Karelitz, R. Abraham Isaiah, 65, 294
Karo, R. Joseph, 84, 106, 126
Kasher, R. Menachem, 273, 288, 300
Katz, R. Judah Leib, 377
Katzenellenbogen, R. Raphael, 169, 226, 242
Kaufman, R. Chaim Saul, 333
Kaufman, Sherwin A., 361
Kav ha-Ta'arikh ha-Yisra'eli, 273
Kav Naki, 54
Kefiyah derekh bereirah, 40
Keigwin, C., 167
Kelly-Hill, Linda, 94
Ke-manḥa be-dikula damya, 297, 299
Keren Orah, 233
Kereti u-Peleti, 294, 295, 296
40.4, 294
Kesef Mishneh, 175, 234, 236, 390
Kessler v. Kessler, 331
Ketav Sofer, 103
Ketubah, 44, 45, 46, 47, 48, 49, 56, 57, 58, 60, 62, 63, 64
Kibush milḥamah, 141, 144, 145, 150, 172
Kiel, J. Michael, 346
King Ahab, 118
King David, 107, 189, 237
King James I, 348
Kirschenbaum, Aaron, 169
Kiryat Sefer, 106
Kleegman, Sophia J., 361
Klein, R. Menasheh, 169, 213
Kluger, R. Shlomoh, 169
Knesset ha-Gedolah, 217, 218, 223, 295
Kobylack v. Kobylack, 69
Koeppel v. Koeppel, 34, 36, 37, 41, 43, 44, 57, 82
Kohler, K., 133
Kol Sifrei Maharaẓ Ḥayes, 126
Kol Ẓofayikh, 266, 288
Kook, R. Abraham Isaac, 201, 202, 218
Korban ha-Edah, 225, 233, 237
Korein, Julius, 259, 260
Kosher, 213, 294, 296, 300, 307, 316, 323, 344, 383, 386, 396
Koveẓ He'arot, 191, 383
Koveẓ Inyanim, 383
Koveẓ Nehora'i, 236
Koveẓ Shi'urim, 293, 383
Krattenmaker, Thomas A., 347
Kraus, R. Gavriel, 292
Krinsky, R. Judah Leib, 364
Kristallnacht, 130
Kuntres Ba'ayot ha-Zeman be-Hashkafat ha-Torah, 292
Kupperman v. Congregation Nusach Sfard, 34
Kurland, Philip B., 75

Lake, Peter, 342
Landau Commission, 181
Landau, R. Ezekiel, 66, 137, 163
Langbein, John H., 175, 177
Lashon ha-ra, 332, 333, 336
Lazerson, R. Simchah Bunim, 266
Leḥem Mishneh, 222, 224, 225, 228, 229, 234
Leḥem Setarim, 341
Leiner, R. Gershon, 375, 382
Leiter, R. Ze'ev Wolf, 212, 213
Lemon v. Kurtzman, 43, 52, 73
Lempert, Richard O., 347
Leon v. Wainwright, 181
Le-Or ha-Halakhah, 198, 209, 218, 219, 229, 233
Lèse majesté, 115, 189
Leshinsky v. Leshinsky, 21
Levi ben Gershon, R., 335
Levinson, Sanford, 180
Levush, 85
Lew, Julian D.M., 31
Lieber v. Operman, 128
Liebes, R. Isaac, 138, 139, 140, 153
Liebmann, Ronald S., 348
Life of Flavius Josephus, The, 213
Life of John Locke, The, 351
Life support, 263, 275, 281, 282, 285, 295, 297, 324
Lifnim mishurat ha-din, 150, 173
Likkutei He'arot, 380
Likkutei Ḥever ben Ḥayyim, 380
Livingston v. Jefferson, 318
Locke, John, 204, 321, 350, 351
Louisell, David W., 347
Loving v. Virginia, 54

Ma'adanei Ereẓ, 107
Ma'amar Teḥiyat ha-Metim, 292, 293
Mabit, 86, 87
Machesky v. Bizzell, 55
Machransky v. Machransky, 21
Magar v. Arkansas, 353
Magen Avraham, 65, 261, 334
Maḥanayim, 232, 233, 237

Maharal of Prague, 212, 245, 366, 373, 380
Maharam of Rothenberg, 149
Maharaz Ḥayes, 126, 127
Mahari Asad, 378
Mahari bei Rav, 378
Maharsha, 289, 334, 335, 370, 379, 382
Maḥazik Berakhah, 273, 375, 378, 379, 380
Maidment, Susan, 23
Maimonides, Moses, 16, 28, 89. *See also* Rambam
Maitland, Frederic W., 176
Malbim, R. Meir Leibush, 381
Mammana, Robert B., 286
Mandel, S., 274
Manheim, Ralph, 370
Mar'it he-Ayin, 375, 376, 378, 379
Mareh Panim, 233
Margaliyot ha-Yam, 237, 243
Margaliyot Tovah, 364
Margulies v. Margulies, 37, 38, 39, 41, 43, 44, 48, 52, 82
Margulies, R. Reuben, 237, 243
Maritime law, 148, 149
Marriage. *See Chapter Two*
Martyrdom, 109, 110, 193, 205, 277
Mashuaḥ milḥamah, 241
Mauritz, W., 258
Mayer-Kolker v. Kolker, 62, 63
McConnell, Michael W., 349, 351
McDonald v. McDonald, 331
McKale, D., 132
McLaughlin v. McLaughlin, 45
Me'iri, R. Menachem ha-, 65, 82, 84, 106, 161, 216, 217, 218, 224, 227, 228, 229, 230, 231, 273, 289, 299, 301, 302, 308, 335, 345, 368
Mecklenberg, R. Jacob Zevi, 11, 367
Medini, R. Chaim Chizkiyahu, 198
Megillat Esther, 221
Megillat Sefer, 374
Meir Simchah ha-Kohen of Dvinsk, R., 191
Meir, R., 387
Mekhilta, 236
Mekom Shmu'el, 219
Mekor Ḥayyim, 364
Meltzer, R. Iser Zalman, 123, 222
Meshekh Ḥokhmah, 236
Meshovev Netivot, 194
Meyer v. Nebraska, 54, 73
Michelson, R. Zevi Yecheskel, 289
Midrash Rabbah, 366
Midrash Shohar Tov, 9
Midrash Tanḥuma, 233
Midrash Tehillim, 369
Mielziner, Moses, 37, 52
Mi-Gei ha-Hareigah, 187
Migo, 159, 164, 165, 166, 167, 168
Milḥemet ḥovah, 214, 222, 223, 227, 233
Milḥemet mizvah, 211, 214, 217, 218, 220, 221, 222, 223, 224, 226, 227, 229, 230, 231, 232, 233, 234, 237, 241, 243, 244, 245, 247, 248
Milḥemet reshut, 207, 211, 214, 217, 218, 220, 222, 223, 224, 225, 226, 227, 228, 229, 230, 231, 232, 233, 234, 237, 238, 240, 241, 243, 244, 245, 247, 248
Miller v. Miller, 21
Miller, Jeffery H., 352
Minḥat Ḥinnukh, 194, 198, 207, 208, 209, 220, 236, 243, 266, 386
Minḥat Shlomoh, 243
Minḥat Yizḥak, 83, 266
Minkin v. Minkin, 58, 59, 60, 62, 64, 66
Minyan, 373, 376, 377, 378, 379, 380, 388, 393
Mishkenot Ya'akov, 85, 295
Mishnah Berurah, 195, 213, 378
Mishnat ḥasidim, 190
Mishnat Ḥayyei Sha'ah, 266
Mishneh le-Melekh, 213, 339
Mishneh Torah, 15, 16, 28, 40, 65, 66, 112, 124, 196, 220, 222, 226, 227, 229, 230, 244, 323, 332, 337, 339
Mishpat ha-Melukhah, 220, 221, 233
Mishpat Kohen, 201, 218, 229, 241
Mishpetei ha-melekh, 175
Mitchell, Mary Harter, 346
Mitpaḥat Sefarim, 374
Mo'adim u-Zemanim, 169, 221, 381
Mohandas, A., 263
Montefiore, Sir Moses, 178
Mordekhai, 148, 149, 150, 194
Morio, M., 259
Morris v. Morris, 56, 58, 62, 64, 82
Mosaf Shabbat, 254
Moses, 5, 6, 10, 16, 53, 56, 57, 62, 64, 65, 89, 93, 100, 194, 334, 335, 336, 340, 341, 379
Mu'tazila, 280
Muḥzak, 157, 158, 159, 160, 164, 165
Mullen v. United States, 353

Naamani, Israel T., 31
Nabot, 118
Nagar, R. Maimon, 84
Nathanson, R. Joseph Saul, 113, 272, 295

National Bioethics Advisory Commission, 361
National Endowment of the Arts v. Finley, 325
Natural law, 2, 3, 93, 122, 125, 126, 128, 204, 362, 365
Nebenzahl, R. Avigdor, 388
Nebuchadnezzar, 193
Nefesh ha-Rav, 333
Netivot ha-Mishpat, 166, 194
Netivot La-Shevet, 65
Netter, R. Shlomo Zalman, 364
Neugroschel, J., 373
Nifla'ot Maharal, 373
Nineteen Letters of Ben Uziel, The, 364, 367
Nishmat Avraham, 266, 279, 388
Nishtaneh ha-teva, 251, 261
Nissim, Rabbenu, 106, 170, 190, 299, 300, 301, 307, 308
Niv ha-Midrashiyah, 241
Nizozei Or, 237, 243
No'am, 169, 226, 300
Noah, 208, 376
Noahide Code, 101, 102, 103, 112, 113, 117, 122, 123, 124, 125, 128, 176, 197, 198, 205, 207, 208, 210, 211, 212, 245, 249, 250, 375, 376
Noda bi-Yehudah, 66, 163, 236, 266
Noe, R. Abraham Chaim, 49
Norris, Martin J., 149

Oakes, Dallin H., 55
Ogunyemi, A., 261
Ohel Yosef, 364
Old, S., 259
Oolygamy, 95
Or ha-Ḥayyim, 334, 335
Or ḥa-Mizraḥ, 112, 233, 235, 236, 255, 266, 273, 274, 275, 288
Or Sameaḥ, 191
Or Zaru'a, 213, 231, 232
Oshia, R., 298, 368, 371, 379
Oshry, R. Ephraim, 138, 139, 143, 154, 155
Ouakine, G.F., 256
ousia, 277
Outwater, K.M., 258
Over, P.E., 286
Ozar ha-Poskim, 65, 66, 389, 390

Pal v. Pal, 40, 42, 43, 44, 47, 48, 70
Pallis, Christopher, 258, 261, 264
Panim Yafot, 237
Papa, R., 269, 303, 304
Pardes Rimmonim, 370, 374, 380, 381
Paris, John, 361
Parise, Joseph F., 256
Parry, John T., 181
Passamaneck, Stephen M., 134
Paul v. Davis, 329, 347
Paulsen, Monrad, 54, 55
Pearson, J., 260
Peirushei Ivra, 145, 147
Pelaggi, R. Chaim, 377
Pennsylvania v. Musolina, 353
People ex rel. Chitty v. Fitzgerald, 331
People ex rel. DeMauro v. Gavin, 285
People ex rel. Fields v. Kaufman, 331
People v. Eulo, 281, 282
People v. Phillips, 349
People v. Smith, 350
Perashat Derakhim, 236
Peretz, Rabbenu, 84
Perl v. Perl, 82
Perlin, Michael L., 342
Petur, 29, 31, 32, 53, 54
Philbrick, Francis I., 149
Philipson, David, 37
Philosophical Quest, The, 283, 384
Pines, R. Zalman, 202
Pirkei Yesod, 372
Pirkus, 270, 274, 295, 297, 305, 308
Piskei ha-Din ha-Rabbaniyim, 124, 146
Pithei Teshuvah, 16, 19, 73
Plato, 355
Plaut, Wolf Gunther, 53
Plessy v. Ferguson, 9
Plocki, R. Meir Dan, 109, 198, 209
Pnei Mosheh, 233, 387
Polish, David, 37
Pollack, Sir Frederick, 176
Polygamy, 19, 20, 66, 95, 96
Posner, R. Meir, 85
Powner, D.J., 259
Prader, Joseph, 30
Preger v. Preger, 23
Preil, Eleazer Meir, 169
Presbyterian Church v. Mary Elizabeth Blue Hull Memorial Presbyterian Church, 43
Pri Malkah, 213
Pri Megadim, 234
Price v. Price, 47, 62
Price, Robert H., 261
Privacy, 329, 333, 336, 347

Property, 50, 51, 94, 114, 115, 122, 126, 131, 133, 136, 138, 141, 142, 144, 146, 147, 173, 241
Prostitution, 39, 98
Purim, 289

Quantum meruit, 149

Ra'avan, 236
Rabbah, 168, 289
Rabbinic confidentiality. *See Chapter Eight*
Rabinowitz-Teumim, R. Benjamin, 107
Radecki v. Schuckardt, 353
Radvaz, 214, 273
Radzyner Rebbe, 375
Ralbag, 335
Rambam, 15, 16, 65, 66, 70, 89, 102, 103, 105, 106, 112, 113, 116, 117, 119, 120, 122, 124, 125, 127, 141, 142, 146, 147, 160, 168, 170, 175, 189, 190, 191, 196, 197, 198, 199, 210, 211, 214, 215, 216, 217, 218, 219, 220, 221, 222, 223, 224, 225, 226, 227, 228, 229, 230, 232, 233, 234, 239, 241, 242, 244, 247, 253, 254, 270, 273, 274, 280, 292, 293, 294, 304, 308, 310, 311, 314, 315, 323, 324, 332, 337, 339, 357, 365, 372, 389, 390
Ramban, 106, 110, 113, 114, 122, 123, 218, 219, 220, 221, 234, 244, 292, 293, 364, 365
Ramon v. Ramon, 45
Ramsey, Paul, 362, 388
Ran, 109
Rape, 39, 208
Rappaport, R. Yitzchak Meir, 138, 155
Rashba, 84, 85, 106, 110, 111, 112, 117, 118, 126, 142, 144, 145, 169, 170, 297
Rashbam, 104, 105, 106, 337
Rashi, 5, 109, 121, 122, 123, 124, 125, 126, 130, 141, 142, 152, 161, 169, 175, 215, 216, 217, 219, 220, 221, 222, 223, 234, 235, 236, 243, 245, 254, 270, 271, 272, 274, 289, 291, 299, 304, 305, 306, 310, 313, 334, 336, 341, 363, 364, 369, 376, 383, 384
Rastafarians, 6, 253
Rava, 161, 216, 217, 218, 309, 369, 370, 371, 374, 377, 378, 379
Redl, G., 258
Reese, Seward, 347, 350, 351, 353
Reid, Thomas, 321
Reitz, Bruce A., 286
Reliance, 83, 104, 106, 119
Religious Freedom Restoration Act, 284
Rema, 23, 31, 32, 39, 65, 66, 83, 84, 119, 120, 121, 123, 137, 138, 150, 151, 152, 153, 155, 156, 159, 160, 161, 162, 164, 168, 190, 195, 213, 227, 230, 231, 232, 336
Remarriage, 19, 20, 22, 24, 25, 26, 29, 30, 32, 33, 36, 37, 38, 40, 41, 48, 51, 53, 54, 56, 57, 61, 63, 64, 65, 67, 68, 71, 72, 73, 76, 77, 78, 79, 80, 83, 87, 94, 97, 98, 253, 282, 283, 287, 290, 291, 292, 322, 323, 390
Resh Lakish, 189
Resisei Lailah, 378
Respiration, 252, 253, 255, 256, 260, 265, 267, 268, 269, 270, 271, 272, 273, 274, 275, 301, 303, 304, 305, 306
Resurrection, 288, 290, 291, 292, 293, 294, 295, 296, 322, 323
Rheinstein, Max, 52
Riegenfeld v. Jacobson, 35
Rif, 160
Right of conquest, 142, 143, 144, 145, 146, 151, 153, 155, 250. *See also Kibush milḥamah*
Ritual murder, 178
Ritva, 65, 106, 107, 109, 110, 111, 112, 117, 118, 120, 121, 390
Rivash, 85, 86
Robin Hood, 204
Robl, Dr. James, 360
Rockoff, M.A., 258
Rodef, 119, 128, 185, 186, 188, 189, 190, 207, 234
Ropper, Allen H., 274
Rosen, R. Joseph, 374
Rosenbaum v. Consolidated Prods, 133
Rosenbaum, R. Yehudah, 207, 211
Rosenberg v. Rosenberg, 50
Rosenberg, Alfred, 154
Rosenberg, Yudl, 373
Rosh, 125, 147, 161, 170, 254, 279, 280, 310, 313, 381
Rosner, Fred, 255, 285
Roth v. Roth, 50, 53, 54, 69, 70, 71, 72, 76, 82
Rozanes, R. Judah, 339
Ruaḥ Ḥayyim, 377, 380, 381
Ruaḥ memallela, 380
Rubin v. Rubin, 38, 42, 43, 44, 50, 59, 70
Rudner, Abraham R., 44

S. S. & B. Live Poultry Corp. v. Kashruth Association, 45, 70
Sa'adia, Ga'on, 89, 280, 292, 293, 380
Saltzburg, Stephen A., 347
Sampson, William, 349

Samuel ben Meir, R., 104
Samuel, R., 104
Sanhedrin, 13, 105, 107, 126, 201, 202, 211, 218, 219, 220, 222, 223, 224, 225, 229, 237, 238, 240, 242, 243, 247, 250, 310, 385
Saperstone v. Saperstone, 30, 31
Scarry, Elaine, 180
Schachter, R. Herschel, 333
Schick, Maharam, 112
Schmelkes, R. Isaac, 210, 390
Schneider, Sanford, 260
Schneiderman, H., 373
Scholem, Gershom G., 370, 372, 373, 374, 379, 380, 381
Scholl v. Scholl, 44
Schorr, R. Isaac, 198, 210
Schwadron, R. Shalom Mordecai, 274, 295
Schwartz v. Schwartz, 68, 69, 99
Scott v. Hammock, 353
Seasta, D., 274
Sedei Ḥemed, 198, 211
Seder ha-Get, 29, 53, 54
Seed, G. Richard, 361
Sefer ha-Agudah, 39
Sefer ha-Bahir, 380
Sefer ha-Bitaḥon, 372
Sefer ha-Gematri'ot, 379
Sefer ha-Ḥinnukh, 217, 220, 221, 236, 244, 311, 338
Sefer ha-Ma'or, 169
Sefer ha-Miẓvot, 214, 219, 220, 221, 241, 244, 294, 337
Sefer Ḥasidim, 112, 125
Sefer Miẓvot Gadol, 334, 336
Sefer Yeẓirah, 368, 370, 371, 372, 374, 379, 380, 381, 387
Segal v. Segal, 82
Seidman v. Fishburne-Hudgin Foundation, Inc., 353
Seifer ha-Gematri'ot, 371, 372
Self-defense, 6, 128, 185, 186, 207, 209, 214, 232, 233, 234, 237, 244, 245, 247, 249
Sema, 137
Separation of Church and State, 52, 54, 69, 70, 73, 74, 98, 326
Seridei Esh, 139, 140, 146, 151, 155, 156, 170
Seven Nations, 220, 221, 222, 223, 226, 237, 241, 244, 245, 246
Sha'ar Efrayim, 377
Sha'ar ha-Gemul, 292
Sha'ar ha-Shamayim, 271
Sha'atnez, 364
Shabbetai ben Meir ha-Kohen, R., 39
Shabtai, David, 276
Shach, R. Eleazar Menachem, 198
Shahnez v. Rizwan, 50
Shakh, 137, 145, 151, 152, 153, 165, 385
Shalom ha-Galil, 227
Shapira, R. Chaim Eleazar, 377, 381
Shapiro v. Shapiro, 55, 56
She'elot u-Teshuvot mi-Ma'amakim, 138, 154
She'ilat Ya'aveẓ, 374, 377, 378, 379, 380, 381
She'iltot de-Rav Aha'i Ga'on, 191
Shechem, 199, 212, 245
Shekhinah, 341, 378
Shelah, 381
Shelley v. Kraemer, 33
Sherbert v. Verner, 284
Sheridan v. Garrison, 55
Shev Shemateta, 168
Shi'urei Torah, 49
Shikoh v. Murff, 32
Shilman v. Shilman, 23, 24
Shiloh, Isaac S., 31
Shimon ben Lakish, R., 108, 190, 297, 299
Shimshon, Rabbenu, 387
Shitah Mekubbeẓet, 106, 107, 109, 141, 161, 193
Shiyurei Korban, 225, 228, 229, 234
Shlomoh Zalman Auerbach, R., 107, 169, 243, 262, 266, 275, 276, 292
Shmelkes, R. Isaac, 198
Sho'el u-Meshiv, 295
Shue, Henry, 179
Shulḥan Arukh, 23, 28, 29, 31, 32, 36, 39, 40, 53, 54, 57, 65, 66, 83, 100, 101, 137, 147, 148, 158, 159, 160, 164, 168, 230, 234, 239, 254, 270, 290, 304, 310, 314, 336, 337, 378, 385, 386, 389
Shulḥan Arukh ha-Rav, 234
Shustal, R. Simchah, 236
Siaḥ ha-Sadeh, 291, 294
Sidrei Taharot, 375
Siegel v. Ribak, 46
Sifra, 294, 337
Sifrei, 241
Silver, Dr. Lee, 358
Simḥat Kohen, 86, 87
Skillings v. Allen, 342
Skornik v. Skornik, 132, 133, 173
Smilow v. United States, 128
Snyder v. Evangelical Orthodox, 327
Snyder, J.V., 259

Sodom, 152, 339, 341
Sofer, R. Abraham Benjamin, 103
Sofer, R. Moses, 6, 65, 92, 113, 123, 212, 245, 272, 304. *See also Ḥatam Sofer*
Solomon, 115
Soloveichik, R. Aaron, 233, 264, 275, 285
Soloveitchik, R. Chaim, 198, 210, 382
Soloveitchik, R. Joseph Ber of Brisk, 319
Soloveitchik, R. Joseph Dov, 11, 333, 365, 366
Spendings, J., 177
Sporn, P., 258
Steinberg v. Steinberg, 43, 59, 70
Steinberg, Dr. Abraham, 266, 267
Stern v. Stern, 48, 49, 50, 56, 58, 62, 64, 66, 67, 82
Sternbuch, R. Moshe, 169, 221, 292, 381
Stice, Dr. Steven L., 360
Stillman, Dr. Robert, 359
Stinson, Edward B., 286
Stone, Scott N., 348
Swift, Morris, 30

Taguchi, H., 259
Takkanah, 15, 19, 96, 137, 319
Talaq, 33, 77
Talebearing, 332, 333, 335, 337, 338, 342, 356
Talpiyot, 226, 233
Tam, Rabbenu, 160
Tamar, R. Issachar, 333
Tanḥuma, 233
Tarasoff v. Regents of University of California, 342
Tarfon, Rabbi, 125, 126
Targum Onkelos, 380
Tashbaẓ, 84, 85, 86, 110, 111, 142
Ta-Shma, Israel Moses, 149
Taxes, 90, 104, 105, 106, 128, 239, 241
Taz, 254, 378
55.4, 378
Teḥumin, 265, 266, 336, 339
Teitz, R. Pinchas, 138, 141, 143, 147, 150, 151
Temple, 13, 15
Tendler, R. Moses D., 255
Tennenbaum, R. Malkiel Zevi, 290
Terumah, 35, 279
Terumat ha-Deshen, 145
Teshuvot Aḥi'ezer, 121
Teshuvot Avkat Rokhel, 106
Teshuvot Ben Yehudah, 198, 207, 211
Teshuvot Bet Avi, 138, 139, 153
Teshuvot Bet David, 212
Teshuvot Bet Shlomoh, 390
Teshuvot Bet Yiẓḥak, 198, 210, 390
Teshuvot Bnei Banim, 333
Teshuvot Divrei Malki'el, 290
Teshuvot Divrei Menaḥem, 288, 300
Teshuvot Dovev Meisharim, 107
Teshuvot Dvar Avraham, 118
Teshuvot Ge'onei Batra'i, 65
Teshuvot Ḥakham Ẓevi, 39, 67, 271, 276, 374, 380
Teshuvot ha-Rashba, 65, 84, 110, 111, 345, 379
Teshuvot ha-Rashbaẓ, 84, 85
Teshuvot ha-Rosh, 65
Teshuvot Ḥatam Sofer, 65, 92, 113, 114, 115, 116, 117, 123, 212, 213, 245, 268, 272, 304, 311, 313, 381
Teshuvot Ḥatan Sofer, 389, 391
Teshuvot Ḥavvot Ya'ir, 333, 340
Teshuvot Ḥelkat Ya'akov, 136, 139, 169, 338
Teshuvot Hemdat Shlomoh, 66
Teshuvot Imrei Esh, 213, 239
Teshuvot Imrei Yosher, 83, 137
Teshuvot Kerem Ḥemed, 381
Teshuvot Ketav Sofer, 390
Teshuvot Koaḥ Shor, 198, 235
Teshuvot Kol Aryeh, 83
Teshuvot Mabit, 86, 87
Teshuvot Maharam Rothenberg, 161
Teshuvot Maharam Shik, 112, 169
Teshuvot Mahari Basan, 65
Teshuvot Maharil Diskin, 113
Teshuvot Maharsham, 274
Teshuvot Maharya, 378
Teshuvot Maimuni, 67
Teshuvot Malbushei Tom Tov, 168
Teshuvot Minḥat Yiẓḥak, 169
Teshuvot Noda bi-Yehudah, 39, 66, 137, 163
Teshuvot Pe'er ha-Dor, 390
Teshuvot R. Akiva Eger, 66
Teshuvot Ra'anaḥ, 86
Teshuvot Radvaz, 65, 234, 272, 292
Teshuvot Rema, 123
Teshuvot Rivash, 85
Teshuvot Sedei ha-Areẓ, 381
Teshuvot Shevet ha-Levi, 109
Teshuvot Sho'el u-Meshiv, 113
Teshuvot Tashbaẓ, 110
Teshuvot Tevu'ot Shor, 210
Teshuvot Tirosh ve-Yiẓhar, 289
Teshuvot Yad Yiẓḥak, 381
Teshuvot Ẓofnat Pa'aneaḥ, 374

Tiemann, William H., 348
Tiferet Yisra'el, 236, 261
Tiferet Yonatan, 366
Toldot Adam, 394
Toledano, Rabbi Jacob Moses, 66
Torah she-be-al Peh, 218, 220, 242, 255, 270
Torah Temimmah, 334, 335
Torat ha-Bayit he-Arukh, 297
Torat ha-Mo'adim, 221, 237, 243
Torat ha-Shabbat ve-ha-Mo'ed, 232, 233, 237
Torat Nevi'im, 126
Torture. *See Chapter Five*
Torture préalable, 179
Totten v. United States, 353
Trachtenberg, Joshua, 394
Trammel v. United States, 347, 348
Trani, R. Daniel, 378
Treifah, 254, 257, 266, 267, 272, 273, 294, 299, 302, 307, 308, 309, 310, 312, 314, 315, 323, 324
Tribe, Laurence H., 70, 71, 73, 74, 75, 76
Tur Shulḥan Arukh, 84, 100, 126, 161, 389, 390
Turk, R. Samuel, 213
Turner v. Turner, 69
Tussman, Joseph, 73

Ula bar Kushav, 108
Uniform Determination of Death Act, 262, 280
United States v. Seeger, 96
Uozumi, T., 259
Urim ve-tumim, 113, 123, 165, 207, 211, 218, 219, 220, 224, 225, 229, 233, 234, 238, 240, 244, 245, 246, 247, 250
Uziel, R. Ben-Zion, 65, 66

Vaihinger, Hans, 316
Va-Yomer Yitzḥak, 67
Veatch, Robert, 262, 280
Veit Simon, Dr. Heinrich, 133, 134, 135, 157, 158
Vermes, M., 258
Victor v. Victor, 63
Vigorney, Robert P., 256

Wachtel v. Wachtel, 68
Wakayama, T., 360
Wald, Michael, 347
Waldenberg, R. Eliezer, 216, 217, 236, 266, 271, 276, 336, 387
Walker, A. Earl, 255, 258
Wallace v. Brewer, 55
Walz v. Tax Commission of New York, 43, 52, 75
War, 141, 145, 151, 152, 153, 155. *See Chapter Six*
Wasserman, R. Elchanan, 191, 293, 383
Wasserman, R. Yitzchak, 169
Waxstein v. Waxstein, 43
Weidenfeld, R. Dov Berish, 107
Weinberg, R. Yechiel Ya'akov, 139, 151, 155, 156
Weinberger v. Van Hessen, 33
Weingurt, R. Saul, 169
Weisburg, Robert, 347
Weisz, R. Yitzchak Ya'akov, 83, 169, 266
Wener v. Wener, 44, 45, 49
Wilde, Jenny, 134
Willadsen, Dr. Steen, 359, 361
Williams, James, 177
Williams, John C., 342
Wilmut, I., 359
Winkler, Gershon, 373
Witness, 28, 39, 42, 53, 65, 66, 67, 100, 101, 103, 107, 113, 122, 124, 166, 167, 175, 176, 177, 294, 337
Wolpo, R. Shalom Dov, 189, 190
Woody, R., 258
Worthington v. District Court, 72
Woszner, R. Samuel ha-Levi, 109
Wrape, V., 258

Yad Sha'ul, 169, 272
Yan'ai, Rabbi, 10
Yanagimachi, Dr. Ryuzo, 358
Yated Ne'eman, 254
Yavneh, 169
Ye'ush, 136, 137, 138, 139, 140, 141, 142, 143, 145, 146, 147, 148, 150, 151, 152, 154, 155, 156, 157, 172, 173
Yellin, Jacob M., 348, 350
Yere'im, 194
Yitzchak Aharon of Vilkomir, R., 120
Yoḥanan, R., 189, 216, 217, 218, 309, 340, 341
Yom Kippur, 177, 279
Yosef, Rav, 168
Yoẓei, 383, 384, 385, 386, 387

Ẓeruf, 372
Za'ar ba'alei ḥayyim, 374
Zablocki v. Redhail, 54
Ẓadok ha-Kohen of Lublin, R., 377, 378, 379, 380, 381, 382
Zagouri, Abraham, 30

Zeira, R., 289, 290, 369, 370, 371, 374, 375, 376, 378, 379, 380
Zekhuta de-Avraham, 209
Zera Avraham, 245
Zevi Ashkenazi, R., 67, 271, 294, 374
Zevin, R. Shlomoh Yosef, 92, 198, 209, 218
Ziemba, R. Menachem, 212, 245
Zilberstein, R. Yitzchak, 254, 341
Zimbler v. Felber, 34
Zimra, R. David ibn, 292
Ẓiẓ Eli'ezer, 236, 266, 271, 276, 336, 387, 388
Ẓofnat Pa'aneaḥ, 382
Zohar, 357, 378
Ẓohar, 341
Zolti, R. Betzalel, 124, 144
Zorach v. Clauson, 73, 76
Zuto shel yam, 146, 147, 148, 149, 150, 152, 154, 156, 166, 168

www.ingramcontent.com/pod-product-compliance
Lightning Source LLC
LaVergne TN
LVHW011531200926
848484LV00001B/225
9780521765473